GOVERNMENT AND POLITICS
IN SOUTH ASIA

SIXTH EDITION

GOVERNMENT *and* POLITICS *in* SOUTH ASIA

Yogendra K. Malik

Charles H. Kennedy

Robert C. Oberst

Ashok Kapur

Mahendra Lawoti

Syedur Rahman

Westview Press
A Member of the Perseus Books Group

Published by Westview Press,
A Member of the Perseus Books Group

Parts of this publication were originally published in East-West Center *Policy Studies* 43, titled "Looking Back, Looking Forward: Centralization, Multiple Conflicts, and Democratic State Building in Nepal," and also in *Contentious Politics and Democratization in Nepal* (Sage, 2007), edited by Mahendra Lawoti.

Find us on the World Wide Web at www.westviewpress.com.

Every effort has been made to secure required permissions to use all images, maps, and other art included in this volume.

Westview Press books are available at special discounts for bulk purchases in the United States by corporations, institutions, and other organizations. For more information, please contact the Special Markets Department at the Perseus Books Group, 2300 Chestnut Street, Suite 200, Philadelphia, PA 19103, or call (800) 810-4145, extension 5000, or e-mail special.markets@perseusbooks.com.

Designed by Brent Wilcox

A CIP data record for this title is available from the Library of Congress.
ISBN-13: 978-0-8133-4389-1
10 9 8 7 6 5 4 3

As in the past editions, this book is dedicated to our wives:

Usha Malik

Patricia A. Poe (Kennedy)

Kathy Shellogg (Oberst)

Deepika Kapur

Tannaz Khosrowshahi (Rahman)

Geeta G. Lawoti

However, we also want to make a special dedication to Craig Baxter, who passed away on February 7, 2008.

Craig Baxter 1929–2008, Diplomat, Scholar, and Friend

CONTENTS

LIST OF TABLES
AND ILLUSTRATIONS

TABLES

MAPS

FIGURES

PREFACE TO
THE SIXTH EDITION

The sixth edition of this book marks the first significant change in the book since it was first published in 1987. The first and foremost change is the loss of our colleague and friend Craig Baxter, who died on February 7, 2008. Without Craig this book would never have been published. His tireless effort and determination ensured that the first and later editions went to press. We will miss him dearly.

The second change is the addition of chapters on Nepal. We are finally acknowledging the importance of Nepal in the region. While this omission remains the responsibility of the original authors, we have undone our omission and have included Nepal in this edition.

Finally, the primary authorship of the Bangladesh chapters has passed from Craig Baxter to Syedur Rahman and the Indian chapters are a collaborative effort by Ashok Kapur and Yogendra Malik.

With these changes the book enters a second generation of authors. Twenty years ago, none of us ever expected the book to last as long as it has. The original four authors believed that there was a need for a book that examined all of South Asia rather than just India. Our original optimism has been reinforced by the support for the book over the first five editions. The South Asia we wrote about in 1987 no longer exists. It has been transformed by the changes that are sweeping across Asia. We have tried to keep up with those changes.

We wish to thank especially those at Westview Press. While we have worked with many at Westview Press over the years, we wish to thank Steve Catalano and Karl Yambert, who worked with us on this edition. In addition, we would like to offer a special thanks to Will Falla for his work in preparing the tables for the book.

Our thanks and appreciation for the patience and encouragement of our wives is shown in the dedication of this work to them.

Yogendra K. Malik
Charles H. Kennedy
Robert C. Oberst
Ashok Kapur
Mahendra Lawoti
Syedur Rahman

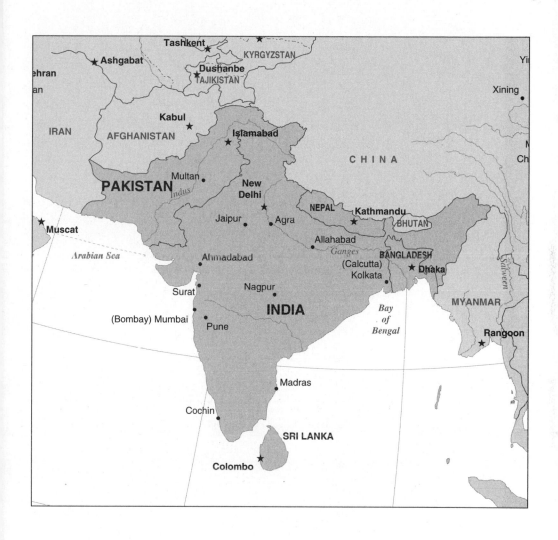

1

Introduction

To most people in North America the Indian subcontinent is an exotic land of maharajas and sadhus. It holds a special place as part of the remote and distant orient. However, while our quaint stereotypes continue to dominate the way we view the subcontinent, India and its neighbors have increasingly begun to play a major role in international affairs and the international economy, and thus are an important subject for study and better understanding.

The region can no longer be dismissed as remote or unimportant. It may still seem exotic, but it is increasingly becoming a part of the mainstream of world affairs. First of all, the subcontinent's population makes it important. With a population of 1.5 billion, or nearly one out of every four people on earth, the Indian subcontinent cannot be ignored.[1] Second, its role in the world economy as a South Asian nation has become increasingly important. Indian telephone service personnel have become a staple of late night television comedians, but the growth of the information technology industry and the subcontinent's role in it is important. Finally, the region has become important to North American strategic interests. The events of 9/11 thrust the region into the awareness of every citizen of North America and Europe. Pakistan's remote hill territories are no longer harmless exotic lands hidden away in remote mountains with no importance to the rest of the world. They are the alleged hiding place of U.S. enemies, and the millions of poor people in South Asia a potential breeding ground of a new uprising against Western societies.

The following chapters will describe the countries of South Asia and examine the reason for their successes and failures. Each of these nations is struggling to create stable political environments which will allow for rapid economic growth and the resolution of their most serious problems.

South Asia is home to one of the world's oldest civilizations. The Harappan (or Indus Valley civilization) was the birthplace of one of the world's oldest cultures. Existing more than 3,500 years ago, the society was not only a marvel among the

1

societies of that era but also laid the groundwork for the civilization that would become India. The region's geography would protect the subcontinent for nearly 2,000 years. The land routes to the west required travel across the Hindu Kush range of mountains or across the great desert of Baluchistan. To the north was the natural wall of the Himalayas and to the east, the narrow ranges and jungles of Burma. The only accessible route was the seas to the south, which would become the preferred route of invasion as waves of Europeans would come.

Although Alexander the Great came to Pakistan in the fourth century B.C., the first permanent colonies were created by the Portuguese, followed by the Dutch, French, and British. Among them, the British would prevail and rule India for nearly 200 years.

Before the Europeans, there had been sporadic streams of invaders who came and conquered for a brief time. The residents of the subcontinent would absorb some elements of the cultures of each wave of invaders. The first Muslim invaders came in the eighth century; however, the Mughal empire, established in 1504, created some of the world's most important architectural treasures, including the Taj Mahal. They would also leave a remarkable administrative legacy which the British eventually would adopt.

When the subcontinent is compared with other former European colonies, it stands out as a refuge of democratic and stable political development. Although some of the countries of the region are struggling with democracy, democratic values have taken hold in most of them. Each of these countries is also evolving as a major source of scientific research and development. India and Pakistan have both exploded nuclear bombs while their scientists have flocked to richer Western nations. The rise of information technology has opened up South Asia in a way that no other event could have done. Today, it is a center of software development and Internet call centers for service lines of Western products.

The attack on the World Trade Center in New York City forced the Western nations to focus on Afghanistan and Pakistan. The spread of a more militant version of Islam than what was known in South Asia for nearly a millennia has begun to split and transform the region's 400 million Muslims. It has also brought increased concern and scrutiny from the military planners in the United States and western Europe.

Each of the states of South Asia faces five critical areas of political development: nation building, state building, participation, economy building, and distribution. Although India, Pakistan, and Sri Lanka inherited fairly effective state apparatuses, they are facing different challenges.

After discussing the political heritage of the British era, we will examine the five largest countries of the region in Parts 1–5: Part 1, India; Part 2, Pakistan; Part 3, Bangladesh; Part 4, Sri Lanka; and Part 5, Nepal. Chapter 30 addresses the interrelationships among the states in the region and the roles they play in the international system and ties the themes of the book to a discussion of the political development of the region as a whole.

European and British Expansion

The South Asian political systems and societies of the twenty-first century owe much of their existence to the influence of British colonial rule. While colonialism destroyed the right of the people to govern themselves and placed an alien ruler located 5,000 miles away in charge of their destinies, it did leave some positive and lasting effects.

While other former colonies in Asia and Africa have struggled in their efforts to create democratic governments, the South Asian nation-states have been much more successful. Although we will discuss the countries of the subcontinent separately, it is important to understand their common historical experience and the important influence that the British colonial experience had on the nations that they have become today. The British did not rule the region as a single colony. The countries of India, Pakistan, and Bangladesh were part of the British colony of India, while Sri Lanka was a separate crown colony and Nepal was never a formal colony but rather a protectorate under British control. While we discuss the countries individually, the common British experience has helped to shape the success the nations have experienced in nation building. Although the British influence has been important in shaping the independent nations of the region, the experience was not all positive. The success of the people of the subcontinent in taking advantage of the positive contributions of the British and overcoming the negative influences is a testament to the resiliency of South Asian culture and its people.

It is easy to forget that the British were not the first Europeans to arrive on the subcontinent. Vasco da Gama visited it on his voyage of discovery around the Cape of Good Hope in Africa in 1498. He left a few Portuguese representatives behind to set up a trading post. In 1503, the Portuguese would set up the first European outpost in South Asia at Cochin, in what is now the southern Indian state of Kerala. The Portuguese would spend the next century expanding their control of South Asia along India's western coast and Sri Lanka. For the next 150 years the trading language of the region would be Portuguese. However, in 1600, Queen Elizabeth I presented a charter forming the British East India Company, with the British arriving at Surat (in present-day Gujarat) in 1612. However, the British would slowly establish their control of India in the face of the Portuguese who were already there and the Mughal empire, ruled from Delhi, that challenged their ability to control India. The Dutch East India Company, formed in 1602, also coveted the riches of South Asia and began to establish trading outposts along the coast of India and Sri Lanka. In 1608, it would establish its headquarters on the Coromondal coast near Madras. After a series of failed attempts, the French established their first factory in India in 1668 at Surat.[2]

The British East India Company would be given a monopoly over all British trade with India. As the company expanded, they were forced to set up more administration and government functions, including an army for protection. The company would create the city of Calcutta in eastern India and establish its headquarters there until the British government would dissolve the company and rule India directly in 1862.

The first European efforts to establish economic and political control over South Asia encountered one major obstacle—the Mughal empire. The Mughals were western and central Asians who conquered India in 1526 and established a remarkable record of architectural, artistic, educational, and political accomplishments during their rule. The Mughals did not rule all of India, since several southern Hindu kingdoms resisted conquest. However, the Mughals ruled from the Khyber Pass to Bengal across the north and as far south as the Deccan plateau. The Mughals were the last of a series of Muslim dynasties that ruled India from the eleventh century onward.

Mughal rule was marked by great decentralization. The Mughals allowed a number of Hindu kingdoms to exist autonomously as long as they pledged to support the Mughal leadership. The first Europeans arrived as the Mughal empire was founded (1526) and began establishing outposts as the empire peaked in its power and influence in the seventeenth century under the leadership of Jahangir and Shah Jahan. The overthrow of Shah Jehan by his son in 1657 marked the beginning of the decline of the empire. The decline would be hastened by the Europeans, especially the British, who would make alliances with Hindu kings seeking more autonomy from the Mughal leadership. The Mughal empire would decline in power after 1750. The last emperor was exiled to Burma in 1858 after participating in the revolt of 1857 against the British.

In the last years of the empire, the British and the Europeans would control the coastal areas of the country while the Mughals would gradually be left with control of only the Gangetic plain (modern-day Uttar Pradesh) and finally the city of Delhi. After the collapse of the Mughals, the British would maintain most of the Mughal administration and would gradually impose their rule. Their piecemeal approach would result in two forms of control over the subcontinent. Some of the territory acquired by the British East India Company would be ruled directly by the British governor-general and described as "British India." It comprised 60 percent of the territory of India and two-thirds of the population.

The other territories were obtained through agreements with local rulers. These areas are usually called "princely states." At the time of independence in 1947, there were more than 500 of them. The British negotiated a separate agreement with each princely state, although they usually granted autonomy while maintaining control over their foreign affairs, defense, and other matters.

The Mutiny and Its Aftermath

A defining moment of British rule was the Indian Revolt, or Sepoy Mutiny (which many Indian nationalists refer to as the first war of independence). The causes of the uprising are too complex to discuss here, but it resulted from the British East India Company's arrogance in its dealings with the princely states and the Indian people. The revolt was a carefully coordinated uprising led by the sepoys, who were the foot soldiers of the British East India Company's army in India. Initially the Indians captured many important urban centers of British rule and killed many British people living in the country. Ultimately the British forces would regain control of the country and British rule would continue.

In the end, the British East India Company would be dissolved on September 1, 1858, and the British Crown would assume control of India. The British government realized that there was a need to be more responsive to the Indian population and began a series of reforms to avoid any future rebellion by the Indians.

The Indian Councils Act of 1861, passed by the British Parliament, created a legislative council that would advise the executive council (cabinet of the Viceroy). It included a number of appointed "nonofficial" members who could be Indians. While the legislative councils did not provide effective representation to the Indian people, it was a beginning that would lead to greater demands for more representation.

The Indian National Congress was founded in 1885 and became an outspoken representative of the Indian people and an important force for greater Indian representation in the colonial government. Later, in 1906, the Muslim League would be founded and the two organizations would both work to pressure the British to provide more representation.

In 1906, Viceroy Lord Minto endorsed a plan which would become the Government of India Act of 1909. The act, more commonly called the Morley-Minto reforms, allowed for elected representatives on the legislative council. It also allowed one Indian to be named to the Executive Council. However, its significance was the provision of twenty-seven elected Indian members and five appointed Indian members of the Legislative Council in addition to the thirty-six appointed members who were almost all British. This provision provided for nearly equal representation for Indian and British members on the legislative body.

The other unique feature of the Morley-Minto reforms was the creation of separate representation for religious groups. Each seat on the council was designated for one of the major religious groups in India (Hindus, Sikhs, and Muslims), and only the members of that group could vote for the seat. The seats were apportioned roughly on the basis of the population; thus, most went to Hindus.

The Indian National Congress opposed separate electorates for religious groups when it was first demanded in 1906. However, in 1916 both the Congress and the Muslim League held their annual meeting in Lucknow, India, at the same time. During the meetings the two groups signed an agreement (the Lucknow Agreement) in which the Congress accepted the demand for separate Muslim and Sikh representation in the Legislative Council. The agreement was negotiated by two of the most important figures during the colonial era and the march to Indian independence. The Muslim League was represented by Mohammed Ali Jinnah (1876–1948), who was the primary architect of the pact; among the Indian National Congress negotiators was Motilal Nehru (1861–1931), who would become president of the Congress in 1919. His son (Jawaharlal Nehru, 1889–1964), granddaughter (Indira Gandhi, 1917–1984), and great-grandson (Rajiv Gandhi, 1944–1991) would all serve as prime ministers of independent India. Both the League and the Congress believed that the British were about to grant further reforms.

While Lord Morley stated that the British had no intention of granting self-government to India, the British secretary of state for India, Edwin Montagu, would state in the British Parliament in 1917 that the policy of the British government was to gradually develop self-government. In consultation Viceroy Lord Chelmsford and Montagu would present what would become the Government of India Act of 1919. More commonly called the Montagu-Chelmsford reforms, the act would increase Indian representation on the Legislative Council to a majority. It would also create a bicameral system with a Council of State with sixty members and a Central Legislative Assembly with 145 members. Thirty-two of the sixty Council of State members would be elected Indians, and 97 of the 145 Central Legislative Assembly members would be elected Indians. The Executive Council of the Viceroy would now have four British and three Indian members. While the act expanded the powers of the councils, ultimate power rested in the hands of the British viceroy, who could declare any act to be of paramount importance and override the assembly's decision.

Administratively, the British had divided India into provinces and princely states.[3] The Montagu-Chelmsford reforms created councils at the provincial level. Control over nation-building departments was left with the provincial legislature. These included agriculture, public works, health, and education. Finance, revenue, and security were maintained directly under the control of the

British governor. This system, called dyarchy or dual rule, would allow a substantial amount of self-rule for the Indians and much more than the British had granted to any of its other colonies.

The Indian National Congress rejected the Montagu-Chelmsford reforms because they did not go far enough in moving India toward self-government. This rejection led to a split within the movement. Mohandas K. Gandhi (1869–1948), who had begun a mass movement of nonviolent resistance against the British, wanted more power granted to the Indians. His movement had broadened the Congress from its original roots of elitist British-educated intellectuals. The early leaders of the movement came from a British-speaking elite of the country who, for the most part, supported cooperation with the British. This wing was led by Motilal Nehru. This wing of the Congress would contest the Legislative Council elections and become the largest bloc in the council. Both groups were severely affected by the Amritsar massacre of April 13, 1919, when British troops opened fire on unarmed peaceful demonstrators, killing 379 and wounding 1200. The event galvanized both wings of the party and convinced many that independence was the only option for India.

The Montagu-Chelmsford reforms called for a review of the act to determine its effectiveness, which would lead to even greater dissatisfaction. A commission was created in 1927 to evaluate the movement to self-government by the Montagu-Chelmsford reforms but failed to include an Indian member. In anger, the Indian National Congress prepared a constitution for India. The British rejected the constitutional proposal, and the Indian National Congress, at its 1929 annual meeting, demanded complete independence from Britain.

To slow down the growing dissatisfaction with their rule, the British held a roundtable conference in London in 1930. These efforts would fail as differences between the Muslims and Hindus would emerge and prevent the two groups from presenting a united front. The Indian nationalist leadership was beginning to sense that British rule in India was destined to end and increased its pressure on the British.

The British would try one more time to offer reforms leading to self-government. The Government of India Act of 1935 was an effort to create dyarchy at the national level and thus provide more power and influence to the Indians. The act also sought to make India into a federal system by giving some autonomy to the provincial (state) governments. However, the act would not be implemented at the national level and the federal provisions would be blocked by the leaders of the princely states, who saw the reforms eroding their limited autonomy.

British efforts for reform were stalled with the advent of World War II. The British restricted freedoms for the Indians and incurred the wrath of the Indian

National Congress leadership. The viceroy unilaterally declared India at war without consulting the provincial or princely leaders. The Indian National Congress boycotted the government while one nationalist, Subhas Chandra Bose, formed the Indian National Army and fought with the Japanese in Burma to overthrow the British. In response, the British jailed most of the Congress leadership for the duration of the war.

During the war, opposition to the war would weaken the Indian National Congress and its influence with the British. Meanwhile, the Muslim League would pledge its full support to the British war effort and gain influence with the British.

Independence and Partition

At the end of World War II, the British were ready to give India its independence. They also appeared to support a united India. A British cabinet mission was sent to India in 1946 and proposed a loose federation for independent India. Under the proposal, the provinces would hold the most power while the central government would be limited to defense, foreign affairs, currency, taxation, and communication. They also proposed that the provinces could come together into three regional groups One group would comprise the Punjab, Sindh, the North-West Frontier Province, and Baluchistan. These provinces roughly correspond to modern-day Pakistan and would have been a Muslim majority region. A second group would have been Bengal and Assam in India's east. It too would be a Muslim majority group. The rest of India would comprise the third group and would be Hindu majority. The plan was accepted by the Muslim League but rejected by the Congress. As a result, the proposal was abandoned.

Support for the creation of Hindu and Muslim Indias would gain strength after the 1946 cabinet mission collapsed. The Congress would reluctantly agree to the partition while the Muslim League would actively advocate for it. Lord Mountbatten arrived in India in 1947 as the new viceroy and on June 3, 1947, would announce his partition plan. The Indian provinces were divided on the basis of their religious makeup, one in the west and the other in the east. As a result, two noncontiguous sections were drawn for Pakistan. The other provinces would become India. The 565 princely states were given the choice of which country to join. Seventy-two days later, India was divided and on August 15, 1947, both countries were granted independence from Great Britain.

The partition became one of the greatest humanly made tragedies in history. Fifteen million people would be displaced and forced to flee to lands where they had never lived. Hundreds of thousands would die in the violence that each side would exact against the other. The wounds caused by the division have taken many decades to heal. More importantly, as the following chapters will present, the trauma from the partition has helped define the challenges faced by modern India, Pakistan, and Bangladesh. All three countries have sought to define their national identities and to overcome the anger and resentment left by the partition.

The Crown Colony of Ceylon

Ceylon (now Sri Lanka) was governed separately by the British. After the Portuguese arrived in 1505, they were forced out by the Dutch, and in 1802 the British would establish it as a crown colony. Initially, the British controlled the coastal areas only. The Sri Lankan kingdom of Kandy continued to exist in the central hill country of the island and resisted efforts by each of the colonial powers to conquer it until the British finally succeeded in 1818.

Ceylon adapted more quickly to Western education and the British system of administration. As a result, the British were more willing to let the local population join the civil service of the colony. In addition, an executive council and legislative council were created in 1833 as a result of the Colebrooke Commission. In the 1920s, the council was given a Sri Lankan majority and the councils were given more power over finances than the Indian Legislative Council. Self-rule in Ceylon advanced more rapidly than it did in India. In 1931, a state council elected by the people took over much of the power of government. Although the governor still retained control, Ceylon was, for all practical purposes, self-governing.

As in India, a cabinet commission was sent to discuss independence in 1945. A constitution was modeled on the British Westminster system of government and on February 4, 1948, Ceylon would become an independent member of the British Commonwealth. Independence was achieved without the violence or conflict that accompanied Indian independence.

Nepal

Nepal's history during the British era differed from that of the other countries of the region. The Himalaya mountains formed a barrier that blocked British expansion into the Himalayan countries (Tibet, Sikkim, Nepal, and Bhutan). However, the mountains did not completely eliminate British influence.

The modern era of Nepal begins with the conquest of the country under the king of Gurkha, Prithyi Narayan Shah. He captured the Kathmandu valley in 1768 and established the Shah dynasty. Before the defeat of the kingdom of the Kathmandu valley, his opponents had sought and received the assistance of the British East India Company. On his way to victory, Prithyi Narayan defeated the British in 1767.

The Nepalese would go to war with the British from 1814 to 1816 over the low-land strip of land at the foot of the Himalayas, the Terai region. Although the Nepalese inflicted large losses on the British, the Nepalese would be forced to cede large segments of the Terai to the British and to allow a British representative to be housed in Kathmandu. The loss in the war would increase British influence over Nepal but did not lead to the British colonization of Nepal. In 1923, the British signed an agreement with the Nepalese to accept their independence.

The modern political systems of South Asia are a product of their past along with the events since the British left. The following chapters will describe and analyze the events and reasons for the creation of the current political affairs in the region.

NOTES

1. Data in this introduction are taken from World Bank, *World Development Report, 2007* (New York: Oxford University Press, 2007); and United Nations Development Program, *Human Development Report, 2007/2008* (New York: Oxford University Press, 2007); or online at World Bank, *Human Development Report 2007/2008,* http://hdr.undp.org/en.

2. The term "factory" referred to a place where traders and merchants gathered to carry on business in a foreign country.

3. The territorial divisions of British India were termed "provinces." The term is still used in Pakistan and was used in India until the 1950 constitution was enacted. Since then, in India, the major divisions have been termed "states."

SUGGESTED READINGS

A useful overview of Indian history is Stanley Wolpert, *A New History of India,* 5th ed. (New York: Oxford University Press, 1997). For nearly encyclopedic coverage of the British period, see the venerable *Oxford History of India,* 3d ed. (New York: Oxford University Press, 1958); this is an update of the original work by Vincent A. Smith. A new, multivolume Cambridge history of India is under preparation, with many volumes already in print. Still a standard work is Arthur Berriedale Keith, *A Constitutional History of India* (Allahabad: Central Book Depot, 1961).

For information on Ceylon (Sri Lanka), see W. Howard Wriggins, *Ceylon: Dilemmas of a New Nation* (Princeton: Princeton University Press, 1960). For Nepal, see Leo E. Rose and John T. Scholz, *Nepal: Profile of a Himalayan Kingdom* (Boulder: Westview, 1980).

For further discussions of specific topics in this chapter as well as others in this book, see Maureen L.P. Patterson, *South Asian Civilizations: A Bibliographic Synthesis* (Chicago: University of Chicago Press, 1981), which can be supplemented by the annual Bibliography of Asian Studies, published by the Association for Asian Studies, now online.

PART I

INDIA

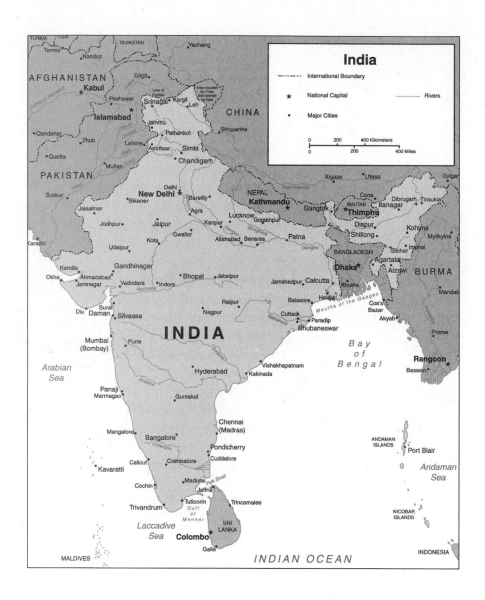

2

Political Culture and Heritage

India's difficulties in nation building, economic development, and political stability have been strongly influenced by a host of complex factors, most prominently its geographical setting, its sociocultural history, and a pattern of continuous external interventions. India is the largest state on the South Asian subcontinent. One-third the size of the United States—about 1,266,595 square miles—it is a country of great distances. From the Himalayan mountains in the north to the Indian Ocean in the south, the distance is 2,000 miles, and it is some 1,700 miles from the western border with Pakistan to the eastern border with Burma. These distances and elevational changes mean that India has a wide variety of climates and landscapes, from snow-covered mountains and lush green forests to dry brown plains and sandy deserts.

Geographically, India is divided into three main regions, each having its own culture, traditions, and history. The various subregions add to the country's variety of lifestyles and traditions. The first region consists of the vast plains of north India, irrigated by the Ganges River and its tributaries. Originating in the Himalayas, the sacred Ganges runs more than 1,500 miles through several states of India until it reaches the Bay of Bengal. The silt deposited by the river enriches the soil of the vast northern plains, where agriculture is the main livelihood of the people. It was in the Ganges valley in ancient times that the Hindu civilization flourished.

The second region, the Deccan plateau, is separated from the north by the Vindhya mountains and from the coastal areas by the Eastern and Western Ghats, which form a kind of mountain wall. Although rich in mineral resources, the plateau receives little rainfall; hence it is not heavily populated, in contrast to the other regions of India. In this region the people and the cultures of north and south intermingle.

The third region, farther south near the port city of Chennai (formerly Madras), is the ancient land of the Tamils and the heartland of the Dravidian people. This southern peninsula has been free from any extended domination by invaders and has preserved the ancient traditions of Hinduism.

India's society is basically agrarian. Despite rapid strides in industrialization since 1947, when India became independent, 80 percent of its population still relies on agriculture for a living. The fortunes of Indian farmers, who live in thousands of tiny villages, depend on the erratic monsoon, which can cause disastrous floods or droughts. Although with recent improvements in irrigation, varieties of seeds, and petroleum-based fertilizer the government has succeeded in increasing the country's agricultural output, the majority of Indian farmers remain untouched by these developments. Efforts by India's political elites to raise the standard of living of the country's more than a billion people and to bring them into the modern age are complicated by sociocultural practices, rural poverty, and economic policies that favor industrialization, the middle class, economic growth, and rigid labor laws. The 2004 elections gave a new emphasis to a commitment to develop the countryside and build infrastructure to help economic growth and the rural poor.

Sociocultural Plurality: Historical Roots

Historians often divide Indian history into three distinct periods: Hindu, Muslim, and British. Each period left its impact on the cultural and sociopolitical structure of the country, leading to a composite culture enriched by these diverse sources.

Ancient Hindu Heritage

The origins of Hindu India may be traced back to the Indus Valley civilization of Harappa and Mohenjodaro. The civilization was highly developed and thrived from 2000 to 1500 B.C. It is now believed to be the source of many elements of Indian society and Hinduism. Archeological evidence discovered in the Indus Valley since the 1970s has challenged an earlier theory of Indian development which attributed Hinduism and Indian culture to the Aryans, who migrated to India from central Asia around 1500 B.C., entering India through Afghanistan and the Hindu Kush mountains. The Aryans, who have been described as sharp featured, handsome, tall, and fair skinned, were nomadic. Their early settlements were located in northwest India, particularly in the Punjab (which means the "land of five rivers").

While the theory of the Aryan invasion attributes much of Indian culture and development to the Aryans, the archeological evidence from the Indus Valley has revealed that many of the contributions originally attributed to the Aryans existed before they arrived. In any case, the Sanskrit language developed. Sanskrit was subsequently discovered by philologists to be Indo-European, or similar to the languages spoken by the people who settled in Iran and various parts of Europe. The languages spoken in present-day north India and in the western states of Maharashtra and Gujarat (along with the Sinhala Language of Sri Lanka) belong to this Indo-European family of languages.

The development of Hinduism took centuries; the religion is evolutionary in nature and reflects a great deal of local and regional variation. Around 1200 B.C. the followers of Hinduism started composing hymns that were collected into the Vedas, the early Hindu scripture. The Vedas are the "oldest known literature in any Indo-European language."[1] Later, in the post-Vedic period, the early Indians began discussing fundamental philosophical questions and speculating about the nature of the universe and the meaning of human life. These discussions have been summed up in the Darshanas, the literature that provides the intellectual heritage of Hindus.

Although there is no one source of Hindu religious thought, the two great epics composed in Sanskrit, the Ramayana and the Mahabharata, have profoundly influenced the religious, cultural, and literary worlds of the Hindus. These two epics describe the period between 1000 and 700 B.C., and their heroes and heroines have been the subjects of writings in all Indian languages, including the languages of south India. Even today the stories in these two epics are told to children in Hindu families. The Bhagavadgita (Song of God), which is a part of the Mahabharata, is the most frequently cited Hindu sacred work.

During the Vedic period a complex social structure developed. It is based on the caste system, in which the priests (Brahmins) and the warriors (Kshatriyas) occupied the highest positions, the traders (Vaishyas) the middle, and the menials (Sudras) the lowest. Despite repeated attacks on the caste system by subsequent reform-oriented social and religious movements, it still exists in India and has a strong impact on the sociopolitical behavior of Hindus. (This aspect of Hindu society is discussed in detail in the following chapter.)

Although ancient Hinduism was not egalitarian—it asserted that different classes are needed to perform different social functions—it nevertheless emphasized kindliness and tolerance of other human beings. The ethics of Hinduism required ritualistic sacrifices but also emphasized such personal virtues as honesty, hospitality, and "piety, in the sense of such religious acts as worship, pilgrimage, and the feeding of cows and brahmans."[2]

The most important challenge to the teachings of Hinduism and its hierarchical social order in ancient India came from Buddhism and Jainism, which were founded almost at the same time by two princes born into Kshatriya families. In the late sixth and early fifth centuries B.C., Gautama Buddha (563–483 B.C.) turned ascetic, propounded his teachings, and established a new order of followers. These followers emphasized truthfulness, nonviolence, eschewing of hatred, purity of heart, and love for fellow human beings irrespective of caste or class considerations. Vardhaman Mahavir (599–527 B.C.), the founder of Jainism, was equally emphatic on personal virtues as opposed to the ritualistic sacrifices practiced by Hindu Brahmins, but Mahavir placed far greater emphasis on self-discipline and nonviolence than the Buddha had done. Most of the religious writings of Buddhism and Jainism were in vernaculars rather than Sanskrit. Even though royal patronage was extended to Buddhism, Hinduism was able to reassert itself and become the predominant religion of the subcontinent. Buddhists and Jains survive today as small religious minorities.

The cultural heritage of Hindus was also influenced by pre-Islamic Persia and especially by ancient Greece. Even before Alexander the Great invaded India in 326 B.C., it was in touch with Greece through Persia. Many scholars find close parallels between early Greek and Indian schools of philosophy. After the Greek invasion several Greek imperial outposts were set up in India; many were eventually absorbed into the cultural groups of north India.

Although various Hindu kingdoms were founded from time to time in both the north and the south, they never established control over the entire subcontinent of India. Most of these kingdoms were regional in nature, and the founders were unable to build a type of government that could survive the demise of the ruling dynasty.

There was little discussion of the theoretical basis of politics and political institutions in Hindu India. Unlike the ancient Greeks, the ancient Hindus did not develop a formal political philosophy. The authors who wrote on state and government actually expounded the elements of statecraft rather than the theoretical issues of politics.

Evidence suggests the existence of both monarchical and republican forms of government. In some cases monarchs were advised by a council of ministers; in others they were absolute rulers. In essence the Hindu system was authoritarian and feudalistic in structure. Even in republics the power belonged to the elders of the tribes or to the leaders of the guilds and community groups rather than to the ordinary citizens.[3] In any case, the Hindus, who had made rich contributions to the development of civilization in India, largely failed to display a constructive ability to build stable political institutions.[4]

By the end of the tenth century A.D., Hindu civilization had lost its dynamism and creativity. Hindu society had become stagnant and rigid. The rulers of the various Hindu kingdoms displayed no sense of nationalism or patriotism and were unable to withstand the onslaught of hardy Muslim invaders from the northwest.

The Muslim Heritage

The advent of Islam in India proved to be a different story. Broadly speaking, the interaction between Muslims and Hindus in India followed three patterns. The first was terrorism: Muslim invaders came to plunder and slaughter the native population, leaving in their wake a trail of death and destruction. Mahmud of Ghazni, a Turk by descent, typifies this early aspect of India's contact with Islam. In A.D. 1000, he repeatedly invaded India in order to plunder its wealthy towns and cities and particularly the fabulous offerings of gold and cash stored in Hindu temples. A devout Muslim, Mahmud concentrated his destructive tactics on nonbelievers. His example was later followed by Tamerlane, Nadir Shah of Persia, and Ahmad Shah Abdali of Afghanistan, although they were less religiously motivated than Mahmud and discriminated little between Muslim and Hindu gentry while looting. Most of these invaders went back to their native lands and did not settle in India.

The second pattern of Muslim invasion was characterized by the Muslim conquest, settlement, and founding of kingdoms in parts of western and northern India. This pattern is evident, for example, in the Arab conquest of Sindh in 712 by Muhammad bin Qasim, who founded an Arab kingdom and forced the Hindus to convert to Islam. This pattern of conquest was followed from the twelfth to the sixteenth centuries until the establishment of the Mughal empire. During this period, divided Hindu kingdoms fell, one after another, to the Muslim invaders of Turkish, Persian, and Afghan origin. Although the Muslims left a majority of the resident Hindu population alone, some were subjected to humiliation and discrimination, and occasionally to torture and forcible conversion to Islam. Many of these Muslim kingdoms were short-lived and ruled by transient dynasties, and most of them were unstable. The early Muslim rulers failed to build an efficient system of administration, and the organizational abilities they displayed were no better than those of their Hindu predecessors.

The founding of the Mughal empire in the sixteenth century represented the third pattern of interactions. Not only did the Mughal rulers conquer most of India, but they also established a stable and centralized administration directed from Lahore, Agra, and Delhi. The founder of the Mughal empire was Babur, who conquered Delhi in 1526. But it was Babur's grandson, Akbar, who during his long rule (1556–1605) laid the foundation of the Mughal empire in north India. During his reign and those of his three successors, India achieved political stability unmatched in the history of Muslim India.

The Mughals were not only the new rulers; they were also the newest settlers in India. In the process they actively integrated the Hindus into both the civil and military administrations. In addition, they tried to reach across the religious divide to create a more coherent society by making matrimonial alliances with the Hindu princely houses of Rajasthan. Many of the Mughals, especially Akbar (who was highly rationalist in his orientation), were opposed to the orthodox and dogmatic Islamic traditions. They tried to create a composite Indian culture incorporating both Hindu and Muslim values. But Islam, unlike many other religious movements of the past, was a young, vibrant, and aggressive religious force that could not be absorbed by Hinduism.

Some progress was made during this period in uniting Hindus and Muslims in a composite culture. A powerful part of the Bhakti (devotional) movement criticized the orthodoxies of both Hindu Brahmins and Muslim ulema (religious scholars). Nanak, Kabir, and many other saint poets emphasized a devotee's personal relationship with his god and tried to synthesize the teachings of Islam and Hinduism. Among the Muslims, similar efforts were made by the Sufis, who were influenced by Hindu mysticism.[5] As a result, many places of worship were established that were frequented by both Muslims and Hindus. Yet despite these efforts, the fundamental division and a sense of latent hostility continued between Hindus and Muslims throughout India. No religious or social movement was able to bridge the deep gulf between the two religious communities.

The Mughal empire brought progress in other areas, however. In addition to building forts and beautiful palaces and mausoleums, the Persian-speaking Mughal rulers patronized Urdu, which is written in Persian script. As a language it is rich in literary traditions, and it was spoken by cultivated people in and around Delhi, the principal seat of the Mughal empire. But even though both Hindus and Muslims contributed to the development of Urdu literature, a majority of Hindus considered Urdu and its literature to be symbols of Muslim culture.

In contemporary India Hindu nationalists regard the Muslim period of Indian history as a period of alien rule and subjugation. For them the desecration of Hindu temples and the slaughter of innocent followers of Hinduism are too painful to be forgotten, and the defeats of Hindu kings at the hands of Muslim invaders are shameful episodes of Indian history. The religious tolerance of Akbar, they assert, was only an exception, for his successors gave up this policy. Instead, following Islamic orthodoxy, they prohibited interreligious marriages, pulled down Hindu temples, and even imposed jizya (poll tax) on Hindus. Hindu nationalists today have disowned Urdu language and literature and instead consider Hindi to be the language of north India.

In contrast, secularist Hindus and nationalist Indian Muslims emphasize the positive side of the Muslim rule in India. They look upon the Mughal empire, its architectural achievements, and Urdu literary traditions as an important part of India's cultural heritage. For example, Jawaharlal Nehru, a leader of the freedom movement and the first prime minister of India, displayed a high regard for the Muslim contributions to Indian civilization. Nevertheless, the two contradictory attitudes toward the Muslim period persist in the contemporary politics of India.

British Rule and the Contact with the West

In the third period of Indian history, British supremacy was firmly established in 1858, when the queen-in-council took over the direct administration of India, replacing the East India Company (see Chapter 1). British rule brought India face-to-face with a dynamic, creative, and vibrant culture. The British displayed far better administrative and organizational skills than did any of the earlier ruling classes of India. Not only did they establish control over India and achieve territorial integration, but they also founded a centralized administration that could not be challenged easily.

The territorial integration of the country was strengthened by the building of an extensive network of highways, railroads, and post and telegraph systems. Such a system not only enabled the British to exploit India as a vast market for the sale of its manufactured goods, but it also gave the Indians a mobility within their own country that they had never before experienced. Trade between different parts of India expanded rapidly, and by the time the British left, India had developed a national economy that strengthened the unity among different regions of the country.

The efficient administrative machinery built by the British and the merit-based system of recruitment to bureaucracy they introduced are two of the important traditions inherited by the Indians from this period. The foundation of this system of administration at the district level had been laid earlier by the Mughals, in which the local and the provincial administrators would act as the agents of the central government. But the British introduced a high degree of uniformity in both the civil and the judicial administration; in addition, the administrative system possessed objectivity and impersonality, qualities not found in the previous system of administration. Such a system established rule of law, respect for personal liberty, and equality of all persons of Indian origin, regardless of religion. Administratively, India became one—an achievement unparalleled in the political history of India.

The Western system of education brought a slow though radical transformation of the value structure and behavior patterns of Indian intellectuals. The new system of civil and judicial administration made the English language and education a valuable avenue for achieving political influence, economic power, and social mobility. Thus it came as no surprise when thousands of Indians started flocking to the newly established institutions of higher learning that provided instruction in English. This system of education produced a new class of professionals and enlarged the size of the urban middle class; it also exposed Indian elites to the constitutional liberalism and democratic socialism propounded by English utilitarians and Fabian socialists. The democratic ideals of liberty, equality, and social justice gradually took root among the members of the intellectual establishment of the country. In short, the knowledge of English brought the upper classes of India in contact with the West, thus injecting a new dynamism into an ancient civilization.

The British impact, however, was not uniform throughout India. Princely India, with a few notable exceptions, remained feudal and isolated, and many regions of the country were slow to respond to the new ideas and values. In some parts of the subcontinent the feudal order was dismantled, but in other areas it survived.

In the nation-building and modernization process, the unevenness of the British impact created problems for the elites in the post-independence period. The pace of modernization and development of a national identity has been faster in those communities that had a higher exposure to the Western impact.

Quest for National Identity: The Cultural Revival and the Nationalist Movement

One of the most remarkable developments of the British period of Indian history was the growth of a national sense of unity among the elites from urban areas who practiced law or medicine or other professional occupations. These professionals had received their training in English, but although they were as qualified as their English counterparts, they were never considered their equals. The average British ruler in India looked down on the native culture and its practitioners. The resultant sense of humiliation and status deprivation brought these Indian people together and forced them, despite their diverse ethnic and religious origins, to think about the political issues in all-India terms.

The English system of education and contact with the West brought the Indian elites in touch with nationalism as an ideological force at a time when it was at its zenith in Europe. Moreover, the English language provided communication links among the urban elites, who originated from different provinces and therefore spoke different native languages. Members of this elite class rose above the ascriptive and primordial ties characteristic of traditional India and propagated a national vision of India.

Nationalism as a movement was preceded by cultural revivalism and a social reform movement. Contact with the West through the British forced Indians, especially Hindus, to examine critically the structure of Hindu society. Through this process of self-examination, Hindu elites became painfully aware of the deficiencies of Hindu society, which was permeated with social customs that could not be justified on rational or even religious grounds. The elites saw Hindu society as dominated by superstitions, idolatry, magical myths, and many reprehensible social customs. If Hinduism was to save itself from the onslaught of Western culture and proselytizing Christian missions supported by the British Empire, its critical need was not only to get rid of social evils but also to reorganize its structure on a more rational basis. Consequently, an upsurge of social reform movements occurred in different parts of the country. Some reformers sought a synthesis of Hinduism, Western liberalism, and selective principles of Christianity while others emphasized the glories of Hindu India and hoped to restore to it the essential Vedic values they felt had been lost in the course of subjugation of Hindus during the Muslim rule. Raja Ram Mohan Roy (1774–1833), a Bengali thinker and reformer, exemplified the first group of reformers. A learned person who had studied the scriptures of Christianity, Islam, and Hinduism and who knew many languages, including Sanskrit, Arabic, English, Hebrew, and Persian, he was deeply influenced by the rationalist philosophies of the West. He strongly disapproved of idol worship, the caste system, the inferior status of women, untouchability, and other social evils of Hinduism. In order to propagate his reformist views he founded the Brahmo Samaj, an organization that contributed a great deal to social reform and to the stimulation of cultural and intellectual activities in Bengal and in several other parts of India.

The second type of social reform movement, seeking social reforms coupled with Hindu revivalism, was reflected in the writings and activities of Swami Dayanand (1824–1883), a Gujarati Brahmin who sought to legitimize the reform of Hindu society on the basis of a reinterpretation of the Vedas. These ancient Hindu scriptures, Dayanand felt, not only contained sacred knowledge but were the source of all philosophical and scientific thought as well. He glorified the Hindu past and sought to purify contemporary Hinduism by getting rid of the caste system, untouchability, idol worship, and other superstitions. Such evil social practices, he stressed, were introduced into Hinduism by selfish Brahmins, who used them to perpetuate their dominance of Hindu society. In his quest to create a sense of pride among Hindus, he virulently attacked both Islam and Christianity. Dayanand was a staunch nationalist who thought social reform should precede swarajya (self-rule).

The Arya Samaj, a social reform movement founded by Dayanand in 1875, became closely associated with educational activities, especially with the spread of English education through the Dayanand Anglo-Vedic (DAV) college movement in northwest India. In subsequent years many leaders of the Arya Samaj movement joined hands with the protagonists of Hindu nationalism.

In south India, the Theosophical Society became instrumental in both cultural revival and social reform among Hindus. The society worked to establish the superiority of Hindu philosophy over Western philosophy. Annie Besant (1847–1933), an Englishwoman who was deeply influenced by Hindu philosophy, became a major spokesperson for the society; she helped popularize its teachings and create a high degree of cultural pride among middle-class Hindus of south India.

But there was another group of reformers, consisting of intellectuals and professionals, who were deeply influenced by the rationalist thinking of the West. Although they were committed to preserve the basic institutions of Hindu society and its value system, they believed that it needed reform and reorganization in order to face the challenge of modern times. They held that patience, endurance, and understanding were needed to accomplish such changes, not a frontal assault on the traditional Hindu leadership. They sought these gradual changes by founding educational institutions, cultural organizations, research foundations, science and religious study groups, reading rooms, libraries, and so on. Justice M. G. Ranade (1842–1901) and R. C. Bhandarkar in Maharashtra and Debendranath Tagore (1817–1905) in Bengal represented this more secular route toward social reform among Hindus.

Originally, contact with the West had created a sense of cultural inferiority among the English-educated Hindus. Swami Vivekanand (1863–1902) and his associates sought to counter this image by comparing Hinduism and Western culture. A powerful speaker and a charismatic personality, Vivekanand called on Hindus to take pride in their spiritual heritage and attacked Western culture as inferior. For him, "the backbone, the foundation and the bedrock of India's national life was India's spiritual genius," which the West did not possess.[6]

The overall consequence was an unprecedented cultural revival among Hindus. Interest in classical Sanskrit writings and Hindu art and philosophy was stimulated by an outpouring of European scholarship in praise of India's cultural heritage. It was not surprising, therefore, that the glorification of Indian history became a staple of writings in various regional languages of India. In addition, literary elites and political leaders used Hindu religious symbols to arouse patriotism. They identified Indian nationalism with Hinduism and deified the motherland. Recollection of the glories of the past was essential to the creation of a sense of national respect and a new national identity.

But in this process of cultural revival and resurgence of Hindu nationalism, Muslims were left out. Initially, the Indian Muslims' reaction to British rule was to withdraw within the shell of their own community and their self-imposed isolation from the new ideas that British rule had generated in Indian society. Sir Syed Ahmad Khan (1817–1898) brought the Muslims into the modern world by establishing in 1875 the Mohammadan Anglo-Oriental College at Aligarh (now known as Aligarh Muslim University). Syed Ahmad Khan strongly emphasized the revival of the Muslims' pride in their heritage, preservation of the Muslim subnational identity, and the reconciliation of the Muslims' interests with British rule in India. Aligarh produced the main elements of the Western-educated Muslim intelligentsia, who became the vanguard of Muslim separatism in Indian politics.

In a politically and administratively united India, the cultural revitalization movement, as in other parts of South Asia, especially in Sri Lanka, led to the rise of a well-organized nationalist movement. The impetus for the organization of a national association that would speak on behalf of all Indians was provided, ironically, by the racially motivated policies of the British government, which discriminated against Indians in their own land. Even though, for instance, recruitment of Indians into the Indian Civil Service (ICS), the most prestigious bureaucratic organization in British India, was promised as early as 1858, all efforts were made to block the Indians' entry into such services. When an Indian such as Surendranath Banerjea (1848–1926) was successful in entering the ICS, he was dismissed on flimsy grounds. Indians faced further humiliation when Englishmen living in India were successful in withdrawing the Ilbert Bill of 1883, which had permitted the trial of a European in a court presided over by an Indian judge. Events such as this forced Indians to seek a national forum not only to articulate their demands and to protest this discrimination but also to consolidate their ranks to force the attention of the British government in India to their needs. The result was the establishment of the Indian National Congress in 1885.

From its very inception, the Indian National Congress became intertwined with the nationalist movement in the country. This movement underwent several phases, however, and revealed considerable tension among its various leaders and factions with respect to both the ultimate goals of the movement and the methods to achieve these goals. Fortunately for India, its struggle for freedom was spread over a long period of time; the leaders of the movement were thus permitted the opportunity to debate openly the kind of society and polity to be built once India achieved independence. By contrast, the Pakistan movement was not only single issue oriented, but it was also dominated by one powerful leader, Muhammad Ali Jinnah, who displayed little tolerance for dissent within his ranks. Not surprisingly, then, the Indian political elites at the time of India's independence were much better prepared to tackle the issues of institution building and economic development than were the leaders of Pakistan.

The first phase of the nationalist movement was dominated by the well-to-do segment of Indian society. The leaders representing this segment were steeped in British traditions and education and depended on the British sense of justice; they sought to ameliorate the conditions of Indians through an appeal to the British sense of fairness. Their main objective was to seek greater representation of educated Indians in the civil services and to introduce representative institutions at the provincial and local levels. They did not entertain the hope of complete independence from British rule; rather, they believed that continued association with the British Empire was in the interests of Indians. Surendranath Banerjea, who was twice elected president of the Indian National Congress, asserted that English civilization was the "noblest the world has ever seen, a civilization fraught with unspeakable blessings to the people of India."[7] These nationalists took pride in their citizenship in the British Empire and sought to propagate values of British liberalism throughout the country. During this period such men as Dadabhai Nauroji (1825–1917), Justice M. G. Ranade, and Pherozshah Mehta (1845–1915), all products of the British system of education, led the Indian National Congress and pressured the British government to address the problems. The British tried to defuse this pressure by passing the Government of India Act of 1909 (known as the Morley-Minto Act; see Chapter 1), which expanded political participation and electoral representation at both the provincial and central government levels. The representatives to the legislative councils were to be elected by voters holding property or having high educational qualifications. This measure also introduced separate representation for the Muslims, who were to elect their representatives from their own community.

In the second nationalist phase, starting in 1905, the struggle for the control of the Indian National Congress was divided between the "moderates," led by Gopal Krishna Gokhale (1866–1915), and the "extremists," led by Bal Gangadhar Tilak (1856–1920). These two leaders, both Maharashtrian Brahmins, differed not only in their personalities and ideological orientations but also in their approaches to achieving self-rule for the country. Gokhale was a disciple of Ranade, a moderate, and even though he was much more vocal in his criticism of British government than Ranade, he believed in constitutional methods. He did not hesitate to work with British rulers, and he tried to represent Indians in the Imperial Legislative Council, where he was a member.

Bal Gangadhar Tilak and his extremist associates, on the other hand, did not trust the British government. Tilak was a Hindu nationalist and an ardent believer in the superiority of Hindu culture over Western culture. In his opposition to the moderates, Tilak was supported by Lala Lajpat Rai of the Punjab and Bipan Chandra Pal and Aurobindo Ghose of Bengal. These extremists were militant and provided philosophical justification for the use of violence against the alien rulers of India. Unlike the moderates, the extremists asserted that political freedom could be won only by waging a war against the enemy. Whereas the moderates believed that they would be able to achieve self-government with the blessings of British rulers, the extremist Tilak declared, "Swaraj [self-rule] is my birthright and I will have it." Also unlike Gokhale and his associates, the extremists openly used Hindu religious symbols and traditions to stimulate nationalist sentiments among the masses. They never stopped attacking the moderates for their subservience to Western culture.

In 1907 the extremists lost out to Gokhale and his moderate associates in their struggle to control the Congress organization. But British suppression, Tilak's confinement in Mandalay, the arrests of Pal and Ghose, and the political exile of Lala Lajpat Rai turned the extremists into popular heroes. By 1915 a reconciliation between the two factions had occurred, and Tilak and his associates once again became active within the Congress party. The united nationalist leadership of the Indian National Congress demanded and was promised by the British a large measure of self-government at the end of World War I.

This second nationalist phase also witnessed the rise of self-assertiveness among the minorities. The emergence of the Hindu-dominated Indian National Congress at center stage in Indian politics and the fear that Hindus would become the rulers of the country owing to their overwhelming majority in the population spurred the Muslims into political activity, resulting in the organization of the All-India Muslim League in 1906. The Muslims demanded separate representation and allied themselves with the British, seeking their favor and protection against what the Muslims perceived as the aggressiveness of the Hindu-dominated Indian National Congress. Given the pluralistic structure of Indian society, the rise of such particularistic movements was not surprising. However, the leaders of the nationalist movement underestimated the strength of these subcultural and regional movements in perceiving the problem of national integration to be primarily a political one.

The end of World War I brought about a radical transformation in the political expectations and aspirations of Indians. The British government responded by enacting the Government of India Act of 1919 (known as the Montagu-Chelmsford reforms; see Chapter 1). This act introduced partial responsible government in the provinces; increased the number of elected representatives in the central legislative assembly; gave separate representation to the Sikhs, the Europeans settled in India, and the Anglo-Indians (Eurasians); and extended voting rights to almost 10 percent of the adult population of the country. Even though these steps provided opportunities for Indians to learn about parliamentary government, to organize voters for electoral purposes, and to gain experience in self-government, they did not satisfy the political aspirations of the nationalist leaders. Their alienation from the British rulers in India was increased by the continuation of the repressive policies that the government had adopted during the war. The British government still possessed enormous powers to restrict civil liberties, to imprison politically active Indians, and to declare martial law. Increased protests against such repressive measures after World War I resulted in the declaration of martial law and in the Amritsar tragedy (April 13, 1919), in which more than 300 Indians were killed and more than a thousand wounded when General R. E. H. Dyer ordered troops to fire on peaceful and unarmed protesters. This brutal action shocked the Indian nationalists, but the House of Lords, ignoring Indian sentiments, passed a resolution in 1920 in appreciation of General Dyer's services to the empire.

The conflict between the Indian extremists and the British left the moderates outside the mainstream of the nationalist movement. As the extremist faction led by Tilak took over the Congress organization in 1917, the moderates withdrew from the party and founded their own organization, the Indian Liberal Federation. Tilak then became the undisputed leader of the nationalists. After Tilak's death in 1920, the leadership passed into the hands of Mohandas Karamchand Gandhi (1869–1948). Gandhi rejected the moderates' gradualist approach to political reforms, but he also rejected the extremists' philosophical justification of violence. His nonviolent approach, using mass mobilization and peaceful defiance of British authority, radicalized Indian politics far beyond the expectations of Tilak's followers.

During the twenty years he lived in South Africa practicing law among the Indian settlers, Gandhi developed his concept of satyagraha (loosely translated as "soul force") and the technique of civil disobedience. On his return to India, before he plunged into Indian politics, Gandhi traveled widely throughout the country, observing the culture, traditions, and living conditions of the people. He felt that the leaders of the nationalist movement were out of touch with the people who lived in India's many villages. He realized that in order to win freedom from Britain, the nationalist movement required a mass base; it needed to involve the people living in the countryside. Accordingly, Gandhi not only established his headquarters in rural India but also sent the nationalist leaders and party workers to live in the villages, to undertake social service, and to lead simple and austere lives. He enforced strict discipline, emphasized nonviolence, and demanded sacrifices from his followers. This pacifist approach, austere and rigorous life, and complete identification with the common man earned Gandhi the saintly title of the Mahatma (the great soul).

Thus it was only after prolonged observation that Gandhi applied his concept of satyagraha and the technique of civil disobedience to the Indian situation. He called for peaceful breaching of unjust laws; protesting through strikes, fasting, and noncooperation with the authorities; and boycotting not only of imported goods but also of British educational institutions. But he insisted on peaceful defiance of authority, seeking arrest by breaking laws. Soon, thanks to his charismatic personality and simple and saintly lifestyle, Gandhi built a formidable nationwide following for himself as well as for the Indian National Congress. Under his leadership the elitist nationalist movement became a mass movement. Although the top leaders of the Congress organization were still English-educated and upper-class Indians, they were nevertheless able to identify with the cause of the common man. In addition, the second tier of leadership at the provincial and local levels was more attuned to the sensitivities of the masses than any other group in the country. A well-organized vernacular press and an articulate vernacular-speaking intelligentsia established strong links between these national leaders in the center of Indian politics and the mass of Indians living on the periphery.

Thus began the third phase of the nationalist movement, in which the nationalist leadership, with an expanded mass base, started to press for complete independence. During its Lahore session in 1929, the Indian National Congress, no longer willing to accept dominion status and membership in the British Commonwealth of nations, adopted a resolution demanding complete independence for India. During this phase of the nationalistic movement, Gandhi launched several mass drives: the noncooperation movement of 1921, the breaking of salt laws (the salt march) in 1930, and the civil disobedience of 1933. Although the sudden suspension of these movements was criticized by many young and leftist leaders, each of them succeeded in enhancing mass political consciousness and demonstrated Gandhi's ability to mobilize the country. The British government responded by passing the Government of India Act of 1935, which established complete provincial autonomy and proposed partial responsible government at the center. These concessions were no doubt a substantial improvement on the institutional setup created by the Government of India Act of 1919, but they were too little and too late. The nationalist movement had planted deep roots in Indian soil, and Gandhi's Indian National Congress had caught the imagination of the masses. The popularity of the Congress became evident when in the elections of 1937 it won the majority of legislative seats in six provinces; it had become the single largest party and formed the government in eight of eleven provinces in British rule. For the next twenty-eight months (1937–1939), when the party's leadership ran the provincial governments, it not only gained administrative experience but also made substantial progress in social and economic programs for the masses.

It should be noted, however, that while the Indian National Congress represented the nationalist aspirations of a majority of Indians, there were several smaller movements representing the aspirations of religious and regional minorities that could not be absorbed by the nationalist group led by Mahatma

Gandhi. The Muslim League, for example, under the able leadership of Muhammad Ali Jinnah, became a powerful rival of the Indian National Congress, claiming to be the sole representative of the Indian Muslims. Similarly, in Kashmir, the National Conference, under the dynamic leadership of Sheikh Muhammad Abdullah, and, in the Punjab, the Akali Dal, led by Master Tara Singh, represented the Kashmiri Muslims and the Punjabi Sikhs, respectively. During the 1940s the subnational movements gained momentum and became a major challenge to the nationalist goals of the leaders of the Indian National Congress.

The final phase of the nationalist movement (1940–1947) was dominated by the Congress leaders' two concerns: complete independence from British rule and preservation of the territorial unity of India through accommodation of the aspirations of these subnationalist movements, especially the leaders of the Muslim League.

By 1942 it had become evident to the leaders of the Indian National Congress that the British government was in no mood to meet its demands for independence despite the Congress' offer to support the British war efforts against Japan and Germany. In August 1942, therefore, Mahatma Gandhi planned to launch a massive "Quit India" movement. But before the leaders could organize this movement, the British government arrested many of the leaders of the Indian National Congress, including Gandhi. The British were always baffled by the success of Gandhi's methods of nonviolence and uncertain as to how to deal with them. However, a preemptive strike by the government in August 1942 saved it from the unpleasant task of brutalizing Gandhi's nonviolent soldiers. Despite some disruption of the administration, order was restored in a short time.

While the Congress leaders were in jail, the leaders of such subnationalist parties as the Muslim League and the Akali party of the Sikhs were able to consolidate their positions within their respective communities. Toward the end of World War II it became evident to the British government that it would not be able to keep India under control and that it would have to reach an agreement with the nationalist leaders. Hence in 1944 Gandhi and later many of his associates were released.

Once out of jail, the nationalist leaders were confronted with the prospect of independence but also with the possibility that the country might become divided on a religious basis. In 1940 the Muslim League had demanded the creation of a Muslim-majority state out of British India consisting of provinces in which the Muslims formed a majority. The Sikhs, for their part, sought the creation of a Sikh homeland in Punjab, where the Sikh religion had originated. The leaders of the Indian National Congress were ill prepared to face the challenges of rival nationalist groups based on religion; their nationalist ideology, in fact, sought to downgrade the importance of religious divisions in the Indian population.

During the 1945–1946 elections the Muslim League emerged as the representative body of the Muslims of India, capturing 446 of 496 provincial seats in the Muslim-majority provinces of the country. In addition, the Muslim League launched a massive campaign to press its demand for the division of the country. This action resulted in widespread Hindu-Muslim rioting; indeed, there emerged a real threat of civil war in India. Ultimately, the Congress leaders agreed in 1947 to a division of the country on the basis of religion. The demand for Pakistan was conceded, Punjab and Bengal were divided, Muslim-majority areas went to Pakistan, and the rest became parts of India. Such religious and ethnic minorities as the Sikhs were not able at the time to manage sovereign states for themselves, but the desire for separate states persists to this day, especially among a section of the Sikh community. On August 15, 1947, India became independent from Britain; the aspirations of the nationalist leaders were realized. Despite this triumph, however, the religious division of the country proved to be a major setback for their ideology of nationalism. Independence and partition were accompanied by massive Hindu-Muslim rioting and migration in which an estimated half million Hindus, Muslims, and Sikhs perished.

The Indian people still have bitter memories of the partition of the subcontinent and the consequent exchange of population between West Pakistan and the East Punjab State of India. Indeed, the independence movement left a smoldering hostility between the Hindus and the Muslims. The Indian leaders' adherence to the principle of a multicultural and multireligious society in India has caused them to become wary of politicians and parties that make religious demands or seek to alter state boundaries along religious lines. The disintegration of the nationalist movement after independence and the experience of the division of the country have made Indian leaders highly sensitive about the territorial integrity and unity of the country.

Quest for Institution Building and Modernization: The Development of New Goals

Even before independence, questions regarding the future setup of an independent India were frequently discussed among the Indian elites. The dominant sector of the Indian National Congress, the modernists, agreed on the form of government they wanted. Their experience with representative government during the British rule and their observation of the parliamentary system in the United Kingdom fixed their choice on the Westminster model of government.

The elites were convinced that if people could participate in the political process, national unity would be consolidated and the national identity that had been nourished by the cultural revival and the nationalist movement would be strengthened. The establishment of a liberal democracy in India thus became the modernists' new goal, reflecting the Indian leaders' desire for citizen participation in the political process. Freedom of speech and expression was also to become an essential attribute. Conscious of the social and economic disparities in Indian society, the leaders believed that the ideals of democratic socialism would help them to achieve some degree of social and economic equality in the society, with the state actively helping the poor, the backward, and the helpless. The ideology of socialism, they believed, would also strengthen the principles of secular nationalism that they had so ardently championed. In subsequent chapters we will see how successful the contemporary political elites have been in adhering to these ideas.

With independence, India needed modernization and economic development. The nationalist leaders inherited from the British rulers a primarily agricultural economy; an overwhelming majority (80 percent) of the population depended on the land to earn their living. Furthermore, Indian agriculture was one of the most inefficient and backward systems in the world. Indians were hardly able to feed themselves. The land was tormented by frequent droughts, famines, floods, and pestilence. Most of the industries the British had set up were established merely to meet consumers' needs for cotton textiles, sugar, and jute. Despite India's possession of certain strategic raw materials, such as iron ore, coal, mica, bauxite, magnesite, chromite, titanium, and refractory materials, the country lacked a significant capital goods industry. It was heavily dependent on Great Britain and other industrialized countries of the West for its machinery and engineering goods.

The elites agreed on the need to end poverty and raise the standard of living of the people. However, they differed as to the approach they should undertake to achieve these goals. There were two main viewpoints—one advocated by Gandhi and his followers, the other by a more modernist and secular-minded group. Gandhi's approach was the product of his moral and religious orientations. He strongly disapproved of the profit motive, favored strict limits on private property, and opposed the tyranny of machines and the ruthless competition of a market economy. He also favored the development of agricultural and consumers' cooperatives. According to Gandhi, India needed to maintain its agricultural, rural-based economy while redeveloping and expanding its traditional cottage and small-scale industries, which would once again make the village society self-sufficient. His vision of India also recognized the need for low consumption of resources and the development of indigenous technologies suitable for its environment and culture. As the society of India was primarily agricultural and rural, Gandhi's strategy of economic development would have resulted in a higher investment of resources in rural India, where 80 percent of its population lives. Although a labor-intensive development process might not have made India an industrial giant, the belief was that such an effort would have generated more jobs for the poorer segment of Indian society. Such a vision of India, however, was incompatible with the model of a modern industrial state.

Jawaharlal Nehru and his modernist and secularist associates, influenced by Marxist and socialist thought, disagreed with the Gandhian approach to the economic development of India. Nehru looked to science and technology as the key elements in the transformation of the character of Indian society. Technology was perceived as the handmaiden of science; when effectively linked together, the two could eradicate poverty and radically change the face of India. These modernists attributed underdevelopment of societies such as that of India to the insufficiency of technological development. They sought to modernize India through the application of science and technology and through heavy investment in capital goods industries. They believed in centralized planning, increased output of technically skilled labor, and importing of technical know-how to make India ultimately a technologically self-sufficient country. In such a system the state would play a key role; it would set the development priorities. Although no wholesale takeover of industries and businesses would occur, and although private initiative and investment would be allowed, the private sector of the economy was to be subservient to the public needs, which the government alone was capable of defining.

Of these two ideological approaches to India's economic and industrial development, it was Nehru's approach rather than Gandhi's that the political elites preferred. As a result, in industrial and economic development the new goal became the development of an extensive scientific and technological infrastructure based on the model of advanced industrialized societies.

In sum, India's sociocultural background, its history, its geographic diversity, and its demographic diversity, and the socialist character of the evolution of its nationalist movement under the influence of J. L. Nehru (Mahatma Gandhi's chosen successor and India's first prime minister) have rendered the task of nation building and modernization extremely difficult for its leaders. Unlike the political leaders of Pakistan, India's leaders were very clear about the direction in which they wanted their newly independent country to move. Reflecting the religious division of the country, India's political leaders—in contrast to those of Pakistan—refused to adopt the religion of the majority as the state religion. Instead, they opted to build a modern nation-state on the twin principles of democracy and socialism. The development of Indian socialism during the Nehru years (1947–1964) and thereafter produced a pattern of extensive state intervention in India's economic life and a system of bureaucratic and political controls that impeded private sector development and India's participation in the global economy. India took the path of economic reforms a decade after China did and the process was inhibited by resistance to reforms by Indian leftists. This shows the influence of current minority government politics and the role of ideology in India's economic development since 1947.

Social Structure and Political Culture

The stability of a political system is dependent upon the support that it enjoys from its citizens. In return, social institutions transmit sociopolitical values and norms of political behavior. They become instrumental in creating support for the system and enhancing its legitimacy. A description of India's social structure and the nature of its political culture can help us understand the conditions under which the system operates.

India is an ancient civilization but a new nation in the making; the values and attitudes of its citizens, the nature of its political culture, and its political processes are influenced by both its traditional past and its contemporary experience. Indians are proud of the operation of their contemporary democratic institutions and of the uniqueness of their culture, which gives its people a distinct identity.

Through a complex network of primary and secondary structures, the people of India have successfully transmitted several key elements of their cultural and political structure from generation to generation. It is through this process of socialization that India has developed its distinct political culture.

The Dominant Cultural Pattern: The Hindu Worldview

Despite the confluence of the various cultures that have affected the Indian people, the Hindu worldview constitutes the dominant cultural force in the society. The religious teachings of Hinduism and its belief system deeply influence the social behavior and political attitudes of its followers.

Hindus have often been described as otherworldly and fatalistic, because Hinduism teaches that an individual is bound in the cycle of birth and death. It is the karma (the actions in one's life) that determines the nature of one's following life. In order to end the earthly cycles of birth and death, an individual needs salvation through an ultimate union of his soul (atman) with the Supreme Reality (parmatman).

Even though acquisition of material wealth and a desire for enjoyment and reproduction are important for the survival of this world, spiritual salvation through this union of the soul with the Supreme Reality is superior to all other life goals. Therefore, to Hindus the quest for political power and secular activities ought to be secondary to spiritual affairs. In actual life, however, there is a considerable gap between religious prescriptions and an individual's behavior. Thus, despite their emphasis on spiritual values, Hindus continue to pursue vigorously material goals in their lives.

Hinduism, however, is known for its flexibility, sectarian organizations, and religious tolerance. Because there is no organized church or clerical authority among the Hindus as there is among the Christians, there is no uniform enforcement of the rules among Hindus. God may be perceived and worshiped in many ways. Not only may individuals choose different paths to reach the Supreme Reality, but also they are free to worship deities of their own choice. Hindus are therefore divided into numerous sects, each having its own deity, temples, and rituals. This kind of flexibility is nowhere more evident than in the villages of India, where the majority of Indians live. Their belief system enables Hindus to live side by side with the followers of such other religions as Buddhism, Jainism, and Christianity without friction. Peaceful coexistence between Hinduism and Islam, however, has been difficult to achieve.

Although Hindus are flexible in their religious practices, they do tend to separate politics from religion. These characteristics of Hinduism have enabled the predominantly Hindu political elites of India to build the political institutions of the new republic on secular principles.

The Caste System

Despite its flexibility in other areas, Hinduism retains one of the world's most highly structured and stratified social orders, the caste system. This traditional social order divides Hindus into a hierarchical structure consisting of four castes: the Brahmins (priests and custodians of sacred knowledge), Kshatriyas (warriors and rulers), Vaishyas (traders), and Sudras (persons performing manual labor and menial jobs). In this hierarchical social order the Brahmins occupy the top position and the Sudras the lowest. Today the caste system has become ascriptive in its nature; high-caste origin and high social status usually go together. Thus a person born into a particular caste rarely has an opportunity to change status within the society, regardless of his or her talent and achievements. In rural India the system has also created a highly segregated residential pattern in which the Sudras live on the outskirts of the villages and towns, away from the high-caste neighborhood. Some sections of Sudras have been treated as "untouchable" by the members of the upper castes because their hereditary occupations (such as scavenging and leather working) have been considered unclean. Even after the legal abolition of untouchability in post independence India, the practice is still prevalent in many sections of Hindu society, especially in rural India. In addition, many native tribes who earlier did not believe in Hinduism have now adopted many of its practices and traditions but are not yet considered part of mainstream Hindu society. Although in theory Hinduism may be one of the most tolerant and flexible religions in the world, in its social order it displays a high degree of rigidity. Still, India's Dalits (formerly untouchables) have gained political power and social mobility in significant ways. Dalits have served as chief ministers, federal government ministers, as a major political party president, as India's president, and chief justice of the Supreme Court. They are influential now in university administrations.[8]

The Hindu caste system in reality, however, does not exist in these simple four-fold divisions. The four main castes are actually formal names for the organizational structure consisting of 3,000 subcastes into which the present Hindu society is divided. In rural India, where the caste system is most pervasive, a close interrelationship exists among social status, economic power, and occupational divisions. In the thousands of villages the landowners traditionally make up the upper castes—the Kshatriyas and the Brahmins. In south India the situation is different in that non-Brahmins constitute the landowning castes. Money lending, banking, and trading are done mostly by the Banias, a term used almost interchangeably with Vaishyas. Landholding and well-to-do castes are traditionally expected to look after the well being of the members of lower castes, who in turn perform services for the upper castes. In this kind of jajmani (superordinate-subordinate) relationship, both the upper and lower castes have rights and obligations toward each other. Both the caste obligations and the occupational differentiations have religious sanctions. In this way each caste group is obligated to fulfill its role within the society, whatever its status and the nature of the work it is obliged to perform.

The status, functions, and organizations of the subcastes (jatis) vary considerably from one region of the country to another. Many of the subcastes are confined to a subregion of the country and others to a locality or village. Yet despite these variations, the caste system is deeply embedded in the subconscious of the individual Hindu. Indeed, caste affiliations influence and often determine the social and political behavior of all citizens.

The organization of the members of one caste to protect and promote their common sociopolitical interests has been a frequent phenomenon. Caste group activity has long been in evidence even before the introduction of representative institutions in India. Since independence in 1947 some castes have become highly politicized. Whether the castes infiltrate the parties or the parties use the existing caste associations to mobilize the voters is a debatable question, but there is little doubt that candidates for public office, regardless of their ideological orientations and party affiliations, are attuned to the sensitivities of caste groups. According to A. H. Somjee, "The fact that a caste is horizontally integrated and continues to hold itself together for the pursuit of its primary social concerns, despite rapid change in all other aspects of Indian life since independence, indicates an effective network of communication integrating its members towards common social goals."[9] It is not surprising, therefore, that in the selection of candidates for political offices the parties are deeply influenced by the caste composition of the population of an electoral district.

In recent years electoral politics has enhanced caste consciousness among the voters and led to the formation of political parties that represent a group of castes with common interests. Such particularistic parties have come to play an important role both in state and national politics.

Castes and subcastes are important instruments of political socialization. In the formation of the political attitudes of young adults and children, the caste affiliation plays an important role. Empirical evidence suggests that persons originating from the upper castes (Brahmins and Kshatriyas) have a higher sense of personal efficacy and interpersonal trust; they also seem to have a stronger commitment to the operation of democracy than do the members of the Jats (an agriculturist subcaste) and the low castes.[10] There is a clear tendency on the part of children and young adults to identify themselves with the national political leaders originating from their own caste rather than with those from other castes. Mahatma Gandhi, for instance, is a political hero more favored by the members of his own caste, the Vaishya, than, say, by the Jats.[11]

Family and Kinship

Along with his or her caste, Indian's sociopolitical and economic behavior is likely to be influenced by family and kinship group. The basic unit of Hindu society in particular and of religious communities of India in general is not the individual but the extended or joint family, which consists of three generations living under the same roof.[12]

Kinship is one of the most important organizational structures in the Indian religious groups—a structure that includes numerous real or supposed uncles, aunts, brothers, sisters, and cousins as well as maternal and paternal grandparents. Each person is accorded a status in the kinship hierarchy and receives due respect. Indian children brought up under this complex structure of kinship relations learn about politics from their families, in which there are frequent exchanges of political views and a high degree of trust between parents and children. Various surveys of Indian children indicate that the process of political socialization in India does indeed reflect familial transmission of party identification and political orientations to the children. An overwhelming majority of the young respondents in one recent study not only were aware of the party affiliations of their parents but also identified with the parties that their parents preferred.[13]

Minority Religions and Subgroup Identities

Although Hinduism is the religion of the majority of Indians (see Table 2.1), there are important religious minorities such as Muslims and Sikhs who have been able to preserve their group identities.

TABLE 2.1   Religious Distribution of the Population of India

Religion	Total	Percentage
Hindus	827,578,868	80.5
Muslims	138,188,244	13.4
Christians	24,080,016	2.3
Sikhs	19,215,730	1.9
Buddhists	7,955,207	0.8
Jains	4,225,053	0.4
Others	7,367,214	0.7

Source: Census of India, 2001, Religious Composition, retrieved February 26, 2008, www.censusindia
.gov.in/Census_Data_2001/India_at_glance/religion.aspx.

In societies such as that of India, minority religions provide "each group with a focal point of identity and social solidarity, and large areas of its culture are associated with its religion."[14] By the same token, religion and aspects of cultural life such as language, art, literature, and social institutions become intertwined and lead to the development of powerful group identities that often inhibit the development of a cohesive political community.

Ideology of Nationalism: Various Versions

There are two dominant versions of the pan-Indian ideology of nationalism: Indian nationalism and Hindu nationalism. Indian nationalism is one of the vital elements of the ideology on which the Indian state was founded. It is basically a liberal and humanitarian force. It recognizes the pluralistic nature of the society and rejects the idea of homogenizing the society by eliminating religious and cultural diversities. Its founders recognized that individuals in India belong to a variety of communities based on caste, religion, occupation, region, and a host of other factors. They were, furthermore, aware that such communities enjoyed a great degree of autonomy. The founders held that even though a majority of the country's population was Hindu, the Hindus have a tradition of tolerance and the capacity to absorb the ideas, values, and norms of behavior as well as groups coming from outside. Hindu religious traditions not only allow a wide variety of sectarian diversity but also teach respect for all religions. These traditions enabled such minority religions as Islam and Christianity and such cultures as Greek, Turkish, Iranian, and others to contribute to the development of the composite culture of the country.

Because it was deeply influenced by European liberal-rationalist thought, Indian nationalism was committed to the reform and the rationalization of the structure and the organization of the society. It held that the state authority could be used to reform a traditional society. Middle-class elites, exponents of Indian nationalism, were wedded to the ideals of scientific temper, industrialization of the country, distributive justice, protection of rights and the cultures of ethnic and religious minorities, and development of a secular democratic polity based on the British system of parliamentary government.

Starting in the 1980s, however, many of the vital elements of Indian nationalism, developed and nurtured both before and after India's independence, came to be challenged by Hindu nationalists on both practical and intellectual bases. Although Hindu nationalism originated in the Hindu cultural revival movement of the nineteenth century and developed as a reaction against Indian nationalism, it is only in the recent past that it has emerged as a major ideological force in the politics of the country. Hindu nationalists advocate a single homogeneous national identity for the whole country, rejecting the idea that India is a multicultural and multinational state. To them the term "Hindu" has geocultural, not religious, connotation. For Hindu nationalists the political-territorial concept of nationalism without its Hindu cultural content, as advocated by Nehru and his associates, is incapable of serving the unity of the country. For them the secular concept of Indian national identity, based on an alien ideology of socialism, is limited to the state and lacks those psychic elements that bind the people as a nation. They argue that it is not the common economic interests that give birth to a nation; people's love for their land is based on common traditions and culture. For the Hindu nationalists, Bharat, or India, is not only their motherland; it is also their holy land. They believe that all Indians, irrespective of their religion, should take pride in India's ancient cultural heritage.

Hindu nationalists are also influenced by British ideologies that emphasize equality before the law, a uniform civil code, democracy, universal suffrage, and the system of representative government. Contrary to the position of Indian nationalists, Hindu nationalists are opposed to providing special rights or protection for the minorities. Although they reject Indian nationalists' version of secularism, they do not believe in the establishment of a theocracy. However, they display considerable hostility toward Muslims as a community as well as to their contributions to the enrichment of Indian culture. Hindu-Muslim polarization has been apparent in some instances of riots as in Gujrat (2002), but there are also instances such as the Mumbai railway blasts (2006) where despite the polarity and the provocation by Muslim terrorists, the two communities helped each other. The Hindu-Muslim question remains dynamic in India's political and social life as a result of adaptation and learning by the leadership and the street on both sides.

New Status Symbols and the Role of Political Power in Social Mobility

Despite the persistence of traditional values, caste stratification, and belief in the superiority of the sacred over the secular, new secular values and status symbols are becoming increasingly important. The criterion for measuring a person's success has become the amount of money that person has, rather than social origin. Higher social origin may help in establishing contacts for material advancement, but social origin alone may not always guarantee higher status and success. Persons of lower social origin who are successful in accumulating wealth may actually be able to earn the respect of their fellow citizens now that social origin is somewhat less significant.

The ongoing industrial and agricultural revolutions and the introduction of the electoral process based on universal suffrage have increased the opportunities for social and economic mobility as well as political participation. Education, knowledge of the English language, political power, material wealth, and higher social status have become interdependent. Higher education, as in other modern societies, is considered one of the primary means of achieving upward social mobility. In India an understanding of English and proficiency in writing and speaking English give a person a head start. Although many people might criticize a westernized Indian, in urban areas they can hardly disguise their eagerness to accept him as their role model. If they cannot adopt his values and lifestyle in their own lives, they would like their children to emulate him. Moreover, the image of such an Indian as an ideal to emulate has been reinforced by television, movies, magazines, and newspapers. Both the politically influential people and the nouveaux riches send their children to the exclusive private schools that provide education in English.

With the diversification of political activity in several areas of national life, the competition for elective positions has increased immensely. Naturally this process has enhanced the demand for and the status of people who are politically ambitious and who possess organizational abilities. As the older generation of leaders who commanded authority because of their age and contributions to the independence movement has almost disappeared, reliance on the new type of political leaders who are willing to use all means to acquire power has increased. In India, the people do not trust most politicians; they are viewed cynically, even though their services are constantly in demand.

At present, social stratification and class divisions in India are based on a mixture of ascription and personal ability. The upper class in India is small and consists of members of the landed aristocracy, former rulers of princely states, industrial proprietors, businesspeople, and English-educated westernized groups holding top positions in the administration as well as in the business and intellectual establishment of the country.

The post-independence period has also witnessed the emergence of a middle class. Aside from the lower echelon of the bureaucracy, the middle class includes the members of the business community, the managerial-political elites, and the powerful, wealthy, and influential farmers of the countryside. According to one estimate, this class constitutes about 20 percent of the population of the country. It is also estimated that the members of this class are gradually "adopting similar life-styles and values and are being steadily woven together by a web of communication, trade and commercial economic development."[15] This growing middle class provides strategic political support for the ruling elites by accepting the legitimacy of the system. The rest of the population constitutes the lower classes, of which approximately 35 percent live below the poverty line.[16] As a result of India's economic boom in the last decade the size of India's middle is expected to grow and gradually reduce the percentage of people at the poverty level.

A Mixed Political Culture

Given the enormous complexity of the Indian sociocultural structure, it is not surprising that Indian political values and norms of behavior often give contradictory signals. There is a considerable intermixing of modern and traditional values. For example, one may find hero worship verging on idolatry along with an expression of strong democratic impulses; supersensitive nationalism along with strong parochialism; egalitarianism along with the existence of a hierarchical social order; a high degree of tolerance and passivity along with occasional outbursts of violence; and so on. These contradictory tendencies may be attributed to the vast size of the country and to its diversity as well as to the uneven levels of exposure to modern values in the different segments of the population.

The introduction of democratic institutions in India, as is well known, was not the result of an internal groundswell. The ordinary person in India has little awareness of the advantages of a democracy. It was the Western-educated and Anglicized elites who made the deliberate choice for democracy over other forms of government. John Osgood Field puts it well: "Indians struggled against Englishmen for the right to run a British system in India."[17] The political elites believed that through the introduction of universal suffrage and the mass political participation that would follow, a traditional society based on an ascriptive oligarchic structure would transform itself into an egalitarian and open society. In addition, the spread of mass media and industrialization would help to internalize democratic values and lead to the development of an egalitarian political culture. Various surveys suggest that these values are in fact becoming increasingly integrated into the personality structure of the newer generations of Indians.[18] However, values of caste, ethnicity, and minority politics exist as well.

The frequent elections held at the state and national levels on the basis of adult franchise have broken the traditional isolation in which most of the villagers of India formerly lived. Many of the groups on the periphery of the village society have developed political awareness and are learning to use their political power, and the members of the so-called backward (lower) castes and former untouchables (now called Dalits) are becoming increasingly restive and challenging the domination of the landowning upper castes. Consequently, electoral participation and voter turnout are impressive. Whereas in the first national election of 1951–1952 the voter turnout was around 45 percent, since then it has consistently risen. In the several most recent national elections about 61 percent of the voters turned out to cast their ballots.

Even though the degree of politicization is higher in urban than in rural areas, issue awareness among the rural poor is increasing. Average citizens, though often illiterate and relatively ill informed, are not ignorant. In fact, they tend to display sound common sense in politics. They have also been highly politicized. They may or may not always be aware of the national issues involved in the elections, but pocketbook issues have a strong impact on their voting behavior.[19] Moreover, they are capable of penalizing politicians and the parties for their high-handedness and insensitivity toward the people. In a village society the elected representative is an easily accessible spokesperson for the citizens, serving as an important link between the citizens and the complex world of administration. By contrast, administrators are often English educated and come from urban areas; hence illiterate villagers do not have easy access to them.

The egalitarian values emphasized by the elites have found expression both in the constitution and in the laws of the country. Strong efforts have been made to provide not only equal voting rights—granted to all citizens regardless of sex and social origin—but also greater educational and job opportunities for India's millions of untouchables, the people Mahatma Gandhi called Harijans (the Children of God), and the members of the backward castes. Despite these efforts, however, the equality of "citizenship in the economic field whereby irrespective of his place in the social hierarchy an individual would be able to claim the right to economic advancement and distributive justice has yet to take place."[20]

The resilience of the Indian system and its capacity to face internal and external challenges seem to be rooted in the strong sense of nationalism that pervades it. This nationalism, rooted in turn in the cultural revival movement of the nineteenth century and nurtured and promoted by the political stalwarts who led the independence movement, has been further consolidated and strengthened by the policies adopted by the elites in the post-independence period. Despite the divisions within Indian society, Indians on the whole display a very positive attitude toward the system as well as its accomplishments. They express pride in the creation and operation of its democratic political institutions; indeed, India's achievements in the area of foreign policy and the emphasis on an independent foreign policy have become symbols of political pride. Nehru's nonaligned position and his defiance of John Foster Dulles (President Dwight Eisenhower's secretary of state) and, by extension, American power, were described as the days of national glory and pride.[21] The system also seems to have "shown a remarkable capability to create several technological, scientific and industrial symbols which evoke a great degree of emotional response" among the elite and nonelite segments of the population.[22] In a 1974 survey that asked college students to list the achievements of the system about which they felt a sense of pride, 96 percent were able to indicate one or more achievements they thought were worthy of their pride. India's nuclear testing, victory in war with Pakistan, the Green Revolution, industrial development, and successful working of democracy under difficult internal and external circumstances were viewed as Indian achievements by college students and the broad masses. Thereafter, confidence among Indians about the country's future and individual well-being has grown as a result of several developments: impressive economic gains, assertiveness in the military and nuclear spheres and the growth of power projection capabilities in space and at sea, growing strategic partnerships with traditional players (Russia, United Kingdom, France, and Germany) and with nontraditional partners (United States, Israel, Japan, and Australia), an ability to manage relations with traditional rivals (Pakistan and China), and the lingering problem of foreign-aided and home-grown terrorism in Kashmir and other parts of India. These achievements and new directions indicate that India is well positioned to join the global economic and strategic mainstream as a major power, and to develop itself as a model of economic and social development and peaceful change in a volatile and disorderly part of the world. Following the growth of global terrorism after September 2001 the value of India as a stabilizing element in the region became apparent to international observers.[23]

An emphasis on consensus, conciliation, compromise, and accommodation is a tradition that Indians have inherited from their past. In particular, conflict management through consensus or arbitration has been widely used by the community and caste leaders. Gandhi employed this method to resolve intraparty disputes as well as a variety of conflicts arising in national politics. In fact, the Gandhian approach to politics based on nonviolence, or ahimsa, was "not only a technique of protest, defiance, and change, but also the major support for consensual decision-making and conflict resolution in inter-group and interpersonal context."[24] This unique Indian tradition of conflict management continued to operate even in the post-independence democratic process. Most of the successful Indian leaders have been conciliators and consensus builders who were able to balance conflicting political interests based on religious, linguistic, and cultural diversities. It is widely believed that India's unity and integrity have been preserved primarily through the practice of the politics of consensus and conciliation as opposed to the politics of confrontation and partisan divisions.

Another dominant trait of Indian political culture, shaped by its religious traditions and literature as well as by the behavior of such political leaders as Mahatma Gandhi and his followers, is a negative attitude toward the assumption of dictatorial powers (as in the case of Indira Gandhi during the emergency in 1975) and toward abuse of power by elected leaders and public servants. Indian civil society groups have grown in numbers and involvement in a variety of social, environmental, legal and political questions. Indian ethics places emphasis on self-negation—that is, on the renunciation of desire for power, money, and status. In general, both repression of desires and cleanliness of mind have been traditionally emphasized in India.[25] According to the ancient Hindu ordering of personal virtues, satogun (purity of heart and absence of desire for power and wealth) ranks higher than rajogun (the desire to acquire power or wealth); a sanyasi (a person who has renounced such desires and devotes himself entirely to social service) is superior to a king. Indians therefore tend to revere those persons who seek to influence politics and public policy without seeking political power. Hence India has witnessed the introduction of what W. H. Morris-Jones has called the "language of saintly politics," a kind of politics that "is important as a language of comment rather than of description of practical behavior."[26] It sets up very high standards of public behavior, with the Mahatma as the role model.

However, starting with the Nehru years (1947–1964), while Indian practitioners have talked in Gandhian terms, in reality traditional Indian utopian and moral principles, including Gandhian ones, have been marginalized, if not made irrelevant, in Indian political behavior. The process of Indian policy making and public policy implementation is driven by politicized compulsions and public pressures rather than moral or ethical principles. Change in Indian politics and government reflects the primacy of entrenched government rules and regulations, ad hoc-ism, consensus building, and "satisfying" behavior as a basis of governance. As politics has become an important avenue of social mobility and political ambition is playing an increasingly important role in the acquisition of political power, Indian politics has become what could be termed "amoral politics." This brand of politics is characterized by a decline of the political values associated with democratic institutions and political leaders during the early stages of independent India. For example, both the elected officials and the people know that the high-sounding moral phrases of politics serve rhetorical purposes only; they are not likely to be put into practice. In addition, the giving and accepting of bribes are normal ways of political life; elected officials frequently seek and receive monetary rewards for the services they render, and persons hoping to acquire elective positions frequently purchase votes and distribute liquor to uneducated voters on or before polling days. Indeed, there is the widespread belief in India that with money and political influence, rules can be bent and laws can be broken. Many politicians and their children are in league with black marketeers or other criminal elements and yet are rarely penalized for their transgressions. Such politicians are considered to be "free looters" interested only in "plunder and power."[27] They have also been called "half-educated, money-making simpletons."[28] Many in India look on the power hungry professional politicians as a new breed of pundits, careerists, and dream merchants who have fooled many people often in the name of democracy and public service but whose motive is self-aggrandizement more than public welfare. Moreover, corruption and the flow of "black money" (undeclared income) is widespread among Indian political parties, businesses, and official circles. In this respect the politicians and political representatives in India are not much different from those characteristic of the early stages of political development in many Western societies. Indeed, the polities based on representation rather than coercion tend in general to develop patron-client relationships rooted in amoral politics. As James Scott has noted, "self-interest thus provides the necessary political cement when neither a traditional governing elite nor a ruling group based upon ideological or class interest is available."[29]

NOTES

1. Percival Griffiths, *The British Impact on India* (London: Archon, 1953), p. 22; F. Max Muller, *India: What Can It Teach Us?* (New Delhi, Rupa Paperback, 2002).

2. A. L. Basham, *The Wonder That Was India* (New York: Grove, 1954), p. 341.

3. Basham, *Wonder That Was India,* pp. 80–137.

4. Griffiths, *British Impact,* p. 26.

5. H. G. Rawlinson, *India: A Short Cultural History* (New York: Praeger, 1968), p. 245.

6. Dennis Dalton, "The Concept of Politics and Power in India: Ideological Traditions," in *The States of South Asia: The Problem of National Integration,* ed. J. R. Wilson and Dennis Dalton (London: C. Hunt, 1982), p. 177.

7. D. Mackenzie Brown, *The Nationalist Movement: Indian Political Thought from Ranade to Bhave* (Berkeley: University of California Press, 1965), p. 15.

8. With respect to representation in legislative bodies, the legal term for "untouchables" is "Scheduled Castes"; the unassimilated tribals are called "Scheduled Tribes." For significant changes in Dalits' political standing, see Christopher Jaffrelot, *Reservations and the Dalits at the Crossroads,* Center for the Advanced Study of India, University of Pennsylvania, May 8, 2007, research note, http://casi.SSC.upenn.edu/India/iit_Jaffrelot.html.

9. A. H. Somjee, "Caste and the Decline of Political Homogeneity," *American Political Science Review,* September 1973, p. 816.

10. Yogendra K. Malik, "Efficacy, Values, and Socialization: A Case Study of North Indian Youth," *Political Science Review,* January–March 1980, p. 84; and Malik, "Trust, Efficacy, and Attitude Toward Democracy: A Case Study from India," *Comparative Education Review,* October 1979, pp. 433–442.

11. Yogendra K. Malik, "Sub-Cultural Variations and Political Socialization: The Case of North Indian Youth," *Journal of Asian and African Studies* 16, no. 1–2 (1981): 230.

12. T. N. Madan, "The Joint Family: A Terminological Clarification," *International Journal of Comparative Sociology,* September 1962, pp. 10–11.

13. Yogendra K. Malik, "Party Identifications and Political Attitudes Among the Secondary School Children of North India," *Asia Quarterly* 4 (1979): 265.

14. Donald E. Smith, "Emerging Patterns of Religion and Politics," in *South Asian Politics and Religion,* ed. Donald E. Smith (Princeton: Princeton University Press, 1966), p. 22.

15. Bhabani Sen Gupta, "Indian Society: An Unromantic Journey," *India Today,* January 15, 1983, p. 50.

16. *Economic and Political Weekly,* August 1979, p. 1220.

17. John Osgood Field, *Consolidating Democracy: Politicization and Participation in India* (New Delhi: Manohar, 1980), p. 347.

18. Yogendra K. Malik, "Attitudinal and Political Implications of Diffusion of Technology: The Case of North Indian Youth," in *Politics, Technology, and Bureaucracy in South Asia,* ed. Yogendra K. Malik (Leiden: E. J. Brill, 1983), pp. 45–73.

19. Rajni Kothari, "The Political Change of 1967," *Economic and Political Weekly* 6 (1971): 250.

20. A. H. Somjee, *Democratic Process in a Developing Society* (New York: St. Martin's 1979), p. 8.

21. Yogendra K. Malik, *North Indian Intellectuals: An Attitudinal Profile* (Leiden: E. J. Brill, 1979), p. 139.

22. Malik, *North Indian Intellectuals.*

23. Note, for example, the significant changes in U.S. attitudes about India's economic, military, and politicosocial importance among the executive branch, congressional leaders, and the business community.

24. Ashis Nandy, "The Culture of Indian Politics: A Stock Taking," *Journal of Asian Studies* 30, no. 1 (1970): 72.

25. Nandy, "Culture of Indian Politics," pp. 57–78.

26. W. H. Morris-Jones, *The Government and Politics of India* (Garden City, N.Y.: Doubleday, 1967), p. 47.

27. Arun Shourie, "The State as Private Property," *Economic and Political Weekly,* March 1980, p. 508.

28. Shourie, "State as Private Property," p. 508.

29. James C. Scott, "Corruption, Machine Politics, and Political Change," *American Political Science Review,* December 1969, p. 1151.

SUGGESTED READINGS

Basham, A. L., ed. *A Cultural History of India.* Oxford: Clarendon, 1975.

Brass, Paul. *Language, Religion, and Politics in North India.* London: Cambridge University Press, 1974.

Brown, D. Mackenzie. *The Nationalist Movement: Indian Political Thought from Ranade to Bhave.* Berkeley: University of California Press, 1965.

Brown, Judith M. *Modern India: The Origins of an Asian Democracy.* New York: Oxford University Press, 1985.

Chand, Tara. *History of the Freedom Movement in India.* Delhi: Publication Division, Ministry of Information and Broadcasting, 1972.

Freitag, Sandria B. *Collective Action and Community: Public Arenas and Emergence of Communalism in North India.* Berkeley: University of California Press, 1989.

Gallagher, John, Gordon Johnson, and Anil Seal. *Locality, Province, and Nation: Essays on Indian Politics, 1870–1940.* Cambridge: Cambridge University Press, 1973.

Gupta, A. K. *Myth and Reality: The Struggle for Freedom in India, 1945–47.* New Delhi: Manohar, 1987.

Hardy, P. *The Muslims of British India.* Cambridge: Cambridge University Press, 1972.

Khare, R. S. *Culture and Democracy: Anthropological Reflections on Modern India.* Lanham, Md.: University Press of America, 1985.

Kohli, Atul, ed. *India's Democracy: An Analysis of Changing State-Society Relations.* Princeton: Princeton University Press, 1988.

Kothari, Rajni. "The Indian Enterprise Today." Daedalus, Fall 1989, pp. 51–67.

Kumar, R. *Essays on Gandhian Politics.* Oxford: Oxford University Press, 1971.

Madan, T. N. "Secularism in Its Place." *Journal of Asian Studies,* November 1987, pp. 745–780.

McLane, John R. *Indian Nationalism and the Early Congress.* Princeton: Princeton University Press, 1977.

Mehrotra, S. R. *The Emergence of the Indian National Congress.* New Delhi: Vikas, 1971.

Menon, V. P. *The Transfer of Power in India.* Princeton: Princeton University Press, 1957.

Moore, R. J. *Escape from Empire: The Attlee Government and the Indian Problem.* Oxford: Clarendon, 1980.

Mujeeb, M. *The Indian Muslims.* Montreal: McGill University Press, 1967.

Muller, F. Max. *India: What Can It Teach Us?* New Delhi: Rupa Paperback, 2002.

Nanda, B. R., ed. *Essays in Modern Indian History.* Delhi: Oxford University Press, 1980.

Nandy, Ashis. "The Culture of Indian Politics: A Stock Taking." *Journal of Asian Studies,* November 1970, pp. 57–78.

_____. *At the Edge of Psychology: Essays in Politics and Culture.* New Delhi: Oxford University Press, 1980.

_____. "The Political Culture of the Indian State." *Daedalus,* Fall 1989, pp. 1–21.

O'Connell, Joseph, Milton Israel, and W. Oxtoby. eds. *Sikh History and Religion in the Twentieth Century.* Toronto: Toronto University Press, 1988.

Radhakrishnan, S. *The Hindu View of Life.* New York: Macmillan, 1962.

Rawlinson, H. G. *India: A Short Cultural History.* New York: Praeger, 1968.

Rudolph, Susanne H. "Consensus and Conflict in Indian Politics." *World Politics,* April 1981, pp. 385–399.

Sankhdher, M. M., ed. *Secularism in India: Dilemmas and Challenges.* New Delhi: Deep & Deep, 1992.

Schwartzberg, Joseph E. *A Historical Atlas of South Asia.* Chicago: University of Chicago Press, 1978.

Smith, Donald E. *South Asian Politics and Religion.* Princeton: Princeton University Press, 1966.

Spear, Percival, ed. *The Oxford History of India.* 3d ed. London: Oxford University Press, 1967.

Srinivas, M. N. *Caste in Modern India and Other Essays.* Bombay: Asia Publishing House, 1962.

Upadhyaya, Prakash Chandra. "The Politics of Indian Secularism." *Modern Asian Studies* 26, no. 4 (1992): 816–853.

Vanaik, Achin. "Situating Threat of Hindu Nationalism." *Economic and Political Weekly,* July 9, 1994, pp. 1729–1748.

Varshney, Ashutosh. "Contested Meanings: India's National Identity, Hindu Nationalism, and the Politics of Anxiety." *Daedalus,* Summer 1993, pp. 227–261.

Weiner, Myron. "India: Two Political Cultures." In *Political Culture and Political Development,* ed. Lucian W. Pye and Sidney Verba. Princeton: Princeton University Press, 1965.

Wolpert, Stanley. *A New History of India.* New York: Oxford University Press, 1982.

3

Political Institutions, Governmental Processes, and Changing Policies

One of the major problems facing the leaders of third world countries is creating stable political institutions capable of governing effectively, accomplishing sociopolitical changes peacefully, and providing smooth transitions of power. Events preceding Indian independence and the widespread religious rioting that accompanied the partition of the country had convinced the leaders of the Indian National Congress, who inherited power from the British government, that India needed a powerful, effective set of political institutions at the national level to provide stability in a vast land. Sardar Vallabhbhai Patel, deputy prime minister and home minister, summed up their position when he said that "the first requirement of any progressive country is internal and external security. It is impossible to make progress unless you first restore order in the country."[1]

The assembly that deliberated the institutional structure for the new nation and undertook the task of framing a new constitution was created by the British government. An overwhelming majority of its members were elected indirectly by the legislative bodies existing in the provinces of British India. Although elections to the provincial legislative bodies, before the creation of a Constituent Assembly, were not held on the basis of universal suffrage, as many as 46 million voters participated in the 1946 elections. The Constituent Assembly convened in December 1946 was thus a representative body of Indians. Its membership, dominated by the Indian National Congress, consisted of intellectuals, lawyers, constitutional experts, and administrators as well as ideologues. In short, it was a representative body from which emanated the different shades of opinion to be found in the India of the 1940s.[2] Three years of discussion, debate, and deliberation on the draft of the constitution were required before it was adopted in November 1949.

The new constitution, which came into effect on January 26, 1950, when India became a republic, is a lengthy, complex document consisting of 395 articles and schedules. Despite some shortcomings, it has provided India with a stable system of government.

The Nature of the Constitutional System

The Indian constitution represents a triumph of the modernists over the neo-traditionalist element. It represents the viewpoint of the nationalist leaders who envisioned India as a modern nation-state. Such leaders drew freely from the U.S. and British constitutional systems and were deeply influenced by the experience of the liberal democratic societies of Canada and Western Europe. They also drew heavily from the Government of India Act of 1935.

The neotraditionalists, represented by hard-core followers of Mohandas Gandhi, pressed for the creation of a highly decentralized, party-less system of government based on the village panchayats (councils). Not seeing much wisdom in building a modern state system based on a Western model, they had suggested that the village, in which direct election would prevail, should constitute the core of the system. The rest of the political institutions would be elected indirectly. The neotraditionalists, however, lost out to the modernists.

During the colonial period Indian leaders, while waging a war against the arbitrary exercise of power by British rulers, had learned to value civil liberties. The incorporation of a detailed list of fundamental rights into the constitution reflected their determination to safeguard the civil rights and individual freedom of the common people. This list includes the rights to equality, to freedom of religion, to constitutional remedies, and against exploitation. The list also includes certain cultural and educational rights.

The constitution, with its impressive list of rights, seeks to alter the traditional Indian system of social stratification based on ascriptive assignment of status. Its various articles abolish untouchability, provide equality of opportunity for jobs, and ensure equality of individuals in the eyes of the law. Recognizing that a democratic polity cannot operate without freedoms, Articles 19–22 provide such basic rights as freedom of speech and expression, freedom to form associations, freedom of movement, and freedom to assemble peacefully without arms. The division of the country on the basis of religion had created a sense of insecurity among the minorities, especially the Muslims. To assuage their fears and guarantee their security, the constitution provides for freedom of religion and worship and prohibits discrimination in administrative, political, and social life on the basis of caste, creed, sex, or social origins.

All of these rights are protected by the courts, and judicial procedures are provided to ensure their enforcement. The Indian judiciary, especially the Supreme Court, has been active in protecting the basic rights of citizens.

These rights are not absolute or unlimited, however. The framers of the constitution, though committed to fundamental rights and freedoms of citizens, were also concerned about India's unity and territorial integrity. Strong centrifugal tendencies have always been present in India. Many great subcontinental empires were broken up in the past as a result of the divisive forces existing within the region, most recently exemplified by the creation of Pakistan. In keeping with these fears, the framers incorporated certain emergency provisions into the constitution to safeguard the unity of India. During periods of emergency caused by foreign aggression and internal civil disorders, civil rights can be suspended. Through such laws as the Preventive Detention Act (1950), the Defense of Internal Security of India Act (1971), and the Maintenance of Internal Security Act, or MISA (1971), great authority has been left in the hands of the executive and administrative branches of the government. Under these acts the government can limit personal freedom to maintain civil order, and persons can be arrested without specification of the charges. Such limitations on individual rights have often been criticized by advocates of civil liberty.

The Directive Principles of State Policy, another distinguishing feature of the Indian constitutional system, is a statement of certain principles, goals, and ideals to be pursued by the state and the national governments in their policy formulations. The declaration was borrowed from the constitution of the Irish Republic. Many of the goals and principles constitute the wishes and various shades of ideology and opinion represented in the Constituent Assembly, which could not be incorporated into the fundamental rights section or other parts of the constitution. The Principles of State Policy direct the state to provide satisfactory means for people to earn their living, to obtain proper distribution of material resources of the community, to protect children and youth against exploitation, to promote the interest of the weaker sections of society, and to ban alcohol and cow slaughter. As they have no force of law, however, they cannot be enforced by the courts.

For purposes of amendment, the constitution has been divided into three sections. The section that deals with such important matters as the creation of new states out of existing states and the creation and abolition of the second chambers for the state legislatures can be amended by a simple parliamentary majority. A second section, dealing primarily with fundamental rights, can be amended by a two-thirds majority vote in parliament. Amendment of the last section of the constitution, which deals with the fundamentals of government

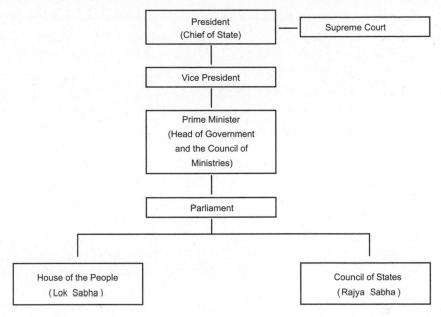

FIGURE 3.1   Organization of the Central Government of India

such as the offices of the president or prime minister and the powers of the Supreme Court, requires not only a two-thirds majority of parliament but also ratification by a majority of the state legislative assemblies.[3]

The President, the Prime Minister, and the Cabinet

The government in India is headed by the president, the executive by the prime minister, and the judiciary by the Supreme Court, and the parliament is entrusted with the exercise of legislative power (see Figure 3.1). It should be noted that India has adopted the British system of parliamentary democracy. Unlike in the United States, where the president is the chief of state as well as the head of government, in India the two are distinct. The president in India, like the queen in the United Kingdom, is a ceremonial chief of state. The executive powers lie with the prime minister, who heads the government. The prime minister is closely linked to the lower house of parliament, to which he or she is responsible. It is through the members of parliament that the people exercise control over the prime minister. The Indian prime minister, unlike the U.S. president, does not have a fixed term of office. The prime minister can be removed from office by the lower house of parliament by a vote of no confidence.

The President

Though endowed with many executive powers, the president is the chief of state rather than the head of government. He or she is elected for a term of five years, with no restrictions on reelection (although no president of India has ever been elected for a third consecutive term). The president is chosen by an electoral college consisting of all elected members of the legislative assemblies existing in each one of India's twenty-eight states, along with the elected members of the two chambers of the Indian parliament. A single transferable ballot is used, and the members of the electoral college are allowed to give their first and second preferences. If no candidate wins a clear majority of the votes, the second-preference votes cast for the candidate with the lowest number of votes are transferred to other candidates. Such vote transferences continue until one candidate secures an absolute majority of votes and is declared the president of the country. This process of election, while complex, gives substantial voice to the states in the choice of who will be the chief of state. As the presidential election is conducted by an electoral college, there is no popular participation, and the event is not one of national excitement. A president may be removed by a process of impeachment conducted in the parliament.

Although the president of India is vested with many executive powers, in actual practice he or she acts only at the advice of the prime minister and the cabinet. During periods of national crisis, such as an attack on the country by a foreign power, internal insurrection, or acute financial crisis, the president may declare a state of emergency. In such situations, the powers of the national government are enormously enlarged. Fundamental rights and freedoms may be suspended, and the country may be brought under a kind of authoritarian rule. The president also may declare a state of emergency in a particular state where the constitutional machinery has failed and take over its administration for a limited period. However, the exercise of such drastic powers by the president is subject to control by both the cabinet and parliament.

The president of India has powers normally exercised by the ceremonial chiefs of state in other countries, such as the right of addressing the joint sessions of parliament, the right of signing bills with a limited veto, the right to appoint the justices of the Supreme Court and other high public officials, the right to receive ambassadors from other countries, and the right to grant pardon. He or she also serves as the head of the nation's armed forces. All of these powers are exercised only at the advice of the prime minister, however.

A majority of the twelve persons who have been elected president were drawn from active politics. Their backgrounds have been diverse (see Table 3.1). Rajendra Prasad, the first president of India and a stalwart of the freedom

TABLE 3.1 Presidents of India

Year of Election	Name of President	Religion	Party	Region/State	Native Language
1952	Rajendra Prasad	Hindu	Congress	North (Bihar)	Hindi
1957	Rajendra Prasad	Hindu	Congress	North (Bihar)	Hindi
1962	S. Radhakrishnan	Hindu	Congress	South (Tamil Nadu)	Tamil
1967	Zakir Hussain (died in office)	Muslim	Congress	North (Uttar Pradesh)	Urdu/Hindi
1969	V. V. Giri	Hindu	Independent (supported by Indira Gandhi)	South (Andrha Pradesh)	Kannada
1974	Fakhruddin Ali Ahmad (died in office)	Muslim	Congress (I)	Northeast (Assam)	Assamese/Urdu
1977	N. Sanjiva Reddy	Hindu	Janata	South (Andrha Pradesh)	Telugu
1982	G. Zail Singh	Sikh	Congress (I)	Northwest (Punjab)	Punjabi
1987	R. Venkataraman	Hindu	Congress (I)	South (Tamil Nadu)	Tamil
1992	Shankar Dayal Sharma	Hindu	Congress (I)	Central India	Hindi
1997	K. R. Narayanan	Hindu	Independent	South (Kerala)	Malayaam
2002	A. P. J. Abdul Kalam	Muslim	Independent (Supported by BJP)	South (Tamil Nadu)	Tamil
2007	Pratibha Patil	Hindu	Congress (I)	Central (Maharastra)	Marathi

movement, held the position from 1952 to 1962. A person with strong views on sociopolitical issues and a strong base in the conservative sector of the Congress party, he had constant political differences with Jawaharlal Nehru, the first prime minister of the country, although these differences were rarely made public. Nehru, however, treated him as the constitutional head of state.

Prasad was succeeded by Sarvapalli Radhakrishnan (1962–1967), an academician and philosopher of international stature. Although Radhakrishnan had no independent power base in national politics, he did not hesitate to express his disagreement with Nehru's policies. Both Prasad and Radhakrishnan were elected as the nominees of the Congress party, but they were able to rise above party politics and meet frequently with the leaders of the opposition parties.

In 1967 Zakir Hussain, another academician, a Muslim and a favorite of Indira Gandhi, was elected to the presidency as a nominee of the Congress party. With Hussain's election the presidency became more partisan than it had been in previous years. In 1969 Hussain died of a heart attack. Indira Gandhi then supported V. V. Giri, an independent trade union leader, in opposition to the official Congress party candidate, Neelam Sanjiva Reddy. (Reddy was a nominee of the syndicate, an informal body of party bosses.) Giri was elected, defeating the official Congress party nominee. Even though Giri rarely showed any partisanship and always acted on the advice of the prime minister, he never saw himself as Indira Gandhi's protégé. Hence in later presidential elections Gandhi became very careful in the selection of candidates and sought to elevate to the office only persons who would not defy her and would not show even nominal independence.

When Giri's term expired in 1974, Fakhruddin Ali Ahmad, a member of the cabinet and a staunch supporter of Indira Gandhi, was elected. It was Fakhruddin who signed the 1975 declaration of emergency proposed by Indira Gandhi that resulted in the suspension of democracy and established, for a time, what amounted to an authoritarian system in India. Indira Gandhi's manipulation of the presidency made it evident that the occupant of this high office could play a key role in the operation of the country's institutional structure, as in the selection of the prime minister and the declaration of a state of emergency. This implication was further reinforced by the actions of Neelam Sanjiva Reddy, who was elected president in 1977 after Ahmad died and the Janata Party captured power by defeating the Congress party at the polls. Even though Reddy was a member of the Janata Party, he was elected as a consensus candidate. During his term (1977–1982) he played a controversial role in the selection of the prime minister, especially when the Janata Party lost its majority and no party had an absolute majority in parliament. Generally outspoken on public issues, he did not hesitate to criticize a prime minister when he felt it was needed.

In 1982, when Reddy's term expired, Indira Gandhi, who had won the parliamentary election in 1980, successfully installed Giani Zail Singh, a Sikh, as the seventh president of India, instead of asking Reddy to seek a second term. As Zail Singh had neither the educational background nor the intellectual stature of his predecessors, his elevation to the presidency was not acclaimed by the country's upper-class establishment. He was viewed as an unabashed Indira loyalist who would faithfully carry out her bidding to prove his loyalty. Singh remained loyal to Indira and later helped in the smooth succession of Rajiv Gandhi to the position of prime minister after his mother's assassination. Nevertheless, Singh brought his high office close to the people. He was termed "the people's president" because he was one of the most accessible presidents of the country.[4]

R. Venkataraman, a senior statesman and experienced administrator elected in 1987, proved to be more impartial and nonpartisan than his immediate predecessor. Shankar Dayal Sharma, the highly respected elder statesman who succeeded him in 1992, followed the traditions set by Venkataraman. In 1997, while celebrating fifty years of independence, Indian political parties elected the former diplomat K. R. Narayanan to the presidency, marking the first time a Dalit (former untouchable) has been elected to the office. Dr. A. P. J. Abdul Kalam became the eleventh president of India on July 25, 2002, having been nominated by the rightist, Hindu-oriented BJP prime minister A. B. Vajpayee. Kalam is a distinguished scientist of Muslim faith, the first Indian president with a string of achievements in the development of India's space and missile programs. He is committed to using science and technology for India's development and transforming India into a developed nation by 2020. His choice was a signal event in Indian politics because he was chosen for his distinguished record in the defense sector and his literary pursuits rather than personal loyalty to the ruling party or the Nehru-Gandhi dynasty.

In 2007, Pratibha Patil was elected president. As the first woman elected president, she has an impressive party résumé. She has been a Congress party member of parliament and the first woman governor of Rajasthan. Her background reflects a continuation of using the office to advance partisan objectives as well as the interests of underrepresented groups in Indian society.

The Vice President

India's vice presidency is not very different from its counterpart in the United States. Though elected by the two chambers of parliament in a joint session rather than by an electoral college, the vice president performs some of the same functions as those of a U.S. vice president. In addition to presiding over the sessions of the Council of States, the upper house of Indian parliament, the vice president succeeds the president in the event of the latter's resignation, death, or incapacity. Unlike the U.S. vice president, however, the Indian vice president does not complete his predecessor's term. He acts as president only until a new president is elected—an event that must take place within six months. Under normal circumstances, the vice president is elected for a term of five years. Some of the vice presidents (such as Radhakrishnan, Zakir Hussain, and Giri) were subsequently elevated to the office of the presidency. The president and vice president are traditionally expected to come from different regions of the country.

The Prime Minister and the Cabinet

The real executive of the country is made up of the prime minister and the cabinet. Despite the constitutional provision of the Westminster model of cabinet government in India, the prime minister has emerged as the undisputed chief of the executive branch. The personality of the prime minister determines the nature of the authority that he or she is likely to exercise. Such prime ministers as Lal Bahadur Shastri and Morarji Desai served as firsts among equals, but this was not the case with Jawaharlal Nehru and his daughter, Indira Gandhi. Longtime domination of government by charismatic and powerful personalities such as Nehru and Indira Gandhi, and particularly the centralization of political power by Gandhi in her office, has rendered the Indian executive a prime ministerial government rather than a cabinet government.

Theoretically the prime minister is selected by the president of India. In reality, the president invites the leader of the majority party in parliament to form the council of ministers. Usually major political parties go to the parliamentary polls with a clear choice of leaders. For the most part, the voters know who is likely to be the prime minister if a particular party wins a majority in the lower house of parliament. The Congress party has always entered the parliamentary election with a nationally known leader as its head—a strategy that has often given the voters the opportunity to elect the prime minister of the country. In the 1984 and 1989 parliamentary elections, for instance, the Congress (I) party (i.e., the Indira Congress, originally dominated by Indira Gandhi) went to the polls with Rajiv Gandhi as its leader. In the 1996 elections the Bharatiya Janata Party (BJP) followed the same process when it contested the elections, with Atal Bihari Vajpayee as its leader, and projected him as the future prime minister of the country in case the party won a majority in parliament.

The president can exercise some discretion in the selection of the prime minister when no party commands a clear majority in the lower house of parliament. When a party leader has clear majority support in the lower house of parliament, the president has no choice but to call on him to form the council of ministers.

With the decline of the Congress (I) as the dominant party, and no political party having a clear majority in the Lok Sabha (House of the People, the lower house of the parliament), in 1989 and 1991 President R. Venkataraman invited the leader of the single largest party to form the government. In 1996, when no political party had an absolute majority, President Shankar Dayal Sharma, following the convention set by his predecessor, invited Atal Bihari Vajpayee, the leader of the BJP, the single largest party in the Lok Sabha, to form the government and set a limit of thirteen days for the party to win a vote of confidence in the Lok Sabha. When he failed to do so, he called on the leader of the National Front-Left Front (NF-LF), a thirteen-party alliance, to form the new government. Given the increased possibilities of a hung parliament, the president now can play a more critical role in the selection of a prime minister and the formation of a new government than in the past.

If the voters are not satisfied with the performance of a prime minister and his or her government, they can vote the party out of power in the next parliamentary elections. In 1977 the voters defeated Indira Gandhi and her party for the excesses committed during her emergency rule and gave a majority of seats to the Janata Party in the lower house of parliament. When the Janata Party leaders were unable to maintain unity within their ranks, however, the voters replaced them in the 1980 parliamentary elections and Indira Gandhi was brought back to the prime ministership. In 1989 Rajiv Gandhi was ousted from office for his nonperformance. Similarly, in the 1996 elections P. V. Narasimha Rao's government, plagued with charges of widespread ministerial corruption, was routed at the polls despite the success of its economic policies.

The prime minister determines the composition of the council of ministers as well as its inner core, the cabinet. Members of the cabinet occupy the highest position within the council of ministers, and they meet regularly under the chairmanship of the prime minister. The prime minister also distributes the portfolios, deciding who should get which department.

Members of the council of ministers are generally appointed from the prime minister's own party, and they must be or become members of parliament. The council of ministers represents a cross-section of India's different states, regions, religions, and language groups. The nature and composition of the council of ministers also varies according to the prime minister in power.

With the advent of coalition governments, however, both the prime minister's freedom in forming the council of ministers and his or her control over the cabinet have declined. Not only were H. D. Deve Gowda and I. K. Gujral, the two prime ministers belonging to the NF-LF government of the post–1996 elections, unable to constitute their governments according to their wishes but their authority was often undermined by their cabinet colleagues.

Ever present in the cabinet have been organizations and committees, formal and informal, that serve as the prime minister's inner core of advisers. According to Michael Brecher, in the early period of Nehru's prime ministership major policy decisions were made by an informal supercabinet consisting of Nehru and Patel, the two stalwarts of the freedom movement. Such decisions were subsequently submitted to the regular cabinet for approval.[5] After Patel's death in 1950 an informal kitchen cabinet consisting of Maulana Abdul Kalam Azad and Rafi Ahmad Kidwai, later joined by Govind Ballabh Pant, became Nehru's main advisory body. Since Nehru's time the cabinet has always contained many subcommittees consisting of important cabinet members. Indira Gandhi, for example, chaired the Political Affairs Committee, a small subcommittee consisting of senior members of the cabinet that came to be known as a cabinet within a cabinet.

In 1996, when the NF-LF government came to power, in an unprecedented move, the leaders of the parties participating in the government formed a steering committee to supervise the work of the prime minister and the cabinet.

The prime minister is assisted by his secretariat, headed by a principal secretary, a top-ranking bureaucrat. The principal secretary is assisted by several members of the Indian Administrative Service (IAS), the elite bureaucratic organization of India. This top echelon of the prime minister's secretariat also includes technocrats, economists, politicians, and personal assistants.[6] In some ways the prime minister's secretariat resembles the U.S. president's executive office. It prepares the agenda for cabinet meetings, maintains the records of cabinet proceedings, and coordinates the administration of different departments of the government headed by the members of the council of ministers. The prime minister and his or her secretariat also stay in close touch with the chief ministers of the states and with the members of the Planning Commission and the National Development Council, the two bodies entrusted with the job of shaping the economic and development policies for the country.

A majority of Indian prime ministers have come from the Hindi-speaking states of north India. All of them have been upper-caste Hindus, with only one exception. There has been no prime minister from the Scheduled Castes, consisting of former untouchables, now known as Dalits (see Table 3.2).

Outstanding Prime Ministers

Jawaharlal Nehru: Charismatic but Flawed and Modernist

Whereas Gandhi is called the father of the Indian nation, Nehru (1889–1964) should be credited with building India's modern political institutions and with laying the foundations of its economic and foreign policies. In 1947, Nehru

TABLE 3.2 Prime Ministers of India

Prime Minister	Party Affiliation	Year of Birth	Year of Death	Leadership Dates	Caste/Subcaste (Religion)	Language/Region
Jawaharlal Nehru	Congress	1889	1964	Aug. 1947–May 1964	Brahmin (Hindu)	Hindi-speaking north (U.P.)
Lal Bahadur Shastri	Congress	1904	1966	June 1964–Jan. 1966	Kayastha (Hindu)	Hindi-speaking north (U.P.)
Indira Gandhi	Congress	1917	1984	Jan. 1966–Mar. 1977	Brahmin (Hindu)	Hindi-speaking north (U.P.)
Morarji Desai	Janata	1896	1995	Mar. 1977–July 1979	Brahmin (Hindu)	Gujarati west (Gujarat)
Charan Singh	Janata (Secular)	1902	1987	July 1979–Jan. 1980	Jat (Hindu)	Hindi-speaking north (U.P.)
Indira Gandhi	Congress (I)	1917	1984	Jan. 1980–Oct. 1984	Brahmin (Hindu)	Hindi-speaking north (U.P.)
Rajiv Gandhi	Congress (I)	1944	1991	Nov. 1984–Dec. 1989	Parsi-Brahmin (Hindu)	Hindi-speaking north (U.P.)
V. P. Singh	Janata Dal	1931		Dec. 1989–Nov. 1990	Rajput (Hindu)	Hindi-speaking north (U.P.)
Chandra Shekhar	Janata Dal (S)	1927	2007	Nov. 1990–June 1991	Rajput (Hindu)	Hindi-speaking north (U.P.)
P. V. Narasimha Rao	Congress (IP)	1921	2004	June 1991–May 1996	Brahmin (Hindu)	Telugu south (A.P.)
A. B. Vajpayee	BJP	1926		May 1996–June 1996	Brahmin (Hindu)	Hindi-speaking (Central India)
H. D. Deve Gowda	Janata Dal	1934		June 1996–April 1997	Backward Caste (Hindu)	Kannada (south)
I. K. Gujral	Janata Dal	1920		April 1997–April 1998	Khatri (Hindu)	Punjabi/Urdu/Northwest (Punjab)
A. B. Vajpayee	BJP	1926		April 1998–May 2004	Brahmin (Hindu)	Hindi-speaking (central India)
Manmohan Singh	Congress	1932		May 2004–	Sikh	Punjabi (Punjab)

became independent India's first prime minister, and he held this position and dominated the Indian political scene until his death on May 24, 1964.

Nehru's commitment to democratic institutions and norms of behavior, his unbounded faith in science, technology, and the industrialization of the country, his emphasis on planned economic development in India, and his concern for the poor, the downtrodden, and the minorities all deeply influenced political developments in India. He valued individual freedom and believed that only in a democratic system can an individual realize his or her full potential. Although the introduction of a parliamentary system in India based on the British model may be attributed to the collective efforts of Western-educated elites, it was Nehru, as the first prime minister and the most powerful leader of the country, who put it into practice.

Not only did he adhere to the practice of holding elections for parliament on the basis of universal suffrage, an unusual practice in a third world country, but he also respected the autonomy of the Election Commission and never intervened in its affairs.

Continuing a pre-independence practice, he held regular elections of party officials at all levels and thus maintained interparty democracy. On occasion Nehru was unwilling to tolerate dissent within the Congress party, as in 1951, when he forced Purushottam Das Tandon out of the party presidency because of the latter's commitment to Hindu chauvinistic ideology. But he respected the popular electoral verdict even when it went in favor of his ideological opponents. Nehru, like Gandhi, adhered to constitutional procedures and norms of behavior.

Nehru also permitted the democratic process to operate in the states. He was willing to accommodate the Congress party chief ministers, even when they disagreed with him. He rarely intervened in their affairs as long as they broadly followed the party platform. And he was willing to accommodate the demands of the regional leaders even if they did not belong to his party.

In addition, Nehru withstood pressure from the right wing of the Congress, which, after the creation of Pakistan, was less willing to treat Indian Muslims as equals of the Hindu majority. This right-wing faction wanted to modify Nehru's vision of a secular state in favor of Hindus. Ultimately, however, Nehru prevailed, granting Muslims and other minorities equal rights in the constitution of India. Nehru, like Mohandas Gandhi, had a national support base. He never appealed to regional or religious sentiments to keep himself in power. In addition to his authority based on the constitution, which Jinnah's successors in Pakistan lacked, Nehru had charisma and soon became a folk hero. He enjoyed the support of the masses, but he also had a very large following among intellectuals, especially among the English-educated and westernized intelligentsia who were committed to his ideas of religious tolerance and secular political culture.

As a modernist, Nehru considered science-based technology the key to the future prosperity and transformation of Indian society. He thus initiated policies that resulted in the establishment of a score of scientific institutions in India. For him, the industrialization of the country and scientific and technological development were interrelated goals to achieve economic independence of the country—hence his great emphasis on planned economic development. Although Nehru's ideals were remarkable, his economic and diplomatic record in hindsight shows many failures.

Indira Gandhi: Dynamic, Controversial, and Authoritarian

The period of Indira Gandhi's dominance of Indian politics, from 1966 to 1984, put enormous strain on the country's political institutions as well as on the informal rules used to settle conflicts among elites. Unlike her father, Jawaharlal Nehru, Indira Gandhi (1917–1984) had little regard for established procedure and norms of democratic politics. In 1966 she was brought to power as the prime minister by the party bosses; by 1969 she had become embroiled in a power struggle with the same group of leaders. This power struggle evolved into a conflict between the Young Turks represented by Indira Gandhi and the older, conservative party bosses represented by the syndicate. Gandhi's progressive image resulted from the introduction of her mildly radical program of nationalization of banks, abolition of privy purses (pensions) for the rulers of the former native states, liberal loan terms for the poor sector of the society, and strong denouncement of the monopoly of business and industrial establishments in India. This progressive strategy paid her rich dividends. She earned the support of most of the intellectual establishment in India, particularly the leftists and the Marxists. She was quite successful in projecting the image of a dynamic leader seeking the establishment of an egalitarian social order in an ancient society traditionally dominated by ascriptive values and rigid social stratification. These progressive projects also helped her to ward off any threat to her authority from the Communist or Socialist parties, which claimed to be champions of the poor. Having conducted herself as an accomplished politician, she surprised nobody when she won a massive majority in the 1971 parliamentary elections.

Riding on the wave of popularity generated by India's victory in the war with Pakistan over the issue of the creation of an independent nation of Bangladesh, she carried her Congress party to victory in the 1972 state elections. With these electoral victories she became not only the dominant force within the Congress party but also the undisputed leader of the country. She refused to seek accommodation and compromise with the discredited party bosses who had brought her to power. Instead she followed her own independent course of action, created a new party known as the Congress (I)—I for Indira—and thereby provided herself a new power base.

Indira Gandhi's departure from the established constitutional practices that had been in operation since independence came as a shock, however. One of the most dramatic developments in the post-independence period was her declaration of national emergency. This provision is included in the constitution of India for cases in which the country's security is threatened by internal insurrection or external aggression. Only twice previously had such an emergency been declared, and for external reasons: once in 1962, when India and the People's Republic of China fought a brief war over a border dispute, and again in 1971, when the Indo-Pakistani War broke out over the liberation of Bangladesh. In 1975, however, India witnessed widespread discontent over the failure of Indira Gandhi's economic policies. She was unable to reduce unemployment, control inflation, or cut widespread corruption. The opposition leaders organized mass rallies and protest marches, some demanding the resignation of the state governments led by her party.

Ultimately, it was a crucial court decision against her that led to the declaration of internal emergency. On June 12, 1975, on the basis of an election petition, a judge of the High Court in Allahabad convicted Gandhi of breach of election laws. She lost her seat in parliament and was barred from holding elective office for six years. As the violations were based on minor technicalities of the law, however, she appealed the conviction to the Supreme Court of India, which reversed the decision of the lower court and allowed her to stay in power. But the lower court's verdict had undermined the legitimacy of her office, and it was the fear of losing her office that forced her to declare a national emergency. When the opposition leaders demanded her resignation, she feared widespread disruption and nationwide protests. The declaration of emergency on June 26, 1975, enabled her to arrest all her political opponents, including Jaya Prakash Narayan, a venerable Gandhian leader; Morarji Desai, a former deputy prime minister; Charan Singh, a prominent opposition leader; and thousands of other opposition leaders and party workers.

Indira Gandhi's decision to declare an emergency was made with the support of her family and some of her close associates, rather than in consultation with the cabinet as required by constitutional law. The declaration has been criticized as a violation both of the spirit of the constitution and of the democratic policies in practice since independence.

The eighteen-month period of emergency was the first authoritarian rule experienced by India since the country had attained independence. Indira Gandhi enforced rigid press censorship. Numerous organizations were banned. Furthermore, paramilitary and police organization became arbitrary, creating an atmosphere of widespread oppression and fear. Gandhi also successfully amended the constitution to free the prime minister from judicial control. In the future, electoral disputes involving such high public officials as the president, vice president, and prime minister would not be referred to the courts. She also postponed a parliamentary election.

During this period her younger son, Sanjay, became a center of extra-constitutive authority. Even though he was not a member of the government, he launched his Five Point Program that included, among other projects, forced sterilization—a stipulation limiting families to only two children. His arbitrary and arrogant exercise of political power created widespread discontent and alienation, even among the members of the Congress party and India's widely respected bureaucrats. He arbitrarily transferred many civil servants and even dismissed chief ministers of the states who opposed his policies.

In short, Indira Gandhi not only differed from her predecessors in her style of leadership but also drastically changed even the substance of Indian politics. She sought to exercise state power on a personal level, sometimes disregarding constitutional norms and practices—as when she groomed her son Sanjay Gandhi to be her successor. In March 1977 she called parliamentary elections to legitimize her authority and the constitutional changes made during the period of her emergency role, but she miscalculated. Her party lost the election, and she could not even get herself elected to parliament. Such a humiliating defeat for Nehru's daughter demonstrated that India's illiterate voters had come to value the rules and procedures of a democratic polity. They resented the arbitrary exercise of political power by men such as Sanjay and the members of India's police administration. They also resented the loss of the links with the administration that they had enjoyed earlier through their representatives. Gandhi was brought back into power in the 1980 elections when her opponents could not hold together. She was assassinated on October 31, 1984.

Indira Gandhi was a complex and dynamic personality. During her long term as prime minister she provided political stability in India. During this period India made considerable economic progress, increased its technically skilled manpower, and established itself as the dominant military power in the region.

Indira Gandhi's dedication to a strong and united India was never questioned, but her leadership style left a bitter legacy. She undermined the democratic fabric of India by encouraging the rise of her son, Sanjay Gandhi, as an extra-constitutional center of power and influence in Indian politics and policy making. The Indira Gandhi era set in motion the theory that the Nehru-Gandhi dynasty was critical for India's destiny, and that Indian secularism was tied to the rule by the Nehru dynasty and the Congress party. Sonia Gandhi, currently the leader of the Congress party, is the guardian of this view.

Rajiv Gandhi: Dynastic Rule with Limited Competence

Rajiv Gandhi (1944–1991) became the sixth prime minister of India following Indira Gandhi's assassination on October 31, 1984. His elevation to the position of prime minister followed the established procedure of succession, and his appointment to this position by the president of India was subsequently confirmed by his unanimous election as party leader by 497 Congress (I) members of parliament. Nevertheless, Rajiv was the first person to become the prime minister of this vast land without having held any ministerial position at either national or state level. He was elevated to the high office of prime minister over the protests of many senior cabinet members and party men. Many of these persons had had far more administrative and political experience than Rajiv, whose political experience was limited to two years of organizational work within the Congress (I). A former airline pilot, he was brought into politics by his mother after the accidental death on June 23, 1980, of his younger brother, Sanjay. In 1981 he was elected to the lower house of parliament in a special election to fill the vacancy caused by the death of his brother. Rajiv entered politics reluctantly, his main incentive being to help his mother, Indira Gandhi, who had ceased to trust almost everybody except the members of her immediate family. He kept working under the shadow of his mother until he became prime minister.

There were certainly some cold calculations on the part of the Congress (I) members when they elected Rajiv as the leader of the party. None of the members of Indira Gandhi's cabinet were leaders of national standing. They would have been little help to the party in winning the forthcoming parliamentary elections. However, as a grandson of Jawaharlal Nehru and an heir to the Nehru dynasty, Rajiv had national recognition. In addition, the sympathy generated by the brutal assassination of Indira Gandhi ultimately helped the party, when it was led by Rajiv, to win the election. Furthermore, Indira Gandhi had been grooming Rajiv for succession; by electing him as the leader of the party, her party men were fulfilling the slain leader's wishes. However, Rajiv legitimized his elevation to the position of prime minister when he led his party to a massive victory in the parliamentary elections of 1984.

At the outset of his administration in 1984, the people of India had high expectations of Nehru's grandson. Unlike many of the old guard of Indian politics, Rajiv was blessed with a clean public image, expectations of a new style of management, and a pragmatic approach to politics. Very shortly these high hopes were dashed as Rajiv developed an imperial and arrogant style of governance, becoming inaccessible not only to the people but also to high government and party officials. He lacked consistency and stability in his administrative organization at both the national and state levels.

For instance, Rajiv reshuffled his cabinet twenty-seven times during his five-year term of office, and between 1985 and 1989 he changed Congress (I) party chief ministers in the states twenty times. In addition he surrounded himself with a small number of advisers, primarily civil servants, media experts, and foreign-trained technocrats who did not have roots in traditional Indian society.

Instead of eradicating corruption from the Indian body politic and distancing himself from the Congress (I) party's manipulators, powerbrokers, and influence peddlers, Rajiv's administration became identified in the minds of the public with the pursuit of amoral politics and corrupt politicians. Following the pattern set by his mother, he tended to centralize power in the prime minister's office, both in the party and the government. Although Rajiv liberalized the economy, leading to unprecedented economic and industrial growth, the benefits of such growth were unevenly distributed. The tendency toward arrogance, corruption, and the unequal distribution of new wealth led to public disenchantment with Rajiv, resulting in his electoral defeat in 1989.

In March 1991, after two governments fell in quick succession, general elections were called. In the ensuring elections, Rajiv and his party seemed to have a slight edge over the opposition parties. However, Rajiv's political career was tragically cut short on May 21, 1991, when he was assassinated during an election rally by an alleged member of the Sri Lankan Tamil Tigers. The assassination was said to be in retaliation for Rajiv Gandhi's 1987 deployment of the Indian army in Sri Lanka to help the Sri Lankan government crush the Tamil insurgency in the northern provinces of the island. His death temporarily ended the hold of the Nehru-Gandhi dynasty on both the Congress (I) party and the national government.

Indira Gandhi's tenure marked the start of dynastic rule in Indian politics, but she was known for her ability to outmaneuver Congress party bosses, cut Indian princes down to size, nationalize Indian banks, engineer the Bangladesh War (1971) and the breakup of Pakistan against the fierce opposition of President Richard Nixon, his adviser Henry Kissinger, and China's leaders. India's economy lacked luster and Indian politics were polarized, but her ability to manipulate her opponents and the bureaucracy to protect her position showed her understanding of the weakness of her political opponents and the usefulness of skilled administrators. But if her father's policies did not strike deep roots in Indian society, Indira Gandhi's rule created the foundation of the Indira Gandhi-Rajiv Gandhi-Sonia Gandhi dynasty.

Indira Gandhi's activism was partly self-serving and partly served Indian interests. Rajiv Gandhi's tenure revealed activism in the form of ill-concerned measures. Three examples will suffice. (1) He wanted to develop a nondiscriminatory nuclear nonproliferation treaty—a nonstarter. (2) He wanted to discuss nuclear disarmament with China, only to be reminded by Beijing that he did not have nuclear arms and there was nothing to discuss. (3) He sent the Indian army as peacekeepers in Sri Lanka, and the mission ended in failure. His death in 1991 at the hands of a Sri Lankan Tamil suicide bomber ended his career prematurely and appeared to end the Nehru family dynasty, until the rise of Sonia Gandhi.

Atal Bihari Vajpayee

Atal Bihari Vajpayee was the first genuine non-Congress prime minister of the country. He is one of the best-known national leaders of the BJP. A powerful orator, a versatile and enduring politician, and a charismatic personality, Vajpayee convinced his reluctant party members in the Bombay session of the BJP to accept his Gandhian socialism and humanistic liberalism as the new political creed of the party in order to broaden its base.

A founding member the Bharatiya Jana Sangh, he never gave the impression of being a spokesman for Hindu fundamentalism or Hindu chauvinism despite his long association with the RSS. Vajpayee was the president of the Jana Sangh from 1968 to 1973; earlier he had held the position of general secretary. From 1957 to 1977 he was also the leader of the Jana Sangh parliamentary party.

Born in 1926 to a Brahmin family from Gwalior (Madhya Pradesh), Vajpayee was educated at the Victoria (now Laxmibai) College of Gwalior and D.A.V. (Dayanand Anglo Vedic) College of Kanpur, where he earned a master of arts degree. He started his political career as a journalist and edited various Hindi-language magazines and newspapers, all of them associated with Hindu nationalist organizations.

Vajpayee was first elected to the Lok Sabha, the lower house of the Indian parliament. A skilled parliamentarian gifted with a sense of humor, a rare quality for an Indian politician, Vajpayee has earned the respect of his colleagues in both his own party and the opposition. It was during his term as Janata government minister for external affairs that he displayed his flexibility, diplomatic sophistication, and administrative abilities.

Vajpayee's ideological liberalism, political flexibility, and use of diplomatic skills at home and abroad enabled him to head a multiparty NDA government and move India forward on economic and strategic fronts. In 1998 the Vajpayee-led BJP government, in defiance of international opinion, conducted nuclear tests and embarked on the development of nuclear weapons. In 2000, under his leadership, the NDA government was able to repair the diplomatic damage by reaching understandings with the United States and other major powers. The United States and India became strategic partners, leading to significant military cooperation on land, sea, and air between Indian and American military services as well as economic interactions between the two countries. On the domestic front his government could also claim credit for introducing the second generation of economic reforms, notably relating to opening up the insurance sector to private capital, disinvestment of public sector undertakings, and opening up the telecommunications industry to private investment. Furthermore, it created the three new states of Uttarachal, Jharkhand, and Chattisgarh.

Vajpayee, however, still faced the challenge of removing the feeling of insecurity which often haunts the Christian and Muslim minorities of the country, and meeting the demands of ethnic and various nationalities in Jammu and Kashmir, and northeastern India.

The Vajpayee era was short-lived, yet it introduced major changes in Indian diplomatic and strategic affairs, external relationships, and the approach to internal secessionist movements. The 1998 nuclear tests were justified by the Sino-Pakistani nuclear threats to India, a stance which highlighted the role of nuclear weaponry in India's China and Pakistan policies, and in international conference diplomacy relating to the nuclear nonproliferation treaty (NPT) and the comprehensive test ban (CTBT) issues. In doing so, India was freed of the ambivalence on the nuclear question that had been the basis of India's nuclear policy since the Nehru days. In 2001–2002 Pakistan was threatened by Indian war mobilization, and at the same time a peace process was initiated. Strategic dialogues were opened up with traditional (Russia, France, and United Kingdom) and nontraditional (United States, Japan, Australia, and Germany) partners.

A Look East policy was highlighted to build commercial and strategic ties between India and Southeast Asian countries that were uncomfortable with China's looming presence and sought external balances. Nehru and his successors had ignored the region, while the Vajpayee government projected the South China Sea as India's new frontier and engaged in naval cooperation with the United States and its allies in the region. The region thus became a front of engagement between Indian and Chinese interests. Finally, processes for political dialogue with Kashmiri separatists and insurgents in India's northeast were institutionalized. The new approaches have been resilient, and they survived the defeat of the BJP at national polls in 2004. Observers believe that BJP overconfidence in its "India Shining" slogan and the concern about BJP's secularism led to its defeat and the Congress party's appeal on the grounds that it was the voice of secularism and India's rural poor.

Manmohan Singh

The election of the first Sikh prime minister of India could not have come in a more unusual manner. In 2004 Sonia Gandhi's skilled electioneering brought the Congress party back into power as the head of a minority coalition. In returning the Congress party to power, she restored the Nehru dynasty. Sonia decided to avoid the opportunity and obligation of assuming the prime ministership, which was her right as the party leader. Instead, she decided to concentrate on party work, behind the scenes supervision of the Manmohan Singh government, and the grooming of her son and daughter for public office. Her son is an MP and her daughter is a party organizer.

Sonia's decision to forgo the prime ministership apparently reflected the controversy in India about her Italian birth. She named Dr. Manmohan Singh to assume the responsibility. Singh was educated at Cambridge and Oxford University, held important economic appointments in India, and was acclaimed as an author and architect of the first phase of Indian economic reforms that started in 1991. He is diligent and knows the value of monitoring implementation of policies by India's cumbersome bureaucracy. He has maintained the post-Nehruvian framework of India's external policies that Vajpayee initiated, and with P. Chidambaran, his Harvard-trained finance minister, the minority Congress government has deepened India's economic reforms and ties with the West, China, and Russia, as well as Asian neighbors. The landmark U.S.-India nuclear deal took shape under Singh's lead, as did the buildup of defense ties with Russia and the United States. Singh's prime ministership is a novelty in Indian politics because he is an unelected leader; he sits in India's upper house as a nominated member. India has two coleaders (with Sonia Gandhi as the Congress party leader whose agenda at times differs from that of the government) and a difficult leftist coalition that opposes the United States and in the past advocated India's nuclear disarmament (but not China's).

Parliament and the Legislation

The Indian parliament, entrusted with the power of legislation, consists of two houses, the Lok Sabha (House of the People) and the Rajya Sabha (Council of the States). The first is the lower house and the second, the upper house of India's national legislature.

The Lok Sabha consists of 541 members elected from state and union territories on the basis of population. In addition, two members are appointed to represent the Anglo-Indian (Eurasian) community. Each state is divided into several electoral districts, and each member of parliament (MP) represents around 1.5 million people. India has universal adult suffrage, with all citizens aged eighteen years and older eligible to vote. In 1989 there were 475 million voters. There has been a constant increase in voter participation over the years. The qualifying age for seeking election to the Lok Sabha is twenty-five years. Elections are conducted by an autonomous agency, the Election Commission, headed by a chief election commissioner, who is assisted by two other members.

The members of the Election Commission and its chief enjoy a status and power equivalent to those of Supreme Court judges. They are not subject to political pressure and governmental interference.

Each MP is elected for a term of five years, although that span can be extended for one year during a period of emergency. Election to the Lok Sabha must be held within six months after the termination of such an emergency. Elections are called by the president on the advice of the prime minister, who may ask for the dissolution of the Lok Sabha and call for elections well before the expiration of its term, provided that he or she feels confident that the election can be won by the ruling party.

As India does not enforce a residency requirement for a candidate, a person is free to seek election to the Lok Sabha from any part of the country, whether or not he or she resides in that constituency. In practice, however, most of the members seek election from the areas in which they reside. Quite frequently their choice of an electoral district is influenced by the composition of its population. People tend to vote along caste, community, religious, ethnic, and linguistic lines, and hence even the Communist Party of India puts up candidates of the caste or religion that is dominant in the district.

Elections to the Lok Sabha are vigorously contested. In the 1989 elections, there were 6,084 candidates to fill only 541 elected Lok Sabha seats.[7] Moreover, a substantial amount of money is spent during elections. Even though the limit on campaign spending is around 15 lakhs (1.5 million) of rupees (the ceiling fixed by the Election Commission), actual expenses may run much higher than that.[8] The cost of elections has been going up every year. Political parties select the candidates (there are no party primaries) and also try to meet a substantial part of the campaign expenses.

Indians vote more for the parties than for individual candidates, although, as noted earlier, the caste affiliation, religion, and personality of a candidate tend to influence voters' choices. As a large majority of the voters are illiterate, all of the political parties and independent candidates are allocated visual symbols by the Election Commission, for identification purposes. For example, a hand is the symbol of the Congress (I) party; a hammer and sickle is the symbol of the Communist Party of India; and a wheel is the symbol of the Janata Dal. The candidates and the parties both give extensive exposure to these symbols while campaigning.

Election campaigns run from four to six weeks. The campaign period is colorful, festive, and noisy. Parades, torchlight processions, mass rallies, and public square meetings addressed by the candidates and the nationally known leaders are common. Quite often popular entertainers, folk singers, and film stars join in to promote a party or a candidate. Gaudy billboards and posters with the pictures of nationally known party leaders are prominently displayed, and much door-to-door canvassing is done, especially in urban areas.

Although the political parties issue election manifestos or party platforms, the parliamentary elections have been dominated since 1971 by one or two national issues rather than by a particular party platform. For instance, Indira Gandhi's garabi hatao (remove poverty) in 1971, her emergency rule and suppression of civil rights in 1977, her call for effective national government and political stability in 1980; Rajiv Gandhi's call for territorial integrity and the unity of the country in 1984; and V. P. Singh's pledge to remove corruption in 1989 were major focuses of the elections in those years.

The constituencies from which the candidates are elected to the Lok Sabha are single-member districts. The outcome of each election is determined by simple plurality, as in the United States and the United Kingdom, rather than by an absolute majority. Thus a party may receive 44 percent of the votes and yet bag 73 percent of the seats, as happened in the case of the Congress party in the first three elections of India. In the 1984 parliamentary elections, the Congress (I) party, under the youthful leadership of Rajiv Gandhi, won 80 percent of the seats even though it received only 50 percent of the votes. Such a lopsided outcome results from multiple contests for the Lok Sabha seats.

Survey data indicate that around 95 percent of the voters consider their vote valuable, and 65 percent are satisfied with the type of the candidate seeking election from the constituency.[9] Voters are willing, however, to throw errant politicians out and often switch their parties. According to Robin Jeffery, who studied 1,700 MPs since 1977 through five elections, only twenty-two (1.3 percent) could survive the electoral competition to reelection. Thirteen of twenty-two were elected from reserved constituencies for the Scheduled Castes or Scheduled Tribes. In Hindi-speaking states, where disadvantaged sectors of the society are becoming far more active than in the past, the rate of turnover was far more sweeping than in other states, and there was only one MP who won elections five times.[10]

The organization, powers, and functions of the Lok Sabha are analogous to those of the House of Commons in the United Kingdom. The Lok Sabha's meetings are presided over by the speaker, who, though elected on a party basis, tries to exercise considerable impartiality and to project a nonpartisan profile. He or she maintains order in the house and conducts its proceedings. The office of the speaker may have considerable influence, but the position is much weaker than that of the speaker in the U.S. House of Representatives.

The majority party is headed by a leader who is assisted by whips responsible for maintaining discipline within the party. As there are several small parties in the Lok Sabha, only the leader of a party with more than fifty seats is recognized as the leader of the opposition. Members and the leaders of the minor opposition parties, however, are provided the facilities to perform their role effectively.

The Lok Sabha meets at least twice in a year, with no more than six months between its two sessions. Although the MPs can address the house in any of the recognized languages of the country, a majority of the members speak in English or Hindi. When a member insists on speaking in another native language, English and Hindi translations of the speech are provided.

Votes on bills or other issues in the Lok Sabha are made strictly along party lines. Frequently, however, even the members of the ruling party become critical of their government's policies and programs. Individual MPs try to promote the interests of their constituents. But the district an MP represents in the Lok Sabha may be large and the voters unorganized. A member will tend to give priority to the powerful groups or better organized interests of his or her district over the average voter. On specific policy issues, each member is expected to follow the party line.

Of the two houses of parliament, the Lok Sabha is far more powerful than the Rajya Sabha. The Lok Sabha has effective control over both ordinary legislation and money bills. If a deadlock develops between the two houses over an ordinary bill, a joint session of the two chambers is convened and a decision is made by a majority vote. Money bills can be initiated only in the Lok Sabha. The Rajya Sabha may scrutinize such bills, but it has no power to veto them. Similarly, it is the Lok Sabha that exercises ultimate control over the prime minister and the council of ministers, as only the Lok Sabha can pass a vote of no confidence.[11] The Rajya Sabha has no such power.

Following the British practice, the Lok Sabha devotes the first hour of its business to addressing questions to the ministers. The "question hour," as it is known, gives the MPs an opportunity to seek information from the government, put the ministers on the spot, and cause embarrassment to the government. Such a process keeps the ministers on their toes.

The Rajya Sabha is much smaller than the lower house, consisting of 250 members; 238 are elected from the states roughly on the basis of population, although the smaller states are given slightly higher representation than their population would warrant. Like the U.S. Senate, the Rajya Sabha is a permanent body. Its members are elected for a period of six years, and one-third of them retire every two years, as in the U.S. Senate. The members of the Rajya Sabha are elected indirectly by the state legislative assemblies, to fill the vacancies caused by the retirement of the members. The Rajya Sabha, also referred to as the "house of the elders," is thus a representative body of the states. The remaining twelve members are appointed to the upper house by the president to give representation to individuals who have performed distinctive service in the areas of art, sciences, literature, and social work.

The Rajya Sabha plays a role secondary to that of the Lok Sabha in that it has no control over the executive branch. Nevertheless, during emergencies, if the Lok Sabha is under suspension, the Rajya Sabha can become a forum for the voicing of public concerns and thus serve as a check on any exercise of arbitrary power by the executive.

Supreme Court: The Guardian of the Constitution and Law

The Supreme Court is the highest judicial tribunal of India. It consists of a chief justice and twenty-five associate justices who are appointed by the president in consultation with the judges of the high courts and the prime minister. India has a unified judicial system. There are no separate state supreme courts. Each state has a high court subordinate to the Supreme Court, and at the national level, the Supreme Court sits at the head of an integrated judiciary. The Supreme Court has original as well as appellate jurisdiction. Following the practice existing in most federations, the original jurisdiction of the Supreme Court covers the disputes arising between the national government and the state governments, as well as cases involving two or more states. In significant civil and criminal cases, the Supreme Court serves as the final court of appeal.

Like the Supreme Court of the United States, India's Supreme Court enjoys the right of judicial review, even though its rights are not as extensive as those of its U.S. counterpart. The Indian Supreme Court has been the primary protector of civil liberties and fundamental rights, especially the right to private property. There has been constant conflict between the Supreme Court's right of judicial review and the parliament's claim to legislative sovereignty. The Supreme Court has denied parliament the absolute right to amend the constitution so as to limit the citizens' fundamental rights and civil liberties, particularly where the arbitrary takeover of private property is involved. The Congress party–dominated and Indira Gandhi–led parliament in 1976 passed the Forty-Second Amendment, which asserted parliament's ultimate power to amend the constitution. Gandhi also tried to pack and politicize the court. A balance between the Supreme Court's power of judicial review and parliamentary authority was restored during the rule of the Janata Party government (1977–1979) through the provision of the Forty-Fourth Amendment, which partially modified the absolute power granted to parliament under the Forty-Second Amendment.[12]

In the 1990s the judges of the Supreme Court have assumed an activist role. Through public interest litigation, filed by private citizens and civil liberties organizations, judges have tried to establish the principle of accountability for persons holding high public office, including the prime minister, members of the cabinet, and state chief ministers. As a result, many members of parliament have called for a constitutional amendment to restrict the powers of the judiciary. Thus, the potential for conflict between the two branches of government still persists.

The year 2006 was a landmark for Indian justice against politicians who had hitherto avoided conviction and jail time. For the first time, a serving minister, ally of the ruling Congress party, received life imprisonment for murder. A cricket star and MP were later sent to jail for manslaughter. A sign of the increasing role of crime in Indian politics is that almost 25 percent of Indian MPs have been charged with murder, extortion, and rape.[13]

But still politicians have a privileged status even in prison. They are housed in VIP quarters and can exercise influence from behind bars.[14]

Role of the State Governments

The Indian constitution provides for a federal system of government, with a division of powers between the national and the state governments. Unlike the state governments in the United States, however, those in India have only limited powers. Despite the existence of a powerful central government, the state governments have control over such important subjects as public order, police, administration of justice, agriculture, water supply and irrigation, education, public health, land rights, industries, and mineral development. They have also been given the right to levy taxes to raise revenue for the administration and to determine policies related to land use and land distribution as well as agricultural and industrial development within the states. In short, by capturing political power at the state level, a party or a group of political leaders can exercise control over the distribution of vital goods and services within its area. Because state government is an important source of patronage, there is intense competition among elites to capture elective positions at the state level.

Several important implications are related to the operation of India's federal system. This system provides institutional structures that grant self-government to its diverse people. It also provides the means to satisfy the political ambitions of regional elites as well as regional parties. State-level politics serves as a training ground for the politicians who may subsequently assume important roles in national politics. Many of India's able administrators, and some of its prime ministers, held important elective positions at the state level before they became prominent in national politics. Such former prime ministers as Lal Bahadur Shastri, Morarji Desai, Charan Singh, and V. P. Singh were initially elected to state legislative bodies and served in the state cabinets or were the state chief ministers. There have been many ministers who have previously held ministerial positions at the state level before being elevated to cabinet positions in the national government.

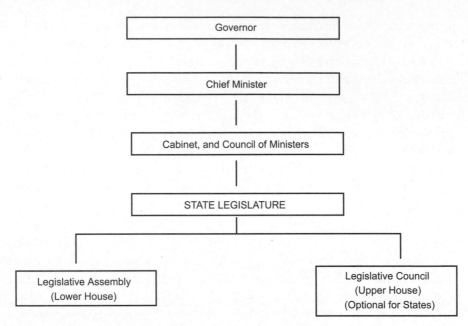

FIGURE 3.2   Organization of the State Governments of India

There are considerable differences in attitude, orientation, and behavior be-tween the national political leaders and the state-level politicians. Politicians at the state or regional level have close ties with caste and community leaders. Often they become intertwined with powerful local interests that are eager to maintain the status quo. The state political leaders keep themselves in power by appealing to the primordial loyalties of caste and religion. Many of them use their positions to benefit the members of their kinship group or community.

National leaders, on the other hand, seek to build national cohesion by play-ing down the traditional divisions existing within the society. Often the differ-ences of approach and orientation between the two sets of politicians aggravate the tension between the state and central governments, especially if they belong to different parties.

There are twenty-eight states in India. The organization of each of the state governments is presented in Figure 3.2.

The governor is appointed by the president for a term of five years and holds office for as long as he or she enjoys the president's confidence. The governor is a representative of the national government in the state and exercises more pow-ers in the state than the president does at the national level. Although the gover-nor was intended to be the constitutional figure in the governmental setup of a state and to act in nonpartisan ways, the office has become politicized in recent years. Many of the governors became embroiled in state politics, especially in those states in which non–Congress party governments were in power. It has been observed that "with the Congress (I) in power at the Center and the variety of homespun regional parties ruling in the states it has suddenly dawned on everyone that the governor may be a Trojan Horse sent by the Union government."[15] The governor invites the leader of the majority party in a state Legislative Assembly to form the government and to assume the office of chief minister. In the event that no party has a majority in the assembly, which happens more frequently at the state level than at the national level, the governors become actively involved in the formation of a state government. The governor also has the power to dismiss a popularly elected state government. He or she can recommend instituting the "president's rule" in a state, thus enabling the national government temporarily to take over the administration of a state. These practices go against both the principles of a federation and the spirit of representative government. Recently, therefore, the office of the governor has come under attack from the leaders of the opposition parties.

The chief minister, the cabinet, and the council of ministers are vested with the exercise of executive power in a state. The institutional setup at the state level is normally under the effective control of the chief minister, who is the most powerful person in state politics. The chief minister also commands a majority in the state Legislative Assembly, determines the size of his or her council of ministers, distributes portfolios among these ministers, and presides over the meeting of his or her cabinet. During Nehru's prime ministership many state chief ministers became powerful regional leaders with considerable influence in national politics. W. H. Morris-Jones has described this stage of the operation of the Indian polity as a "bargaining federalism." In such a federation, he points out, "neither centre nor states can impose decisions on others." Instead, "hard competitive bargaining" would take place in such federally instituted agencies as the Finance Commission and Planning Commission.[16] Chief ministers played a crucial role in the bargaining process until Indira Gandhi, after her 1972 landslide victory, undercut the power of most of the Congress party chief ministers. However, with the rise once again of many regional parties with such chief ministers as M. Karunanidhi and Jayaram Jayalalitha in Tamil Nadu, Jyoti Basu in West Bengal, and Mulayam Singh Yadav in Uttar Pradesh, the office of state chief minister has emerged as an independent and autonomous center of power.

The state legislatures are particularly important to state politics. Some of these legislatures are bicameral, consisting of a Legislative Assembly (lower house) and a Legislative Council (upper house); many, however, have only the assembly. The Legislative Assembly (Vidhan Sabha) has the right to legislate on all state subjects. It also controls the chief minister and the council of ministers, who can be dismissed by the adoption of a vote of no confidence. The state assemblies are elected on the basis of universal adult suffrage. Inasmuch as the elections of state assemblies have generally been separated from parliamentary elections, elections to a Vidhan Sabha is dominated by local and state issues.

The Legislative Councils are elected in part directly and in part indirectly, and some of the members are appointed by the governors on the advice of the chief ministers. The Legislative Council (Vidhan Parishad) plays a role secondary to that of the Legislative Assembly. The state legislative bodies work under almost the same rules of procedure as those followed in the national parliament.

The elections to the state legislative bodies are contested vigorously. On average, there are about five candidates for each seat. People show higher interest in assembly elections than in the elections of national parliament. It is through their representatives in the state Legislative Assembly that ordinary people are able to make political statements. The status of a candidate in the local community, his or her financial resources, and his or her party affiliations are all-important factors contributing to a successful election to the state legislature.

The members of the Legislative Assembly (MLAs) are generally less interested in legislative business or policy formulation than in securing benefits for their constituents or serving as power brokers between the bureaucrats and powerful interests in their constituencies. The services of an MLA are in great demand. Ordinary citizens seek the help of MLAs to intercede with the administration on their behalf. Their easy accessibility makes them an invaluable link between the people, the administration, and the state government.

Local Governments: The Roots of India's Democracy

There are a host of self-governing institutions in India's thousands of villages, towns, and cities. Local self-government in urban areas was, of course, introduced by the British government. Through several acts it established various types of local bodies, town committees, municipalities, and municipal corporations, all endowed with different levels of autonomy and financial power. Whereas corporations exist in the metropolitan areas or large cities, area committees with only limited powers are present in small towns.

Even though the powers of the city government are limited, it is the only representative body that exists in a city. The members of a municipal committee, or a municipal corporation, and its presiding officials are included among the politically influential members of the community. They develop vital links with the MLAs, especially if they belong to the same party. Through various channels they are able to influence the allocation of resources at the state capital.

In rural areas the self-governing institutions are known as the panchayats (village councils), panchayat samithis (association of village councils), and zila parishads (district councils), existing at the village, block, and district levels, respectively. Like the city councils, these rural self-governing institutions are elected on the basis of universal adult suffrage. The zila parishads are the highest self-governing institutions in rural India. Over the years the powers, functions, and financial resources of these institutions have varied greatly. However, with the notable exception of the zila parishads in the states of Karnataka, Maharashtra, and Gujarat, they were never given the powers with which to play an effective role in the development of rural areas.

Local politicians who are elected to these self-governing institutions are able to build horizontal and vertical links with community organizations on the basis of ascriptive and kinship ties, and with state-level politicians who belong to various political parties. Through this kind of informal network of power and influence local politicians and political notables mobilize the voters for the political leaders and also distribute patronage among their clients and supporters. This kind of institutional network, existing as it does at the different levels of Indian society, has integrated diverse elements of its population into a working political order.

The framers of the Indian constitution created a powerful center, believing that this would help in maintaining the unity of the country. Nevertheless, in view of India's cultural diversity, they preferred a federal system of government over a unitary system. Since the adoption of the constitution, however, for various reasons, certain important changes have occurred, resulting in greater centralization of political power than the framers of the constitution had envisioned.

Although no constitutional change took place in India's federal system, Indira Gandhi frequently resorted to its subversion. She made dubious use of some of the constitutional means to undermine the federal structure, especially the authority of the opposition-run state governments.

The office of the state governor, for instance, is a carryover from the days of the Raj. It was left in the post-independence constitutional structure, perhaps with the understanding that the state governor would perform only ceremonial functions and would not play any political role. In recent years, however, the office of the governor has become increasingly politicized. Both the Congress party and the Janata Party (later Janata Dal) governments have appointed their party men as state governors. After her 1980 return to power, Indira Gandhi frequently appointed discredited state politicians and her loyalists as governors of the opposition-run state governments. She also transferred those governors of the states who refused to carry out her instructions. The governor of Jammu and Kashmir, B. K. Nehru, an able administrator and former member of the ICS, refused to dismiss

Farooq Abdullah's government in Kashmir, as demanded by the Congress (I) supporters of Gandhi, on the grounds that such a move would not be in the national interest.[17] He was replaced soon afterward by Jagmohan, a Gandhi loyalist. Jagmohan carried out Indira Gandhi's instructions and dismissed Abdullah's government, disregarding established constitutional practices.

The governors of the opposition-run state governments of West Bengal, Karnataka, Sikkim, and Tamil Nadu had frequently behaved in partisan ways in the past, involving themselves either in dismissing a popularly elected state government or in stalling the implementation of important cabinet decisions.

Nehru was extremely reluctant to impose president's rule (basically a takeover of the state administration by the national government) in the states. In 1949 he is reported to have observed that "so far as I am concerned, I do not propose, nor intend, nor look forward to, nor expect governments falling apart except through a democratic process."[18] The evidence suggests that he never started or encouraged any efforts to topple the opposition-run state government. Under Indira Gandhi, however, the toppling of state governments by encouraging defection from the ranks of the opposition parties became a standard practice. The leaders of the opposition parties alleged that either by outright bribe or by a promise of a cabinet position in the state government, or both, Gandhi encouraged her Congress (I) party leaders to engineer defections and the toppling of the opposition-run governments in the states.

This undermining of the federal structure and state autonomy and the frequent toppling of state governments controlled by the regional parties led to an increase in regional discontent and frustration, which found expression in periodic outbursts of violence and disorder.

The national government has far greater financial resources at its disposal than the states have. In fact, through grants-in-aid, budgetary provisions, and financial institutions, the center has been making inroads into many of the subjects allocated to the state governments.[19] Such encroachments by the national government on states' rights and responsibilities have caused considerable strains in center-state relations.

Center-state relationships and the extent of state autonomy are issues that are likely to be debated in the coming years. Pressure is likely to increase for greater state autonomy.

The chief ministers from several states have already asked for greater legislative and administrative autonomy and have insisted that the "provisions in the Constitution would have to be changed to accommodate and give full play to the new definition of (a) center-state relationships and (b) relationships between the states."[20]

Three shades of opinion reflect the position of different groups on the nature of the Indian federation. One group led by the Sikh party, the Akali Dal of the Punjab, has demanded the transfer of all powers to the states, with the exception of defense, foreign affairs, communications, railways, and currency. Such a demand does not have countrywide support, however. Another group, led by moderate regional leaders, hopes to maintain a distance from the political control of New Delhi and seeks a reassertion of the spirit of federalism as embodied in the constitution. The third group, led by M. Karunanidhi of Tamil Nadu and Jyoti Basu of West Bengal, sought an extensive revision of center-state relations in the light of political experience gained over the fifty years that the Indian constitution has been in effect. All groups, no doubt, seek the revisions within the framework of the Indian constitution. A one-man commission headed by a retired Supreme Court justice, Ranjit Singh Sarkaria, was appointed in March 1983 to look into the issue. In particular, the commission was authorized to examine the center-state relationship and to make recommendations to meet the new demands coming from the non-Congress-run state governments. The commission submitted its report in 1988, though its recommendations have yet to be implemented.

Political leaders in India, such as the Sri Lankan elites, have been successful in building and operating an effective and complex institutional structure. Unlike the systems in neighboring Pakistan and Bangladesh, that in India provides its citizens with ample opportunities to become involved in the political process. Indeed, the citizens of India have frequently used the constitutional process to change the government. The federal system of government, furthermore, provides enough opportunities to state and local politicians to protect their regional interests and to preserve their subnational identities. Even though occasional tensions arise between the national and state governments, the political institutions overall have shown considerable flexibility in defusing these tensions without leading to any breakdown of the system.

The Executive and the Bureaucracy: Policy Formulation and Implementation

Along with political institutions and political parties, the Indian bureaucracy is an important element, in part because it helps to ensure stability and administrative continuity. The bureaucracy of India consists of tenured civil servants who remain in their administrative posts even when the political bosses lose their elective positions. The members of a bureaucracy are expected to make decisions on a rational rather than a political basis. In addition, they must observe certain rules and procedures that are essential for the orderly conduct of administration.

Like other South Asian states, India inherited well-developed traditions of administration from the British Raj. But unlike in Pakistan and Bangladesh, where civil servants and members of the armed forces have in the past taken over the government, in India the elected politicians have remained the top decision makers.

Cabinet and Bureaucracy: Policy Formulation and Implementation

The government of India is a complex network of departments, bureaus, regulatory agencies, boards, and a host of commissions and autonomous organizations. Today there are eighty-one ministries and major departments with an ever-increasing number of employees. Whereas in 1961 the central government had 1.9 million employees, in 1997 there were some 4 million.[21]

Politicians head the departments; bureaucrats assist them in the administration of these departments. Key policy decisions are made by the members of the cabinet, which is also responsible for the coordination of the work of various departments of the government. On the other hand, bureaus, regulatory agencies, and state-run industrial corporations are headed by members of the bureaucracy, whose work is overseen by the ministers.

The Indian bureaucracy is a legacy from the British. Under British rule, however, it served primarily as a regulatory agency whose primary responsibility was to raise revenue and maintain law and order so as to serve the interests of the colonial rulers. Its functions remained limited even when the British government adopted certain benevolent policies directed toward expansion of educational and other public service–related activities. The British did not use the government and bureaucracy as agents of social change. After independence from the British and with the rise of the welfare state in India, however, the government became actively involved in shaping the social and economic life of the country. Today the state has the primary responsibility for rapid development through the democratic process.

Earlier India was committed to an economic structure based on state socialism, economic and technological self-reliance, and a highly state-regulated economy. In recent years the political-administrative leadership of the country has been engaged in deregulation of the economy, making it more responsive to market forces and more open to direct foreign investment than it was in the past. Elected representatives, in order to ensure social justice, also make decisions on social policy, such as the introduction of a quota system in the recruitment of civil servants, reservation of seats in educational institutions for members of the

Hindu backward castes, and adequate representation of women in parliament and state legislative bodies.

Accordingly, the members of parliament and the council of ministers have set development goals. These individuals are not experts, however; it is the bureaucrats who make recommendations for the introduction of appropriate legislation to help achieve those goals.

Under these conditions the responsibilities of the bureaucracy have increased enormously. The actions of the civil servants are expected to reflect the aspirations of elected representatives, and the bureaucrats themselves are expected to mobilize human and material resources to help modernize the society. As a consequence, "thanks to the growth of the governmental activities resulting from the logic of modern nationalism and the increasing complexity of the modern life, the bureaucracy has emerged as the major locus of political power in the central government."[22]

Despite their key administrative positions, however, the bureaucrats are no longer the "masters" that they were during the British period. The real power lies with the ministers, who often remind the members of the bureaucracy that they are public servants.

Organization and Tradition of Indian Bureaucracy

Broadly speaking, the civil services in India can be grouped into three major categories: all-India services, central (union) services, and state civil services.

1. The top echelon of all-India services consists of the Indian Administrative Service (IAS) and the Indian Police Service (IPS), both of which have their roots in the British period of Indian history. The IAS is the successor to the British-designed elite Indian Civil Service (ICS), which is frequently referred to as being "heaven born" because of the high prestige and status bestowed on it by the society and the ruling classes. Contemporary members of the IAS claim to have inherited the traditions of their predecessor. The IPS and other all-India services originating during the British period also carry the glamour inherited from that period. In a country in which the unemployment rate is very high even among university graduates, a government job not only provides security and health benefits but also pays well and offers a good retirement system. Entry into Indian service jobs is all the more desirable because they command the highest status among government jobs.

   The ICS ruled India for a century and, assisted by the IPS, provided the well-known "steel frame" that enabled the British to govern India so

effectively for such a long period. Both the ICS and the IPS were originally staffed by the British, although even before India had achieved its
independence considerable Indianization of these services had occurred.
Because of the services' close association with British rule, there were
many Indian nationalists who sought their abolition after independence.
It was Sardar Patel, however, who defended the services and very wisely
perceived them as institutions of enormous value for the effective administration of a country as vast as India.

After independence, India kept only two all-India services, the IAS
and the IPS; but later on the number of such services increased, to include engineering, health, medicine, agriculture, education, and other
services necessary for the development of the country. The Rajya Sabha
can create a new all-India service by a two-thirds majority vote.

The members of the IAS, the elite component of the bureaucratic system in the country, see themselves as the guardians of the interests, unity,
and territorial integrity of the country. They claim to stand above the linguistic and communal cleavages in Indian society. In this respect they are
the representatives of what Myron Weiner has termed the "elite political
culture" of the country.[23] The members of both the IAS and the IPS are
very conscious of their high status within Indian society, and the traditions
have fostered an esprit de corps among them. This spirit and pride create
a sense of professional independence that may help them to withstand political pressure. The IAS and other all-India services are genuinely national
organizations and are able to reach every part of the country.

2. The central services include such divisions as the Indian Revenue Service, the Postal Service, the Indian Audit and Account Service, the Indian Railways Account Service, and the Indian Customs and Excise
   Service.
3. Finally, there are the cadres of civil services created by the states, which
   perform similar functions at the state level. It is the national IAS and the
   IPS that occupy positions of power and status, however; the state bureaucracies are assigned mostly to subordinate positions.

Recruitment and Training of the Bureaucrats

Recruitment to the services is based on merit, and there is considerable objectivity in the selection process. The Union Public Service Commission, an autonomous body, is entrusted with the job of holding examinations for the
applicants seeking entry into the top echelon of Indian bureaucracy. The examinations, with slight variations for each service, emphasize the applicant's proficiency in English and background in humanities and social sciences. Personality

tests, through extensive interviewing conducted by the members of the Union Public Service Commission, constitute a vital part of the selection process. No candidate is allowed to join the services without being interviewed. Both the tests and the interviews are based on the values and orientations of the upper and middle classes. The recruits are fairly young (twenty-one to twenty-four years old), and only college graduates are allowed to take the test. Every year more than 12,000 college graduates from all parts of the country compete for the 200 or so positions to be filled.

The young recruits are first given one year of extensive training in the National Academy of Administration, located in the hill town of Mussoorie. The new entrants study economics, public administration and government organization, the constitution of India, and Indian criminal law, among other subjects. In recent years the Indian Institute of Public Administration in New Delhi has begun to offer short courses and seminars designed to expose the senior members of the IAS to the newest methods of management and empirical research. However, training on the job is still considered the highest priority.

Each state in India designs its own rules and procedures for the recruitment of state-level bureaucrats; most are modeled on the procedures established at the national level. All states maintain their own public service commissions and use objective criteria to fill positions in the civil services.

The members of both the IAS and the state civil services are trained as "generalists" on the basis of British traditions.[24] As generalists they are expected to be equipped with the knowledge, skills, values, and attitudes to make policy recommendations not only in the area of administration but also in scientific, technical, and educational matters as well. Upward career mobility, enhancement of status, and increased financial rewards are dependent on their performance as well as their obedience to and loyalty to their immediate superiors.

Administrative Responsibilities and Upward Mobility

Upon the completion of his or her training, an IAS or IPS officer is assigned to a state cadre. According to established practice, no more than 50 percent of the recruits of India's elite services will serve in the states of their origin. These officers, then, are recruited and trained on the national level, and a substantial number of them will serve outside of their own states. Through this process they develop a national orientation and become instruments of national integration. The uniformity of values and training of these civil servants is unmatched by any other organization except the armed forces.

New IAS officers usually start their careers at the district level (for administrative purposes each of India's twenty-five states is divided into several districts). IAS officers are put in charge of district administration with the title of collector, district officer, or deputy commissioner. During the British period such officers were given almost full responsibility for the administration of the district; in fact, they were chief magistrates. Not only were they responsible for maintaining law and order, inasmuch as they had control over the police, but they also supervised the administration of local self-government, public health, education, agriculture, irrigation, and other activities.

In the post-independence period, IAS officers have also been assigned duties related to the economic and industrial development of the district. Each officer is assisted by several junior officers who belong to the state civil service cadre. It is during this field assignment that an IAS officer's administrative abilities are tested with respect to "generalism." Many IAS officers spend their entire careers at the district level; others move on to the state secretariat.

In the state secretariat, situated in the state capital, the members of the IAS hold important positions. As secretaries of the departments, they assist state ministers in the performance of their functions. In addition, they make recommendations leading to the formulation of department policies. The highest position an IAS officer can hold in the state is that of chief secretary. A chief secretary is responsible for the coordination of the many departments. He may also influence the postings of younger and junior IAS officers to different positions.

In India the states are required to contribute officers to the central secretariat, which stands at the apex of the national bureaucratic structure. At this level the final policy decisions are made. Positions in the central secretariat carry a great deal of prestige and are therefore desirable to the members of the IAS. Each state prepares a list of those IAS officers it is willing to spare, from which the central government can make its selection. Most of these officers go on deputation to New Delhi, some for a specific number of years, others on a permanent basis. In the central secretariat they start as undersecretaries or deputy secretaries, become joint secretaries, move on to the senior positions of additional secretaries, and then finally become the secretaries of departments. Most serve as the chief administrative aides of the ministers. The brightest and best officers are placed in the prime minister's secretariat or in such key ministries as home, defense, finance, foreign affairs, industries, and commerce. Frequently a state and the central government will compete with each other over the services of intelligent and talented administrators.

The national and state governments have set up several corporations that engage in economic and business activities. The managing heads, who require specialized training, are normally recruited from the private sector. Occasionally, however, an IAS officer is put in charge of such a corporation. In that case he or she would be required to make business decisions and to act as an executive rather than as an administrator. Such a position does not necessarily help the officer's upward mobility, however.

Social Origins and Value Orientations

Despite their key position within the institutional structure of India, the members of India's elite services have a very narrow social base. Because of a quota system, almost 35 percent of the new entrants to the IAS since independence have been members of the low or backward castes; nevertheless, an analysis of the bureaucrats' class origin demonstrates that "the middle and upper middle classes of urban origin have continued to grab the lion's share of the most powerful positions within the society."[25] Evidence collected by another observer shows that the members of these elite organizations "come from relatively high income families, with family income often exceeding Rs 15,000 a year; the father and often both parents are highly educated and enjoy high status in society."[26] The children of "the businessmen and business employees are less well represented than civil servants and professionals and, outside the middle class, the farmers and agricultural laborers forming the bulk of the work force are grossly under-represented in all services even more than the artisans and the industrial workers."[27] Just as the IAS is dominated by the middle class, there are numerous landowners belonging to the Jat subcaste in the Indian Police Service.

During the British rule, the Indian Civil Service was often criticized as being India's new caste system, created to maintain the elitist nature of the colonial system of administration. Today it is not uncommon to hear the IAS referred to as the continuation of the ICS under a new name. It has been said that as elitist organizations, "the services are allowed to restrict their intake and keep their monopoly over strategic positions in the bureaucracy."[28] Despite the elitist nature of Indian bureaucracy, however, it would be hard to deny that its highly intelligent and skilled members stand committed to the goals of modernization and industrialization of the country.

The Bureaucracy and the Changing Political Culture

The bureaucracy in India has been under pressure from various directions. The introduction of representative government has generated tension between the elected representatives and the bureaucrats. These strains result from the differences between the cultures to which the groups belong. Unlike the career of a member of the administrative services, an elective representative's career is dependent on his ability to be responsive to the needs of his constituents. He is guided by what has been termed political rather than administrative rationality. Unlike the administrator, the politician has no tenure; his reelection depends on the results he is able to obtain for his clientele. Hence the more services he is able to provide the electorate, the better his chances for reelection. Bureaucrats, on the other hand, as they are not dependent on voters, are more concerned with rules, regulations, and procedures. The contrast creates tensions between the results-oriented politician and the rule-bound civil servant.

Until 1947 bureaucrats were unaccustomed to taking orders from the elected representatives. Now the situation is dramatically different. Civil servants face far greater pressure at the state and local levels than at the national level. Before independence, for instance, a district officer was not subject to any local control, and his administrative powers were almost unrestrained. Now a local MLA (member of the Legislative Assembly of a state) represents a major restraint on the district officer's administrative authority. An influential MLA of the ruling party frequently intervenes in the administration on behalf of his supporters and allies. And an MLA's easy access to the state chief minister makes him a powerful person in a district and often forces the district officials to yield to his pressure. Despite the tenured position and the protection enjoyed under the civil service regulations, however, the district officer and his associates can be transferred to undesirable locations or to supervisory positions without much power and glamour if they refuse to cooperate with an influential MLA.

The tension between administrators and elected representatives has been aggravated by the growing role of the state in the expansion of social services and the economic and agricultural development of the country. The government has set up numerous elective bodies at the village, town, city, and state levels so that the popular representatives can become involved in the process of economic development. Under these conditions, the cooperation between elective representatives and civil servants becomes important in the mobilization of the masses necessary to achieve the goals set by the planners.

Many recent studies of the interaction between bureaucrats and representatives illustrate the distrust and tension between the two groups. It is believed that "insofar as interrelationships between officials and political leaders were concerned, the former were largely inclined to consult the latter, but only a few were willing to be guided by their advice."[29] The bureaucrats generally look upon the political leaders as irrelevant to the achievement of nationally desirable development goals. They believe that most of the politicians seek benefits only for their supporters, who belong primarily to their caste or community. Indeed, such an assumption on the part of the administrators is not entirely incorrect.

At the national level, the bureaucracy is free from this pressure of parochial interests. Nevertheless, in the post-Nehru era the civil servants and the central secretariat have been constantly subjected to political pressure. Both the Congress (I) and the opposition party ministers have tried to politicize the bureaucracy, such as by rewarding the more pliant and politically loyal bureaucrats with promotion and choice appointments. Of course, such efforts undermine the traditional nonpartisan and independent nature of the IAS.

The bureaucrats of India also feel threatened by the rise of the new class of technocrats. The government's economic and industrial development goals require the services of a host of engineers, scientists, economists, agricultural experts, planners, and other specialists, and the government has accordingly hired thousands of technocrats. These experts not only demand equal status with the administrators but also seek to share power with them. As a result, the new class of technocrats has further undercut the powers of the Indian civil bureaucracy.

Bureaucratic Corruption

While corruption among the bureaucrats and among the members of the law enforcement agencies occurred even during the British period, it was never as widespread as it is today. Traditionally, status within the society was assigned on an ascriptive basis, social mobility was limited, and social stratification was rigid. Even though these ascriptive principles persist, money and material wealth are now becoming the basis on which one can achieve higher status. The far greater social acceptance of corruption today than in previous periods can be attributed to the decline in the Indian value system.

At the same time, wide disparities have developed since independence in the incomes of bureaucrats, business people, and manufacturers. The existence of a sheltered market as well as the growing middle-class demand for consumer goods account for the tremendous rise in income of business people and manufacturers of consumer goods. By contrast, the pay scales of the top-level bureaucrats have not correspondingly increased; indeed, today the bureaucrats are paid far less than their counterparts in the private industries and businesses. Moreover, the often excessive and vulgar displays of wealth on the part of the business people may in part account for the civil servants' vulnerability to accepting bribes.

The chances of bureaucratic corruption are further aggravated by the multiplicity of rules and regulations dealing with economic and industrial expansion and granting of licenses.[30] Alleged widespread corruption in the civil services has led to many a cynical attitude toward the integrity and honesty of the bureaucrats.[31]

Assessment

Despite increased political pressure, the relations between the members of the civil services and the representatives and ministers have been improving. Both groups are learning to respect each other's contributions to the governance of the country. Moreover, there is now a far smaller social gap between a minister and a civil servant than existed at independence in 1947. Most civil servants and ministers are drawn from the middle classes. The members of the administrative services are also adapting themselves to the country's democratic government. District officers now value the local politician as an important link with the masses. During periods of emergency they seek the help of local representatives to mobilize the people to help achieve administrative goals.

As noted, bureaucratic corruption is a fact of political life. A highly centralized system of administration and an overregulated economy certainly add to the bureaucratic corruption. Civil servants enjoy considerable legal immunities. No officer of the Indian civil service, for instance, can be punished without the permission of the Indian Public Service Commission. Courts also have limited jurisdiction, since no legal proceedings can be instituted against senior officers without the permission of the government.[32]

NOTES

1. Quoted in Granville Austin, *The Indian Constitution: Cornerstone of a Nation* (London: Oxford University Press, 1966), p. 45.

2. Austin, *Indian Constitution,* p. 13.

3. M. V. Pylee, *Constitutional Government in India,* 3d ed. (Bombay: Asia Publishing House, 1977), pp. 761–762.

4. *India Today,* April 15, 1984, pp. 22–23.

5. Michael Brecher, *Nehru: A Political Biography* (London: Oxford University Press, 1959), p. 395.

6. *India Today,* January 31, 1985, pp. 8–17.

7. *The Hindu: International Edition,* December 8, 1989.

8. *The Tribune,* November 1, 1997, p. 1.

9. *India Today,* August 18, 1997, p. 28.

10. Robin Jeffery, "The Right Stuff: Leadership, Representation, and India's Parliamentary System," *Journal of Commonwealth and Comparative Politics,* July 1995, p. 259.

11. Pylee, *Constitutional Government,* p. 403.

12. Lloyd I. Rudolph and Susanne Hoeber Rudolph, "Judicial Review Versus Parliamentary Sovereignty: The Struggle over Stateness in India," *Journal of Commonwealth and Comparative Politics,* November 1981, pp. 231–255.

13. Samuel Paul and M. Vivekananda. "Knowing our Legislators," *India Together,* October 2004. http://www.indiatogether.org/2004/oct/gov-knowmps.htm.

14. BBC News/South Asia, "Watershed Year for Indian Law," updated January 5, 2007.

15. *India Today,* February 15, 1984, p. 74.

16. W. H. Morris-Jones, *The Government and Politics of India,* 3d ed. (London: Hutchinson University Library, 1971), p. 152.

17. *Economic and Political Weekly,* March 31, 1985, p. 231.

18. Quoted in Henry C. Hart, "Indira Gandhi: Determined Not to Be Hurt," in *Indira Gandhi's India: A Political System Reappraised,* ed. Henry C. Hart (Boulder: Westview, 1976), p. 256.

19. K. K. George and I. S. Gulati, "Central Inroads into State Subjects: An Analysis of Economic Services," *Economic and Political Weekly,* April 6, 1985, pp. 592–602.

20. *India Today,* April 15, 1983, p. 9.

21. Manoj Joshi, N. K. Singh, and S. Rekhi, "Bureaucracy: The Babus We Can't Afford," *India Today,* August 4, 1997, p. 30; O. P. Dwevidi and R. B. Jain, *India's Administrative State* (New Delhi: Gitanjli Publishing House, 1985), table 2.

22. Dennis Encarnation, "The Indian Central Bureaucracy: Responsive to Whom?" *Asian Survey,* November 1979, p. 1126. Also see O. P. Dwevidi and B. D. Dua, "Imperial Legacy, Bureaucracy, and Administrative Changes: India, 1947–1987," *Public Administration and Development* 9 (1989): 253–269.

23. Myron Weiner, "India: Two Political Cultures," in *Political Culture and Political Development,* ed. Lucian W. Pye and Sidney Verba (Princeton: Princeton University Press, 1965), pp. 199–244.

24. Asok Chanda, *Indian Administration* (London: George Allen & Unwin, 1967), pp. 97–134; Richard P. Taub, *Bureaucrats Under Stress* (Berkeley: University of California Press, 1969), p. 191.

25. Ram D. R. Sharma, "Selection of Civil Services," *Economic and Political Weekly,* January 27, 1979, p. 141.

26. Shreekant Garg and Palin K. Garg, "Brave New World of Young Indian Decision-Making Elite," *Economic and Political Weekly,* August 25, 1979, p. M95.

27. V. Subramaniam, *Social Background of India's Administrators* (New Delhi: Public Division, Ministry of Information Broadcasting, 1971), p. 124.

28. Harry W. Blair, "Mrs. Indira Gandhi's Emergency—The Indian Election of 1977, Pluralism and Marxism: Problems and Paradigms," *Modern Asian Studies,* April 1980, p. 280.

29. H. R. Chaturvedi, *Bureaucracy and the Local Community* (Columbia, Mo.: South Asia Books, 1977), p. 149.

30. Surjit Singh, "Political and Bureaucratic Corruption in India," *Journal of Government and Political Studies,* September–March 1978–1979, p. 65.

31. Samuel J. Eldersveld, V. Jagannadham, and A. P. Barnabas, *The Citizens and the Administrator in a Developing Democracy* (Glenview, Ill.: Scott, Foresman, 1968), pp. 29–30.

32. *India Today,* August 4, 1997, p. 35; O. P. Dwevidi and R. B. Jain, "Bureaucratic Morality in India," *International Political Science Review* 9, no. 3 (1988): 205–213.

SUGGESTED READINGS

Austin, Granville. *The Indian Constitution: Cornerstone of a Nation.* New York: Oxford University Press, 1966.

Basu, Durga Das. *Introduction to the Indian Constitution.* 9th ed. New Delhi: Prentice-Hall, 1984.

Baxi, Upendra. *The Supreme Court and Politics.* Lucknow: Eastern Book House, 1980.

Baxi, Upendra, and Bhikhu Parekh. *Crisis and Change in Contemporary India.* New Delhi: Sage, 1995.

Bayley, David H. *The Police and Political Development in India.* Princeton: Princeton University Press, 1969.

Bhambhri, C. P. *Bureaucracy and Politics in India.* Delhi: Vikas, 1971.

Braibanti, Ralph, ed. *Asian Bureaucratic Systems Emergent from the British Imperial Tradition.* Durham, N.C.: Duke University Press, 1966.

Chanda, Asok. *Federalism in India.* London: Allen and Unwin, 1965.

_____. *Indian Administration.* London: Allen & Unwin, 1967.

Choudhry, Nanda K., and Salim Mansur. eds. *The Indira-Rajiv Years: The Indian Economy and Polity, 1966–1991.* Toronto: Centre for South Asian Studies, University of Toronto, 1994.

Dwevidi, O. P., and R. B. Jain. *India's Administrative State*. New Delhi: Geetanjali, 1985.

Gadbois, George H., Jr. "The Indian Superior Judiciary: Help Wanted: Any Good People Willing to Be Judges." In *Law, Politics, and Society in India,* ed. Yogendra K. Malik and Dhirendra K. Vajpeyi, pp. 16–51. Delhi: Chanakya, 1990.

Heginbothan, Stanley. *Cultures in Conflict: The Four Faces of Indian Bureaucracy.* Berkeley: University of California Press, 1975.

Jain, R. B. ed. *Public Services in Democratic Context.* New Delhi: Indian Institute of Public Administration, 1983.

Kashyap, Subhash C. *The Ten Lok Sabhas: From the First to the Tenth. 1952–1991.* Delhi: Shipra, 1992.

Maheshwari, S. R. *Local Government in India.* New Delhi: Orient Longman, 1971.

_____. *Indian Administration.* New Delhi: Orient Longman, 1974.

_____. *State Government in India.* Delhi: Macmillan, 1979.

Malik, Yogendra K. "Political Finance in India." *Political Quarterly,* January 1989, pp. 75–94.

Manor, James. ed. *Nehru to the Nineties: The Changing Office of Prime Minister in India.* Vancouver: University of British Columbia Press, 1994.

Mishra, B. B. *The Government and Bureaucracy in India.* New Delhi: Oxford University Press, 1986.

Morris-Jones, W. H. *Parliament in India.* Philadelphia: University of Pennsylvania Press, 1957.

_____. *The Government and Politics of India.* Garden City, N.Y.: Doubleday, 1967.

Pal, R. N. *The Office of the Prime Minister of India.* New Delhi: Ghanshyam, 1983.

Palmier, L. *The Control of Bureaucratic Corruption.* Delhi: Allied, 1985.

Potter, D. C. *India's Administrators, 1919–1983.* Oxford: Oxford University Press, 1986.

Pylee, M. V. *Constitutional Government in India.* 4th ed. Bombay: Asia Publishing House, 1984.

Shukla, J. D. *State and District Administration in India.* New Delhi: National Publications, 1976.

Singh, M. P. *Lok Sabha Elections 1989: Indian Politics in 1990s.* Delhi: Kalinga Publications, 1992.

Venkateswaran, R. J. *Cabinet Government in India.* London: Allen & Unwin, 1967.

Weidner, Edward W., ed. *Development Administration in India.* Durham, N.C.: Duke University Press, 1970.

4

Political Parties and Political Leaders

Characteristics of the Indian Party System

Some parties and political factions were present in India before independence, but it was the Indian National Congress that dominated the political scene. As an umbrella organization leading the freedom movement, it attracted persons of diverse ideological persuasions and political goals who were willing to work toward achieving independence for the country. Whereas the Muslim League in Pakistan disintegrated soon after the creation of a Muslim majority state, in India the Congress not only survived but was converted from a loosely organized freedom movement into a cadre-based mass party. In 1948, at the urging of Sardar Vallabhbhai Patel, the Congress party Working Committee (the party's top executive organization) passed a resolution banning factions that had their own constitutions or organizational structure and had previously been allowed to operate within the Indian National Congress. This action led to the exit of various factions, which then converted themselves into new political parties. When the Congress became the ruling party of India, for many dissidents the only course left open was to form opposition parties.

The Common Socioeconomic Background of Party Leaders

The first generation of Indian leaders originated from the politically conscious stratum of Indian society and shared the experience of the freedom movement. Most of them were members of the upper or upper-middle classes. Most were educated in the West or in schools in India that followed a Western curriculum. This was true for the leadership of both the Congress and the parties of the ideological left and right. The middle class and the landowning upper and middle castes still dominate the parties, although an

89

English-language education may no longer be the common background. Lately the Dalits and Scheduled Castes have emerged as political players in Indian politics and they are demanding social and educational reforms and better employment opportunities.

Reliance on Powerful Personalities

Although the parties have built organizational structures, they rely heavily on charismatic and powerful personalities or community and religious leaders. But this tradition has its disadvantages. For example, a party that depends on one leader tends to disappear with his or her demise. In addition, influential persons sometimes change parties in search of power and position and bring their followers into the party of their choice. Domination of parties by small oligarchies is common. In the parties that have captured power at the national or state level, parliamentary wings under these strong leaders become dominant, and organizational or mass wings are relegated to a secondary position, used primarily for the mobilization of the voters. For years India's Congress party was the dominant party and was identified with the independence movement, nationalism, and governance. As a result of manipulation of the party by Indira Gandhi, her sons Sanjay and Rajiv, and her daughter-in-law Sonia Gandhi, the party lost its moral and political status and legitimacy as a mass national party, and as a progressive builder of party norms and national policies.

Factions Within the Parties

All political parties tend to be factionalized. In noncommunist parties the faction leaders tend to be community caste or religious leaders who have skillfully built patron-client relationships among the members of different castes or communities. Such factional leaders vie among themselves for political influence within the party and the government, entering into political alliances with one another in order to keep their political rivals out of power. Most of these factional alliances are not ideological; they also tend to shift and keep the parties in a state of flux. In rural areas, moreover, traditional hostilities based on caste and kinship are transformed into factional fights that lead to interparty and intraparty power struggles. In order to maintain unity, party leaders must constantly try to balance the interests of different factions.

In the Communist or Socialist parties, on the other hand, ideological considerations frequently lead to faction formation, although personality, caste, or regional affiliations can also play divisive roles despite the adherence of these parties to a common ideology. Political parties have also created various auxiliary organizations in an effort to mobilize different sectors of the society. More specifically, most of the prominent parties have organized youth wings, student unions, women's organizations, and peasant and labor groups. In addition, parties with the necessary strength and resources hold camps, seminars, and conferences for the different wings of the party.

The Use of Nonparliamentary Means to Power

Although electioneering and campaigning in an effort to capture a maximum number of seats in public offices are said to be the main functions of the parties, very few parties are able to make a respectable showing using only these legitimate methods. As a result, political parties of all ideological persuasions frequently try to exploit political or social discontent to their advantage. They do not hesitate to use such nonparliamentary means as civil disobedience, mass demonstrations, strikes, and protest rallies to embarrass the party or group in power. Sometimes the use of these tactics leads to violence.

The use of mob violence, however, has an unfortunate association with the method of the Congress party. As Crocker points out,

> He [Nehru] must take his share of the blame too for a spirit of violence which the Independence movement brought into Indian life. The Independence movement was dedicated to the purpose of breaking the British Government in India by all means possible (though Gandhi would have added, not quite convincingly, 'by all means short of terrorism') . . . The Nationalist agitators called in the mob to sabotage the British Government; but in doing that they risked destroying the principle of government itself, the principle of authority.[1]

The growth of Naxalite "gherao" and illegal strikes became widespread in the Bengal and other areas. In the 1980s they represented the mob mentality that India's independence leaders had encouraged. The BJP government was tarnished by its tolerance of mob violence in Gujrat between Hindus and Muslims in 2002, when Muslims burned a train carrying Hindu pilgrims, and Muslims suffered mob violence. A Congress government was also associated with killings of innocent Sikhs in 1984 as a result of Indira Gandhi's assassination. So tolerance of mob violence has emerged as a sub-rosa aspect of Indian party politics and society.

A Multiparty System

Since the disintegration of the consensus-based Congress system in 1967, the Indian parties have comprised a multiparty system. The Congress party itself is a coalition of diverse interests, factions, groups, and individuals. It has rarely been able to capture more than 50 percent of the votes, the remainder of which have been won by the opposition parties and independents. In the 1989 elections no political party won a majority in the lower house of parliament. At the state level, the dominance of the Congress party is frequently contested by regional and local parties.

Indian parties are divided into four major groups. First, All-India political parties have been officially defined as those national parties with broad-based national support that win a minimum of 4 percent of the votes or more than 3 percent of the seats in at least four state legislative assemblies. Also considered All-India political parties are those able to win 4 percent of the votes or 4 percent of the seats in the Lok Sabha. These parties present national platforms and emphasize national issues in the parliamentary elections.

On the basis of the results of the 1984 and 1989 elections, the following parties are classified as All-India parties: the Congress (I), the Bharatiya Janata Party (BJP), the Janata Dal, the Communist Party of India, and the Communist Party of India (Marxist). These parties draw support from different segments of the society and put up their candidates across state lines.

The second group consists of regional parties that clearly represent subregional nationalism based on the common languages, culture, and history of a region. Given the pluralist nature of Indian society, the rise of such parties is not surprising. These parties try to aggregate regional interests regardless of the caste and religious affiliations of their members. Their power base and voting strength are confined to a particular geographic area. The following are the best-known regional parties: the Dravida Munnetra Kazhagam (DMK) and the All-India Anna DMK of Tamil Nadu, the Telugu Desam Party (TDP) of Andhra Pradesh, the National Conference of Jammu and Kashmir, and Asom Gana Parishad (AGP) of Assam.

The third group includes those parties and organizations that are exclusive in their membership; that is, they accept as members only members of a particular religious or ethnic community. They seek to protect and promote the interests of that community alone, are basically nonaggregative, and generally mobilize their supporters by appealing to their particularist sentiments. The following parties fall into this category: the Shiromani Akali Dal of the Punjab, the Muslim League in Kerala, and the Shiv Sena in Bombay.

The fourth group of parties consists of those organized around powerful persons or local and state issues. Such parties may appear for a short period and then disappear completely or merge into other parties. There are currently several such parties existing in various states.

The Congress System and the Congress (I)

The Congress system emerged after India had attained independence. From 1947 until it broke down in 1967, this system was at the center of Indian politics, spanning three distinct stages in its post-independence development. The first phase (1947–1967) was the period of the Congress system; the second (1967–1977) was characterized by the decline and disintegration of the Congress system and the consolidation of power by a small oligarchy; and the third and current phase (from 1977 on) witnessed the development of a new system, which because of its domination by Indira Gandhi became known as the Indira Congress or Congress (I). The third phase is now entrenched. It highlights a political culture that openly flaunts the dominance of a single Congress leader who controls the power of patronage, the party's treasury, and the power to nominate loyalists to ministerial and party posts and for elections as MPs. Indira Gandhi started this system, and Sanjay and Rajiv Gandhi built on it; Sonia Gandhi inherited it and used her popularity to continue it.

Rajni Kothari, who developed the model of the Congress system, asserts that the Congress party, based on a broad consensus, was able to accommodate diverse interests and factions within its fold. These factions competed with each other but usually reached compromises that avoided any breakdown of the system. The opposition parties worked outside the system and used the factional leaders of the Congress party to influence its policy decisions. These parties acted as pressure groups and frequently created informal alliances with the factional leaders of the ruling party. The Congress system showed remarkable flexibility and accommodation in withstanding the pressure from within its own ranks as well as from the opposition groups. Often the programs, policies, and even personnel of the opposition parties were absorbed by the Congress system, thus leading to the strengthening of the one-party system in India.[2] This system operated during Nehru's leadership of the Congress party.[3]

The second phase in its development started with the critical elections of 1967, when the Congress lost its predominant position at both the state and national levels. The social and political mobilization resulting from two decades of independence had increased subgroup awareness in Indian society. Many new groups were brought into politics, and there was an increase in the polarization among different castes, communities, and religious minorities. In addition, several dissident groups became active, leading to increased competition at the state level for power and prestige within the Congress party. When the party became incapable of satisfying their aspirations, factional leaders sought to form alliances with the leaders of the opposition parties, thus contributing to the disintegration of local and state Congress party organizations. As Nehru's authority in national and international affairs diminished in the latter part of his tenure, the growing power and policy vacuum in Indian politics and government presented opportunities for others to occupy the space at times by coopting Nehru to their agenda(s). Nehru's indecisiveness, his political loneliness or aloofness from a coterie of peers, and the burden of governing a complex society helped others to influence Nehru's decisions and thinking. Nehru became a leader, the best known in India and abroad, but he was not the most effective decision maker.

At the national level, the death of Nehru and the rise of Kamaraj Nadar as the president of the organizational wing of the party led to the weakening of its parliamentary wing. The renewed conflict between the two sides was ultimately settled by the 1969 split within the party. Indira Gandhi, who was the leader of the parliamentary wing and the prime minister of the country, defied and defeated the party bosses by successfully supporting the election of V. V. Giri to the presidency. She thus became the dominant force within the party. The Congress was no longer a party based on broad consensus. Instead, it became dependent on the charismatic personality and populist policies of Indira Gandhi for electoral victories. Party and Indian norms suffered when Indira Gandhi and her supporters propagated the view that "Indira was India" (and vice versa). As the cult of personality grew, party norms suffered, and the system of checks and balances in a constitutional government—involving all branches of the Indian government and various segments of attentive Indian publics outside the government—broke down.

The parliamentary victories in the 1971 elections and the subsequent party sweep of the state legislative assembly elections in 1972 not only made Indira Gandhi the undisputed leader of the party but also transformed the nature of the party. The new members recruited into the parliament and state legislative assemblies were not always part of the local party organizations and often lacked an independent power base. Moreover, the autonomy of the state party units was subverted by Indira Gandhi's policy of creating divisions between the organizational and legislative wings of the party.

Indira Gandhi intervened in state elections and was known for dismissing state governments she did not like. This was not Nehru's approach. She adopted a divide-and-rule approach to state politics and was reinforced in this attitude by Sanjay Gandhi's determination to teach opponents a lesson. Her declaration of national emergency and the suspension of fundamental rights in 1975 reflected Sanjay Gandhi's influence and the rise of an extra-constitutional power center in the prime minister's household. As a result Indian politics acquired a dual character. While elections were free and fair under supervision of the Indian Election Commission and international observers, the decision-making process in the political and policy spheres had a secretive and manipulative character. In general, the central leadership became highly oligarchic and autocratic. But in 1975, unable to contain the unrest caused by economic and social discontent and challenged by the opposition leader and total collapse of the party organizations in various states, Indira Gandhi declared a state of emergency and suspended democratic activities. With this period of emergency ended the second phase of the Congress party's history.

The third phase commenced after Indira Gandhi's defeat in the 1977 election, which was held after the termination of her emergency rule. In this election for the Lok Sabha, the Congress won 34.5 percent of the votes and 153 seats, in contrast to the 43.6 percent of the votes and 352 seats it had won in the 1971 elections. Indira Gandhi even lost her own seat in parliament. This defeat resulted in another split within the party, leading to the emergence of the Congress (I). Many of the old and experienced leaders left the party, blaming Gandhi for its humiliating defeat in the elections. As a result, the new Congress (I) became completely identified with her personality. Many of the party's top decision-making agencies, such as the Congress Working Committee and the All-India Congress Committee, lost their powers. Similarly, state party organizations were brought under her direct control, as was the presidency of the Congress party, since she handpicked the top functionaries. She built a pyramid-like organization that was run by her or her henchmen.[4] When the 1980 elections were held after the collapse of the Janata government, the Congress (I), led by Indira Gandhi, returned to power by winning a massive majority. Assisted by her son Sanjay Gandhi, she selected only persons of proven loyalty to the Nehru/Gandhi family to run for parliament. She especially sought to reward political cronies who had stood by her during the period in which she had been out of power; administrative experience and parliamentary skill did not matter. In the 1980 Lok Sabha elections, the Congress (I) captured 43 percent of the votes and won 351 of 539 seats.[5] In June of the same year, Gandhi called elections for state legislatures, and the Congress (I) captured power in fifteen of twenty-two states.

The return of the Congress (I) to power in 1980 was attributed to the failure and eventual disintegration of the Janata Party coalition that had captured power in 1977. In the 1980 elections the opposition leaders who had become discredited failed either to put up a joint front against the Congress or to build electoral alliances to give it a tough fight. Starting in 1971 a dramatic change in the composition of the Congress party elites took place. In that year a large number of political careerists and opportunists joined the party. In 1980, in addition to these elements, many persons of dubious character and even criminal backgrounds entered into the Congress party.[6] Under Indira's leadership the Congress party simply became an instrument of personal power. She also sought to use the organization for dynastic succession. First she groomed Sanjay, her younger son, to take over the leadership of the party, but after his accidental death in June 1980, she brought in her elder son, Rajiv.[7] In the 1984 parliamentary elections after the assassination of Indira Gandhi, the Congress (I) won with a record-setting vote, capturing around 50 percent of the popular vote and 396 Lok Sabha seats—a feat unmatched in the history of free India. The relentless campaign mounted soon after Rajiv's mother's assassination brought him a great many sympathy votes. His victory was made easier by a fragmented opposition led by old-guard politicians who had failed to establish their credibility with the masses.

The key issue in the 1984 election was the threat to national unity. The events in the Punjab and the separatist movement led by the Sikh extremists were alarming enough to persuade the people to vote for the Congress (I), a party that possessed a national image. The election result was perceived as the "clearest mandate possible on the central issue of national unity and the rejection of Janata, DMK and BJP opposition."[8] The Congress (I) under the leadership of Rajiv Gandhi swept all the states in the country except Andhra Pradesh, Jammu and Kashmir, and Sikkim.

In the 1989 parliamentary elections the Congress (I) was able to capture only 193 of 525 seats, however, losing power at the center. The party was routed in the densely populated Hindi-speaking states of north India. In the 1991 May–June parliamentary elections, after the assassination of Rajiv Gandhi, the Congress (I) was able to improve its position when it won 226 seats. Its new leader, P. V. Narasimha Rao, became prime minister with the support of some regional and minor parties and independent members of the Lok Sabha. In 1992 it further increased its strength when it won twelve of thirteen seats from the state of Punjab. In the 1990 elections for the state legislative bodies, once again the Congress (I) suffered humiliating defeat at the hands of the Janata Dal and BJP and lost power in important states like Madhya Pradesh, Bihar, Rajasthan, Gujarat, Orissa, Himachal Pradesh, and Uttar Pradesh.

The constitution of the Congress party provides for an elaborate organization headed by a president, assisted by a Working Committee (the executive of the party) and supplemented by the All-India Congress Committee (AICC), the deliberative branch of the party. Its central office in New Delhi supervises the work of the Pradesh (state) Congress committees (PCCs) as well as other subordinate organizations. However, when she had control of the party, Indira Gandhi stifled intraparty democracy and did not hold party elections after 1972. Under the leadership of Rao, who became the party president after the May 1991 assassination of Rajiv Gandhi, efforts were made to revitalize the party organization. In 1992 Rao held party elections, which, though not flawless, introduced a considerable degree of democracy into the internal functioning of the party.

The Congress party's program and policies have been generally moderate and reform oriented rather than radical, seeking to bring about gradual changes in the basic structure of Indian society. During the period of Nehru-Gandhi family domination of the Congress party, the party was committed to democratic socialism and planned economic development. It gave the dominant role to the state in running such key industries as steel, heavy chemicals, and fertilizers. However, in the 1992 session of the All-India Congress Committee held at Tirupati, the party accepted the Rao government's private enterprise–oriented policies of economic liberalization. While paying lip service to the Nehru legacy of democratic socialism and planned economic development, it stressed efficiency and productivity, even if it required the privatization of public sector industries. Thus in the post–1991 period the Congress party has opted for much more pragmatic and flexible economic policies than in previous periods. This was a turning point which set in motion a series of economic reforms in India.

In the 1996 elections for the Lok Sabha, with the party bereft of charisma and vision and plagued by charges of widespread corruption, the Congress (I) suffered its worst defeat ever and lost power (see Table 4.1). Consequently, the party went through a leadership change. Rao had to quit as both the president of the organizational wing and the leader of the party in the parliament. Subsequently the party went through several leadership changes without much electoral success; eventually, in 1998 it installed Sonia Gandhi, the widow of Rajiv and heir to the Nehru-Gandhi dynasty, as the president of the Congress party. Initially, Sonia helped the Congress party win elections in such states as Rajasthan, Madhya Pradesh, Karnataka, and Delhi. However, in the 1999 national elections it suffered the worst defeat in its history despite vigorous campaigning by Sonia Gandhi. Sonia was, however, for the first time elected to the lower house of the Indian parliament and became the leader of the opposition.

The stunning defeat in 1999 became a lesson for Sonia, who began to rebuild the party. In 2004, in the middle of a strong economic boom, she led the Congress party into national elections which almost all analysts believed would return the BJP to power. However, the Congress targeted its appeal to the rural population and to the inhabitants of the regional cities. The economic boom of the BJP years had largely ignored these constituencies and focused on the larger urban areas such as Mumbai and Delhi. The Congress appeal received very strong support and returned the party to power in a coalition government.

The Congress party won the largest number of seats in parliament, 145, and their allies another 76 seats to the BJP's and its allies' 186 seats. Because the Congress and their allies did not win a majority, they formed a minority coalition with smaller independent parties.

TABLE 4.1   Lok Sabha Elections, 2004

Name of Party	Seats Contested	Seats Won	2004 vote %	1999 vote %
CONGRESS AND ALLIES				
Congress	400	145	26.5	28.3
Rashtriya Janatha Dal	42	24	2.4	2.8
Dravida Munnetra Kazhagam	16	16	1.8	1.7
Nationalist Congress Party	32	9	1.8	2.3
Pattali Makkal Katdchi	6	6	.6	.6
Telangana Rashtra Samithi	22	5	.6	0
Jharkhand Mukti Morcha	9	5	.5	.3
Marumaralarchi Dravida				
Munnetra Kazhagam	4	4	.4	.4
Lok Jan Shakti	40	4	.7	0
Jammu & Kashmir People's				
Democratic	3	1	.1	0
Republican Party of India				
(Athvale)	7	1	.1	0
Indian Union Muslim League	10	1	.2	.2
2 Others	19	0	.1	.3
Total: Congress and Allies	610	221	35.7	36.8
BJP AND ALLIES				
Bharatiya Janata Party	364	138	22.2	23.8
Shiv Sena	56	12	1.8	1.6
Biju Janata Dal	12	11	1.3	1.2
Shiromani Akali Dal	10	8	.9	.7
Janata Dal (United)	73	8	2.4	3.1
Telugu Desam Party	33	5	3	3.6
Nationalist Trinamool Congress	33	2	2.1	2.6
Nagaland Peoples Front	3	1	.2	0
Mizo National Front	1	1	.05	0
All-India Anna Daravida				
Munneetra Kazhagam	33	0	2.2	1.9
Total: BJP and Allies	618	186	36.1	38.4
PARTIES NOT ALLIED TO				
BJP OR CONGRESS				
Communist Party of India				
(Marxist)	69	43	5.7	5.4
Samajwadi	237	36	4.3	3.8
Bahujan Samaj	435	19	5.3	4.2
Communist Party of India	34	10	1.4	1.5
Ind	2385	5	4.2	2.7
Janata Dal (Secular)	43	3	1.5	1
Revolutionary Socialist	6	3	.4	.4
Rashtriya Lok Dal	32	3	.6	.4

(continues)

TABLE 4.1   *(continued)*

Name of Party	Seats Contested	Seats Won	2004 vote %	1999 vote %
All-India Forward Bloc	10	3	.4	.4
Asom Gana Parishad	12	2	.5	.3
Jammu & Kashmir National				
Conference	6	2	.1	.1
Indian Federal Democratic	1	1	.1	0
Kerala Congress	1	1	.1	.1
All-India Majilis-e-ittehadul				
Muslimeen	2	1	.1	.1
Bharatiya Navshakti	4	1	.04	0
National Loktantrik	18	1	.1	.04
Sikkim Democratic Front	1	1	.04	.03
Samajwadi Janata Party (Rashtriya)	10	1	.1	.1
161 Others	867	0	2.9	4.25

Source: Election Commission of India, www.eci.gov.in/StatisticalReports/ElectionStatistics.asp.

The 2004 election solidified the new nature of national party politics in India. The Congress party's decline as a national party has left the country with coalitions which form over local issues and stay together as long as the local, smaller parties gain their objectives from the coalition. At the moment, it appears unlikely that either the Congress party or the BJP will emerge as a truly national party capable of winning an outright majority nationally. The Congress party victory was slim and the party needs to solidify its base of strength before the next national elections.

In the twelve state Legislative Assembly elections in 2006 and 2007, the Congress and its allies won control of only three assemblies (Goa, Assam, and Manipur). However, the BJP won only four (Himachal Pradesh, Gujarat, and Uttarakhand). The other SLAs were won by regional parties, including the BSP, a Dalit party, in India's largest state, Uttar Pradesh. There appears to be no end to the decline of national parties in India.

Non-Congress Parties: Janata Dal and the National Front—Ad Hoc Coalitions of Factional Leaders

Non-Congress centrist parties constitute an important segment of India's polarized multiparty system. Of the different constituents of India's party system none show more remarkable tendencies toward frequent fusion and fragmentation than these. The non-Congress ideological center contains certain inherent contradictions and tensions, which lead to political instability and ultimately to its fragmentation or disintegration. This constellation consists of influential caste and community leaders and other frustrated politicians seeking to dislodge

India's entrenched political elite. Many of these groups have been recently mobilized, for example, the Jats, the peasant proprietors of western Uttar Pradesh, the Yadavs, the Kurmis and the members of Other Backward Castes (OBCs) of Hindus, Scheduled Castes, and Muslim minorities. Their disparity of interests tends to be overridden by their common disenchantment and disillusionment with the Congress (I) and other major parties. Members of these groups are mostly rural, and in the post-independence period they have produced an educated middle class seeking jobs and a share in India's increasing prosperity.

While the non-Congress political parties tend to organize themselves around the leaders of these groups, it is tempting to analyze the efforts of the centrist political leaders to organize parties on the basis of common class interests. It has been argued that these groups are pitted against the high-caste and westernized upper-class elites originating from landowning gentry or the older urban middle class represented by the Congress (I) and the BJP.[9] It is doubtful whether such a class-based explanation would have much validity, however.

It is very difficult, if not impossible, to create class consciousness among groups divided by status and other conflicts of interest. For instance, there is intense competition between the Jats, Yadavs, Kurmis, and other members of OBCs for status in the highly stratified Hindu social structure. On the other hand, in rural India, members of Scheduled Castes are frequently the victims of violence perpetrated on them by the Yadavs or the Jats. There is also frequent hostility between Muslims and Jats or Yadavs, who are Hindus, on the basis of religion. Such internal tensions and contradictions lead to the formation of unstable political alliances.

Cultural Disparity of the Factions

In addition, the leaders of these parties are people with dramatically different social and cultural backgrounds. For example, there was little commonality between Raj Narain and Jagjivan Ram or between Charan Singh and Morarji Desai, all leaders of the non-Congress centrist Janata Party founded in 1977. Whereas Raj Narain represented the disruptive and anarchic traditions cultivated by Ram Manohar Lohia, Jagjivan Ram, an able administrator and a shrewd politician, was a leader of the Scheduled Caste establishment, deeply entrenched in the ruling circles of the Congress (I). Similarly, Charan Singh, a representative of the affluent peasant proprietors and a strong supporter of agrarian interests, was an opportunist, whereas his rival, Morarji Desai, a Gujarati Brahmin and a favorite of Indian industrialists and businessmen, was a stickler for principles. Such contradictions in the backgrounds of the actors, significant differences in their attitudes and orientations, all fueled by their political ambitions, often created friction among the coalition partners, finally leading to disintegration of the coalitions. Such a pattern of behavior was repeated in 1989 when V. P. Singh forged an alliance of factions led by Devi Lal, Ajit Singh, Mulayam Singh Yadav, Chandra Shekhar, Arun Nehru, and others. They represented different interests, sociocultural backgrounds, and policy orientations, and were motivated by conflicting political ambitions.

Many of these factional leaders demand absolute loyalty from their followers, equating political dissent with personal betrayal. They constantly seek recognition of their status and authority by their political rivals. Because of this concern with power and status they sometimes pursue strategies to undermine each other's positions within the party or government, rather than focusing on conducting the business of the government or building the organizational structure of the party.

Lacking cohesion and a stable support base, the leaders of these parties are unable to build any viable organizational structure. They are constantly vigilant to protect the integrity of their factions. At the heart of such factionalism is the patron-client relationship existing between the leader and his or her followers. While factional leaders could enter into alliances with other groups if a split in the party took place, their supporters are expected to follow the leaders.

In earlier years, most of the centrist parties depended on the notables of caste and community groups for mobilization of the voters. With the decline of the status of such notables, many leaders of these factions now turn to local thugs and musclemen belonging to a particular caste or community to help them win elections. These characteristics of the centrist parties have contributed to the growing perception of corruption in the party system. In 1965 and 1966 Dr. Ram Manohar Lohia moved to unite the non-Congress opposition parties by adopting a strategy of forming electoral alliances and mutually beneficial seat adjustment to dislodge the Congress from power. To achieve this goal, he pleaded with the opposition parties to set aside their ideological differences and organize United Legislative Parties (Samyukta Vidhyak Dals) to form non-Congress governments at the state level. In many states, such as Uttar Pradesh, Bihar, Haryana, and Punjab, United Legislative Fronts led by the leaders of the centrist parties were able to form governments. Leaders of the right-wing and left-wing parties, such as the Jana Sangh and the Communists, joined the leadership of the centrist parties to form coalition governments as it became evident that the centrist parties could not capture power on their own. However, the cooperation among the leaders of these parties with such different ideological orientations and constituencies did not last long. Within the context of market-oriented politics and fluid political situations, defection became the norm.

After the sweeping electoral victories of the Congress (I) in 1971 reduced the centrist parties to the margins of Indian politics, many of them went through further mergers and name changes in their quest for continuing relevance. They began resorting to agitation, protest movements, and demonstrations for political survival and as a means of maintaining public visibility. By 1975 the centrist parties, first led by Morarji Desai, brought down the corrupt Congress (I) government in Gujarat. Subsequently, under the leadership of Jaya Prakash Narayan, a massive agitation to bring down the central government forced Indira Gandhi to declare a national emergency and arrest most of the leaders of the opposition. The Janata Party, which came into existence in 1977 as a result of the merger of the centrists, socialists, and various other groups, was primarily a collection of former members of the Congress party united in a desire to dislodge the Indira Gandhi–dominated Congress party from power. The only non-Congress group to join the new party was the Jana Sangh, the right-wing Hindu nationalists. The Janata Party was able to capture power nationally in 1977. It was also successful in capturing several state governments, especially in north India. However, lacking a common program, a grassroots organization, and any sense of unity, this coalition of diverse factional leaders could not survive long. Following the patterns set by the Samyukta Vidhyak Dal in the late 1960s and motivated by their personal ambitions and conflicting political orientations, the leaders of the new party became engaged in an intense power struggle, which led to numerous fissures and the fall of its government in 1979.

Unable to devise a common electoral strategy or to plan any meaningful seat adjustment among themselves, the leaders of the centrist parties failed to deny massive majorities to the Congress (I) in both the 1980 and 1984 elections. But in 1989 these factional leaders were once again brought together in the form of the Janata Dal by V. P. Singh and his associates, who either had resigned or were expelled from the Congress (I). As the prospects for an electoral victory looked promising, it was not surprising to see these factional leaders subordinate their personal ambitions to dislodge the Congress (I) from power. After entering into electoral alliances and seat adjustments with such right-wing political parties as the Bharatiya Janata Party and others, in the 1989 Lok Sabha elections the Janata Dal emerged as the second largest party in parliament with 143 seats.

At the national level a loose confederation of national and regional parties founded in 1988 by the late N. T. Rama Rao, with V. P. Singh as its convener, became the center of the new coalition government, with the Janata Dal as its anchor. Under the leadership of V. P. Singh, the Janata Dal/National Front, with the support of the Communists and right-wing Bharatiya Janata Party, was able to form a government. Subsequently, in the 1990 assembly elections held in ten states the Janata Dal was able to capture power in three critical states,

Bihar, Gujarat, and Orissa, having earlier won election in Uttar Pradesh, India's most populous state.

The Janata Dal, as expected, undermined the support base of the Congress party built by Indira Gandhi, especially in Uttar Pradesh and Bihar. It attracted the votes of well-to-do peasant proprietors such as the Jats, who traditionally voted for the Lok Dal, and also received the votes of Muslims, Scheduled Castes, and backward castes such as Yadavs and Kurmis. However, state and local party units rarely depended on the national leadership or its organization, because they were controlled primarily by the state party bosses. Since the Janata Dal had no grassroots organization and was based on a precarious and unstable alliance of disparate factions at the national level, the survival of not only the government but even the party itself was doubtful.

In its public policies and programs, the Janata Dal occupied a centrist position, placing greater emphasis on rural development, decentralization of power both in the economy and in politics, restoration of civil liberties, and accommodation of the demands of India's various religious and linguistic minorities. In foreign policy, it sought understanding and accommodation with India's neighbors rather than confrontation, as the Congress (I) governments often did.

Search for Social Justice or a Strategy for Votes?

During the eleven months (December 1989–November 1990) that the Janata Dal/National Front government held office it was plagued with factional conflicts, defections, and political intrigues. However, the major challenge to V. P. Singh's leadership came from Devi Lal, an old-guard politician with support among the Jats. Having no power base of his own and with no organization to mobilize the voters, in August 1990 Singh announced his intention to implement the recommendations of the Mandal Commission report. The commission recommended that in addition to the Scheduled Castes and Scheduled Tribes who were the beneficiaries of previously established quotas, now Other Backward Castes (OBCs) of Hindu society, who were deemed to be socially and economically deprived, would also be entitled to reservation of jobs in government and public sector industries as well as seats in educational and professional institutions. Consequently, 52 percent of these jobs would have been reserved for these segments of the population, leaving members of the upper castes high and dry. V. P. Singh's decision unleashed unprecedented violence, leading to the deaths of more than 100 students.[10]

It was a clever electoral strategy disguised as a revolutionary policy decision to achieve social justice. Assured of Muslim support, Singh's hope was, as Paul Brass observed, that "the Mandal decision would prevent the consolidation of the Hindu community behind the BJP, and would instead divide the Hindus and consolidate the support of the backward castes behind the Janata Dal."11 Subsequent election results show that the Janata Dal was unable to improve its electoral fortunes despite its efforts to woo the OBCs and the Scheduled Castes. More significantly, however, this strategy did not prevent splits within the party. As in the past, with its leaders guided by their own political interests, the party fragmented into state-level or regional parties, using slightly different names. The result was that in the 1991 Lok Sabha elections two factions of the Janata Dal, one led by V. P. Singh and the other by his rival, Chandra Shekhar, and called Samajwadi Janata Dal, both performed poorly, securing just sixty seats for the faction led by Singh and five seats for Shekhar. In the 1993 state elections the Janata Dal suffered additional erosion of support in such crucial states of north India as Uttar Pradesh, Rajasthan, Himachal Pradesh, Madhya Pradesh, and Delhi, losing control of the Uttar Pradesh state government.

In the October 1996 legislative assembly elections held in Uttar Pradesh, the Janata Dal could capture only seven of 424 seats. It supported Mulayam Singh Yadav, the leader of the Samajwadi Party (SP), for the position of chief minister. He was able to capture 110 seats. In this instance, the Samajwadi Party, which represents primarily OBCs in the state, was the main beneficiary of the implementation of the recommendations of the Mandal Commission. In the 1999 and 2004 national elections the Janata Dal was split into three parties. The first was called Rashtriya Janata Dal, led by Laloo Prasad Yadav; the second was Janata Dal United, led by Sharad Yadav; and the third, known as the Janata Dal Secular, led by H. D. Deve Gowda. While Rashtriya Janata Dal formed an electoral alliance with the Congress party and won twenty-four seats out of the forty-two which it contested in 2004, the Janata Dal United, led by Sharad Yadav, joined by the National Democratic Alliance, led by the BJP, and won eight seats out of the seventy-three contested. The Janata Dal Secular, led by Deve Gowda, contested forty-three seats on its own and was able to win only three seats (see Table 4.1).

The Party of the Right: Bharatiya Janata Party (BJP)

The Bharatiya Janata Party, a proponent of right-wing Hindu nationalism, suddenly emerged as the second-largest party in the Lok Sabha by winning unexpected electoral victories in 1991 and again in 1996–1997 and 1999. It virtually eliminated the Congress party in the Hindi-speaking states of north India. The BJP poses a major challenge to secularist political ideology and to the Congress and other centrist parties that have ruled India since independence in 1947.

A Strategy to Consolidate Hindu Votes

The BJP represents an important version of nationalism in India that originated in the nineteenth century but was rendered peripheral when the Indian
nationalist movement of Gandhi and Nehru dominated Indian politics. The
basic premise of the BJP's ideology is that India's national identity is rooted in
Hindu culture, for the obvious reason that Hindus are a majority in the country and nations are built on the basis of common culture and historic traditions. To the BJP, genuine Indian nationhood should incorporate the Hindu
heritage along with the traditions, practices, and beliefs that flow through the
ancient history of the country. It holds that the groups which make up a nation come together for a purpose represented by a community of projects, desires, and historic undertakings. Such essentials for nation building are
provided by a culture based on a people's shared experience. According to this
view, minorities must reconcile themselves to the political reality of Hinduism
and its social values, its centrality in the formation of India's national identity.
By thus appealing to the majority community's religious and cultural sentiments and a distaste of minority Muslim politics which the Congress leaders
favored, the leadership of the BJP sought to build and consolidate its base of
support. It was perceived to hold an anti-Muslim bias, but our discussion can
be broadened. Was the BJP advocacy a plea to recognize the political vitality of
Hinduism and its relevance to Indian politics, or was it only a rigid anti-Muslim
position?

Repudiation of Centralized, State-Controlled Economic Planning

The BJP repudiates not only the secular version of Indian nationalism as propagated by Nehru and the Congress party and support of special Muslim rights
but also the concept of centralized and state-directed economic planning and
socialism in favor of free enterprise and a market economy. Earlier it advocated
drastic liberalization of the economy, lifting of state control, abolition of the
system of permits and licenses, and turning over most public sector enterprises
to private business. Many of the BJP's economic policy pronouncements were
adopted by the Rao government. This stratagem forced the BJP leadership to
modify some of its earlier economic positions. At one point it was protectionist
and opposed the entry of multinationals in Indian markets except in the area of
high technology. This attitude changed after 1997 when the centrist Vajpayee
government, in opposition to the extreme rightist Rashtriya Swayamsevak
Sangh (RSS) leaders and extremist Indian leftists, cautiously embraced globalization, favored a tilt toward the United States in economic and strategic affairs,
and pushed selective economic reforms in India. The BJP, like the Congress

party, seeks rapid industrialization of the country and planned to see India emerge as a major economic and military power in the world.

Despite advocating economic decentralization and greater state autonomy, the BJP is unwilling to accommodate the demands of religious and ethnic minorities for political and economic rewards based on their minority status. In its foreign and security policies the BJP adopted a more aggressive nationalist and militant posture than the Congress or other centrist parties. The BJP government under Vajpayee had an anti-Nehruvian orientation and adopted a set of economic, diplomatic, and military policies at odds with the Nehruvian paradigm of socialism, nonalignment with a pro-Soviet tilt, and peace diplomacy. The BJP policies enabled India to join the global economic and strategic mainstream by tilting toward the United States and Israel, by balancing and broadening India's search for relations with traditional and nontraditional partners, and by adopting coercive diplomacy as a method of action with Pakistan.

The BJP inherited the traditions and ideology of the Jana Sangh, founded in 1951 by Dr. Shyama Prasad Mookerjee (1901–1953). In 1977 it merged into the Janata Party. The party came into existence in its present form in 1980, under the leadership of Atal Bihari Vajpayee, a former president of the Jana Sangh. To join the mainstream of Indian politics and to expand its popularity, the party adopted Gandhian socialism as its political ideology. In 1986, failing in its efforts to expand its electoral base and shunned by the centrist parties, under the leadership of L. K. Advani the party adopted Hindutva, militant Hindu nationalism, in place of Gandhian socialism, as its political ideology. However, while in power from 1997 to 2004, the BJP faced internal controversies. Vajpayee represented the pragmatic side of the BJP in economic and strategic affairs while Vajpayee's deputy, L. K. Advani, expressed an ideological view of Hindutva and was associated with events like the mob attack in the demolition of the old Muslim Babri Masjid in 1992.

Changing Strategies: Electoral Alliances and Religious Symbols for Voter Mobilization

Advani cleverly used religious symbols to mobilize the masses by exploiting Hindu resentment against the Protection of Rights on Divorce Act passed by the Rajiv Gandhi government. In its pursuit of political power the BJP leadership adopted a strategy of making electoral deals with the centrist parties. Thus in 1989, to avoid multiple contests and to split the votes of the opposition parties, the party under Advani's leadership made an electoral agreement with the Janata Dal in which they did not oppose each other for the same seats, and they captured eighty-six seats in the Lok Sabha, emerging as the third largest party in parliament. In contrast, in 1984 it had won only two seats.

In the February 1990 state elections the BJP not only improved its electoral performance in key states but also outdistanced the Congress (I). The Congress and the BJP had fielded 1,559 and 1,000 candidates, respectively, winning 417 and 569 seats in the states. The Congress (I) lost 350 seats, and the BJP gained 479 seats.[12] Even though the BJP lost its foothold in the south, where it had made some gains in the 1985 elections, it emerged as the dominant party in key states like Madhya Pradesh, Rajasthan, and Himachal Pradesh and as a major contender in the western states. Such an achievement was all the more significant since the BJP had made only a limited seat adjustment with the Janata Dal.

Subsequently, when V. P. Singh decided to implement the Mandal Commission report to build his party's popular support, the BJP leadership, realizing that such a move would deeply divide Hindu society and hurt its chances of capturing political power, decided to use religious issues as a means to unite Hindus, irrespective of caste or class. The decision was made to mobilize Hindus on the basis of the highly emotional issue of reestablishing their control over Hindu sacred places that were converted to mosques during Muslim rule. This strategy resulted in Advani's rath yatra, a journey in an air-conditioned Toyota converted into a chariot, through hundreds of miles of Hindu-majority states. Although this move caused extensive Hindu-Muslim riots, involving massive loss of life and property, the electoral strategy paid rich dividends in the 1991 parliamentary elections, in which the BJP emerged as the second largest party in the Lok Sabha. It also won a majority of seats in the Uttar Pradesh state Legislative Assembly, forming the government in India's most populous state.

The Inability of the Party to Demonstrate Administrative Responsibility

The BJP had an opportunity to act as a responsible political party and to demonstrate its administrative capabilities in the states under its rule. Large states like Uttar Pradesh, Madhya Pradesh, and Rajasthan faced many developmental problems. They were plagued by poverty rooted in an economy based on backward agricultural practices and sluggish industrialization. People were looking for a clean government with a capacity to uplift the sagging morale of the bureaucracy and to rein in disorderly behavior by the police establishment.

Instead, the December 1992 destruction of the Babri mosque by Hindu militants and the inability of the BJP government in Uttar Pradesh to protect the lives and the property of the minority community raised serious concerns about the responsible behavior of its leadership. The result was the dismissal of the BJP-led state governments and imposition of president's rule by the central government.

In the 1993 elections in the key states of Uttar Pradesh, Rajasthan, Madhya Pradesh, Himachal Pradesh, and Delhi, the BJP captured only Rajasthan and

Delhi, losing control of other states. The BJP was able to maintain its popular support (it actually increased its share of votes in Uttar Pradesh, Delhi, and Madhya Pradesh and lost marginally in Rajasthan), but its capacity to win seats declined. In most cases, this was because of the consolidation of Hindu backward castes and the Dalits with the Muslims, which tilted the balance against the BJP. An aggregate analysis of votes polled by parties in all five states (Uttar Pradesh, Madhya Pradesh, Himachal Pradesh, Rajasthan, and Delhi) shows that the BJP secured 36.2 percent as against 26.2 percent, 9.1 percent, and 16.6 percent by the Congress, Janata Dal, and the combined Socialist party–Bahujan Samaj Party.[13]

The BJP has been gradually extending its support in the south, especially in Karnataka, where it improved its yield from five seats in 1989 to eighty-four in the 2004 state legislative assembly elections, where it was able to form a coalition government. The dramatic electoral victories that the BJP scored over its main opponents, Congress and Janata Dal, in the two western states of Gujarat and Maharashtra established it as a major contender for power at the national level. While in Maharashtra the BJP formed the government with Shiv Sena as its senior partner, in Gujarat it formed the government on its own. In the May–June 1996 elections to the Lok Sabha the BJP emerged as the largest single party, with 162 seats, leaving Congress behind with only 141 seats. Supported by some of the regional parties as well as ideological allies, with a total of 192 seats in the Lok Sabha, and led by a moderate and well-known national leader, Atal Bihari Vajpayee, it staked its claim to form the government at the national level. However, it was unable to win support from other parties and failed in its efforts to come to power at the center.

The rise of the BJP was stopped by the 2004 general elections. The overwhelming defeat led the party to reassess its electoral strategy. Many within the party felt that the leadership may have assumed that they were going to win and failed to adequately campaign. This criticism included a belief that they relied too heavily on television and cell phone campaign ads. In any case, the party has attempted to reestablish its electoral majority since the 2004 loss.

The party has continued to be successful at the elections to the state Legislative Assemblies and rebuilt much of its electoral base. However, at the national level, the Congress can rule until 2009 and the BJP's aging leadership may no longer be in a position to lead the country unless the next national election is carried out with a new generation of leaders.

National Democratic Alliance (NDA)

Since the late 1980s both the national parties, Congress and the BJP, have been unable to win absolute majorities and thus form a government on their own.

The importance of the regional and minor parties has increased. Their support became essential to achieve a stable government at the national level. Atal Bihari Vajpayee and his associates in the BJP were quick to understand the imperatives of coalition politics. Therefore, in the 1999 elections Vajpayee actively sought an electoral and political alliance with important regional parties. The result was the formation of the National Democratic Alliance, consisting of such parties as DMK of Tamil Nadu; Telugu Desam of Andhra Pradesh; Janata Dal United; Akali Dal of Punjab; Shiv Sena of Maharashtra; the Manipur State Congress party; the Trinmool Congress of West Bengal; the Biju Janata Dal of Orrisa and Jammu; the Kashmir National Conference; and various others. Led by the BJP, with mutual seat adjustment, the NDA contested elections on a common political platform. Such an electoral strategy paid rich electoral dividends (see Table 4.1) and gave the regional parties a stake in national politics; it also forced the BJP to dilute its ideology of militant Hindu nationalism. With the support of important constituents of the NDA, the BJP has been able to keep Congress, its main rival, out of power at the national level.

Limitations of BJP Ideological and Electoral Strategies

Between 1997 and 2004 the BJP emerged as an alternative to Congress party rule. But despite its extensive cadre-based organization and links with RSS, and despite its good record in the economic and strategic spheres during its tenure as a minority government, its RSS links and ideology and events in Babri Masjid (1992) and Gujrat (2002) generated a belief in the Indian public that the BJP was antisecular and anti-Muslim. This view, and its overconfidence in 2004, led to its defeat in the polls. However, the 2004 election results led to the replacement of the BJP minority government with a Congress-led minority government (2004 to present). It showed that Indian voters were unwilling to trust either party with majority status.

After its unexpected electoral defeat in 2004, the BJP lost its sense of direction. Supported by poll numbers before the election, the BJP felt confident that a booming economy, elevation of India as a major global player and power, stability despite a coalition government during its five-year rule, and an improved relationship with Pakistan before the election would lead to their return to power. Overconfidence, growing inequality despite a booming economy, and disenchantment of its core extremist Hindu base toward the party's government for adopting a more moderate attitude are some of the explanations given for the loss. After the loss some sections of the party began to question its more moderate policies and called for going back to its previous exclusionary posture.

In its attempts to gain direction, the party has changed leadership several times. Venkaiah Naidu quit and Lal Krishna Advani became the president of the party again in 2004. Advani had to quit the party presidency in 2005 after a furor broke out in the party over a remark he made while visiting Pakistan that Muhammed Ali Jinnah, the founder of Pakistan, was secular. Rajnath Singh, former union minister and Uttar Pradesh chief minister, became president of the party in January 2006. In 2007, the BJP declared Lal Krishna Advani as its prime ministerial candidate, perhaps preparing groundwork for the 2009 general elections. The party also set a quota of 33 percent female members to attract women to join its organizations.

The BJP's performance in state elections has been mixed after 2004. It regained power in Uttarkhand and Himachal Pradesh from the Congress while retaining Gujarat in 2007. It also formed coalition governments in Punjab and Karnataka. However, the party faced a major electoral setback in Uttar Pradesh, the most populous state. Likewise, several prominent leaders like Uma Bharati and Madan Lal Khurana left the party to form their own political fronts.

Which alliance would form a government at the center after the next union elections would depend on what type of alliance the BJP and Congress formed as both alliances received nearly equal percentages of votes. In 2004, the Congress-led alliance won 219 seats with 34.51 percent votes while the BJP-led alliance won 185 seats with 34.83 percent of votes. Thus BJP's path to power in the center may depend on whether it is able to form a winning coalition while retaining support among its core supporters, who were not happy with the party's moderate posture to form alliances with regional and other parties.

Despite its organizational efficiency, the party is plagued by factional divisions and ideological conflicts. Anecdotal evidence indicates that factionalism is rampant in many state units of the BJP, especially in Madhya Pradesh, Maharashtra, Rajasthan, and Delhi. Following the Congress party model of organization, the BJP's central leadership is unwilling to grant autonomy to the state party units. Given the complexity of the variations existing in the regional subcultures, the central leadership of the BJP cannot impose its will on the state party organizations with any greater hope of success than the centrist parties have had since the 1970s.

The questionable practices of Congress and other centrist parties have also left their impact on the BJP. For instance, the BJP has within its roster of MPs and MLAs persons with alleged criminal backgrounds, even some charged with serious crimes. In addition, the BJP's associations with the Bajrang Dal, representing the lumpen elements of Hindu militants, and the Vishwa Hindu Parishad (VHP), the Hindu revivalist organization, along with its tendency to take to the streets to settle political scores with the ruling party, do not enhance its image as a responsible political party ready to rule as vast a country as India.

Bahujan Samaj Party: Dalits as a Swing Element

Caste-based politics has been embedded in the Indian political process since independence. Although earlier caste-based political parties, such as the Republican Party organized by Dr. B. R. Ambedkar, were not successful in electoral politics, this was largely because the Congress party was able to win Scheduled Caste votes and to coopt many of their leaders within its ranks. The leadership of the Congress (I) appeared unable to bring about significant improvement in the lot of the lower castes and the Scheduled Castes, who during the past fifty years have produced a middle class of their own. It is thus not surprising that starting in the 1980s leaders of the Scheduled Castes decided to create a party of their own in order to be active players in state and national politics.

In 1984 the Bahujan Samaj Party (BSP) was launched by Kanshi Ram, a Sikh Chamar leader from Punjab. With the decline of the Congress party and the continuing inability of the upper-caste leadership of the major political parties to satisfy the rising expectations of the educated middle class of the Scheduled Castes, the BSP sought to challenge their political domination and electoral exploitation of the lower castes. The BSP entered the electoral arena in 1985 when it competed in the special election to fill vacancies in the legislative assemblies. However, it was only in the 1989 Lok Sabha elections that the BSP made earnest efforts in the states of Uttar Pradesh, Punjab, and Madhya Pradesh. Although the party did not win any seats in Madhya Pradesh, polling only 4.3 percent of the votes, it won two seats in Uttar Pradesh with 9 percent and one seat in Punjab with 8.6 percent. In addition to selecting the Scheduled Caste candidate, it also put up candidates from among Muslims as well as from the backward castes. From then on, the BSP became a political force to reckon with in these states and began to expand its base in other states as well.

Meanwhile, a short spell of power in Uttar Pradesh (June–October 1995), with outside support from the BJP, played an instrumental role in softening the BSP attitude toward the upper castes. In the 1996 Lok Sabha elections the BSP included some upper-caste candidates in its electoral list. This strategy improved its electoral performance; it was able to win eleven seats (six from Uttar Pradesh, three from Punjab, and two from Madhya Pradesh) in the Lok Sabha. The party made especially impressive gains in Uttar Pradesh, improving its popular vote tally from 9.9 percent in the 1989 elections to 20 percent in 1996. In the 1996 legislative assembly elections in Uttar Pradesh, the Congress (I) was forced to enter into electoral alliance with the BSP as a junior partner. In this election, held in October, the BSP captured sixty-seven seats, and the Congress was able to win only thirty-three seats. However, the BSP won a majority in the

2007 state legislative elections with 206 out of 402 seats. Thus in north India the BSP is emerging as the sole representative body of the Dalits RO and showing its ability to reach out to higher castes to generate electoral victories.

The Communist Party of India (CPI)

The communist movement in India has undergone various strategic and ideological transformations. It has always been plagued with factional conflicts and has experienced several splits. The Communist Party of India, which held its first all-India session in 1927, faced serious problems in its effort to create a suitable balance between the political realities of India and the foreign policy goals of the Soviet Union. Its leadership's ideological subservience to Moscow frequently led it into conflicts with the nationalist aspirations of the people of India. Thus in 1942, when the Indian National Congress under the leadership of Mahatma Gandhi launched the Quit India movement and sought freedom from British rule in exchange for India's support for British war efforts, the CPI decided to join with the British government and denounced Gandhi's movement. Britain and the Soviet Union had formed a common front against Nazi Germany, so the communists supported the "people's war" while ignoring the dominant Indian national aspirations. Similarly, in 1947 they supported the Muslim League on the issue of Pakistan and thus alienated the majority of Indians, who opposed the division of the country on a religious basis.

After independence in 1947, the CPI followed the Stalinist line by denouncing Congress party leaders as slaves of imperialist interests. Under the leftist leadership of B. T. Ranadive, the CPI launched a movement of terrorism and incited peasant uprisings, which were suppressed by the national government. But with the new political leadership in the Soviet Union and the ongoing process of de-Stalinization under Khrushchev, the Soviets decided to befriend the Nehru government. This change in Soviet foreign policy forced the CPI to alter its course. Thus in 1958 it adopted the Amritsar resolution pledging to seek power and social change through parliamentary means. The dominant faction within the party supported Nehru's "progressive" policies, especially his foreign policy.

During the 1969 split in the Congress party, and later during the national emergency, the CPI consistently supported Indira Gandhi and her government. Only after the 1977 defeat did it try to chart an independent course. The more radical Marxists in India view the CPI as primarily a "revisionist" party that has lost its revolutionary direction. The CPI has pockets of support in different parts of the country, primarily Andhra Pradesh, Bihar, eastern Uttar Pradesh, Kerala, and West Bengal. In the 1989 national elections the CPI captured twelve seats, twice the number it won in 1984. Again in 2004, the party retained its level of support by winning ten seats.

The Communist Party of India (Marxist): An Indian Road to Marxism-Leninism?

A 1964 split in the CPI led to the founding of India's second communist party, called the Communist Party of India (Marxist) (CPI[M]). The split resulted from a clash of ideologies between the pro-Moscow faction led by S. A. Dange and the allegedly pro-Chinese faction headed by Jyoti Basu, Hare Krishna Konar, and E. M. S. Namboodiripad. Subsequently, however, the new party modified its pro-Chinese stance and sought to direct the communist movement in accordance with the political and historical realities of India. Under the able leadership of Basu and Namboodiripad, the party adopted an independent course for Indian communists, maintaining distance from both the Chinese and the Soviet communist parties. For example, it staunchly opposed Indira Gandhi's emergency rule as well as her subversion of the federal system in India. At the same time, it favored the formation of selective electoral alliances with ideologically similar parties, excluding such rightist parties as the BJP.

At present, the CPI(M) holds power in West Bengal, where it commands a considerable following among intellectuals, students, industrial workers, landless laborers, and poor farmers. Since 1967, when it first contested the elections, it has maintained steady support among voters, receiving around 6 percent of popular votes. In the 1989 elections, the CPI(M) supported anti-Congress parties, capturing thirty-two seats, in contrast to the twenty-two seats it had won in 1984. The CPI and the CPI(M) supported the National Front government led by V. P. Singh.

In the May–June 1991 elections the communists improved their position in parliament slightly. In the 1996 elections both communist parties had informal anti-Congress electoral alliances with the Janata Dal. The CPI(M) won thirty-one seats in the Lok Sabha, in contrast to the thirty-five it had won in the 1991 elections; the CPI was able to win twelve seats, thus suffering a loss of one seat. In 2004 the party captured forty-three seats and increased its national vote total to 5.7 percent (see Table 4.1).

Both communist parties have adopted moderate land reform programs and seek central government-directed economic planning and industrial development of the country. Both the parties initially opposed the economic liberalization introduced by the Rao government in 1991. However, the frequent overseas visits of West Bengal's Marxist chief minister, Jyoti Basu, to seek foreign investments as well as his efforts to woo Indian industrialists to invest in his home state show that the CPI(M) was gradually, though reluctantly, willing to accept the essence of the Rao government economic reforms. It appears that the communists have given up their ideological stance based on the Marxist theory of class struggle and instead have embraced electoral politics as a political strategy of empowerment of the poorer segments of Indian society.

The Communist Party of India (Marxist-Leninist)

When the communist movement in India became involved in electoral politics, some of the young generation of communists became disenchanted with the older generation of leaders. Renouncing the parliamentary methods of their elders and following the Maoist line of radicalization of the peasantry, they launched a peasant revolution in the Naxalbari area of rural northern West Bengal.

In 1969, under the leadership of such young and idealistic people as Kanu Sanyal and Charu Mazumdar, a third communist party was founded, the Communist Party of India (Marxist-Leninist) (CPI(M)L). The party immediately called for an armed uprising.[14] The Communist Party of the People's Republic of China extended recognition to the new party and provided considerable propaganda support. But the leftist state government led by the Marxists in West Bengal, with the support of the national government, was able to suppress the revolt and contain the peasant uprising. Although the CPI(M) is still left with some pockets of support among youth groups, many of its leaders have either given up political activity or started flirting with electoral politics.[15] The "Naxalites," as most of the left-wing radicals and the extremists were formerly called, are split into several small factions and splinter groups.

Regional Parties in Search of a National Role

Regional parties existed even before the 1967 elections; however, with the decline of the aggregative capacity of the Congress party and the subversion of the autonomy of the state-and local-level Congress party elites, there has been an increase in the number of parties representing regional and subnational interests. The rise of such parties has further strengthened the multiparty nature of Indian politics.

The Dravida Munnetra Kazhagam (DMK) and the All-India Anna DMK (AIADMK) represent the cultural nationalism of the people of Tamil Nadu, who speak the Tamil language and take pride in their Dravidian (non-Aryan) heritage. The Dravidian cultural revival movement and the DMK are closely intertwined.[16] C. N. Annadurai, the charismatic leader of the DMK, transformed this social-cultural revival movement into a political party. Initially the party sought creation of a sovereign state in the south; later on, however, it gave up its separatist demand. Now the DMK seeks only greater state autonomy and an end to the domination of the south by the Hindi-speaking north.

In the 1967 election the DMK defeated the Congress party at the polls and became the ruling party in Madras, a state that the DMK renamed Tamil Nadu (meaning "a country of Tamils"). After the death of Annadurai in 1969, a power struggle developed between M. Karunanidhi and M. G. Ramchandran (known by his initials, MGR), leading to MGR's forming the AIADMK in 1972. Soon thereafter the AIADMK came to dominate the state's politics; its success in the elections of 1977 resulted in MGR's assumption of the chief ministership.

AIADMK, under MGR and, after his death, under his successor, Jayaram Jayalalitha, became closely allied with the Congress (I) in national politics. Since 1967 Tamil Nadu has been ruled by either AIADMK or DMK, to the exclusion of the Congress (I). In the 1996 state elections, the DMK, led by M. Karunanidhi, defeated Jayalalitha and her AIADMK. In the 2004 parliamentary elections the DMK allied itself with the Congress party and won each of the sixteen seats it contested (see Table 4.1) while the BJP-allied AIADMK lost every one of the thirty-three seats it contested.

The Telugu Desam Party (TDP) is a comparatively new political party that in 1982 gained dominance in Andhra Pradesh's politics under the leadership of the late N. T. Rama Rao, a former matinee idol (just as M. G. Ramchandran had been in Tamil Nadu). The party originated in reaction to Indira Gandhi's frequent imposition of unpopular Congress party chief ministers on the people of Andhra Pradesh. Most of these chief ministers did not last very long, and the faction-ridden state Congress party failed to deliver on its promises. Rama Rao had only to appeal to the subnational pride of the Telugu people; the TDP denounced the New Delhi domination of the state's politics and in 1983 won an impressive majority in the state election, defeating the Congress party.

Since its formation, the TDP has faced various challenges from the Congress party. In both the 1984 parliamentary elections and the March 1985 state elections, however, it routed the Congress (I) at the polls: for the Lok Sabha it won twenty-eight of forty-nine seats, and in the state elections it won 202 of 287 seats. In the 1989 parliamentary and state elections, the TDP suffered a humiliating defeat at the hands of the Congress (I), losing control of the state government.

In the 1993 Andhra Pradesh Legislative Assembly elections, however, the TDP defeated the Congress (I) and returned to power in the state. After Rama Rao's death, his son-in-law Chandrababu Naidu became the chairman of the National Front. After the decline of the National Front and subsequent disintegration of the non-Congress Third Front, the TDP, led by Naidu, became allied with the BJP. In the 1999 parliamentary elections the party was able to win twenty-nine out of thirty-four Lok Sabha seats which it contested, but in 2004 it won only five seats (see Table 4.1).

The Jammu and Kashmir National Conference was founded in 1939 by Sheikh Muhammad Abdullah, a Kashmiri freedom fighter. His efforts resulted in the development of Kashmiri self-respect and a strong sense of subnational identity. The National Conference under his leadership was able to secure for Jammu and Kashmir a special status in the Indian union not given to any other Indian state.

After Sheikh Abdullah's death in 1982, however, the party became divided into two factions—one led by the sheikh's son, Dr. Farooq Abdullah, and the other by the sheikh's son-in-law, G. M. Shah. Abdullah's government, which won a clear majority in the 1982 state election, was dismissed through Congress (I) manipulation. In its place Indira Gandhi installed a government led by G. M. Shah's faction of the National Conference, which was supported by the Congress (I) members. However, in the 1984 elections the Farooq-led National Conference once again swept the parliamentary election in Kashmir Valley.

In January 1990, when Jagmohan was appointed governor of the state, Dr. Abdullah and his ministry resigned, protesting the failure of V. P. Singh's government to consult them before his appointment. In July 1990 the state of Jammu and Kashmir was placed under president's rule: faced with insurgency, the state was deprived of the democratic process by the central government. Political activity came to a virtual halt, and the National Conference went into a political wilderness. It was only with the restoration of the democratic process in 1996 that the National Conference became active again in state politics.

Elections for the state legislative assembly were held in September 1996 in Jammu and Kashmir. While the All-Party Hurriyat Conference, a conglomerate of parties seeking secession from India, boycotted the elections, eight major parties of the state, along with several independent candidates, participated. There were 505 candidates vying for 87 seats. The Jammu and Kashmir National Conference, which had earlier stayed away from the Lok Sabha elections, won a majority of the seats. Farooq Abdullah, the leader of the National Conference, became the chief minister. However, both Abdullah and his Jammu and Kashmir National Conference still have to prove their ability to pacify the state and to satisfy the aspirations of its people. In the 2004 parliamentary elections the National Conference contested six and won two Lok Sabha seats.

In addition to the major parties, there are such minor regional parties as Jharkhand Mukti Morcha in Bihar; Sikkim Sangram Parishad (SSP), led by N. B. Bhandari; and Asom Gana Parishad, led by Prafulla Mahanta, in Assam.

Communal or Sectarian Parties

Of all the sectarian and communal parties in India in the post-independence period, the most successful in promoting the cause of a particular religious community has been the Shiromani Akali Dal. The Akali Dal is a militant political organization with religious appeal; it claims to be the exclusive representative of the Sikhs, who constitute a majority in the state of Punjab. The Akali Dal is closely associated with the educational, cultural, and religious life of the Sikhs. For example, it is the Akali party that has a monopoly over the Shiromani Gurudwara Prabhandak Committee (SGPC), the management body for the Sikh temples. The SGPC not only exercises control over the Sikh temples but also possesses huge revenues from the offerings made by Sikh devotees. Through its skillful use of SGPC funds, the Akali Dal manages several Sikh educational, cultural, and religious institutions. Thus the Sikh denominational schools, colleges, and other societies not only employ Sikh intellectuals and party workers but also try to create a distinct subnational identity among the Sikhs.[17]

From time to time the Akali party has been in power in the Punjab, but until the 1985 election it was able to maintain itself in power only in coalition with other parties. Such coalitions are usually unstable, and the Akali party governments collapsed frequently. Akalis have therefore often resorted to agitation in seeking to achieve their political goals. In 1982 the Akalis launched a mass agitation against the national government, seeking, along with certain religious concessions, greater autonomy for the Sikh-dominated state of Punjab. When the party lost control of the agitation to the religious fundamentalists and Sikh extremists, a bloody confrontation with the national government resulted. In 1985 the majority faction of the Akali party, led by Harcharan Singh Longowal, reached an agreement with the national government and terminated its agitation. Subsequently it won elections in the state and was brought back to power in the Punjab.[18]

NOTES

1. W. R. Crocker, *Nehru* (London: George Allen & Unwin, 1967), pp. 166–167.

2. W. H. Morris-Jones, "Parliament and Dominant Party: Indian Experience," *Parliamentary Affairs,* Summer 1964, pp. 296–307; Gopal Krishna, "One Party Dominance: Development and Trends," in *Party System and Election Studies: Occasional Papers of the Centre for the Study of Development Societies,* no. 1, ed. Rajni Kothari (Bombay: Allied, 1967), pp. 19–98.

3. Bhagwan D. Dua, "India: A Study in the Pathology of a Federal System," *Journal of Commonwealth and Comparative Politics,* November 1981, p. 261.

4. Stanley A. Kochanek, "Mrs. Gandhi's Pyramid: The New Congress," in *Indira Gandhi's India: A Political System Reappraised,* ed. Henry C. Hart (Boulder: Westview, 1967), pp. 93–124.

5. Richard Sisson and William Vanderbock, "Mapping the Indian Electorate: Trends in Party Support in Seven National Elections," *Asian Survey,* October 1983, p. 1142; Javeed Alam, "The Vote for Political Stability and the Implications: An Analysis of 1980 Election Results," *Political Science Review* 21, no. 4 (1983): 313.

6. Paul R. Brass, "National Power and Local Politics in India: A Twenty-Year Perspective," *Modern Asian Studies* 18, no. 1 (1984): 89–118; James Manor, "Anomie in Indian Politics: Origins and Potential Impact," *Economic and Political Weekly,* May 1983, pp. 225–234.

7. Robert L. Hardgrave Jr., "India on the Eve of Elections: Congress and the Opposition," *Pacific Affairs,* Fall 1984, pp. 404–428.

8. Gopal Krishna, "A Nation State to Defend," *Times of India,* January 7, 1985.

9. Javeed Alam, "In Defence of Their Alternative," *Economic and Political Weekly,* March 1966, pp. 510–512.

10. Dharma Kumar, "The Affirmative Action Debate in India," *Asian Survey,* March 1992, p. 290. Also see Lewis P. Fickett Jr., "The Rise and Fall of the Janata Dal," *Asian Survey,* December 1993, p. 1152.

11. Paul Brass, "The Rise of the BJP and the Future of Party Politics in Uttar Pradesh," in *India Votes: Alliance Politics and the Ninth and Tenth General Elections,* ed. Harold A. Gould and Sumit Ganguly (Boulder: Westview, 1993), p. 258.

12. Yogendra K. Malik and V. B. Singh, "Bharatiya Janata Party: An Alternative to the Congress (I)?" *Asian Survey,* April 1992, p. 331.

13. Yogendra K. Malik and V. B. Singh, *Hindu Nationalists in India: The Rise of the Bharatiya Janata Party* (Boulder: Westview, 1994), p. 211.

14. Marcus F. Franda, "India's Third Communist Party," *Asian Survey,* November 1969, pp. 797–818.

15. *India Today,* January 13, 1985, p. 28.

16. Marguerite Ross Barnett, *The Politics of Cultural Nationalism in South India* (Princeton: Princeton University Press, 1976).

17. Baldev Raj Nayar, *Minority Politics in the Punjab* (Princeton: Princeton University Press, 1966); Paul R. Brass, "Ethnic Cleavages and the Punjab Party System, 1952–1972," in *Electoral Politics in the Indian States,* ed. Myron Weiner and John Osgood Field (New Delhi: Manohar, 1974), 4:7–61.

18. Gopal Singh, "Socio-Economic Basis of Punjab Crisis," *Economic and Political Weekly,* January 1984, pp. 402–507; Sucha Singh Gill and K. C. Singhal, "The Punjab Problem: Its Historical Roots," *Economic and Political Weekly,* April 1984, pp. 603–608; Yogendra K. Malik, "Sikh Militancy and the Akali Party in Punjab: Move for Secessionism or Greater Autonomy?" *Asian Survey,* March 1986, pp. 344–362.

SUGGESTED READINGS

Barnett, Marguerite Ross. *The Politics of Cultural Nationalism in South India.* Princeton: Princeton University Press, 1976.

Baxter, Craig. *The Jana Sangh: A Biography of an Indian Political Party.* Philadelphia: University of Pennsylvania Press, 1969.

Bhambri, C. P. *The Janata Party: A Profile.* New Delhi: National, 1982.

Brass, Paul R. *Factional Politics in an Indian State: The Congress Party in Uttar Pradesh.* Berkeley: University of California Press, 1966.

Brass, Paul R., and Marcus Franda. eds. *Radical Politics in South Asia.* Cambridge, Mass.: MIT Press, 1973.

Dasgupta, B. *The Naxalite Movement.* Bombay: Allied, 1974.

Erdman, Howard. *The Swatantra Party and Indian Conservatism.* Cambridge: Cambridge University Press, 1967.

Fickett, Lewis P., Jr. *The Major Socialist Parties of India: A Study in Leftist Fragmentation.* Syracuse, N.Y.: Maxwell School, Syracuse University, 1970.

Graham, B. D. *Hindu Nationalism and Indian Politics: The Origins and the Development of the Bharatiya Jan Sangh.* Cambridge: Cambridge University Press, 1990.

Hardgrave, Robert L., Jr. *The Dravidian Movement.* Bombay: Popular Prakash, 1965.

Hartmann, Horst. *Political Parties in India.* New Delhi: Meenakshi Prakash, 1982.

Kochanek, Stanley A. *The Congress Party of India: The Dynamics of One-Party Democracy.* Princeton: Princeton University Press, 1968.

Ludden, David. ed. *Making India Hindu: Religion, Community, and the Politics of Democracy in India.* Delhi: Oxford University Press, 1996.

Malik, Yogendra K., and V. B. Singh. *Hindu Nationalists in India: The Rise of the Bharatiya Janata Party.* Boulder: Westview, 1994.

Naik, J. A. *The Opposition in India and the Future of Democracy.* New Delhi: S. Chand, 1983.

Nayar, Baldev Raj. *Minority Politics in the Punjab.* Princeton: Princeton University Press, 1966.

Ram, Mohan. *Indian Communism: Split Within Split.* Delhi: Vikas, 1969.

Sen Gupta, Bhabani. *Communism in Indian Politics.* New York: Columbia University Press, 1972.

Weiner, Myron. *Party Politics in India: The Development of a Multi-party System.* Princeton: Princeton University Press, 1957.

_____. *Party Building in a New Nation: The Indian National Congress.* Chicago: University of Chicago Press, 1967.

5

Groups and Multiple Demands on the System

The segmented nature of Indian society tends to stimulate diverse group activity. Before India came under British control, traditional and ascriptive ties based on kinship and community provided easy avenues for people to organize to protect their common interests. With the advent of British rule, competition for jobs and the need to obtain economic and business concessions encouraged Indians to organize themselves. The subsequent introduction of representative institutions and electoral politics after independence provided the incentive to politically ambitious people to organize all kinds of groups and associations.[1]

The British Raj was replaced by the Nehru/Congress party/Indian bureaucracy Raj. India's new political rulers became the objects of group demands in the highly politicized and bureaucratic environment of independent India. After 1947 India was "new" in the sense that a new political class came into power and the foreign ruler was expelled. With the establishment of a new political elite came a new style and rhetoric that emphasized nationalism and modernity, nation building and populism, and a new foreign and military policy. In this frame of reference the group demands of the Indian armed forces were marginalized, and the demands of political and business groups such as Indian leftists, trade unions, and the Birla businesses were highlighted along with a buildup of state planning groups that expressed the political values of Nehruvian socialist economy. The new Indian political orientation of Indian socialism and democracy built a superstructure of more bureaucratic and political controls on the structure of the British-origin government of India. The "new" government of India adopted en masse the rules, procedures, laws, and political organizations of British India.

Group Activity

The complex post-independence institutional network created by the new constitution of India provided a new focus for interest groups. Multiple power centers have emerged since 1947. The village councils, municipal governments, district administrations, state legislative bodies, the council of ministers, and a host of bureaucratic organizations and administrative agencies have become subject to various kinds of pressure, thus intensifying group activity.

The competition for power and influence among rival groups is both a divisive and an integrative process. On the one hand, the activities of religious minorities such as the Muslims, Sikhs, and Christians evoke protest from the members of the majority religion and tend to aggravate intercommunal tension and reinforce the religious divisions. On the other hand, many nontraditional economic groups such as the Chamber of Commerce and Industry, the trade unions, and the peasants' and farmers' organizations tend to play an integrative role. These are open groups that draw their membership from people of all segments of Indian society engaged in the same trade.

After independence interest groups in India did not enjoy much autonomy. Interest in civil society, child labor, disarmament, environment, and women's rights emerged later. They have a voice now in national debates but their effect on policy making is limited. Many are dominated by Indian political parties or funded by foreign institutions which use them to advance their partisan goals rather than promote the interests of group members.

Business

Business and commercial classes long had a poor image in Indian society. In the Hindu social system, the trading and commercial classes represented by the Vaishya caste occupy a lower status than the Brahmin, the carriers of sacred knowledge, and the Kshatriya, the administrators and the warriors. The Banias and Marwaris, leading members of India's trading community, also had a poor image.[2] British Administrators shared a similar jaundiced view of the "commercial classes" and often distanced themselves from the "box-wallahs." Moreover, as Stanley Kochanek has pointed out, modern political ideologies such as Marxism and Gandhism, to which many Indian leaders subscribe, depict businesspeople as exploiters.[3]

By the late 1980s this situation began to change. A new breed of enterprising businesspeople with considerable business and political sophistication arose, and the political parties, in order to meet the escalating cost of electioneering, became dependent on business donations. These developments have given the world of business a new respectability and political clout.

This in part is owing to the introduction of economic liberalization by the Rao government in 1991 which led to a dramatic change in the environment surrounding the business organizations. Since liberalization business organizations have assumed greater importance. Party leaders and government ministers now seek to address their gatherings, assuring them of their cooperation in the economic growth of the country. Leading businessmen often are included in the government delegations visiting foreign countries looking for direct foreign investment.

Students

Students constitute one of the most politicized segments of Indian society. The political development of the student community is attributed partly to the freedom movement and partly to the behavior of the political leaders in the post-independence period. Before India achieved its independence, the leaders of the Indian National Congress frequently called on students to give up their studies to participate in the civil disobedience movement. Since independence, the leaders and the political parties have vied with each other both to capture the student unions existing on the campuses of more than 105 universities and thousands of colleges and to recruit the student leaders into political parties. Many students are ready to use even minor grievances as reasons to stage protests, strikes, and demonstrations against unresponsive school administrations.

Only a small minority of the more than a half million university graduates each year obtain gainful employment. With few or no job possibilities, many ambitious students look to parties and political leaders to advance their careers. For this reason, student politics in India tends to be special interest and issue oriented rather than ideologically oriented.[4] It is not surprising, therefore, that students have become an influential pressure group in Indian politics.

The Congress minority government's decision in 2006 to allow a policy of 50 percent reservations in university admissions (including all professional schools) and jobs emerged as a new and powerful issue in India's political system. It was seen as undermining the merit basis of university recruitment, a principle that enabled top Indian academic institutions and graduates to gain worldwide recognition. Indian political parties have viewed the issue in political and electoral terms, and deem it politically incorrect to criticize the new policy. However, a new element has taken shape. In 2007 India's Supreme Court suspended the reservation policy pending a decision on its legality, and it was critical of the government's decision to use the 1931 census as the database for this policy. The emergence of an activist Supreme Court and student agitation against the reservation policy indicates that Indian political parties no longer dominate Indian education.

The Military

India's military establishment is not politicized as in Pakistan and Bangladesh. It is subordinate to and controlled by the country's civilian rulers. This is not to say that India's military establishment is devoid of influence, however. The rise of a national security state in India has facilitated the enormous growth of influence of the Indian armed forces in policy making, in shaping the limits of policy action by Indian politicians and bureaucrats (e.g., in Kashmir and the India-China border), and in resource allocations by government to all branches of the armed forces. The position of the Indian military in India today differs radically from the Nehru-Menon days (1950–1962).

Nehru relied on diplomacy to promote Indian interests and the Indian armed forces were starved of funds in the belief that no power would dare attack India. If it were attacked, other powers were expected to come to India's rescue. Krishna Menon felt that Pakistan, not China, was India's main enemy. As a result of Nehru-Gandhi-Menon faith in pacifism and disarmament, the development of conventional and nuclear military capabilities was ignored.

At present India maintains one of the largest armies in the world, with over 1 million people in uniform.[5] It is a well disciplined and thoroughly professional body. Since 1962 the Indian defense ministry has been headed by politicians with national stature and distinguished administrative abilities who have effectively advanced the needs of India's military establishment. Now the chiefs of staff of the three armed forces have been granted both a voice in defense policy formulation and easy access to the higher echelons of political decision-making agencies. India also has a growing and modern air force and navy equipped with modern weapons. The modernization of India's navy is noteworthy because it was historically the poor cousin of the Indian army in resource allocation, and yet today, it must deal with a large part of the complicated Indian Ocean area with challenges that emerge from growing Chinese and Pakistani navies, with a focus on the Persian Gulf, the Bay of Bengal, and the sea lanes between the South China Sea and the Indian Ocean. The navy must also deal with arms trading and the voluntary and involuntary movement of insurgents and refugees into southern India as a result of insurgency in Sri Lanka. The coast guard is responsible for monitoring drug trade and illegal infiltration from hostile neighbors into India's vast and generally unpoliced coastline. With growing competition for energy resources in Africa, Persian Gulf, Middle Eastern, and Indian Ocean areas, the role of the Indian navy is likely to grow in importance.

Three other defense-oriented constituencies form a wide and deep foundation of India's national security structure. (1) The Department of Atomic Energy (DAE) was established in 1947 to promote "peaceful uses" of atomic energy.

With India's formal declaration of its nuclear weapon status in 1998, DAE's facilities have become a key part of India's nuclear deterrent. (2) With the growth of India's short-range and long-range missile capabilities, India's defense research and space organization now have a military and a civilian rationale. Space is India's new frontier and the growth of its capacities reveal the marriage between space technology, military power projection capacity, and civil applications of such technology. (3) Finally, the proliferation of India's paramilitary forces under the ministries of defense and home affairs show the importance of managing long and porous borders, and signal the threat of internal insurgencies.

The Intelligentsia

India possesses a well-established, articulate intelligentsia.[6] India's technocrats include engineers, doctors, agronomists, scientists, and computer engineers. This group provides highly skilled technical services but its political influence was limited in the past. Indians with science and engineering backgrounds have entered different branches of the central and state governments, and with an official platform they are able to influence policy making and its implementation. Indians with legal and financial credentials (e.g., Arun Shourie, lawyer, BJP; P. C. Chidambaran and Manmohan Singh, finance and prime minister respectively, Congress party) have also joined political parties; as ministers, they are now decision makers. So the stranglehold over Indian politics by the nontechnical but professional politician who dominated Indian political life from the 1930s to the turn of the century is broken by the rise of the knowledge sector of Indian society and its participation in political and government activity. As India's problems with agriculture, water, electricity, and environment loom large, the role of the scientific experts in each area is bound to grow. The strength of India's technically qualified manpower is estimated to be over 2.5 million, the third largest in the world.[7] More than 2,000 research units employ thousands of scientists and researchers.

India's national newspapers, such as *The Times of India, Indian Express, Hindustan Times, The Statesman,* and *The Hindu,* are known for their high standards. In recent years such English periodicals as *Sunday, Frontline,* and *India Today* have also emerged as major sources of information. The investigative news reporting in *India Today,* in particular, has earned widespread acclaim. Many young reporters and journalists have successfully exposed scandals involving politicians and public officials. India's business press has emerged quickly and professionally. Papers like *Economic Times* and *Business Standard* offer timely reporting of market trends and developments and policy analysis relating to India. With growing acceptance of capitalism by India's middle class, the role of India's business press is likely to grow.

The vernacular intellectual establishment occupies a less prestigious position than its English counterpart, but it has a larger readership. Although their impact at the national level is limited, vernacular-speaking intellectuals exercise considerable influence in the state capitals. And even though writings in regional languages (with few exceptions) have yet to develop the national press tradition of cogent analysis of political and economic issues, the regional press has frequently demonstrated the courage to withstand heavy political pressure. Often they provide a better measure of Indian public opinion in contrast to the expression of elite opinion—by the elites for the elites—in the English language medium.

Caste and Religious Groups

Indian groups organized on the basis of social origin or groups whose membership is "drawn from the community in which individuals are born" may be referred to as community associations.[8] These groups date back to nineteenth-century British India. It was the English-educated Indians who took the initiative to form these organizations. As Anil Seal has pointed out, "the membership of these bodies was restricted to one caste or community. Their sole reason for existence was to better the lot of these members."[9] However, with intermarriage and migration of individual caste members, caste characteristics have evolved and diluted into "intermediate castes." Castes articulate their demands through politics in several ways. The relationship between caste groups and politics can be summarized as follows:

1. The people of the same caste are organized on an associational basis to seek political concessions.
2. Persons of the same caste may line up support behind a particular party and try to use it to seek political influence.
3. A caste group may organize a party of its own. For example, B. R. Ambedkar, a well-known leader of the untouchables, organized the Republican party of India.
4. A group of castes may come together to form a common organization or federation to protect their interests and to advance the political fortunes of their leaders.
5. Political parties may select a candidate for an electoral office at the local or state level who belongs to the dominant caste. If elected, he or she may serve to advance its members' interests.
6. Caste-based alliances may be formed between powerful leaders within the same party.

In contrast to caste associations, India's various religious groups tend to organize on an all-India basis.

Hindu Groups.   Many Hindus have grievances to voice. In the first place, they have long felt that even though Hindus constitute an overwhelming majority in the country, their interests have been ignored by the politicians. Some Hindus blame the Congress party's leadership for the division of their "motherland" by the creation of the Muslim state of Pakistan on India's western border. In addition, some Hindus object to their treatment by Muslims: they point out that in neighboring Pakistan the majority's religion, Islam, has become the state religion and the Hindus have been driven out. In Bangladesh, another neighboring country in which Muslims are a majority, Hindus have little representation and feel that they are treated as second-class citizens. The ruling political elite of India, they assert, have put the interests of religious minorities before those of the majority in order to win elections.

There are several Hindu sectarian organizations. The most active and articulate is the Rashtriya Swayamsevak Sangh (RSS), which provides an important channel for the expression of militant Hindu nationalism. The RSS was founded in 1925 by a Maharashtrian Brahmin, Keshav Baliram Hedgewar, in Nagpur, where it still maintains its headquarters. Slowly and steadily it established its branches in all parts of India, although its largest following is in the Hindi heartland of north India.

The RSS has built an effective paramilitary organization and possesses a large, active, and well-disciplined membership. Although it claims to be a cultural rather than a political organization, the RSS became a major force behind the Jana Sangh, a militant Hindu nationalist party. Since 1979, with the formation of the Bharatiya Janata Party, the RSS seems to have achieved a degree of autonomy, and it supports the parties and candidates that it believes are committed to the interests of Hindus. It has maintained a militant anti-Muslim posture, and its workers are frequently blamed for inciting anti-Muslim rioting in urban areas. [10]

Muslim Groups.   The creation of a Muslim-majority state out of British India against the strong opposition of the Hindu majority left India's more than 100 million Muslims in a state of confusion. A large number of the educated, well-to-do, and politically conscious Muslims went to Pakistan, leaving behind millions of their coreligionists without leaders or a well-knit political organization. The present-day Muslim population in India consists mostly of "smaller peasantry, landless laborers, the artisans in the villages and lower middle class in the cities."[11]

NOTES

1. Anil Seal, "Imperialism and Nationalism in India," in *Locality, Province, and Nation: Essays on Indian Politics, 1870 to 1940,* ed. John Gallagher, Gordon Johnson, and Anil Seal (London: Cambridge University Press, 1973), p. 21.

2. The Banias and Marwaris are important subcastes among the Vaishyas known for their enterprising skills. India's largest industrialist family, Birla, is Marwari.

3. Stanley A. Kochanek, "The Federation of Indian Chambers of Commerce and Industry and Indian Politics," *Asian Survey,* September 1971, pp. 866–885; Kochanek, *Business and Politics in India* (Berkeley: University of California Press, 1974).

4. Lloyd I. Rudolph, Susanne H. Rudolph, and Karuna Ahmed, "Student Politics and National Politics in India," in *The Context of Education in Indian Development,* ed. Joseph Di Bona (Durham, N.C.: Program in Comparative Studies on Southern Asia, 1974), p. 206.

5. International Institute for Strategic Studies (London), *Annual Military Balance and Strategic Survey for Military Data and Assessments.*

6. Edward Shils, *The Intellectuals Between Traditions and Modernity: The Indian Situation,* Supplement 1, Comparative Studies in Society and History (The Hague: Mouton, 1961).

7. Government of India, *Sixth Five-Year Plan* (Delhi: Government of India Press, 1981), p. 318.

8. Myron Weiner, *The Politics of Scarcity* (Chicago: University of Chicago Press, 1962), p. 36.

9. Anil Seal, *The Emergence of Indian Nationalism* (London: Cambridge University Press, 1968), p. 15.

10. Craig Baxter, *The Jana Sangh: A Biography of an Indian Political Party* (Philadelphia: University of Pennsylvania Press, 1969), is a pioneering study.

11. M. J. Akbar, *India: The Siege Within* (New York: Viking Penguin, 1985), p. 309.

SUGGESTED READINGS

Altbach, Philip, ed. *Turmoil and Transition: Higher Education and Student Politics in India.* New York: Basic, 1968.

Andersen, Walter K., and Shridhar D. Damle. *The Brotherhood in Saffron: The Rashtriya Swayamsevak Sangh and Hindu Revivalism.* Boulder: Westview, 1977.

Calman, Leslie. *Protest in Democratic India: Authority's Response to Challenge.* Boulder: Westview, 1985.

Chatterji, R. *Union Politics and the State: A Study of Indian Labor Politics.* New Delhi: South Indian Publishers, 1980.

CIA World Fact Book, India. https://www.cia.gov/library/publications/the-world-factbook/geos/in.html.

Cohen, Steven P. *The Indian Army: Its Contributions to the Development of a Nation.* Berkeley: University of California Press, 1971.

Crouch, Harold. *Trade Union and Politics in India.* Bombay: Manaktalas, 1966.

Das Gupta, Jyotirindra. *Language Conflict and National Development: Group Politics and National Language Policy in India.* Berkeley: University of California Press, 1970.

Engineer, A. Ali, ed. *Communal Riots in Post-Independence India.* Hyderabad: Sangram, 1984.

Erdman, Howard L. *Political Attitudes of Indian Industry.* London: Athlove, 1971.

Giri, V. V. *Labor Problems in Indian Industry.* 3d ed. New York: Asia Publishing House, 1972.

Hardgrave, Robert L., Jr. *The Nadars of Tamilnadu: Political Culture of a Community in Change.* Berkeley: University of California Press, 1960.

Kochanek, Stanley A. *Business and Politics in India.* Berkeley: University of California Press, 1974.

Kothari, Rajni, ed. *Caste in Indian Politics.* New Delhi: Orient Longman, 1970.
Rao, A. V. Raman. *Indian Trade Unions.* Honolulu: University of Hawaii Press, 1967.
Rao, M. S. A. *Social Movements in India.* New Delhi: Manohar, 1979.
Weiner, Myron. *The Politics of Scarcity: Public Pressure and Political Response in India.* Chicago: University of Chicago Press, 1962.

6

Conflict Management

The ongoing process of sociopolitical change in India and the increased competition for scarce resources and political power are placing enormous pressure on the political system. The central government is being pressured to effectively redistribute political and economic power among emerging regions in India and to strengthen the Indian union with a strong national political center that projects pan-Indian values and policies for the common good. At the same time, it is expected to lay the foundation for strong regional power and policy development. Indian regionalism expresses issues of identity, language, regional economic grievances, and quests for power by local elites. The fear that strong regional power centers may dilute the strength of a center that is needed to hold India together is balanced by the view that by satisfying regional ambitions, the cost of managing regional agitations and insurgencies may be reduced and the process of developing the culture and means to advance peaceful economic, political, and social change is enhanced. The relationship between India's central government and its regional authorities is not a zero-sum game. It is a unique experiment that contrasts with the emphasis on excessive central controls in Russia and in China. At the same time, the success of the Indian political experiment is not guaranteed because excessive regionalism or localism could lead to a reversion to the British India system of India as a sum of small and large principalities and kingdoms and states ruled directly by the center (then British India, now India). The worst-case scenario is based on the premise that political disunity among Indian peoples is the dominant theme in Indian history and politics (pre–1947 and post-independence). If the space for divisive tendencies grows, and that of unifying tendencies decreases as a result of minority governments and coalition governments at the center, India's experiment to secure major change in its institutions and values could be undermined. Moreover, increased mass expectations as well as enhanced sectarian and caste/class consciousness are creating stresses and strains on the society that hitherto have not been experienced. The following sections describe the main areas of concern.

Danger of Hindu-Muslim Tension

Muslim religious doctrine is based on the belief that the Quran contains the ultimate truth and the revelation of the divine will. Muslims believe in the establishment of a divinely ordained social order. In institutional structures and value systems, Hinduism and Islam seem incompatible.

As Islamist terrorism has grown in Kashmir, Afghanistan, Pakistan, and other parts of India and the subcontinent since the 1980s, two Muslim types or styles of political action have emerged. The first one emphasizes Hindu-Muslim polarity, citing Indian/Hindu oppression of Muslims in Kashmir and religious rioting in Gujrat, and the importance of jihad to liberate the Muslims in India. This is premised on a fear of numerical Hindu majority by a numerical Muslim minority. (An extreme version of this approach suggests the existence of a Hindu-Christian-American Jewish conspiracy against the Muslims.) The second view among Muslims is that the Indian theory of secularism and Indian constitutional arrangements are entrenched in India's political system and society (especially in the media, national party politics, and judiciary), and Indian Muslims have used the legal, political, and social space to survive and to prosper in India. Millions of Muslims voted with their feet after partition by refusing to leave India for Pakistan. In this view, more needs to be done to enhance the political, economic, and social mobility of Indian Muslims by improved access to educational opportunities and employment in the government and private sectors.

India today is a tale of both stories.

In post-independence India, Muslims have freely participated in the political process of the country. They have used their votes as leverage for political bargaining in seeking accommodation for themselves. The fear of majority Hindu domination persists even though Hindus have never functioned as a political majority, as rulers in Indian history, or in post–1947 politics. Caste, ethnicity, regionalism, right-wing and left-wing ideologies, and the Gandhian nonviolent versus armed struggle divide have prevented the possible rise of monolithic Hindu majority rule in India. The development of Hindu-Muslim political integration is problematic because Muslim (and many others) voters see themselves as a swing element in party politics and elections, and, second, with the robust growth of Islamist, Hindu, and leftist extremism and insurgencies (e.g., movements in Telengana, Kashmir, Uttarakhand, Gorkhaland, northeast Indian states, and central India since 1947), strong polarities exist between extremists (seeking violent change) and moderates (seeking peaceful change) among all major constituencies: Muslim, Hindu, and leftist. In other words, Indian moderates are under pressure from the extremists and advocates of Indian development and reform through peaceful change are under pressure from advocates of revolution through violent change. Recent years have also witnessed greater polarization between the members of the two communities than in the past, resulting in frequent Hindu-Muslim riots. Despite the fact that the Muslims constitute the largest minority of the country, they form one of the depressed segments of Indian society. Nevertheless, they have displayed greater assertiveness as well as group awareness in recent years. The orthodox and traditional Muslim leaders have been joined by the more educated and younger members in seeking to mobilize the community in order to preserve its cultural identity and to acquire a greater share of the society's goods and services.

Communal divisions have resulted in religious rioting. Religious fundamentalism verging on fanaticism is on the rise because the modernization process has eroded traditional values and religious identities. To counter this trend, religious minorities are increasingly turning to their scriptures, reasserting their symbols, and organizing themselves on a communal basis. The result has been an increase in religious hostility among different communal groups. According to data, communal hostility has increased in both intensity and geographic reach.[1] On the other hand, as communal riots occur, Indian state and social elements respond by political and social action to dampen the tensions. The fear of a communal civil war is a deterrent against the spread of communal fights. In short, just as the political space of extremists on all sides has grown since the 1980s, the voice of secular elements has also grown along with a growing capacity to police the extremists, and a commitment to negotiate such tensions.

Communal violence springs not only from religious conflict but from political and sociological problems as well. Gangs of unemployed, rootless, and alienated youths often roam the streets of towns and cities that have experienced an influx of migrants from the rural areas and other parts of the country. These migrants have no neighborhood ties or kinship bonds. Frequently divided along religious or caste lines, the gang leaders are on the lookout for opportunities to indulge in violence. They often enjoy the protection of local party bosses or communal leaders who use them for political purposes. With weak government administrations at the central and state levels, poor quality intelligence, and corruption, criminal elements too have gained space in India's political system and criminal-state and criminal-communal nexuses have emerged. As well, external forces have stimulated political violence in India. Pakistan's ISI is widely believed to have stimulated political violence in Kashmir, Punjab, and eastern India in order to provide opposition to Indian government rule and authority in these areas. India has large and porous borders with Pakistan, Nepal, Bangladesh, China, Myanmar, and Sri Lanka, and transnational ethnic ties facilitate militancy against India.

Sikhs

Another example of the assertion of religious identity is in the rise of Sikh fundamentalism. Sikhism, which was born out of a fusion of Hinduism and Islam, is a young and vibrant religion. Guru Nanak Dev (1469–1539), who founded Sikhism, advocated monotheism and opposed the idolatry and caste system practiced by Hindus. He was followed by nine gurus (teachers). It was Guru Gobind Singh (1666–1708), the tenth guru, who gave the Sikhs a distinct organization and turned them into militant fighters against the Muslim rulers. The Sikhs believe in one sacred book, the Adi Granth, a collection of hymns written mainly by Nanak, Kabir, and Hindu and Muslim saints. The practice of the caste system is still prevalent among them despite its denunciation by the Sikh gurus. An overwhelming majority of the followers of Sikhism came from the fold of Hinduism. Sikhs and Hindus intermarried and celebrated each other's religious festivals. But the early part of the twentieth century witnessed the rise of numerous Sikh sectarian organizations that emphasized the distinct Sikh identity. Claiming Punjabi as their religious language and looking upon Punjab, a northwestern state in India, as their homeland, the Sikhs have developed a very strong subnational identity.

In 1982 the members of the Akali Dal, a moderate Sikh political party, launched a peaceful agitation in which they demanded certain religious concessions. They also wanted greater political autonomy for the Sikh majority state of Punjab than had been granted by the constitution of India. Soon, however, the militant Sikhs, led by a fundamentalist preacher, Sant Jarnail Singh Bhindranwale (1947–1984), resorted to terrorism. They converted the Golden Temple, the holiest shrine of the Sikhs, into an armed fortress. In June 1984 Prime Minister Indira Gandhi sent the army to flush out the terrorists from the temple. The result was considerable loss of life: in addition to the large number of terrorists killed, many innocent pilgrims were fatally trapped in the temple. The Sikhs as a community felt humiliated and angered. They became alienated from the national government, and some even sought the establishment of an independent and sovereign Sikh state called Khalistan. The subsequent assassination of Indira Gandhi by two Sikh bodyguards, on October 31, 1984, resulted in widespread Hindu retaliation against the Sikhs.

Punjab emerged as a major center of Hindu-Sikh and Sikh-Congress party polarity in the 1980s. Following a bitter campaign, the Khalistan movement was crushed by coercive state action and by a campaign to rebuild Punjab's political and economic institutions and processes. Here Sikh grievances and Pakistani intervention communalized the state, but again the moderate-extremist polarity among the Sikhs was settled in favor of the moderates as of 2006. Punjab's political space revealed a pattern of stability if the Sikh political class was given power, and furthermore, Punjab politicians showed maturity to share power with the BJP. The pattern of Akali-BJP coalition politics was repeated in state elections in 2007 when this coalition defeated the incumbent Congress party government and formed a new government. Here Sikh ethnicity and coalition politics, Punjab's regionalism, and BJP alliance politics combined to create a winning coalition in a key Indian border state that adjoins Pakistan and Kashmir.

Subnational Solidarities: Linguistic and Cultural Divisions

India's problems in attaining national integration and political cohesion have been further complicated by the existence of strong subnational identities formed along linguistic-cultural lines. The Indian constitution recognizes fourteen major languages spoken by a large majority of the people, and hundreds of other languages and dialects are spoken by the people in rural areas. Many people can speak more than two or three languages, and in urban areas bilingualism is common.

Linguistic and cultural identities are very strong among the regions that are far removed from the Hindi heartland of north India. Even though they are listed separately in the constitution, the Hindi, Urdu, and Punjabi languages are closely related. People are often able to shift speaking from one language to another without much difficulty. Hindi, the plurality language, was chosen in 1950 by the body that framed the constitution of free India as the official language of the country; then, in 1965, after the constitution had been in force for fifteen years, Hindi was to become the sole official language of the country. But there was strong cultural and practical opposition to Hindi in the south, because Hindi is a north Indian language and a language of Indo-European origin. To south Indians, the adoption of Hindi symbolized the domination of the Dravidian south by the Aryan north. Hindi is as foreign to the people in south India as English is. Hindi remains only a regional language, however; it is not yet well enough developed to take the place of English as the interregional and commercial language of India. As English is a global language, knowledge of English enhances job opportunities for educated persons in India as well as in other parts of the world. Preferring English, the south Indians therefore resented the

TABLE 6.1　　Languages Specified in the Constitution of India and Their Speakers

Languages	Number of Speakers	Percentage of Total
Hindi	422,048,642	41.7
Bengali	83,369,769	8.1
Telugu	74,002,856	7.2
Marathi	71,936,894	7.0
Tamil	60,793,814	5.9
Urdu	51,536,111	5.0
Gujarati	46,091,617	4.5
Kannada	37,924,011	3.7
Malayalam	33,066,392	3.2
Oriya	33,017,446	3.2
Punjabi	29,102,477	2.8
Assamese	13,168,484	1.3
Kashmiri	5,527,698	0.5

Source: Census of India, 2001, "Statement 1." www.censusindia.gov.in/Census_Data_2001/
Census_Data_Online/Language/Statement1.htm

forced imposition of Hindi. As a result of violent opposition to Hindi in the south, the government of India agreed in 1965 to an indefinite continuation of English as the second official language of the country.

Regional divisions solidified by common language, literary traditions, and culture have deep historical roots in India. Even though various vernacular literary traditions took shape in the thirteenth and fourteenth centuries, such regional identities were politically diffused and unorganized until recent times. It was only during the British period that vernacular literary traditions matured; the literary elite chose native symbols and myths and glorified the history, the land, and the people who spoke their own languages. In this way they became instrumental in developing subnational identities. Many of the literary elite became torn between pan-Indian nationalism and regional loyalties based on cultural-linguistic identities. But when India became independent, the regional elite became the strongest protagonists of the subnational movements, immediately putting strong pressure on the national government to reorganize the states on a linguistic basis. They sought equal treatment and status for all regional languages. The national political elites initially resisted these demands, fearing the balkanization of the country. However, Indian political elites showed political flexibility by meeting the aspirations of the leaders of linguistic groups. In 1956 the government of India agreed to their demands and carried out a vast reorganization of the state boundaries on a linguistic basis. In each of the unilingual states of India today, the regional language is used for both administrative and educational purposes. The creation of unilingual states, however, has further strengthened regional identities; it has also led to an increase in interstate conflict and enhanced the tension between the state and national governments.

To facilitate interstate communication as well as population mobility, the national government recommended the adoption of a three-language formula. Under this agreement, the states were expected to provide instruction in both Hindi and English in addition to instruction in the local language. It was hoped that in the Hindi-speaking states of the north the students would learn some of the languages of the non-Hindi-speaking regions of India, but this hope has not been borne out.

Given the vast size of the country and the existence of strong subnational identities, the emergence of various types of strong subnationalist movements would not be considered an unusual development. Maintenance of political stability in a multiethnic society, however, depends on the skills of the national leaders in dealing with the aspirations of leaders of regional or subnationalist movements. So long as the territorial unity and integrity of the country are not threatened, the leaders of regional and subnationalist movements have been allowed to pursue their goals through peaceful means. This is not to say, however, that no tension has existed between them and the national government. On several occasions the agitation and protests of such movements have resulted in political violence, the arrest of the leaders, and the suspension of civil liberties in these areas. Eventually, however, compromise and conciliation have prevailed. The successful resolution of the Tamil subnationalist movement of south India is a case in point.

The protagonists of Sikh and Kashmiri subnationalist movements pose other important challenges to the concept of pan-Indian nationalism. The Sikh nationalist movement was contained, but the ongoing insurgencies in the Muslim-majority states of Jammu and Kashmir and in northeastern states and central India have yet to be resolved. These subnationalist movements either seek greater autonomy or wish to establish independent states of their own. These movements and insurgencies pose challenges to the belief that despite its diversity or because of it, India's political system has the capacity to adjust to conflicting demands within the framework of its constitutional and political norms.

Other Sources of Stress and Strains

1. Caste/class-based conflicts have become more frequent and are erupting into ghastly violence as well. Earlier, the landowning dominant castes in the rural areas had been able to mobilize the low-caste voters for the Congress party in addition to the voters of their own castes; in other words, the low castes followed the leadership of the dominant castes. But this relationship in the countryside has changed; the low-caste voters are

no longer willing to submit to the dictates of traditional rural leaders.[2] Younger, better-educated low-caste leaders seem determined now to assert their independence. The assertion of independence, however, has not always brought them positive results; on the contrary, such actions have invited retaliation by the landowning castes. Supported by the middle castes, the upper castes have resorted to brute force to teach their former subordinates a "lesson." Uttar Pradesh and Bihar have witnessed some of the worst incidents of caste violence in recent years.

2. Caste riots in urban areas have been directed against both the quota system used for government jobs and the practice of reserving seats in professional colleges for the members of backward castes. This system of "reverse discrimination" has been resented by upper-caste Hindus and recently by students who feel threatened by the new government policy to allot 50 percent of the seats for the Scheduled Castes and Scheduled Tribes.

3. In addition, uneven distribution of the gains from the green revolution in such states as Punjab and Haryana has increased the tension between the landowning and the landless castes. Unwilling to work for the wages offered to them by the landowning castes, the landless labor groups increasingly have organized unions. As there is a seasonal shortage of labor and, more important, as unionization on the part of the low castes is looked upon as an affront to the dominant castes, the latter have frequently resorted to the use of force against the Scheduled Castes.

4. The introduction of criminal elements into politics has paralleled the rise of a new breed of politicians who find enormous opportunities for social mobility in democratic politics: "Unlike the gentlemen politicians of earlier years, they know that the difference between being and not being in power is vital in their lives."[3] Because these politicians depend on politics for their social status as well as their income, in urban areas they are often willing to form alliances with criminals, smugglers, and other antisocial elements as well as with the police establishment to stay in power.

5. Similarly, in rural areas the politicians, the landowning castes, and the police establishment often work together openly to suppress landless labor.[4] Until 1967 criminals were used to help politicians get elected, and subsequently they sought and got elected to public offices. It was the development of the "culture of lumpenisation introduced by Sanjay Gandhi during the Emergency" that encouraged them to seek election to legislative bodies.[5] The development of a nexus of criminals, politicians, and political parties led the *Economist* to comment on the 1991 electoral

contest that "Indian voters now believe that virtually all politicians are crooks. They may take the view that the Gandhi mafia can provide the stability that small-time crooks cannot."[6]

6. Uttar Pradesh and Bihar, the two north Indian states, rank at the top in the percentage of members of legislative bodies with criminal records. According to one estimate, whereas in 1984 only 7 percent of the Uttar Pradesh legislature had criminal records, by 1990 the proportion had gone up to 30 percent.[7] In fact, no political party in Uttar Pradesh can claim that it does not shelter criminals. And this situation is not confined to Bihar and Uttar Pradesh; no state legislative body in India can claim to have no criminal elements within its ranks.[8]

7. Ethnic unrest has resulted from the mobilization of small ethnic or tribal groups. Until recently such groups were only marginally relevant to national politics. Now, however, they are becoming increasingly fearful of losing their subgroup identity as well as their land and ways of life, leading them to use violent methods to protect themselves against outsiders. The continuation of ethnic and tribal unrest in the northeastern hill states of Nagaland, Meghalaya, Mizoram, and Tripura is a testament to the unresolved issue of subnational and regional autonomy in that part of the country.

8. Regional competition for scarce resources has emerged as another major source of national concern in states with non-Congress (I) governments. Disparities in the distribution of natural resources are inevitable in a country the size of India. However, the ongoing process of industrialization and modernization has further accentuated these disparities, resulting in gross regional imbalances in wealth, living standards, and general prosperity. Whereas Punjab and Haryana have reaped enormous benefits from the green revolution and have become granaries of the country, other states such as Bihar, Orissa, and Uttar Pradesh, particularly eastern Uttar Pradesh, have hardly been touched by the prosperity. India's economic growth rate is 8–9 percent per year, but as a result the disparities between the rich and poor classes are growing, as are the strains between the classes.

Despite government efforts to achieve a balance, regional inequalities have become even more pronounced. W. Kirk, after carefully analyzing the subject, has concluded that "if one examines what has happened in India since independence as opposed to what has been planned there is little evidence of the reduction of spatial inequalities."[9]

NOTES

1. Shekhar Gupta, The "Gathering Storm," *India Briefing,* ed. Marshall M. Bouton and Philip Oldenburg (Boulder: Westview, 1990), p. 27.

2. Duncan B. Forrester, "Electoral Politics and Social Change," *Economic and Political Weekly,* July 1969, p. 1079; Peter Lyon and James Manor, eds., *Transfer and Transformation: Political Institutions in the New Commonwealth* (Leicester, U.K.: Leicester University Press, 1983).

3. Ashis Nandy, "Myths, Persons, and Politics," seminar, October 1979, p. 19.

4. Paul R. Brass, "National Power and Local Politics in India: A Twenty-Year Perspective," *Modern Asian Studies* 18, no. 1 (1984): 93; editorial, *Political Weekly,* July 1968, p. 1079; Lyon and Manor, eds., *Transfer and Transformation.*

5. *India Today,* August 31, 1995, p. 32.

6. Quoted in Inder Malhotra, *India: Trapped in Uncertainty* (New Delhi: UPBSD, 1992), p. 88.

7. *Indian Express Sunday Magazine,* May 2, 1992, p. 2.

8. *Times of India,* May 10, 1992, p. 14.

9. W. Kirk, "Core and Peripheries: The Problems of Regional Inequality in the Development of Southern Asia," *Geography* 66 (1981): 188.

SUGGESTED READINGS

Akbar, M. J. *India: The Siege Within.* New York: Viking Penguin, 1985.

Bonner, Arthur, et al. *Democracy in India: A Hollow Shell.* Washington, D.C.: American University Press, 1994.

Das, Veena, ed. *Mirrors of Violence: Communities, Riots, and Survivors in South Asia.* Delhi: Oxford University Press, 1990.

Galanter, Marc. *Competing Equalities: Law and Backward Classes in India.* Delhi: Oxford University Press, 1984.

Library of Congress county studies.

Rajgopal, P. R. *Communal Violence in India* New Delhi: Uppal, 1987.

Wright, Theodore P., Jr. "The Indian State and Its Muslim Minority: From Dependency to Self-Reliance?" In *India: Fifty Years of Democracy and Development,* ed. Yogendra K. Malik and Ashok Kapur. New Delhi: Ashish, 1997.

Zakaria, Rafique. *Widening Divide: An Insight into Hindu-Muslim Relations.* New Delhi: Viking, 1995.

Zelliot, Eleanor. "Fifty Years of Dalit Politics." In *India: Fifty Years of Democracy and Development,* ed. Yogendra K. Malik and Ashok Kapur. New Delhi: Ashish, 1997.

7

Modernization and Development: Prospects and Problems

Traditionalism and Modernism: Coexistence and Conflict

Since the end of World War II, societies have sought modernization and development. Modernization refers to the assertion of secular rather than sacred, rational rather than mythical, universal rather than parochial, and achievement-oriented rather than ascriptive norms.[1] In a modern society, then, the individual, no longer just a member of the parochial world, is inducted into the larger world of state and national society.

To bring about a transformation Indian elites chose a path of political moderation, economic socialism, and bureaucratic controls over India's political and economic life (1947–1991). But India's record of modernization has been mixed at best. Although granting voting rights to all citizens has ensured equal political participation, the electoral process also revitalized the caste system, thus enabling caste politicians to consolidate their hold on both economic and political power, especially in northern and rural India. While participatory politics has created a new group identity and sense of assertiveness among the members of the lower castes, India's urban and rural poor remain impoverished, even though the total number of people below the poverty line is gradually shrinking. Allegations that many Indian politicians have amassed wealth beyond their known sources of income suggest that India has yet to develop a corruption-free political culture among ruling elite members.

In fact, since the 1980s the members of the backward and lowest castes of the Hindu social structure, who were previously on the periphery of India's power structure, have assumed influential positions in the politics of the country. They are gradually displacing the upper caste/class elites. India's participatory democracy is ushering in a silent but fundamental social and especially political change in the sociological background and political character of India's rulers at various state levels in the country.

In each national election since 1971 voters have demonstrated awareness of national and regional issues. The right to vote seems to have integrated the average Indian into the mainstream of national life, leading one political analyst to assert, "We have now a national electorate which is responsive to national concerns. In the slow and uncertain process of nation-building the development of a national electorate represents a great achievement."[2] Empirical evidence leaves little doubt that Indians are as "supportive of their system as people in any Western society."[3] Indeed, the voters' political awareness is evident in the election results. In 1971 the voters gave a massive mandate to Indira Gandhi when she presented herself as a progressive politician fighting against discredited party bosses; but in 1977 they voted her out of office for denying their democratic rights during her authoritarian rule (June 1975 to March 1977). In the 1980 elections they dislodged the leaders of the Janata Party–led government for their failure to maintain order in their ranks, and in 1984 they gave a massive majority to Rajiv Gandhi to preserve national unity against the secessionist movement launched by the Sikh extremists in the state of Punjab. In 1997–1998 they voted in a minority BJP-regional parties coalition, but in 2004 they voted in a minority Congress-left coalition government. A pattern of anti-incumbency has emerged as a predictable element in Indian national and state politics that shows mass-level frustration with Indian leaders.

Six decades of democracy in India have enhanced the capacity of the political system, so that astute observers of Indian politics find it hard to envision the country's actually breaking apart, as was predicted fifty years ago.[4] Nevertheless, frequent outbreaks of communal rioting, violent expressions of linguistic subnationalism, and territorial claims made by regional elites against one another amply demonstrate the strength of primordial loyalties and the continuing conflict between the traditional and modern elements in Indian society. For example, demographic change of India's northeastern states as a result of higher Muslim birth rates and mass migration of Bangladeshi Muslims into the northeast areas, the growth of Islamic militancy and the prospect of Islamization of India's northeast as well as the Kashmir region (and the possible Talibanization of Pakistan and Afghanistan), and growth of armed insurgencies in Bihar, northeast India, Chattisgarh, Jharkhand, Orissa, and Andhra Pradesh that reject political accommodation with the Indian union and state politicians are signs of growing radicalism in India. This is not to imply an imminent breakup of India or the failure of India's tradition of political compromise, but it suggests that the vitality of Indian democratic elections does not guarantee a rosy future for the Indian union.[5]

Institutional Stability

As noted earlier, Indian leaders, in contrast to those of its neighbors and many other third world countries, drafted, adopted, and implemented a constitution rapidly. Under the guidance of its charismatic leaders in the twentieth century, the Indian political system developed an institutional structure capable of facilitating the peaceful resolution of conflicts. Three key institutions—the Congress party, the federal structure of the government, and an apolitical bureaucracy—aided the smooth transition of India from its colonial stage to political maturity since 1947. In the 1950s and the 1960s the Congress party functioned as a federal organization, with a consistent accommodative interplay of power politics between the regional and national elite and with strong grassroots support. Moreover, regional political leaders, especially after the states were reorganized along linguistic lines, were able to get their regional demands conceded at the national level. A combination of regional political pressure and mass agitation worked to produce political accommodation within the framework of Indian constitutional arrangements and its political nationalism. That way, subnational tendencies were contained by political means rather than by armed struggle, and Indian leaders have experience and convictions to resolve disputes.

This situation, however, underwent a dramatic change with the slow, steady rise of Indira Gandhi to a dominant position in national politics. Even if one does not agree with James Manor that a complete disintegration of the Congress party organization occurred, one must concede that Gandhi transformed the Congress party beyond recognition. She stripped such party agencies as the Congress Working Committee, the parliamentary board, and the All-India Congress Committee (AICC) of their power and reduced them to nonentities. She reduced the state party organizations to the extent that they no longer played an independent role in the regions they were supposed to represent. In addition, Gandhi tried to subvert federalism in India by undermining the authority of state governments.

Indira Gandhi demanded personal, not institutional, loyalty. As a result, there was considerable politicization of the Indian civil services, once famed for their professional independence and integrity. She created a personality cult and the Indira-centric Congress party and governmental system. This approach continued with Rajiv Gandhi when he succeeded his mother as prime minister. Following the 2004 elections, which brought the Congress party back to power, Sonia Gandhi as party chief stayed outside government but continues to dominate the MPs, who are beholden to her for support and resources for fighting elections. She also exercises enormous influence over her appointee, Manmohan Singh, the prime minister (Singh has never won an election and does not have an independent political base or legitimacy as an elected MP). Without Sonia Gandhi's leadership, the

Congress party is a hollow shell because the party lacks a pool of strong independent leaders. Lately, Sonia Gandhi and Manmohan Singh have projected Sonia's son, Rahul Gandhi, as the next generation's party leader. These actions continue India's pattern of dynastic rule which is now at the core of Congress party culture.

Yet despite Gandhi's efforts to manipulate the country's political institutions to achieve her personal and partisan goals, the constitutional system has remained intact. Political institutions have already started to reassert themselves. India's civil service still attracts highly qualified, intelligent, and talented young persons from all parts of the country, and the bureaucracy still possesses the organizational structure to reassert its autonomy. Despite the asymmetry in the distribution of political power in favor of the Gandhi family, checks and balances exist in the Indian political system as a result of work by the judiciary, media, the BJP and other opposition parties, regional state administrations and parties, civil society groups, and occasionally the president, who maintains the right to refer decisions for review and is not a rubber stamp.

The stability and strength of India's system have been tested by the peaceful transition of power not only from one leader to another but also from one political party to another. Even when two prime ministers of the country, Indira Gandhi in 1984 and Rajiv Gandhi in 1991, were assassinated in office, the new prime ministers were sworn in smoothly and without any constitutional crisis. Part of the explanation for this orderly transfer of power may be found in the institutional framework created by India's political system, but another important factor is the informal rules and procedures developed by the leaders to resolve succession struggles and intraelite conflicts.

Finally, the operation of an independent judiciary headed by the Supreme Court of India, the administrative workings at the district, local, and village levels, and the operation of several autonomous commissions and agencies also point to the strength of India's institutional structure.

Planning for Industrial and Agricultural Development

India's leaders perceived the consolidation of the state through territorial integration and the establishment of effective political institutions as preconditions for steady economic growth. The leaders also realized that the country needed industrial and agricultural revolutions if it was to emerge as a modern country. Applied science and technology were seen as the keys to mobilize the material and human resources of the country for the common good. At the initiative of Jawaharlal Nehru, a Planning Commission was created in 1950. The commission is basically an advisory body consisting of economists, technocrats, statisticians, and ministers for planning and finance. Chaired by the prime minister, it established India's five-year plans to develop the agricultural and industrial sectors of the economy. It also makes frequent assessments of the country's progress and recommends changes in its development strategies. The five-year plans are submitted to the National Development Council, the members of which include the prime minister, the union cabinet staff, and the state chief ministers. Both the commission and the council direct the economic development of the country, first through the mobilization of the country's internal resources by means of taxation, and later on through the investment of funds in specific projects.

India's planned economic development has been directed toward (1) achieving a high economic growth rate, (2) building the country's industrial and technological self-reliance, (3) creating full employment, and (4) achieving social justice by removing gross social inequalities. These aims are constant ones in India's political history and there is a consensus among different political parties in the left-centrist-right political and ideological spectrum in India. Controversies, however, existed about policies and methods to secure these aims. Nehru's Congress Party relied on socialist policies, economic nationalism, autarchy, limited dependence on economic links with Western powers, and an abiding suspicion about Western economic colonialism following India's independence. Hence economic planning had a strong bias toward state regulations and a preference for public sector enterprises, checks on private sector development, and development of a vast bureaucracy to exercise the controls and direct economic activity. Since the economic culture was statist and socialist, market principles and globalization imperatives took the back seat to Nehruvian prescriptions. The first crack in this approach occurred when Prime Minister Narashimha Rao shifted toward partial economic reforms. He recognized that India was lagging behind China, a socialist country that had accepted capitalist principles as the basis of its development, while India, a liberal democracy, remained tied to the principles of a socialist economy. However, the contention between the capitalist and socialist mode of production persisted. Still, with the acceptance of free market/private sector/globalization imperatives, the contention between "economic nationalists" and "economic rationalists" was joined, irrevocably so. Under the BJP, the reform process was pushed further and India became a part of the global economic mainstream. BJP's acceptance of the necessity and the value of strong U.S.-India, India-West, and India-Israel strategic and economic partnerships increased the political space of private sector voices in India and the West. The Manmohan Singh government (2004 to present) strengthened the process and the space for reformers despite resistance by their leftist coalition partner. But Indian leftists bark worse than they bite; leftists in West Bengal have no ideological problems in adopting capitalism as the basis of the state's development when they are in power. Still, minority governments—BJP and Congress—have been weak and hence dependent on negotiating the common ground in the area of economic reforms. As a result of a rising trend of weak minority government leaders, the debate between economic nationalists and economic rationalists is likely to continue with a reactive, zigzagging approach to economic reforms.

Prior to the recent upsurge in India's economic activity, commentators differed in their assessment of India's economic performance. According to some economists, whereas in 1950, with a population of 360 million, India "produced $50 billion of goods and services; in 1995, 925 million Indians produced $250 billion."[6] Thus since independence the Indian economy has achieved a fivefold increase. Some thought that such growth was admirable since India was able to maintain itself as a functional democracy during the period when it was undergoing rapid social and economic transformations.

Other groups of economists held that even though India's economy has at times been estimated to be the sixth largest in the world, and even though India has a rapidly growing middle class, compared to the economies of the People's Republic of China and Southeast Asian nations such as South Korea, Taiwan, Singapore, and Indonesia, India's economic performance has been dismal.[7] In 1990 India's gross domestic product (GDP) grew at a poor 1.2 percent and India was faced with a serious economic crisis and an acute shortage of foreign exchange because of mismanagement of the national economy. In comparison, the economies of China and the nations of Southeast Asia had a healthy growth rate with robust foreign exchange reserves. This view was valid with reference to India's anemic economic performance from the 1950s through the 1980s (with food shortages and dependence on foreign aid), but it is not relevant now. India has poverty but no famine or food shortage. It has strong foreign exchange reserves. In 2006 its GDP grew by 9.2 percent—a one-year performance that equaled India's total economy thirty-five years ago. In 2006–2007 foreign direct investment into India grew by 44 percent ($16.0 billion, up from $2.2 billion in 2003–2004). India also has a pool of 500 million young, well-trained people who can engage the world and mobilize India.[8]

At the end of World War II, India and the Southeast Asian states started with similar economic structures; all were primarily agrarian economies. Only recently has India started to catch up in terms of economic growth and international trade, and it is still behind China, especially in terms of infrastructure development. Prime Minister Manmohan Singh indicated that India requires about $320 billion to secure its infrastructure requirements. The FDI coming to India is about $16–19 billion, far below its infrastructure development needs. India still has significant limits against FDI and ownership rules. Ironically, China shed its fixation against capitalism and massive economic links with the United States. India's pro-China leftists, who are coalition partners of the ruling Congress party coalition, however, still have an ideological fixation against Indo-U.S. economic ties, which is a major engine of India's economic growth and international trade. Here domestic politics and weak minority coalition governance and the theory of state controls and bureaucratic rule trumps economic rationality of the Indian and global marketplace and the social and economic needs of India's poor. Furthermore, despite significant growth in India's middle class and a slight reduction in the population pool that lives below the poverty line, almost 30 percent of the population lives below the poverty line. "Two-thirds of all women are illiterate. Clean water, adequate sanitation, and basic health care are absent from many villages and urban slums."[9] This observation is still relevant today. Evidently, in the areas of social justice and the elimination of poverty and economic disparities, despite the goals established by the Planning Commission, the Indian economy does not have much to boast about. India's socialistic experiment has failed; today India's private sector produces far more goods than the public sector, which suffers from both waste and inefficiency. India's large bureaucracy emerged on the theory of state controls and socialism and it is difficult for careerists and ideologues to abandon their interests and beliefs in statism.

By the early 1980s India's ruling elites became aware of the limitations of the state-controlled economic development strategy, and they were willing to undertake piecemeal economic reforms. To its credit, the Rao government in 1991 introduced massive economic reforms and freed the Indian economy from excessive state regulations.[10] By the end of 1996 India's economy achieved a 6.5 percent growth rate. India also became an attractive market for direct foreign investment despite significant government limits. As a result of economic liberalization there was a steady increase in direct foreign investment, "from a paltry $30 million in 1990 to around $5 billion by the second quarter of 1995."[11] India's foreign exchange reserve also grew from $1 billion in 1991 to $35 billion in October 2000. Many blue chip corporations—Procter & Gamble, General Motors, General Electric, Siemens, Enron, Daimler Benz, and others—are either establishing new plants or expanding existing operations.[12]

NOTES

1. Lloyd I. Rudolph and Susanne H. Rudolph, *The Modernity of Traditions* (Chicago: University of Chicago Press, 1967), p. 3.

2. Gopal Krishna, "A Nation-State to Defend," *Times of India,* January 7, 1985.

3. Samuel J. Eldersveld and Bashiruddin Ahmed, *Citizens and Politics: Mass Political Behavior in India* (Chicago: University of Chicago Press, 1978), p. 292.

4. Paul H. Kreisberg, "India's Inside Threat," *New York Times,* November 4, 1984.

5. James J. Manor, "Anomie in Indian Politics: Origins and Potential Wider Impact," *Economic and Political Weekly* 18, no. 1–2 (1983): 725; Manor, "Party Decay and Political Crisis in India," *Washington Quarterly,* Summer 1981, pp. 24–40. Since the mid-1990s the Indian government at center and state levels has dealt with a growing list of insurgencies in Assam and the northeast,

Jammu and Kashmir, Punjab, and central and south India. The growth of these insurgencies shows a rising faith in armed struggle as the revolutionary way to economic, social, and political reforms; the growing interaction between internal grievances and external stimulation by Pakistani, Nepalese, Bangladeshi, and Sri Lankan groups is indicated. For origins of the major movements, see Library of Congress Country Studies on India, Public Order and Internal Security.

6. John Adams, "Reforming India's Economy in an Era of Global Change," *Current History,* April 1996, p. 151.

7. Shalendra D. Sharma, "India's Economic Liberalization: The Elephant Comes of Age," *Current History,* December 1996, pp. 414–418.

8. See Aziz Hanifta citing U.S. undersecretary of commerce Frank Lavin, "India's Growth Totally Dependent on U.S.," *India Abroad,* April 27, 2007, p. 24; Hanifta, "India's Middle Class Is Set to Bust Out, but the Masses Must Buy into Reform," *Globe & Mail,* May 9, 2007, p. B10.

9. Adams, "Reforming India's Economy," p. 151.

10. Vijay Joshi and I. M. D. Little, *India's Economic Reforms: 1991–2001* (Oxford: Clarendon, 1996), chap. 7. Also see Jagdish Bhagwati, *India in Transition: Freeing the Economy* (Oxford: Clarendon, 1993), chaps. 1–3.

11. Shalendra D. Sharma, "Staying on Course to Be a Colossus," *World Today,* April 1996, p. 109.

12. Sharma, "Staying on Course."

SUGGESTED READINGS

Barddhan, Pranab. *The Political Economy of Development in India.* New York: Basil Blackwell, 1984.

Brass, Paul. *The New Cambridge History of India: The Politics of India Since Independence.* Cambridge: Cambridge University Press, 1990.

Eldersveld, Samuel J., and Bashiruddin Ahmed. *Citizens and Politics: Mass Political Behavior in India.* Chicago: University of Chicago Press, 1978.

Frankel, Francine R. *India's Political Economy, 1947–1977.* Princeton: Princeton University Press, 1978.

Hardgrave, Robert L., Jr. *India Under Pressure: Prospects for Political Stability.* Boulder: Westview, 1984.

Kohli, Atul. ed. *India's Democracy: An Analysis of Changing State-Society Relations.* Princeton: Princeton University Press, 1988.

Manor, James. "Anomie in Indian Politics: Origins and Potential Wider Impact." *Economic and Political Weekly* 18, no. 1–2 (1983): 725–734.

Mellor, John W., ed. *India: A Rising Middle Power.* Boulder: Westview, 1979.

Nayar, Baldev Raj. *India's Quest for Technological Independence.* Vols. 1–2. New Delhi: Lancers, 1983.

_____. *India's Mixed Economy: The Role of Ideology and Interests in Its Development.* Bombay: Popular Prakashan, 1989.

Rosen, George. *Industrial Change in India: 1970–2000.* Riverdale, Md.: Riverdale, 1986.

Rudolph, Lloyd, and Susanne H. Rudolph. *In Pursuit of Lakshmi: The Political Economy of the Indian State.* Chicago: University of Chicago Press, 1987.

Thomas, Raju. *India's Security Policy.* Princeton: Princeton University Press, 1986.

Vajpeyi, Dhirendra K., and Yogendra K. Malik, eds. *Religious and Ethnic Minority Politics in South Asia.* New Delhi: Manohar, 1989.

Wilson, A. Jayaratnan, and Dennis Dalton. eds. *The States of South Asia: Problems of National Integration.* London: Hunt, 1982.

Wood, J. R. *State Politics in Contemporary India: Crisis or Continuity?* Boulder: Westview, 1985.

PART II

PAKISTAN

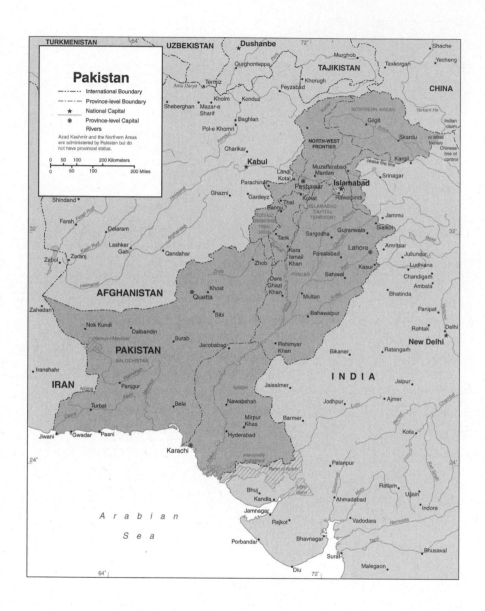

8

Political Culture and Heritage

Dominant Political Values and Beliefs

Pakistan came into existence as the fulfillment of a dream to create a Muslim homeland in South Asia. Consequently, Pakistan's dominant political values and beliefs have revolved around alternative interpretations of the meaning of "Muslim nationalism," which advocates understand as the ideal of pursuing a stable democratic polity that represents the people who reside within the territorial confines of Pakistan. In this context Muslim nationalism is indistinguishable from Pakistani nationalism, which in turn is functionally equivalent to the expression of other state nationalisms in South Asia (e.g., Indian nationalism). To so-called Islamists, on the other hand, Muslim nationalism has a different meaning. Islamists favor the expansion of Islamic law in various spheres of Pakistani national life—in regard to punishments and the style of dispensing justice or as the source of provisions of law, the method of training judges, or the final arbiter of legislation. They may also favor the expansion of Islamic practices such as the abolition of financial interest *(riba)*, prohibition of alcohol, gender segregation, Islamic taxation, and so forth. Finally, they may favor severing ties with Western society and culture. The basic thrust of such Islamist thought is not conservative in the sense of preserving institutions; rather, it is activist. The goal is to restructure Pakistan in a form more in accord with perceptions of what an Islamic state should be. Conversely, nationalists restrict the role of Islam in a Muslim state. They may oppose the expansion of Islamic law and the enforcement of Islamic practices, and they may favor development along the secularist lines of the West.

Pakistan's founders were ambivalent with respect to the meaning of Muslim nationalism. For instance, renowned Pakistani poet and philosopher Muhammad

149

Iqbal (1876–1938) made an important early proposal for a separate state based on the principle of Muslim nationalism. In December 1930 he stated, "I would like to see the Punjab, North West Frontier Province, Sind and Baluchistan amalgamated into a single state. Self-government within the British Empire or without the British Empire, the formation of a consolidated North-West Indian state appears to me to be the final destiny of the Muslims of at least North-West India."[1] Another founding father of the state, Chaudhury Rehmat Ali (1897–1951), is credited with having coined the name "Pakistan" as an acronym created from the names of the territories proposed to be included in the new state: Punjab, Afghania (North-West Frontier Province), Kashmir, Iran, Sindh, Tukharistan, Afghanistan, and Balochistan.[2] As Pakistan also literally translates as "land of the pure," the selection of the acronym was doubly meaningful.

Despite the yearnings for a separate Muslim state, however, mainstream Muslim opinion, represented by the Muslim League and its leader, Muhammad Ali Jinnah (1876–1948), pursued a policy of cooperation with the Congress party and favored a loose federal relationship among provinces within a united India once independence from Britain was achieved. By 1937, however, Jinnah and the Muslim League had a change of heart. Two explanations are usually given for this volte-face: (1) Jinnah and his colleagues were growing increasingly impatient with the Congress party's insistence on a strong central government wholly independent from Britain (prospectively dominated by Hindus) at the expense of minority community (i.e., Muslim) interests. This development, the Muslim League argued, ran counter to the intent of the Government of India Act of 1935. Therefore, the demand for a separate state was portrayed essentially as a defensive strategy to preserve the rights of minority Muslims. (2) In 1937 the Muslim League, running on the platform of an undivided India in the elections to the provincial assemblies sanctioned by the Government of India Act of 1935, was handed an unexpected and overwhelming defeat. Of the 489 Muslim seats, only 104 were won by the Muslim League.[3] Given this rebuff at the polls, the Muslim League was forced to change tactics. The strategy eventually adopted was to invoke the specter of Hindu domination in an undivided India by stressing the theme of "Islam in danger" and the consequent "solution" of a separate Muslim state.

Accordingly, the Muslim League adopted a resolution at its annual meeting on March 23, 1940—the so-called Lahore Resolution—calling for the creation of a separate Muslim state. The substantive passage reads:

Geographically contiguous units of British India are to be demarcated into regions which should be so constituted, with such territorial adjustments as may be necessary, that the areas in which the Muslims are numerically in a majority as in the North-Western and Eastern zones of India should be grouped to constitute *Independent States* in which the constituent units shall be autonomous and sovereign.[4]

After the Lahore Resolution was presented, sentiment for a divided India grew rapidly. The popularity of the Muslim League and Jinnah soared now that they represented an easily identifiable platform and the time of partition neared.[5]

Ethnic Makeup and Social Divisions

Since the separation of Bangladesh in 1971, truncated Pakistan has contained five major politically significant ethnic groups/nations: Punjabis, Sindhis, Pakhtuns (Pathans), muhajirs (the Indian Muslims who opted for Pakistan during partition; the term has been extended to their descendants as well), and Baloch. Each nation is defined by an admixture of linguistic and regional attributes. Generally speaking, the Punjabis are centered in Punjab and their ostensible mother language is Punjabi; the Sindhis are domiciled in Sindh and speak Sindhi; the Pakhtuns live in the North-West Frontier Province and speak Pushto; the muhajirs live in the urban areas of Pakistan (particularly Karachi and Hyderabad) and are usually native speakers of Urdu; and the Baloch live in Balochistan and speak Balochi or Brohi.

There is significant slippage in these definitions of ethnic identity, however. Pakistan's ethnic composition has been deeply affected by external and internal migration. Most obvious is the case of the muhajirs, who settled for the most part in Karachi and other urban areas. Furthermore, after partition around 4 million international migrants, primarily from India and East Pakistan, later Bangladesh, have settled in Pakistan. Not included in the above are approximately (2006) 2.6 million "temporary migrants" or "refugees" from Afghanistan. Most such individuals are Pushto speaking and are close ethnic relatives of the Pakhtuns. Accordingly, most have taken residence in border communities or refugee camps in the North-West Frontier Province (1.6 million) and northern Balochistan (0.7 million).[6]

In addition to such international migration, significant interprovincial and intraprovincial migration has taken place. Two patterns are noteworthy. One has been the phenomenon of rural-to-urban migration, spurred by brighter employment prospects in the cities. The urban population of Pakistan grew by 19.2 million (83 percent from 1981 to 1998; Table 8.1). A second phenomenon beginning as early as the 1950s, also largely fueled by employment prospects,

TABLE 8.1   Pakistan Population by Province/Region, 1998; 1981

Area	1998	1981	% Change 1981–1998	% Urban 1998
Punjab	73,621	47,292	55.7	31.3
Islamabad	805	340	236.7	100.0
NWFP	17,744	11,061	60.4	16.9
FATA	3,176	2,198	44.5	2.7
Sindh (ex. Karachi)	21,170	13,821	65.2	26.3
Karachi	9,269	5,208	78.0	100.0
Balochistan	6,566	4,332	51.6	23.8
Pakistan	132,352	84,254	57.1	32.5

Populations are expressed in thousands.
NWFP = North West Frontier Province; FATA = Federally Administered Tribal Areas
The last Pakistan census was conducted in 1998; before that 1981. A fresh census is scheduled for 2008.
Derived from Population Census Organization, 1998 Census (2000).

has been the interprovincial shifting of Punjabis and Pakhtuns throughout the state. These phenomena have had two major consequences. First, the major urban areas of Pakistan (Karachi, Lahore, and Rawalpindi/Islamabad) have become more ethnically diverse, and the indigenous population of the smaller provinces, particularly Balochistan and Sindh, has become threatened by the prospect of outside domination. For instance, Quetta, the capital of Balochistan, has more Pakhtun and Punjabi residents than local Baloch; and Sindhis constitute less than 10 percent of the inhabitants of the four districts of Karachi (Sindh's largest city).[7]

Pakistan has a national language, Urdu, and an overwhelming majority of the population can speak it or at least understand it. Less than 5 percent of the population can speak or understand English, yet it has remained the predominant language of higher education, the courts, and government since independence. Although numerous attempts have been made to enhance the significance of Urdu in the national life of Pakistan, along with parallel attempts to limit the importance of English, such efforts have been blunted from two directions. Some have argued, on the one hand, that increasing the use of Urdu will detract from the importance of provincial languages, particularly Sindhi and Pushto. Many argue, on the other hand, that discarding English would limit the international prospects of Pakistanis, and that such a policy would favor native speakers of Urdu and closely related Punjabi at the expense of other linguistic communities. Underlying the debate regarding the enhancement of Urdu in Pakistan is the fact that Urdu, though the link language of the state, is the primary language of a small minority of the population. The 1998 census disclosed that Urdu was "usually spoken" by only 7.8 percent of the households in Pakistan (mostly muhajirs, and primarily in Karachi and Islam-

TABLE 8.2   Major Mother Language by Province/Region, 1998 (percentage)

	Urdu	Punjabi	Pashto	Sindhi	Balochi	Siraiki
Punjab	4.5	75.2	1.1	0.1	0.7	17.4
Islamabad	10.1	71.7	9.5	.6	—	1.1
NWFP	0.8	1.0	73.9	—	—	3.9
FATA	0.2	0.2	99.1	—	—	—
Rural Sindh	1.6	2.7	0.6	92.0	1.5	0.3
Urban Sindh	41.5	11.5	8.0	25.8	2.7	1.7
Balochistan	1.6	2.9	23.0	6.8	58.6	2.6
Pakistan	7.8	45.4	13.0	14.6	3.5	5.5

Compiled by Charles H. Kennedy from Government of Pakistan, *Population Census Organisation*, 1998. Provincial Census Reports (various dates, 2000–2002).

abad), compared to the percentages for other languages (see Table 8.2). A further complicating factor is that such linguistic diversity is not related exclusively to provincial domicile. For instance, only 75 percent of those domiciled in Punjab speak Punjabi in their homes; 74 percent of those domiciled in the North-West Frontier Province speak Pushto; 59 percent of Balochistan-domiciled people speak either Balochi or Brohi; and only 60 percent of those domiciled in Sindh speak Sindhi.[8]

Given the diversity of communities, ethnic stereotypes are plentiful and widely held in Pakistan. Punjabis view themselves as civilized heirs of the martial tradition, providing the society with fine soldiers, efficient administrators, yeoman agriculturalists, and pious Muslims. Outside communities view Punjabis as arrogant, deceitful, and domineering—and resist their political and social domination. Muhajirs (at least those who live in urban areas) consider themselves the intellectual leaders of the society—and indeed they are disproportionately represented in the universities, professions, administration, and big business. Other communities view the muhajirs as an effete and somewhat illicit commercial class, doubting both their sincerity as true Muslims and their patriotism, owing to their former ties to India. The Pakhtuns consider themselves to be a pure tribe of consummate warriors, following the manly path of the Pakhtunwali, which prizes the virtues of hospitality, honor, and revenge. Outside communities view the Pakhtun as lawless, rough, and anti-intellectual. Sindhis take great pride in the antiquity of their culture and the purity and beauty of their language. They also claim a connection to the font of mystical Islam and Sufi orders. Outside communities view the Sindhis as dominated by perverse feudal chieftains. Finally, the Baloch are proud of their accomplishments as warriors and independent survivors of their harsh environment. Outside communities view the Baloch as archetypical provincials.

Religious Factors

Islamic identity is at the core of Pakistani beliefs and values. Islam, one of the world's great religious traditions, is based on the teachings and life experiences of the Prophet Muhammad. The basic teachings of Islam were revealed to Muhammad through divine inspiration and are found in the Quran. The life experiences of the Prophet (Sunnah) were compiled by his early followers and are codified in the books of traditions (Hadith). The Quran and the Sunnah are inseparably linked components of the corpus of Islam. Islam is both a religious doctrine and a code of social and political organization. Accordingly, there is no contradiction involved in seeking an Islamic solution to the secular ills of society. This fact is crucial to understanding Pakistan's development. As already noted, in many ways Pakistan's existence is predicated on Islam. In addition, its population is composed overwhelmingly of Muslims, who were found to constitute over 97 percent of the total population in the 1998 census.[9] Given this confluence of factors, Pakistan has possessed an Islamic mandate—a basis for the creation of an Islamic state. This mandate is given great emphasis by Islamists in Pakistan, although it is contested, at times bitterly, by others.

After partition Pakistan took nine years to adopt its first constitution. One major reason for the delay was contention over prospective Islamic provisions in the document. The first task of the Constituent Assembly was to define the basic directive principles of the new state, and in March 1949 the fruit of this exercise, the Objectives Resolution, was passed. It contained the following provisions dealing with Islam:

> The Government of Pakistan will be a state . . .
> Wherein the principles of democracy, freedom, equality, tolerance and social justice, as enunciated by Islam, shall be fully observed; Wherein the Muslims of Pakistan shall be enabled individually and collectively to order their lives in accordance with the teachings and requirements of Islam, as set out in the Holy Quran and Sunnah; Wherein adequate provision shall be made for the minorities freely to profess and practice their religion and develop their culture.[10]

Once established, these provisions have remained virtually unchanged in the otherwise fluid environment of constitutional law that has characterized Pakistan's statehood. Indeed, in 1985 the Objectives Resolution was incorporated into Pakistan's constitution. However, the new state ran into difficulty when it attempted to frame the basic principles to be implemented by the Constituent Assembly, and the Basic Principles Committee took nearly three years to complete its report. Regarding Islam, it recommended—at the urging of the ulema (religious scholars)—that the head of state be constituted of a Board of Ulema consisting of not more than five persons "well-versed in Islamic law" to review all provisions passed by the national legislature. If it was the unanimous opinion of this board that any pending legislation was "repugnant to the Holy Quran or Sunnah," the legislation would be referred back to the legislature for amendments. Excluded from the purview of such a board would be all fiscal legislation.[11] This recommendation received a cold response when it was released to the general public, and the final *Basic Principles Report* eventually adopted by the Constituent Assembly in 1955 contained no mention of the board.[12]

Provisions for the establishment of such an institution were also not included in the final draft of the 1956 constitution. In its place the president was empowered to appoint a committee that would look into the question of "bringing existing law into conformity with the Holy Quran and Sunnah." Other Islamic provisions of the 1956 constitution were similarly without teeth. The preamble adopted the vague wording of the Objectives Resolution. The "directive principles of state policy" provided that the "state shall endeavor . . . to make the teaching of the Holy Quran compulsory for Muslims; to promote the unity and observance of Islamic moral standards; and to secure the proper organization of *zakat* (charitable tax), *wakfs* (religious endowments), and mosques." The state was also to "endeavor" to "prevent prostitution, gambling, the taking of injurious drugs; and . . . the consumption of alcoholic liquor other than for medicinal . . . purposes." The preamble also called upon the state to "eliminate *riba* as soon as possible."[13] One outcome of the nine-year process of constitution formation in Pakistan, then, was a dilution of the Islamist position. Pakistan was designed to be a Muslim state, but the constitutional mechanisms to implement such a vision were intentionally weak, vague, or ill defined.

The 1956 constitution was short-lived, abrogated two and a half years after its adoption as a consequence of the military coup that brought General Muhammad Ayub Khan (1907–1974) to power in 1958. During the discussion preceding the adoption of the 1962 constitution, the status of Islam in Pakistan was again debated, and once again the nationalists prevailed. And when it came time to write the 1973 constitution (the 1962 constitution was suspended in 1969 and abrogated in 1972), the outcome was similar. Each of Pakistan's constitutions defined Pakistan as an "Islamic state," but determining what that meant in terms of law or practice was left for later.

General Muhammad Zia-ul-Haq (1922–1988) assumed power after a military coup in July 1977. Eighteen months later he announced a series of reforms termed nizam-i-Mustafa (Islamic political system, literally, rule of the Prophet), proclaimed to bring all laws into conformity with Islamic tenets and values. The main thrust of such reforms was directed at legal and economic institutions and practices in the state.

Most important, Zia created two new courts and assigned them extensive jurisdiction to examine existing laws in light of the injunctions of Islam. The most activist of these has been the Federal Shariat Court (FSC). Since 1979 the FSC has addressed hundreds of Shariat petitions (petitions challenging the validity of laws on the basis of Islam) and has completed a monumental review of all civil and criminal laws in Pakistan, testing for "repugnancy" to Islam. Indeed, the FSC has assumed many of the functions envisaged by the Basic Principles Committee for the Board of Ulema. Appeals from the FSC are heard by Zia's second creation, the Shariat Appellate Bench of the Supreme Court (SAB).

Since the early 1990s the pace of such legal change has slowed and the role played by the FSC and SAB has been reduced. But the cumulative effect of the earlier hectic legal activity has been significant. Findings by the FSC and SAB have prompted the rewriting of numerous provisions pertaining to criminal law, land transfer, financial transactions, laws of bodily hurt, standards of evidence, and inheritance.[14]

Numerous groups in Pakistan have voiced opposition to the Islamization process, including women's organizations and the Pakistan People's Party (PPP). Indeed, Prime Minister Benazir Bhutto (1953–2007) promised to dismantle Zia's Islamic policies, claiming that Zia's nizam-i-Mustafa was barbaric, reactionary, undemocratic, and discriminatory toward women. But she was unable or unwilling to deliver on her promise during either of her tenures as prime minister (1988–1990; 1993–1996). Conversely, her main political rival, Mian Nawaz Sharif (b. 1949), pressed for the passage of a Shariat bill during his first administration in 1991.[15] Its passage, however, raised more questions than it answered. Islamists argued that the bill was too weak; nationalists, that it usurped Pakistan's democratic constitutional structure. Nawaz addressed these concerns during his second administration, and in August 1998 he proposed the introduction of a constitutional amendment (Fifteenth Amendment) which would guarantee the supremacy of the Quran and Sunnah over other provisions of the constitution.[16] The Fifteenth Amendment failed to gain passage, however, during the remainder of his regime, which ended abruptly when General Parvez Musharraf (b. 1943) led a military coup that dislodged his government in October 1998. During the subsequent decade, Musharraf (now president), championing the image of "enlightened moderation," gradually rolled back the Islamist project: the Fifteenth Amendment was abandoned; Islamist judicial activism was discouraged and weakened; and Zia's much maligned hudood ordinances were rescinded through the passage of the

Protection of Women Act in 2006. Despite such actions, determining what form Islam should take in the Islamic state of Pakistan is likely to remain problematic and contested for the foreseeable future. Indeed, the turmoil that has gripped Pakistan since mid–2007 is inextricably associated with the still unresolved issue of Pakistan's identity.

Geographical and Social Factors

Pakistan possesses one of the most varied geographical settings in the world. Sindh, the southernmost province of the state, boasts the fine white sand beaches of the Arabian Sea and Karachi, a large natural port and the largest city in the country. Inland Sindh is a semidesert region in which the population is clustered along the winding banks of the Indus River. Balochistan, Pakistan's largest province, presents a startlingly forbidding landscape. Eastern Balochistan is dominated by the Sindhi Desert, and the western part of the province is composed of surreal-looking mountains. Except for the area surrounding Quetta, Balochistan is sparsely settled. Punjab, fed by five major rivers (the Indus and its four tributaries—the Jhelum, Chenab, Ravi, and Sutlej), is the breadbasket of Pakistan and its most densely populated province. Depending on the availability of water, Punjab varies from the semiarid regions in the south to the lush, irrigated plains near Lahore and the foothills surrounding Islamabad and Rawalpindi. The North-West Frontier Province presents the most varied landscape of all. In the south the province is indistinguishable from the plains of Sindh or Balochistan, and in the west the mountains, particularly in the Khyber Pass region, are reminiscent of Balochistan's mountains. In the north, however, the North-West Frontier Province features breathtaking scenery that, depending on rainfall and local ecology, varies from arid, forbidding mounds to deciduous Alpine slopes to lush, river-fed valleys. The Northern Areas (Gilgit, Hunza, Baltistan) and Azad Kashmir possess some of the highest mountains in the world, including the legendary Karakorum 2 (K2). The region also defines the ostensible site of the mythical kingdom of Shangri-la.

Pakistan's economic performance has been very impressive during the past twenty years. Indeed, the GDP has increased at a rate of approximately 4.6 percent per year (1986–2006), and the value of exports has risen by over 8 percent per year during the same time span. Pakistan is rapidly transitioning from an economy based on agriculture (which contributed 28 percent of the GDP in 1986, 19 percent in 2006) to one dominated by industry (27 percent of GDP in 2006) and services (54 percent of GDP in 2006).[17] Despite such rapid aggregate economic growth and change, however, the state of human development in

Pakistan remains woeful. The most recent UNDP Human Development Index ranks Pakistan 136th of 177 countries overall on the HDI index—123rd in life expectancy at birth (64.6 years); 124th on adult literacy (49.8 percent); 158th on combined primary, secondary, and tertiary school enrollment (40 percent); and 127th on GDP per capita ($2,270).[18]

The limitations preventing rapid improvement of the quality of life in Pakistan are demographic and political. First, Pakistan suffers the effects of rapid population growth, around 2.4 percent per year. Pakistan's current population (2008) is estimated to be 162 million; by 2025 its population will likely exceed 220 million. Given current trends, it is estimated that Pakistan's population will stabilize around 400 million, at which point Pakistan will be the third largest state in the world, trailing only China and India. Such rapid growth exerts extreme pressure on social services (e.g., health, education, transportation); it also swells the ranks of the underemployed labor force. Such demographic problems have been compounded by the influx of Afghan refugees owing to continuing wars in Afghanistan. Although millions of Afghans have been repatriated since hostilities began in 1979, over 2.6 million Afghans remain in Pakistan, primarily in the North-West Frontier Province. Second, there are political limitations. Pakistan faces one of the most difficult security environments in the world. Partially as a consequence of this, defense expenditures command the lion's share of the annual budget. Also, the demands of servicing Pakistan's international debt are staggering and rising.

Many daunting challenges continue to face Pakistan. The following chapter outlines Pakistan's numerous attempts to structure political institutions to meet such challenges.

NOTES

1. Khalid bin Sayeed, *Pakistan: The Formative Phase, 1857–1948* (Karachi: Oxford University Press, 1968), pp. 103–104.

2. Sayeed, *Pakistan*, p. 104.

3. Sayeed, *Pakistan*, p. 83. Also see Stanley Wolpert, *Jinnah of Pakistan* (New York: Oxford University Press, 1984).

4. Quoted in Muhammed A. Quddus, *Pakistan: A Case Study of a Plural Society* (Columbia, Mo.: South Asia Books, 1982), p. 24.

5. See David Gilmartin, *Empire and Islam: Punjab and the Making of Pakistan* (Berkeley: University of California Press, 1988).

6. UNHCR, *Afghan Population in Pakistan (2007)*, www.unhcr.org/country/pak.html.

7. Calculated by author from relevant census data. Government of Pakistan, Population Census Organization, *1998 Census* (2000). Provincial and district census reports were also consulted.

8. For details on language origins and the politics of language movements, see Tariq Rahman, *Language and Politics in Pakistan* (Karachi: Oxford University Press, 1996).

9. Hindus constitute around 1.5 percent of the population and reside primarily in Sindh province; Christians around 1 percent and reside primarily in Punjab province.

10. Adapted from GOP, Ministry of Justice and Parliamentary Affairs, *The Constitution of the Islamic Republic of Pakistan as Amended up to March 1999* (Lahore: PLD Publishers, 2000), Article 2(a).

11. GOP, *Report of the Basic Principles Committee* (Karachi: Government of Pakistan Press, 1952), chap. 3, nos. 3–8.

12. GOP, *Report of the Basic Principles Committee As Adopted by the Constituent Assembly of Pakistan on the 21st September 1954* (Karachi: GOP Press, 1954). A detailed account of the formation of the 1956 constitution is found in Herbert Feldman, *A Constitution for Pakistan* (Karachi: Oxford University Press, 1956); Leonard Binder, *Religion and Politics in Pakistan* (Berkeley: University of California Press, 1961).

13. The Constitution of the Islamic Republic of Pakistan (1956), Articles 25, 28, 29, and 198.

14. For details, see Charles H. Kennedy, "Repugnancy to Islam—Who Decides? Islam and Legal Reform in Pakistan," *International and Comparative Law Quarterly*, October 1992, pp. 769–787; Charles H. Kennedy, "Islamization and Legal Reform in Pakistan, 1979–1989," *Pacific Affairs*, Spring 1990, pp. 62–77.

15. Enforcement of Shariah Act, 1991 (Act of 1991), *PLD* 1991, Central Statutes 373. For discussion, see Kennedy, "Repugnancy," pp. 60–64.

16. Constitution (Fifteenth Amendment) Act, 1998. Text found in *Dawn*, August 29, 1998.

17. *World Bank World Development Indicators (2007)*, worldbank.org.

18. UNDP, *Human Development Report: Pakistan*, hdrstats.undp.org.

SUGGESTED READINGS

Gilmartin, David. *Empire and Islam: Punjab and the Making of Pakistan.* Berkeley: University of California Press, 1988.

Hayat, Sikandar. *Aspects of the Pakistan Movement.* Lahore: Progressive, 1991.

Jalal, Ayesha. *The Sole Spokesman: Jinnah, the Muslim League, and the Dream of Pakistan.* New York: Cambridge University Press, 1985.

Kennedy, Charles H. "Pakistan: Ethnic Diversity and Colonial Legacy." In John Coakley, ed., *The Territorial Management of Ethnic Conflict.* 2d ed. London: Frank Cass, 2003.

Malik, Ifttikhar H. *State and Civil Society in Pakistan: Politics of Authority, Ideology and Ethnicity.* New York: Macmillan, 1997.

Rehman, Tariq. *Language and Politics in Pakistan.* Karachi: Oxford University Press, 1996.

Syed, Anwar Hussain. *Pakistan: Islam, Politics, and National Solidarity.* New York: Praeger, 1982.

Talbot, Ian. *Pakistan: A Modern History.* London: Hurst, 1998.

Wolpert, Stanley. *Jinnah of Pakistan.* New York: Oxford University Press, 1984.

Ziring, Lawrence. *Pakistan in the Twentieth Century: A Political History.* Karachi: Oxford University Press, 1997.

9

Constitutional Structure

Pakistan's record as an independent nation-state is not a happy one. The litany of failures includes the inability to compose a constitution until nine years after independence; the abrogation of that constitution and two others during the next twenty years; three wars with India, one of which was a clear defeat for Pakistan; the failure to gain Kashmir; the inability to form stable democratic institutions; the failure either to sustain economic development or to effect meaningful redistribution of wealth to the impoverished masses; the loss of a majority of the population when the state of Bangladesh was formed; the inability to silence regional and sectarian disputes; and, finally, the inability to sustain a clear concept of and direction to Pakistan's nationalism.

Constitutional government in Pakistan has been more sham than substance. Pakistan has had five constitutions in its brief history: one inherited at independence (the Government of India Act of 1935, as modified by the India Independence Act of 1947, and four indigenous creations, in 1956, 1962, 1972, and 1973). Pakistan has also been governed at times without the benefit of a written constitution (1958–1962, 1969–1971), under a suspended constitution (1977–1985), and under a "modified" though "restored" constitution (1985–1997)—the latter having been wholly altered by the passage of the Thirteenth Amendment (1977–1999). Since October 1999 the state has been dominated by the military under various legal devices, including two Provisional Constitution Orders (PCOs 1999, 2007), a Legal Framework Order, and a significantly modified constitution revised by the Seventeenth Amendment. Ideally, a constitution is the framework of a government's intentions; it describes structural arrangements, allocates functional powers, and establishes limits to political authority. But constitutions, however artfully drafted, always reflect the state they represent. A state cannot overcome its problems solely through constitution making. Pakistan is a case in point. This chapter outlines the characteristics of Pakistan's twelve constitutional phases since independence.

Phase One: 1947–1956

At partition in 1947 Pakistan was declared a free, sovereign dominion to be governed until a constitution could be formulated by the Constituent Assembly acting under the Government of India Act of 1935, as amended by the Indian Independence Act. Until the new constitution could be drafted, the Constituent Assembly (CA) doubled as a National Assembly, and in this role it was empowered to enact legislation. Therefore, the combination of prepartition enactments and CA legislation constituted the effective law of the state. The duties of the governor-general, however, were ambiguous. At the core of the ambiguity were two questions: whether the CA could pass laws without the consent of the governor-general, and whether the governor-general had the legal authority to disband the CA. This ambiguity remained unchallenged until 1954.

The task of constitution making facing the CA proved to be so difficult that Governor-General Ghulam Muhammad (1895–1956) tested the aforementioned constitutional ambiguity by disbanding the CA on October 24, 1954. He argued that since the CA was unable to produce a constitution, it was prolonging its existence at the expense of the nation. Ghulam Muhammad's action was upheld by the Supreme Court of Pakistan in 1955. The court argued that the governor-general had the power not only to disband the CA but also to veto any legislation passed by it. Therefore, when the second Constituent Assembly was convened, it could do little more than follow the framework established by the governor-general. Instead of a decentralized legislature-dominated system, a form of presidential government emerged. The viceregal tradition of a strong executive set apart from and superior to other political machinery had been reestablished.

Phase Two: 1956–1958

Pakistan's first indigenous constitution was promulgated on March 23, 1956. It established Pakistan as an Islamic republic and replaced the governor-general with a president. The constitution was described as "federal in form and parliamentary in composition," but objective circumstances in the state made both claims dubious. First, as a means of muting the question of representation for East Pakistan, Iskandar Mirza (1899–1969), the new governor-general, amalgamated the provinces of West Pakistan into one unit in October 1955. This arrangement, which persisted until 1970, negated any federal solution to Pakistan's problems of regionalism. With only two units in the federation and with one holding effective control, the possibility of meaningful federalism was nil. Second, by 1956, the prospects of parliamentary democracy had become bleak.

The Muslim League, the only party of national unity, was in disarray. It commanded almost no support in East Pakistan, and its platform was virtually nonexistent. The only other significant party was the Awami League (its strength limited to East Pakistan), a party that ultimately repented its decision to support the 1956 constitution. Such party weakness led to extreme governmental instability. From August 1955 to October 1958, Pakistan had four separate governments. Under such circumstances, it is no wonder that the promised general elections to the National Assembly were never held, and that President Iskander Mirza (governor-general, 1955–1956; president, 1956–1958) was encouraged to suspend political activity, disband the legislative assembly, and declare martial law, thus abrogating the constitution less than three years after its promulgation.

Phase Three: 1958–1969

Pakistan was governed under martial law, without the benefit of a written constitution, from 1958 to 1962. General Ayub Khan (1967–1974), commander in chief of the army since 1951, staged a military coup in association with Iskander Mirza, but then forced Mirza out of the presidency and assumed the post himself in October 1958. From Ayub's vantage point as a soldier, the politicians had brought Pakistan to the brink of collapse. He believed that a centralized government with strong leadership was required. These views were embodied in the institutions he created (discussed later) as well as in Pakistan's second indigenous constitution, the latter largely a creation of Ayub.

Ayub's constitution, promulgated on March 1, 1962, established a presidential form of government. Pakistan's president (Ayub) was to be both head of state and head of government. Essential decisions were to flow to and from his office, implemented by powerful civilian bureaucrats (members of the executive). The constitution also established the Basic Democrats (elected local officials) as an electoral college to select the president and members of the National Assembly and provincial legislatures. The 1962 constitution created a National Assembly, but its powers were weak; it was designed more to legitimize the decisions made by the executive than to act as an independent lawmaking body.

Phase Four: 1969–1971

Ayub resigned in March 1969. General Agha Muhammad Yahya Khan (1917–1980), his successor, suspended the 1962 constitution, ended the electoral role of the Basic Democrats, and reestablished martial law. Yahya also held national elections in December 1970. But the results of these elections proved unacceptable to Pakistan's ruling elite, and martial law, now termed "emergency rule," remained in force. Eventually General Yahya sent additional troops to East Pakistan, thereby precipitating the civil war and the dismemberment of the state.

Phase Five: 1972–1977

After the civil war, Pakistan's military was in a shambles and saw no choice but to hand over authority to the most successful candidate in West Pakistan in the 1970 election, Zulfiqar Ali Bhutto (1928–1979). Bhutto governed until 1973 under military-sponsored emergency legislation; indeed, Bhutto was originally installed as civilian chief martial law administrator (CMLA) and president.

Within four months Bhutto lifted martial law and institutionalized his regime in the context of an interim constitution in April 1972. Under the terms of this document, Bhutto as president was granted broad powers reminiscent of the powers granted viceroys under the British Raj. For instance, provincial governors were appointed by the president and were solely responsible to him, and the powers of the National Assembly were left weak and ineffective.

Once secure in office, Bhutto presided over the drafting of Pakistan's fourth constitution, which was promulgated on April 10, 1973. Unlike the interim constitution, the 1973 constitution called for the establishment of a parliamentary system. The prime minister (a post Bhutto assumed after resigning as president) would be the effective head of government, with the president consigned to the role of a figurehead. Although the 1973 constitution established that the prime minister was to be elected by a majority of the National Assembly, many restrictions were placed on this provision. For instance, votes of no confidence could not be passed unless the assembly had already named the prospective successor to the prime minister, and for a no-confidence vote to be accepted, a majority of the prime minister's party had to cast votes of no-confidence. Functionally, the powers granted Bhutto under the 1973 constitution were as broad as those delegated to Ayub under the 1962 constitution. Again, the viceregal tradition of Pakistani politics had prevailed.

Phase Six: 1977–1985

Bhutto was removed from office after mass disturbances led by the Pakistan National Alliance (PNA), and alleged voting irregularities presaged a military coup on July 5, 1977. The successor regime under Zia-ul-Haq (1924–1988), however, chose not to abrogate the 1973 constitution. Rather, Zia's government suspended the operation of the constitution and governed directly through the promulgation of martial law regulations. Such regulations were defined by the courts as functionally equivalent to constitutional precepts. Between 1977 and 1981, Pakistan did not have legislative institutions. In 1981, Zia appointed the Majlis-i-Shura (Federal Council), but its functions were wholly advisory to the chief martial law administrator. In December 1984 Zia was elected through a referendum to the position of president. Nonpartisan elections (political parties were not allowed to compete, although members of the "defunct" parties could do so as individuals) were held in February 1985 to choose members of the newly established national and provincial assemblies.

Phase Seven: 1985–1988

Before the newly elected assemblies could meet, President Zia announced long-expected modifications in Pakistan's constitution. Accordingly, on March 2, 1985, Zia promulgated the Revival of the Constitution of 1973 Order. This document ushered in the seventh phase of Pakistan's checkered constitutional history. Although nominally a revival of the 1973 constitution, the presidential order fundamentally altered the terms of that constitution. Most important, the revival order dramatically increased the powers of the president. First, it reversed the lines of functional authority between the prime minister and the president. The president was given the power to appoint and dismiss the prime minister, and the prime minister's role was defined as largely advisory to the president. Second, it gave the president authority to appoint and dismiss the governors of the provinces and the federal ministers. Third, the president was given the functional authority to dissolve the National Assembly and the provincial assemblies.

In November 1985 the National Assembly passed the Constitution (Eighth Amendment) Act, which further legitimized Zia's constitutional order. Indeed, the Eighth Amendment protected actions taken during Zia's martial law regime with a retrospective constitutional justification. Article 270(A)(2) states:

All orders made, proceedings taken and acts done, by any authority or by any person, which were made, taken or done, or purported to have been made, taken or done, between the fifth day of July 1977, and the date on which this Article comes in force, in exercise of the powers derived from any Proclamation, President's Orders, Ordinances, Martial Law Regulations, Martial Law Orders, Enactments, notifications, rules, orders, or bylaws, or in execution of or in compliance with any order made or sentence passed by any authority in the exercise or purported exercise of powers as aforesaid, shall, notwithstanding any judgment of any Court, be deemed to be and always to have been validly made, taken or done and shall not be called in question in any Court on any ground whatsoever.[1]

In short, the revival order coupled with the Eighth Amendment substantially modified the 1973 constitution by concentrating predominant political authority in the hands of the president.

Despite such constitutional safeguards, the government under Prime Minister Muhammad Khan Junejo (1932–1993) proved too independent for President Zia's liking, and on May 29, 1988, Zia dissolved the National Assembly and the provincial assemblies and promised to hold new elections by November. Before such elections could be held, however, Zia died in an airplane crash on August 17. His sudden death left Pakistan without a president, prime minister, National Assembly, chief ministers, or provincial assemblies. The chairman of the senate (not dissolved by Zia's order), Ghulam Ishaq Khan (1915–2006), became interim president. Under Ghulam Ishaq, elections were held in November 1988 and resulted in Benazir Bhutto's emergence as prime minister. In December Ghulam Ishaq was elected to a five-year term in office as president.

Phase Eight: 1988–1997

The election of Benazir Bhutto did not in itself change Zia's constitutional system. Although Benazir campaigned on a platform calling for the restoration of the 1973 constitution, her electoral mandate was too narrow to engineer the two-thirds majority necessary to amend the constitution or to rescind the Eighth Amendment. Moreover, Ghulam Ishaq Khan pursued policies that jealously safeguarded the powers of the presidency.

For instance, on August 27, 1990, the president, exercising his powers under Article 58(2)(b) of the constitution, dismissed Benazir Bhutto's government and called for new elections to be held under the caretaker administration of Ghulam Mustapha Jatoi (b. 1931). Pakistan's four provincial governments were also dismissed. The superior courts upheld the actions of the president, and elections were held that resulted in the victory of the *Islami Jamhoori Ittehad* (IJI) [Islamic Democratic Alliance] and Mian Nawaz Sharif.[2]

Relations between President Ghulam Ishaq Khan and Prime Minister Nawaz Sharif soured during the next three years, and on April 17, 1993, the president dismissed Nawaz Sharif's government. This time, however, in a landmark decision, the Supreme Court accepted the appeal by the ousted prime minister and ordered that his government be restored.[3] The court reasoned that the president's power to dissolve governments was limited to cases in which there were compelling reasons to dismiss a standing government. That is, it drew a distinction between the 1990 and 1993 dissolutions. The 1990 dissolution was a proper exercise of presidential authority because it had been prompted by the extra-constitutional actions of Benazir Bhutto's government, whereas the 1993 dissolution had been prompted solely by a personal rift between the prime minister and the president. The Nawaz Sharif case established the important principle that the president's power was limited by the Supreme Court. This was a profound departure from the president-dominated system envisioned by President Zia and marked a new phase in Pakistan's confusing constitutional history.[4]

The remedy afforded to the Nawaz Sharif government proved short-lived. Barely three months after the restoration of his government, the military establishment, concerned with the deteriorating order in the state, brokered (some say forced) the resignation of both Ghulam Ishaq Khan and Nawaz Sharif. An interim government was established, and general elections were held in December, which returned Benazir Bhutto to power. Shortly thereafter Farooq Leghari (b. 1940), a Pakistan People's Party (PPP) loyalist, was elected as president.

Although relations between Benazir Bhutto and the new president were cooperative at first, they deteriorated in 1996, particularly after the death of Mir Murtaza Bhutto (1954–1996) in September. In a widely publicized speech, Benazir charged that Leghari was behind the plot to "murder" her brother. In fact, there was no evidence linking Leghari with the death.[5] Reluctantly, Leghari moved on Benazir's government, dissolving the National Assembly on November.[5] Again such actions were challenged before the Supreme Court. But the court, citing numerous examples of misrule by the Benazir government, upheld the actions of the president.[6] Elections were held in February 1997, and Nawaz Sharif and the Pakistan Muslim League–Nawaz Sharif faction (PML[N]) routed the PPP.

Phase eight, then, can be characterized as a period of checks and balances, of competing institutional authority. The prime minister effectively ran the government, while the president retained the ultimate power to dissolve the national and provincial assemblies. But such presidential authority was circumscribed by the superior judiciary, which could reverse the actions of the president and restore the assemblies. However ingenious and/or democratic, the system proved untidy. Between 1988 and 1997 Pakistan had eight prime ministers and four presidents. The system also proved short-lived.

Phase Nine: 1997–1999

Nawaz Sharif and the Pakistan Muslim League (PML) had received a convincing majority of seats in the 1997 election, far more than the two-thirds necessary to revise the constitution. This he did in a rapid and forceful manner. In April he orchestrated the unanimous passage of the Thirteenth Amendment. This amendment repealed articles 58(2)(b) and 112(2)(b) of the constitution which had respectively empowered the president to suspend the National Assembly and the governors to suspend the provincial assemblies. These articles served as the basis of presidential control of the government. Obviously the passage of the Thirteenth Amendment was an attack on the authority of the president, but it was also a frontal assault on the authority of the superior judiciary. Before the introduction of the Thirteenth Amendment (1988–1997), the Supreme Court served (for all intents and purposes) as the power broker between the president and the prime minister.

In one stroke the passage of the Thirteenth Amendment undid years of work by the superior judiciary. If this wasn't enough, Nawaz Sharif further signaled his intention to consolidate power by pushing through the Fourteenth Amendment to the constitution in July. This amendment prohibited "floor crossing" (changing party affiliation or voting against party policy) by members of Pakistan's parliament. Combined, the two amendments left the office of prime minister (read: Nawaz Sharif) functionally insulated from any challenges. The president had been reduced to a figurehead, the Fourteenth Amendment had left the opposition powerless to introduce a vote of no-confidence, and the Supreme Court had been stripped of its powers to referee the succession process.

The superior judiciary was obliged to strike back and found its vehicle in writ petitions filed before the Supreme Court that challenged provisions of the Fourteenth Amendment. Accordingly, on October 29, 1997, a three-judge bench of the Supreme Court, headed by Chief Justice Sajjad Ali Shah (b. 1933), admitted a petition challenging the amendment and suspended the operation of the amendment while the case was *sub judice*.[7] Nawaz Sharif, angered by the court's action, issued an intemperate public diatribe against the Supreme Court and its chief justice. On November 2, Sajjad Ali Shah responded in kind by citing Nawaz Sharif for contempt of court.

Earlier, two other judges of the Supreme Court (Sharif appointees) had issued an order declaring that the original appointment of Sajjad Ali Shah as chief justice (made by Benazir Bhutto) was illegal as Justice Shah at his time of appointment to the position was not the senior-most jurist on the bench.[8] Upon learning of this order, Sajjad Ali Shah issued his own order (November 26) directing that no more cases be sent to the two offending judges. The next day the two latter justices, joined by one of their colleagues, issued a counterorder contending that Sajjad Ali Shah was not competent to hold the post of chief justice and consequently any orders he made in that capacity were null and void. Before these warring judicial orders could be resolved, a mob (encouraged, if not directed, by Nawaz Sharif and the leadership of the PML) occupied the Supreme Court building, disrupting the first day of the contempt hearing of the prime minister. The hearing was postponed.

Subsequently, the full bench of the Supreme Court (December 23) passed an order declaring that the original appointment of Sajjad Ali Shah was illegal and unconstitutional. Justice Ajmal Mian (b. 1934), as the most senior judge, was duly sworn in as the new chief justice.[9]

During the factional wrangling Sajjad Ali Shah had issued an order suspending the Thirteenth Amendment, undoubtedly with the support of President Leghari. There was considerable speculation at the time that a constitutional crisis was imminent and that the military would be obliged to intervene in order to reestablish the pre–Thirteenth Amendment system, that is, to reintroduce Article 58(2)(b). However, the military chose not to intervene.[10] Left hanging, President Leghari resigned and was replaced in December by Nawaz Sharif's choice, Rafiq Ahmed Tarar (b. 1929). With Sajjad Ali Shah out of the picture, the Ajmal Mian–led Supreme Court dismissed the contempt charges against the prime minister and rejected petitions challenging the constitutionality of the Fourteenth Amendment.

When the dust had finally settled by the end of 1997, Nawaz Sharif stood triumphant. The Thirteenth and Fourteenth Amendments were law and had withstood legal challenge; the Supreme Court (without Sajjad Ali Shah) was behaving itself; Farooq Leghari had been replaced by the more Nawaz-friendly Rafiq Tarar; and the military had decided, at least for the time being, to stay in the barracks. But they wouldn't remain there for long.

Phase Ten: 1999–2000

General Parvez Musharraf (b. 1943), chief of staff, seized power on October 12, 1999, in a bloodless coup after Nawaz Sharif dismissed the chief of army staff (COAS) while Musharraf was abroad in Sri Lanka. The prime minister then allegedly attempted to prevent General Musharraf's return to Pakistan by ordering the hijacking of his airplane on its return flight from Colombo. The coup was undoubtedly motivated by the earlier authoritarian actions of Nawaz Sharif as detailed above. In any case, General Musharraf (now the self-styled "chief executive") moved quickly to legitimize his takeover by promulgating the Provisional Constitution Order of 1999 (PCO). Curiously, it neither suspends the constitution nor limits the power of the judiciary except insofar as the constitution or courts may intrude on the actions of the chief executive (read: Parvez Musharraf):

> Notwithstanding the abeyance of the provisions of the constitution of the Islamic Republic of Pakistan, hereinafter referred to as the constitution, Pakistan shall, subject to this Order and any other Orders made by the Chief Executive, be governed, as nearly as may be, in accordance with the constitution.
>
> Subject as aforesaid, all courts in existence immediately before the commencement of the Order, shall continue to function and to exercise their respective

powers and jurisdiction provided that the Supreme Court or High Courts and any other court shall not have the powers to make any order against the Chief Executive or any other person exercising powers or jurisdiction under his authority.

The Fundamental Rights conferred by Chapter I of Part II of the constitution not in conflict with the Proclamation of Emergency or any other Order made thereunder from time to time, shall continue to be in force.

The PCO also directs that "no judgment, decree writ, order or process whatsoever shall be made or issued by any court or tribunal against the Chief Executive or any authority designated by the Chief Executive."[11]

To remove any possible remaining loopholes in this order, the military regime deemed it expedient for members of the superior judiciary to take a fresh oath of office under the terms of the PCO. Accordingly, on January 28, 2000, the jurists were required to take an oath promising to uphold the PCO. Such jurists had previously taken an oath promising to "uphold the constitution."[12] Six justices of the Supreme Court, including the chief justice, refused to take the oath and hence stood retired; nine High Court judges also refused to take the oath.[13]

The chief executive also employed the Anti-Terrorism Courts (ironically introduced and championed by Nawaz Sharif) to try those accused of "hijacking" the airplane carrying Musharraf to Karachi. In April 2000 a Karachi-based Anti-Terrorism Court convicted Nawaz Sharif of hijacking and ordered him imprisoned for life. In December 2000 Nawaz Sharif and his family members were allowed to leave the country for Saudi Arabia. It was reported that the Sharif family was fined over Rps. 20 million ($400,000) and agreed to the forfeiture of property worth in excess of Rps. 500 million ($10 million) as part of the deal. At the time this deal was thought to effectively end Nawaz Sharif's political career.[14]

The military's actions, including the coup, the issuance of the PCO, the dissolution of the national and provincial assemblies, and the introduction of the new oath for the superior judiciary, were validated by the Supreme Court in the *Zafar Ali Shah* case handed down in May 2000. However, the court ordered that the national and provincial assemblies be reconstituted and that fresh elections to such institutions be held no later than three years from the date of the coup—October 12, 2002.[15]

Phase Eleven: 2000–2007

Perhaps Chief Executive Musharraf actually intended, as he had often promised, to hold elections as soon as practicable and return the military to the barracks. But such plans were dashed following the events of September 11,

2001, and the subsequent targeting of Afghanistan and al-Qaeda by the U.S.-led coalition. Pakistan was obliged to become a key U.S. ally in the "global war against terror," with Musharraf and the Pakistan military the key players in the alliance. It was hardly time to place global security in the hands of weak, corrupt, and discredited civilian leaders. But Musharraf faced four obstacles to the continuation of his regime: (1) he had to assume the presidency; (2) he had to significantly revise the constitution in order to remove Nawaz Sharif's amendments; (3) he had to hold and "win" elections by October 12, 2002; and (4) he had to get the newly constituted National Assembly to validate his reengineering of Pakistan's political and constitutional structure.

Musharraf proved adept at such tasks.

First, on May 1, 2002, borrowing from the playbook of his military predecessors (Ayub and Zia), he held a referendum. The chief executive asked the voters to elect him for a five-year term as president in order to consolidate his "reforms and reconstruction of institutions of state for the establishment of genuine and sustainable democracy . . . and to combat extremism and sectarianism."[16] It was reported that 97.5 percent of Pakistan's electorate voted yes.[17]

Second, Musharraf directed the National Reconstruction Bureau (NRB) to craft a package of constitutional revisions and publish them online for public discussion in June 2002. Such suggested revisions were far-reaching and became the basis of the Legal Framework Order (LFO) promulgated by President Musharraf on August 22, 2002.[18] Among its many provisions the LFO legitimized Musharraf's five-year term as president; altered the electoral system to disfavor candidates from the opposition and conversely to favor candidates supporting Musharraf and the Pakistan Muslim League (Qaid-i-Azam–PML[Q]); abrogated the Thirteenth and Fourteenth Amendments (i.e., restoring the power of the president to dissolve the national and provincial assemblies); and validated all laws and actions taken by Musharraf since he assumed power.

Third, elections were held on schedule under the terms of the LFO. Not surprisingly, given the electoral reforms and the absence of the two main opposition candidates (both in exile), the PML(Q) was able to win a plurality of seats and Mir Zafarullah Khan Jamali (b. 1944) was asked to form a government (see Chapter 10).

Fourth, the newly elected National Assembly eventually agreed to validate Musharraf's new constitutional system, for a price. In exchange for support of the LFO, which was presented to parliament as the Seventeenth Amendment, the loyal opposition insisted that Musharraf relinquish his position as COAS by the end of December 2004.[19] On the basis of this deal the Seventeenth Amendment was passed on December 30, 2003; and on January 1, 2004, Musharraf was provided with a vote of confidence by the elected assemblies

confirming his continuation as president. Reluctant to keep his promise to relinquish his position as COAS, in October 2004, Musharraf cobbled together
a majority to gain passage of the President to Hold Another Office Act, 2004
in the National Assembly. Although this bought him time it did not obviate
the objection that Musharraf's continuation as COAS (the so-called Uniform
Issue) ran afoul of Article 63 of the constitution, which mandates that no one
can hold at any one time more than one "properly paid position in the service
of Pakistan."[20]

Nonetheless, Musharraf, subsequent to the passage of the Seventeenth
Amendment, established a new constitutional order—a system with a strong
president, a weak and generally ineffective if occasionally raucous National Assembly, and a relatively effective, if depoliticized, government. In Musharraf's
system there was little scope for politicians. Indeed in 2004 he arranged the selection of a new prime minister, replacing Muhammad Jamali with the econo-
mist-technocrat and former executive of Citibank Shaukat Aziz (b. 1949), who
had served as Pakistan's finance minister since 1999.

But in 2007 Musharraf's carefully crafted system unraveled. Before embarking
on a campaign to seek a second five-year term as president, he decided to take
preemptive action against the "unreliable" chief justice of the Supreme Court
Iftikhar Muhammad Chaudhury (b. 1948) by suspending him on March 9. Justice Chaudhury contested his suspension (a superior court judge cannot be suspended without cause) and he filed a petition to the Supreme Court challenging
Musharraf's actions. His refusal to resign, typified by his supporters as "heroic,"
galvanized the support of many who objected to Musharraf's system and took to
the streets. Playing a prominent role in the street demonstrations were lawyers
and opposition political party workers of the Pakistan People's Party (PPP) and
the Pakistan Muslim League (Nawaz) (PML[N]). On May 12, Justice Chaudhury, at the invitation of the Karachi Bar Association, visited Karachi. But before
he could reach the venue of the rally his motorcade and supporters were attacked, ostensibly by party workers of the Muttahida Qaumi Mahaz (United National Movement, MQM; long-term rivals of the PPP). When the dust settled
42 people had died and over 150 had been injured. The Sindh government, allied with Musharraf, was generally blamed for providing inadequate security.[21]
Ten weeks later, on July 20, a full bench of the Supreme Court ruled that
Musharraf's suspension of Chaudhury was illegal, and it reinstated him as chief
justice. Chastened by the Supreme Court, Musharraf sought another remedy to
his dilemma. On October 5, he promulgated the National Reconciliation Ordinance (NRO). Among other things the NRO withdrew and terminated all
pending legal proceedings related to financial improprieties initiated before October 12, 1999. Benazir Bhutto, who had been forced into exile in 1998 to avoid

prosecution on numerous charges of corruption and impropriety allegedly committed during her two terms as prime minister, was thus cleared to return to Pakistan and not risk going to jail. On October 6, one day after the NRO was promulgated, President Musharraf was reelected by the members of the National Assembly, senate, and provincial assemblies by a narrow vote of 55 percent. The PPP (Benazir's party), unlike other opposition parties, did not boycott the polls but rather contested the election by putting up Makhdoom Amim Fahim (b. 1939) as a candidate. Therefore, the PPP's actions had the effect of legitimizing the election. It was generally assumed that Benazir and Musharraf had struck a deal, which some claimed had been brokered by U.S. officials.

Unfortunately, Musharraf's woes were not over. The Supreme Court, emboldened and perhaps angered over the attempt to suspend the chief justice, began to hear arguments challenging the legality of Musharraf's election on various grounds, including the uniform issue. Before they could issue their findings, which many thought would go against Musharraf, the latter struck by declaring a state of emergency and issuing a new Provisional Constitution Order (PCO) on November 3, thus ending the eleventh phase of Pakistan's constitutional history.

Phase Twelve: 2007–

Musharraf's actions were a first in Pakistan's quite turbulent and creative constitutional history. In effect the suspension of the constitution was a military coup by a standing COAS against the president where the COAS and the president were one and the same person. That is, Muharraf dismissed his own government and replaced it with his own government. Although Musharraf legitimized his actions as based on a breakdown of law and order "posing a grave threat to the life and property of the citizens of Pakistan," the real target of the coup was Pakistan's superior judiciary who were, according to Musharraf, "working at cross purposes with the executive and legislature in the fight against terrorism and extremism."[22] The remedy proposed to correct this deficiency was to require that all superior court judges would have to take a fresh oath of office under the terms of the 2007 PCO in order to continue to hold their seats; otherwise they would stand retired. The PCO in turn suspended numerous fundamental rights and mandated that the superior courts had no power to "make any order against the President or Prime Minister or any person exercising powers or jurisdiction under their authority." For good measure the PCO also mandated that no court could challenge the validity of the PCO. [23]

Sixty-three superior court judges ultimately refused or were not invited to take the new oath under the terms of the PCO, including Chief Justice Iftikhar

Chaudhury and all but four of the standing judges of the Supreme Court. Subsequently, Justice Abdul Hameed Dogar (b. 1944), the most senior judge taking the fresh oath, was sworn in as the new chief justice. The government moved rapidly to fill the vacancies in the Supreme Court and the High Courts, detaining some justices who had refused to take the fresh oath, including former Chief Justice Chaudhury.[24] The government also cracked down on prominent members of the legal community, most notably Aitzaz Ahsan (b. 1945), and imposed draconian restrictions on the press.

On November 13 the newly constituted Supreme Court issued an order dismissing the challenges to Musharraf's election as president, which paved the way for President Musharraf to dismiss the National Assembly (having completed its five-year term) and name a caretaker cabinet headed by the chair of the Senate, Mohammadmian Soomro (b. 1950). The Supreme Court's order also paved the way for Musharraf to finally resolve the uniform issue by stepping down as COAS on November 28 and naming General Ashfaq Parvez Kayani (b. 1952) the new COAS, which in turn enabled Musharraf to announce that elections to the new national and provincial assemblies would be held on January 8, 2008. Finally, on December 15 Musharraf revoked the emergency and repealed the PCO, mandating that the current justices of the superior courts (those who had taken an oath under the PCO) would now take oaths under the restored constitution.[25]

As 2007 was coming to an end, Musharraf had weathered a constitutional storm. He had arranged to be elected for a second five-year term as president; he had defused the judicial crisis by changing the composition of the superior courts; and he had finessed the uniform issue. Following the December 10 announcement that the PML(N) would contest the general elections, thus joining the PPP, he effectively ended the political boycott of the elections and emasculated the opposition to his regime and the 2007 PCO. Then on December 27, following a campaign rally in Rawalpindi, Benazir Bhutto was assassinated.

Benazir's death has deeply challenged Musharraf's carefully orchestrated plans to extend his tenure as president. First, the elections had to be postponed ultimately until February 18. Second, Musharraf and his administration were blamed directly or indirectly for Benazir's death. Some prominent members of the PPP charged that Pakistan's military intelligence (ISI) was responsible for the murder and called for a UN-led investigation into Benazir's death; others blamed Musharraf's regime for not providing adequate security for her campaign motorcade. Third, the alleged deal between Benazir and Musharraf became null and void. Following Benazir's death the PPP (ostensibly following the wishes of Benazir) named her son Bilawal (b. 1988) and her widowed husband Asif Zardari (b. 1954) as co-chairs of the party. Neither had made a "deal" with

Musharraf, and Zardari and the PPP proved quite adept at pushing the advantage afforded by a sympathy vote for the party's fallen martyr. Fourth, Nawaz Sharif, making the most of the changed circumstances and skillfully championing the cause of the retired superior court judges, led a resurgent PML(N) in the general election campaign.

The combination proved a perfect storm for Musharraf. His party, the PML(Q), was routed in the February 2008 election and his future as president as well as the constitutional order he established has now become quite uncertain.

NOTES

1. Act VIII of 1985, Constitution (Eighth Amendment) Act, 1985–1986 *PLD,* Central Statutes, p. 6.

2. The president's dissolution was upheld by *Ahmad Tariq Rahim v. Federation of Pakistan PLD* 1991 Lahore 78; *Ahmad Tariq Rahim v. Federation of Pakistan PLD* 1992 SC 646.

3. *Mian Nawaz Sharif v. President of Pakistan PLD* SC 473.

4. For a detailed discussion, see Charles H. Kennedy, "Presidential–Prime Ministerial Relations: The Role of the Superior Courts," in *Pakistan: 1995,* ed. Charles H. Kennedy and Rasul B. Rais (Boulder: Westview, 1995), pp. 17–30.

5. Ironically, Benazir Bhutto's husband, Asif Ali Zardari (b. 1954), was implicated in Murtaza Bhutto's murder. He was indicted for this crime in July 1997. This charge was finally dropped in March 2008.

6. *Benazir Bhutto v. President of Pakistan PLD* 1998 SC 388.

7. *Dastoor v. Federation of Pakistan PLD* 1998 SC 1263. Also, see S. M. Zafar, "Constitutional Developments in Pakistan 1997–99," in *Pakistan: 2000,* ed. Charles H. Kennedy and Craig Baxter (Lanham, Md.: Lexington, 2000), pp. 1–23.

8. As per the Supreme Court's dicta in *Jehad Trust v. Federation of Pakistan PLD* 1996 SC 324.

9. For additional details, see S. M. Zafar in Charles H. Kennedy and Craig Baxter, eds., *Pakistan: 2000* (Lanham, Md.: Lexington, 2000).

10. COAS General Jehangir Karamat, after failing to establish a National Security Council against the objections of Nawaz Sharif (an institution designed to institutionalize the power of the military), had resigned on October 6. That is, the military had already decided to not intervene prior to the Supreme Court crisis.

11. Provisional Constitution Order no. 1 of 1999 *PLD* 1999 Central Statutes 446.

12. Oath of Office (Judges) Order, 1999 (Order no. 10 of 1999) *PLD* 2000 Central Statutes 38.

13. Those on the Supreme Court refusing to take the oath were Chief Justice Saeeduzzzman Siddiqui and Justices Mamoon Kazi, Khalilur Rehman Khan, Nasir Aslam Zahid, Wajihuddin Ahmad, and Kamal Mansur Alam. Justice Irshad Hasan Khan became the new chief justice.

14. *Dawn,* December 10, 1999, www.Dawn.com.

15. *Zafar Ali Shah v. Parvez Musharraf PLD* 2000 SC 869.

16. International Crisis Group, "Pakistan: Transition to Democracy?" *ICG Asia Report 40* (Islamabad: ICG, 2002), p. 3.

17. Ayub's (1960) referendum garnered only 95.6 percent affirmation; Zia's (1984) referendum drew 97.7 percent support. See Charles H. Kennedy, "A User's Guide to Guided Democracy: Musharraf and the Pakistani Military Governance Paradigm," in *Pakistan: 2005,* ed. Charles H. Kennedy and Cynthia Botteron (Karachi: Oxford University Press, 2006), pp. 120–157.

18. Government of Pakistan, Chief Executive Secretariat, National Reconstruction Bureau, *Conceptual Framework of Proposals on the Government of Pakistan on the Establishment of Sustainable Democracy,* June 26, 2002. The text of the Legal Framework Order is found in *Dawn,* August 22, 2002, dawn.com

19. "Text of the 17th Amendment Bill," *Dawn,* January 5, 2004, dawn.com.

20. For details see Charles H. Kennedy, "Pakistan 2005: Running Very Fast to Stay in the Same Place," *Asian Survey,* January 2005.

21. Massoud Ansari, "The Day Karachi Died," *Newsline,* June 2007.

22. The text of the Proclamation of the Emergency is found in *Dawn,* November 4, 2007, dawn.com.

23. The text of the Provisional Constitution Order is found in *Dawn,* November 4, 2007, dawn.com. The fundamental rights suspended by the PCO related to security of persons (Article 9), safeguard as to arrest and detention (Article 10), freedom of movement (Article 15), freedom of assembly (Article 16), freedom of association (Article 17), freedom of speech (Article 19), and equality of citizens (Article 25).

24. Fifteen justices on a bench of nineteen did not take a fresh oath in the Supreme Court. The four justices who took the fresh oath were Abdul Hameed Dogar, Muhammad Nawaz Abbasi, Faqir Muhammad Khokhar, and M. Javed Buttar. In the Lahore High Court thirteen of thirty-one; in the Sindh High Court twenty-three of twenty-seven; and in the Peshawar High Court five of thirteen did not take the fresh oath. All five of the justices of the Balochistan High Court took the fresh oath.

25. "Revocation of Proclamation of Emergency Order, 2007," Pakistan.org/constitution.

SUGGESTED READINGS

Hamid Khan. *Constitutional and Political History of Pakistan.* Karachi: Oxford University Press, 2001.

Kennedy, Charles H., and Craig Baxter, eds. *Pakistan: 2000.* Lanham, Md.: Lexington, 2000.

Kennedy, Charles H., and Cynthia Botteron. *Pakistan: 2005.* Karachi: Oxford University Press, 2006.

Maluka, Zulfikar Khalid. *The Myth of Constitutionalism in Pakistan.* Karachi: Oxford University Press, 1995.

Newberg, Paula. *Judging the State: Courts and Constitutional Politics in Pakistan.* New York: Cambridge University Press, 1995.

Saeed Shafqat, ed. *New Perspectives on Pakistan.* Karachi: Oxford University Press, 2007.

10

Political Parties and Political Leaders

Political Parties

Political parties have not worked very well in Pakistan—though not for want of trying. Literally hundreds of political parties have existed during Pakistan's brief history, but, with a few short-lived exceptions, they have been ineffective in performing the functions usually associated with such institutions—interest articulation, interest aggregation, and policy formulation. Of course, other institutions have taken up the slack. The policy process in Pakistan has typically bypassed political parties, with effective power going to unelected advisers of heads of government, civil and military bureaucrats, and the courts.

There are four explanations for such ineffectiveness. The first is personalism. Pakistan's political parties have served as the vehicles of their respective founders and then disintegrated on their death. For instance, the Muslim League dispersed into warring factions after its leader and motive force, Muhammad Ali Jinnah, died in 1948, and disintegrated after Liaquat Ali Khan's (1895–1951) assassination three years later. The Pakistan People's Party (PPP) survived the death of its founder, Zulfiqar Ali Bhutto, but only through the transfer of authority to his daughter Benazir Bhutto. The latter's assassination in December 2007 has made the future of the party problematic, as evidenced by the unlikely transfer of party leadership to her nineteen-year-old son Bilawal Bhutto Zardari (b. 1988) and her controversial husband Asif Ali Zardari, bypassing more experienced and qualified members of the party. But clearly personalism continues as a strong force in Pakistani politics.

Second, political parties in Pakistan typically derive most of their support from a specific region of the state. For instance, in the 2002 and 2008 general elections (see Tables 10.1–10.4)[1] the PML(Q) and the PML(N) derived most of their support

TABLE 10.1   General Election Results, National Assembly, 2002, Number of Seats Won

Party	Punjab	Sindh	NWFP	Balochistan	FATA	Total
PML(Q)	68	4	4	2		78
PML(N)	14			1		15
PPP(P)	36	27				63
MMA	4	6	29	6		45
MQM		13				13
NA	7	5		1		13
Others	6	5	2	3		16
Independents	15	1		1	12	29
Total Seats	148	61	35	14	12	272

Key: PML(Q)–Pakistan Muslim League (Qaid-i-Azam); PML(N)—Pakistan Muslim League (Nawaz); PPP(P)—Pakistan People's Party, Parliamentarians; MMA—Muttahida Majlis Amal; MQM—Muttahida Qaumi Mahaz; NA—National Alliance; Others—eleven other parties won at least one seat; Independents—FATA's elections are nonpartisan.

Additionally as mandated by the Legal Framework Order (2002), 60 National Assembly seats were reserved for women and 10 for minorities, which were allotted to the parties following the election. The PML(Q) was allotted 26 "reserved seats" (22 women; 4 minorities); the PML(N) 4 (3 women; 1 minority); the PPP(P) 17 (15 women; 2 minorities); the MMA 14 (12 women, 2 minorities); the MQM 4 (3 women; 1 minority); the NA 3 (3 women); and two minor parties: the Pakistan Muslim League Functional and the Pakistan Muslim League–Junejo were allotted 1 women's seat each.

Source: Derived from Mohammad Waseem, *Democratization in Pakistan: A Study of the 2002 Elections* (Karachi: Oxford University Press, 2006), pp. 164; 167.

from the Punjab; the constituent parties of the MMA from their respective bases of support; and the MQM from Sindh (and then almost entirely from Karachi and Hyderabad). The only major party with significant strength in more than one province was the PPP with support in both Sindh and the Punjab, although the core of its support remains centered in Sindh. This is not a new phenomenon; regionalism has dominated party politics in Pakistan since independence.

A third explanation for the ineffectiveness of political parties in Pakistan is factionalism. This factor is primarily attributable to the operation of kinship (biradari) politics. In Pakistan politics is often viewed as a struggle between competing kinship groups for scarce resources and for prestige and honor. Political parties, then, become loose confederations of kinship groups, and political leaders are typically prominent members of important families. Loyalty to such parties, therefore, is generated by neither doctrinal nor ideological allegiance to a program but rather by individuals within the party. When personal considerations or rivalries intervene (and they often do), leaders typically abandon the party and take their followers with them.

Finally, party politics in Pakistan has been subject to a history of repression. Martial law during civilian regimes (in which curbs are placed on political

TABLE 10.2 General Election Provincial Assemblies, 2002; Seats Won

Party	Punjab	Sindh	NWFP	Balochistan
PML(Q)	131	11	6	11
PML(N)	38		4	
PPP(P)	63	51	8	2
MMA	9	8	48	13
MQM		32		
NA	12	12		5
ANP			8	
BNM				5
JWP				3
PKMAP				4
PPP-S			9	
PML(J)	3			
PML(F)		10		
Others	3	1	1	3
Independents	38	5	15	7
Total Seats	297	130	99	53

Key: See Table 10.1, additionally ANP—Awami National Party; BNM—Balochistan National Movement; JWP—Jamhoori Watan Party; PKMAP—Pakhtun Khwa Milli Awami Party; PPP(S)—Pakistan People's Party, Sherpao; PML(J)—Pakistan Muslim League (Junejo); PML(F)—Pakistan Muslim League (Functional).

Source: Mohammad Waseem, *Democratization in Pakistan: A Study of the 2002 Elections* (Karachi: Oxford University Press, 2006), p. 171.

activities) and direct military government (in which political parties are typically banned) have been the rule and not the exception of Pakistan's political process.

Muslim League

The Muslim League was the only major political party in existence in Pakistan at independence, and it possessed all of the advantages a party could wish for. Nearly every Muslim in Pakistan claimed allegiance to the party (sixty-two of seventy-six members of the First Constituent Assembly were members of the Muslim League; most of the others were Hindus). The party was associated with the dynamic and exceedingly popular Muhammad Ali Jinnah, who was the governor-general and president of the Constituent Assembly. Finally, the Muslim League had few institutional rivals. Yet less than ten years later the party had disintegrated into numerous warring factions. Why? First, the two individuals most closely associated with the party, Jinnah and Liaquat, died shortly after independence. With the death of these party stalwarts went the image of the Muslim League as the party of all of Pakistan. Second, the Muslim League never developed a coherent ideology. The party had been formed to secure the independence of the Muslim state from British India. After independence, however,

TABLE 10.3   General Election Results, National Assembly, 2008, Number of Seats Won

Party	Punjab	Sindh	NWFP	Balochistan	FATA	Total
PML(Q)	28	5	6	3		42
PML(N)	61		4	1		66
PPP(P)	45	29	10	4		88
MMA			3	2		5
MQM		19				19
ANP			10			10
Others	1	5	1	3		10
Independents	15	3	1	1	12	32
Total Seats	150	61	35	14	12	272

Key: PML(Q)—Pakistan Muslim League (Qaid-i-Azam); PML(N)—Pakistan Muslim League (Nawaz); PPP(P)—Pakistan People's Party, Parliamentarians; MMA—Muttahida Majlis Amal; MQM—Muttahida Qaumi Mahaz; ANP—Awami National Party; Others—four other parties won at least one seat; Independents—FATA's elections are nonpartisan. "Punjab" includes two Islamabad seats both won by the PML(N).

Additionally as mandated by the Legal Framework Order (2002), 60 National Assembly seats were reserved for women and 10 for minorities, which were allotted to the parties following the election. The PML(Q) was allotted 13 "reserved seats" (11 women; 2 minorities); the PML(N) 19 (16 women; 3 minority); the PPP(P) 25 (22 women; 3 minorities); the MMA 2 (2 women); the MQM 6 (5 women; 1 minority); the ANP 4 (3 women; 1 minority); and the Pakistan Muslim League(Functional) was allotted 1 women's seat.

Source: Derived from Raja Asghar, "PPP-PML-N in Sight of Magical Number," *Dawn*, February 20, 2008; and "Pakistan Election 2007-8," elections.com.pk.

TABLE 10.4   General Election Provincial Assemblies, 2008; Seats Won

Party	Punjab	Sindh	NWFP	Balochistan
PML(Q)	66	9	6	17
PML(N)	101		5	
PPP(P)	78	65	17	7
MMA	2		9	6
MQM		38		
PML(F)	3	7		
ANP		2	31	2
BNP				5
PPP(S)		5		
NPP		3		1
PML(Z)				1
Independents	35	1	18	12
Not finalized*	12	5	8	
Total seats	297	130	99	51

Key: See Table 10.1, additionally ANP—Awami National Party; BNP—Balochistan Nationalist Party; PML(F) Pakistan Muslim League (Functional); PPP(S) Pakistan People's Party—Sherpao; NPP National People's Party; PML(Z) Pakistan Muslim League (Zia-ul-Haq).

*As of April 1, 2008.

Source: Derived from "Pakistan Elections 2007-8," elections.com.pk.

its task was much less clear. These difficulties were compounded by the party's continued attempts to be a party of national unity (a vestige of Jinnah's influence), integrating diverse shades of opinion under its mantle. Such attempts rendered the remnants of the Muslim League's platform vague and platitudinous. Third, the constitutional impasse, peculiar to the formation of the new state and caused by the unresolved issues of political representation and the status of Islam, proved to be beyond the organizational capabilities of the party.

Accordingly, in 1954 the Muslim League was routed in the East Pakistan provincial election, winning only 10 of 309 seats, and in 1955 it lost its majority in the West Pakistan Legislative Assembly to the landlord-dominated, Punjab-centered Republican Party.[2] Between 1955 and 1958 the fortunes of the party continued to decline. In 1957 the Muslim League lost control of the national government, and in 1958 Ayub Khan staged a bloodless military coup. Since 1958 the Muslim League has remained defunct, although several parties have borrowed its name, including most prominently the political parties associated with Parvez Musharraf and Nawaz Sharif.

Pakistan Muslim League (N)

The Pakistan Muslim League (Nawaz) is a lineal descendant of the Islami Jamhoori Ittehad (IJI, Islamic Democratic Alliance), the latter a composite party that formed in 1988 to contest the general elections. Originally the IJI consisted of nine parties, but two parties predominated—the Pakistan Muslim League (Forward Bloc) and the Jamaat-i-Islami (Islamic Party, JI). The former was a faction of the PML that remained loyal to Zia after he dissolved the national assembly on May 29, 1988. The JI severed its official ties with the IJI in 1991. Under the leadership of Mian Nawaz Sharif, the IJI won 32 percent of the votes in the 1988 National Assembly election but, more significantly, won a plurality of seats in the Punjab provincial assembly election and accordingly formed the government. From his position as chief minister of Punjab, Nawaz Sharif and his IJI emerged as the main opposition to Benazir Bhutto's government. On November 1, 1989, Sharif led a no-confidence motion against Benazir's government in the national assembly. It failed by only twelve votes. Nine months later, on August 2, 1990, this goal of the IJI was accomplished when President Ghulam Ishaq Khan dismissed Benazir's government and named Ghulam Mustapha Jatoi as caretaker prime minister pending elections announced for October. The 1990 elections resulted in a sweeping victory for the IJI, which won 105 seats in the national assembly, and Nawaz Sharif became prime minister.

The IJI disintegrated in 1992 as both the JI and the MQM deserted the coalition. Weakened, Nawaz Sharif's government was dismissed by President

Ghulam Ishaq Khan in April 1993, but it was later restored by the Supreme Court.[3] The damage had been done, however, and Nawaz Sharif was obliged to hold general elections in November. This time the election was close and the PPP emerged as the winner with eighty-six seats to the PML(N)'s seventy-three and was able to form the government. However, the PPP received fewer popular votes than the PML(N). After another round of presidential dissolutions of assemblies and early general elections the PML(N) won a resounding victory in the February 1997 polls, capturing 134 seats in the National Assembly compared to the PPP's eighteen. This overwhelming majority allowed Nawaz Sharif and the PML(N) to restructure Pakistan's constitution. Nawaz's government was removed by a military coup in October 1999. Following the coup Nawaz fled to Saudi Arabia to avoid imprisonment in Pakistan. With its leader exiled, the PML(N) contested the 2002 election but won only fifteen seats in the National Assembly elections. In November 2007 Nawaz was allowed to return to Pakistan (following a decision by the Supreme Court) in order to lead his party in the prospective 2008 elections, although he was still banned from contesting the election himself. In the general elections the PML(N) made a very strong showing, winning the second largest number of seats in the National Assembly and commanding a plurality in the Punjab Provincial Assembly. At the national level the PML(N) joined the coalition government in March, and the PML(N) was able to form the Punjab government in April. (See Tables 10.3 and 10.4). The PML(N) is a centrist party which advocates the resignation of Musharraf, the restoration of parliamentary supremacy in the government, the restoration of the judges who failed to take a fresh oath of office under the 2007 PCO, and a distancing from U.S.-led policy in Afghanistan and Iraq.

Pakistan Muslim League (Q)

The Pakistan Muslim League (Quaid-i-Azam) began as a faction of the PML(N) when several prominent MNAs, including Mian Muhammad Azhar, Syeda Abida Hussain, and Syed Fakr Imam, broke from the leadership of Nawaz Sharif following the 1997 election. In 1999 the faction threw its support behind Parvez Musharraf, earning its pejorative nickname of "king's party." In 2001 the faction formally organized and contested the 2002 elections. It gained a plurality of seats in the National Assembly and the Punjab Assembly and formed coalition governments in each. Accordingly, the PML(Q) headed three governments between 2002 and November 2007, led respectively by Zafarullah Jamali, Chaudhury Shujaat Hussain, and Shaukat Aziz. The PML(Q) is a centrist party which favors the policies followed by Musharraf: to combat "terrorism and extremism" and devolution, and to provide continuing support for U.S. policies in the region. The PML(Q) was routed in the 2008 elections, winning only 42 seats in the National Assembly, and is not part of the coalition government which was formed in March.

Pakistan People's Party (PPP)

The PPP was largely the creation of one man, Zulfiqar Ali Bhutto. As such, the party was as enigmatic, complex, and full of contradictions as the man himself. On the one hand, the party represented a left-leaning populist movement: Bhutto espoused the cause of "Islamic socialism," which attempted to blend the spirit of Islam with socialism. The resulting policies included land reform to favor the peasants; the nationalization of industry to limit the power of the industrialists; and administrative reforms to curb the power of the unelected bureaucratic elite. Indeed, in its early days the PPP counted many leftist intellectuals among its members. On the other hand, the PPP was built on the foundations of the old ruling class of Pakistan (the landed gentry), and Bhutto's political style was reminiscent of biradari factionalism, replete with personal vendettas and periodic purges of PPP members. Moreover, as many analysts of PPP policies have argued, the outcomes of the reforms contemplated by the party fell far short of its ambitious platform.

The PPP came to power by capturing a majority of the West Pakistan seats in the 1970 election; it won with an even greater margin in 1977. However, the nine-party alliance that formed to contest the 1977 election, the Pakistan National Alliance (PNA), claimed the election had been rigged. Civil unrest ensued during the spring and early summer, and General Zia staged a coup in July. Bhutto was eventually imprisoned on the charge of complicity in the attempted murder of a political rival (Ahmad Raza Kasuri, whose father was mistakenly murdered). After a lengthy trial he was hanged on April 4, 1979.

Zia banned the PPP along with other parties in 1979, but after party restrictions were lifted in early 1986 the party reemerged as a potent political force under the dynamic leadership of Benazir Bhutto, Zulfiqar's daughter. Although the PPP secured a plurality in the National Assembly elections of 1988, the party's mandate was much narrower than it had been during the elder Bhutto's regime. The PPP entered into a coalition with the MQM and several independent members of the National Assembly (MNAs) to form the government in December 1988. Benazir's government was dismissed in 1990 and it lost the ensuing general election to the PML(N). The PPP and Benazir returned to power in 1993, but her government was dismissed again in 1996. The resultant 1997 election was a disaster for the PPP. It won only eighteen seats in the National Assembly—all from Sindh province. Moreover, the party was shaken by charges of corruption and criminality. Numerous indictments were issued against both Benazir Bhutto and her husband, Asif Ali Zardari, charging them with, inter alia, corruption and financial impropriety. Zardari was also indicted for complicity in the 1996 murder of Murtaza Bhutto (Benazir's brother).[4] Convicted in absentia for misappropriation of funds in 1998 and facing a five-year jail sentence, Benazir went into self-imposed exile, dividing her time between Dubai and England. In her absence her party, called the PPP(P) (Pakistan People's Party [Parliamentarians]), did remarkably well in the 2002 elections. In October 2007, President Musharraf promulgated the National Reconstruction Ordinance which vacated her conviction and allowed her to return to Pakistan. While campaigning for her party in Rawalpindi she was assassinated on December 27, leaving the party in the shaky hands of her teenage son, Bilawal, and her widowed husband, Asif Ali Zardari.

Nonetheless the PPP did very well in the 2008 general elections, winning a plurality in the National Assembly and becoming the largest component of the coalition government. Accordingly a Punjabi member of the PPP, Yusuf Raza Gilani (b. 1952), was selected as prime minister in March. The PPP has also been able to form the government in Sindh province.

Islamist Parties: The Jamaat-i-Islami and the Jamiat Ulema Islam

Islamist parties have been the most ideologically consistent parties in Pakistan, and the largest and most articulate of these has been the Jamaat-i-Islami (JI), or Association of Islam. The JI was founded in 1941 in Lahore by Maulana Maududi (1903–1974). Its general aim, shared by all Islamist parties in Pakistan, has been to promote Islamic policies, practices, and politicians. Moreover, the JI has opposed westernization by campaigning, for example, against capitalism, socialism, and party-based representative government. It has also opposed the adoption of corrupt Western social practices such as bank interest, birth control, relaxed sexual mores, and Western-style feminism. In the place of Western institutions and practices it foresees the adoption of a state ruled by Sharia (Islamic law). In such a state a pious amir (nonhereditary king) will rule with the consent of learned Islamic legal scholars (i.e., ulema). Members of the JI have been prominent in Pakistan's politics since independence. The JI was the dominant voice for ulema interests in the debates preceding the adoption of Pakistan's first constitution and was active in the anti-Ahmadi communal disturbances of 1953. The JI also led the opposition to the Family Law Ordinance (1961) and participated in opposition politics from 1950 to 1977 and during Benazir Bhutto's two governments. The JI is organized around party cells in universities, and membership in the party is based solely on selection by the leadership. Consequently, most of its members are university educated, although socially they represent the urban lower middle class. Despite its ideological prominence, the JI has generally enjoyed only limited electoral success in Pakistan.[5]

The Jamiat Ulema Islam (JUI), or Association of Ulema, is a Deobandi party which derives its support almost exclusively from Pakhtuns in the North-West Frontier Province and Balochistan. It was founded by Mufti Mahmood (1919–1980). His son is the current leader of the dominant faction of the current JUI, the JUI(F), Fazl Rahman—a consummate politician having been allied in one capacity or other with every government in Pakistan since Zia's military coup. A much smaller faction of the party, the JUI(S), is led by Sami ul-Haq. Like the JI, the JUI advocates Islamist issues, but its particular interest is Afghanistan. The JUI was closely affiliated with the Taliban, and in recent years it has criticized the U.S.-led occupation of the state. Also like the JI, the JUI has enjoyed little electoral success in Pakistan.

In the 2002 elections six Islamist parties united under the rubric of the Muttahida Majlis-i-Amal (MMA, United Action Council) to contest the elections.[6] Partially owing to the weakness of the PML(N), LFO-inspired electoral rules which favored candidates of the Islamist parties, and seat distribution agreements between the various Islamist parties, the MMA emerged as the third largest party in the National Assembly and gained a plurality of seats in the NWFP and Balochistan provincial assemblies.[7] Subsequently, the MMA alliance has largely broken down over the issue of whether to boycott the 2008 elections, with the JUI(F) deciding to contest the elections and the other five members of the MMA deciding to boycott. Largely as a consequence of this disunity the MMA suffered a devastating setback in the 2008 elections, winning only 5 seats in the National Assembly (they had won 45 in 2002).

Regional Parties

As previously noted, national parties in Pakistan have derived the bulk of their support from particular regions of the state, but their platforms have typically attempted to attract all of Pakistan's voters. The two most successful Pakistani parties—the Muslim League (with strongholds in West Pakistan, particularly Punjab and Sindh) and the PPP (Sindh and Punjab)—were no exceptions to this rule; neither were the Islamist parties: JI (Punjab and Karachi), Jamiat Ulema-i-Islam (JUI, North-West Frontier Province and Balochistan), and Jamaat-i-Islami (JI, urban Sindh and Punjab). However, numerous other parties have focused their appeal on regional autonomy. The National Awami Party (NAP) and its successors, the National Democratic Party (NDP) and the Awami National Party (ANP), have derived the bulk of their strength from Pakhtun voters in the North-West Frontier Province and Balochistan. Similarly, Baloch autonomist interests have been voiced by the Balochistan National Movement (BNM); Sindhi separatist sentiments by the Jiye Sindh; and expatriate Punjab and Pakhtun community interests in Sindh and Balochistan by the

PKMAP (Pakhtun Khwa Milli Awami Party). The ANP under the leadership of Asfandyar Wali Khan (b. 1949) did very well in the 2008 elections and was able to form the provincial government in the NWFP. The ANP is also a member of the coalition government formed in March.

The most significant ethnoregionalist party to emerge since 1988 has been the Muhajir Qaumi Mahaz (MQM, Muhajir National Movement, but since 1997, Muttahida, United Qaumi Mahaz). The MQM represents the interests of Pakistan's muhajir community. In the 1988 National Assembly elections the MQM won thirteen seats; in 1990, it won fifteen seats; it refused to contest the 1993 election but returned in 1997 to win twelve seats; in the 2002 and 2008 elections it won thirteen seats. Far more important than its role in national politics, however, is the authority the MQM holds in Pakistan's largest city, Karachi. The MQM dominates street politics in the city, and it has been deeply involved in numerous incidents of ethnonational violence over the years. The leader of the MQM, Altaf Hussain, directs the affairs of the party from exile in England.

Leaders

It is beyond the scope of this section to present a detailed treatment of the political careers of Pakistan's leaders. It is useful, however, to look briefly at the political backgrounds of nine of Pakistan's most significant leaders: Muhammad Ali Jinnah, Liaquat Ali Khan, Ayub Khan, Yahya Khan, Zulfiqar Ali Bhutto, Zia ul Haq, Benazir Bhutto, Mian Nawaz Sharif, and Parvez Musharraf. Table 10.5 presents a list of Pakistan's heads of state and government since partition.

Muhammad Ali Jinnah: The Father of Pakistan
Jinnah (1876–1948) was the son of a wealthy Khoja Ishmaili Shia merchant. His father, who expected the young Jinnah to take over the family business, sent him to London to study commerce. Jinnah found the study of law more congenial to his tastes, however, and in 1895 he was admitted to the bar at Lincoln's Inn. Already a member of the Congress party, Jinnah in 1913 also joined the Muslim League with the intention of merging the league with the programs of the larger and longer-established Indian National Congress. His efforts helped to pave the way toward the Lucknow Pact (1916), a cooperative agreement between the Muslim League and the Congress party that later led to the Government of India Act of 1919. But Muslim League–Congress party unity proved short-lived, and Jinnah resigned his Congress party membership in 1920 after disagreeing with Mahatma Gandhi's tactics of satyagraha (truth force/nonviolent resistance). Between 1920 and 1937, Jinnah waged an uphill battle against the forces of Hindu-Muslim disunity, but his political strategy

TABLE 10.5   Heads of State and Government Since Independence

Leader	Position	Duties
Muhammad Ali Jinnah	Governor-general	August 1947–September 1948
Linquat Ali Kahn	Prime minister	August 1947–October 1951
Khwaja Nazimmudin	Governor-general	September 1948–October 1951
Ghulam Muhammad	Governor-general	October 1951–August 1955
Khwaja Nazimmuddin	Prime minister	October 1951–April 1953
Muhammad Ali Bogra	Prime minister	April 1953–August 1955
Iskander Mirza	Governor-general/President	August 1955–October 1958
Chaudury Muhammad Ali	Prime minister	August 1955–September 1956
H. S. Suhrawardy	Prime minister	September 1956–October 1957
I. I. Chundrigar	Prime minister	October 1957–December 1957
Firoz Khan Noon	Prime minister	December 1957–October 1958
Muhammad Ayub Khan	CMLA/President	October 1958–March 1969
Muhammad Yahya Khan	President	March 1969–December 1971
Zulfiqar Ali Bhutto	President	December 1971–August 1973
Zulfiqar Ali Bhutto	Prime minister	August 1973–July 1977
Fazl Illahi Chaudhry	President	August 1973–September 1978
Muhammad Zia-ul-Haq	CMLA/President	July 1977–August 1988
Muhammad Khan Junejo	Prime minister	March 1985–May 1988
Ghulam Ishaq Khan	President	August 1988–July 1993
Benazir Bhutto	Prime minister	December 1988–August 1990
Ghulam Mustapha Jatoi	Prime minister (caretaker)	August 1990–December 1990
Mian Nawaz Sharif	Prime minister	December 1990–April 1993
Balkh Sher Mazari	Prime minister (caretaker)	April 1993–May 1993
Mian Nawaz Sharif	Prime minister	May 1993–July 1993
Moeen Qureshi	Prime minister (caretaker)	July 1993–October 1993
Wasim Sajjad	President (caretaker)	July 1993–November 1993
Benazir Bhutto	Prime minister	October 1993–November 1996
Farooq Leghari	President	November 1993–December 1997
Meraj Khalid	Prime minister (caretaker)	November 1996–February 1997
Wasim Sajjad	President (caretaker)	December 1997
Mian Nawaz Sharif	Prime minister	February 1997–October 1999
Rafiq Ahmed Tarar	President	December 1997–June 2001
Parvez Musharraf	Chief executive	October 1999–June 2001
Parvez Musharraf	President	June 2001–
Zafarullah Khan Jamali	Prime minister	November 2002–June 2004
Chaudhury Shujaat Hussain	Prime minister (caretaker)	June 2004–August 2004
Shaukat Aziz	Prime minister	August 2004–November 2007
Mohammadmian Soomro	Prime minister (caretaker)	November 2007–March 2008
Syed Yusuf Raza Gilani	Prime minister	March 2008–

changed after the Muslim League's humiliating defeat in the provincial elections of 1937. Accordingly, Jinnah came to espouse the Two Nation Theory and eventually sponsored the Lahore Resolution of 1940. His argument was twofold: (1) In a united India, Muslim interests would be dominated by the majority community Hindus, and (2) the prospects of an Islamic state were in danger of subversion by such an outcome. Under this plank the Muslim League came to dominate Muslim politics on the subcontinent, and Jinnah, as president of the party (1934–1948), emerged as its unchallenged leader.

Jinnah was an unlikely figure to assume such a role. He was an aloof, haughty, elitist intellectual. He never learned Urdu or Bengali, and his personal life was quite secular. However, Jinnah was brilliant and tireless, and his ability to deal with the British as well as with the legal complexities engendered by the prospects of partition made him an indispensable vehicle of Muslim nationalism.

The Quaid-i-Azam (great leader) died on September 11, 1948, within thirteen months of becoming governor-general of Pakistan. Although he accomplished much during his lifetime, his legacy is mixed. His dominance of the Muslim League and his assumption of the governor-generalship, perhaps necessary for pursuing the goal of Pakistan and preserving unity after independence, nevertheless retarded the growth of representative democracy in the state by providing a precedent for one-man rule. Similarly, Jinnah's Muslim League, crafted to secure its nationalist demands, proved ineffective as a political party after independence.

Liaquat Ali Khan: The Lieutenant

Liaquat's political career was mainly undertaken in the shadow of Jinnah. Liaquat (1895–1951) was born in Karnal, Punjab, the son of an important landlord. Like Jinnah, he was liberally educated, at Aligarh, Allahabad, and finally Oxford; also like Jinnah, he was a lawyer. Unlike Jinnah, however, Liaquat lacked personal charisma, and his political constituency was small. A younger son, he pursued his political career in the United Provinces (now Uttar Pradesh) rather than in Punjab.

The basis of Liaquat's power was his close relationship to Jinnah, who had selected the young, inexperienced lawyer to be general secretary of the Muslim League in 1936. The choice was propitious, as Liaquat proved an astute organizer who was able to hold the disparate factions of the party together. In 1947 Liaquat became Pakistan's first prime minister, although he remained in the background while Jinnah effectively ran the government from the post of governor-general.

After Jinnah's death, Liaquat became the dominant personality in the government, but most analysts agree that his performance in office was ineffectual. First, his leadership was challenged by the Bengali Khwaja Nazimuddin (1894–1964), who served as governor-general from 1948 to 1951 and later as prime minister. Second, the unresolved issues of political representation and the status of Islam, muted as long as Jinnah lived, were joined during Liaquat's tenure. Finally, Liaquat could not accomplish the critical task of drafting a constitution. Perhaps such issues would have been resolved if Liaquat had lived, but the Quaid-i-Millat (leader of the nation) was felled by an assassin's bullet in Rawalpindi on October 16, 1951.

Muhammad Ayub Khan: Soldier-Statesman

Ayub Khan (1907–1970) was the quintessential "British generation" military officer. Ayub was born in the village of Rehana, fifty miles north of Rawalpindi; his father was a subedar major (noncommissioned officer) in the British Indian army. Ayub was never a good student (admitting in his autobiography that he failed the sixth grade), but he worked hard and was eventually admitted to the Mohammadan Anglo-Oriental College at Aligarh. Ayub's teachers, impressed by his "sporting ability" and family background, encouraged him to undertake studies at Sandhurst (the British military academy), where he graduated with a commission in 1929. Ayub fought with British forces in Burma during World War II. After the war, as one of a handful of Muslim Sandhurst-trained graduates, his rise was meteoric. In 1951 he was selected by Liaquat as Pakistan's first Pakistani army commander in chief (a post previously held by British officers under contract).

From his background and training Ayub internalized two characteristics that would greatly influence the course of Pakistan's history. First, Ayub was firmly wedded to the integrity of the Pakistan army. Second, Ayub distrusted the loyalty and vacillations of Pakistan's politicians. Therefore, when (according to Ayub) he was offered control of the government in 1954 (by Governor-General Ghulam Muhammad), he turned it down because it would damage the prestige of the armed forces. But four years later, in the midst of the civil unrest caused by "self-serving politicians, wrangling over portfolios" and Iskander Mirza's abrogation of the 1956 constitution, Ayub moved.[8] On October 5, 1958, through the strategic repositioning of two brigades of troops, and without a single shot being fired, Ayub became chief martial law administrator. Ayub remained head of state and head of government (after February 1960 as a "civilian" president) until his forced resignation on March 25, 1969.

Agha Muhammad Yahya Khan: The Unwitting Architect of Pakistan's Dismemberment

Yahya (1917–1980) was born in Chakwal, a town in the Jhelum district of the Punjab. He was the son of a police superintendent, and after his education at Punjab University he was commissioned in 1938. He underwent military training at the Indian Military Academy in Dehra Dun. After partition he rose rapidly through the ranks, becoming chief of general staff in 1957 and commander in chief in 1966. When Ayub resigned, Yahya replaced him as president, a post he held until December 1971.

Yahya's presidency was brief but eventful. Following the disturbances that led to Ayub's resignation, Yahya was perceived as a caretaker until a civilian regime was established. Accordingly, Yahya dissolved the One Unit Scheme in 1970 and oversaw

Pakistan's first national election including universal adult suffrage. However well meaning, the 1970 election proved a disaster for unified Pakistan. Sheikh Mujibur Rahman (1920–1975), leader of the Awami League, won an overwhelming victory in East Pakistan and as a consequence a commanding majority of the National Assembly seats. Zulfiqar Ali Bhutto, head of the Pakistan People's Party (PPP), came in a distant second, winning all of his seats in West Pakistan. Yahya attempted to forge a compromise between Bhutto and Mujib in which there would ostensibly have been some form of power sharing between East and West Pakistan.[9] But his efforts were thwarted by Mujib's demand to be prime minister of an undivided state and Bhutto's unwillingness to merely head up the opposition. On March 25, 1971 (the second anniversary of Ayub's resignation), Yahya ordered the catastrophic military crackdown on East Pakistani nationalists which led in turn to the horrors of the civil war, the capture of Dhaka by the invading (liberating?) Indian army, and the unconditional surrender of the Pakistan army. It also led to the secession of East Pakistan and the formation of Bangladesh. Yahya resigned from office and served five years under house arrest for his role in the debacle.

Zulfiqar Ali Bhutto: Islamic Socialist

Bhutto (1927–1979) was perhaps the most enigmatic of all of Pakistan's leaders. He was the son of Sir Shahnawaz Bhutto, a wealthy, well-known landlord from central Sindh. Sir Shahnawaz was very active in politics, and he bequeathed to his son the task of looking after the landed interests of his family as well as those of other landed aristocrats in the province. This influence contrasted with Bhutto's earned status as a member of the urban intelligentsia. Bhutto attended Oxford University and the University of California–Berkeley. The tensions between these interests were to shape the political career of Pakistan's most skilled politician.[10]

At the age of thirty-one Bhutto was made minister of fuel and natural resources in Ayub's first cabinet; later he became foreign minister. Bhutto used these positions as a base for developing his own political constituency, increasingly espousing a leftist position in the process. Accordingly, as minister of fuels he worked out an oil exploration agreement with the Soviet Union, and as foreign minister he worked toward strengthening Pakistan-China relations. After the 1965 war with India, and perhaps sensing that Ayub's hold on the government was slipping, Bhutto broke with Ayub and became openly critical of Ayub's foreign policy. He was dismissed from the cabinet in 1967 and set about building a national following through extensive travel, speechmaking, and the publication of several books. Bhutto's support for third world causes, his socialist rhetoric, and his outspoken criticism of the unpopular Ayub regime won him many followers, particularly among students and intellectuals in West Pakistan's urban areas. He also organized the Pakistan People's Party (PPP).

After the 1970 election and the civil war, Bhutto emerged in the anomalous position of civilian head of a military regime; his official title on assuming office was president and chief martial law administrator. The termination of martial law and the promulgation of the 1973 constitution redefined his position as prime minister.

Bhutto's leadership style was greatly influenced by his feudal background. Although he espoused a populist egalitarian domestic program and a liberal nonaligned foreign policy, Bhutto's approach to politics was autocratic. He perceived opposition to his policies as a personal affront, and the history of his rule is replete with the political repression of his rivals. Ironically perhaps, Bhutto fell victim to a comparatively minor gaffe (i.e., minor relative to the enormity of other alleged crimes)—complicity in the bungled assassination of a former member of the PPP turned political opponent.[11] Bhutto was eventually convicted of murder, and his appeal was rejected by a 4 to 3 decision of the Supreme Court; he was hanged on April 4, 1979.

Muhammad Zia-ul-Haq: "Reluctant" Leader and Martial Islamist

Like Ayub, Zia (1924–1988) was a career military officer who served with British Indian forces during World War II. He received his commission in 1945 from the Indian Military Academy at Dehra Dun. Zia was born in Jullundur, East Punjab (India). After twenty years in the lower ranks of Pakistan's officer corps, he was promoted to colonel in 1968, brigadier in 1969, and major general in 1972; in 1975 he was appointed lieutenant general and corps commander. Up to this point, his military career had been unexceptional. He had a deserved reputation as a devout Muslim, he avoided political intrigue, and on many occasions he had proven his loyalty to the state and to the chain of command. These characteristics attracted Bhutto (who since assuming office had feared another military coup), and he appointed Zia chief of army staff over the heads of several more senior generals in 1976.

Thus the military coup of 1977 headed by General Zia came as a surprise to Bhutto. Perhaps Zia was a reluctant participant in the coup, his hand forced by the military's long-standing grievances with the Bhutto regime and by the deteriorating law-and-order situation after the 1977 election. Regardless of motive, Zia maintained power for over eleven years, as chief martial law administrator (1977–1985) and as president (1979–1988).

Zia is perhaps best remembered for shaping Pakistan's foreign policy during the Afghan War and for initiating the Islamization process. His role in both proved controversial, and his legacy consequently remains mixed.[12]

Within months of dismissing the government of Muhammad Khan Junejo, Zia died along with several senior military officers and the U.S. ambassador to

Pakistan, Arnold Raphel, when his military plane was targeted by unknown assassins on August 17, 1988.

Benazir Bhutto: Daughter of Destiny and Martyr

Benazir Bhutto's (1953–2007) life was shaped by her role as the daughter of Zulfiqar Ali Bhutto. At his insistence, Benazir was educated abroad (Radcliffe College and Oxford University). He had entertained hopes that his daughter would undertake a career in the foreign service. His plans were derailed, however, after Zia's military coup in 1977 and Bhutto's execution in 1979. To Benazir, the military's actions were illegal and the execution of her father "murder." In her eyes his wrongful death made him a martyr (shaheed). Accordingly, she became obsessed with avenging her father's death, restoring the PPP to power, and reestablishing her father's 1973 constitution.[13]

Through a series of propitious circumstances, including Zia's dissolution of the National Assembly in May 1988 and the sudden death of Zia and several senior military officers before a new National Assembly could be elected, she managed partially to accomplish her goals in December 1988. At that time Benazir led the PPP to a narrow victory in the National Assembly elections and became prime minister. Subsequently Benazir was at the center of national politics in Pakistan either as prime minister (1988–1990; 1993–1996) or as opposition leader (1990–1993; 1997–2007).

Unfortunately, her performance as prime minister is generally acknowledged as disappointing. In 1990 her first government was dismissed by Ghulam Ishaq Khan. Her second government was dismissed by fellow PPP member Farooq Leghari in 1996. In both instances the Supreme Court upheld charges of corruption and mismanagement by her respective governments. Ironically, the vehicle for the "restoration" of the 1973 constitution ("Zulfiqar's constitution"), a longtime PPP demand, was the humiliating defeat of the PPP in the 1997 general election, which gave the PML the requisite two-thirds majority to amend the constitution. After that defeat, Benazir's fortunes waned. She was convicted in absentia on charges of corruption in 1998 and lived in self-imposed exile until October 2007, when she was encouraged to return to Pakistan by the promulgation of Musharraf's National Reconciliation Ordinance. As tragic and senseless as her December 27 assassination was, it is somehow fitting that she died while campaigning for her party in Rawalpindi at Liaquat Bagh, a site named to honor the memory of another martyr of Pakistan who like Benazir was felled by an assassin's bullet.

Mian Nawaz Sharif: Industrialist Turned Politician and Statesman

Mian Nawaz Sharif was born near Lahore in 1949, the eldest son of a prominent industrialist family that owned Ittefaq Foundry, the largest steel mill in the Punjab. The young Nawaz Sharif was groomed by his parents to take over the family business, and unlike his forebears, who were self-taught, he received his bachelor's degree from Government College, Lahore, and his bachelor of laws degree (LLB) from Punjab University. In 1973 Zulfiqar Ali Bhutto nationalized the bulk of the Sharif family holdings, but in 1978 Zia-ul-Haq restored the Ittefaq group of industries to their original owners. Under the able and dynamic leadership of Nawaz Sharif and his brother Shahbaz, and with the help of numerous lucrative government contracts, the Ittefaq group rapidly became one of Pakistan's largest and most successful industrial houses. Nawaz first entered politics in 1981 as finance and sports minister in General Ghulam Jilani's Punjab provincial cabinet. In 1985 Zia appointed Nawaz chief minister of the province, a position he held until his election as prime minister in 1990. He remained in that position until 1993, and he returned to power in the February 1997 general election. During his two tenures as prime minister he boldly launched several policy initiatives, including privatization of public enterprises, the "yellow taxi scheme," and the construction of the Pakistan motorway. But his boldest stroke was the passage of the Thirteenth and Fourteenth Amendments in 1997, which led to the dismantling of the controlled democratic system of 1988–1997, and the full restoration of the 1973 constitution. Subsequently he attempted to restrict the authority of Pakistan's military, which proved his undoing. On October 12, 1999, his government was toppled by a military coup led by the Nawaz-appointed COAS, Parvez Musharraf. Reminiscent of the fate that befell Zulfiqar Ali Bhutto following Zia's coup in 1977, Nawaz was arrested and charged with a capital crime. Also like Bhutto, Nawaz was convicted. But instead of being executed he was sentenced to life imprisonment. In December 2000, Nawaz and his family were allowed to leave Pakistan to avoid imprisonment. In August 2007 the Supreme Court, led by the restored Chief Justice Iftikhar Chaudhury, showing its defiance and activism, accepted Nawaz Sharif's long-standing petition to allow him to end his exile and return to Pakistan. However, his "triumphant return" on September 10 was aborted when he was met at the Karachi airport by Pakistani security officials and put on a commercial flight back to Saudi Arabia. In the fullness of time, most likely at the urging of the Saudi government, Nawaz was allowed to return to Pakistan on November 21. At first he called for a boycott of the elections but later, bowing to pragmatic considerations (the PPP was not boycotting the elections), he announced that the PML(N) would contest the elections. Following the stunning success of the PML(N) in the 2008 elections, Nawaz Sharif is once again at the forefront of Pakistani politics, arguably assuming the role of the elder statesman in the coalition government.

Parvez Musharraf: Enlightened Moderate or Military Dictator

Parvez Musharraf was born in New Delhi in 1943. His family was originally from Allahabad and moved to Pakistan after partition, making him a muhajir. As a child, Musharraf spent six years in Turkey, where his father was posted as Pakistan's ambassador. Back in Pakistan, Musharraf completed his Intermediate from St. Patrick's College, Karachi, and after spending a year at Forman Christian College, Lahore, he entered the Pakistan Military Academy in 1962. He was commissioned into the artillery in 1964. Soon thereafter he joined the elite commando unit of the Pakistan army—the Special Services Group. In his thirty-five-year career with the army, Musharraf held several important posts including director-general military operations and corps commander, Mangla. He also taught at the Staff College in Quetta and attended the Royal College of Defence Studies in the U.K. In 1998 Nawaz Sharif appointed him chief of army staff, and following a military coup in 1999, he assumed the role of Pakistan's head of state—defining himself as the chief executive.

Musharraf's long tenure has been dominated by three main policy concerns: accountability and good governance; devolution and the development of institutions of local government; and maintenance of security in light of the global threats from terrorism and extremism. In pursuing these goals Musharraf has styled himself as an "enlightened moderate" dedicated to the cause of restoring democracy to Pakistan and combating religious obscurantism. Over the years his enemies have grown and his carefully crafted image, always easier to accept in the West, has been tarnished. Indeed, in the aftermath of his orchestrated re-election as president, the accompanying emasculation of the superior judiciary, the fallout from the untimely death of Benazir Bhutto, and the PML(Q)'s debacle in the 2008 election, Musharraf finds himself isolated and weak.

NOTES

1. The results of all previous general elections can be found in Craig Baxter et al., *Government and Politics in South Asia,* 5th ed. (Boulder: Westview, 2002), pp. 196–199.

2. K. K. Aziz, *Party Politics in Pakistan, 1947–1958* (Islamabad: National Commission on Historical and Cultural Research, 1976), pp. 105–110.

3. *Mian Nawaz Sharif v. President of Pakistan PLD* SC 473. For details, see Charles H. Kennedy, "Presidential–Prime Ministerial Relations: The Role of the Superior Courts," in *Pakistan: 1995,* ed. Charles H. Kennedy and Rasul B. Rais (Boulder: Westview, 1995), pp. 17–30.

4. Murtaza Bhutto, politically estranged from his sister, had formed a rival faction of the PPP, the PPP(Shaheed Bhutto), in alliance with his and Benazir's mother, Nusrat Bhutto. The PPP(SB) fielded candidates in the 1997 elections.

5. For details, see Seyyed Vali Reza Nasr, *The Vanguard of the Islamic Revolution: The Jama'at-i Islami of Pakistan* (Berkeley: University of California Press, 1994).

6. The six parties that joined the alliance were Jamaat-i-Islami; Jamiat Ulema Islam—Fazl Rahman (F); Jamiat Ulema Islam Sami-ul Haq (S); Jamiat Ulema-i-Pakistan (JUP); Tehrik Jafaria

Pakistan (TJP); and Jamiat ahl-e-Hadith. Only candidates of the first three parties won seats in the 2002 National Assembly elections. The JUI(S) broke from the MMA in 2005, and the MMA has become defunct.

7. For discussion, see Cynthia Botteron, "Validating Educational Qualifications as a Prerequisite to Hold Elective Office: The Supreme Court and the Pakistan Muslim League (Q) Decision," in *Pakistan: 2005,* ed. Charles H. Kennedy and Cynthia Botteron (Karachi: Oxford University Press, 2006), pp. 158–197.

8. Mohammed Ayub Khan, *Friends, Not Masters: A Political Autobiography* (Karachi: Oxford University Press, 1967), pp. 4, 52, 70–76. Also see Altaf Gauhar, *Ayub Khan: Pakistan's First Military Ruler* (Lahore: Sang-e-Meel, 1993).

9. See G. W. Choudhury, *The Last Days of United Pakistan* (Bloomington: Indiana University Press, 1974).

10. This theme is developed fully in Shahid Javed Burki, *Pakistan Under Bhutto, 1971–1977* (New York: St. Martin's, 1980). Also see Anwar H. Syed, *The Discourse and Politics of Zulfikar Ali Bhutto* (New York: St. Martin's, 1991); Stanley Wolpert, *Zulfi Bhutto of Pakistan* (New York: Oxford University Press, 1993).

11. After Bhutto was removed from office, the Zia regime published a three-volume white paper exposing in great detail Bhutto's alleged excesses. See Government of Pakistan, *White Paper of the Misuses of the Media; White Paper on the Conduct of the General Elections of 1977; White Paper on the Performance of the Bhutto Regime* (Islamabad: Printing Corporation of Pakistan Press, 1978).

12. For analysis of the Zia years, see Shahid Javed Burki and Craig Baxter, eds., *Pakistan Under the Military: Eleven Years of Zia ul-Haq* (Boulder: Westview, 1991); Robert Wirsing, *Pakistan's Security Under Zia, 1977–1988: The Policy Imperatives of a Peripheral State* (New York: St. Martin's, 1991).

13. See Benazir Bhutto, *Daughter of Destiny* (New York: Simon & Schuster, 1989).

Suggested Readings

Bhutto, Benazir. *Daughter of Destiny.* New York: Simon & Schuster, 1989.

Bhutto, Zulfikar Ali. *If I Am Assassinated.* Delhi: Vikas, 1979.

Kennedy, Charles H. *Bureaucracy in Pakistan.* Karachi: Oxford University Press, 1987.

Nasr, Seyyed Vali Reza. *Mawdudi and the Making of Islamic Revivalism.* New York: Oxford University Press, 1996.

Rais, Rasul B, ed. *State, Society, and Democratic Change in Pakistan.* Karachi: Oxford University Press, 1996.

Syed, Anwar H. *The Discourse and Politics of Zulfikar Ali Bhutto.* New York: St. Martin's, 1991.

Talbot, Ian. *Pakistan: A Modern History.* London: Hurst, 1998.

Waseem, Mohammad. *Politics and the State in Pakistan.* Lahore: Progressive, 1989.

_____. *Democratization in Pakistan: A Study of the 2002 Elections.* Karachi: Oxford University Press, 2006.

Wilder, Andrew R. *The Pakistani Voter: Electoral Politics and Voting Behaviour in the Punjab.* Karachi: Oxford University Press, 1999.

Wirsing, Robert. *Pakistan's Security Under Zia, 1977–1988: The Policy Imperatives of a Peripheral Asian State.* New York: St. Martin's, 1991.

Wolpert, Stanley. *Jinnah of Pakistan.* New York: Oxford University Press, 1984.

_____. *Zulfi Bhutto of Pakistan.* New York: Oxford University Press, 1993.

Ziring, Lawrence. *The Ayub Khan Era.* Syracuse, N.Y.: Syracuse University Press, 1971.

11

Conflict and Mediation

Since independence Pakistan has suffered from internal conflict stemming from ethnonationalism and sectarianism. The former characterized the dismemberment of the state in 1971 and has helped define competing nationalisms in the truncated state ever since. The latter encompasses conflict within Islam (Sunni-Shia conflict) and conflict involved in defining who is a Muslim (Muslim-Ahmadi conflict). This chapter details such conflicts.

Ethnonationalism

As we have seen, the homeland for the Muslims of South Asia was formed with little concern for the ethnic homogeneity of its people. Today Pakistan encompasses five major politically significant ethnic groups, and eight major languages are spoken by its population. Ethnonational identifications roughly correspond with provincial domiciles, but the fit is imperfect owing to the effects of partition and internal migration. Perhaps more important than the objective differences between peoples, however, are the *perceptions* of ethnonational differences held by Pakistan's population. Indeed, the perception of ethnic discrimination against Bengalis that resulted in the eventual secession of Bangladesh was spawned in the contentious ethnonational environment of Pakistan.[1] Unfortunately Pakistan is still beset with such perceived grievances, and the threat of additional "Bangladeshes" is real.

Punjabi Dominance

At the core of ethnoregional sentiment in Pakistan is the perception by Punjabis and non-Punjabis alike that the Punjabi community dominates the politics and society of the state. There is considerable objective support for this perception. First, Punjabis constitute a majority of the population when one includes closely affiliated Siraiki speakers in the nation (see Table 8.2). Second, Punjabis have

195

long dominated membership in the civil and military bureaucracies.[2] Third, Punjab is by far the wealthiest and most developed province in the state. Indicators of such advantage include differentials in per capita income, life expectancy, levels of industrialization and urbanization, and literacy rate. In the face of such facts, nationals of the smaller provinces perceive themselves as underrepresented or even dominated by the larger ethnoregional group. The issue of Punjabi domination was particularly contentious during Nawaz Sharif's second government (1997–1999), as the president (Rafiq Tarar), COAS (Jehangir Karamat), and prime minister were Punjabis. This ethnic monopoly was broken in 1999 when Parvez Musharraf, a muhajir, took over as chief executive and later as president.

Sindhi Regionalism

Sindh, to a greater extent than any other province in Pakistan, has experienced an extensive influx of inhabitants, first from India (the muhajirs) and, after partition, from the other provinces of Pakistan. More often than not, these non-Sindhis have continued to cling to their original culture and language, ignoring local traditions and often failing to learn the Sindhi language. In addition, such newcomers were often better educated, wealthier, more cosmopolitan, and better able to compete in a modernizing state than the Sindhi sons of the soil.[3] Particularly galling to the indigenous Sindhis has been the rapid commercial growth of Karachi, fueled by refugees and later by Punjabi money and talent, with relatively little corresponding benefit to the indigenous Sindhis. Indeed, the rural areas of Sindh have remained largely unaffected by the rapid growth of Karachi, and the social patterns that have prevailed in Sindh for centuries have remained largely unchanged. Rural Sindh is still largely dominated by a semi-feudal system in which rich landlords, who often hold hereditary religious offices as well, dominate nearly destitute peasants. Government policies that award tracts of reclaimed agricultural land in Sindh to retired civil and military officers, the majority of whom are Punjabi or Pakhtun, have exacerbated the perception of Sindhi subordination in the rural areas.

Originally the demand for "Sindhu desh" (Sindhi homeland) was directed primarily at the muhajir community, which controlled the commercial and industrial life of Karachi. Aggravating such sentiments in the early years of Pakistan's statehood were the successive attempts by Muhammad Ali Jinnah and Liaquat Ali Khan (both muhajirs) to make Urdu the national language of Pakistan. Also aggravating Sindhi grievances was the One Unit Plan (1955–1970), which integrated Pakistan's four western provinces into one administrative unit with its capital in Punjab at Lahore. Sindh was further isolated when the federal capital was moved from Karachi to Islamabad.

But the greatest impetus for Sindhi regionalism is inextricably linked with the career and demise of the late Prime Minister Zulfiqar Ali Bhutto. Bhutto was the scion of a prominent landholding family based in Larkana, Sindh. During his regime he encouraged Sindhi sentiments by empathizing with the grievances of the Sindhis and by promising to rectify past injustices. Among the policies pursued by his government were land reforms, intended to weaken the power of the landlords in Sindh and end non-Sindhi ownership of Sindhi agricultural land. Bhutto also nationalized heavy industry, banks, and insurance. Each of these actions was perceived in Sindh as a challenge to the interests of the muhajirs and the Punjabis; similarly, Bhutto's civil and military reforms were perceived as detrimental to non-Sindhi interests. In the aftermath of Bhutto's overthrow by a military coup and his eventual execution, Sindhi regionalism gained a focal point, perhaps even a martyr, and has correspondingly proliferated.[4]

During President Zia-ul-Haq's regime (1977–1988), Sindh became the most disaffected of Pakistan's provinces. Many Sindhis perceived Zia's government as Punjabi inspired—at best oblivious to the grievances of Sindhis, at worst conspiring to further strengthen Punjabis at the expense of Sindhis. Perhaps the most serious challenge to Zia's rule was the Movement for the Restoration of Democracy (MRD), which inspired the disturbances of 1983 that originated in, and for the most part remained confined to, rural Sindh. At the heyday of the 1983 disturbances, Sindhi separatists voiced grievances reminiscent of Bengali leader Mujibur Rahman's Six Points (see Chapter 16). These dissidents called for increased provincial autonomy; insisted on reducing disparities in economic development; charged the federal government with inadequate allocation of federal government funds; claimed underrepresentation in the military, bureaucratic, entrepreneurial, and political elites of the state; and charged that Sindhis were treated as second-class citizens, even in their own province. The assassination of President Zia in August 1988 and the subsequent election of Benazir Bhutto to the prime ministership dramatically changed such perceptions. Sindhi grievances remained, but there was widespread confidence that Benazir's regime, led by the daughter of Zulfiqar, would be more accommodative of Sindhi interests.

As the daughter of the late prime minister, Benazir inherited the mantle of Sindhi leadership. Partially as a consequence, competing nationalisms (Sindhi, Punjabi, and muhajir) have largely come to define the Pakistani political arena since 1988. Benazir Bhutto and the PPP have become increasingly associated with Sindhi interests, Nawaz Sharif and the PML(N) with Punjabi interests, and Parvez Musharraf representing the interests of the military and the PML(Q) with Punjabi and muhajir interests. Such ethnonational considerations have come to dominate electoral outcomes in the state (see Chapter 10).[5]

The strength of Sindhi regionalism and discontent was demonstrated forcefully subsequent to the assassination of Benazir on December 27, 2007. Massive crowds expressed their collective grief through chaotic riots that targeted government institutions and MQM and PML(Q) workers throughout the Sindh. Such riots destroyed hundreds of millions of dollars worth of property and claimed over a hundred lives.

Muhajir Nationalism

The recent emergence of muhajirs as a full-fledged ethnic group constitutes a pure case of what could be termed the creation of an "acquired" as opposed to a "primordial" ethnic identity. For most of Pakistan's history, muhajirs were a residual category, in effect newcomers to the country who had abandoned their respective primordial ethnicities when they opted for Pakistan. It is true that nonmuhajir communities, particularly Sindhis, defined muhajirs as a group that took unfair advantage of state policies. But the overwhelming majority of so-called muhajirs rejected such definitions, preferring rather to be called Pakistanis. Such self-definition underwent rapid transformation following the communal riots in Karachi in late 1986.

During the riots, muhajirs organized by the fledgling muhajir national movement (Muhajir Qaumi Mahaz, MQM) and its leader Altaf Hussain participated on the side of "indigenous Sindhis" (defined in 1986 to include both muhajirs and Sindhis) against "outsiders" (Pakhtuns, Punjabis, and Afghans). Muhajir militancy continued after the riots and resulted in the forceful expression of several demands by the MQM on the central government. Four demands are salient. The first was a call for the repeal or significant revision of Pakistan's ethnic quota system for government employment. According to the MQM, the size of the "urban Sindh" quota (7.6 percent) unfairly restricts muhajir entry into Pakistan's elites. Second, the MQM demanded the repatriation of the approximately 300,000 Urdu-speaking Biharis, many of whom languish as stateless people in refugee camps in Bangladesh. Third, Altaf Hussain also advocated the idea that muhajirs should be treated as a "fifth nationality," a status commensurate with that of the Punjabis, Sindhis, Pakhtuns, and Baloch. Fourth, the MQM insisted on holding a fair national census, as earlier censuses had underreported the muhajir population. Each of these demands was clearly anathema to Sindhi nationalist interests.[6]

Despite such obvious conflicts of interest, the MQM joined the PPP's coalition government following the national elections of 1988. The PPP had promised to pursue the MQM's demands in exchange for its support. Benazir's government, however, proved unable or unwilling to keep its promises. The immediate consequence was that the MQM left the coalition government and joined the opposition Islami Jamhoori Ittehad (IJI) led by Nawaz Sharif. The IJI-MQM accord held firm throughout the course of the 1990 elections; MQM candidates swept the polls in both Karachi and Hyderabad; and the MQM helped to form the government both at the center and in the Sindh provincial assembly. However, following a military crackdown in Sindh province during the summer of 1992 which targeted the illegal activities of MQM activists (including torture cells, kidnapping and extortion gangs, and drug running), the MQM severed ties with the IJI. Consequently, Altaf Hussain and other prominent MQM leaders have either absented themselves from Pakistan or gone underground to escape arrest.

Since then, MQM-Sindhi as well as MQM-Punjabi relations have continued to deteriorate and were major contributors to the ethnonational violence that plagued urban Sindh during the 1990s. Ethnic violence reached its peak between 1994 and 1996, claiming over 5,000 lives according to official figures. During Muharraf's regime muhjair-related violence has quieted. This trend is related to the MQM's joining the PML(Q)-led governing coalition since 2002; it is also related to Musharraf's local government system, which has empowered the MQM in Karachi's metropolitan districts. Nonetheless, violence is still endemic to Karachi, as evidenced by the melee related to Benazir Bhutto's attempted assassination during a campaign rally in Karachi on October 18, 2007, and the ethnic violence which swept Sindh following her tragic assassination two months later.

Pakhtun Provincialism

In the North-West Frontier Province (NWFP) the call for an independent entity, Pakhtunistan, predates independence. Pakhtunistan means different things to different people, ranging from the demand for the formation of a new state incorporating Pakhtun (Pathan) areas on both sides of the Afghanistan-Pakistan border, to a mere change of nomenclature for the NWFP. Near consensus has emerged, at least among Pushto speakers, that the NWFP should be renamed "Pakhtunkhwa." In any event, the call for a Pakhtun entity stems from the perception of the common ethnic, cultural, and linguistic background of the Pakhtun communities on both sides of the border.

Before partition, the demand for a separate Muslim state was weaker in the frontier regions of Pakistan than in the more settled areas. Undoubtedly, one reason was the fact that few Hindus lived in the frontier regions. Hence the grievances of the Pakhtuns at that time were with the British and not with the confluence of British and Hindu domination, as in Sindh or Punjab. Consequently, the prepartition sentiments of the Pakhtun leaders found a natural ally in the policies of the Indian National Congress, and few took part in the Pakistan movement. Indeed, Khan Abdul Ghaffar Khan (1890–1988), the most prominent prepartition Pakhtun leader, was referred to as the "frontier Gandhi" for espousing an undivided India and supporting nonviolent civil disobedience.

After partition, development in the NWFP was slow and uneven. Khan Abdul Ghaffar Khan built on a similar foundation of grievances engendered by the status of a minority backward province that eventually resulted in Mujibur Rahman's Six Points and the secession of Bangladesh. He founded the West Pakistan portion of what in 1957 became the National Awami Party (NAP). This party never amounted to much in Sindh or Punjab, but it took firm root in the NWFP and Balochistan. Indeed, in the 1970 election the NAP emerged as the most significant party in the NWFP; and with the co-operation of the Jamiat Ulema Islam (JUI), it was able to form the provincial government. Khan Abdul Wali Khan (1917–2006—the leader of the NAP and son of Ghaffar Khan) and Zulfiqar Ali Bhutto were natural rivals; both were ambitious politicians who saw their rivalry in zero-sum terms. Between 1971 and 1974, relations between the two became increasingly acrimonious, and after the assassination in early 1975 of NWFP minister and Pakistan People's Party (PPP) member H. M. Sherpao, allegedly perpetrated by NAP sympathizers, Bhutto arrested Wali Khan, dissolved the provincial government, and banned the NAP. Wali Khan was subsequently tried for murder. Bhutto was ousted before a verdict could be reached, however, and the charges against Wali Khan were dropped.[7]

The Soviet-Afghan war and its aftermath complicated issues connected with Pakhtun provincialism. Afghanistan has never accepted the validity of the Durand Line, which demarcates the Afghan-Pakistan border. Cross-border raids by Soviet-Afghan airplanes, common during the period of the Soviet occupation (1979–1989), highlighted this fact. A further complication is the status of the Afghan refugees who have taken up residence in the NWFP. Several sectarian clashes between the two main groups of Muslims—the Shias and Sunnis—have been exacerbated by the influx of Afghans, most of whom are Sunnis. There is considerable sentiment in the NWFP (particularly in the urban areas) that the Afghans also constitute a drain on the already limited resources of the province. From the Soviet withdrawal in 1989 until the war in 2001, these issues were finessed by successive regimes through a combination of tacit noninterference in Pakhtun tribal affairs and extensive domestic and international financial subsidies to the refugee communities.

The U.S.-Afghan war that began in 2001 has exacerbated Pakhtun-Pakistan relations. The U.S. target, the Taliban regime, was primarily made up of and supported by Pushto-speaking Afghans, close ethnic affiliates of the Pakhtuns on the Pakistan side of the border. The defeat of the Taliban, coupled with President Musharraf's support for U.S. actions, has created the impression that Pakistan, in league with the United States, "is fighting against Pakhtun nationals." But such considerations, albeit serious, paled into insignificance following the U.S. decision to invade Iraq in 2003.

Since that time Pakistan has been obliged to be a more active participant in the global U.S. war against terror and as a consequence Pakistani military and paramilitary units have come into direct conflict with local insurgents in the Federally Administered Tribal Areas (FATA). At first (2003–2004) the scale and scope of such operations was limited to the two Waziristan Agencies (North and South), and the goal was clearly designed to allay international concerns that Pakistan was not doing enough to combat international terror. However, the scale of the insurgency has widened to other FATA agencies, and most alarmingly to settled areas of the NWFP. During October and November 2007 insurgents under the titular leadership of Maulana Fazlullah established a self-styled "parallel government" in the Swat valley. After the Frontier Corps suffered humiliating loses and defections, Pakistan's regular military was forced to subject the area to shelling and bombardment. Fazlullah's forces have fled to the surrounding mountains, where they continue to wage a guerrilla war against the government. It is important to note that much of the insurgency is driven by a jihadist sentiment, designed to establish Islamic law (Sharia) in the province. It is also important to note that Pakhtun identity, particularly in the FATA and the rural areas of the frontier, is inextricably linked to, if not indistinguishable from, such Islamist sentiments. Musharraf's government is an ideal target for jihad, as Musharraf espouses a secular approach to politics and his government is perceived as doing the bidding of the United States. In any case, the scale of violence in the NWFP and the FATA escalated rapidly in 2007.[8]

Baloch Marginalism

Balochistan is Pakistan's largest, poorest, and most sparsely settled province. It constitutes roughly 40 percent of Pakistan's area but has less than 5 percent of its population. Furthermore, a majority of Balochistan's population is non-Baloch. Balochi speakers are a minority in eight of Balochistan's twenty-two districts. Pashto speakers predominate in six of these and Brohi speakers in the other two districts. In Quetta, Balochistan's capital and largest city, Balochi speakers constitute only around 5 percent of the population. These figures do not include the three-quarters of a million or more Afghan refugees (mostly Pushto speakers) who live in the province, their camps clustered near Quetta. [9]

At the time of partition, Balochistan was only partially incorporated into Pakistan. British policy before independence had treated Balochistan as a large buffer zone and granted local Baloch leaders wide autonomy within their traditional sphere of influence. In 1955 Pakistan moved to incorporate the territories as part of the One Unit Plan, and the tribal leaders, in "merger agreements," ceded their territories to Pakistan. In practice, however, the Baloch tribal leaders maintained considerable autonomy over their former domains.[10] But the merger sparked demands by the masses for major social change. Such incipient politicization found expression in the 1970 elections, and Balochistan, like the NWFP, elected the NAP to power.

Tensions between the Baloch NAP government and the federal government came to a head on February 12, 1973, when a cache of arms allegedly destined for Baloch separatists was discovered in the residence of the Iraqi military attaché in Islamabad. The government reacted by confiscating the arms, dismissing the Baloch government, and arresting its leaders. As a result of such "provocations," Baloch guerrillas began to ambush army convoys. The war rapidly escalated; at its peak, between 80,000 and 100,000 Pakistani army personnel were in Balochistan. Despite considerable loss of life, the results of the conflict were inconclusive. Fighting continued intermittently until Bhutto was removed from government in 1977. Upon assuming power, General Zia released from 6,000 to 11,000 Baloch from jails and declared amnesty for the guerrillas who had taken refuge in Afghanistan or Iran.[11]

Since the civil war, most Baloch nationalists have tempered their demands for separation from the state but have continued to stress the need for greater provincial autonomy. Such autonomist demands have been countered with increasing fervor during the 1990s by Balochistan-domiciled Pakhtuns who call for the partition of Balochistan along ethnic lines. Small-scale violence between the two communities has become endemic since the late 1990s, which has been exacerbated by the ethnic pressures related to the Afghan war and the continuing flow of refugees and insurgents (mostly Pushto speaking) into the province. Baloch nationalists increasingly see their interests being neglected by ethnic outsiders who are ignoring the needs of the indigenous people to favor their own developmental agenda, most notably the exploitation of oil and gas reserves in the province and the development of Gwadur as a major commercial port. Such dangerous perceptions were brought to a boiling point following the assassination of prominent Baloch leader Nawab Akbar Khan Bugti (1927–2006) in August 2006, allegedly by the military. Since that time the Pakistan military and intelligence agencies have adopted harsh measures to quiet the ensuing uprising. Such measures have included the arrests and disappearances of hundreds of Baloch insurgents. Such "missing persons" (as the detainees were dubbed in the Pakistani press) became the object of a highly publicized Supreme Court decision, which may in turn have played a significant role in the subsequent suspension of Chief Justice Iftikhar Chaudhury and the ensuing constitutional crisis (see Chapter 9). In any case, significant violence continues to plague Balochistan.[12]

Azad Kashmir: Disputed Partition and Conflict Unending

Technically, Azad Kashmir (Free Kashmir) is not part of Pakistan.[13] Azad Kashmir has its own political institutions: its own constitution; its own court system; and its own legislature. However, in a de facto sense the "state" is hardly sovereign with respect to Pakistan, though its independence is a logical consequence of the long-standing Pakistani claim that Kashmir is disputed territory. This dispute can only be settled, according to Pakistan, when a U.N.-sponsored referendum is held in the "whole of Kashmir," including the Indian state of Jammu and Kashmir, to determine the status of the entire territory. In lieu of holding such a referendum, which was sanctioned by the United Nations in 1949 and has little chance of being implemented sixty years later, Kashmir will remain the focal point of the Pakistan-Indian conflict.

At first the conflict was seen in its original terms—wholly between India and Pakistan. Kashmir could either become part of India or part of Pakistan, the outcome to be decided by the aforementioned referendum, rather than being partitioned between the two countries. Since the mid-1980s, however, the issue has become far more complicated as the so-called third option of Kashmiri independence has gained increasing salience. What such independence would entail remains problematic. The minimal boundaries of such an independent state could be confined to Srinagar and the Vale of Kashmir (wholly within India); the maximal boundaries could encompass the whole of Jammu and Kashmir (including Ladakh), Azad Kashmir, and Pakistan's Northern Areas.

Nevertheless, the conflict in Kashmir has become increasingly violent in recent years owing to the Indian government's brutally repressive policies, as well as Pakistan's complicity in supporting Kashmiri "nationalist" (India would use the term "terrorist") activities in the Vale of Kashmir. Conservatively, more than 50,000 people have died in the conflict since 1988, the overwhelming majority Muslims.

The long-standing Indian position that the conflict is at heart a terrorist uprising led by Pakistan has been given theoretical support by actions of the United States and its coalition partners during the ongoing "war against terror."

That is, if the justification for regime change in Afghanistan and later Iraq is that such regimes "harbored terrorists" it follows that Pakistan should be obliged to crack down on those supporting the Kashmiri uprising. If Pakistan fails to follow through, the Indian government argues, Pakistan's government should suffer the same fate as the Taliban. Pakistan rejects such a comparison, claiming that the Kashmiri uprising is a legitimate indigenous national movement, not akin to the Taliban's relation with external terrorists. Such Indian claims and Pakistani counterclaims led to the mass mobilization of troops along the India-Pakistan border following the December 13, 2001, attempted attack on the Indian parliament, which India blamed on Pakistani-supported Kashmiri insurgents. Since that time both India and Pakistan have stepped back from the precipice of war: Pakistan has taken steps to ban Kashmiri jihadist groups; India has taken steps to reduce the repression in the Vale; the international community has been supportive of their efforts. But the Kashmir conflict remains endemic, and far from conclusion.

Sectarianism

Conflict Within Islam: Sunni and Shia

Sectarian differences within Islam have widened the gulf between Islamists and nationalists in Pakistan. Most Muslims in Pakistan are Sunni followers of the Hanafi legal system. But there are significant numbers of Shias as well—both Ithna Asharis (the Twelvers, the branch of Shiism dominant in Iran) and Ismailis (followers of the Agha Khan). Census data do not exist on the size of each group, although it is generally acknowledged that Ithna Asharis constitute 10–15 percent and Ismailis 2–3 percent of the population.

The potential for Sunni-Shia violence is endemic to Pakistan, as it is in many Islamic states, but for the most part Pakistan was spared such conflict until 1979. At that time the confluence of two factors exacerbated the Sunni-Shia rift—the rise of a militant and expansionist Shia regime in Iran and the promulgation of President Zia's Islamization program. The former was perceived as a threat to Sunni interests throughout the Muslim world; the latter was generally viewed, at least among the Shia community in Pakistan, as an attempt to enforce Sunni orthodoxy in the state. Such developments, international and domestic, alarmed both the Shia and Sunni communities.[14]

In 1980 the Shias formed the Tehrik-e-Nifaz-e-Fiqh-e-Jafariya (TNFJ, Movement for the Enforcement of the Jafariya Fiqh) to counter the effects of Zia's Islamization program and to defend their community. Sunni activists countered by forming the Sipah-e-Sahaba-e-Pakistan (SSP, Pakistan Army of the Prophet's Companions). Militant factions of both soon developed, and violence has proliferated. Since 1985 there have been over 2,500 victims (around 75 percent Shia) associated with Sunni-Shia sectarian violence in the state. Most of the killing has been in southern Punjab (particularly in the Jhang district), in Parichinar (in the FATA), in the Northern Areas (particularly near Gilgit), and in Karachi. This conflict has almost certainly been exacerbated by the actions of neighboring states. It is generally acknowledged that Iran channels funds and other support to the TNFJ, and Saudi Arabia to the SSP. It is also generally believed in Pakistan that India supports militants in both groups.

Unfortunately, incidents of sectarian conflict have risen since the Afghan and Iraq wars have been joined, and they reached unprecedented levels in 2007, which saw 341 Sunni-Shia related incidents in the state, with 441 killed and 630 injured.[15]

The Ahmadiyya: Who Is a Muslim?

The Ahmadiyya are members of a religious sect who follow the teachings of the late-nineteenth-century religious leader and self-proclaimed "prophet" Mirza Ghulam Ahmad (c. 1840–1908). Ahmad was a prolific polemicist, the author of hundreds of pamphlets and religious tracts. The targets of his writing were primarily Christian missionaries, but he often ran afoul of orthodox Islamic groups as well. Between 1892 and 1906 Ghulam Ahmad made a confusing and contradictory set of claims that were considered heretical by orthodox Islamic groups but were interpreted by his followers as constituting proof of Ahmad's prophet status. Such claims, contended orthodox Muslims, violated a central tenet of Islam that Muhammad was the final prophet.[16]

Consequently, clashes between the Ahmadi community and the politico-religious groups of ulema have been frequent. The most violent confrontation occurred in 1953.[17] One outcome of these disturbances was the discrediting of the ulema (who were blamed by the inquiry commission as being responsible for instigating the violence) and, by implication, their demands for an Islamic constitution. Indeed, with many of their leaders in jail, opposition to the secular nature of the proposed 1956 constitution evaporated. In 1973 the issue was resurrected, and in the aftermath of the resultant bloodbath an amendment was made to the 1973 constitution that designated the Ahmadiyya as a "non-Muslim minority" community.[18] Similarly, President Zia, reacting in 1984 to threats of potential violence against the Ahmadiyya by disaffected ulema, placed further legal restrictions on the community that have resulted in widespread discrimination against the Ahmadi community.[19] It is likely that the Ahmadi question will continue to haunt decision makers in Pakistan for the foreseeable future. In an Islamic state the question of who is a Muslim is of crucial importance—and, as Pakistan's experience has demonstrated, the determination of that fact is not always easy.

*   *   *

In sum, Pakistan, like India and Sri Lanka, was formed through the amalgamation of several "nations"—groups with distinctive languages, cultures, and ethnicity. For the states of South Asia such an outcome was partially a consequence of British colonial policy, which paid only slight attention to the ethnic homogeneity of its administrative units. But in Pakistan it was also the consequence of the ideological demand for an Islamic state. The ideal of Pakistan envisioned the creation of a state that would transcend the national particularisms of its population. Pakistan was to form a community of Muslims. Unfortunately, the integrative effects of Islam proved too weak to prevent the dismemberment of the state in 1971. Consequently, Pakistan has the dubious distinction of being the first state in the twentieth century to suffer a successful violent separatist movement. Therefore, unlike its neighbors (although they too must contend with the deleterious effects of competing nationalisms and religions), Pakistan carries the double burden of precedent: Pakistan has been the victim of a successful secessionist movement, and would-be opponents of the continued integrity of Pakistan are encouraged by their predecessors' success.

NOTES

1. Among the best known and most useful works are Rounaq Jahan, *Pakistan: Failure of National Integration* (New York: Columbia University Press, 1972); Leo Rose and Richard Sisson, *War and Secession: Pakistan, India, and the Creation of Bangladesh* (Berkeley: University of California Press, 1991); and Feroz Ahmed, *Ethnicity and Politics in Pakistan* (Karachi: Oxford University Press, 1998).

2. Charles H. Kennedy, "Pakistan: Ethnic Diversity and Colonial Legacy," in *The Territorial Management of Ethnic Conflict,* ed. John Coakley, 2nd ed. (London: Frank Cass, 2003), pp. 143–172. The approximate numbers of senior officers in the Secretariat Group (core of civil bureaucracy) in 2001 broke down as follows: Punjab 67.4 percent; NWFP 11.4 percent; rural Sindh 7.6 percent; urban Sindh 6.0 percent; Balochistan 3.3 percent; FATA 2.2 percent; and Azad Kashmir 2.2 percent. Similarly, over 75 percent of all ex-servicemen come from only three districts in Punjab (Rawalpindi, Jhelum, and Campbellpur Attock) and from two adjoining districts in the North-West Frontier Province (Kohat and Mardan). Stephen Cohen, *The Pakistan Army* (Berkeley: University of California Press, 1994), p. 45.

3. For details of Sindhi-Muhajir communal relations, see Theodore P. Wright, "Center-Periphery Relations in Pakistan: Sindhis, Muhajirs, and Punjabis," *Comparative Politics,* April 1991, pp. 299–312; Charles H. Kennedy, "The Politics of Ethnicity in Sindh," *Asian Survey,* October 1991, pp. 938–955; and Feroz Ahmed, *Ethnicity and Politics in Pakistan* (Karachi: Oxford University Press, 1998), pp. 41–158.

4. For the most complete treatment of Bhutto's term in office, see Shahid Javed Burki, *Pakistan Under Bhutto, 1971–1977* (New York: St. Martin's, 1980); for the most comprehensive treatment

of the land reforms, see Ronald J. Herring, *Land to the Tiller: The Political Economy of Agrarian Reforms in South Asia* (New Haven: Yale University Press, 1983).

5. Mohammad Waseem, "Pakistan Elections 1997: One Step Forward," in *Pakistan: 1997,* ed. Craig Baxter and Charles H. Kennedy (Boulder: Westview, 1998). Also see Mohammad Waseem, *Democratization in Pakistan: A Study of the 2002 Elections* (Karachi: Oxford University Press, 2006).

6. Indeed, a major reason for the delay in holding a national census in Pakistan was concern over prospective Sindhi/muhajir enumeration. Accordingly, the census originally scheduled for 1991 was delayed until 1998, and then was held only under pressure from the international community and administered by the military.

7. Lawrence Ziring, *Pakistan: The Enigma of Political Development* (London: Dawson, 1980), pp. 148–159; Tahir Amin, *Ethno-National Movements of Pakistan: Domestic and International Factors* (Islamabad: Institute of Policy Sciences, 1988), pp. 88–92.

8. According to the India-based *South Asia Intelligence Review,* a total of 3,549 people were killed in terrorism-related violence in Pakistan during 2007: 1,523 "civilians," 597 security or military personnel, and 1,479 terrorists/insurgents. Of these, 1,681 deaths occurred in the FATA and 1,190 in the NWFP: 80 percent of all terrorism-related deaths during 2007. Kancham Lakshman, "Pakistan: Chronic Failure," *SAIR,* January 7, 2008.

9. Figures are derived from district census reports 1998 issued by the Population Census Organization (various dates).

10. Ziring, *Pakistan,* p. 160. Privy purses were granted to rulers (as in the princely states of India and Pakistan) and to tribal leaders as compensation for their loss of revenue when the territories were incorporated into India or Pakistan.

11. For a more complete description of the war, see Selig Harrison, *In Afghanistan's Shadow: Baluch Nationalism and Soviet Temptations* (New York: Carnegie Endowment for International Peace, 1981), pp. 35–40; Tariq Ali, *Can Pakistan Survive? The Death of a State* (London: Penguin, 1983), pp. 115–123.

12. International Crisis Group, *Pakistan: The Forgotten Conflict in Balochistan,* Asia Briefing no. 69, October 22, 2007.

13. Robert Wirsing, *India, Pakistan, and the Kashmir Dispute: On Regional Conflict Resolution* (New York: St. Martin's, 1994); Ainslee Embree, Charles H. Kennedy, Howard Schaffer, Joseph Swartzberg, and Robert Wirsing, *The Kashmir Dispute at Fifty: Charting Paths to Peace* (New York: Kashmir Study Group, 1997); Robert Wirsing, *Kashmir in the Shadow of War: Regional Rivalries in a Nuclear Age* (New York: Sharpe, 2003).

14. For context, see Afak Haydar, "The Politicization of the Shias and the Development of the Tehrik-e-Nifaz-e-Fiqh-e-Jafaria in Pakistan," in *Pakistan: 1992,* ed. Charles H. Kennedy (Boulder: Westview, 1993), pp. 75–94.

15. Lakshman, "Pakistan."

16. Yohanan Friedmann, *Prophecy Continuous: Aspects of Ahmadi Religious Thought and Its Medieval Background* (Berkeley: University of California Press, 1989); Spencer Lavan, *The Ahmadiyya Movement: A History and Perspective* (Delhi: Manohar, 1974); and Charles H. Kennedy, "Towards the Definition of a Muslim in an Islamic State: The Case of the Ahmadiyya in Pakistan," in *Religious and Ethnic Minorities in South Asia,* ed. Dhirendra Vajpeyi and Yogendra Malik (Riverdale, Md.: Riverdale, 1989), pp. 71–108.

17. Government of Punjab, *Report of the Court of Inquiry Constituted Under Punjab Act II of 1954 to Enquire into the Punjab Disturbances of 1953* (Lahore: Superintendent Government Printing, 1954).

18. Articles 106(3) and 260.

19. Anti-Islamic activities of the Qadiani Group, Lahori Group, and Ahmadis (Prohibition and Punishment) Ordinance, 1984, *PLD* 1984 Central Statutes, 102.

SUGGESTED READINGS

Ahmed, Feroz. *Ethnicity and Politics in Pakistan.* Karachi: Oxford University Press, 1998.

Amin, Tahir. *Ethno-national Movements of Pakistan: Domestic and International Factors.* Islamabad: Institute of Policy Sciences, 1988.

Iqbal, Muhammed. *The Reconstruction of Religious Thought in Islam.* Lahore: Ashraf, 1962.

Jahan, Rounaq. *Pakistan: Failure of National Integration.* New York: Columbia University Press, 1972.

Kennedy, Charles H. "The Politics of Ethnicity in Sindh." *Asian Survey,* October 1991, pp. 938–955.

————. *Islamization of Laws and Economy: Case Studies on Pakistan.* Islamabad: Institute of Policy Studies, 1997.

Kennedy, Charles H., and Cynthia Botteron, eds. *Pakistan: 2005.* Karachi: Oxford University Press, 2006.

Nasr, Seyyed Vali Reza. *The Vanguard of the Islamic Revolution: The Jama'at-i Islami of Pakistan.* Berkeley: University of California Press, 1994.

Shafqat, Saeed, ed. *New Perspectives on Pakistan.* Karachi: Oxford University Press, 2007.

Wirsing, Robert. *Kashmir in the Shadow of War: Regional Rivalries in a Nuclear Age.* New York: Sharpe, 2003.

12

Policy Issues

The policies that Pakistan's leaders have pursued are as important as the constitutional forms of government the country has had. This chapter traces the policies of six of Pakistan's most important leaders (from 1958) and the effects these policies had on state institutions.

Ayub's Regime (1958–1969): The Military as Praetorians

Ayub believed in centralized authoritarian government. He was convinced that the people of Pakistan were too uneducated, divided, impoverished, and unsophisticated to form democratic institutions. He was also convinced that Pakistan's politicians were self-serving parasites on the body politic. The institutions established and the policies pursued by Ayub reflected these biases.

The system of government established by Ayub placed great reliance on Pakistan's civilian bureaucrats. To Ayub, bureaucrats were the ideal ruling elite. They were intelligent, well educated, loyal to the state, and experienced in administration. Therefore, the majority of Ayub's advisers and cabinet ministers were civilians with administrative, legal, financial, or agricultural experience. The most prominent group of such bureaucrats was the Civil Service of Pakistan (CSP), the lineal descendent of the Indian Civil Service (ICS). During Ayub's regime the 400-odd members of the CSP came to dominate virtually every locus of authority in government.[1]

Despite his military background, Ayub chose relatively few military officers to staff political or administrative posts.[2] The military served in Ayub's government (especially after 1962) as loyal "praetorians" (the emperor's loyal personal guards during the Roman Empire). Their role was to support the regime from the barracks. Ayub accordingly consciously downplayed his military origins.

Given Ayub's distrust of politicians, it should come as no surprise that his regime limited the importance of the legislature, political parties, and elections.

There was no National Assembly during the period of martial law, and the 1962 constitution established a very weak legislature. Although Ayub reluctantly allowed the operation of political parties, he placed restraints on the political activities of many politicians and restrictions on the freedom of the press. Ayub's own party, the Convention Muslim League, was a creation of its leader and never amounted to more than a label for Ayub's colleagues in government. Ayub held four national elections, but every one of them had a severely restricted franchise. In each case, the electors were the 80,000 Basic Democrats. During the first election, a referendum in 1960, the following question was asked: "Do you have confidence in the President, Field Marshal Ayub Khan?" Of the total electorate, 96 percent answered yes.[3] During the second, in 1962, members of the National Assembly and the provincial assemblies were elected by the Basic Democrats. The third, the 1965 presidential election, followed a new election for Basic Democrats and involved a contest between Ayub and the Combined Opposition party's candidate, Fatima Jinnah (Muhammad Ali Jinnah's sister, 1893–1967). Given the nature of the franchise, Jinnah did surprisingly well, winning 34 percent of the total vote and 47 percent of the vote in East Pakistan.[4] The fourth, also in 1965, elected new assemblies at the national and provincial levels.

Ayub believed that Pakistan was not ready for democracy.[5] Therefore, in 1959 he established the Basic Democracies (BD) Scheme, a program designed to teach democracy from the grass roots. Under the BD program, local councils were constituted at the union, tehsil (subdistrict), and district levels. Such councils were partially constituted by direct election, but above the union level a majority of each council's membership was appointed. Functionally, the BD program was dominated by civilian bureaucrats. The functions performed by the councils were also severely constrained. As noted above, the Basic Democrats also served as an electoral college for members of the provincial and national assemblies and the president. Under Ayub, therefore, local government became increasingly dominated by bureaucrats, especially by the CSP. Ayub's government also introduced land reforms touted to reduce the power of landlords. The reforms placed ceilings on the individual holdings of agricultural land, but most analysts agree that the reforms were ineffective.[6]

Ayub believed that capitalism would be the most direct path to economic development in Pakistan. Accordingly, he pursued industrial policies that favored business and capital-intensive investment. Indeed, Pakistan's gross domestic product grew rapidly (approximately 6 percent per year) during Ayub's regime. However, Ayub's policies also resulted in increased economic inequalities between East and West Pakistan, as most foreign aid and industrial investment were channeled to West Pakistan. His policies also increased the inequalities of income distribution within the population—the rich got richer, but the poor remained poor.

The two most important accomplishments of Ayub's foreign policy were the settlement in 1962 of the boundary dispute with the People's Republic of China, which paved the way for a lasting Sino-Pakistani friendship; and the Indus Basin Treaty of 1960, which provided for the division of waters with India. Ayub's greatest failure was the 1965 war with India. At least before 1965, Ayub had cultivated the image of the most trusted ally of the United States. However, during the 1965 war the United States (Pakistan's only major arms supplier), in an effort to appear neutral, cut off military supplies to both Pakistan and India. This action, viewed as a betrayal of trust by Ayub, gravely damaged U.S.-Pakistani relations. In addition, the cutoff of arms forced Pakistan to the peace table. The Tashkent Agreement of 1966, negotiated by Ayub, ended the war but was viewed by many in Pakistan (including Foreign Minister Zulfiqar Ali Bhutto, a member of the negotiating party) as a sellout to India.

Many factors led to Ayub's resignation in March 1969. Among them were Ayub's deteriorating health (he had suffered a pulmonary embolism in 1968); the alleged corruption of his son, Captain Gohar Ayub; Ayub Khan's increasing unpopularity in East Pakistan; and growing internal military disenchantment with his regime after the 1965 war. Pakistan's economy also suffered a downturn in the late 1960s. In addition, West Pakistan's urban masses took to the streets in 1968 and 1969 calling for the breakup of Ayub's system. The disturbances were spearheaded in West Pakistan by the gifted orator Zulfiqar Ali Bhutto. After some delay, East Pakistan joined the protests.

Bhutto and Reforms (1971–1977)

Bhutto had agitated since 1968 for the ending of Ayub's system of government. As a consequence, his task upon assuming office was to restructure institutions while increasing his personal authority.

One of the main targets of Bhutto's restructuring was the civil bureaucracy. In 1973 he purged 1,303 civil bureaucrats from the government and announced his administrative reforms. The reforms abolished all service cadres (semifunctional groups that had represented bureaucratic interests), including the CSP; modified the pay structure to weaken the advantage enjoyed by CSP officers; enlarged the Civil Service Academy by forming the Academy for Administrative Training; eliminated reservation of administrative posts (a practice that favored CSP officers); and began a program of lateral recruitment (political appointment of administrators).[7] One consequence of the reforms was the dilution of the power of civil bureaucrats and their replacement with members of Bhutto's Pakistan People's Party (PPP) and with those personally loyal to Bhutto.

Like all other leaders of Pakistan, Bhutto ruled with the consent of the military. The civil war had left the military establishment weak and unpopular. In this context, Bhutto took the opportunity to dismiss some senior military officers and to promote others who were personally loyal to him. He also abolished the position of commander in chief, replacing it with chief of staff (General Zia was appointed to this position in 1976). Ultimate authority, therefore, was transferred to the prime minister. In addition, a clause was inserted into the 1973 constitution stating that any abrogation of the constitution, as had happened in the 1958 coup, would constitute an act of high treason against the state.

Bhutto, as an elected civilian and as leader of the PPP, personally favored increasing the importance of the legislature and of political parties. However, his authoritarian leadership style and his image of party politics allowed for little dissent from his positions. Accordingly, Bhutto placed restrictions on, and later banned, the principal opposition party, the National Awami Party (NAP), and periodically purged his own party of members who did not agree with his policies. Bhutto had hundreds of political opponents arrested during his regime and, like Ayub, restricted freedom of the press.

Yahya Khan, Bhutto's immediate predecessor, had abolished the electoral college aspect of the Basic Democracies program upon assuming office in 1969. Bhutto introduced a modified form of local government, the People's Works Program, which called for the establishment of four tiers of elected officials; like the BD program, however, such councils were functionally dominated by civil bureaucrats. The only significant change was that Bhutto had replaced some of the career bureaucrats with personally loyal party faithful.

More important than Bhutto's local government institutions were his land reforms. Bhutto, the self-styled champion of Pakistan's peasant masses, dubbed himself the Quaid-i-Awam (leader of the masses). He also campaigned on the slogan of kapra, makaan, and roti (clothing, housing, and food) for the rural and urban masses. Bhutto introduced two land reform policies (1972 and 1977). Both, like Ayub's policy, placed ceilings on the ownership of agricultural land, although Bhutto's ceilings were lower than Ayub's. In practice, however, Bhutto's land reforms were no more successful than Ayub's in curbing the power of the landlords or in distributing land to the landless.[8]

Whereas Ayub believed in capitalism, Bhutto espoused Islamic socialism. Thus in 1972 he nationalized insurance, banking, and a number of heavy industries.

During Bhutto's regime the economy performed poorly; analysts disagree as to whether this was the result of Bhutto's economic policies or a combination of unfortunate circumstances (e.g., the increased price of oil after 1973, disastrous harvests, and floods).

Perhaps Bhutto's greatest achievements were in foreign policy. When Bhutto assumed office, Pakistan was a virtual international pariah because of the highly publicized atrocities of the Pakistan army during the civil war. In this context, Bhutto's achievements are remarkable. Bhutto successfully negotiated for the return of Pakistan's prisoners of war from India and Bangladesh through the Shimla agreement with India of 1972; greatly strengthened relations with China; established stable détente with Pakistan's historical foes, India and the Soviet Union; improved relations with the United States (the latter reestablished military aid agreements with Pakistan during Bhutto's regime); and in 1974 convened the Islamic summit, a meeting of the heads of the Islamic world.

But Bhutto's regime collapsed because his reforms made many enemies, especially the military and the opposition politicians. As already noted, Bhutto introduced several reforms that affected the military. The most important motives underlying the coup of 1977 were the establishment of the Federal Security Force (FSF) and the Balochistan War. The FSF, a paramilitary security organization, preempted the authority of the military. The undeclared civil war in Balochistan also proved very unpopular among Pakistan's military officers, particularly as it occurred on the heels of the debacle in East Pakistan.

After the 1977 election, in which the PPP was returned in a landslide but tainted victory, the Pakistan National Alliance took its grievances to the streets. The military, led by General Zia-ul-Haq, intervened—ostensibly to maintain order.

Back to the Military with Zia (1977–1988)

General Zia promised to relinquish power and hold a general election within ninety days of the military coup that brought him to power. However, Zia held office for over eleven years, and only his death prevented him from continuing longer. Zia's was a military regime and demonstrated much in common with Pakistan's other military regimes (those of Ayub and Yahya), but there were important differences as well.

Like Ayub, Zia believed in centralized, authoritarian government. But whereas Ayub came to this conclusion reluctantly, aware as he was of the weakness of the state and its institutions, Zia justified his continued role as a matter of accommodating the necessities of Islam. Zia increasingly viewed his role as that of an Islamic head of state who legitimately holds power and deserves the loyalty and support of his subjects as long as he governs the state according to the precepts of Islam.[9] Central to the ideology of his regime, therefore, was the establishment of a nizam-i-Mustafa (rule of the Prophet).

The Zia regime took a position somewhere between those of Ayub and Bhutto on the question of the significance and importance of the civilian bureaucracy. One of Zia's first acts after assuming office was to abolish the lateral recruitment program of his predecessor and to subject Bhutto's bureaucratic appointees to review by the Federal Public Service Commission. In addition, Zia reappointed several former CSP officers and other senior bureaucrats whom Bhutto had dismissed. Zia also appointed many civilian bureaucrats as close personal advisers. Zia did not reestablish the CSP, however, nor was the civilian bureaucracy as central to the policy-making process as it had been under Ayub.[10]

Unlike Ayub or Bhutto, Zia relied greatly on the military to fill administrative posts, since Pakistan remained under martial law between 1977 and 1985. Under Zia's system of martial law, Pakistan was divided into several zones, each of which was governed by a deputy chief martial law administrator drawn from the military and carrying the rank of lieutenant general. Further, Zia established martial law tribunals, which possessed jurisdiction parallel to Pakistan's civil courts and were staffed by senior military officers. Finally, Zia established a 10 percent quota for retired military officers at all officer-level ranks in the civilian bureaucracy. As a consequence, many important posts in the bureaucracy were held by active and retired military officers.[11]

Zia's distrust of politicians exceeded that of other Pakistani leaders, and his regime placed severe restraints on political activity. In 1979 a martial law regulation banned all political parties and prohibited the future electoral activity of any party that failed to register with the Election Commission. Most of Pakistan's parties failed to register. In addition, specially constituted Disqualification Tribunals (1970) barred hundreds of politicians on a case-by-case basis from contesting future elections. Finally, amendments in 1979 and 1984 to the Political Parties Act (1962) barred former national and provincial office bearers and former federal ministers who had held office during the Bhutto years (1971–1977) from contesting elections. Such restrictions were lifted shortly before the 1985 elections, although most of those barred chose not to participate. Most remaining restrictions on political party activity were lifted in 1986. Zia failed to hold national elections in Pakistan until December 1984. At that time, he held a referendum (reminiscent of Ayub's) asking the people of Pakistan whether they supported Zia's policies of Islamization and the ideology of Pakistan, with a yes vote interpreted as giving Zia an additional five-year term as president (March 1985–March 1990). Zia was said to have received a 98 percent affirmative vote. In February 1985 "partyless" elections for the national and provincial assemblies were held. Although many of the political restrictions were partially lifted for the election, few prominent politicians took part in the poll. However, campaigning for the elections was brisk, and the turnout at the polls was surprisingly high (53 percent). Moreover, the polls themselves may have been among the fairest in Pakistan's history. Nevertheless, the national and provincial assemblies that were elected remained weak, and they were dissolved by presidential fiat in May 1988.

Zia revived many aspects of Ayub's Basic Democracies through the establishment of local-bodies programs in each province. Elections to local bodies (a four-tiered system of subprovincial government) were held in 1979, 1983, and 1987. Unlike the Basic Democracies, however, Zia's system did not use the local body representatives as an electoral college, nor were civilian bureaucrats as dominant in the system as in the BD system or in Bhutto's system. The elections were nonpartisan and the local bodies were dominated by rural notables (members of the landholding elite). Whatever their shortcomings, the local bodies institutions constituted the most representative and effective form of local government ever implemented in Pakistan up until that time. Although Zia did not abolish the land reform legislation of his predecessors, he also took no steps to implement it.

Zia followed a capitalist line in economic policy, although he was reluctant to denationalize the industries that had been nationalized by Bhutto. In fact, the number of "autonomous corporations" and "public enterprises" actually increased during the Zia regime. The performance of Pakistan's economy under Zia was impressive, although it must also be stressed that the Pakistani economy benefited greatly from remittances from Pakistanis working abroad.

Zia's foreign policy centered on the Soviet presence in Afghanistan, and Zia's crowning achievement was the Soviet withdrawal in February 1989. Indeed, Pakistan's foreign policy was influenced by Afghanistan in several regards. First, the Soviet-Afghan War created many refugees who took sanctuary in Pakistan. The presence of the Afghan refugees and their sympathizers precipitated several Soviet-Afghan reprisals, including bombings, directed at refugee camps within Pakistan's border. Second, the Soviet presence in Afghanistan prompted the resumption of U.S. aid to Pakistan. In 1981 the United States signed a six-year, $3.2 billion military aid and economic credits package with Pakistan. In addition, the United States sold Pakistan forty F-16s. Third, the combination of the foregoing factors moved Pakistan toward a de facto alignment with the United States. It also affected relations with India, although, on balance, these relations improved under Zia.[12]

PPP Part Two: Benazir Bhutto (1988–1990)

Those who anticipated rapid change under Pakistan's first democratically elected government since 1977 were disappointed by Benazir's initial term in office. First, Benazir's government was unable to restore the 1973 constitution, nor did it rescind the Eighth Amendment. Second, the PPP-led National Assembly passed no new legislative bill during its tenure; in fact, only ten bills, all minor amendments to existing legislation, passed the assembly. Third, center-provincial relations deteriorated markedly during Benazir's tenure, as evidenced by the widening rift between the PPP and IJI in Punjab and by the proliferation of ethnic violence in Sindh. Fourth, the Afghan civil war remained unresolved.

Of course, Benazir's government operated under severe disadvantages from the start. The PPP gained a very narrow plurality in the 1988 election and consequently was forced to enter into a shaky coalition with the MQM and several independent MNAs in order to form the government. As a result, PPP leaders expended great energy in efforts to maintain power. Such efforts were complicated when the MQM decided to withdraw from the government in October 1989. Moreover, Benazir's government, like all civilian regimes in Pakistan, served at the sufferance of the military.

Despite such disappointments and inherent weaknesses, the accomplishments of Benazir's government were not inconsiderable. Benazir's greatest accomplishment was to further democratize the society. Also, Benazir improved Pakistan's relations with the United States, the Commonwealth nations, and India, at least until the Kashmir dispute was rekindled in February 1990.

Capitalist Caretaker: Nawaz Sharif (1990–1993)

Nawaz Sharif's first administration entered power with decided advantages over his predecessor's regime. First, the IJI enjoyed a comfortable majority in the National Assembly, and it was able to form governments in each of Pakistan's four provinces. Second, Nawaz and his party were the obvious favorites of both the military and President Ghulam Ishaq Khan. Nawaz was thus able to act decisively during his first few months in office by implementing significant economic reforms, including the privatization of many of the firms that had been nationalized during Zulfiqar Ali Bhutto's regime. He also shepherded a Shariat bill through the National Assembly and sponsored the Twelfth Amendment to the constitution, which was designed to address the deteriorating law-and-order situation in Sindh province.

Unfortunately, his administration's effectiveness proved short-lived. Alleged involvement in financial misdeeds, including the Bank of Commerce and

Credit International (BCCI) scandal and the collapse of several Punjab-based cooperative societies, plagued his regime during 1991 and 1992. The United States applied additional pressure to the government by withdrawing economic and military assistance to Pakistan, an action linked to the alleged continuation of Pakistan's nuclear weapons program. Communal unrest in Sindh was quieted somewhat, but at the cost of massive repression under the tenure of chief minister Jam Sadiq Ali and later by recourse to direct military involvement. Moreover, political support for Nawaz Sharif and the IJI quickly evaporated. In 1992 the MQM and the JI deserted the IJI coalition, further weakening the government.

In April 1993 President Ghulam Ishaq Khan dismissed Nawaz Sharif's government. Sharif challenged the dismissal in the Supreme Court and was reinstated in May. But his reprieve was short-lived. Under pressure from the military and in the shadow of continuing civil unrest in Karachi, Sharif resigned in July, and soon Benazir Bhutto was returned to power.

PPP Part Three: Benazir Bhutto (1993–1996)

Benazir's second term in office was even more disappointing than her first. The policy accomplishments of her government were modest by any standard. She did establish a women's police force, designed in part to improve women's conditions in Pakistan's legal system; she also continued the privatization policy of her predecessor. In foreign policy her greatest accomplishment was a partial relaxation of the rigors of the U.S. Pressler amendment, thus allowing some arms shipments from the United States already "in the pipeline" to be delivered to Pakistan.

As in her first administration, Benazir's government was hampered by the effects of a narrow mandate (the PPP had won by a razor-thin margin in 1993), and she was unable to dismantle Zia's constitutional system. Partially as a consequence, her administration was often consumed by petty political disputes with the opposition. For instance, during her second tenure Benazir's government brought hundreds of charges (mostly groundless) against members of the Sharif family. Of course, from the perspective of the PPP these were taken in retaliation for the actions that the Sharif regime had taken against the Bhutto family during the 1990–1993 period. Also, her administration spent an inordinate amount of time trying to prevent the PML(N) from gaining control over the Punjab provincial government.

Benazir ran afoul of the superior judiciary too. Her government attempted to put pressure on the superior judiciary by manipulating the appointments, promotions, and assignments of judges. Benazir's administration also employed transfers or the threat of transfers to intimidate recalcitrant jurists. The Supreme Court eventually fought back, in the so-called judges case, in which the court severely limited the power of the prime minister to make judicial appointments.[13] The publicity generated by this case, in which Benazir's government was portrayed as having attempted to "usurp the judiciary," further weakened the government.

Unprecedented levels of ethnonational conflict raged in Karachi during her second term as well. Operation Clean-up, in which the Pakistan army was called in to quiet such violence, was a signal failure. Several thousand casualties resulted from the three-sided conflict between the army, muhajir nationalists, and Sindhis. The Sunni-Shia conflict, largely dormant during most of Pakistan's history, raged during the mid-1990s as well.

Underscoring her government's difficulties was the growing perception that her administration was "the most corrupt in Pakistan's history." The flamboyant lifestyle and enormous wealth of Asif Ali Zardari, Bhutto's husband, was generally believed to be the fruit of widespread kickbacks and influence peddling.

But the last straw came after Murtaza Bhutto's death in a police encounter in September 1996. Benazir's first reaction was to claim that President Farooq Leghari was behind the "murder." The president, perhaps encouraged by the military establishment, dissolved her government; the Supreme Court, still smarting from the effects of her judicial policies, quickly legitimized his action.[14]

The Triumphant Return and Devastating Fall of Nawaz (1997–1999)

Nawaz entered his second administration with an overwhelming majority in the National Assembly and moved quickly to consolidate his position. In April, he orchestrated the passage of the Thirteenth Amendment, which eliminated the power of the president to dissolve elected governments. In May, he pushed through the Fourteenth Amendment, which prohibited party defection, thus ensuring his unchallenged control of the parliament from the threat of a vote of no-confidence. During the remainder of the year he fended off challenges to his actions by the Supreme Court and the presidency, ultimately securing the resignation of President Farooq Leghari and Chief Justice Sajjad Ali Shah. (See Chapter 9.)

He also targeted his enemies. Building on the accountability process initiated by the caretaker regime of interim prime minister Meraj Khalid, Nawaz revised the Ehtesab (Accountability) Ordinance, 1996, by introducing the Ehtesab Act, 1997.[15] The latter act had the effect of stopping legal procedures filed during Nawaz's absence from power against corrupt practices that had allegedly taken place during his first regime, and it strengthened and stream-lined procedures to target Benazir's administrations. The fruit of his exercise was the April 15, 1999, conviction of Benazir and Asif Ali Zardari for "corruption and corrupt practices" resulting in a five-year jail term and a fine of $8.6 million. This conviction disqualified Benazir from holding future elected office.[16]

In the context of increasing Shia-Sunni sectarian violence, Nawaz also introduced an Anti-Terrorism Act in 1997 which established anti-terrorism courts to dispense speedy justice.[17] The newly introduced courts bypassed the normal judicial system. In 1998, Nawaz went even further by establishing military courts in Sindh province which had jurisdiction to try civilians for acts of terrorism. In 1999 the Supreme Court ruled that the establishment of military courts with civilian jurisdiction was extra-constitutional; earlier they had limited the authority of the antiterrorism courts by making their convictions subject to direct High Court appeal.[18]

Nawaz also used his overwhelming mandate to attempt to downsize government by offering attractive buyouts to government servants—the so-called golden handshake scheme. He also dismissed hundreds of Benazir's political appointees. Against great odds, Nawaz completed the first section of the Pakistan motorway—the link between Lahore and Islamabad—a project he had initiated during his first administration.

But his boldest policy shifts came with respect to foreign policy. In 1997, the Nawaz government sought to diffuse the Kashmir issue and improve, if not normalize, relations with India. Nawaz met with Indian prime minister Deve Gowda in February and with his successor, Inder Gujral, in June. But India's United Front government was in no position to take bold steps on the Indian side, and the talks were put on hold when the hard-line BJP assumed power in January 1998. In May, fulfilling a campaign pledge, the new Indian prime minister, Atal Behari Vajpayee, ordered the testing of nuclear weapons. The effect was chilling in Pakistan, and Nawaz Sharif, particularly in the light of jingoistic statements made by prominent Indian politicians, was compelled to order a similar round of nuclear tests in June.[19] But despite such setbacks, or perhaps because of the perceived danger of allowing relations between India and Pakistan to deteriorate, Nawaz continued to pursue a peaceful dialog with India. Surprisingly, when Nawaz extended an invitation to Prime Minister Vajpayee for a state visit, the latter not only accepted but decided to travel by bus on the inaugural run of a new bus service between Lahore and Delhi. Vajpayee's highly publicized visit, the first by an Indian prime minister to Pakistan since 1951,

was a remarkable success and the resultant policy statement—the so-called Lahore Declaration—promised that the two sides:

> shall intensify their efforts to resolve all issues, including the issue of Jammu and
> Kashmir; shall refrain from intervention and interference in each other's internal
> affairs . . . shall take immediate steps for reducing the risk of accidental or unau-
> thorized use of nuclear weapons and discuss concepts and doctrines with a view
> to elaborating measures for confidence building in the nuclear and conventional
> fields, aimed at prevention of conflict.[20]

As pleasantries were being exchanged, however, plans were being perfected
for the Pakistan military's incursion into Indian-occupied Kashmir—the so-
called Kargil Operation. Pakistani forces along with Kashmiri nationalists
crossed the Line of Control, entering Indian territory in April and May and occupying the strategic heights north of Kargil. From such heights Pakistani
forces threatened to cut the main road from Srinagar to Leh. The Kargil Operation was a carefully planned attempt to seize the advantage offered Pakistan in
light of nuclear parity. Unlike the 1965 Pakistani incursion, which had been re-
pulsed by a massive Indian conventional response, Pakistani military strategists
assumed India would not risk nuclear war over such a provocation. They were
also counting on the reluctance of the international community to intervene.
Pakistani defense strategists miscalculated on both scores. India soon proved
willing to take significant casualties to regain the heights, and the international
community was appalled at what was interpreted as Pakistani aggression. Facing
insuperable international pressure, Nawaz ordered the forces to leave on July 4
as a prelude to his visit to the United States. The retreating Pakistani forces suffered severe losses.

It remains uncertain who originally ordered the Kargil Operation. But it is
certain that the operation proved a humiliating defeat for Pakistan. It is also certain that the fallout from Kargil poisoned the already unhealthy relations between the military and Nawaz. Whether or not the operation was originally
sanctioned by the military, the precipitate withdrawal of Pakistani forces was
clearly a disaster and it was openly opposed by the Pakistani COAS, General
Parvez Musharraf. [21]

The consequent military coup was hardly a surprise. Nawaz had made his government impervious to change from civilian sources and his actions had angered
and humiliated the military. The last straw came when Nawaz attempted to sack
General Musharraf. When Musharraf refused to be dismissed, the military chose
to follow the deposed COAS rather than their civilian commander in chief.

Musharraf's Enlightened Moderation (1999–)

Musharraf's first and most important task after seizing power was to restore a modicum of domestic and international confidence in his regime and in Pakistan. During the sixteen months before he seized power Pakistan had tested nuclear weapons, breaking the long-standing strictures of the nonproliferation regime. It had also prompted a dangerous war with India threatening, in the worst case, a nuclear war. And its much heralded democratic transition had been interrupted by Musharraf's coup.

Accordingly, his first act was to issue a Provisional Constitution Order, which hedged on the issue of whether Musharraf's regime was really a martial law regime. He insisted on taking the title "chief executive" and not "chief martial law administrator" (as had been the title of his military predecessors Ayub, Yahya, and Zia) (Chapter 9).

He also moved quickly to clean up the corruption left by his civilian predecessors. In November he established the National Accountability Bureau (NAB), an extension of Nawaz's Ehtesab Bureau. The NAB was granted extensive powers to seize assets and detain those suspected of corruption. The NAB initiated hundreds of cases against loan defaulters and others who had engaged in corrupt practices since 1988, although it avoided implicating judicial or military officials. This had the immediate effect of weakening his political rivals, especially Nawaz Sharif, who eventually had to leave Pakistan to avoid imprisonment. But it is generally acknowledged that Musharraf's anticorruption policies introduced with such fanfare and fervor have proven at best partially successful and selectively implemented. Indeed, in 2007 as part of a political arrangement with Benazir Bhutto, Musharraf promulgated the National Reconciliation Ordinance which vacated all pending proceedings initiated by Nawaz Sharif's Ehtesab Ordinance. This had the effect of allowing Benazir Bhutto and her husband Asif Ali Zardari, both convicted in absentia, to return to Pakistan. Also, eight years after the NAB regime was introduced, Pakistan still ranks very badly in terms of corruption when compared to other states.[22]

Also, Musharraf attempted to convey the message to his domestic and international critics that his government was eager to restore democracy in Pakistan—not the "sham democracy" of his civilian predecessors but rather a "true democracy" based on the establishment of meaningful elected local government institutions. The vehicle for this transformation was the Local Government Plan (LGP), the brainchild of the National Reconstruction Bureau (NRB). Reminiscent of Zia's Local Bodies and Ayub's Basic Democracies, it called for the reestablishment of a three-tiered system of elected councils established at the union, tehsil (subdistrict), and zila (district) levels. But, unlike its predecessors, the LGP provided that such councils be given extensive authority and comparable budgetary resources to address such additional responsibilities. Even more revolutionary the LGP called for the elected nazims (mayors; chairs of zila councils) to be accorded authority to transfer or dismiss deputy commissioners (senior civil servants in the district; this provision was later weakened). Therefore, the LGP envisaged the reversal of the relationship between civil bureaucrats and elected politicians, a relationship that has been a dominant feature of local government in South Asia since the mid-nineteenth century. The LGP also called for a wholesale revision of the local government departments, creating new departments and eliminating or merging others. It also called for the reservation of one-half (later revised to one-third) of all seats in the union councils for women. Some of the more radical features of the original LGP were worn away as the program was implemented. But the thrust of the reform has remained intact. Nazims still maintain formal authority over civilian bureaucrats; district councils were provided significant funds to enable them to meet, at least partially, their expanded functions; district-level departments were significantly restructured; and women were elected in unprecedented numbers to the union, tehsil, and zila councils.[23] The first series of elections to local government councils were held in 2001; the second in 2005.[24]

Like his military predecessors, Musharraf was obliged to legitimize his extra-constitutional seizure of power. Accordingly, following the well-established traditions of his forebears, he held a referendum to get himself elected as a civilian president, intimidated the judiciary into legitimizing his election, rewrote the constitution in order to hold elections and reconvene national and provincial assemblies, and convinced the newly elected assembly members to subsequently pass a constitutional amendment (the Seventeenth Amendment) to complete the transformation from martial law to a restored constitutional order.[25] But, as was chronicled in Chapter 9, Musharraf's carefully crafted system broke down, a victim of an unsympathetic chief justice of the Supreme Court. Following the unsuccessful attempt to suspend the chief justice, Musharraf had to depart from Pakistan's military governance paradigm by taking the unprecedented action of staging a second military coup, this time against his own government, in November 2007.

Musharraf's regime has been deeply affected by international events and foreign policy concerns. This has been both a blessing and curse. Following the U.S. decision to respond to the horrors of September 11 with regime change in Afghanistan, Musharraf quickly abandoned Pakistan's support for the Taliban and became a front-line participant in the U.S.-led global war against terrorism. Pakistan's new role had several immediate benefits, including begrudging international acceptance of the military coup and Musharraf's authoritarian domestic policies. It also provided Pakistan space with India, blunting the latter's claims that Pakistan had provoked the Kargil Operation and that Pakistan was responsible for "cross-border terrorism" with respect to Kashmir. Pakistan's participation in the coalition also ended the halfhearted sanctions that had been imposed on Pakistan following its nuclear weapons testing. In other words, Musharraf's government was able to extricate itself from the international disabilities that faced it in the months immediately following the coup.

But the war in Afghanistan was deeply unpopular in Pakistan. Indeed, since joining the GWAT, the Musharraf government has walked a tightrope between meeting U.S. and international expectations while maintaining at least the semblance of an independent foreign policy. This task has become ever more difficult as the Bush administration's foreign policy, particularly with respect to the invasion and occupation of Iraq, has become increasingly unpopular in Pakistan. President Musharraf has proven incredibly adept at walking this tightrope, and in 2005 he coined, perhaps facetiously, a term which characterized his foreign policy strategy, "enlightened moderation." The core of such a strategy is to adopt policies which respond to international perceptions and pressure but are implemented or crafted in a way that provides only minimal challenges to domestic interests. For instance, bowing to international pressure, Musharraf outlawed several Kashmiri jihadi organizations that the international community deemed as "terrorist" but later allowed them to continue operating in Pakistan under different names.[26] Musharraf adopted a similar strategy with respect to Waziristan in 2003–2004. Responding to international pressure that Pakistan had been less than attentive to cross-border violations of the Afghan-Pakistan border, he authorized raids by paramilitary units into the Waziristan Agencies that resulted in highly publicized successes, as defined by numbers of militants killed. But such operations were limited and prudent, and when the occasion arose he negotiated cease-fire agreements with the insurgent leadership.[27] The Waziristan policy was designed to demonstrate that Pakistan was being proactive with respect to pursuing the goals of the GWAT, but at the same time it was designed to be limited in scope and confined to the remote and largely inaccessible FATA. As long as military action is confined to Wana and Miramshah, as opposed to Peshawar and Lahore, few care. But enlightened moderation is a fragile and dangerous policy, as the multifaceted turmoil that has bedeviled Pakistan in 2007 demonstrates. Most of the violence is related to Pakistan's support or tacit acceptance of U.S. policy in Afghanistan, Iraq, and Israel. But Musharraf's regime and Pakistan's foreign policy is conditioned by maintaining close relations with the United States. Ultimately any policy, even if "enlightened" and "moderate," cannot survive such an inherent contradiction.

NOTES

1. For details, see Charles H. Kennedy, *Bureaucracy in Pakistan* (Karachi: Oxford University Press, 1987), esp. pp. 213–214.

2. Lawrence Ziring, *Pakistan: The Enigma of Political Development* (London: Dawson, 1980), p. 88.

3. Altaf Gauhar, "Pakistan: Ayub Khan's Abdication," *Third World Quarterly,* January 1985, p. 108.

4. Asaf Hussain, *Elite Politics in an Ideological State: The Case of Pakistan* (London: Dawson, 1979), p. 137.

5. See, for instance, Mohammad Ayub Khan, *Friends, Not Masters: A Political Autobiography* (Karachi: Oxford University Press, 1967).

6. For details, see Ronald J. Herring, *Land to the Tiller: The Political Economy of Land Reform in South Asia* (New Haven: Yale University Press, 1983).

7. For details, see Kennedy, *Bureaucracy in Pakistan,* pp. 129–152.

8. Herring, *Land to the Tiller,* pp. 100–103, 117–125.

9. See Government of Pakistan, Cabinet Division, *Ansari Commission's Report on Form of Government 4th August 1983* (Islamabad: Printing Corporation of Pakistan Press, 1984).

10. Kennedy, *Bureaucracy in Pakistan,* pp. 122–125, 145–150.

11. Kennedy, *Bureaucracy in Pakistan,* pp. 122–125.

12. For details of the Zia years, see Robert Wirsing, *Pakistan's Security Under Zia, 1977–1988: The Policy Imperatives of a Peripheral Asian State* (New York: St. Martin's, 1991); Shahid Javed Burki and Craig Baxter, *Pakistan Under the Military: Eleven Years of Zia ul-Haq* (Boulder: Westview, 1991).

13. *Al-Jehad Trust v. Federation of Pakistan and others PLD* 1996 SC 324. For a discussion, see Nasim Hasan Shah, "Judiciary in Pakistan: A Quest for Independence," in *Pakistan: 1997,* ed. Craig Baxter and Charles H. Kennedy (Boulder: Westview, 1998).

14. *Benazir Bhutto v. President of Pakistan PLD* 1998 SC 388.

15. Respectively Ehtesab Ordinance, no. CXI of 1996 (November 18, 1996) and Ehtesab Act (Act IX) of 1997 (May 31, 1997). See discussion in S. M. Zafar, "Constitutional Developments in Pakistan, 1997–99," in *Pakistan: 2000,* ed. Charles H. Kennedy and Craig Baxter (Lanham, Md,, Lexington, 2000), pp. 1–23.

16. *State v. Benazir Bhutto PLD* 1999 SC 535.

17. Anti-Terrorism Act (XXVI) of 1997 (August 20, 1997).

18. Respectively *Liaquat Hussain v. Federation of Pakistan PLD* 1999 SC 504 and *Mehram Ali v. Federation of Pakistan PLD* 1998 SC 1445.

19. See Devin T. Hagerty, "Kashmir and Nuclear Question Revisited"; and Thomas P. Thornton, "Long Way to Lahore: Pakistan and India Negotiate," in *Pakistan: 2000,* pp. 81–106; 45–62.

20. The complete text of the Lahore Declaration and its attendant memorandum of understanding is found in Thornton, "Long Way to Lahore," pp. 58–60.

21. See V. P. Malik, *Kargil* (Delhi: Harper, 2006); and Parvez Musharraf, *In the Line of Fire: A Memoir* (New York: Free Press, 2006).

22. Pakistan is ranked (2007) as 138 of 181 most corrupt states in Transparency International's corruption perceptions index. India ranks 72, Sri Lanka 94, Nepal 131, and Bangladesh 162 on the index.

23. In the 2005 local government elections 6,132 union councils were selected (each council has 13 members). Therefore, 79,716 union councilors were elected and one-third of these seats (26,306) were reserved for women. Pakistan has 110 districts.

24. For an analysis of the first local government election, see Farzana Bari, *Local Government Elections December 2000 (Phase One)* (Islamabad: Pattan Development Corporation, 2001); and Mohammad Waseem, *Democratization in Pakistan: A Study of the 2002 Elections* (Karachi: Oxford University Press, 2006).

25. See Charles H. Kennedy, "A User's Guide to Guided Democracy: Musharraf and the Pakistani Military Governance Paradigm," in *Pakistan: 2005,* ed. Charles H. Kennedy and Cynthia Botteron (Karachi: Oxford University Press, 2006), pp. 120–157.

26. Charles H. Kennedy, "The Creation and Development of Pakistan's Anti-terrorism Regime, 1997–2002," in *Religious Radicalism and Security in South Asia,* ed. Robert Wirsing and Mohan Malik (Honolulu: Asia-Pacific Centre for Security Studies, 2004), pp. 387–411.

27. See International Crisis Group, *Pakistan's Tribal Areas: Appeasing the Militants,* Asia Report no. 125, December 11, 2006.

Suggested Readings

Baxter, Craig, and Charles H. Kennedy, eds. *Pakistan: 1997.* Boulder: Westview, 1998.

Kennedy, Charles H. *Bureaucracy in Pakistan.* Karachi: Oxford University Press, 1987.

Kennedy, Charles H., and Craig Baxter, eds. *Pakistan: 2000.* Lanham, Md., Lexington, 2000.

Kennedy, Charles H., and Cynthia Botteron, eds. *Pakistan: 2005.* Karachi: Oxford University Press, 2006.

Khan, Hamid. *Constitutional and Political History of Pakistan.* Karachi: Oxford University Press, 2004.

Siddiqa, Ayesha. *Military Inc.: Inside Pakistan's Military.* New York: Pluto, 2007.

Talbot, Ian. *Pakistan: A Modern History.* London: Hurst, 1998.

Waseem, Mohammad. *Democratization in Pakistan: A Study of the 2002 Elections.* Karachi: Oxford University Press, 2006.

Ziring, Lawrence. *Pakistan in the Twentieth Century: A Political History.* Karachi: Oxford University Press, 1997.

13

Problems and Prospects

Pakistan faces an uncertain future. Six decades after independence, it is still confronted with profound challenges to its integrity as an independent nation-state, stemming from numerous domestic shortcomings as well as its hazardous international security environment. This chapter presents a brief discussion of the three most intractable challenges currently facing the state.

Institution Building

Pakistan's greatest shortcoming since partition has been its inability to establish stable, effective political institutions. The litany of its failures is long: numerous constitutions, dormant legislatures, ineffective political parties, and persistent military rule. From the perspective of political development, Pakistan is a signal failure. Unfortunately, such difficulties are likely to continue into the foreseeable future.

First, there is the question of national unity. For a state to build effective political institutions, a broad agreement on the fundamentals of the state is required. As demonstrated numerous times in Pakistan's history, however, no such agreement exists. Pakistan is torn by ethnonationalism. Even the potentially unifying effects of a shared religion, Islam, have at times constituted an additional source of ideological or sectarian disunity throughout Pakistan's troubled history.

Second, Pakistan's failures of institution building have been both a cause and a consequence of additional failures. Pakistan's policy makers have often sought the quick-fix solution to problems of institution building, scuttling existing programs or institutions when they encountered resistance. Pakistan's checkered history of local government is a case in point. None of the numerous local government programs established over the decades since partition has survived a change of regime; many have not lasted long enough for that. The current local government system, introduced by Musharraf in 2001, may break this pattern, however. Clearly it has been the most carefully planned and most fully implemented local government system to date. But the ultimate test is whether the program can survive Musharraf's departure, whenever that occurs. Indeed, leaders of the coalition government which came to power in March 2008 have already begun to talk about plans to restore provincial autonomy and correspondingly weaken the local government system.

Third, the stakes of politics in Pakistan have become high. The groups in control share the considerable perquisites of office; those out of power are often consigned to prison or exile. In such a setting, the emphasis is not on creating long-lasting institutions but rather on gaining and maintaining power. Also, at regime change the winners tend to adopt policies which discredit and disestablish the accomplishments of their predecessors.

Finally, like many new states, Pakistan faces the problem of chronic military rule. It has become an axiom of political science that once the threshold of military involvement in civilian politics has been crossed, it becomes increasingly easy to do so again. Indeed Pakistani politics has been dominated by the military for fifty years, since 1958. The country has been under martial law for fourteen years, and military leaders or former military leaders have been the head of government for thirty-two years. Military regimes are notoriously inept at creating representative political institutions, as Pakistan's experience with military regimes has clearly demonstrated.

External Threats

Pakistan faces one of the most difficult security environments in the world. On the east is India; on the west is war-torn Afghanistan. India is Pakistan's oldest and most troublesome opponent. Pakistan has fought three major wars with India (1948, 1965, and 1971), and came perilously close to a fourth in 1999 owing to the Pakistan-inspired Kargil Operation. The Kashmiri nationalist struggle, the source of much Indo-Pak conflict, continues to defy solution. Accordingly, many Pakistanis view Indians as implacable foes and vice versa. And since the summer of 1998 both states have had nuclear weapons arsenals. During winter 2001–2002 in the aftermath of the December 13 attack on the Lok Sabha in Delhi by militants which India claimed were Pakistani-inspired Kashmiri jihadists, tensions nearly reached the breaking point between the two states. War was averted only by skillful diplomatic intervention from the international community and rare prudence on the part of Indian and Pakistani decision makers. Since that time the atmospherics of the India-Pakistan relationship have improved dramatically. Nonetheless, there remains considerable tension between the two states fueled by the unresolved issue of Kashmir, chronic Indian claims that Pakistan continues to inspire "cross-border terrorism," and the firm belief among many Pakistanis, particularly in the establishment, that India still has hegemonic designs on its western neighbor.

Pakistan's difficulties with Afghanistan, also not of recent origin, were exacerbated by the Soviet occupation of that country (1979–1989). The Soviet invasion of Afghanistan caused millions to flee to Pakistan as refugees. Their presence placed severe demands on Pakistan's economy and significantly increased underemployment, particularly in the NWFP and Balochistan. Their presence also encouraged continuing Pakistani involvement in the Afghan civil war (1989–2001). Segments of the Pakistani military (particularly the Inter-Services Intelligence, ISI) became deeply involved in Afghan politics. The ISI is generally acknowledged to have been crucial to the organization, training, and arming of the Taliban, the Islam-oriented Afghan military regime that eventually controlled most of the state from the late 1990s until its ouster in 2001. Moreover, thousands of Pakistani young men and boys, joined by Afghan youth from the refugee camps, mostly Pakhtun, fought with mujahideen groups contesting the Soviet occupation, and later the Taliban after the Soviet withdrawal.

The events of September 11, and the U.S. decision to target the Taliban for its role in harboring Osama bin Laden, which resulted in Operation Enduring Freedom and all that followed, have had a remarkably deleterious effect on Pakistan, which was deemed crucial to the U.S.-led war and the eventual occupation of Afghanistan. Although benefits were associated with assuming the role of the U.S. strategic partner in the global war on terror, in recent years the costs associated with the blowback from Afghanistan have far exceeded such benefits. First, the events in Afghanistan have destabilized Pakistan's border areas, most particularly FATA. As a consequence Pakistan has been obliged to conduct military raids into the agencies, most significantly the two Waziristans, to flush out "terrorist insurgents" who have used the border areas to launch attacks against the Karzai government. These attacks have resulted in many casualties. Second, Pakistan's role in Afghanistan has become increasingly unpopular in Pakistan, particularly following the U.S.-led invasion and occupation of Iraq. The legitimacy of the Musharraf regime, the symbol of such an unpopular policy, has suffered as a consequence. But most importantly, during 2007, the war in Afghanistan seemed to spread to the "settled" areas of Pakistan. Thousands have died in terrorist violence, which is mostly traceable to Pakistan's involvement in Afghanistan and its support for U.S. policies.[1]

Pakistan's policy makers, understandably, have been very concerned with the security of the state. One indicator of such concern is military spending. Pakistan (2007) has a standing army of 1.5 million and spends nearly $4.2 billion per year on defense. Moreover, its per capita military expenditures are greater than those of any other state in South Asia. Yet Pakistan's military is dwarfed by India's, which has 3.7 million soldiers. India spends over $19 billion per year on its military.[2]

A second consequence of uncertain security has been Pakistan's nuclear weapons program. After India exploded a nuclear device in 1974, Prime Minister Zulfiqar Ali Bhutto launched a heavily publicized nuclear development program in Pakistan. However, the international community, and particularly the United States, disapproved of Pakistan's attempt at nuclear proliferation, and the United States subsequently applied pressure on France (which had agreed in 1976 to sell a nuclear reprocessing plant to Pakistan) to withdraw from nuclear agreements with Pakistan. When Pakistan continued clandestinely to seek nuclear capability, the United States invoked provisions of the Symington amendment to the Foreign Assistance Act in 1977 and cut all assistance except food aid to Pakistan, although this amendment was interpreted in 1981 as permitting the provision of new economic and military assistance. For the next seventeen years, the question of whether Pakistan possessed nuclear weapons capability generated much speculation. Successive governments consistently stated that Pakistan did not have the bomb but was seeking nuclear capability solely for peaceful purposes. Despite these assurances, the George H. W. Bush administration, invoking the Pressler amendment, failed to certify that Pakistan was not seeking to develop a nuclear weapons capability and in October 1990 suspended military and economic aid to Pakistan. The effects of the Pressler amendment were relaxed in September 1995 by the passage of the Brown amendment to the Foreign Assistance Act. Uncertainty with respect to Pakistan's nuclear weapons capability was dispelled when Pakistan tested five nuclear devices in June 1998, following similar tests by India. This action violated the main tenet of the nuclear nonproliferation regime. Attendant with such a violation were a host of international economic and military sanctions on the state, which were eventually lifted fully subsequent to Pakistan's joining the international coalition targeting the Taliban in 2001. In 2004 there was considerable international perturbation associated with the confession by Dr. Abdul Qadeer Khan (the architect of Pakistan's nuclear program) that he had sold nuclear secrets to Libya, Iran, and North Korea. Musharraf contained the fallout from this crisis by placing Khan under house arrest, although pardoning him from prosecution by Pakistani courts.[3]

Pakistani-U.S. Relations

Pakistan's most important ally is the United States. But the relationship can be likened to a stormy love affair in which one of the participants is serious and wants to settle down (Pakistan) while the other (the United States) wants to keep its options open and play the field. Pakistan's initial foreign policy called for nonalignment, but that stance began to change in the mid-1950s as the United States sought allies to combat the spread of communism. The United States found its most ardent South Asian support in the person of Ayub Khan, and until 1965 Pakistan was its "most allied ally." But this arrangement ended when the United States stopped arms shipments to Pakistan during the 1965 Pakistani-Indian war. Until such aid was discontinued, the United States had been Pakistan's primary arms supplier, providing $1.2 billion in military aid from 1954 to 1965. The United States viewed the stoppage of arms as conducive to peace in South Asia; Pakistan viewed it as a betrayal by an ally. Between 1965 and 1979, relations between the two states remained cordial and the United States periodically resumed limited arms sales to Pakistan, but never close to the levels prevailing before 1965. Indeed, during the 1971 war the United States provided little material assistance to Pakistan despite the well-publicized "tilt toward Pakistan."

U.S-Pakistani relations reached their nadir in 1979, when the U.S. embassy in Islamabad was burned by an angry mob instigated by alleged U.S. involvement in a plot to occupy the Ka'aba in Mecca. However, this trend of events was reversed when the Soviet Union launched its invasion of Afghanistan in December 1979. After a change of administration in Washington and a year of negotiations, Pakistan emerged with a six-year, $3.2 billion arms sale and economic assistance package in 1981. This agreement was renewed for a three-year period in 1988 at $600 million per year. These agreements made Pakistan the third largest recipient of U.S. security aid in the world (after Israel and Egypt). In October 1990 the United States suspended economic and military aid to Pakistan, charging that Pakistan was continuing attempts to acquire nuclear weapons. This aid was partially restored in 1995, but it was halted again following Pakistan's 1998 nuclear testing.[4]

But again events in Afghanistan reversed this trend. Pakistan, after assuming the role of front-line state in the war against terror, once again became the recipient of significant U.S. military and economic aid, which rose from $3 million in 2001 to over $1.5 billion in 2002. Since then the total U.S. assistance to Pakistan has exceeded $10 billion, $6 billion of which has been distributed under the Coalition Support Fund designed to aid countries associated with the global war against terror. Pakistan has paid dearly for this financial assistance.

Pakistan has allowed the United States to use its airbases in antiterrorism operations, has shared intelligence, and has captured, detained, and in many instances transported to U.S. authorities hundreds of suspects implicated in terrorist activities. It has taken steps to secure Pakistan's porous borders with Afghanistan, including the aforementioned Waziristan operations, and has continued to house nearly 2 million Afghan refugees. Pakistan has also paid dearly with respect to its internal security; in 2007 Pakistan suffered the effects of over fifty suicide bombings and the deaths of over 3,500 in acts associated with terrorism, most such incidents related to Pakistan's role in the war against terror and its alliance with the United States. Nonetheless, there is considerable U.S. sentiment that supporting Pakistan, and particularly a military regime in Pakistan, is a mistake. In 2005, prompted by the AQ Khan affair, Congress passed the Ackerman amendment, reminiscent of the Pressler amendment, which requires the CIA to make annual reports to Congress about Pakistan's nuclear activities, democratic development, and counterterrorism efforts. Similarly, following Benazir Bhutto's assassination in December 2007, several prominent legislators, including Hillary Clinton, Nancy Pelosi, and Harry Reid, have called on the United Nations to conduct an investigation into her death. The implication is clear: Pakistan and the Musharraf regime (the most important U.S. ally in its war against terror) cannot be trusted.

*   *   *

Today Pakistan continues to grapple with the same problems it faced in 1947. First, Pakistan remains a relatively poor country. Although its economy has expanded rapidly since independence, the population has grown at an almost equal rate. Furthermore, the inequalities in distribution of resources have remained largely unaffected by such economic growth. Second, Pakistan still struggles with the problems of choosing a structure of government acceptable to its people and of forming stable and effective institutions. Third, Pakistan faces an insecure international environment. Finally, Pakistan is still searching for a distinctive national identity.

Pakistan's survival will require a combination of luck, dynamic and skillful leadership, an acceptable settlement of its long-standing constitutional and representational disabilities, and the cooperation of its diverse population.

NOTES

1. Rasul B. Rais, *Recovering the Frontier State: War, Ethnicity, and State in Afghanistan* (New York: Longman, 2008); Larry Goodson, *Afghanistan's Endless War* (Seattle: University of Washington Press, 2002).

2. globalfirepower.org (accessed January 10, 2008).

3. Devin Hagerty, *The Consequences of Nuclear Proliferation: Lessons from South Asia* (Cambridge: MIT Press, 1998).

4. Denis Kux, *The United States and Pakistan, 1947–2000: Disenchanted Allies* (Baltimore: Johns Hopkins Press, 2001).

SUGGESTED READINGS

Ganguly, Sumit, and Devin Hagerty. *Fearful Symmetry: India-Pakistan Crises in the Shadow of Nuclear Weapons.* Seattle: University of Washington Press, 2006.

Hagerty, Devin. *South Asia in World Politics.* Lanham, Md.: Rowman & Littlefield, 2005.

Kux, Denis. *The United States and Pakistan, 1997–2000: Disenchanted Allies.* Baltimore: John Hopkins University Press, 2001.

Rais, Rasul B. *Recovering the Frontier State: War, Ethnicity, and State in Afghanistan.* New York: Longmans, 2008.

Rizvi, Hassan Askari. *Military, State, and Security in Pakistan.* New York: St. Martin's, 2000.

PART III

BANGLADESH

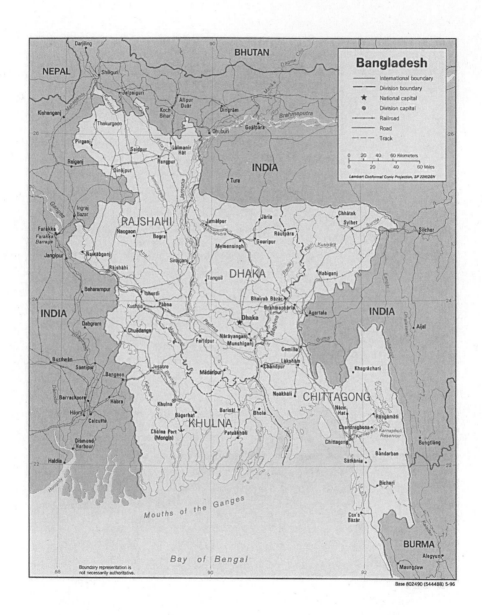

14

Political Culture and Heritage

Recognizing itself as an independent country, war-torn Bangladesh in December 1971 righted itself through a *muktijuddho* (war of liberation) or *shadhinothar juddho* (war of independence). Western countries, pursuing their own geopolitical agenda, view events in Bangladesh from March 24 through December 16, 1971, as a civil war, thereby absolving themselves of any complicity they may have had in the mass killings that took place in Bangladesh. Radical scholars interpret what happened in Bangladesh in those nine months in 1971 as something close to genocide. Bangladesh is usually represented as a country prone to natural disaster where poverty is rampant. A Muslim-majority country with one of the highest population densities in the world and a political system that is continually embroiled in street politicking, Bangladesh is sometimes viewed as a country teetering on the precipice of internal implosion. Others view the country as heading toward radicalism, fundamentalism, and terrorism, both national and global.

Bangladesh in the first decade of the twenty-first century is one of the largest contributors to United Nations peacekeeping operations, and the country is transforming itself through small group creations. Its microcredit enterprise initiative is recognized as having a global impact and constituting a major new instrument in the fight to eradicate poverty throughout the world. Bangladesh has made such progress toward its millennium goals that many predict Bangladesh will become a medium-income country within fifty years. In this chapter we will examine the emergence of Bangladesh, its historical evolution and challenges, and the nature of its society and culture.

The Bangladesh Heritage

Bangladesh, East Pakistan, East Bengal, Bengal, Varendra, Vanga, Samatata, and Harikela are entities that have played a role in defining Bangladeshi cultural and political heritage. Buddhism, Hinduism, and Islam define the cultural heritage of Bangladesh. Dravidian, Mongol, Aryan, Persian, and Arab define Bangladesh heritage. Nationalism and secularism, democracy and authoritarianism define the political heritage of Bangladesh.

The physical boundary of Bangladesh is located between latitude 20°34' and 26°38' north and between longitude 88°01' and 92°41' east. The country is bordered on the west, north, and east by India. On the east it is also bordered by Myanmar and on the south by the Bay of Bengal. Ancient Bengal was primarily composed of Varendra, Vanga, Samatata, Harikela, Radha, Gauda, Anga, Vardhamana, Suhma, and Videha. Bangladesh today is composed of Varendra, Gauda, Radha, a part of Vardhamana, Vanga, Samatata, and Harikela.

Two major rivers, the Ganges and Brahmaputra, originate in the Himalayas and traverse Bangladesh. A third major river is the Meghna, originating in the Assam province of India. These three rivers form the Bangladesh delta. The comparative data of the Bangladesh delta with others around the world confirms its distinctiveness. The implications of this phenomenon for the social, economic, and political life of Bangladesh is immense.

The combined catchment basin of the Ganges, the Brahmaputra, and Meghna measures 1,758,000 square kilometers, which is more than twelve times the size of Bangladesh. The amount of rainfall in the catchment basin of the Bengal rivers is more than four times the rainfall in the Mississippi basin, although in terms of area the former is less than half of the latter.

The amount of sediment carried annually by the rivers of the Bengal delta is about 2 billion tons. This is far more than any other river system anywhere in the world. Under average conditions, from June to September, 775 billion cubic meters of water flow into Bangladesh through the main rivers, and an additional 184 billion cubic meters of stream flow is generated by rainfall in Bangladesh. This may be compared with the annual flow of only 12 billion cubic meters of the Colorado River at Yuma, Arizona. The combined channel of the Ganges, Brahmaputra, and Meghna is about three times the size of the Mississippi channel.[1]

Bangladesh Ancient Heritage

Not much is known about prehistoric Bangladesh. Information can be gleaned from copper and stone inscriptions and *prasastis* (eulogies). There is a general agreement among scholars that a non-Aryan tribe inhabited the Mahastan area in Bogra district as early as the third century B.C. The village of Mahasthan entrenches the remains of one of the oldest cities of Bangladesh, known in the pre-Muslim period as Pundranagara ("the city of the Pundra," a tribe mentioned in the Veda). In the modern period (thirteenth to fifteenth centuries), the name changed to Mahasthan ("great or sacred place"). In 2007, a 1,500-year-old temple was discovered in Bogra about four kilometers west of Mahasthangarh. By the fifth century B.C. Indo-Aryan tribes moved into Bengal. The interaction between the non-Aryan and the Indo-Aryan peoples of Bengal is central to understanding the heritage of Bangladesh. Over many centuries the Indo-Aryan culture became dominant in the delta as the non-Indo-Aryan peoples moved to the periphery of the Bengal delta. During this period the Bengali language and literature were sanscritized (Aryanized). Prior to that the people used the Buddhist-Sanskrit Magadh-Prakrit. The descendants of the Indo-Aryan people speak modern Bengali. However, modern Bengali has incorporated many non-Aryan language groups, such as Austroasiatic, Dravidian, and Sino-Tibetan.[2]

Bangladesh Hindu and Buddhist Period

The earliest written records of the Bangladesh region can be traced to the tenth century A.D. The earliest existing work is *Ramacharitam*, by Sandhyâkaranandi. It provides the genealogy of the Pala dynasty of Bengal and references the Raghu people of Bengal. Other scholarly works mention the Radha and Suhma peoples living in western and southwestern Bengal and the Vanga people living in central and eastern Bengal. Two dynasties, the Palas and the Senas, have played an important role in the sociocultural development of Bangladesh. While the Palas were Buddhists, the Senas were primarily Hindus. The Pala dynasty lasted from A.D. 750 to 1155. The Sena dynasty began around A.D. 1095 and collapsed in A.D. 1202, when the Sena capital Nadia fell to the Gurid dynasty of the Delhi sultanate.

Prior to A.D. 750, parts of Bangladesh were ruled by the Gupta dynasty. During the more than four centuries of Pala rule, there were eighteen rulers. The Pala dynasty began with Gopala and ended when Govindapala lost the Indian province of Bihar to the Delhi sultanate. The much shorter rule of the Senas, which lasted only 128 years, began with the rule of Vijayasena. Four other rulers followed. The last dynastic ruler was Kesavasena, who governed for only three years. The Pala rulers were ardent Buddhists and their seat of power was located near modern-day Vikrampur, which is not far from Dhaka. The Senas were a Hindu dynasty that revived Brahmanism in Bengal. Records are sparse, but two anthologies, *Subhâsitaratnakosa,* consisting of verses from 275 authors from the seventh to the eleventh centuries, and *Saduktikarnâmtra,* also a compilation of verses in Sanskrit, provide a representation of the society, culture, religion, and economics of ancient Bangladesh. Many of the authors of the two anthologies are Bengalis. Two poems, one by Yogesvara about life and another by Vasukalpa in praise of rulers, provide a portrait of ancient Bangladesh.[3]

Verse 291

The days are sweet with ripening of sugar cane;
The autumn rice is high;
And Brahmins, being overfed at feasts
To which the leading families invite them,
Find the heat grows hard to bear.

Verse 1381

O King Kamboja, when your victorious army marches forth,
From the flood of dust raised by the hoofs of afghan steeds
And spreading to kiss the sky
The horses of the sun seem decked with rouge
And the lotuses that grow in heaven's stream
Anticipate the closing of their sunset sleep.

Bangladesh: The Muslim Period

If the ancient culture of modern Bangladesh was more Buddhist than Hindu, the advent of Islam in the thirteenth century further transformed the country and posed the challenge of how to merge the social customs of the region with the religious practices of Islam.[4] Although Islam is generally thought to have been introduced in the thirteenth century, there is some evidence that Arab merchants visited the coastal areas of Bangladesh, especially Chittagong, as early as the eighth century. A silver coin found in an archeological site at the Paharpur monastery identified as issued by Abbasid Caliph Harun al-Rashid dates to A.D. 788 and is used as evidence of such interaction.

How Islam spread in the area of Bangladesh is highly debatable. It arrived in Bengal in 1204 as a Muslim force conquered the area, and maintained its grasp on the leadership for over four hundred years. While the rulers fought for supremacy over the domain, Islam spread among the people of modern Bangladesh. Prior to the advent of Islam, the people of the region were non-Aryan and primarily Buddhist. But Buddhism was relegated to the background when the tantric practices of the Hindu Sena became dominant. Lower-caste Hindus and the Buddhist ruling nobility were relegated to the background. The British explained the dominance of Islam in Bengal by having the lower-caste Hindus convert to the Islamic message of equality and fraternity. Whatever the social conditions of people of the region may have been, other factors must be considered in relation to the spread of Islam in Bengal. First, the role of the expatriates who came to the region has to be considered. In A.D 1204 Ikhtiyaruddin Muhammad Khalji, a son of Bakhtiyar, a general of the Delhi Sultan Qutuddin Aibak, forced the Sena king to flee and took over Bengal. This rule lasted till

1227, when Prince Nasiruddin, son of the Delhi Sultan Iltutmish, defeated the ruler of Bengal Sultan Ghiyasuddin Iwaz Khalji. The new rule lasted for sixty years, and fifteen Mamluk sultans occupied the governorship of Bengal, ten of whom were originally slaves in the imperial court of Delhi. The last governor of Bengal of this period was named Tughral. When he declared his independence from Delhi, Sultan Balban of Delhi defeated him and divided Bengal into four political divisions, one of which was eastern Bengal with its capital at Sonargoan. An armor bearer of the governor of Sonargoan took over the region, rebelled against the Delhi sultan, and assumed the title Sultan Fakhruddin Mubarak Shah in 1388. In 1342, Haji Shamsuddin Ilyas Shah set up an independent dynasty in Bengal. For the next two centuries three independent dynasties—Ilyas Shahis (1342–1487), the Sayyid dynasty of Alauddin Hussain Shah (1493–1538), and the Afghan Karranis (1564–1575)—ruled Bengal with some Hindu kings and Abbyssinian Habshi eunuchs. It was not until the reign of the Mughal King Akbar that Bengal was once again brought under the rule of Delhi in 1575. In 1612 Bengal was finally consolidated into the Mughal empire during the reign of the Jahangir. Further consolidation of Bengal into the Mughal empire took place during the reign of Emperor Aurangzeb. However, upon his death in 1707, Bengal once again moved away from Delhi and established its independence under Murshid Quli Khan in 1717. This rule lasted till 1757, when the British East India Company defeated the Nawab of Bengal Sirajuddaula at the battle of Plassey. Since the rulers were all Muslims, the role they played in promoting Islam must be factored.

As the different regimes were established, different groups like soldiers, traders, fortune seekers, and administrators came to populate the area. The first Muslim immigrants to come to Bengal were Turkish. The Arab immigrants came after the Sayad Alauddin Hussain Shah dynasty (1493–1519) was established. The Abbyssinian Habshi came to Bengal during the Ilyas Shahi reign. Sufficient evidence is available to establish that people from Arabia, Herat, Samarkhand, Tabriz, Bukhara, Balkh, and Abyssinia came to Bengal and settled there. These groups are identified as those who systematically came to Bengal. There is also evidence that prior to the systematic immigration of Muslims to Bengal, sporadic contact and individual settlement took place in Bengal prior to the Turkish invasion. As settlers came to the region and integrated into the community, they also helped transform the region into a Muslim society. Another group that helped spread Islam was composed of Muslim holy men who settled in the different parts of Bengal. The names most prominently associated with the spread of Islam in the different regions of modern Bangladesh are Shaikh Jalaluddin Tabrizi, Sufi-saint Hazrat Sharfuddin Abu Tawwammah of Sonargoan, Shaikh Akhi Serajuddin Uthman, Shaikh Alaul Huq, Hazrat

Shaikh Nur Qutb Alam, Makhdum Sharfuddin Yahya Maneri, Khan Jahan Ali, and Shah Jalal of Syhlet. They settled near present-day Dhaka, Rajshahi, Dinajpur, Khulna-Jessore, Chittagong, and Sylhet. In effect they covered all the critical regions of Bangladesh.

Most assertions about the spread of Islam in Bengal focus on personal conversion. However, for a society to become immersed in a new religion, as was the case in Bangladesh, an institutional structure is needed. During the sixth century, the first institutional structure was the gifting of land (jagirs), which allowed for the permanent settlement of people associated with those in power. A second institutional structure was the rulers' patronage of their religion, Islam. Many of the rulers built beautiful mosques and other structures. In these structures Islamic architecture merged with Bengali architecture, producing the distinctive Bengal tughra architectural calligraphy. Surface decoration, curvilipear roofs, and covered domes are other aspects of the merger of the two cultures, which helped Islam permeate Bengali society.

The third institutional structure was the development of literary works on Islam. The early leaders of Muslim Bengal were known for their scholarship. Mawlana Sharfuddin Abu Tawwammah compiled a work on Islamic mysticism entitled *Maqamat*. Makhdum Sharfuddin Yahya Maneri composed many works on Islamic theology and mysticism, among which *Ajiba, Fawaid I-Rukmi,* is noteworthy. Haji Gharib Yamani wrote a book of Islamic knowledge entitled *Lataif-i-Ashraf.* The Islamization of Bangladesh also corresponded with the enrichment of Bengali art and literature with the steady input of Arabic and Persian into Bengali songs, folklore, poetry, and works of fiction. Islamic thought and practices were not only being written in Arabic or Persian but also in Bengali, which demonstrates that people in Muslim Bengal not only had control over the vernacular language but also mastered the religious language as well as the language of the conquering forces. Such works as Shaikh Jalal Mujarrad's *Shar Nuzhat-i-Arwah;* the *Nasihat Nama,* written by Afdal Ali during the reign of Sultan Nusrat Shah (1519–1532), which is a manual of instruction to Muslims in religious matters; or *Rasul-Vijaya,* another book on religious practices written during the reign of Sultan Yusuf Shah (1474–1481) by Zainuddin, all suggest that the local population also contributed heavily to the spread of Islam in modern Bangladesh.

The name "Bengal" came into existence during the beginning of the Muslim period.[5] Prior to twelfth century A.D. the area was known as Vanga, Gauda, Samatata, Harikela, and other names.

Clearly during the Islamic period from the thirteenth century to the middle of the eighteenth century, the rulers of Bangladesh were outsiders and at times maintained their independence from Delhi. The culture of Bangladesh was a mix-

TABLE 14.1   The Origin of the Name "Bangladesh"

During the Muslim period the whole country received the name "Bangalah" (twelfth century A.D.).

Minhaj in Tabuqut-i-Nasiri, p. 151, uses the term "Bang," meaning eastern and southern Bengal (A.D. 1242–1244).

Barani, p. 53, uses "Banglalh" to refer to eastern and southern Bengal.

Fakhr-al-Din was the king of Bangalah, and Bangali extended to embrace the territories and people of northern and western Bengal. During the time of sultan Shams-uddin Ilyas Shah (1342–1357) this expansion of the name took place and the whole of Bengal came to be known as Bangalah. Ilyas Shah united the two territories Laknawti and Bangalah under his sole authority and founded an independent sultanate in Bengal.

Although his capital was at Pandua in northern Bengal, Ilyas Shah preferred to style himself as Shah-I-Bangalah, Shah-I-Bangaliyan, and Sultan-I-Bangalah. This contrasts with the practice of Hindu kings who called themselves as Gaureswar or the king of Gaur, even though a large portion of Bangalah formed part of their kingdom.

Table developed from Mohammed Anisuzzaman, Bangladesh Public Administration and Society (Dhaka: Bangladesh Books International, 1979), pp. 22–23, 34.

ture of Hindu, Buddhist, and Muslim religions, with Islam becoming more dominant. There were undertones of societal tension as the new and the old regimes merged.

Bangladesh: The British Period

It is generally accepted that the British rule of India started with the defeat of Nawab Sirajuddullah of Bengal in June 1757. However, the British formally entered India when the Nawabs of Murshidabad gave the British East India Company permission to establish a trading post in Calcutta in 1690. One hundred years later a conflict known as the Sepoy Mutiny of 1857 shook the foundations of British authority in India. The Bengal Regiment organized the Sepoy Mutiny. While the main battleground was in the Uttar Pradesh province of India, the mutiny impacted the Dhaka and Chittagong areas of Bangladesh. The British sent the last mughal ruler of India to present-day Myanmar (Burma). As a result of the Sepoy Mutiny, power in India was transferred from the British East India Company to the British government, and British authority was moved from Calcutta to New Delhi.

A census finding in 1872 continues to have a major impact on the psyche of the people of Bangladesh. The census found a large Muslim population in Bengal, which could not be explained by the British. What baffled the British further was the fact the Muslims were not concentrated in the center city but were mostly located in the rural areas of eastern Bengal, suggesting a mass conversion from lower-caste Hindu. An alternative explanation offered by some Muslim

Bengalis was that the Muslims of Bengal were descendants of foreign soldiers who settled in Bengal. The British point of view, however, prevailed. After Pakistan became independent, the conversion theory became a major source of ill will between the peoples of East and West Pakistan, since it had major social and political implications.

During the British rule in India two other events that took place prior to the partition of India in 1947 impacted modern-day Bangladesh. The first was the partition of Bengal in 1905, essentially as an administrative restructuring with Calcutta and Dacca being the principal cities centering the two parts. Unfortunately, because of the religious divide, Calcutta solidified as the center of Hindu culture and society and Dacca emerged as the cultural center for the Muslims. Continued opposition made it difficult for the British to implement partition smoothly, and subsequently they had to merge the two divisions into one in 1912. The second was the great famine of 1943. The two most common explanations for the 1943 famine are shortage of food and the scorched earth policy of the Allied forces in India during World War II. Amartya Sen in his book *Poverty and Famine: An Essay on Entitlement and Poverty* challenges the food shortage rationale. The scorched earth policy remains a potent explanation for the famine. While the cause is debated, it is estimated that approximately 5 million people died in the great famine of Bengal. The famine resulted in severe socioeconomic devastation in Bengal and its consequences continue to be felt in Bangladesh.

Politically, the last five decades of the British rule of India witnessed the emergence of the Muslim League, which was founded in 1906 in Dhaka as a counterweight to the Indian National Congress. The role of the Muslim League became progressively more important as the British firmed up their plans to leave India. The formation of the Muslim League in Dhaka, and the two provincial elections, one in 1937 and the other in 1945–1946, changed the dynamics of political negotiations between the Muslims, the dominant Hindus, and the British rulers of India. The election of 1937 in the Indian provinces resulted in the highest number of Muslim delegates in Bengal. In the other Muslim-majority provinces the Muslims did not win as many delegates, nor were they able to form the provincial government. Bengal provided a special role to the Muslim members representing Bengal in the negotiation between the British, the Indian National Congress, and the Muslim League toward the partition of India. By the 1945–1946 election, the nature of representation changed dramatically. In Bengal and Sind provinces, the Muslim League won a majority to form a government. In other Muslim-dominated provinces they won the largest number of seats but did not form the government as a coalition of other parties formed the government. While in 1937 the Muslim League won only 109 out of 492 reserved seats allocated to the Muslims of India, by 1945–1946, the Muslim League won 445 out of 490 Muslim seats.

Embedded in the Muslim representation of Bengal was a major social phenomenon, which was at the heart of differences between the two wings of Pakistan. The Muslim members who represented Bengal were primarily derived from the nonvernacular elites of Bengal, who can be traced to the Mughal period, when Mughal officials were posted in Bengal and were given landholdings. While the vernacular Muslims were more interested in social issues impacting the Muslims of Bengal, the nonvernacular elites were more interested in nation building. Another issue of the British period that was at the heart of the differences between the two wings of Pakistan was the Lahore Declaration of 1940, which formally proposed separate Muslim homelands. The declaration, made on March 23, 1940, wanted the Muslim-majority areas of India, those of northwestern India and eastern India, to be grouped into "independent states." However, the Delhi Declaration of 1946, made prior to a visit by an official British negotiation team known as the Cabinet Mission, changed the word "independent states" to "independent state," through which India was divided into two countries—India and Pakistan.

Bangladesh: The Pakistan Period

Prior to the Pakistan period, Bengal was an ethnically separate region of India and the ebb and flow of its "independence" from those in power in India (Mughals and Great Britain) depended on Bengal's ability to ward off the central authority in India. With the amalgamation of eastern Bengal as a part of Pakistan, modern-day Bangladesh became for the first time part of a nation-state based on religion and not ethnicity and or regional identity. This dual identity of religion and ethnicity came to the forefront of the political development of Pakistan soon after the partition of India in 1947. Pakistan was comprised of a western part composed of four provinces–North West Frontier, Sind, Baluchistan, and Punjab. Together they became known as West Pakistan. Eastern Bengal, which was renamed East Pakistan, was the fifth province of Pakistan and separated from West Pakistan by approximately 1,000 miles.

The euphoria of a separate homeland for the Muslims of India did not last long, as the social and cultural differences between the two wings of Pakistan started to emerge. Ethnically the peoples of the two wings are different. However, the immediate principal irritant was the issue of national language. The relationship between West Pakistan and East Pakistan took a negative turn when the Pakistani leadership decided to make Urdu, at that time spoken by 7 percent of the population of Pakistan, the sole national language of Pakistan (English being the official language). East Pakistan's demand that Bengali, which was a majority language, be declared a national language was denied. This led to major protests in East Pakistan. The leadership of the protest movement came from the students enrolled in higher education institutions in East Pakistan, especially the University of Dhaka. On February 21, 1952, several students from the University of Dhaka were killed by the police trying to disperse the crowd demanding that Bengali be made a national language. February 21 became known as National Language Movement Day and was celebrated each year to remember those who gave their lives for the cause of making Bengali a national language. Bangladesh facilitated a global effort to recognize February 21 as International Mother Language Day, and in 1999 the United Nations Educational and Cultural Organization (UNESCO) declared February 21, International Mother Language Day. The discord over the national language played a major role in the separation of the two wings of Pakistan and the formation of independent Bangladesh.

Disputes over power sharing between the two wings and the five provinces of Pakistan emerged soon after independence. In the first Pakistani cabinet, East Pakistan found itself represented by a Scheduled Caste Hindu and an Urdu-speaking representative of the national elite. None of the Bengalis who were instrumental in the Muslim electoral victories of 1937 and 1946 were included. Representation thus became a major issue during the constitution-making process. East Pakistan had 7 percent of the total area of Pakistan but had 54 percent of the population. The three major issues that needed to be addressed in formulating the constitution were (1) structure of governance and the composition of the national assembly, (2) the division of powers between the central government and the provincial governments, and (3) the national language. There was general agreement that both Bengali and Urdu should be accepted as national languages, although the bitterness of 1952 was to remain in the hearts of the Bengalis. The representation issue was to be resolved by providing East Pakistan with a majority in the lower house. However, in the upper house representation was to be based on area. The end result was that the total number of combined seats was to be equally distributed between East and West Pakistan. The debate over power sharing between the central government and provincial governments was very controversial. Although the general consensus supported a federal list of powers, a provincial list, and a concurrent list, the operational modalities were difficult to formulate. Just as the three issues were generally resolved, the constitution-making process was abruptly stopped in favor of a new process, which established the first constitution of Pakistan in 1956. Many of the earlier consensus provisions, such as a bicameral legislature and representation based on population size and land mass size, were taken out of the constitution of 1956. However, the 1956 constitution did not last long as a military coup took place in 1958 and Pakistan's experiment with democratic rule came to an abrupt halt.

East Pakistan had a major economic grievance with West Pakistan. Economically, East Pakistan was the major foreign exchange earner from independence until the 1960s. However, only a small percentage of the foreign exchange was being reinvested in East Pakistan. In addition, international assistance was being directed toward West Pakistan. An inability to resolve these economic disparities led to a further separation of interest between the wings of Pakistan. Increasingly the economic disparity coupled with the political disparity of not being provided majority representation in the parliament started to generate discontentment and added to the importance of East Pakistan's demand for greater political autonomy. Along with the political and economic issues that raised tensions between the two wings were other structural disparities. The two principal ones were representation in the civil service and in the armed forces. In both sectors, East Pakistan's representation was negligible. In both sectors efforts to increase the representation of East Pakistan were weak, further strengthening the sense that independence did not bring the benefits expected and whatever benefits came accrued significantly more to West Pakistan than East Pakistan.

Within East Pakistan major political changes also took place. The Muslim League, which provided leadership during the prepartition phase, started to lose its base. Bengali nationalism and social issues came to the forefront of East Pakistan's political culture. Issues such as the role of landlords in society, addressing poverty issues, and minority relationships along with the demand for political autonomy led leaders of the Muslim League like Hussain Shahid Suhurawardy to leave and to join up with A. K. Fazlul Huq, a prominent Bengali political leader, to form the United Front, which defeated the Muslim League in the provincial parliamentary election of 1954. H. S. Shurawardy formed the Awami Muslim League that became the Awami League.

A decade of military rule started to unravel in the aftermath of the India-Pakistan war of 1965. Although no war was fought on the eastern front, East Pakistan felt its vulnerability. Politically, the war pointed out the inherent weakness of military rule, and opposition to the rule began to grow and expand. In a 1966 meeting of the opposition in Lahore, West Pakistan, the Awami League, one of the principal grass roots–based political parties in East Pakistan, floated a power-sharing scheme known as the Six Point Program. The six points were as follows: (1) The constitution should provide for a Federation of Pakistan in the true sense on the basis of the Lahore Resolution and for a parliamentary form of government based on the supremacy of a directly elected legislature on the basis of universal adult franchise. (2) The federal government will deal with only two issues—defense and foreign affairs. All residuary subjects will be vested in the federating states. (3) There should be either two separate, freely convertible currencies for the two wings, or one currency with two separate reserve banks to prevent interwing flight of capital. (4) The power of taxation and revenue collection shall be vested in the federating units; the federal government will receive a share to meet its financial obligations. (5) Economic disparities between the two wings shall disappear through a series of economic, fiscal, and legal reforms. (6) A militia or paramilitary force must be created in East Pakistan, which at present has no defense of it own. To Mujibur Rahman, the Awami League, and East Pakistan it was a political correction to underlying issues of the Lahore Declaration of 1940 where Muslim states were to be created. The six points were placed as issues of provincial autonomy and not separation, although effectively it would have brought about major separation between the two wings. The ruling class of Pakistan, mainly led by the political leaders of West Pakistan and the military leaders, saw the six points as a covert attempt by East Pakistan and the Bengalis to go their separate way. A consequence of the six point program was that charges were brought against Sheikh Mujibur Rahman in 1968, known as the Agartala conspiracy case for sedition and treason to declare East Pakistan as an independent state.

Popular agitation against military rule resulted in the fall of Ayub in 1969. General Agha Muhammad Yahya Khan replaced Ayub. Yahya described himself as a caretaker whose primary task, after restoring law and order, was to hold elections to determine the wishes of the people of Pakistan. He also set out his requirements regarding the nature of a new constitution and in doing so paid lip service to the principle of provincial autonomy. Of Mujib's six points, he particularly opposed the fourth, which would deny the power of taxation to the central government. To determine the return of civilian rule in Pakistan, elections were held in December 1970 after nearly a year of open campaigning by all political parties. Yahya had decided that elections should be held on a system of joint electorates and on the basis of population rather than parity. In a 300-member house (313 with the addition of seven indirectly elected women members from the east and six from the west), the east would directly elect 162 members and the west 138, from single-member constituencies. In the east wing, the Awami League won 160 of the 162 seats, with more than three-quarters of the vote. Yahya reverted the west wing from one unit into the original four provinces of Punjab, Sind, the North-West Frontier Province, and Baluchistan. The Pakistan People's Party, led by Zulfiqar Ali Bhutto, won a majority in West Pakistan as a whole, with 81 seats of the 138, but a majority in only two provinces, Punjab and Sind. Similar results were recorded for the provincial assemblies; the Awami League won 288 of 300 in East Pakistan.[6]

Mujibur Rahman claimed victory as well as the right to frame a new constitution on the basis of the six points and the right to form a government for Pakistan. At one point Yahya hailed Mujib as the "future prime minister of Pakistan." But the military was not pleased with the outcome, seeing, if nothing else, a diminution of its power and its budget. Bhutto, too, was dissatisfied, inasmuch as he saw himself playing second fiddle to a Bengali. Negotiations on a constitution and the transfer of power from the military to the civilians continued through January, February, and early March 1971, with the greater opposition from Bhutto and responsive stonewalling by the Awami League. Bhutto claimed that there were two majorities in Pakistan and that he led one of them and would have to be accommodated in any arrangements made. Mujib came under increasing pressure to separate from Pakistan and allow Bangladesh (the name then being used) to go its own independent way. Meanwhile, Yahya had sworn to hold the unity of Pakistan. It was clear that Yahya's troops, consisting mostly of Punjabis and Pathans, would prefer to repress Mujib and the Bengalis before they attempted to put down Bhutto and the Punjabis if force were necessary. In the early part of March, a civil disobedience movement began on a wide scale in East Pakistan and clashes between the Pakistan army and Awami Leaguers escalated.[7]

Bangladesh: The Birth of a New State

On the night of March 25, 1971, the Pakistan army, strengthened by 80,000 troops flown from West Pakistan, struck at Awami Leaguers and others in Bangladesh (especially Dhaka) in an effort to end the resistance the military had met. In the past, police and military measures had broken the Bengali opposition, but the attack on the Bengalis was so brutal that it stiffened their resolve to become an independent state. On March 27, 1971, an independent state was declared by a Major Ziaur Rahman at Chittagong. Ziaur Rahman would later become one of the heroes of the war and eventually president of independent Bangladesh.[8] While precise figures are not available, Pakistani armed forces killed between 1 million and 3 million people in Bangladesh.

Suffice it to say here that India assisted Bangladesh's Mukti Bahini (national army) and intervened in the war against Pakistan in November and December 1971. Pakistan army units surrendered to a Joint Bangladesh-Indian command on December 16, 1971, and Bangladesh became an independent, sovereign nation. Mujibur Rahman, who had been arrested on the night of the Pakistan army crackdown, taken to West Pakistan, and charged with treason, was released by the new Pakistan government headed by Bhutto, who had succeeded Yahya after the latter resigned in disgrace following the surrender. Mujib returned to

Bangladesh in January and assumed the reins of government as prime minister. The fall of united Pakistan seems to many observers to have been the final act in a play that began in 1947. There was little hope for a final act that would be anything but tragic for Pakistan and triumphant (even in tragic circumstances) for Bangladesh. Who should be placed in the dock? Many would say that Bhutto was responsible for the final act, but others would maintain that Jinnah may have played the key role in the first act.

In sum, the political culture of Bangladesh cannot be understood apart from the events of the period beginning with the Mughal period, followed by the British and finally the Pakistanis. A number of factors are paramount. A constant desire for independence brought about by people's struggle, whether it is through the Sepoy Mutiny of 1857, the language movement of 1948, or the war of liberation of 1971, Bangladeshis have always seen themselves as a separate entity. For a while the Muslim struggle coalesced to form a larger community but in the long run autonomy and independence overrode cooperation with the Muslim community. Built into this idea of what some call "Bengalness" in the importance of language, arts and literature, social rituals, and religion, where none is superior and where all are practiced in accordance with the needs of the individual rather than being dictated by the state. Bangladeshis tend not to recognize their lack of economic resources but carry with them the concept that different peoples over the ages have plundered their national wealth, bringing about the poverty that exists in Bangladesh. That rulers are plunderers and have systematically destroyed the economic advancements is part of the political culture of Bangladesh. Built into the political culture is a concept of negotiation in which the rulers trade their rights and privileges in response to a set of "demands." This has led to a socialization process that is more conducive to the establishment of liberal democracy and has resulted in democratic institution building that has been more successful than in Pakistan.

NOTES

1. Nazrul Islam, "Let the Delta Be a Delta: An Essay in Dissent on the Flood Problem in Bangladesh," *Journal of Social Studies* 48 (1990).

2. Craig Baxter and Syedur Rahman, *Historical Dictionary of Bangladesh* (Lanham, Md.: Scarecrow, 2003); Mohammed Anisuzzaman, *Bangladesh Public Administration and Society* (Dhaka: Bangladesh Books International, 1979).

3. The poems are taken from two works of translation by Daniel H. H. Ingalls: *Sanskrit Poetry from VidyGkara's Treasury* (1965); and *An Anthology of Sanskrit Court Poetry: VidyGkara's "Subh-Gsitaratnakosa"* (1968).

4. The primary sources consulted for the section on the Muslim period are *Richard M. Eaton, The Rise of Islam and the Bengal Frontier, 1204–1860* (1993); Rafiuddin Ahmed, ed., *Understanding the Bengal Muslim: Interpretative Essays* (2001); Nizamuddin Ahmed, *Islamic Heritage of Bangladesh* (1980); Nazimuddin Ahmed, *Discover the Monuments of Bangladesh* (1984); Siddiq,

Mohammad Yusuf (1997); Masjids Madrasah, "Khanqah and Bridge: Reflections on Some Islamic Inscriptions of Bengal," *Journal of the Asiatic Society of Bangladesh* 42, no. 2 (1998): 231–286.

5. Muhammad A. Rahim, *Muslim Society and Politics in Bengal, A.D. 1757–1947* (1994); Mohammed Anisuzzaman, *Bangladesh Public Administration and Society* (Dhaka: Bangladesh Books International, 1979).

6. For more detailed results, see Craig Baxter, "Pakistan Votes, 1970," *Asian Survey*, March 1971, pp. 197–218.

7. For more information, see David Dunbar, "Pakistan, the Failure of Political Negotiations," *Asian Survey*, May 1972, pp. 444–461; Craig Baxter, "Pakistan and Bangladesh," in *Ethnic Separatism and World Politics*, ed. Frederick L. Shiels (Lanham, Md.: University Press of America, 1984), pp. 209–262.

8. For a discussion of the war, see Shiels, ed., *Ethnic Separatism*; A. M. A. Muhith, *Bangladesh: Emergence of a Nation* (Dhaka: Bangladesh Books International, 1978); and Mizanur Rahman Shelley, *Emergence of a New Nation in a Bipolar World: Bangladesh* (Dhaka: University Press, 1979). For the diplomacy of the period, see Richard Sisson and Leo E. Rose, *War and Secession: Pakistan, India, and the Creation of Bangladesh* (Berkeley: University of California Press, 1990). On December 31, 2000, the government of Pakistan released the report of the Hamoodur Rahman Commission, which was set up in 1972 to review the causes and conduct of the war. See *Dawn* (Karachi), January 1–6, 2001, for reportage and analysis. The report had been released earlier and was published in 2000 by *India Today*.

SUGGESTED READINGS

Ahmed, Kamruddin. *A Socio-Political History of Bangladesh*. Dhaka: Zahuruddin Ahmed, 1975.

Ahmed, Moudud. *Bangladesh: Constitutional Quest for Autonomy*. Dhaka: University Press, 1979.

Ahmed, Rafiuddin. *The Bengal Muslims, 1871–1906: A Quest for Identity*. New York: Oxford University Press, 1981.

Ahmed, Sufia. *Muslim Community in Bengal, 1884–1912*. Dhaka: University Press, 1974.

Baxter, Craig. *Bangladesh: From a Nation to a State*. Boulder: Westview, 1997.

Baxter, Craig, and Syedur Rahman. *Historical Dictionary of Bangladesh*, 2d ed. Lanham, Md.: Scarecrow, 1996.

Bhuiyan, Muhammad Abdul Wadud. *Emergence of Bangladesh and the Role of the Awami League*. New Delhi: Vikas, 1982.

Choudhury, G.W. *The Last Days of United Pakistan*. London: Hurst, 1974.

Jahan, Rounaq. *Pakistan: Failure in National Integration*. New York: Columbia University Press, 1972.

Karim, A. K. Nazmul. *The Dynamics of Bangladesh Society*. New Delhi: Vikas, 1980.

Maniruzzaman, Talukder. *The Politics of Development: The Case of Pakistan, 1947–1958*. Dhaka: Green Book House, 1971.

Muhith, A. M. A. *Bangladesh: Emergence of a Nation*. Dhaka: Bangladesh Books International, 1978.

O'Donnell, Charles Peter. *Bangladesh: Biography of a Muslim Nation*. Boulder: Westview, 1984.

Rizvi, Hasan Askari. *Internal Strife and External Intervention*. Lahore: Progressive Publishers, 1981.

Shelley, Mizanur Rahman. *Emergence of a New Nation in a Multi-Polar World: Bangladesh*. Dhaka: University Press, 1979.

Zaheer, Hasan. *The Separation of East Pakistan*. Karachi: Oxford University Press, 1994.

SUGGESTED READINGS ON ANCIENT, MEDIEVAL, AND MUGHAL PERIODS IN BENGAL

TABLE 14.2 Authoritative Works on Bengal

Text	Author	Period Covered
ANCIENT PERIOD		
Râmacharitam	Sandhyâkaranandi	A.D. 1075–1062
Pan Sam Zon Zang	Sumpa Mkhanpo	1747
Aryâsapkasati	Govardhanâchârya	1200 c
ANTHOLOGIES		
Subhâsitaratnakosa	Vidyakara	1178–1206
Saduktikarnâmtra	Shridharadasa	1205
MEDIEVAL PERIOD		
Tabaqat-I-Nasiri	Minhaj-I-Siraj	1246–1266
Tarikh-I-Firuz Shahi	Ziauddin Barawi	1266–1357
Tarikh-I-Firuz Shahi	Shams-I-Siraj Afif	1351–1388
Futuh-Us-Salatin	Khwaja Abdul Malik Isami	1349
Tarikh-I-Mubarak Shahi	Yahya bin Ahmed bin Abdullah Sarhindi	1421–1434
Qiran-Us-Sadain	Amir Khausraus	1280–1325
Rehlâ	Ibn Batuta	1346–1347
Yin Yai Sheng Lan	Mahuan	1390–1411
Tarikh-I-Sher Shahi	Abbas Khan Sherwani	1538–1576
Tarikh-I-Khan Jahani	Khwaja Niamatullah	1538–1576
Makhjan-I-Aghani	Khwaja Niamatullah	
Tarikh-I-Shahi	Ahmed Yadgar	1538–1576
Tarikh-I-Daudi	Abdullah	1572–1576
Tabaqat-I-Akbari	Nizamuddin Ahmed Bakhshi	1592–1593
Tarikh-I-Frishta	Abul Qasim Firishta	1570–1623
Baharistan-I-Ghaybi	Mirza Nathan	1632
Sabh-I-Sadiq	Muhammad Sadiq	1628–1660
Ajiba-I-Ghariba	Shihabuddin Talish	1660–1688
Tarikh-I-Mulk Assam	Shihabuddin Talish	1660–1688
AFTER THE FALL OF THE EMPEROR AURANGZEB		
Naubahar-I-Murshid Guli Khan	Azad Husain	1707+
Ahwal-I-Mahabat Jang	Yusuk Ali	1740–1752
Muzaffar Namah	Karam Ali	1722–1772
Tarikh-I-Bangala	Salimullah	1760–1764
Wariat-I-Fath Bangala	Muhammad Wafa	
Siyar-Ul-Mutakhkherin	Ghulam Husain Tabatabai	
Riaz-Us-Salatin	Ghulam Husain Salim Zaidpuri	1788

Source: "Historiography," in *Banglapedia* (Dhaka: Asiatic Society of Bangladesh 2003), 5:93–104.

15

Government Institutions

Bangladesh has undergone a variety of regimes since it became independent in 1971. Amendments to the constitution of 1972 have changed the form of government from the original parliamentary system to a presidential system in 1975 and back to a parliamentary system in 1991. The goal of the newly independent state was to establish a socialist, democratic regime, but Mujibur Rahman became increasingly authoritarian and the experiment ended in a one-party, single-leader government under him. His assassination in 1975 brought a weak government for a brief period, followed by a military government that gradually liberalized the political system under Ziaur Rahman ("Zia"). In turn, a weak government and a further period of military rule that lasted for nearly a decade was unable to transform itself into something resembling an open democratic system following Zia's assassination in 1981. The collapse of that government in 1990 was followed by free and fair elections and the return to a parliamentary system in 1991, although there has been much turmoil since 1991. The president of Bangladesh declared a state of emergency on January 11, 2007, and a reconstituted caretaker government backed by the armed forces of Bangladesh was formed with a stated goal of holding a free and fair election by the end of 2008. Table 15.1 presents a list of heads of government in Bangladesh along with their respective titles.

The Progress of Government

The Democratic Regime of Mujibur Rahman

On December 16, 1971, the Pakistan armed forces in East Pakistan surrendered to a joint India-Bangladesh armed force, leading to the creation of Bangladesh as a state. Absent from Bangladesh during the initial weeks of independence was Mujibur Rahman (Mujib), who was a prisoner of the Pakistanis. Under international pressure Pakistan released Mujib, who arrived in Dhaka on January 10,

TABLE 15.1   Heads of Government of Bangladesh

Date	Name	Title
April 1971–January 1972	Syed Nazrul Islam	Acting Prime Minister
January 1972–January 1975	Sheikh Mujibur Rahman	Prime Minister
January 1975–August 1975	Sheikh Mujibur Rahman	President
August 1975–November 1975	Khondakar Mushtaq Ahmed	President
November 1975–April 1977	Abu Sadat Muhammad Sayem	President and CMLA
April 1977–May 1981	Ziaur Rahman	President and CMLA
May 1981–March 1982	Abdus Sattar	Acting President and President
March 1982–December 1990	Husain Muhammad Ershad	CMLA and President
December 1990–March 1991	Shahabuddin Ahmed	Acting President
March 1991–February 1996	Begum Khaleda Zia	Prime Minister
February 1996–June 1996	Habibur Rahman	Chief Adviser
June 1996–July 2001	Sheikh Hasina Wajid	Prime Minister
July 2001–October 2001	Latifur Raahman	Chief Adviser
October 2001–October 2006	Begum Khaleda Zia	Prime Minister
October 2006–January 2007	Iajuddin Ahmed	President, Chief Adviser
January 2007–January 2007	Fazlul Huque	Acting Chief Adviser
January 2007–	Fakhruddin Ahmed	Chief Adviser

1972. Mujib immediately stepped down from the post of president, which had been assigned to him by the government in exile, to become prime minister of the new state. Mujib piloted the constitution of 1972 through the parliament, a body comprising members of the provincial assembly elected in 1970 along with those members of the National Assembly who had been elected from what was then East Pakistan.[1] The new constitution followed a parliamentary model. The document provided for the basic rights of the people and contained "directive principles" that do not have the force of law but would, if they were followed, set the tone for the new regime. These basic principles were often described as Mujibism or, in Bengali, Mujibbad. There were four components to this political philosophy: nationalism, democracy, socialism, and secularism. Mujib's Bangladesh would not Islamize its polity.

Problems of Reconstruction, Authoritarian Leadership, and Development Failures

The new government was soon overwhelmed by the enormous reconstruction and rehabilitation challenges facing it after the immensely destructive conflict for independence. The social and economic fabric of the nation was mostly destroyed.

Aid arrived in the form of food and medicine as well as assistance in reconstructing the severely damaged infrastructure. In the international arena, the Soviets made themselves too conspicuous and the Indians stayed on long enough that many Bangladeshis suspected their intentions. The Americans, who were accused of being pro-Pakistani during the liberation war, provided much of the assistance along with other Western nations, even though the Americans (and the Chinese) delayed full recognition of the new government longer than seemed necessary.

Few members of the new government had experience in governing. Mujib had been a minister briefly, and a rather unsuccessful one at that. His leadership is almost universally judged to have been ineffective. Like many other leaders of independence movements, he was unable to adapt to being the decision maker. Mujib failed to use the talents of many senior politicians and civil servants who, he thought, had opposed the freedom movement. Consequently many persons qualified only by political persuasion were appointed to key positions, thereby adding to both inefficiency and corruption. Rehabilitation had to take precedence over development. Bangladesh faced critical food shortages and suffered famines during Mujib's administration, despite assistance from the developed world. Much of the industrial sector was nationalized.

Still basking in the glow of being a liberation hero, Mujib and the Awami League went to the polls in 1973 to elect a new parliament. The party won almost all of the seats (307 of 315), and it appeared that, despite some grumbling, Mujib's government would be firmly in office for the ensuing five-year term of parliament. Parties opposed to the creation of Bangladesh such as the Muslim League and the Jamaat-i-Islam were barred from contesting. The challenge came mainly from the left, and it was weak.

The challenges became greater, however, as the law-and-order situation deteriorated, the economy failed to return to pre-independence levels, and corruption became rampant. Liberation of the nation also meant liberation of public opinion. The press began to attack the policies and methods of the government. Members of the opposition and even some members of the Awami League in parliament began to join the press in criticism. Mujib declared a state of emergency in December 1974 and suspended fundamental rights. A month later the constitution was amended to a presidential system with himself as president. In June 1975 Mujib made Bangladesh a single-party state and, for all practical purposes, gave himself absolute power. These steps did not alter the situation. The demands on the political system continued to be far greater than Mujib, his system, or the resources of the country could meet. On August 15, 1975, Mujib and much of his family were assassinated in a plot led by a group of officers in the Bangladesh army. His system collapsed with his death.

The First Interregnum

With the death of Mujib and the arrest of several of his associates, the presidency was assumed by the next senior person in the cabinet, Khondakar Mushtaq

Ahmad, a politician thought to be one of the most conservative of Awami Leaguers. He is also viewed as one who betrayed Mujib and in effect the liberation
movement. Mushtaq promised elections and a return to a parliamentary system. He disbanded the single party and promised to allow other parties to resume activities as elections approached. However, he did not take steps to
prosecute Mujib's assassins.

In November 1975 a series of coups and attempted coups dislodged Mushtaq
but did not permit pro-Mujib forces to regain power. Mushtaq yielded the office of president to the chief justice, A. S. M. Sayem, who also became chief
martial law administrator. The key person, however, was one of the deputy chief
martial law administrators, Major General Ziaur Rahman.

The Regime of Ziaur Rahman: Gradual Liberalization

Ziaur Rahman, the chief of the army staff, quickly emerged as the leading
member of the ruling group. On November 30, 1976, he replaced Sayem as
chief martial law administrator, and on April 21, 1977, he assumed the presidency when Sayem resigned on grounds of "ill health." He was confirmed as
president in May 1977, when a referendum approved his holding the office.
The referendum, however, did not confer legitimacy on him or his system if for
no other reason than that no alternatives had been presented. In June 1978 Zia
was elected president for a five-year term in a contested election.

Beyond these steps toward power, Zia developed a program that might be
called the "politics of hope." The nineteen points of this program called for a revitalization of Bangladesh, both economically and socially. Zia emphasized such
measures as family planning and proposed expanding agricultural production,
with the goal of reaching self-sufficiency in food grains as soon as possible. Considerable progress was made during his tenure in office. Zia also had a vision of
a subcontinent that worked as a unit to find solutions to economic, social, and
technological problems affecting the entire region. Zia, a war hero, soon became
a charismatic figure of the stature of a Fazlul Haq or Mujibur Rahman.

As he prepared to campaign for the elected presidency, Zia had sanctioned
the formation of a political party dedicated to his program and to his candidacy.
After the election the party was reformed into the Bangladesh Nationalist Party,
which became Zia's vehicle for obtaining a majority in the parliamentary election held in February 1979. The BNP won 207 of the 300 directly elected seats;
the Awami League was a distant second with 39 seats.

Zia was not without opponents. The Awami League opposed his military
rule, his failure to punish the assassins of Mujib, and his less than socialist economic policies. Its members believed that the principles of Mujibism were
being sacrificed, even though Zia's program represented for others a pragmatic

stance toward the many problems of Bangladesh. Zia restored to office the civil servants Mujib had discarded. He also rehabilitated the military officers who had been forced to remain in Pakistan in 1971. A split in the army took place between the groups roughly termed "freedom fighters" and "returnees."

Considerable economic progress was made during the Zia regime. A series of appropriate economic policy directives and a severe curtailment of corruption and corrupt practices, coupled with relatively good weather conditions and extensive foreign assistance, led to an economic upturn. Zia's career was terminated on May 30, 1981, when he was assassinated in Chittagong by conspirators led by a disgruntled freedom fighter.

The Second Interregnum

Vice President Abdus Sattar became the acting president when Zia was killed. The constitution stated that a new election for president must be held within 180 days. The election was held in November 1981, and Sattar was elected president. The chief of the army staff, Lieutenant General Husain Muhammad Ershad, demanded a constitutional role for the military in the governance of the country; Sattar refused to comply with the demand. On March 24, 1982, Ershad led a coup and dismissed Sattar and his government.

Authoritarianism Returns: H. M. Ershad

With Ershad's assumption of power, the state returned to the political point it had left with the gradual liberalization under Zia. Parties were banned, the press controlled, channels of access were closed or narrowed, and martial law was reimposed. Ershad, following the pattern of many military leaders, said that conditions required the only organized force in the nation to assume power, temporarily, to set the government in order.

He further declared that elections would be held to restore representative government. In March 1985 Ershad had asked approval for his policies through a referendum. Although the government reported that he won overwhelming support, it was widely believed that the count had been rigged and the turnout vastly overstated. The "approval" obtained did not add legitimacy to the Ershad regime. An election was finally held for parliament in May 1986, but the results were inconclusive, and there were reports of polling irregularities. The Jatiya Party, which had been organized to support Ershad, won a slim majority of the 300 seats contested, whereas the opposition Awami League, now led by Mujib's daughter, Sheikh Hasina Wajid, and its allies won just under 100 seats. The other major opposition group, the BNP, led by Begum Khaleda Zia, refused to participate in the election.

In the fall of 1987 widespread demonstrations against the Ershad regime, led by the BNP and the Awami League, caused Ershad to dissolve parliament and

call for a new election, which was held in March 1988. The Jatiya Party won almost all the seats, as both the BNP and the Awami League boycotted the election. The undercurrent of opposition to Ershad reached its peak in November
1990 as the BNP and the Awami League joined forces again to demand Ershad's resignation and a free and fair election. Ershad resigned, and a caretaker
government was established.[2]

The Caretaker Government and Elections

A temporary government was established without any constitutional premise to
assist Bangladesh in transitioning from an authoritarian system to a democratic
one. Ruling power was transferred to the chief justice of Bangladesh, Sha-
habuddin Ahmed, who became the head of government and conducted the
election of 1991 to elect a new government. In order to legitimize the process,
the elected members of the national assembly (Fifth Jatiya Sangsad) ratified all
measures taken by the caretaker government.

The caretaker government was the subject of intense negotiations between
the opposition political parties and the government as Bangladesh was com-
pleting the first full term of a democratically elected government. In 1996 the
Thirteenth Amendment of the Constitution was enacted that allowed for a
constitutional caretaker government to be formed to conduct a national election at the conclusion of any five-year term of office. Specific modalities were
enacted to ensure the neutrality of the caretaker government. In June 1996 a
caretaker government headed by former chief justice Habibur Rahman conducted the election that returned the Awami League to power after two
decades in opposition.

In 2001 a third caretaker government was led by former chief justice Latifur
Rahman. The BNP was returned to power. Continuing mistrust among the
major political parties, attempts to manipulate the administrative structure responsible for conducting elections, questioning the process of choosing the
chief adviser, and intense desire to hold on to power severely stressed the concept of a caretaker government. When the time came for the establishment of
the fourth caretaker government in October 2006, it essentially imploded.

A caretaker government was formed under President Iajuddin Ahmed when
the political parties could not agree on the chief adviser. And when four of the
advisers under President Iajuddin Ahmed resigned due to lack of transparency,
Bangladesh was at a point of state failure. With the assistance of the armed
forces a state of emergency was declared in January 2007 and a principled caretaker government was established. Instead of conducting a free and fair election
in three months as specified in the constitution, however, the caretaker government of 2007 is likely to hold a national election by the end of 2008.

BNP and Prime Minister Khalida Zia (1991–1996)

Outside observers declared the February 1991 election free and fair. The BNP won a plurality of seats in parliament and, by joining hands with the Jamaat-i-Islam (JI) in the indirect election for the seats reserved for women, achieved a majority.[3] Khaleda Zia became prime minister. The BNP, which had wanted to continue the presidential system, reversed its stand on this issue and joined with the Awami League to pass a constitutional amendment restoring the parliamentary system of the 1972 constitution.[4] During its tenure BNP, with support from the Awami League, democratized the office of the mayor in four principal cities by ensuring that the position became an elected one.

Two events led to increased political tensions during the BNP regime. First, in 1993, when JI elected Gholam Azam as its party chair, it propelled a political debate on national identity. It resurfaced the sensitive issue of the role of religion in the governance of the state and the role of parties opposed to the formation of Bangladesh.[5] Second, in 1994, a by-election resulted in the BNP candidate winning in what was considered to be a "safe" Awami League seat, leading to allegation of election rigging and fraud.

The two main parties have not cooperated since the national election. Consequently the government has been stormy since 1991 and was further polarized as the by-election result only confirmed in the mind of the Awami League that they could not trust the BNP government. The Awami League, joined by the Jatiya Party and the Jamaat-i-Islam, began a series of strikes and demonstrations against the government demanding that for each general election the government resign and a caretaker government be appointed by the president to conduct the poll. Members of parliament from the three parties resigned in December 1994, ending the possibility that some compromise might be reached, as the resignations deprived the parliament of more than one-third of its members, making the passage of a constitutional amendment impossible. The opposition strikes harmed the economy, but the BNP government remained in office until November 1995. An election in February 1996 was boycotted by the opposition alliance, but the new parliament, overwhelmingly dominated by the BNP, passed an amendment that fully met the opposition's demands. Having done so, that parliament was dissolved and another election was held in June 1996.

The Return of the Awami League: Prime Minister Sheikh Hasina Wajed (1996–2001)

The electorate decided to give the Awami League an opportunity to lead due to the policy and programmatic dishonesty of BNP. The Awami League won

nearly 49 percent of the vote and was the majority party in the parliament having won 146 seats. An informal coalition among the Awami League, the Jatiya
Party of Ershad (who was in prison but won 33 seats), and the Jatiyo Saajtantric
Dal with one seat formed the government. In early 1997 Ershad was released
from prison suggesting that a tacit agreement was worked out between the
Awami League and Jatiya Party for gaining his support and subsequently releas-
ing him from jail.

The election of 1996 was considered relatively free and fair. The Awami
League regime was targeted by the same types of strategies and tactics it had used
against the BNP. The opposition joined the parliament but left it at the end of
1996, rejoined in early 1997, left in fall 1997, and returned again in March
1998. A year later the opposition left again. This back-and-forth strategy in parliament was accompanied by street agitation and strikes that debilitated the
economy. The primary rationale was the opposition's inability to present its
views and be a partner in the governance of the country, particularly its inability
to ensure that local and municipal elections were held in a free and fair environment. Violence of all types became endemic during the tenure of the Awami
League, as was the perception of corruption. A caretaker government took over
in July 2001 and held the parliamentary election in a timely way.

Back to BNP: Prime Minister for a Third Time Khalida Zia (2001–2006)

An interesting development during this period of a transitional government was
the visit by former president Jimmy Carter. He got the principal political parties, the Awami League and BNP, to renounce violent street agitation or strikes,
thus facilitating the work of governance. The electorate viewed the political ran-
cor with trepidation, but as in the earlier election of 1996 was also alert to the
policy and programmatic dishonesty of the government. It also noted the increasingly corrupt practices and the rise of corruption in society. The election
was determined to be fair and free, although the Awami League, having lost the
election, charged that it was rigged in favor of the BNP.

BNP won a two-thirds majority in the parliament, much to its own surprise
and that of the Awami League. The results showed the maturity of the
Bangladesh electorate and its ability to punish government for wrongdoing
and reward the opposition for exposing it. It also showed that the Bangladesh
electorate is looking for ways to facilitate good governance practices. The BNP
regime began with high expectations, but within two years it started to show
signs of internal dissension that resulted in a power struggle between the old
guards of BNP and the younger generation led by the son of the prime minister. As internal strife became more intense, the work of governance became

less important and corrupt practices became once again the hallmark of the reigning political party. The depth and intensity of the corrupt practices only became evident when the state of emergency was promulgated in January 2007. A serious attempt is currently being made to root out corruption in Bangladesh politics.

Parliamentary Government

Bangladesh has an emotional attachment to a parliamentary form of governance. But its experiment with parliamentary government resulted in massive official stagnation if not outright failure. Parliamentary government, which requires working closely with the opposition and working through committees, has not been institutionalized in Bangladesh.

The first experiment in 1972–1973 ended when the major proponent of parliamentary government, Mujib, converted the political system to a presidential one in 1975. The second experiment (1991–2006) was not able to develop any sound practices, as the opposition hardly participated in the operations of the parliament.

When they formed the government, neither the Awami League nor the BNP actively sought to integrate the opposition into the committee system of operation but actually disrupted government operation by a combination of street violence and boycott of the parliament.

In 2007 questions were once again raised as to whether the parliamentary system of government is the most suitable one for Bangladesh, which seems to be heading toward a system in which the head of state (president) and the head of government (prime minister) have shared power, rather than the presidency being ceremonial and the prime minister possessing real power and authority. While shared power has its challenges, this mixed parliamentary and presidential form may have to be in place for a period of time during which trust in critical institutions of governance (judicial independence, free and fair election process, an impartial public bureaucracy, regularized process of leadership change, and an equitable sharing of power between the different levels of state power) becomes institutionalized.

The Institutions of Government

The Central Government

The constitution of Bangladesh provides for a president elected by parliament but lacking executive powers, although some presidents have had executive powers. The speaker of the parliament serves as a temporary successor until a new president is elected within 180 days.

The head of government is the prime minister, who is commissioned by the president, but the president, in practice, must select the leader of the majority party or of a coalition if no party has a majority. Mujib, Khalida Zia, and Hasina Wajed were elected prime ministers. The prime minister must win a vote of confidence from the parliament to be confirmed in office. The prime minister selects the members of the cabinet, no more than 5 percent of whom can be chosen from outside the members of parliament. The 300 directly elected members of parliament are elected from single-member constituencies; the first past the post voting system is used, that is, the candidate with the most votes is elected and a majority is not required. There are thirty additional seats for women (although women can and do contest the directly elected seats as well: witness the present and immediate past prime ministers). These are filled by election by the directly elected members as soon as the newly elected parliament meets. Laws are passed by the parliament and approved by the president. Should the president not approve a law, a further passage by the parliament overrides what is, in effect, a suspensory veto.

The government at the center is organized into a number of ministries and departments. At the head of each is a political minister who is a member of the cabinet and may have authority over more than one department. Some ministries and departments have junior political persons who have the title of state minister. The nonpolitical head of a department or ministry, the secretary, is usually drawn from the civil service, although occasionally secretaries are drawn from the police service or, during military rule, even from the military service. Although the secretary is responsible, under the minister, for the operation of the department as a whole, he or she is assisted by a range of subordinate officers who have lower-level responsibility for segments of the department's work.

The members of the higher civil service (i.e., those who enter at a level that will allow them to aspire to the rank of secretary) are selected through examination, and there is a prescribed course of training at entrance and during service. The unified Bangladesh Civil Service, established in 1980, features fourteen "cadres" designed to bring together a number of separate services inherited from Pakistan (and British India). The foreign service operates as a semiautonomous cadre, although the examination procedures are the same as those for the civil service. The police constitute a service separate from the civil service. Senior police officers also enter by examination; the highest level for a police officer is inspector general. There are also a number of boards, commissions, and corporations on an all-Bangladesh level that draw a substantial number of their senior officers from the civil service.

The Supreme Court of Bangladesh has two divisions. The Appellate Division, as its name indicates, has only appellate jurisdiction and is the final court of appeal. The High Court Division has both appellate jurisdiction and some original jurisdiction. However, the point of original jurisdiction in most cases is the district court. The Fourth Amendment of the 1972 constitution placed the judiciary under the president of the country, and therefore Bangladesh did not have full separation of the executive and judicial branches.

In June 2007, the caretaker government took measures to separate the judiciary from the executive. Critical to effective separation are the rules that place the judicial services under the direct supervision of the Supreme Court. Even more important is the fact that in case of a dispute between the Supreme Court and the presidency, the opinion of the court will take precedence. District officers are also magistrates and serve as hearing officers in many cases and perform the role of judges in lesser matters. Here too as the separation of the judiciary from the executive takes place at the national level, it will correspondingly change the role of the district officers as magistrates of the court. The appropriate modalities have yet to be worked out to the satisfaction of the courts and the civil service from where the magistrates are appointed.

Local Government

Administratively, Bangladesh is divided into six divisions (Dhaka, Chittagong, Khulna, Rajshahi Barisal, and Sylhet). Each division is headed by a commissioner. Below the division are 64 districts that are subdivided into 460 Thanas (at times known as the Upazillas). Below the Thana level are the 4,451 unions and 80,000 villages. Tinkering with the form of local government has been a pastime of each regime, as it had been before independence by the regimes of Pakistan. Although both the BNP and the Awami League have stated their intention to change the local government system instituted by Ershad, neither so far has done so. Ershad's goal was to move decision-making power closer to the people. Thus his local government system focused on the Upazilla level rather than the district level. The four-tier system is the foundation of the local government system. The government of Hasina wanted to make the village level the most operational level of the local government system. The third Khalida government was thinking about moving away from the village and back to the Thana or Upazilla level. The caretaker government of Fakhruddin Admed, based on a local government study report, expects to have local bodies elected prior to or in tandem with the national parliamentary election. The salient features are direct election to the district council, direct revenue under the control of the local government, and reserved seats for women increased from 30 percent to 40 percent for the next three elections.

Each district is headed administratively by a deputy commissioner drawn from the civil service. He or she also has the titles of district collector (of revenue) and district magistrate (responsible for law and order and some judicial functions). In a "minicabinet" the deputy commissioner has representatives of most of the central government departments (e.g., a superintendent of police, a district judge, a district public health officer). He or she is charged with the overall administration and development of the district. The task is not an easy one, as the other government representatives have a dual loyalty: to the deputy commissioner, but, more important, to the head of the central government department in Dhaka, where assignments and promotions are controlled. Coordination can be difficult.

Below the district is the Upazilla (literally, subdistrict), of which there are 460. Elections are held to the Upazilla councils, which are intended to be the voice of the people at this level depending on the government of the day. (There are also indirectly elected district councils, the electors being the members of the Upazilla councils.) The Upazilla is meant to be the focal point of administration and development. Below the Upazilla are unions that comprise one or more villages and also have elected councils. The executive at the Upzilla is the Upazilla Nirbahi officer.

Urban coordinating bodies cover entire cities. In the largest urban areas (Dhaka, Chittagong, Khulna, and Rajshahi) there are municipal corporations with mayors and elected councils. Each also has a government-appointed administrator, roughly the equivalent of a city manager. Smaller urban areas have city or town councils. There are twenty such urban areas, also known as Pourashavas.

Police administration is headed by the inspector general of police, who serves nominally under the authority of the Home Ministry. At the district level there is a superintendent of police, and at the Upazilla level, an inspector of police. Commissioners of police direct the work in major urban areas and report directly to the inspector general.

*   *   *

In sum, Bangladesh is developing a structure of government for the long term. The place of a freely elected parliament in the governmental system has perhaps been ensured by the success of free and fair elections in June 1996 and October 2001. Local government is weak, primarily because the system is viewed as the power base of the political party forming the government. The evolving system of government also appears to lessen the specter of direct military intervention. The danger to the system has been the sharp differences among parties and individual leaders, especially between Hasina Wajid and Khaleda Zia. The aggressive approach to good governance undertaken by the caretaker government of Fakhruddin Ahmed bodes well for Bangladesh and comes at a time when the institutional weaknesses in the political institution building process were about to overwhelm Bangladesh and force it toward an undemocratic system. Developments since January 2007 have arrested the backward slide, and systems being put in place will strengthen Bangladesh as it marches toward democratic governance.

NOTES

1. Two members of the National Assembly chose to remain in Pakistan.

2. Craig Baxter, "Bangladesh in 1990: Another New Beginning," *Asian Survey,* February 1991, pp. 146–152.

3. Craig Baxter and Syedur Rahman, "Bangladesh Votes—1991: Building Democratic Institutions," *Asian Survey,* August 1991, pp. 683–693.

4. Craig Baxter, "Bangladesh in 1991: A Parliamentary System," *Asian Survey,* February 1992, pp. 162–167.

5. Zillur Rahman Khan, "Bangladesh in 1993: Values, Identity, and Development," *Asian Survey,* February 1992, pp. 160–167.

SUGGESTED READINGS

Ahamed, Emajuddin. *Military Rule and the Myth of Independence.* Dhaka: University Press, 1994.

Ahmed, Moudud. *Democracy and the Challenge of Development: A Study of Politics and Military Interventions in Bangladesh.* Dhaka: University Press, 1995.

Ali, Shawakat A. M. M. *Bangladesh Civil Service: A Political-Administrative Perspective.* Dhaka: University Press 2004.

Anisuzzaman, Muhammad. *Bangladesh Public Administration and Society.* Dhaka: Bangladesh Books International, 1979.

Chakravarty, S. R., ed. *Bangladesh Under Mujib, Zia, and Ershad.* New Delhi: Har-Anand, 1995.

Choudhury, Dilara, *Constitutional Development in Bangladesh.* Karachi: Oxford, 1994.

Franda, Marcus. *Bangladesh: The First Decade.* New Delhi: South Asian Publishers, 1982.

Islam, Mahmudul. *Constitutional Law of Bangladesh.* Dhaka: Bangladesh Institute of Law and International Affairs, 1995.

Khan, Zillur Rahman. *Leadership in the Least Developed Nation: Bangladesh.* Syracuse, N.Y.: Maxwell School, 1983.

Maniruzzaman, Talukder. *The Bangladesh Revolution and Its Aftermath.* Dhaka: Bangladesh Books International, 1980.

Rahman, M. Shamsur. *Administrative Elite in Bangladesh.* New Delhi: Manka, 1991.

Rahman, Rafiqur A. T. *Reforming the Civil Service for Government Performance.* Dhaka: University Press 2001.

Zafarullah, H. *Government and Politics in Bangladesh.* Dhaka: Centre for Administrative Studies, 1981.

16

Elections, Parties, and Interest Groups

The 1991, 1996, and 2001 elections in Bangladesh may indicate a marginal change, but the earlier tendency of the electorate in Bengal, since the beginning of mass politics in about 1905, was to support a single leader and a single issue. This tendency has been a major factor in Bangladeshi politics, as will be seen in the review of elections below. In the next parliamentary election scheduled sometime between October and December 2008, however, the electorate is likely to shift away from the single-leader single-issue strategy.

Elections

Two elections during the British India period impacted Bangladesh. The first was held in 1936–1937 for the Bengal Legislative Council and Legislative Assembly. Much of the eastern Bengal electorate gave its support to Fazlul Haq and his Krishak Praja Party (KPP), or Farmers and Peoples Party. KPP supported the cause of the smaller farmers, who were primarily Muslims, against *zamindars* (landlords), who were generally Hindus.[1] The second election was held in 1945–1946, and the issue was a national one: the separation of Muslim-majority areas of undivided India from the Hindu-majority territories. The Muslim voters in Bengal gave their support to the Muslim League, which won overwhelmingly, gaining all six seats in the Central Legislative Assembly of India with 94.01 percent of the vote and winning 112 of the 119 Muslim seats in the provincial assembly with 82.04 percent of the vote.[2] The outcome, however, was both regional and national, for at the time that the poll was held the concept of a Muslim homeland in India was based on the plural "independent states" of the Lahore Resolution of 1940.

The first election under the Pakistan period was held in 1954. The national positions taken by the ruling Muslim League had alienated most Bengalis. The Muslim League was routed by the United Front, which consisted principally of Fazlul Haq's party, now renamed the Krishak Sramik (Peasants and Workers) Party (KSP) and the Awami League of Husain Shaheed Suhrawardy. In this election two regional elite leaders combined forces and had the cooperation of a third, Maulana Abdul Hamid Khan Bhashani. The single issue in 1954 was greater participation in the governance of the state that was dominated by West Pakistan. These demands were embodied in the twenty-one points. Demands included the designation of Bengali as one of the official languages of Pakistan along with other issues that would give Bengalis, in the eyes of the East Pakistanis, greater participation in governing the state. The election result was an overwhelming victory for the United Front of the KSP and the Awami League over the Muslim League.[3] Direct elections were suspended during the period of rule by Ayub Khan (1958–1969), but direct elections with open and free campaigning were restored by the decrees of Yahya Khan, and elections were held in 1970.[4] Sheikh Mujibur Rahman was the leader of the Awami League, and the issue was provincial autonomy as demanded in his Six Points. Again, the issue and the leader combined to produce a large-scale victory.

The first election in Bangladesh was held in 1973. The issue at the forefront, which once more resulted in Mujib's victory, was a request for a confirmation that the four pillars of Mujibism were those desired by the people. After the elections there was no doubt, despite a measure of tinkering with the results, that the people supported Mujib. The Awami League won 291 seats of the 300 contested and took 73.18 percent of the popular vote.

Elections were not held again until 1978, under the regime headed by Major General Ziaur Rahman. Zia won the presidential election that year with 76.63 percent of the vote, whereas his nearest rival, General M. A. G. Osmany, who had the support of the major faction of the Awami League, won only 21.70 percent.[5] Zia followed this outcome with a major victory in the parliamentary elections held in 1979 when his party, the Bangladesh Nationalist Party (BNP), won 207 of 300 seats. The percentage of the popular vote (41.16 percent), however, was lower than that of the winners in previous elections because of the extraordinarily large number of candidates running.[6] The leader was clearly the charismatic Zia, and the issue was economic stabilization and advancement. Like Mujib, Zia wanted a confirmation of his nineteen-point program for Bangladesh. In 1981 the BNP successfully elected a successor to Zia, Abdus Sattar, but his term ended when H. M. Ershad led a military coup in March 1982. Parliamentary elections held by Ershad's regime in 1987 and 1988 were

TABLE 16.1   Bangladesh Parliamentary Elections 1991, 1996, and 2001

	1991		1996		2001	
Party	Seats	Percentage of Vote	Seats	Percentage of Vote	Seats	Percentage of Vote
Awami League	88	30.6	146	37.4	62	40.97
Bangladesh Nationalist Party	140	31.0	116	33.6	193	40.13
Jamaat-e-Islami	18	12.1	3	8.6	17	4.28
Jatiya Party	35	11.8	32	16.4	14	7.25
Independents and others*	19	14.4	3	3.9	15	6.03

Independents and others:

1991: Bangladesh Communist Party, 5; Bangladesh Awami Krishak Sramik League, 5; National Awami Party (Muzzafar), 1; Workers Party, 1; Jatiya Samajtantrik Party (Seraj), 1; Islamic Unity Group, 1; National Democratic Party, 1; Ganotantrik Dal, 1; Independents 3.

1996: Jatiyo Samajtantrik Dal, 1; Islamic Unity Group, 1; Independents, 1.

2001: Jatiya Party (Naziur), 1; Jaitya Party (Monju), 1; Islamic Unity Group, 2, Krishak Sramik Janata Party, 2; Independents, 6.

also one-sided, largely because the BNP boycotted the election in 1986, and both the BNP and the Awami League boycotted in 1988.

"Free and fair" elections were not held again until February 27, 1991, after the fall of Ershad. The principal contestants were the BNP, now led by Khaleda Zia (the widow of former president Ziaur Rahman), and the Awami League, led by Sheikh Hasina Wajid (the daughter of former president Mujibur Rahman). A close contest ensued when the two parties, which had joined hands in the demonstrations leading to Ershad's removal in December 1990, resumed their rivalry. The BNP stood for a presidential system, private enterprise, recognition of the place of Islam, and a sense of *Bangladeshi* nationalism. The Awami League favored a parliamentary system, some continuation of the socialist policies of Mujib, secularism, and a vaguely defined concept of *Bengali* nationalism that was sometimes interpreted to mean a "pro-India" stance. For the first time, there were clearly divisive issues. In the end, the BNP won 140 of 300 seats, short of a majority, but increased this to 168 of 330 by winning 28 of the 30 women's seats in alliance with the Jamaat-i-Islam. The Awami League and its allies, with 99 seats, formed the principal opposition. The Jatiya Party of Ershad won 35 seats, despite the fact that its leader was in jail, and the Jamaat-i-Islam won 18. Nonetheless, perhaps demonstrating the lack of a dominant leader and the presence of multiple issues, the popular vote gave the BNP 31.0 percent and the Awami League a close 30.6 percent (see Table 16.1).[7]

When the Khaleda Zia government's five-year term ended, an election was held in February 1996. The opposition parties, mainly the Awami League, the Jatiya Party, and the Jamaat, boycotted the election because they did not feel that the election authority would conduct a "free and fair" election. The Zia

TABLE 16.2   Parliamentary Elections and Votes Cast

Years	Number of Parties and Alliances Contesting Election	Total Votes Cast
1973	14	35,205,642
1979	29	38,363,858
1986	28	47,876,979
1988	08	49,863,829
1991	96	62,181,743
1996	41	56,149,182
1996	81	56,716,935
2001	41	75,000,656

Source: Bangladesh Election Commission Secretariat.

government again resigned but passed a constitutional amendment requiring elections to be held under a neutral caretaker government. With this in place, the opposition contested the June 1996 election. The Awami League won 146 seats; the BNP, 116; the Jatiya Party, 32; and the Jamaat, 3. In terms of votes received, the Awami League garnered 37.4; the BNP, 33.6 percent; the Jatiya Party, 16.4 percent; and the Jamaat, 8.6 percent. The remaining 4.0 percent went to independents and candidates of other parties. After the Awami League completed its five-year term of office, the transitional system of the caretaker government conducted the election of 2001. The single defining issue—the abuse and misuse of power and authority—put the BNP back in power with an overwhelming majority. BNP won 193 seats, with 40.97 percent of the votes. The Awami League won only 62 seats but received 40.13 percent of the votes. Jamaat won 17 seats, the Jatiya 4 seats.[8]

January 2007 was the next scheduled election, but a state of emergency was declared on January 11, 2007, postponing the election. Clashes within the BNP during its 2001–2006 tenure, extreme politicization of the major institutions of governance (bureaucracy, caretaker government, judiciary), continued mismanagement and abuse of power and authority, and a blatant attempt to hold on to power by the BNP by manipulating the election agencies produced chaos in Bangladesh. The Awami League during this period was able to systematically disrupt and stymie the normal operations of government and governance. The tipping point that started the chaos during the 2001 to 2006 period and during the caretaker period between October 2006 and January 2007 was the Twelfth Amendment, which changed the retirement age of judges on the Supreme Court of Bangladesh and its corresponding impact on who would head the caretaker government. The opposition parties led by the Awami League coalesced against it and countered BNP's hold onto power strategy with street politics and demonstrations, mass strikes, work stoppages, and economic disruptions, bringing Bangladesh to near collapse. Similar to events that had monumental impact on the political development of Bangladesh like 1971, when Bangladesh became independent, or 1975, when Sheikh Mujibur Rahman was assassinated, or in 1990, when Ershad was overthrown, the declaration of the state of emergency on January 11, 2007, would unquestionably bring a sea change in the evolution of Bangladesh as a democratic state.

Charismatic personalities, factionalism, and ineffective leadership tend to define the political party system of Bangladesh. None is particularly known for democratic zeal. Mujib, Zia, and Ershad were leaders by their own capacities. Hasina became a leader as representative of her father and Khaleda of her husband. All five leaders have failed to develop and nurture alternate leaders within the party, and they show an inability to withdraw from an active party position. Almost like sheep, party members and officials follow the leader and are unable to see beyond. Another aspect of Bangladeshi politics is factionalism. It caused the victorious Muslim League in 1946 to reject Nazimuddin and replace him with the urbane emerging regional elitist Suhrawardy, although Jinnah's intervention reversed this decision once independence had been won. After the 1954 election the United Front was unable to remain united, and from then until 1958, when Ayub took over, there was a constant tussle between Fazlul Haq's KSP and Suhrawardy's Awami League for control of the provincial government. Bhashani's defection from the Awami League also hurt the party. Through the imposition of emergency rule, Mujib kept most but not all of the Awami League together after 1973. But he was merely sweeping factionalism under the rug, and it reemerged after Mujib was assassinated in 1975. Zia's party was also factionalized, but this became evident only after he was assassinated in 1981. Ershad's Jatiya Party split into rival factions in 1996. To curtail factionalism, especially during Ershad's authoritarian rule, both the BNP and the Awami League selected leaders, Khaleda Zia and Hasina Wajid, respectively, who were considered neutral and were related to the fallen leaders. However, in 2007 both the Awami League and BNP are for the first time being challenged sufficiently to require them to carefully examine their party organization for transparency and accountability. Factions are emerging that may change the nature of the Awami League and are likely to split the BNP.

Mujib was effective in bringing a people together to rise in anger against injustice but was ineffective in the day-to-day management of a country. Zia proved to be effective in bringing diverse and often countervailing forces within Bangladesh to work together but was unable to institutionalize the process so that these forces would continue to work together. Ershad decentralized part of the government structure to make it more accessible to the people but could not bring together sufficient forces to transform his regime into a civilian one.

Ineffective leadership by both Hasina and Khaleda led to mismanagement in government, abuse of power and authority, fear of dynastic leadership, politicization of major institutions of government, and a culture of corruption, which in two decades completely permeated Bangladesh society.

Political Leaders

Some of the Bengali Muslim political leaders mentioned in this discussion began their careers during the British period, some in the Pakistan period, and those of Ziaur Rahman and H. M. Ershad in the post-independence period. Only Mujibur Rahman's spanned all three periods. It will be useful to look briefly at some of these key figures and analyze their political skills.

Maulvi A.K. Fazlul Haq: The Regional Elite

Maulvi Abul Kasim Fazlul Haq (1873–1962) came from the coastal district of Barisal (then called Bakerganj) in eastern Bengal.[9] He was truly a vernacular Bengali in that he had neither the landed aristocracy background of Nazimuddin nor the urbane Muslim intellectual background of Suhrawardy. He completed his education in college and law school in Calcutta, where he qualified to become a vakil (local lawyer) and was called maulvi (a learned person) by his contemporaries. He set out to serve people and thereby built up his political reputation. He entered elective politics in 1913, when he was elected to the Bengal Legislative Council, serving until the council ended in 1937. He was a member of the Indian National Congress and the Muslim League (served as president), and formed his own party, the Krishak Praja Party, in 1927 (renamed the Krishak Sramik Party in 1947) and then led it to victory in the United Front alliance with the Awami League in the 1954 election. He was the first prime minister of Bengal.[10] After independence; he served briefly as chief minister of East Bengal in 1954, as a central minister in 1955 and 1956, and as governor of East Pakistan from 1956 to 1958. He was the prime mover of the 1940 Lahore Resolution that called for separate *states* for the Muslims of India. He worked at the national and regional level with equal diligence. He knew the problems of his fellow Bengalis and worked diligently to solve them. He supported land reform legislation and greater expenditures on education and health. His legacy of the KSP as a party has all but disappeared, but the policies oriented toward rural development have been incorporated into the platforms of the Awami League and Zia's and Ershad's parties. Given his distinguished and active career, Fazlul Haq clearly earned the title Sher-i-Bangla (Lion of Bengal), by which he is still known.

Khwaja Sir Nazimuddin: The National Elite

Throughout much of his career Khwaja Sir Nazimuddin (1894–1964) was the principal rival of Fazlul Haq. Nazimuddin, a member of the wealthy landed Nawab of Dhaka family, was a part of the national elite. He attended Aligarh Muslim University and then continued his studies at Cambridge University. Nazimuddin too was elected to the Bengal Legislative Council and served as a minister (1929–1934). He was home minister (1937–1941) and became opposition leader (1941–1943) before being chosen prime minister (1943–1945). Nazimuddin, after the independence of Pakistan, was named chief minister of East Bengal in 1947. He succeeded as governor-general of Pakistan on Jinnah's death in 1948 and then stepped down from that position to succeed Liaquat Ali Khan as prime minister when Liaquat was assassinated in 1951. He was dismissed from office in 1953. Under Ayub Khan, Nazimuddin reorganized the Muslim League (council faction) and headed the combined opposition against Ayub until his (Nazimuddin's) death in 1964.

Despite Nazimuddin's long service in high positions, Bengali Muslims never viewed him as representing them and their interests. He was a member of the national elite and spoke for all-India and later all-Pakistan interests. Although Nazimuddin did not represent the aspirations of the regional elite and the mass of Bengali Muslims, his skills were recognized in Dhaka. He, Fazlul Haq, and Suhrawardy are buried in adjacent graves in a Dhaka park.

Husain Shaheed Suhrawardy; National Elite

Suhrawardy (1893–1963) represented a Muslim Bengali family of exceptional intellectual and artistic talents. Suhrawardy was educated at Calcutta and Oxford and entered the bar from Gray's Inn in London. He achieved prominence as deputy mayor of Calcutta in the 1920s and later on for his presumed support of Muslims in the Great Calcutta Killing in 1946 and then for his close work with Mohandas Gandhi to calm communal disturbances in 1947. In 1937 he was elected to the Bengal assembly and served as a minister during the coalition with Fazlul Haq and during the premiership of Nazimuddin, with whom he developed a rivalry. He moved the resolution that amended the Lahore Resolution to provide for a single Muslim state. Shortly afterward, he proposed a united Bengal as a third dominion in India.

Suhrawardy was a member of the Pakistan Constituent Assembly. He opposed the Muslim League policy of continuing the party's exclusive Muslim membership and proposed the establishment of a new party open to all Pakistanis. He subsequently broke with the Muslim League to form what became the Awami League, a party primarily based in East Pakistan that became the voice of Bengali interests. Suhrawardy canvassed the entire province and led the party, in alliance with the KSP, to victory in 1954.

Suhrawardy agreed with Fazlul Haq that the KSP would govern in East Pakistan while Suhrawardy went to West Pakistan to represent Bengali interests there. He served as prime minister of Pakistan in 1956 and 1957, and in the eyes of many was the most skilled prime minister in the pre-Ayub period.

Suhrawardy was a convert to regional elitism. Although his own skills were best used at the national level, he chose a group of locally skilled political figures who built the Awami League into the best organized party in Pakistan (albeit only in the east). His political lieutenant in Dhaka was Ataur Rahman Khan (1907–1991), who was several times chief minister of East Pakistan before Ayub and prime minister of Bangladesh (1984–1985). His organizational lieutenant was Sheikh Mujibur Rahman. At Suhrawardy's death in 1963, the party leadership fell to Mujib, who represented the regional elite to an even greater extent.

Sheikh Mujibur Rahman

Mujib (1920–1975) was born far from the centers of power, in Tungipara in Faridpur district. He attended but did not graduate from a college in Calcutta, having become involved in politics through the All-India Muslim Students Federation in 1940. He was a member of the Muslim League but joined Suhrawardy and others in what became the Awami League in 1949. He was general secretary in 1952 after gaining experience at lower levels of the organization and was elected to the East Bengal assembly in 1954. He did brief stints in the cabinet at Dhaka and Karachi, but his skills were more appropriate to party organization and campaigning. Having become the de facto successor to Suhrawardy in 1963, Mujib was jailed on several occasions during the Ayub period. After he stated the Six Points in Lahore in 1966 (see Chapter 14), he was accused of collaborating with India to set East Pakistan free in what was known as the Agartala conspiracy case.[11] During the agitation against Ayub in 1968 and 1969, demands were made for his release. He was freed in 1969, and the case was never completed.

He led the Awami League to victory in 1970 and was arrested in 1971 and taken to prison in West Pakistan, but he returned to lead Bangladesh in 1972—first as prime minister and then as president. He was assassinated on August 15, 1975, under circumstances that will be described in Chapter 17. Mujib's skills were clearly those of an organizer at the party level and of a haranguer of the crowds at public meetings. His roots were in the countryside, and in this respect he was more the successor of Fazlul Haq than the urbane Suhrawardy. The traditions of both the Awami League and the KSP seemed to merge in Mujib, but the KSP strand was probably stronger. At the beginning of the independent era in Bangladesh, he was adored by the masses and was given the title Banga-bandhu (Friend of Bengal). His skills, however, could not be transferred to the running of an independent government—hence his failure in that realm. His charismatic ability to lead was adaptable only to a movement, and in this he was equaled perhaps only by Fazlul Haq and Ziaur Rahman.

Maulana Abdul Hamid Khan Bhashani

Bhashani (1885–1976) is an enigma in Bangladeshi politics. Born in a small vil-lage in Tangail district, he was a Bengali by birth and first achieved political fame when he wandered as a barely trained Islamic leader (hence his title Maulana) to Assam and there took up the cause of tenant farmers against land-lords. His views were often considered radical within the Assam Muslim League inasmuch as he espoused the needs of the downtrodden, at least as he defined them. After independence he moved back to East Bengal and continued to sup-port those causes. He joined Suhrawardy in founding the Awami League. Party discipline and Bhashani were strangers. He stood well to the left of the conser-vative Suhrawardy and worked poorly with the populist Mujib. Bhashani broke with the Awami League to form what became the National Awami Party in 1957, and under that umbrella he associated with groups ranging from the rem-nants of the banned Communist Party of Pakistan to moderates who fought for the restoration of democracy to others whose principal demands were the un-doing of the single province of West Pakistan. Bhashani supported Ayub to the extent of endorsing Ayub's policy of closer relations with China, but in the end he was one of Ayub's outspoken opponents, as he later would be of Mujib. Bhashani represented another element in the regional elite, often a group to whom the word "elite" can barely be applied. He and his party never gained sig-nificant electoral support, but he was expected to take up the cause of the less fortunate—whether it was against the West Pakistanis or the Awami League in Bangladesh, or even against India on the Farakka water question (see Chapter 26). No one has ever replaced him, as all potential claimants lack his charisma.

Ziaur Rahman

Major General Ziaur Rahman (1936–1981) was the principal leader of Bangladesh from 1975 until his death. He was born in Bogra district and at-tended the Pakistan Military Academy. His military career was uneventful until he found himself in control of Chittagong on March 27, 1971, and broadcast a Bangladeshi declaration of independence. He was a hero of the liberation war but was not a favorite of Mujib, and he had risen only to the position of deputy chief of the army staff by the time Mujib was assassinated. The sepoys (soldiers) claimed him as their leader in the series of attempted revolutions in November 1975 and he emerged then as the army leader in the martial law government. He subsequently became chief martial law administrator and then assumed the presidency in 1977, a post to which he was elected in 1978.

Despite his war record, Zia seemed an unlikely person to achieve a high degree of popularity. He was quietly efficient but propelled himself into the public image by a seemingly unending whirl of tours throughout Bangladesh.

He exhorted the Bangladeshis to work together—a key demand in a factionalized nation—to develop the resources of the country, limited though they were. Indeed, he preached the politics of hope, winning his position of leadership by this means and through his ability to make quick decisions. There was no reconciliation between Zia and the Awami League, but his nineteen-point program drew on the demands of the regional elite and advocated rural development ideas that could be traced to Fazlul Haq. From his start as a shy, almost retiring person, Ziaur Rahman grew to be the most successful of the post-independence Bangladeshi leaders.

Like the Awami League, the Bangladesh Nationalist Party, founded by Zia, factionalized after the loss of its leader. The aged vice president, Abdus Sattar, was chosen as the party's candidate to succeed Zia in order to avoid rivalries among other contenders. However, the ultimate result was the choice of Zia's widow, Khaleda Zia, to lead the party. As noted earlier, she campaigned successfully in the 1991 and 2001 elections and became prime minister.

Husain Muhammad Ershad

Lieutenant General H. M. Ershad (b. 1930) led a military coup on March 24, 1982, against the regime headed by Abdus Sattar, who had been elected to succeed Ziaur Rahman. Ershad, like Zia, was a career military man. As he was in Pakistan during the civil war, he was unable to participate in the liberation campaign. Upon his repatriation to Bangladesh in 1973, he was appointed adjutant general, and in 1975, after a year at the Indian National Defence College in New Delhi, he was named deputy chief of staff of the army. When Zia relinquished his chief of staff post in 1978, Ershad replaced him and thereby became the principal military person on active duty. After Zia's assassination and Sattar's election, Ershad stated that the military should have a defined role in the governance of Bangladesh, a position that the civilian Sattar opposed.

As a leader Ershad (first as chief martial law administrator and then combining that position with the presidency) was unable to develop the charisma that characterized Zia. Ershad did not hold elections until 1986, first for parliament and then for the presidency. His party, Jatiya, won the first and he the second, in both cases without the BNP participating and in the second with no significant organized opposition. The withdrawal of the Awami League from parliament caused another election for that body in 1988 and the Jatiya Party won overwhelmingly against little opposition.

While Ershad continued the foreign policy set out by Zia and built on Zia's program of economic and social development, he never gained the popular support that the preceding military president achieved. His authoritarian rule often curtailed the freedoms provided by the constitution of 1972. He faced a serious uprising in the fall of 1987 but was able to put it down. In the fall of 1990 he was not successful in repressing renewed demonstrations against him and was forced to resign in December of that year. However, his party, as noted earlier, did win seats in the 1991, 1996, and 2001 elections. Although he was jailed during the Khaleda Zia regime, he was permitted bail and the right to take his parliamentary seat during the Sheikh Hasina government. He even supported the Awami League to the extent that one of the party's leaders joined the cabinet. He was convicted of corruption and returned to jail in November 2000. In 2007 he announced his retirement from active politics, and Jatiya will likely become a minor party.

Begum Khaleda Zia

The widow of Ziaur Rahman, who became the leader of the BNP in 1984, was born in 1945. She worked to keep the factionalized party together and firmly opposed Ershad. Under her leadership, the BNP refused to contest either of the two elections held during Ershad's presidency. After the February 1991 election she became prime minister and, despite her previously expressed views, agreed to a return to a parliamentary system. She and her party were defeated in the June 1996 election, and she became leader of the opposition. In 2001 she returned to power but within two years acceded to sharing the reigns of public authority with her son. The caretaker government that came to power after the declaration of emergency has arrested her and charged her with corruption and graft.

Sheikh Hasina Wajid

The daughter of Sheikh Mujibur Rahman, Hasina Wajid was out of Bangladesh when her father was assassinated. With competition for leadership in the Awami League, she was called back to Bangladesh in 1981 to lead the party. She led a change in the party's platform by dropping the socialism adopted by Mujib. She led the opposition after the 1986 election but withdrew her party from the parliament and did not contest the resulting 1988 election. In 1991 she again became leader of the opposition and in June 1996, prime minister. In July 2007 the caretaker government arrested her, alleging corruption and extortion. She has had domestic and foreign policy successes during her tenure as prime minister, but they are overshadowed by her inability to overcome the family tragedy of 1975.

Political Parties

The Awami League

Having observed the sharp division between the all-Pakistan goals of the Muslim League and the aspirations of the East Pakistanis, two prominent pre-independence political figures returned to politics in the early 1950s (see Chapter 15). One of them was Fazlul Haq and the other was Husain Shaheed Suhrawardy, who strongly held the view that the Muslim League had accomplished its goal with the partition of India and should be dissolved in favor of a new national party that would include non-Muslims. In 1951 Suhrawardy and some others from East Pakistan formed the Awami (People's) Muslim League as an opposition group. This was renamed simply the Awami League, and membership was open to all Pakistani citizens. The new Awami League was unable to make serious inroads into the west wing of Pakistan, although it formed alliances with short-lived opposition groups in the west.

Suhrawardy's intellectual leadership was a major asset to the new party. He was joined by a large number of vernacular elite Muslim League members, but only a few members of the highest echelons of the East Pakistan Muslim League. Among the former were Ataur Rahman Khan and Sheikh Mujibur Rahman, who eventually succeeded Suhrawardy in the leadership of the party.[12] Still another was the religious and political leader Maulana Abdul Hamid Khan Bhashani. The Awami League's first venture in electoral politics came in 1954 when it joined hands with KPP and other smaller parties to form the United Front, which defeated the Muslim League in the East Pakistan provincial election. The United Front government was dissolved within three months of its formation. The key election issue was the status of Bengali language. During the Ayub period the Awami League consistently opposed military rule even when it attempted to provide itself some legitimacy.

The Awami League remained the focus of opposition to Ayub and contested the indirect elections of the president's Basic Democrats system. Several of the leaders, especially Mujibur Rahman, were jailed for significant periods. The quiet work of strengthening the organization continued. When Ayub was dismissed and replaced by Yahya Khan, who promised free politicking and direct elections, the Awami League was ready to resume full and open activity. In the December 1970 election for the National Assembly, the Awami League swept the polls in East Pakistan by winning 160 of the 162 seats at stake and garnering about three-quarters of the popular vote. In the election for the provincial assembly it all but duplicated this feat, winning 288 of the 300 directly elected seats.

The Awami League leaders who were able to escape arrest by Pakistan authorities in March 1971 set up a government in exile in Calcutta. Syed Nazrul Islam was designated acting president in the absence of Mujibur Rahman, who was in jail in West Pakistan. The Awami League coordinated the resistance to the Pakistan army, joined by several small leftist parties, although it remained a party of the center. It took over the reins of government after the Pakistani surrender in December 1971.

Mujib's one-party decree in 1975 led to the formation of the Bangladesh Krishak Sramik Awami League (BAKSAL), an amalgamation of the names of the two principal parties in the United Front of 1954. With the assassination of Mujib, BAKSAL was ordered dissolved. The Awami League was revived when parties were permitted to function again in 1976. It contested the presidential election of 1978 but lost. A split in the Awami League did not hurt the party in the parliamentary election of 1979, when it finished a distant second to the Bangladesh Nationalist Party. In the presidential election of 1981 the Awami League ran Kamal Hussain, a former foreign minister, against the incumbent acting president, Abdus Sattar, and again was soundly defeated.

The party is now under the leadership of Sheikh Hasina Wajid, the daughter of Sheikh Mujibur Rahman. The party opposed elections under Ershad's martial law regime but reversed that position and participated in the May 1986 election, winning about seventy seats. Sheikh Hasina Wajid became leader of the opposition in parliament. However, in the fall of 1987, the party left the parliament, causing its dissolution, and did not participate in the 1988 election. It had returned to the "no vote under Ershad" stance. In the 1991 election it finished behind the BNP and was formally designated the opposition, won the 1996 election and lost the 2001 election. The Awami League in 1972 strongly supported the four pillars of Mujibism: democracy, nationalism, socialism, and secularism. Despite the deviation to authoritarianism in the latter Mujib period, the party campaigned in 1991 for a return to a parliamentary system with regular free and fair elections. It has abandoned the socialism pillar of Mujibism, however, and its present economic platform differs little from that of the BNP and the Jatiya Party. It opposes the steps taken by Zia and Ershad away from what the party might describe as "pure secularism." Some feel that the party takes a more favorable attitude toward India, but this stance might not be given support by the elites or the people in general.

In 2006 the Awami League effectively counteracted the BNP's attempt to ensure electoral successes but also damaged its most sacred pillar of secularism by signing a coalition agreement with a fringe religious party, Bangladesh Khelafat

Majlish. The memorandum of agreement dealt with who can issue a fatwa (religious edict) ban on laws that go against Quranic values, recognition of degrees awarded by Madrasas, and a ban on criticism of the Prophet Muhammad. Under the current state of emergency of 2007, the Awami League is having to undertake a self-analysis of its organizational structure and administrative and managerial procedures. Given its grassroots permeation in Bangladesh, it is less likely to split into factions, although there is every likelihood that its leadership identification and selection process is going to be radically changed.

Bangladesh Nationalist Party

The Bangladesh Nationalist Party (BNP) was formed in 1978 in support of President Ziaur Rahman. It was built partly on the basis of its predecessor, which used the acronym JAGODAL (National Democratic Party). To the JAGODAL were added splinter groups from a wide variety of parties, ranging from a portion of the conservative Muslim League to several leftist fragments; collectively these now form the BNP. Abdus Sattar was appointed head of the BNP, although Zia was the real leader. The party supported the nineteen-point program for the reconstruction and development of Bangladesh (see Chapter 15). As the JAGODAL the party was behind Zia's successful election for the presidency; as the BNP it won about two-thirds of the seats in the parliamentary election of 1979. After Zia's assassination, the BNP successfully supported Abdus Sattar in his election to the presidency in 1981.

After Zia's death and even before the Sattar campaign, there were signs of factionalism in the party. Some younger members thought that a younger candidate for the presidency than Sattar should be chosen, but the party was unable to agree on any other candidate. After Ershad took over, the party further factionalized. It coopted as party leader Zia's widow, Khaleda Zia—a woman who was very much in the background during her husband's term of office. Like the Awami League, the BNP opposed the holding of elections under Ershad's martial law. Unlike the Awami League, the BNP boycotted the election of May 1986 and also that of March 1988, a course that placed its future in question. But its position was consolidated when it joined the Awami League in demonstrations that resulted in Ershad's fall. In the 1991 election after the fall of Ershad, the BNP won a small majority of the seats and formed the government, but it lost the June 1996 election and now forms the leading opposition party.

The policies of the BNP were a moderate reversal of those of the Awami League. It supported a freer economy, maintained the present formulation of "absolute faith and trust in Almighty Allah," and stood for a presidential form of government. This position changed after the 1991 election, when the BNP agreed to a reversion to the parliamentary form. In foreign policy, the Zia government built close relations with the United States, China, and the Arab states—relations it wishes to maintain. It also prefers to carry out subcontinental politics in the context of the South Asian Association for Regional Cooperation (see Chapter 27) and holds a more distant position toward India than the Awami League.

In 2001 BNP returned to form the government with an absolute majority but soon after lost its traction because of internal dissension. Khaleda Zia allowed her son Tarique Zia to become increasingly the real power broker in the government. In effect, under the BNP rule of 2001–2006, the formal government was headed by Khaleda Zia and a parallel government was led by Tarique Rahman Zia. He initially held the post of joint secretary general and leading up to the expected January 2007 parliamentary election became the senior secretary general of BNP. He was instrumental in a somewhat systematic removal of the BNP old guards like former president of Bangladesh Dr. Badruddoza Chowdhury, who went on to form a political forum and later a political party, the Liberal Democratic Party. Since January 2007, BNP has been challenged to democratize its internal operations and is in the midst of reform and leadership bickering and eventual factions.

Jatiya Party

The party formed in 1983 to support the program and person of Ershad, which at that time used the acronym JANODAL (People's Party), is now known as the Jatiya Party (also meaning People's Party). It is composed largely of defectors from the BNP, a few former Awami Leaguers, and certain others from smaller parties as well as some who previously were inactive in politics. Ershad was unable to generate enthusiasm for himself or for his program as Zia had been able to mobilize. But Ershad, having won confirmation in office in the March 1985 referendum, proceeded to a parliamentary poll in May 1986. The Jatiya Party did not achieve a large majority; rather, it squeaked by with a bare majority of 152 of 300 seats. It won a large majority in the almost uncontested 1988 election and won thirty-five seats and 11.8 percent in the 1991 poll despite the fact that much of its leadership, including Ershad, was in jail. After the June 1996 election in which it won thirty-two seats and 16.4 percent of the vote, Ershad was permitted bail and took his seat in parliament. One of the members of the Jatiya Party took a seat in the Awami League cabinet, but Ershad maintains that his party's support is subject to review on each issue. As mentioned above, Ershad later broke with the Awami League and joined forces with the BNP and the Jamaat as the opposition. However, a faction of the Jatiya Party led by a minister remains supportive of the Awami League. In the 2001 election the Jatiya Party won only fourteen seats. Internal dissension caused the party to split into two, and with Ershad's announcement in 2007 that he is retiring from politics, the Jatiya Party is likely to become insignificant, although for the time being it will remain active in the northern areas of Bangladesh, especially Rangpur, Ershad's birthplace.

The Islamic Right

Islamic fundamentalism is a noisy—but not important—factor in Bangladeshi politics. The only party of any size is the Jamaat-i-Islam, an offshoot of the party by the same name in Pakistan. It stands for the adoption of an Islamic state in Bangladesh. The party polled 12.1 percent of the vote and won twenty seats in the 1991 election. Its support for the BNP in the voting for the women's seats permitted the BNP to gain a majority in the parliament. It was embroiled in 1992 in a controversy over its leader, Golam Azam, who opponents claim is not a Bangladeshi citizen and who was allegedly responsible for the deaths of Bangladeshi nationalists while working with the Pakistan army in 1971. He has since retired from the position and has been replaced by Matiur Rahman Nizami, who is also accused of anti-Bangladesh actions during 1971. The party's performance in the June 1996 election was poorer than in 1991; it won only three seats and 8.6 percent of the vote. In the 2001 election Jamaat won seventeen seats and could garner only 4.28 percent of the vote. The Jamaat was part of the 2001–2006 BNP-led government that also included the Islamic Okiyo Jote, which won two seats. Another Islamic party, the Islamic Jatiya Party, which won fourteen seats, did not participate in the BNP government.

The Left

Nowhere is the Bengali penchant for factionalism more evident than in the fragmentation of the already small left wing of politics. There is a veritable multitude of such parties, often local groups gathered around a single leader. Although these parties can occasionally win a single seat in parliament, they cannot seriously affect the outcome of elections.

Other than the East Pakistan offshoot of the pre-independence Communist Party of India, the organized left can best be traced to the split in the Awami League in 1955. Bhashani and certain others withdrew, combined with groups in West Pakistan, and formed the National Awami Party (NAP). The power of the new party in East Pakistan was attributed to the fact that it held the balance between the contending Krishak Sramik Party and Awami League in the provincial assembly after the breakup of the United Front.[13]

Like the other parties, the NAP was unable to work in a free environment during the Ayub period, although Bhashani strongly supported Pakistan's

opening to China. The party began to fragment; indeed, the major division occurred in the mid-1960s, when a Bhashani faction competed in East Pakistan
with one led by Muzaffar Ahmad. The former was often described as "pro-
Peking" and the latter as "pro-Moscow," the designation of the Bhashani group
having been highly exaggerated. The tiny Muzaffar group continues to exist, as
it has for some time, as a leftist hanger-on of the Awami League. The Bhashani
group has experienced continued and repeated fragmentation, to the extent that
Bhashani's son was briefly in Ershad's cabinet.

Bureaucrats

The highly selective nature of recruitment for the upper level of the civilian and
military services makes the two groups an elite one with interests it is sure to
pursue. The civilian bureaucracy was merit based but became increasingly
politicized, first in 1970 and later on in 1990, such that their performance was
severely downgraded while their political activities became unethical and went
against all norms of public service rules and regulations. The military bureaucracy was more professionalized but in 1970 was actively political. In the latter
part of the twentieth century it was less prone to participating in the direct political process unless there was an emergency of the kind that emerged in 2007.
The military bureaucracy increasingly views itself as an international peacekeeping force and its strategic interest lies outside of Bangladesh today.

Students and Universities

The university community has long been a political force. Many Muslim
League and Awami League leaders gained their first political experience at Calcutta or Dhaka before 1947. After 1947, students and some professors were in
the forefront of the movements for recognition of Bengali, parity for East Pakistan, and eventually autonomy and freedom for the east wing of Pakistan. The
most vicious attack by the Pakistan army in March 1971 was made against
Dhaka University, and there was another round of killings of intellectuals just
before the army surrendered, in December 1971.

Student groups today are generally aligned with one or another of the political parties.[14] Students have become radicalized and there is equal strength between the left and the fundamentalists. Nonetheless, the fact that most student
groups are located in key urban areas, Dhaka Chittagong and Rajshahi, causes
concern to whatever government is in power. The students are capable of
demonstrations, some of which are violent and can tie up the city, and they
often support general strikes (hartals).

Trade Unions

In nations with surplus labor, trade unions are unlikely to have a major impact on politics. Although Bangladesh has large numbers of potential laborers, many of them are unskilled; hence there have been examples in the country of skilled and specialized groups of workers being able to exercise some influence on political and economic policies. Furthermore, the migration of some specialized groups to employment in the Middle East has created shortages in some areas. Bangladesh earns over US$5 billion from migrant workers' remittances.[15] Unions are often closely tied to political parties, although there are also some factory unions. Strikes are generally discouraged by the government. Workers will, however, join other groups in demonstrations, especially when economic matters, such as changes in the subsidized price of food grains, are at issue. If and when significant industrial growth takes place, more trade union activity can be expected.

Rural Elites: Secular and Religious

In a land-poor country such as Bangladesh, the holder of as little as five acres of land can be an influential person in his village area. Those with the land ceiling of thirty acres are very influential. Landlordism in the traditional sense of large estates disappeared in several stages, beginning with the Fazlul Haq ministry in united Bengal and culminating in land reforms during the early years after Pakistan's independence. Nonetheless, there are the traditional elite families to whom respect is given and whose members can draw on vote banks, though to a much more limited degree than earlier. Such elites are likely to oppose further land reform, support government programs that provide agricultural assistance, and look for higher government purchase prices for commodities. Until the landless and very small landholders and tenant farmers are better organized, these elites are likely to continue to exercise a high degree of domination in the rural areas.

Bangladesh has not yet followed the path of many Islamic-majority countries in demanding the establishment of an Islamic state. The constitution was amended by Zia to give recognition to the Muslim majority by amending the "secularist" fundamental principle of state policy to read that the Bangladeshis had "absolute trust and faith in Almighty Allah," and that the Muslims could order their lives according to the Sunnah. However, he also made it clear that the rights of the minorities to practice and preach their faith would not be inhibited. The reason behind the Zia move seems to have been an attempt to assuage the Middle Eastern states that had complained that Bangladesh was not sufficiently Islamic to warrant large assistance packages from the oil-rich nations. During his regime, Ershad declared Bangladesh an "Islamic state," but this seems not to have affected the role of non-Muslims.

The religious leaders, the pirs, have not played an important role in either East Pakistani or Bangladeshi politics. Although many are respected by their followers, a demarcation seems to have occurred between religion (viewed generally as a private matter) and politics—a demarcation that has become increasingly atypical of Muslim-majority nations. Early in his rule, Ershad had the constitution amended to declare Islam the state religion, but no further steps have been taken. There is an emerging fundamentalism in Bangladesh supported indirectly by the Islamic right. Jama'atul Mujahideen Bangladesh (JMB) is an insignificant fringe party but was able to provide a distorted leadership to radicalism in Bangladesh. The party's public face was Bangla Bhai, who was involved in religious vigilantism with an intent to propel Bangladesh toward fundamentalism. In the waning hours of the 2001–2006 BNP rule the extent of their plans to radicalize Bangladesh became known and effective steps were taken to reduce this threat. Bangladesh under the caretaker government of Fakhruddin Ahmed executed Bangla Bhai and JMB's leading members after an open and fair trial, significantly reducing such threat.

NOTES

1. For more detailed results, see Craig Baxter, *Bangladesh: From a Nation to a State* (Boulder: Westview, 1997), p. 51.

2. Baxter, *Bangladesh*, p. 54.

3. Baxter, *Bangladesh*, pp. 74–75.

4. Baxter, *Bangladesh*, p. 79.

5. Baxter, *Bangladesh*, pp. 99–100, also presents the detailed results of the 1981 presidential election.

6. Baxter, *Bangladesh*, pp. 101–102.

7. Baxter, *Bangladesh*, p. 113.

8. Baxter, *Bangladesh*, pp. 118–120, and Eighth Parliamentary Election, *Statistical Report*, Bangladesh Election Commission, April 2002.

9. Baxter, *Bangladesh*, pp. 128–129.

10. Biographies in English of Bengali leaders are scarce. See A. S. M. Abdur Rab, *A. K. Fazlul Haq: His Life and Achievements* (Lahore: Firozsons, 1966). Kazi Ahmed Kamal, *Politics and Inside Stories* (Dhaka: Kazi Giasuddin Ahmed, 1970), discusses Fazlul Haq, Suhrawardy, and Bhashani.

11. Under the Government of India Act of 1935, and until independence in 1947, the heads of government in the provinces were designated prime ministers (premiers). After independence the title in both India and Pakistan was changed to chief minister; the title of prime minister was reserved for the head of the central government.

12. So named from Agartala, the capital of the Indian state of Tripura, where the plot was allegedly hatched.

13. The actual head of the All-Pakistan Awami League was a West Pakistani, but Mujib controlled the bulk of the party through his leadership of the East Pakistan party.

14. The West Pakistan NAP held a similar balancing position in that wing between the Muslim League and the Republican party.

15. Talukder Maniruzzaman, *The Bangladesh Revolution and Its Aftermath* (Dhaka: Bangladesh Books International, 1980), esp. chap. 4.

SUGGESTED READINGS

Ahamed, Emajuddin. *Military Rule and the Myth of Democracy.* Dhaka: University Press, 1988.

Ahmed, Moudud. *Bangladesh: Era of Sheikh Mujibur Rahman.* Dhaka: University Press, 1983.

Ahmed, Rafiuddin, ed. *Religion, Nationalism, and Politics in Bangladesh.* New Delhi: South Asia Publications, 1990.

Banu, U. A. B. Razia Akhter. *Islam in Bangladesh.* Leiden: E. J. Brill, 1991.

Bhuiyan, Muhammad Abdul Wadud. *Emergence of Bangladesh and the Role of the Awami League.* New Delhi: Vikas, 1982.

Chakravarty, S. R. *Bangladesh: The Nineteen Seventy-nine Elections.* New Delhi: South Asian Publishers, 1988.

Ghosh, Shyamali, *The Awami League, 1949–1971.* Dhaka: Academic, 1990.

Hossain, Golam. *General Ziaur Rahman and the BNP.* Dhaka: University Press, 1988.

Kochanek, Stanley A. *Patron-Client Politics and Business in Bangladesh.* Thousand Oaks, Calif.: Sage, 1993.

Maniruzzaman, Talukder. *Radical Politics and the Emergence of Bangladesh.* Dhaka: Bangladesh Books International, 1975.

_____. *The Bangladesh Revolution and Its Aftermath.* Dhaka: Bangladesh Books International, 1980.

Mohaimen, M. A. *The Awami League in the Politics of Bangladesh.* Dhaka: Pioneer, 1990.

O'Donnell, Charles P. *Bangladesh: Biography of a Muslim Nation.* Boulder: Westview, 1984.

Rashiduzzaman, M. "The National Awami Party of Pakistan: Leftist Politics in Crisis." *Pacific Affairs,* Fall 1970.

Westergaard, Kirsten. *State and Rural Society in Bangladesh.* London: Curzon, 1985.

17

Conflicts and Resolution

Bangladesh has seen a number of conflicts. Some have already been discussed, such as the dispute between the parliamentary and the presidential forms of government. In this chapter we will focus on three conflicts in particular. First, the military has played an extra-constitutional role, has at times been politicized, and at one time demanded a permanent role in the operation of the government. Second, Bangladesh has been involved in a lasting struggle with the tribes in the Chittagong Hill Tracts that may be coming to an end. Third, there has been a lack of cooperation between the government party and the opposition, for which Bangladesh has incurred at times significant political and economic costs. Finally, as an aftermath of September 11, extremism and terrorism are emerging issues.

The Military

The roots of the Bangladesh military history can be traced back to the Sepoy Mutiny of 1857 (also known as the first war of liberation), when the Bengal army of British India rebelled against British rule. The Bengal army was defeated and then disbanded. The upshot was that the British made a determination not to recruit Bengalis into the Indian army. The British had introduced the doctrine specifying the Punjabis and Sikhs as "martial races" who could be recruited. Thus at the time of Pakistan independence, Bangladesh, then East Pakistan, did not have a large representation in the Pakistan armed force. Between 1947 and 1972, no systematic attempt was made to significantly increase the representation of Bengalis in the Pakistan armed forces. Thus when the war of liberation began, Bengalis were approximately 6 percent of the total armed forces of Pakistan. In March 1971 the Pakistan military took brutal and aggressive actions against civilians in East Pakistan and required all Bengali members of the armed forces to surrender their arms. The small force of trained Bengalis left, taking their arms, and became the source from which the armed forces of Bangladesh emerged. During the war of liberation, the Bangladesh military, known as the Mukti Bahini (Freedom Force), was composed of trained Bengali military personnel, the civilian police and Ansar brigades (a paramilitary force of Bengalis), and border guards and hundreds and thousands of civilians who took up arms in the defense of their country.[1] With their gallantry and war exploits, they were able to neutralize the well-equipped armed forces of Pakistan. When India interceded directly in the war in late November 1971, the Pakistan forces were defeated and Bangladesh became independent in December 1971. Trained Bengali military personnel who were in West Pakistan at the beginning of the war of liberation were relieved of their duties and detained and isolated in camps in West Pakistan. Those who fought the war are known as the "freedom fighters," and those who were in West Pakistan and came back to a free Bangladesh became known as the "returnees."

The immediate problem facing the Mujib era (1972–1975) was how to integrate the regular army personnel with the civilians who fought during the war of liberation as well the regular military forces who returned from Pakistan. Mujib distrusted the military officers trained during the Pakistan period and especially Zia, who announced the independence of Bangladesh over the radio on March 27, 1971.

Mujib also did not want the Bangladesh military to be involved in the political process and consequently kept it isolated and ill-equipped. At the same time, Mujib was keenly aware that he needed a praetorian guard that would be loyal to him first, and then the country. He built up such a force known as the Jatiya Rakhi Bahini (National Security Force), composed of regular military personnel he could trust and the civilian fighters. He provided them with modern facilities, equipment, and advanced training. This force rivaled the regular military force. This action, followed by an attempt to concentrate all political power in himself, cost Mujib popular support. Eventually the military engineered a coup and assassinated him and most members of his family.

Zia, who replaced him, disbanded the Jatiya Rakhi Bahini and quickly integrated the returnees into higher-level posts in the military previously denied to them, causing a split between the freedom fighters and the returnees. Up until the late 1980s, this split in the military led to several coups and countercoups. But as the military officers and other personnel are becoming solely recruited and trained in Bangladesh, the negative impact of the split is fading rapidly. A more serious internal conflict was the radicalization of the soldiers who firmly believed in the concept of a people's army, patterned after the People's Liberation Army of China.[2] Such groups, led by the leftist Jatiyo Smajtantrik Dal (JSD, National Socialist Party), were behind serious mutinies at Bogra and Dhaka in

1977. Careful selection and retention programs seem to have reduced the danger of mutiny, and the increasing role of the Bangladesh military in United Nations peacekeeping operations has further discouraged radical breakdown.

A Praetorian Army?

Reviewing the period from the assassination of Mujib until the assassination of Zia (August 1975–May 1981) and the period of Ershad's rule (March 1982–December 1990), we find that Bangladesh has been under military rule or domination by the military for much of the time since its independence. Zia, of course, liberalized his regime and ended martial law, but the people never forgot that he came to power through the military and that the military would supply his ultimate support. Ershad too took steps toward liberalization and ended martial law, but the people did not overlook his military connection either. However, when demonstrations led to his downfall in December 1990, the military did not come to his assistance.

Clearly the military has been a major force in Bangladeshi politics. In order to meet Ershad's desire, the military would have required being given the constitutional status to play that role. Before he assumed power, Ershad demanded a role for the military through a national security council, invoking what is often called the "Turkish model."

When the government in 1990 returned to a civilian rule, in which the military was constitutionally subordinated to the government and a national security council was not created, the potential for military intervention remained. Indeed, as history has shown, military establishments that have taken power demonstrate a high propensity for repeating the exercise.[3]

In 2007 the assessment of high propensity to intervene held, as Bangladesh stood on the brink of political and social disaster and the armed forces once again stepped in but, given the context of the twenty-first century, did not directly assume power. The major contextual differences resulted from a transformation of the Bangladesh armed forces as a principal international peacekeeping force. A second factor is the primacy of its role as a disaster management force. These two factors, when added to its informal role as a supporting element to the caretaker government in the conduct of a free and fair election in Bangladesh, provides the Bangladesh military sufficient responsibilities in the functioning of the state without the need to be formally in charge of the country.

Rebellion in the Chittagong Hill Tracts

In Chapter 14 it was noted that the Bangladesh population includes several tribal groups. The tribes that live in the plains have settled into the general population, but those in the Chittagong Hill Tracts (CHT) rebelled against the established government in Dhaka, whether Pakistani or Bangladeshi.[6] The Hill Tracts tribals have usually demanded autonomy, although some leaders have demanded independence, however impractical that may be. Autonomy usually means local self-government and restoration of land rights that have been taken by migrating Bengalis from the plains. An agreement (sometimes referred to as a treaty) signed in December 1997, if actually accepted by the tribals and the government, may herald a new era of peace and cooperation.

In the eighteenth century the land of the Chakmas (the largest tribe) was an independent kingdom, although it paid revenue to the Mughal and later to the British rulers. Various measures passed by the British in the nineteenth century recognized the separateness of the Hill Tracts and its people from the territory directly administered by the British. By 1900 it was described as an "excluded area," meaning that it was excluded not only from direct British rule but also from settlement by nontribals. Although there was some question about the fate of the Hill Tracts at the time of Indian and Pakistani independence in 1947, the area was eventually assigned to Pakistan. In response, some tribals, mainly Chakmas, crossed into Indian territory.

The Pakistani government was not certain that the tribals would give full allegiance to Pakistan. It withdrew an 1881 regulation that permitted the tribals to police themselves and assigned regular Pakistani police to the task. By 1950 the government allowed the settlement of several hundred Muslim families in the Hill Tracts, a direct violation of the 1900 regulation, although the regulation would be confirmed later in the 1956 constitution of Pakistan. The building of the Kaptai hydroelectric station on the Karnaphuli River displaced a large number of tribals whose land was submerged by the reservoir.

With Bangladeshi independence in 1971 Mujibur Rahman assured the tribals that agreements limiting land acquisition by nontribals would be enforced, but enforcement over the years has been lax, and tribal leaders formally demanded autonomy, as described above. Mujib, however, on a tour of the Hill Tracts on February 13, 1973, proclaimed, "From today, there are no more tribal subgroups in Bangladesh; everyone is a Bengalee." In the election that year, the Solidarity Party of the tribals won two seats in the parliament. After Mujib's assassination in 1975, the Solidarity Party created an armed wing, the Shanti Bahini.

In 1976, under Ziaur Rahman, a plan was made to resettle poor Bangladeshis from Chittagong district to the Hill Tracts. The tribals responded with attacks on the settlers, and the government in turn responded with military action against the tribals, many of whom fled to India as refugees and set up a government in absentia. Throughout the Sattar, Ershad, and Khaleda Zia periods armed conflicts alternated with meetings between the tribals and government officials. No settlement could be reached, and the problem seemed intractable.[4]

Nonetheless, the government and the tribals continued their negotiations. Finally, on December 2, 1997, a treaty was signed between the government and the political wing of the Shanti Bahini. The agreement envisages a high level of autonomy for each of the three districts that comprise the Hill Tracts, which includes taxing authority and the maintenance of law and order. Nontribal residents, who compose almost half of the population, have objected to the agreement, as their representatives will compose only one-third of the membership of the new regional council. Some of the nontribals who have improperly obtained land will presumably be expelled. In short, most of the demands of the tribals have been met. Some have concluded that the treaty is unconstitutional, as it creates a level of autonomy that does not exist elsewhere in Bangladesh and is also not subject to ratification by parliament.

But if implemented in full, it will be a major step toward the settlement of a long-standing sore in civil relations in Bangladesh. A decade later in 2007 the treaty, according to scholars and practitioners, remains partially implemented. In terms of the implementation of local autonomy, in the regional council and the three districts the head is a tribal person. However, the tribal demand for the removal of Bengali settlers and the redeployment of the military in a limited number of bases remains to be implemented. The region, on the other hand, continues to be of great strategic and economic importance to Bangladesh. CHT is the primary source of hydroelectric power for the country. Some of the rivers flow into the port of Chittagong and are a breeding ground for the local fish population, and CHT supplies timber for the country. For all practical purposes the CHT will continue to witness low-level violence, sometimes between the tribals and the settlers and the government and sometimes among themselves, unless changes in the Indian eastern provinces spill over and trigger more violence.

Government Versus Opposition and Vice Versa

Until the fall of Husain Muhammad Ershad in December 1990 and the free and fair election that followed in February 1991, governments had overwhelming power, including the parliamentary and presidential regimes of Mujibur Rahman and the military-dominated regimes of Ziaur Rahman and Ershad. There was opposition, but rules inherited from the British, the Special Powers Act enacted by Mujib, and martial law ordinances allowed the government to detain dissidents. Statements and demonstrations were thus dealt with harshly.

The election of February 1991 brought about a large opposition in parliament, capable of hindering the operation of the ministry. However, there was an early period of cooperation. The Bangladesh Nationalist Party preferred to retain a presidential system for Bangladesh, whereas the Awami League wished to change the system back to the parliamentary system prescribed in Bangladesh's original constitution. (The Awami League held this view despite the fact that the presidential system had been instituted by the Awami League and its leader, Mujibur Rahman.) After the election the BNP modified its stance and was willing to change to a parliamentary system. The BNP won fewer votes than the Awami League and its allies, and this brought into question Khaleda Zia's election as president by direct vote. A joint committee was set up, agreement was reached on changing the system, and it was confirmed by a constitutional amendment.[5]

The major event leading up to the opposition boycott of parliament was a by-election held in Magura district on March 20, 1994. The seat had been considered safe by the Awami League, but the BNP candidate was declared the winner. The Awami League immediately called foul and demanded a re-polling. It is not at all clear that there was any electoral rigging, and in fact the Election Commission declared that there was not. On May 5 the opposition, including the Awami League, the Jatiya Party, and the Jamaat-i-Islam, began a boycott of parliament, which grew into regular demonstrations and general strikes. Under the constitution, a member's absence from parliament (without excuse) for ninety days would result in the loss of his or her seat. The opposition demanded a change in the constitution to provide that future elections be held under a "neutral caretaker government," a body to be appointed by the president. The BNP refused to accept this demand on the basis that parliamentary systems do not work this way.

Nonetheless, Prime Minister Khaleda Zia said she would resign thirty days before the election. This did not suit the opposition, as it would not set a precedent that would have to be followed in the future—only a constitutional amendment would be binding—and the demonstrations and general strikes continued. A prominent commentator wrote, "The lack of a worldwide civil society . . . is why people of struggling Bangladesh are caged by 72- and 96-hour *hartals* [general strikes] that virtually closed down the impoverished country. The reason for their predicament is the impractical stubbornness of their leaders as to how a civil society should resolve its problems in a civilized manner."[6] A "civilized manner" was not found. On December 28, 1994, the opposition resigned from parliament. The speaker found a technicality that allowed him to reject the resignations, but on June 20, 1995, the seats were declared vacant under the ninety-day rule. Consequently it would be impossible to pass a constitutional amendment, as many more than one-third of the parliamentary seats were vacated. The Khaleda government held on for a while but resigned on November 24.

A new election was held on February 15, 1996, with the opposition boy-cotting. The BNP won almost all seats and immediately passed a constitutional amendment incorporating exactly what the opposition had demanded. It there-upon resigned and turned the government over to a "neutral caretaker govern-ment." The Awami League won a plurality in the June election and made an agreement with the Jatiya Party that permitted the Awami League under Sheikh Hasina Wajid to form a government.

The BNP soon found issues it could use to begin strikes and demonstrations. Among these were the treaty with India on the sharing of the Ganges water. The BNP said the treaty was biased toward India, which demonstrated the pro-India tilt of the Awami League. The government was also discussing with India transit rights across Bangladesh territory—to the BNP more "proof" of the pro-India policy. Demonstrations ensued, and a number of BNP members were arrested. To this was added the alleged desire of the Awami League to export natural gas ("our birthright") to India and grant transit rights to India for crossing Bangladesh ter-ritory to reach the northeastern areas of India. The BNP and its allies, the Ershad faction of the Jatiya Party and the Jamaat, also boycotted parliament and thus the legislature operated without a sitting opposition. The first attorney general has commented on this pattern of behavior: "Even if one party cannot show respect to the convictions of the other party, mutual tolerance is essential."[7]

At the end of the Hasina government, a duly constituted caretaker government took over the governance of Bangladesh and conducted a relatively free and fair election on October 1, 2001. A BNP government came to power and the oppo-sition Awami League soon found issues to boycott the parliament and go to the street to demand a fair share of participation in executive and legislative decision making. The tipping point for opposition distrust was the constitutional amend-ment to raise the retirement age of judges from sixty-five to sixty-seven years. This change provided the elements of the opposition common ground and raised sus-picion in regard to the intention of the BNP government toward a smooth tran-sition of power. Events associated with the formation of the caretaker government in October 2006 for the next election confirmed their suspicion. The system broke down to such an extent that a state of emergency was declared and a military-backed caretaker government was established in January 2007.

The culture of material greed and violence that permeated Bangladesh politics since 1971 was so debilitating that the caretaker government was unable to con-duct its constitutionally determined role of supporting the Election Commission and conducting the parliamentary election within the stated ninety-day period. The caretaker government of 2007 has provided itself an extra-constitutional role of transforming the fundamental institutions of governance that it expects to complete by holding a free and fair election by December 2008.

Nonetheless, the conflict between government and opposition is by no means over. With institutional changes such as an autonomous election commission, an independent anticorruption commission, and the separation of the judiciary from the executive, the conflict may be reduced. One of the prerequisites of a functioning parliamentary democracy is a high level of cooperation between the government and the opposition. In Bangladesh neither side practiced cooperation. Moreover, absence from parliament deprives the members' constituents of representation in what is supposed to be a representative government. This behavior does not bode well for a smoothly running democracy.

Assessing the outcome of the reforms being undertaken by the caretaker government of 2007 is difficult. Suffice to say, the longer officials take to carry out the reforms they deem vital to transfer power to an elected government, the higher the risk of social unrest leading to political demonstrations and street violence, which Bangladesh can least afford. The longer the caretaker government takes to separate the judiciary from the executive branch, the greater the risk that entrenched groups like the bureaucracy and the political parties will be able to significantly slow down the process and maintain the status quo. The caretaker government's ability to bring corruption charges against people of significance provided the initial legitimacy for their action. However, should they fail to proceed effectively, the people are likely to turn against them. At the beginning of 2008 there are some signs that the people doubt the effectiveness of the caretaker system of temporary government. The two main political parties seem to be uniting in their demand for elections much earlier than the December 2008 election scheduled by the Election Commission. The two main parties are far apart in their position on the trials of collaborators and the role of the Islamic political parties. Unless the two main political parties and the caretaker government sit together and work out all the modalities of transfer of power, Bangladesh at the end of 2008 may face a far worse crisis and conflict than it witnessed during October 2006 and January 2007.

The Rise and Fall of Extremism and Terrorism

The fundamental question facing Bangladesh in regard to extremism and terrorism is whether either is internal to the system or is linked to global terrorism. In Bangladesh there are three types of extremism. The first is linked to the rise of Islamic fundamentalism and the second, to left-wing extremism. The third, on the eastern border of Bangladesh, is an evolving extremism linked to events in India and Burma. Islam has always played a role in the body politics of east Bengal, East Pakistan, and Bangladesh. In the early nineteenth century, political Islam supported the unity of the Muslims of India and the foundation of a separate Muslim nation. In the 1950s, Islam in East Pakistan was for social justice and equity. In the 1970s, Islam became a force of evil, as Pakistan used Islam as an excuse to systematically kill Bangladeshis during the liberation war of 1971. During that war two types of people collaborated with the Pakistani regime to try to fend off an independent Bangladesh. The first group were the political and social elites who took on the role of defending the actions of the Pakistani army in international forums and national and regional forums. The political party primarily associated with the Pakistani effort to deny the independence of Bangladesh was Jaamat-e-Islami.

The second group associated with collaboration were members of the Al-Badr, Al-Shams, which were religious groups, and Razakar and Peace committees that were formed in each neighborhood of Bangladesh to act as informers to the Pakistani regime. In the mid–1970s there was a return to Islam principally through the Eighth Amendment, which declared Islam the state religion of Bangladesh. Over time Islamic religious-based political parties like the Jamaat-e-Islami, Islamic Oyiko Party, and others were slowly permitted to become a regular part of the political process. While the Islamic parties never received any significant popular vote, in the last political government the Islamic parties had less than twenty seats in a 300-member parliament and two ministers of the national government. During the Afghanistan–Russian war period of the 1980s Bangladeshi Muslims participated in the war in support of Islam. Though few in number, the returned Bangladeshis had a role in radicalizing small, isolated segments of society. Three groups—the Jama'atul Mujaheddin Bangladesh (JMB), Harkat-ul-jihad-al-Islam (Huji-BD), and the Jagrata Muslim Janata Bangladesh (JMJB)—are principal proponents of Islamic radicalism in Bangladesh. After the Russian defeat in Afghanistan, the first Gulf War, September 11, and the Iraq war, these groups took on a more violent role in Bangladesh society, culminating in the explosion of over 450 small bombs in a coordinated attack on sixty-three of the sixty-four districts of Bangladesh on August 17, 2005. Many have opined that the Bangladesh government of Khaleda Zia, because of its electoral alliance with Islamic parties, turned a deaf ear to the growing Islamic extremism. With mounting international pressure to control extremism, the government of Khaleda Zia took steps to ban the radical parties, and by May 2006 arrested the principals, put them on trial, and sentenced them to death. The caretaker government carried out the death sentences in April 2007 and gained control over the radical elements. But it is too early to know whether there are sleeper groups waiting for their turn.[8] Smaller radical groups like Harkat-ul-Jihad-e-Islami Bangladesh (HuJI[B]) and Allahr Dal (Allah's Party) have also been cornered and isolated.

One of the spillover effects of extremism, especially since January 2007, is the underlying conflict within the Bangladesh political culture of the role of collaborators during the war of liberation. Since the middle 1970s, the Islamic parties, especially Jamaat, have been supporting the BNP. To counter their growing influence, the Awami League in late 2006 formed an unfortunate alliance with the Khelafat Andolon Party, another Islamic political party, in preparation for the national election of January 2007, losing its well-earned reputation as a secular party. The caretaker government formed on January 12, 2007, has undertaken major reforms to transform the fundamental institutions in Bangladesh to propel Bangladesh toward democracy. In doing so, however, it has unwittingly opened up the sensitive issue of collaborators, who they were and what their role will be in the political development of Bangladesh.[9]

One way that Bangladesh society in general and those who fought for the liberation of the country in particular are attempting to curb the rising role of Islam in the Bangladesh political system is to have individuals and parties declared unfit for political participation. Following the liberation war Bangladesh was unable to bring to trial the Pakistani war criminals and their Bengali and Bihari collaborators. International pressure and a weak Bangladesh declined to try the leadership of the Pakistan armed forces, who committed not just criminal but genocidal acts. In the process Bengali collaborators also escaped trial and over a period of years were slowly reintegrated and reinstated in the political structure of Bangladesh. With systemic reform in Bangladesh today, the divisive question of collaborators has once again resurfaced. Although the Bangladesh Collaborators (Special Tribunal) Act of 1972 was repealed in 1975, the International Crimes Act of 1972, which remains on the books, is being considered as the legal framework for trying the collaborators. There is no question that collaborators must be tried. However, due diligence must be given to its impact on the overall welfare of the society. Will it lead to mass violence? Will it further radicalize the culture and society of Bangladesh?

An even weaker form of radicalism and extremism is often linked to the Gono Mukti Fouz (GMF), Purbo Banglar Communist Party (PBCP), and the New Biplobi Communist Party (NBCP). Located in the western districts of Bangladesh, they sometimes want to establish a Hindu enclave within Bangladesh but are primarily involved in power plays with other factions loyal to establishing communist rule in Bangladesh. As mentioned earlier in this chapter, the Chittagong Hill Tracts area of Bangladesh continues to have a low-level insurgency movement seeking autonomy for tribal people. Because of the proximity of CHT to some eastern provinces of India and also Burma, extremists from these two countries have found refuge in CHT. Two identified groups from India are the National Liberation Front of Tripura and the United Liberation Front of Assam. These two organizations undertake terroristic actions in India, stressing the relationship between Bangladesh and India. Burmese groups taking refuge in CHT include the National United Party of Arakan, the Arakan Rohingya National Organization, and the Rohingya Solidarity Organization. While all these organizations oppose the military junta of Burma, some are linked to the wider Islamic extremism of Southeast Asia.

The current global strategic scenario nourishes the development of terrorism, especially in a country like Bangladesh. If regional political machinations are factored out and national political positioning for power is held in check, the likelihood of radicalism and extremism in Bangladesh is limited. However, holding it in check will require constant vigilance. Bangladeshi organizations such as the National Security Intelligence and the Armed Forces Intelligence, as well as the intelligence gathering capacity of the Home Ministry, police, and other security forces, must be constantly upgraded. Presently, while these agencies have performed credibly, significant modernization must take place in order for them to stop the rise of radicalism, extremism, and terrorism in Bangladesh.

NOTES

1. For an interesting account by the mother of a civilian volunteer, see Jahanara Imam, *Of Blood and Fire* (Dhaka: Academic Publishers, 1990), translated from Bengali by Mustafizur Rahman.

2. For the text of a statement purportedly made by Taher, see Lawrence Lifschultz, *Bangladesh: The Unfinished Revolution* (London: Zed, 1979).

3. See Talukder Maniruzzaman, *Military Withdrawal from Politics: A Comparative Study* (Cambridge, Mass.: Ballinger, 1987).

4. The source for much of the material in this section is Naeem Mohaiemen, "A History of the Chittagong Hill Tracts," *Daily Star* (Dhaka), November 26, 1997.

5. For more detail, see Craig Baxter, "Bangladesh: Can Democracy Survive?" *Current History,* April 1996, pp. 182–186. See also Golam Hossain, "Bangladesh in 1995: Politics of Intransigence," *Asian Survey* 36, no. 2 (TK): 196–203; and Stanley A. Kochanek, "Bangladesh in 1996: The 25th Year of Independence," *Asian Survey* 37, no. 2 (TK): 136–142.

6. Mizanur Rahman Shelley, *Independent* (Dhaka), October 24, 1995.

7. Syed Ishtiaq Ahmed, *Dhaka Courier*, November 24, 2000, p. 19.

8. See also an assessment of Islamic radicalism by Rohan Gunaratna, director of the International Center for Political Violence and Terrorism, Nanyang Technological University, Singapore to the *Daily Star,* January 19, 2008.

9. The South Asia Terrorism Portal (SAP) has a weekly assessment of terrorism in South Asia. SAP did an assessment of terrorism in Bangladesh in 2006.

SUGGESTED READINGS

Ahamed, Emajuddin. *Military Rule and the Myth of Democracy.* Dhaka: University Press, 1988.

Ahmed, A. F. Salahuddin. *Bengali Nationalism and the Emergence of Bangladesh.* Dhaka: University Press, 2001.

Baxter, Craig. *Bangladesh: From a Nation to a State.* Boulder: Westview, 1997.

Bleie, Tone. *Tribal Peoples, Nationalism, and the Human Rights Challenge: The Advance of Bangladesh.* Dhaka: University Press, 2005.

Cohen, Stephen P. *The Indian Army.* Berkeley: University of California Press, 1971.

_____. *The Pakistan Army.* Berkeley: University of California Press, 1984.

Dhaka Courier, November 10, 2000, supplement, "Rule of Law and Democratic Accountability," contains a number of articles by Bangladeshi scholars and commentators on the subject.

Hossain, Golam. *General Ziaur Rahman and the BNP*. Dhaka: University Press, 1988.

Kabir, Bhuian Md. Monoar. *The Politics and Development of the Jamaat-E-Islami Bangladesh*. Dhaka: A. H. Development Publishers, 2006.

Kennedy, Charles H., and David J. Louscher. eds. *Civil and Military Interaction in Asia and Africa*. Leiden: E. J. Brill, 1991. Includes chapters on Bangladesh by Craig Baxter and Syedur Rahman and on Pakistan by Hasan-Askari Rizvi.

Khan, Zillur Rahman. *Leadership in the Least Developed Nation: Bangladesh*. Syracuse, N.Y.: Maxwell School, Syracuse University, 1983.

Maniruzzaman, Talukder. *The Bangladesh Revolution and Its Aftermath*. Dhaka: Bangladesh Books International, 1980.

_____. *Military Withdrawal from Politics: A Comparative Study*. Cambridge, Mass.: Ballinger, 1987.

Mason, Philip. *A Matter of Honour: An Account of the Indian Army, Its Officers, and Men*. London: Jonathan Cape, 1974.

Olsen, Edward A., and Stephen Jurika Jr., eds. *The Armed Forces in Contemporary Asian Societies*. Boulder: Westview, 1985. Includes chapters by G. L. Wood on India, S. P. Cohen on Pakistan, and J. Lundstead on Bangladesh.

Shelley, Mizanur Rahman. *The Chittagong Hill Tracts of Bangladesh: The Untold Story*. Dhaka: Centre for Development Research, 1992.

18

Modernization and Development: Prospects and Problems

Bangladesh is often described as the "largest poorest" nation in the world, and the title of a book on Bangladeshi political development refers to the country as "the least developed nation."[1] According to World Bank data, Bangladesh ranks 167 of 206 countries in the usual measures of wealth or poverty. The gross national product (GNP) per capita was only US$370 in 1999 on the purchasing power parity basis. In 2005, a similar data review showed that Bangladesh ranked 155 of 207 countries, with a GNP of $470.[2] In this chapter, we shall look at the economic and social aspects of political development—an especially problematic concern in Bangladesh if the soaring and geometrically compounding pressure of population on resources is not abated, and soon.

The World's Largest Poorest Nation: Economic Challenges

The two principal goals of Bangladesh, as propounded by Zia, Ershad, and the parliamentary governments of Hasina Wajed and Khaleda Zia, have been attaining self-sufficiency in food grains and reducing the rate of population growth. The two are intimately related. The amount of land available for cultivation is basically constant, changing favorably only to the extent that it can be double- or triple-cropped through better water management, including irrigation. Hence, as the population increases, the amount of land per capita decreases. The challenge is to increase production per unit of land at a faster rate than population growth.

The pattern of land ownership is critical to agricultural productivity, and here the picture is quite dismal and unlikely to change. Small farms, defined as those owning less than 2.49 acres, compose 80 percent of total holdings. In addition, 50 percent of rural households involved in agricultural production are landless, defined as those having less than 0.05 hectares of land. Out of a total of 14 million agricultural households 11 million are landless. For agricultural production to increase, double and triple cropping is essential. In 2003–2004, 51 percent of land was double cropped and only 13 percent triple cropped. Fertilizer use has correspondingly gone up from 1.2 metric tons in 1984–1985 to 2.8 million tons in 1999–2000. In the ten-year period from 1983–1984 to 1993–1994, rice production rose from 14 million tons to more than 18 million tons. The nature of farm credit is also changing. Where once it was more tilted toward the traditional village moneylenders, today it is more identified with government-backed agencies. The development of microlending has shifted the nature of farm credit toward the private sector. By 2003–2004 the production of rice rose to 26 million tons, prompting claims of a high degree of self-sufficiency in food grains. Despite increased food production, there are serious shortages in the average diet, in terms of quantity as well as quality of nutrients.

Much of the protein consumed is derived from lentils. Production of fish, another important part of the traditional Bengali diet, has declined. Total production of meat and poultry has increased, but on a per capita basis it has declined. Bangladesh is always subject to disaster (floods tend to destroy approximately 10 percent of total crop production), and food stocks are depleted rapidly, requiring international assistance.

Industrial production in Bangladesh is primarily driven by the garment industry. Between 2004 and 2005 it grew at a rate of over 20 percent, making it the seventh largest exporter to the United States. This labor-intensive industry has provided a significant boost to female employment in Bangladesh. Overall, the rate of growth of the Bangladesh economy hovered around 5 percent for much of the 1990s and into the first decade of the twenty-first century. Part of this growth rate may be attributed to remittances by Bangladeshi workers. In 2001–2002, Bangladeshi expatriates remitted $2.5 billion, which increased to $4.4 billion in 2006–2007. The GDP is led by the service sector, which contributed 49 percent of growth in 2000 and 52 percent in 2006. The industrial sector contributed 25 percent in 2000 and 28 percent in 2006. The agricultural sector provided 25 percent in 2000 and only 21 percent in 2006.

The world largest poorest nation, however, has serious problems. It has an external debt of over $20 billion and imports 28 percent more than it exports. In 2000, 36 percent of its population had a standard of living of less than $1 a day and an overwhelming 82.8 percent has a standard of living of less than $2 a day. Fifty-five percent of its rural population lives below the national poverty line and 29.4 percent of its urban population lives below the national poverty line. The political implications of this picture are very serious for the public sector and the economic well-being of the country.[3]

Limitations on Resources, Human and Natural

Bangladesh is a nation with few natural resources beyond its fertile soil and abundant natural gas. Much of the soil is replenished each year with silt deposited by rivers during annual floods. The delta on which most of the country is situated serves as an interconnected outlet for much of the flow of the Ganges River system and is the only outlet for the Brahmaputra and the Meghna. Other rivers include the Teesta, which falls into the Ganges in northwest Bangladesh, and the Karnaphuli in the southeast. The Karnaphuli has been harnessed as Bangladesh's only hydroelectric station.

As already noted, a major source of power for Bangladesh is the abundant natural gas found in much of the country. Currently Bangladesh has 24.75 trillion cubic feet of gas reserve. With Jumuna River bridge construction completed, the entire country can be served by gas and electrical power but is dependent on foreign oil for power generation. Bangladesh produces approximately 3,000 megawatts of electrical power, but the total need for the country is more than 6,000 megawatts. Although there has been much searching, hopes for the discovery of oil have thus far gone unmet. The government has opened international investment for the development of gas fields, with the hope that some petroleum may be turned up as well. Limited supplies of coal are known to exist, but mining them at present would not be cost-effective. There are no other known exploitable mineral deposits.

The rivers of Bangladesh are essential for the water supply and serve as an intricate transportation system. But they also divide the country and sometimes are so wide that they create hazards for travelers in storms; moreover, river flooding can be devastating, as was seen especially in 1988, 1998, and 2004.

In 1988, 61 percent of Bangladesh was inundated. In 1998 the figure was 68 percent and in 2004 it was 38 percent. Approximately 48 million people were impacted by the flood in 1988, 31 million in 1998, and 30 million in 2004. In 2007, although floods inundated only 7 percent of the land, 16 million people were affected. Although significant improvements have been made in flood control in Bangladesh, until India and Bangladesh resolve questions in regard to dividing the waters of the Ganges and establishing regional flood control strategies, Bangladesh will continue to be subject to flood disaster.

Bangladesh is also beset by problems in the area of human resources. In 1998 about 60 percent of Bangladeshi adults were estimated to be illiterate—

75 percent of females and 50 percent of males—high figures even with the rel-atively low standards by which literacy is measured. The government main-tains that all eligible students are attending primary school, but this figure is probably inflated inasmuch as it represents the number attending at some time during the reporting year. Female literacy rates and school attendance rates are lower than those for males. The World Bank Indicator database 2007 shows that for the year 2000, ninth grade completion rate was only 40 percent. It is interesting to note that the female completion rate was 41 percent while the male rate was 38 percent. Furthermore, 40 percent of those aged 15 to 24 years were not at school or work. Of those only 11.8 percent were males and an incredible 68.9 percent, females.

In 2003 over 18 million students were in the primary school system, another 7 million in secondary schools. Students attending higher secondary schools numbered more than 1.6 million and those attending universities totaled 1.1 million, with approximately 38 thousand in the private universities. About 37 percent of the university students were women. Many Bangladeshi students take culturally enriching courses of study that, however, are not likely to con-tribute directly to development; technical education lags behind the liberal arts. With the private sector taking a more active role in higher education, computer science and business administration leads recent development in higher educa-tion in Bangladesh. Both fields are market driven. In 2001 the participation rate for primary schools (5–9 years) was 86 percent, for secondary schools (10–14 years) 19 percent, and for higher education (15–24 years) 30 percent.

The average population growth rate was 2.4 percent from 1980 to 1990. In 2000 the population growth rate was 1.5 percent, and it is estimated that the growth rate will continue to be 1.5 percent until 2015. Considerable effort is being given to population planning programs, with sizable contributions from foreign governments and public and private organizations. Population growth, which places heavy pressure on development programs as well as on education, employment, food, and health, has been significantly lowered. The growth of the urban population has been significant: from 9.3 percent in 1975 to 24.0 percent in 1998 and an estimated 30.8 percent in 2015, thus placing further strain on such things as food delivery, transportation, and housing. The com-pletion of a rail-cum-road bridge across the Jamuna River has enabled the con-nection of gas-generated electric power to the southwest region that once depended primarily on imported oil. The bridge, of course, has also improved the movement of goods and people.

Bangladesh is host to a wide range of endemic and potentially epidemic trop-ical diseases. Malaria, cholera, and other intestinal diseases are chief among them. Coupled with malnutrition, these diseases seriously debilitate much of the population, which in turn lowers the level of human resources. Fortunately, international groups have provided aid in the form of health delivery systems and drinking water. Dhaka itself is the site of the largest laboratory in the world studying cholera and other intestinal diseases. Rapid urbanization has also caused both economic and political problems. With good reason, governments in Bangladesh, as elsewhere, are concerned about the potential for urban unrest. Accordingly, urban areas receive greater attention than rural from political leaders and economic planners.[4]

Political Uncertainty

The frequent changes of government in Bangladesh and the swings in economic policy have acted as disincentives to investors, both domestic and foreign. The Zia and Ershad regimes moved far from the doctrinaire socialism espoused (even if not fully implemented) by the Mujib government. The divestitures of some government-held enterprises during the Ershad period encouraged local entrepreneurs. The Awami League government under Sheikh Hasina Wajid has decidedly forsworn the socialist program and follows an economic program hardly different from that of the Bangladesh Nationalist Party under Khaleda Zia, but much needed divestiture of state-owned enterprises has been painfully slow.

Entrepreneurship was not a widely held skill in Bangladesh before 1971. Before independence, many of the small shops in the urban areas were owned and a percentage of the skilled labor provided by the small Bihari group, which comprised about 0.6 percent of the population. This group of Urdu speakers migrated in 1947 mainly from the Indian province of Bihar to East Pakistan, rather than West Pakistan. The group generally supported Pakistan in 1971 and has paid an internationally publicized penalty. Some Biharis have been transported to Pakistan and some remain in camps, but many, though they may live separately, have integrated themselves into the Bangladeshi economy and speak Bengali rather than Urdu.

Two sectors have driven the Bangladeshi interest in business—garment production and expatriate labor. The more traditional private sector was involved in the film industry as well as import and export, especially chemicals and pharmaceuticals. Profits in the garment sector have largely contributed to the development of investment in higher education. Children of government employees and military men often join retirees from both groups in entrepreneurship. The political uncertainty facing the country, however, inhibits many of these people from making large investments that may have slower returns—a problem for foreign investors. Added to this has been the feeling that Bangladesh has little to offer in labor, markets, and resources, especially when compared with the huge potential of neighboring India. Finally, recent revelations of corruption have negated the limited advantages Bangladesh has to attract foreign investors.

The Future

Bangladesh has received large amounts of foreign assistance in efforts to ease its immediate problems and build for the future. Almost all of the aid in the period just after independence came in the form of relief and rehabilitation for an economy and society shattered by the experience of civil war. In more recent years too, a substantial portion of foreign aid has been received in the form of food supplies rather than assistance for long-term development. Aid received from members of the Aid to Bangladesh consortium in 1998 amounted to about $1.3 billion.

Almost every nation and public and private international organization in existence has assisted Bangladesh. The United States, the European Community, and a few other countries have supplied food for survival, and the Islamic oil states have lent funds to help with energy; some, especially Saudi Arabia, have provided money for Islamic religious projects as well. Meanwhile, many of the private nongovernmental organizations (NGOs), such as the U.S. CARE and the British Oxfam, have worked more directly on developmental programs in agriculture, family planning, and health. Japan has become the largest donor, followed by the United States. As noted, however, the economic situation in Bangladesh is such that the immediate problems demand priority. Development receives attention—often well-planned attention—but it must come second.

The economic future for Bangladesh is bleak. The population, unless a miraculous turnabout occurs, will rise from 125 million in 1998 to 161 million by 2015. It is doubtful that agricultural production can continue to advance at a rate to maintain current food supplies, which are already below those considered necessary. It is equally doubtful that nonagricultural employment opportunities will expand at anywhere near the rate needed to provide for a population even now severely afflicted with unemployment and underemployment. But there are bright spots. The mortality rate among children under five has dropped from 148 per 1,000 in 1990 to 77 in 2004 and 73 in 2005. Seventy-four percent of the population now has access to safe water, while 53 percent of the urban population has access to improved sanitation.

Bangladesh's political future is also uncertain. A potential always exists for a mass outbreak of violence in the urban population and increasingly among the rural peoples. However, changes brought about in January 2007 bode well for the country. A caretaker government was formed to conduct a free and fair election, leading to institutional reform and development likely to have a profound impact on the political future of Bangladesh. The reforms currently taking place will impact the political and social infrastructures of Bangladesh. Notable among them are the following:

- Separating the judicial system from the executive will permit a more independent judiciary to apply the rule of law without interference, direct or indirect, from the executive or legislative branches of government.
- An independent Election Commission is focusing on setting up the most appropriate modalities for conducting a free and fair election process through establishing a sound voter registration process and a photo identification card. In addition, it is applying rules of authentication to political parties and their financial and programmatic reporting system.
- An independent Anticorruption Commission now has sufficient power and personnel to aggressively attack pervasive corruption in the economic, political, and social system of Bangladesh. Initial actions taken against the more blatant corruption among the political elites has had a very positive impact on the overall psyche of Bangladesh. It must also move against corrupt individuals, systems, and processes that have impeded economic, business, and administrative advances.
- A reinvigorated Public Service Commission will focus on recruiting civil servants outside of the influence of the executive branch of government. Separating the Public Service Commission from the executive branch will make it possible for the civil service to become more professionalized and true to its mission of serving the political executive. As a move forward to tackling corruption and political interference, the Public Service Commission should emulate the Senior Executive Service of the United States or, alternatively, examine the possibility of establishing a ministerial cabinet similar to the one in France.
- A human rights commission should be established with sufficient checks that does not permit executive interference in its independent action to prevent human rights violations. A narrow definition of human rights is likely to be incompatible with the desires and needs of the people and may be detrimental to the effectiveness of the commission's mission.
- A strong local government system will be able to take a more active role in the development process and distance itself from intrusion by the members of the national parliament or the members of the national executive branch.

The paradox of Bangladesh is that it is a poverty-stricken country prone to natural disasters, with severe population pressure and lack of resources. But Bangladesh has made serious progress toward social, economic, and political development. It is a society where microlending and the garment industry have seriously changed the social network and the role of women in society. It has an economy that, according to the Human Development Index, has impacted the overall life expectancy, educational participation, and standard of living of the average Bangladeshi such that between 2003 and 2006 it moved in the rankings of countries from 177 to 137 and is expected to reach middle income status in the next two decades. It is a country that has had systematic elections for governance worked out as a process of negotiation between the government in power and the opposition and has established a transition process of the caretaker government to bring about trust within the political system. It willingly participates in international peacekeeping and contributes to global development. The challenge for Bangladesh is to build on its successes and to avoid at all cost the smallest step backward towards social, economic, and political instability.

NOTES

1. Zillur Rahman Khan, *Leadership in the Least Developed Country: Bangladesh* (Syracuse, N.Y.: Maxwell School, Syracuse University, 1983).

2. *World Development Report, 2000–2001* (New York: Oxford University Press for the World Bank, 2001), table 1, p. 274.

3. The following sources were utilized to develop the section on the economy: *Agricultural Census, 1977* (Dhaka: Ministry of Agriculture, 1977); A. M. A. Muhith, *Bangladesh in the Twenty-first Century: Towards an Industrial Society* (Dhaka: University Press, 1999); *1993 Statistical Year Book of Bangladesh* (Dhaka: Bangladesh Bureau of Statistics, 1993). Unless otherwise noted, the statistical data in this chapter are taken from the World Bank's *World Development Report, 2000–2001; Human Development Report* (New York: Oxford University Press for United Nations Development Program, 1997); or *1995 Statistical Year Book of Bangladesh* (Dhaka: Bureau of Statistics, 1995); *Statistical Yearbook of Bangladesh 2004; Statistical Pocketbook 2004,* Bangladesh Bureau of Statistics December 2005, January 2006; Md. Habibur Rahman and Somprawin Manprasert, "Landlessness and Its Impact on Economic Development: A Case Study of Bangladesh," *Journal of Social Sciences* 2, no. 2 (2006): 54–60; International Bank for Reconstruction and Development, *Bangladesh: Current Trends and Development Issues* (Washington, D.C.: IBRD, 1979), p. 41. Most data for the remaining part of this segment were taken from the *World Development Report 2007.*

4. Data for the section on human resources are taken from two major sources: *World Development Report* for various years and the *Statistical Yearbook of Bangladesh 2004.*

SUGGESTED READINGS

Ahsan, Abul, and Ahmad. S. Abbasi. *Education in a Rapidly Changing World: Focus on Bangladesh.* Dhaka: Independent University Bangladesh, 2005.

Andaleeb, Syed Saad. *Political Culture of Bangladesh: Perspectives and Analyses.* Dhaka: University Press, 2007.

Baxter, Craig. *Bangladesh: A New Nation in an Old Setting.* Boulder: Westview, 1984.

Faaland, Just, and J. R. Parkinson. *Bangladesh: The Test Case of Development.* London: Hurst, 1976.

Franda, Marcus. *Bangladesh: The First Decade.* New Delhi: South Asian Publishers, 1982. See especially Part 3, "Population and Resources."

Haroun-er-Rashid. *Economic Geography of Bangladesh.* Dhaka: University Press, 2005.

Heitzman, James, and Robert L. Worden, eds. *Bangladesh: A Country Study.* Washington, D.C.: Superintendent of Publications, 1989.

Hossain, Hameeda, ed. *Human Rights in Bangladesh 2005.* Dhaka: Ain-o-Salish, 2006.

Jannuzi, F. Thomasson, and James T. Peach. *The Agrarian Structure of Bangladesh: An Impediment to Development.* Boulder: Westview, 1980.

Khan, Zillur Rahman. *Leadership in the Least Developed Nation: Bangladesh.* Syracuse, N.Y.: Maxwell School, Syracuse University, 1983.

Kochanek, Stanley A. "Governance, Patronage Politics, and Democratic Transition in Bangladesh." *Asian Survey,* May–June 2000, pp. 530–550.

Rahman, Latifur. *The Caretaker Days and My Story.* Dhaka: Mullick, 2002.

Rehman, Sobhan. *Privatization in Bangladesh: An Agenda in Search of a Policy.* Dhaka: University Press, 2005.

PART IV

SRI LANKA

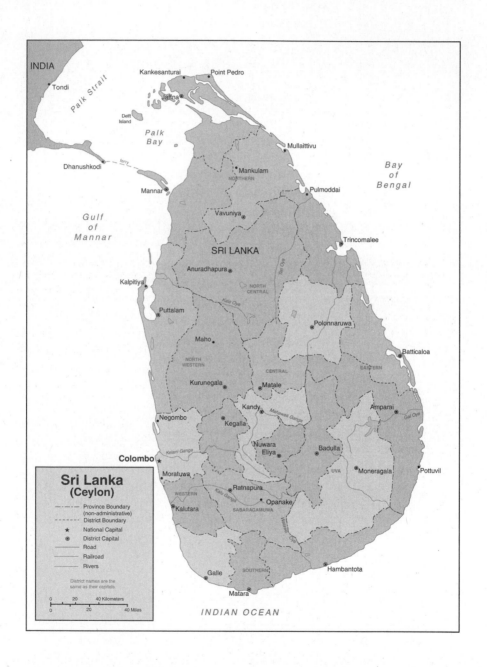

INDIA

Tondi

Palk Strait

Kankesanturai   Point Pedro

Jaffna

Delft
Island

Palk
Bay

Mullaittivu

Dhanushkodi   ferry

Mannar

Mankulam
NORTHERN

Pulmoddai

Bay
of
Bengal

Gulf
of
Mannar

Vavuniya

SRI LANKA

Trincomalee

Anuradhapura

Kalpitiya

Kala Oya

Yan Oya

NORTH
CENTRAL

Puttalam

Polonnaruwa

Maho

Batticaloa

NORTH
WESTERN

CENTRAL

EASTERN

Kurunegala   Matale

Kandy   Mahaweli Ganga   Amparai

Negombo   Gal Oya

Kegalla

Colombo ★   Nuwara
Eliya   Badulla

Kelani Ganga

Moratuwa   Moneragala

UVA   Pottuvil

Ratnapura

WESTERN   Opanake

Kalutara   Kalu Ganga   SABARAGAMUWA

Walawe Ganga

Sri Lanka
(Ceylon)

— ·· — Province Boundary
          (non-administrative)
— — — District Boundary
  ★   National Capital
  ◉   District Capital
————   Road
————   Railroad
————   Rivers

District names are the
same as their capitals.

Galle   SOUTHERN   Hambantota

0   20   40 Kilometers
0   20   40 Miles

Matara

INDIAN OCEAN

19

Political Culture
and Heritage

The political systems of the third world are marked by violent upheaval, revolution, and military intervention. Only a few nations among the developing countries have been able to maintain a system of stable and representative government. From 1948 until the 1980s, Sri Lanka was one of these countries. Even with civil war threatening the unity of the country since 1983, Sri Lanka has maintained its democratic institutions. How has Sri Lanka maintained this record of political stability and representative democracy? It is a poor nation with a gross national product of $1,196 per capita (2005).[1] In addition, a wide gap exists between the rich and the poor. And yet representative government and stability persist. An examination of Sri Lanka reveals many factors that have led to the political stability the country has experienced as well as other factors that would be expected to lead to instability and violence. Despite the violence that Sri Lanka has experienced for more than twenty years, it has been able to maintain its democratic institutions. The chapters in Part 4 explore why Sri Lanka has been successful thus far in establishing stable political institutions while experiencing a civil war; they also describe the threats to that stability. Specifically, they examine the cultural and historical heritage of Sri Lanka, the nature of its political institutions, the style of leadership exhibited by its leaders, and the ethnic problems and divisions in the society that threaten to destabilize it. The present chapter describes some of the basic features of the country, its historical heritage, and the social structure of its society.

Geography

The island now known as Sri Lanka has long been known for its natural beauty and lush vegetation. Located at the foot of the South Asian subcontinent, it is a teardrop-shaped island about the size of West Virginia (25,300 square miles). In mid-2008, its population was estimated to be 21.1 million people, making it one of the most densely populated countries in the world, with over 832 people per square mile.[2] The population density is intensified by the concentration of population in the southwest corner of the island.

Despite its small size, Sri Lanka exhibits great geographic and climatic diversity. The southwest corner of the island, known as the wet zone, normally receives 100 to 200 inches of rain annually. The rest of the island—the north and east—has an arid climate with 50 to 70 inches of rainfall concentrated into a three-month period (October through December) when the northeast monsoons blow rain clouds ashore. The southwest is affected by the monsoon in June and July and receives significant amounts of rainfall throughout the rest of the year.

The island also exhibits sharp topographical differences between regions. The south-central part of the island is marked by mountains and high plateaus, with cities and villages located above the 5,000-foot level. This region is known for its tea plantations; most of the mountains have been stripped of their natural vegetation and replanted with tea. The rest of the island is a relatively level coastal plain with rolling hills and a land mass that rises sharply toward the center of the island.

Cultural and Social History

Amid this environment of geographic diversity and tropical climate, a strong cultural heritage developed. Ancient traders coming to Sri Lanka marveled at the natural beauty and friendly natives of the island they called Taprobane or Serendib, which stood at the crossroads of the Indian Ocean. Over 2,000 years ago a highly developed civilization emerged in the north-central part of the island, an area from which spices and other products were made available to the traders coming from the orient and the Middle East. The arrival of the first Europeans in 1505 marked a change in the nature of life on the island. The Sri Lankans lost their independence, first to the Portuguese in 1505, then to the Dutch in 1656, and finally to the British in 1795, but they did not lose their strong sense of national identity and pride. This national pride, coupled with the political institutions left by the British, helped to create the stable and competitive political system mentioned earlier.

The strong sense of national identity and pride among Sri Lankans today is the result of their deep cultural and historical heritage. The island's inhabitants claim to trace their heritage back more than 2,000 years.[3] Most modern-day Sri Lankans are descended from one of two cultural-linguistic groups and are defined by the language they speak: Sinhalese or Tamil. The Sinhalese are descended from migrants from north India, who are believed to have arrived around 500 B.C., whereas the first Tamil speakers are believed to have come across from south India about the same time.[4] The early Sri Lankans settled in the north-central regions of the country in an area that is now called the dry zone. The original inhabitants of the area, called Veddahs, were an aboriginal people who intermarried with the migrants and largely disappeared from the island as a distinct cultural group. Today, small groups of Veddahs still live in the eastern jungles of Sri Lanka. The dry zone was an arid region that spawned the growth of a major irrigation system to support the agriculture of the area. A great civilization flourished from the third century B.C. until the twelfth century A.D. Two of the major civilizations were centered in the present-day cities of Anuradhapura and Polonnaruwa. In the thirteenth and fourteenth centuries the civilizations began to decline for unknown reasons. Theories suggest such causes as the increase in the prevalence of malaria in the region, caused by the many irrigation tanks that fostered the breeding of mosquitoes; the inability of the society to maintain the thousands of miles of irrigation canals and reservoirs; and the decline of the groundwater levels as a result of the overpopulation of the region.[5]

Buddhism and Hinduism were introduced to the island from India at the time of the development of the great civilizations of the north-central parts of Sri Lanka. Buddhism is believed to have been introduced during the reign of King Devanampiya Tissa (307–267 B.C.);[6] Hinduism appears to have been established even earlier.[7] Hinduism and Buddhism were readily accepted by many of the people, and many Sri Lankan Buddhists today consider themselves to be the protectors of the faith.

These early civilizations thrived in the harsh climate by developing a system of irrigation tanks and canals to support the growing population of the region. With the success of the civilizations came a series of invasions from the Indian empires to the north, and by the thirteenth century, the Sri Lankan civilization of the dry zone was crumbling. While the civilization declined, a Tamil kingdom on the Jaffna peninsula in the north continued to thrive. At the same time, the Sinhalese were abandoning the dry areas of the north-central island and moving into the forested southwest section of the island and the hills of the south-central region.

Socioeconomic Changes with Colonialization

When the Portuguese arrived in 1505, they found the island divided into three kingdoms. Two were Sinhalese, with their capitals at Kotte (near present-day

Colombo) and at Kandy in the central hill country. The third was a Tamil kingdom located on the northern Jaffna peninsula. The Portuguese arrival marked
the beginning of a 300-year period of colonialism on the island. The Portuguese
came with a desire to establish trade and spread the Roman Catholic religion.
They became embroiled in Sri Lankan politics and were ultimately deeded the
Kotte kingdom upon the death of the king in 1597. In 1697 the Portuguese
conquered the Jaffna kingdom and ruled all of the island except the Kandyan
kingdom in the central hills, which repelled all efforts to conquer it.[8]

A desire to control the cinnamon trade of South Asia led the Dutch to challenge the Portuguese for control of the island. Initially the Dutch set up a
trading post in Batticaloa on the east coast of the island in 1602. A series of
battles followed in which the Dutch allied themselves with the king of Kandy
to attack the Portuguese forts on the island. The last fort was overrun in
1658, and the Portuguese were forced off the island. The Dutch turned the
administration of the island over to the Dutch East India Company, which
continued to transform the island into a Christian nation by spreading the
faith of the Dutch Reformed Church and to transform the economy by establishing cinnamon plantations and cultivating coffee, cotton, tobacco, and
sugar for export.[9]

The British arrived in Sri Lanka to head off French influence in South Asia.
In particular, the British were concerned that the port of Trincomalee on the
east coast would fall under French control. As a result, the British began negotiating with the Dutch in the late eighteenth century over the status of the port.
Finally the Dutch were forced from the island in 1795. The British turned the
administration of Sri Lanka (known as Ceylon before 1972) over to the British
East India Company, which ran the country until it became a crown colony in
1802. The British administration soon sought to unify the island by bringing
the Kandyan kingdom under British control. The kingdom had persisted
throughout the Dutch and Portuguese eras, protected from the colonial armies
by the rugged hill country of central Sri Lanka. The armies of the Dutch and
the Portuguese tried to conquer the Kandyan kingdom but the Kandyan
armies, commanding the higher points, were able to turn back armed attacks.
As a result of the isolation of the landlocked Kandyan kingdom, the people of
the region developed a distinct culture and set of traditions that persist today.[10]
The British brought the Kandyan kingdom under their control in 1815 and
consolidated their rule over the whole island. From this time until their voluntary departure in 1948, the British ruled the island with only two serious challenges to their rule—the armed revolts of 1818 and 1848.

The British era was marked by further attempts to transform Sri Lanka into
an export-oriented economy and establish British customs and beliefs in the

country. English became the language of both the government and the Sri Lankan elite, and Christianity, this time in the form of the Anglican Church, was fostered. It became customary for upper-class Sri Lankans to adopt the Christian religion and speak the English language in their homes.

The British made several major changes in the economic life of the country. They used the hill country to establish first a coffee industry and then, after a disease destroyed the coffee plants, a tea industry. At the same time, they established rubber and coconut plantations in the lower elevations of the hill country and in the coastal areas. The development of the plantations led to the growth of a landed aristocracy based on the ownership of the plantations. This aristocracy included British settlers and Sri Lankans who were given the land because of their loyalty and/or service to the British. The development of the plantation economy transformed peasant agriculture by removing land that had once been used for vegetable cultivation from the use of the peasants.[11]

During the period of British rule, Sri Lankan cultural traditions and beliefs were neglected. The Buddhist and Hindu religions were ignored by the British and damaged when traditional temple lands were taken over by the British as "crown" or government lands. The English language was used as the language of government and commerce, and the languages spoken by most of the population—Tamil and Sinhala—were associated with a backward and primitive peasantry. In addition, the government operated with British traditions in mind. Sunday replaced the Buddhist day of prayer (the *poya* day) as the weekly day of rest, and Christian religious holidays were celebrated as national holidays.

After independence, attempts were made to reassert Sri Lankan control over the society. These attempts reflected the influence of the dominant ethnic group in the society—the Sinhalese. In the mid-1950s there was a movement among the rural peasantry to restore the traditional values of the society and to remove the influence of the alien British culture. In 1956 the Official Language Act made Sinhala the national language, thus replacing English as the official language of government. Buddhism was later given special status by a series of laws passed in the 1960s and by the constitution of 1972. These attempts to restore Sinhala and Buddhism to a position of social dominance were accompanied by actions intended to return the traditional culture to a position of respect in the society. The wearing of traditional forms of dress as well as the use of Sinhala in commerce and government soon became popular among politicians.

However, these actions to restore the cultural heritage of Sri Lanka proved to be disruptive to the political system. As discussed in more detail later, Sri Lankans do not agree about what constitutes the traditional Sri Lankan cultural, linguistic, and religious heritage.

Socioeconomic Development

The social and economic environment in which a political system operates can have a great impact on how well the government performs and on how politically stable the government is. In Sri Lanka several features of the socioeconomic environment have influenced the conduct of government and politics.

The quality of life in Sri Lanka is quite high despite the fact that the country is one of the poorest in the world on the basis of per capita gross national product.[12] It also has one of the best educational systems in Asia. The literacy rate in 2005 was estimated to be 90.7 percent, and a very high percentage of school-age children attend school, over 97 percent of primary school age children.[13] Education through the university level is free, and the average Sri Lankan is well aware of the value of education. The university system in the country is well developed, and competition to get into the institutions of higher learning is very stiff; only a small percentage of those taking the entrance examinations actually gain admission.[14]

Health standards in Sri Lanka are quite high. Life expectancy at birth is 71.6 years—only six years lower than life expectancy in the United States and ten years higher than the average of other low-income countries.[15] This high life expectancy reflects the quality of medical services in the country. Medical care is free, and most Sri Lankans have easy access to doctors and hospitals. In addition, the government provides a system of nutritional care. Before 1979, every Sri Lankan was given a free measure of rice each week as well as reduced prices on other commodities. The size of the free measure of rice varied over time but was generally two kilograms. Since 1979, however, the free measure of rice has been replaced with a system of food stamps for the needy. Although the value of food stamp benefits increased very slowly after 1979, the nutritional requirements of the population are still generally met.

Accompanying these high levels of education and health has been a more equitable distribution of income and wealth than is found in other Third World countries. Although there is a wide gap between the rich and the poor in Sri Lanka, the gap is not as large as that in other developing nations.[16] Moreover, the gap decreased throughout much of the 1960s and 1970s. A strong sense of egalitarianism runs through the political culture of Sri Lanka and is reflected in the political behavior of the population.

In addition to this apparent sense of egalitarianism, the Sri Lankan people exhibit strong support for participatory democracy. As will be discussed in Chapter 21, Sri Lankans frequently contact their elected representatives for the resolution of political problems. They also demonstrate widespread interest and involvement in the open and free elections held since independence. Voter turnout in Sri

TABLE 19.1   Voter Turnout Rates in National Elections

Year	Percentage of Electorate Voting	Year	Percentage of Electorate Voting
1947	55.8	1988 (presidential)	55.4
1952	70.7	1989	63.6
1956	69.0	1994	76.2
1960 (March)	77.6	1994 (presidential)	70.5
1960 (July)	75.9	1999 (presidential)	73.3
1965	82.1	2000	75.6
1970	85.2	2001	80.1
1977	86.7	2004	76.0
1982 (presidential)	80.1	2005 (presidential)	73.7
1982 (referendum)	70.8		

All elections are parliamentary unless otherwise noted.

Sources: H. B. W. Abeynaike, Parliament of Sri Lanka (Colombo: Lake House); Island, December 19, 1988, February 18, 1989; W. G. Goonerathne and R. S. Karunaratne, eds., Tenth Parliament of Sri Lanka (Colombo: Associated Newspapers of Ceylon, 1996); and Sri Lankan Election Secretariat.

Lanka has been one of the highest in South Asia, rising from a low of 55.8 percent in the first parliamentary elections shortly before independence in 1947 to a high of 86.7 percent in the 1977 parliamentary elections (see Table 19.1). The turnout rates in the national elections since 1977 have been lower than that year's peak, but they remain relatively high. The parliamentary elections of 2004 resulted in a 71.6 percent turnout rate. The strong commitment to democratic elections by Sri Lankans is reflected in their remarkable turnout rates in the face of political violence and death threats. In the December 1988 presidential election and the February 1989 parliamentary elections, voter turnout was 55.3 percent and 63.6 percent despite death threats by two rebel groups.

The Sri Lankan people exhibit strong support for open and free elections. In 1981 the country celebrated the fiftieth anniversary of universal adult suffrage. Even more impressive is the fact that when the first elections in Sri Lanka permitting universal adult suffrage were held in 1931, it was only two years after Great Britain held its first election with universal adult suffrage.

Ethnicity

Despite its small size, the island of Sri Lanka is marked by a relatively wide diversity of ethnic groups. Two thousand years of invasion and foreign interference have resulted in a highly diverse ethnic structure in which individual Sri Lankans display a strong allegiance to their ethnic groups. The result of this is a great deal of competition and conflict among the groups, which affects the conduct of politics in Sri Lanka. The society is divided by language, culture, religion, and caste.

TABLE 19.2   Ethnic Population of Sri Lanka

Ethnic Group	Percentage of Population
Sinhalese	74.0
Sri Lanka Tamils	12.6
Muslims	7.1
Indian Tamils	5.6
Burghers	0.3
Malays	0.3

Note: Because of the conflict in the north and east, a full national census has not been completed since 1981.

Source: Statistical Pocketbook of the Democratic Socialist Republic of Sri Lanka—1989 (Colombo: Department of Census and Statistics, 1989), p. 14.

TABLE 19.3   Religious Composition of the Sri Lankan Population

Religion	Percentage of Population
Buddhism	69.3
Hinduism	15.5
Islam	7.6
Christianity	7.5
Others	0.1

Source: Statistical Pocketbook of the Democratic Socialist Republic of Sri Lanka—1989 (Colombo: Department of Census and Statistics, 1989), p. 12.

The first three cleavages in particular tend to reinforce each other, as the members of each major linguistic group tend to share the same culture and religion.

The largest ethnic group on the island is the Sinhalese, who compose almost three-fourths of the population (see Table 19.2). They trace their origins to north India, claiming to be the earliest "civilized" inhabitants on the island and to have been responsible for the dry-zone civilizations of Anuradhapura and Polonnaruwa. The Sinhalese speak an Indo-European language similar to Hindi that is not spoken anywhere else in the world. Most Sinhalese practice Buddhism and consider themselves to be the protectors of the faith. Over two-thirds of the population of the island practice Buddhism (see Table 19.3), which was brought to Sri Lanka in the third century B.C. and subsequently spread quickly through the dry-zone civilization. It persisted in Sri Lanka even after Buddhism had lost much of its influence in India. On their arrival the Europeans challenged Buddhism, and a significant minority of the Sinhalese adopted Christianity as its faith. Some of their descendants continue to practice Christianity today, and there are significant numbers of both Roman Catholics and Protestants.

The next largest ethnic community is the Sri Lanka Tamils, who trace their ancestry to the same period as that of the Sinhalese arrival and challenge the Sinhalese versions of the historical origins of Sri Lanka. They are religiously and culturally related to the Tamil community of south India and speak the same Dravidian language, Tamil. Most of the Tamils practice Hinduism, although significant numbers converted to Christianity after the arrival of the Europeans. Thus the religion and the language of the Tamils are distinct from those of the Sinhalese. Although there is a significant population of Sri Lanka Tamils in the capital city of Colombo, most are found in the northern and eastern regions of the island. The northern Jaffna peninsula and the land areas immediately to its south are populated almost exclusively by Sri Lanka Tamils.

The Indian (or Estate) Tamils in Sri Lanka consider themselves to be culturally distinct from the Sri Lanka Tamils, even though most speak the same language, practice the same religion, and trace their cultural origins to south India. The Indian Tamils arrived in Sri Lanka at a much later date than did the Sri Lanka Tamils. The Indian Tamils trace their origins to the coffee and tea estate workers brought from India by the British in the nineteenth and early twentieth centuries. They are found in the estate areas of the Kandyan hill country in central Sri Lanka, where they make up an overwhelming majority of the tea estate workers on the island.

Shortly after independence, the government passed legislation that made it very difficult for Indian Tamils to be Sri Lankan citizens. The rationale behind this act was that even though many of the Indian Tamils were born in Sri Lanka, they were only temporary residents of the island and did not have any long-term ties to the country. The government then sought to deport most of the Indian Tamils and other noncitizens to India and Pakistan. The governments of both of these countries initially resisted this move, and the Indian Tamils remained in Sri Lanka as a stateless body of people. Then an agreement between Sri Lankan Prime Minister Sirimavo Bandaranaike and Indian Prime Minister Lal Bahadur Shastri in 1964 arranged for the granting of citizenship to approximately 300,000 of the 975,000 Indian Tamils in the country and the deportation to India of 525,000 of them. The status of the remaining 150,000 was to be the subject of further negotiations. This agreement has been implemented very slowly, and a significant number of Indian Tamils remain stateless.

An additional ethnic community of importance is the Muslims (also called Moors), who are descended from early Arab traders to the island. The Muslims practice Islam and, for the most part, speak Tamil. They are found in the important trading centers and along the east coast of Sri Lanka. The Moors of the east coast have traditionally constituted a backward community with low levels of income and literacy, while the Moors found in the trading centers tend to be wealthy and often literate in several languages. However, in recent years, there have been large increases in the level of education and income among the east coast Moors.

Several smaller ethnic communities also inhabit Sri Lanka, including the Burghers and the Malays. The Burghers are of mixed European and Sri Lankan descent. Their native tongue is usually English, and most are Christians. The majority are found in the capital city of Colombo and make up part of the economic elite of the island. The Malays are descended from the Malay traders and guards brought to the island during the colonial era. They are largely found in Colombo and practice Islam.

Both the geographic diversity of the island and its colonial history have contributed to the development of subcultures within the two major ethnic groups—the Sinhalese and the Tamils. The Sinhalese are divided between the low-country Sinhalese and the Kandyan Sinhalese. During the 200 years of colonial rule, during which the Kandyan kingdom resisted the European powers, the people in the hill country developed a culture that differs widely from that of the people living in the lowland areas. In recent years, however, the distinction between the two groups of Sinhalese has decreased as contact between them has increased.

The Sri Lanka Tamil community is divided between those Sri Lanka Tamils living on the Jaffna peninsula and those living along the east coast of the island. The east coast Tamils tend to be poorer and less educated than the Jaffna Tamils and are often thought to be more traditional in their outlook.

The Caste System

In recent years the Sri Lankan caste system has been declining in importance. It is similar to that in India (see Chapter 2) in its general structure; however, it is different in two very important respects. In Sri Lanka, unlike in India, the various caste groups generally are concentrated geographically such that an overwhelming majority of the population in any area are members of the same caste. In addition, among both the Tamils and the Sinhalese, who have different caste structures, the highest-status caste is also the largest in size.

Since no census of Sri Lankan castes has been taken since the nineteenth century, the size of the caste groups can only be estimated. It is generally agreed that the Sinhalese caste structure is dominated hierarchically and numerically by the Goyigama (cultivator) caste, which is estimated to comprise about one-half of the Sinhalese population. Beneath the Goyigamas are three castes of lesser status. These are the Karawa (fisherman) caste, the Salagama (cinnamon peeler) caste, and the Durawa (toddy tapper) caste. These three castes are found along the southwest coast of the island and generally constitute a majority in the regions where they are found. Untouchability is rare among the Sinhalese, although several important castes of very low status do exist. Among these are the Wahumpara (jaggery/palm sugar maker) and the Batgam castes (of uncertain occupational origin). These castes, too, are geographically concentrated. Both are found in inland regions in the transition zones between the lowlands and the Kandyan hill country.[17]

The Sri Lanka Tamil caste structure in the northern Jaffna peninsula is also dominated by the cultivator caste, known as the Vellala. The Vellala are believed to comprise about one-half of the Sri Lanka Tamil population in the northern Jaffna peninsula.[18] Beneath the Vellala are several other important castes, including the Koviyar (domestic servants) and two castes associated with fishing—the Karayar, whose members generally live along the northern coast, and the Mukkuvar, whose members generally live along the east coast. Untouchability is much more common among the Tamils than it is among the Sinhalese, and it is estimated that one-fourth of the population of the Jaffna peninsula is composed of members of the untouchable castes. These include the Palla (agricultural laborers), Ambattar (barbers), Valava (toddy tappers), and Paraya (scavengers) castes. With the exception of the Indian Tamils, the Muslims and the other small ethnic groups—like the Muslims in Pakistan, India, and Bangladesh—do not recognize caste distinctions.

The consequence of the ethnic divisions in Sri Lanka has been communal strife. Since independence, the conflict between the Sinhalese and the Tamils has escalated, and smaller conflicts have been waged between the Roman Catholics and the Buddhists as well as among the various caste groups. The most serious conflict is the Sinhalese-Tamil dispute. Both ethnic groups fear the intentions of the other group. The Tamils, as a minority in Sri Lanka, feel that they have not received fair treatment from the Sinhalese and believe that the Sinhalese are trying to turn the country into a Sinhala-speaking Buddhist state. The Sinhalese, on the other hand, despite their majority status in the population, also feel threatened. The Sinhalese culture and language is found only on the island of Sri Lanka and hence is much smaller than the Tamil-speaking culture and society to the north of Sri Lanka in the Indian state of Tamil Nadu. The fear of the Sinhalese has led them to be suspicious of the actions of the Tamil community in Sri Lanka. Some Sinhalese fear that their culture and nation may be absorbed by the Tamils.

This conflict became more violent after 1977 and upset the political stability of the country when it erupted into open civil war in 1984. Since then, the Sri Lanka Tamil regions of the country, especially the Jaffna peninsula, have been in a state of open revolt against the government. Violence and bloodshed increased rapidly in the 1980s and continued until a cease-fire in February 2002. However, the violence has increased sharply since the election of President Rajapakse in November 2005 (see Chapter 22).

Many of the efforts by Sri Lankan leaders to establish a stable society are directed at a resolution of the ethnic conflict facing the country. But government attempts to resolve the conflict have been draining resources that could be used elsewhere to help further develop the economic and social achievements described earlier in this chapter.

NOTES

1. When GNP is computed using purchasing power parity (PPP), Sri Lanka has a GDP per capita of $4,595. United Nations Development Program, *Human Development Report 2007/2008* Table 14, http://hdrstats.undp.org/countries/country_fact_sheets/cty_fs_LKA.html.

2. United States Census Bureau, International Programs Center, "International Data Base," retrieved January 14, 2008, www.census.gov/cgi-bin/ipc/idbagg.

3. K. M. DeSilva, *A History of Sri Lanka* (Berkeley: University of California Press, 1981), chap. 1.

4. Some scholars have argued that the Sinhalese classification as Indo-Aryan was the result of nineteenth-century British politics rather than linguistic research. See Marissa Angel, "Understanding the Aryan Theory: Orientalist Scholarship in Colonial Ceylon and the Structure of Empire," paper presented at the annual conference of the International Centre for Ethnic Studies, March 1997, Colombo.

5. DeSilva, *History of Sri Lanka,* chap. 7.

6. K. M. DeSilva, "Historical Survey," in *Sri Lanka: A Survey* (Honolulu: University Press of Hawaii, 1977), p. 33.

7. C. S. Navarsatnam, *A Short History of Hinduism in Ceylon* (Jaffna: Sri Sanmuganatha Press, 1964). The question of which religion was the first on the island is highly controversial and an important part of the debate concerning the Tamil-Sinhala conflict.

8. See George Davison Winius, *The Fatal History of Portuguese Ceylon: Transition to Dutch Rule* (Cambridge: Harvard University Press, 1971).

9. DeSilva, *History of Sri Lanka,* chaps. 10–14.

10. For a description of the Kandyan kingdom, see Robert Knox, "An Historical Relation of Ceylon," *Ceylon Historical Journal,* July 1956–April 1957.

11. Asoka Bandarage, *Colonialism in Sri Lanka* (New York: Mouton, 1957).

12. United Nations Development Program, *Human Development Report,* "Sri Lanka Data Sheet" http://hdrstats.undp.org/countries/data_sheets/cty_ds_LKA.html.

13. United Nations Development Program, *Human Development Report,* Table 12, http://hdrstats.undp.org/indicators/113.html.

14. Swarna Jayaweera, "Education," in *Modern Sri Lanka: A Society in Transition,* ed. Robert N. Kearney and Tissa Fernando (Syracuse, N.Y.: Maxwell School, Syracuse University, 1979), pp. 147–148; and Sunil Bastian, "University Admission and the National Question," in *Ethnicity and Social Change in Sri Lanka,* ed. Social Scientists Association (Colombo: Social Scientists Association, 1984), p. 174.

15. United Nations Development Program, *Human Development Report,* "Sri Lanka: The Human Development Index—Going Beyond Income," http://hdrstats.undp.org/countries/country_fact_sheets/cty_fs_LKA.html.

16. http://hdrstats.undp.org/countries/country_fact_sheets/cty_fs_LKA.html.

17. Bryce Ryan, *Caste in Modern Ceylon* (New Brunswick, N.J.: Rutgers University Press, 1953).

18. Bryan Pfaffenberger, *Caste in Tamil Culture: The Religious Foundations of Sudra Domination in Tamil Sri Lanka* (Syracuse, N.Y.: Maxwell School, Syracuse University, 1983).

20

Government Structure

Sri Lanka has struggled to create a viable political system that is sensitive to the culture of the country and maintains democratic institutions. There have been three constitutions since 1972, and a fourth has been debated since 1994. Each time a different party has come to power in the past twenty-five years, its members have tried to change the constitution.

Constitutional Development

In their efforts to find a suitable constitutional arrangement, Sri Lankans have gone from a political system modeled on the British Westminster form of government, from 1947 to 1972, to a similar unicameral government from 1972 to 1978, to a French system of government from 1978 to 2008. The unpopularity of the French system has led to calls for a return to a Westminster form of government with significant changes to reflect Sri Lankan society and culture. To date, no changes have been made.

The most drastic change to the constitution came in 1977, when Junius Richard Jayawardene, who was first elected to parliament during the colonial era, became prime minister. He incorporated many of his personal views into the constitution, creating a quasi-presidential arrangement modeled on the French system of government.[1] He of course became the first executive president of Sri Lanka. The overall impact of the new constitution was to concentrate power in the hands of the executive and make the president the dominant figure in the government.[2]

Once Jayawardene left office in 1988, pressure to change the system began to mount. This pressure led to proposals to change the government in the 1990s under the leadership of President Chandrika Bandaranaike Kumaratunga (president, 1994–2006). She was elected to office vowing to abolish the executive presidency. However, once in office, she was unable to obtain a consensus on constitutional change and no action was taken. The current president, Mahinda Rajapakse, has, so far, taken no action to change the constitution.

During the colonial era Sri Lankans were given limited influence in their government. Although there have been many arguments concerning the contribution of the colonial experience in Sri Lanka, most writers agree that two elements of British rule left a major impression on today's Sri Lanka—the structure of government established by the British, and the educational system created during the colonial period.[3] During the colonial era the British created political institutions modeled on their own. They set up a parliamentary system and gave the Sri Lankans a limited degree of self-rule before granting independence. Sri Lanka, along with India, became one of the first British colonies to be allowed elected representatives from the local population in a colonial legislature. In 1912 they were permitted to elect three members of a twenty-one-member legislative council. The number of elected members was increased to four in 1917, and to twenty-three of thirty-seven members in 1920. (These proportions roughly parallel the development of indigenous representation in India.) This experience with self-rule during the colonial era provided Sri Lankans limited experience with self-government.

Just before independence a three-man commission of Englishmen headed by Lord Soulbury wrote a constitution modeled on the British Westminster system of government, which is very similar to India's constitution, though without the federal provisions (see Chapter 3). The Sri Lankans adopted the Soulbury constitution and governed with it until they replaced it in 1972. This original constitution provided for a parliamentary system with a bicameral legislature.[4] The lower house, or House of Representatives, became the dominant chamber of government. It was elected directly by the people in a combination of single-member and multimember electoral districts. The number of multimember districts was limited, never exceeding five districts with either two or three members elected. The House of Representatives was given the responsibility of selecting the prime minister and approving the cabinet. The upper house, or Senate, consisted of thirty members, fifteen nominated by the governor-general on the recommendation of the cabinet and fifteen elected by the lower house by proportional representation. The Senate's power was quite limited, and its main function was to provide the means for political parties to reward their supporters. In addition, the Senate's members could be named to the cabinet of ministers.

The Soulbury constitution generated many criticisms because of its similarity to the governmental structure of Sri Lanka's former colonial ruler, Great Britain. The United Front government led by the Sri Lanka Freedom Party (SLFP) and elected in 1970 was dedicated to changing the structure of government to fit the Sri Lankan society more effectively than the "alien" Soulbury government had done. In 1972 a new constitution was promulgated. It had been written by a constitutional convention consisting of the members of parliament elected in 1970. The fact that the majority of seats had been won by the United Front gave the coalition a free hand in determining the changes in the constitution. The major changes introduced by the constitution included the abolition of the Senate and provisions that not only accorded Buddhism a special place in the society but also affirmed the role of Sinhala in governmental actions.[5]

The 1972 constitution was very unpopular with the two major opposition parties, the United National Party (UNP) and the leading party of the Tamil ethnic group, the Federal Party (FP). The FP opposed the constitution because it designated Sinhala as the official language and bestowed special status on Buddhism. In addition, it did not provide the Tamil language with any special status. The UNP opposed the 1972 constitution because of fears that it would lead to an authoritarian government.

The UNP's 1977 election manifesto promised a new constitution and the creation of a presidential form of government. The new constitution unveiled in 1978 drastically altered the nature of Sri Lankan government.[6] The Westminster-form parliamentary system was replaced by a government modeled after that of France. Its main features were as follows:

1. A provision for an executive presidency that, unlike India's presidency, carries a great deal of power. The position commands many more powers than did the prime ministers under the two previous constitutions. The president is elected by a direct vote of the people for a fixed term of six years. (The Third Amendment to the constitution, passed in 1982, allows the president to call a new presidential election at any time after serving four years of his or her term.) The parliament also has a term of six years, but the president is permitted to dissolve it and call new elections at any time.

2. The president appoints the prime minister and the cabinet, subject to parliamentary approval. In addition, the president rather than the prime minister presides over the cabinet when it meets.

3. The single-member system of electoral constituencies was replaced with a system of proportional representation in the 1989 parliamentary elections.

4. All vacancies in parliament are filled by the party of the member who vacated the seat and not through by-elections, as had been done in the past. In addition, the party has the right to expel any of its members from parliament and to replace them with another member of the party. (The second amendment to the constitution, passed in 1979, allows the

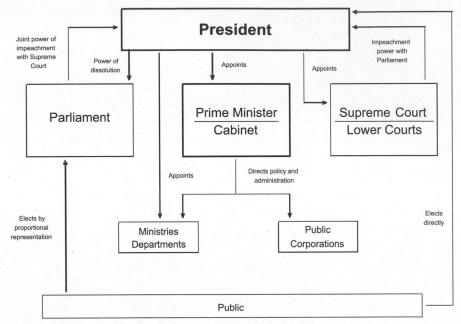

FIGURE 20.1   Structure of Sri Lanka's Government

whole parliament to decide whether a member of parliament can be expelled by his or her party or change his or her party allegiance.)

5. Finally, the constitution provides for national referenda on issues of importance.

The unique feature of the 1978 constitution is the power placed in the office
of the president.[7] On paper, it divides governmental authority among the executive, legislature, and judiciary (see Figure 20.1). The executive president created by the constitution exercises a great deal of power. He or she may declare
war and peace, grant pardons, and carry out any actions approved by the legislature or ordered by the Supreme Court. However, the main powers of the president are, in fact, the informal powers that a president may wield to control the
legislative branch. As the highest elected official of his or her party, the president may exert influence over the members of parliament through the party's
power to replace them. In fact, presidents elected since the system began have
wielded a great deal of influence and power over the parliament through their
control of the members of parliament.

The constitution states that the president is responsible to parliament and
that parliament may impeach the president, with Supreme Court approval.
However, the president also wields a great deal of control over the Supreme

Court, given the presidential power to nominate and remove members. In addition, as a party leader, the president is in a position to remove from parliament any party members he or she does not like or disagrees with. As a result, the parliament may be reduced to little more than a rubber stamp, if the president is in a position to control both the cabinet and the party.

Several other provisions of the constitution help maintain stability and keep one party in power. Before 1978, the governing party had lost each of the previous seven elections. The new constitution created a system of proportional representation that contains an unusual provision. The leading party in each of the electoral districts receives a bonus seat before the seats are distributed on the basis of proportional representation. In addition, 160 seats are distributed on the basis of electoral constituencies while 29 are distributed proportionally on the basis of the national vote. Since Jayawardene's party, the UNP, had been the leading vote getter in almost every election since independence, it forced the SLFP to form electoral alliances or likely face defeat. The successful elections of the SLFP have always involved electoral agreements with smaller parties in which the parties have decided not to contest each other in the same constituencies. Thus it was believed that the provision would aid the UNP.[8] In reality, both leaders of the SLFP since Jayawardene's era, Chandrika Kumaratunga and Mahinda Rajapakse, have arranged an alliance with smaller parties which has successfully defeated the UNP in three of the four parliamentary elections since the early 1990s.

The system of proportional representation also includes provisions for the electoral list of candidates to be determined by the voters. At the ballot box, voters select a party and a candidate from that party. The votes for the party determine how the seats are divided among the parties, and candidate preferences determine who within that party wins the seat. Thus if the SLFP wins eight seats in an electoral district, the top eight vote getters of the SLFP will be elected to parliament. This has created election campaigns in which the parties compete against each other while the individual candidates run against members of their own party. The result has been the generation of ill will between party members.

The most serious area of discussion for changes to the constitutional structure have dealt with changes intended to resolve the civil war. These changes have involved proposals to devolve power to the north and east. President Kumaratunga offered the most detailed proposals to devolve power. She came to power in 1994 with a mandate to end the civil war with the Liberation Tigers of Tamil Eelam (LTTE) and to restructure the government of Sri Lanka. However, she soon found it difficult to make the changes that she had promised. The LTTE opposed her constitutional changes, and there was no consensus among the government and the opposition about what changes were necessary. As a result, the changes were not enacted. However, there have been a number of recurring debates about the constitution. These have included the following discussions:

1. The executive presidency would be abolished and replaced with a ceremonial president with limited power. Executive power would be returned to the prime minister.
2. Members of parliament would be elected by single-member electoral constituencies or a mixed system with some elected by proportional representation and some by single-member districts.
3. The most controversial area deals with the devolution of power from the central government to regional governments. These proposals were made to accommodate Sri Lankan minorities, the Tamils and the Muslims, who felt that their needs were not being met by the highly centralized Sri Lankan political system. There is no consensus about the form that the devolution will take.
4. Among the most controversial proposals are the changes to the current Eastern and Northern provinces. These proposals have included a union of the two provinces, or the creation of a Muslim district or province.

In 2006, President Rajapakse created an All-Party Representative Committee (APRC) to find a political solution to the conflict. The body quickly became deadlocked and was forced to present an interim report to President Rajapakse in January 2008. The interim report called for the implementation of the Thirteenth Amendment to the constitution. This amendment was passed as part of the Indo-Lanka accords and created a system of provincial councils. It was condemned by all important Tamil groups as inadequate when it was proposed in 1987. Beyond this, the Rajapakse administration has separated the Northern and Eastern provinces and announced that the president would not accept a federal solution to the problem of devolving power.

The Sri Lankan parliament, like that of Great Britain, maintains a rigorous separation between government supporters and the opposition. As in most parliamentary systems, the government and opposition benches face each other on opposite sides of the floor of parliament. Constitutional provisions barring crossovers from one party to another have limited what was once common behavior under the provisions of the earlier constitutions. Each side of the parliament chooses a leader: the majority selects the prime minister, and the opposition selects the leader of the opposition. A strict code of party loyalty ensures that the members will vote as the party leaders want them to, unless they are released by the party leadership to vote their consciences—an alternative that does not happen very often. Thus most votes of parliament are highly predictable. Members who do not do as the party leaders wish are often expelled from the party and can be expelled from parliament as well under the provisions of the current constitution. The party leaders hold group meetings of their party's parliamentary members, thus providing the backbenchers—who are otherwise not allowed to express negative opinions about government policy—an opportunity to complain; at the same time, the party leaders are given the chance to determine the sentiment of their members on legislative proposals.[9]

The members of parliament (MPs) represent the privileged elite of the country. Many speak fluent English (especially the more powerful members), and cabinet meetings are often held in English. Most come from the upper economic classes, hence the overrepresentation of the professional occupations and the landowning elite among MPs. The ethnic minorities are fairly well represented as well, although the Indian Tamils had no elected representation from 1952 until 1977, when they elected one representative to parliament. The Indian Tamils had elected six members to the first parliament in 1947, but it was soon afterward that their ethnic group was denied citizenship (see Chapter 19).[10]

The proposal for the elimination of the presidential system in Sri Lanka was largely the result of the abuse of the power that had been placed in the hands of the president. In the first presidential election, held in October 1982, the incumbent president, Jayawardene, won reelection to office.[11] After his election triumph, Jayawardene decided to use the constitutional provision for referenda to ensure for his party the kind of dominance it had exercised from 1977 to 1982. It was generally believed that a parliamentary election might result in a UNP defeat but definitely would not result in the five-sixths majority that the 1977 elections had given the UNP. An election victory with a reduced UNP majority would have taken away the UNP's power to amend the constitution at will, as it had been able to do since the 1977 elections. Hence the first—and thus far only—national referendum in Sri Lankan history was held in December 1982, shortly after the presidential election. The question presented to the voters was whether the parliament elected in 1977 should be allowed to sit until 1989 without general elections.

More than 54 percent of the electorate supported the proposition, and the parliament was allowed to sit until 1989. However, the referendum was the first national election in Sri Lankan history to be marked by allegations of widespread vote fraud.[12] Many voters opposed to the proposal had been intimidated into staying away from the polls. In addition, many poll watchers had been forcibly removed from the polling stations, and irregularities had occurred after they were forced out of the stations.[13]

The election marked the beginning of a cycle of violence, election fraud, and intimidation, which increased during the other elections in the 1980s and returned in the local government elections of 1997 after a relatively fair and free national election in 1994.

In addition, the presidency of Ranasinghe Premadasa was marked by a wide-ranging abuse of power. After being elected president, Premadasa became quite ruthless with his opponents both inside and outside of his party. Many also think he is responsible for unleashing the widespread violence and the death squads that killed many supporters of the leftist Janatha Vimukthi Peramuna (JVP) as well as innocent bystanders in 1989 and 1990.

After his election in 1988, President Premadasa immediately arranged for parliamentary elections to be held in February 1989. This election was also marred by widespread violence and became the bloodiest election in Sri Lankan history. However, it was held, and 63.6 percent of the electorate turned out to vote. The UNP won 125 of the 225 seats contested (see Table 20.1).

The 1994 elections were marked by excessive violence and attacks on supporters of both parties. However, the violence level was considerably less than it had been in 1989. Chandrika Kumaratunga, elected in 1994 on a platform of reforming the system and bringing the violence to an end, was reelected as president in 1999 and her party was reelected to lead parliament in 2000. Both elections were marked by violence levels similar to the 1994 election.

Kumaratunga was unable to run for a third presidential term in 2005 and turned leadership of the party over to Mahinda Rajapakse, a longtime SLFP MP from the southern district of Hambantota. Rajapakse was opposed by the leader of the UNP and former Prime Minister Ranil Wickremasinghe. Ranil was expected to win but the LTTE ordered all Tamils to abstain from the election. Without Tamil votes Ranil was unable to obtain a majority and lost the election by less than 200,000 votes (see Table 20.2).

Since 2005, President Rajapakse's actions have generated a new round of complaints about the presidential system and its power. These have been based on efforts to restrict the media during his administration and other actions of presidential excess, such as attacks against NGOs operating in Sri Lanka and the revocation of the visa issued to the British CEO of Sri Lankan airlines because the CEO would not remove passengers on a flight that the president decided at the last minute to board.

The Public Service and Administration

The national government oversees a large bureaucracy, which is in charge of carrying out the decisions of parliament and the executive. Unlike the U.S. system,

TABLE 20.1 Results of Sri Lanka Parliamentary Elections

	1947		1952		1956		March 1960		July 1960		1965	
	Seats Won	Percent Polled	Seats Won	Percent Polled	Seats Won	Percent Polled	Seats Won	Percent Polled	Seats Won	Percent Polled	Seats Won	Percent Polled
UNP	42	39.8	54	44.1	8	27.9	50	29.4	30	37.6	66	38.9
SLFP	—	—	9	15.5	51	40.0[a]	46	20.9	75	33.6	41	30.2
LSSP	15	16.8[b]	9	13.1	14	10.5	10	10.5	12	7.4	10	7.4
CP	3	3.7[c]	4	5.8	3	4.6	3	4.8	4	3.0	4	2.7
MEP	—	—	—	—	—	—	10	10.6	3	3.4	1	2.7
TC	7	4.4	4	2.8	1	.3	1	1.2	16	7.2	3	2.4
FP	—	—	2	1.9	10	5.4	15	5.7	1	1.5	14	5.4
CIC	6	3.8	—	—	—	—	—	—	—	—	—	—
Others	22	31.4	13	16.9	8	11.4	16	16.7	10	6.4	7	7.0

[a]Results for the Mahajana Eksath Peramuna coalition of S.W.R.D. Bandaranaike and his SLFP.
[b]Includes two LSSP factions contesting the election separately.
[c]Includes the united front of the CP and the VLSSP.

(continues)

TABLE 20.1 (continued)

	1970		1977		1989		1994		2000		2001		2004	
	Seats Won	Percent Polled	Seats Won	Percent Polled	Seats Won	Percent Polled	Seats Won	Percent Polled	Seats Won	Percent Polled	Seats Won	Percent Polled	Seats Won	Percent Polled
UNP	17	37.9	140	50.9	125	50.7	94	44.0	89	40.2	109	47.6	82	37.8
SLFP/PAd	90	36.6	8	29.0	67	31.8	105	48.9	107	45.1	77	38.9	105	45.6
LSSP/USAe	19	8.8	0	3.6	3	2.9	—	—	—	—	—	—	—	—
CPf	6	3.4	0	1.9	—	—	—	—	—	—	—	—	—	—
JVPg	—	—	—	—	—	—	—	1.7	10	6.0	16	9.1	39	—
FP(TULF)	13	5.0	18	6.8	10	3.4	5	.1	5	1.2	15	3.9	22	6.8
EPDP	—	—	—	—	—	—	9	—	4	.6	2	.8	1	.3
EROS	—	—	—	—	13	2.7	—	—	—	—	—	—	—	—
SLMC/NUAh	—	—	—	—	4	3.6	7	1.8	4	2.3	5	1.2	5	2.0
JHU/SU	—	—	—	—	—	—	—	—	—	—	0	.6	9	6.0
Others	5	7.4	2	6.6	0	1.7	5	2.6	6	4.6	1	.7	1	1.5

d The SLFP united with the USA to form the PA in 1994.

e The LSSP, CP, and SLMP united to form the USA in 1989.

f The SLMC ran as the NUA in 2000.

g The JVP with the SLFP; 39 of their members were elected by preference votes.

h The Sinhala Urumaya renamed itself the Jathika Hela Urumaya and ran a slate of Buddhist monks.

The full names of the parties are UNP—United National Party; SLFP—Sri Lanka Freedom Party; LSSP—Lanka Sama Samaja Party; CP—Communist Party; MEP—Mahajana Eksath Peramuna; TC—Tamil Congress; FP—Federal Party; CIC—Ceylon Indian Congress; VLSSP—Viplavakari Lanka Sama Samaja Party; PA—People's Alliance; USA—United Socialist Alliance; TULF—Tamil United Liberation Front; EROS—Eelam Revolutionary Organization of Students; SLMC—Sri Lanka Muslim Congress; NUA—National Unity Alliance; EPDP—Eelam Peoples Democratic Party; SU—Sinhala Urumaya; JHU—Jathika Hela Urumaya.

Source: Sri Lankan Election Secretariat.

TABLE 20.2   2005 Presidential Election Results

Candidate	Party	Total Votes	Percentage Polled
Mahinda Rajapakse	SLFP	4,887,152	50.3
Ranil Wickremasinghe	UNP	4,706,366	48.4
Eleven other candidates		223,521	1.3

Source: Sri Lankan Election Secretariat.

employment as a bureaucrat in most of South Asia confers status, and government jobs are thus highly sought after. The Sri Lankan administrative system is modeled on the British system of administration, and it has been severely criticized by some politicians who attribute Sri Lankan administrative problems to the introduction of an alien system into the country.[14] In particular, the bureaucracy is frequently accused of being partisan, lethargic, and insensitive to public needs.

The administrative system is overseen by cabinet ministries in which political appointees at the very top of the hierarchy make policy decisions. Beneath each of the fifty-six ministries is a system of government departments that carry out functional activities such as irrigation projects, road construction and repair, and statistics gathering. These departments, which are highly centralized, have main offices in Colombo, where most decisions regarding the tasks of field officers are made.

The public service is hierarchical, with an elite corps at the top of the administrative structure. This upper elite is a highly professional and well-trained cadre that carries with it a great deal of social status. Beneath it are subordinate and minor employees who carry out most of the decisions made from above.

At the top of the administrative structure is the Sri Lanka Administrative Service (SLAS), which is similar to the Indian Administrative Service (described in Chapter 3). The SLAS is staffed according to the results of competitive examinations and has three levels of hierarchy. Promotion in the SLAS is handled by the secretaries of the ministry in charge of the SLAS position. The secretaries are the highest-ranking public officials in the ministry. Under the constitutions of 1972 and 1978 they have been political appointees rather than being drawn from the civil service, as had been done from 1947 until 1972.[15]

In addition, a significant number of public corporations oversee government businesses and industries. The government of Sri Lanka has operated many corporations in such industries as tea, rubber, coconut estates, leather, and chemicals. Since the early 1980s the government has been selling the corporations to private investors as part of a vigorous privatization program.

Despite criticisms about the performance of the public service, however, few efforts have been made to change the system of administration since Sri Lanka became independent. The only major change has occurred in the administrative apparatus, which has been politicized: all of the governing parties have been guilty of trying to bring the civil service under their political control; as a result, promotion and hiring decisions are often handled on the basis of political criteria.

Local Government

Since Sri Lanka is a unitary state, its local government has been very weak. Government decisions are made in Colombo and are sent to the rural areas of the country. In addition, the national government has control over most of the revenues generated by the government.

The country is divided into nine provinces, which were significant units of local governmental administration during the colonial era. Today, the system of local government is in a state of change. The district, which had been the main unit of local administration, has been partially replaced by provincial governments created in 1988. Each province has a popularly elected council with a chief minister and ministers approved by the council. The first elections to provincial councils were held in 1988.

The councils have not received adequate funding authority since their creation. Despite efforts by President Premadasa to strengthen them, they failed to meet the expectation that they would decentralize power to local governments. This led later governments to propose a more widespread transfer of power to regional governments.

The creation of the provincial councils has started the removal of the former system of local administration, the *kachcheri* system. Each province is divided into two or three administrative districts, which add up to a total of twenty-five on the island. Each district has a set of government offices called a *kachcheri*, which occupies the center of government administration in each district. Most government departments have district offices in the *kachcheri*, and the highest official in each *kachcheri* is the government agent (GA).[16] The GA is supposed to be the chief coordinator of government activities in the district in addition to overseeing development projects.

Government agents were very important figures in the colonial administration of Great Britain. They were the most powerful officials in the provinces of their administration (during the colonial administration, the GAs oversaw the provinces rather than the districts). Although they were primarily revenue agents, they were soon given extensive powers to control almost all government activities in their regions. After independence, however, the influence of the GAs declined, as they now had to compete with the members of parliament and the main offices of the departments in Colombo for influence over the running of government activities in the district.[17] Because of the high degree of centralization in most government departments, the officials in the departments have been more likely to listen and respond to those who make the decisions about their promotions and transfers, namely, the department heads in the main offices in Colombo rather than the GAs.

The members of parliament also eroded some of the power of the GAs. The development of a patronage system in which the members of parliament are the main distributors of benefits has focused citizen interest on the MPs and away from the GAs. The GAs no longer have the power and influence to resolve complaints. Rather, the MPs have sought this power in order to enhance their position with their electorates. In addition, the MPs have much more influence with the bureaucracy and are better able than the GAs to resolve citizen problems with government departments and agencies.[18] The future of the *kachcheri* system and the government agent is in doubt as the government tries to strengthen the provincial councils.

In addition to the *kachcheri* and the provincial councils, there are several elected local government councils in each district. Before 1981, local government revolved around a system of councils at the village, town, urban, and municipal levels. These governments carried out a relatively small number of functions. With limited tax revenues to work with, they were reduced to overseeing public works in the city or village under their jurisdiction.

In 1981 the government abolished the village and town councils and replaced them with district development councils (DDCs), with the intention of replacing the village and town council system with one council for every administrative district.[19] These councils were not very successful and were eventually replaced with a system of Pradeshya Sabhas, which provided local councils for larger areas that comprised several of the former village council areas.

The creation of the 270 Pradeshya Sabhas did not affect the urban and municipal councils. The eighteen municipal councils function in most of the largest cities on the island, and the forty-two urban councils preside over the medium-size cities. Both types of councils are elected by proportional representation, and both select the mayor and deputy mayor of the city from among the council members.

The creation of the DDCs in 1981 and the provincial councils in 1988 was part of a broader attempt to decentralize the administrative process in Sri Lanka. Since Sri Lanka is a unitary state, most of its important decisions are made in the capital city of Colombo. In recent years the idea of decentralization has become quite popular among Sri Lankan and international experts of development and governmental administration.[20] Decentralization involves a transfer of decision-making authority from the central government machinery to local units of government or citizen groups. It is generally believed that the people who will be affected by administrative and development decisions should have more power to affect what happens to them. In other words, decentralization is conceptualized as a means of providing these people with the power to affect the decisions that directly affect their lives.

In sum, the Sri Lankan government has been structured in a way that provides the people with opportunities to become involved in government decisions. The highly partisan nature of politics (discussed in Chapter 21) has led to a strong patronage system in which the members of parliament try to please the people by meeting their demands. Both the high level of citizen input into the government and the open structure of the government have contributed to Sri Lanka's political stability.

NOTES

1. J. R. Jayawardene, "Parliamentary Democracy: The Role of the Opposition in a Developing Nation," *Parliamentarian,* July 1971, pp. 191–194.

2. A. Jeyaratnam, *The Gaullist System in Asia: The Constitution of Sri Lanka (1978)* (London: Macmillan, 1980), p. 62.

3. James Jupp, *Sri Lanka: Third World Democracy* (London: Frank Cass, 1978), pp. 28, 218.

4. See Jupp, *Sri Lanka,* pp. 258–271, for a discussion of the constitution.

5. See K. M. DeSilva, "The Constitution and Constitutional Reform Since 1948," in *Sri Lanka: A Survey,* ed. K. M. DeSilva (Honolulu: University Press of Hawaii, 1977), pp. 312–329.

6. See Wilson, *Gaullist System in Asia,* for a thorough discussion of the constitution.

7. Wilson, *Gaullist System in Asia,* p. 62.

8. Robert C. Oberst, "Proportional Representation and Electoral System Change in Sri Lanka," in *Sri Lanka in Change and Crisis,* ed. James Manor (London: Croon Helm, 1984), pp. 118–134.

9. Robert C. Oberst, *Legislators and Representation in Sri Lanka: The Decentralization of Development Planning* (Boulder: Westview, 1985), pp. 77–81.

10. Under the Donoughmore Constitution of 1931 there were provisions for naming appointed members of parliament. During this time one Indian Tamil was appointed to parliament.

11. For a discussion of the 1982 election, see W. A. Wiswa Warnapala and L. Dias Hewagama, *Recent Politics in Sri Lanka: The Presidential Election and the Referendum of 1982* (New Delhi: Navrang, 1983); Manor, ed., *Sri Lanka in Change and Crisis,* chaps. 2–5; and Robert C. Oberst and Amy Weilage, "Quantitative Tests of Electoral Fraud: The 1982 Sri Lankan Referendum," *Corruption and Reform,* Spring 1990, pp. 49–62.

12. Warnapala and Hewagama, *Recent Politics in Sri Lanka,* chap. 8; Priya Samarakone, "The Conduct of the Referendum," in *Sri Lanka in Change and Crisis,* ed. Manor, pp. 84–117.

13. Government of Sri Lanka, Sessional Paper No. II, *Report on the First Referendum in Sri Lanka* (Colombo: Department of Government Printing, 1987).

14. For the best description of the development of the administrative system, see W. A. Wiswa Warnapala, *Civil Service Administration in Ceylon: A Study in Bureaucratic Adaptation* (Colombo: Department of Cultural Affairs, 1974).

15. Wilson, *Gaullist System in Asia,* pp. 138–139.

16. For a description of government agents, see G. R. Tressie Leitan, *Local Government and Decentralized Administration in Sri Lanka* (Colombo: Lake House, 1979), chap. 6.

17. Neil Fernando, *Regional Administration in Sri Lanka* (Colombo: Academy of Administrative Studies, 1973), pp. 12–14; Robert C. Oberst, "Administrative Conflict and Decentralization: The Case of Sri Lanka," *Public Administration and Development* 5, no. 4 (1986): 163–174.

18. Oberst, *Legislators and Representation in Sri Lanka,* chap. 4.

19. Bruce Matthews, "District Development Councils in Sri Lanka," *Asian Survey*, November 1982, pp. 1117–1134.

20. See Dennis Rondinelli, John R. Nellis, and G. Shabbir Cheema, *Decentralization in Developing Countries: A Review of Recent Experience* (Washington, D.C.: World Bank, 1983).

21

Political Parties and Interest Groups

Constituent demands in a political system are a way of linking the governed with the governors. In every successful democracy, there is a considerable amount of communication between the constituents who bring their needs to their representatives and the representatives who, because of their accountability in elections, must respond to the demands.

Demands may be presented to the government by two broad categories of constituents—individuals and groups such as political parties and interest groups. As discussed later in this chapter, Sri Lankan members of parliament receive a large number of individual requests from their constituents. In addition, government officials are approached by various groups in the society.

The Political Party Systems

National politics in Sri Lanka has been dominated by two parties, the United National Party and the Sri Lanka Freedom Party. In nine of the last eleven parliamentary elections the parties have replaced each other as the governing party. Despite the national dominance of the UNP and the SLFP, Sri Lanka has had three party systems: one for the Tamil-speaking minority in the north and the east, one for the Muslims, and one for the rest of the Sinhalese. Neither the SLFP nor the UNP has won significant support from the Tamils of the north and east.

The Sinhalese Party System
The Sri Lanka Freedom Party.   The Sri Lanka Freedom Party is the dominant party in the governing People's Alliance. The party of the moderate left has always had a difficult time holding its leftist supporters together. The party was

damaged by factional infighting that led to its collapse after it governed from 1970 to 1977. However, its current leader, Mahinda Rajapakse, has brought together a diverse collection of parties that have allowed it to control the government since 2004.

The party was formed by S.W.R.D. Bandaranaike in 1951. Bandaranaike had been a popular minister in the UNP government formed in 1947 but chose to challenge the political dominance of the UNP. His first attempt was a failure. The party received relatively limited support in 1952 when it elected only nine members to parliament. In 1956, however, Bandaranaike put together a strong coalition of leftist and anti-UNP parties and personalities. (For a list of Sri Lankan heads of government, see Table 21.1.) The party was swept overwhelmingly into power in the 1956 elections. It tapped a strong sense of discontent among the rural Sinhalese, who felt that they had been discriminated against by the British and the first two governments of independent Sri Lanka. The party therefore committed itself to restoring the Sinhalese culture, language, and religion (Buddhism) to a position of dominance in the society. As a result, the government's first act was to make Sinhala the language of government, thus replacing English.

The coalition was held together until Bandaranaike was assassinated in 1959. After his death the coalition fell apart, and the SLFP was unable to provide a cohesive force in the March 1960 elections. Many small parties emerged out of Bandaranaike's 1956 coalition and split the party's support. By the July 1960 elections, the SLFP pulled its supporters together under the leadership of Bandaranaike's widow, Sirimavo Bandaranaike, who became the first woman ever elected as head of a democratic government. She was prime minister until 1965 and again from 1970 until 1977. In 1994 she was once again named prime minister and ruled in the executive presidency system under her daughter, President Chandrika Kumaratunga, until her death on October 10, 2000.

Under the guidance of Chandrika and her mother, the SLFP remained the party of the moderate left, although its membership includes both leftists and rightists. This pattern was continued by her successor, Mahinda Rajapakse. In 2004, his party formed a minority government and has survived with the support of the Maoist/nationalist Janatha Vimukthi Peramuna (JVP). In order to do this, he has been forced to accept the demands of the JVP.

The SLFP's success in elections has always been accompanied by electoral agreements with the major parties of the left. This was the case in 1956, 1960, 1970, 1994, 2000, and 2004. After its stunning loss in 1977 the SLFP underwent a split, with a number of factions emerging at different times.

TABLE 21.1 Heads of Government of Sri Lanka

	Party	Date of Birth	Date of Death	Term of Office	Caste
Don Stephen Senanayake	UNP	10/20/1884	3/22/1952	Sept. 1947–Mar. 1952	Goyigama
Dudley Senanayake	UNP	6/19/1911	4/13/1973	Mar. 1952–Sept. 1953 Mar. 1960–July 1960 Mar. 1965–May 1970	Goyigama
John Kotelawala	UNP	4/04/1897	10/02/1980	Sept. 1953–Apr. 1956	Goyigama
S.W.R.D. Bandaranaike	SLFP	1/08/1899	9/26/1959	Apr. 1956–Sept. 1959	Goyigama
Wijayananda Dahanayake	SLFP	10/22/1902	3/15/1997	Sept. 1959–Mar. 1960	Goyigama
Sirimavo Bandaranaike	SLFP	4/17/1916	10/10/2000	July 1960–Mar. 1965 May 1970–July 1977	Goyigama
J. R. Jayawardene	UNP	9/17/1906	11/1/1996	July 1977–Dec. 1988	Goyigama
Ranasinghe Premadasa	UNP	6/23/1924	5/1/1993	Dec. 1988–May 1993	Hinna
D. B. Wijetunga	UNP	2/15/1922	—	May 1993–Nov. 1994	Goyigama
Chandrika Kumaratunga	PA(SLFP)	6/29/1945	—	Nov. 1994–Nov. 2005	Goyigama
Mahinda Rajapakse	PA(SLFP)	11/18/1945	—	Nov. 2005–present	Goyigama

Note: Through September 1978 the head of government was the prime minister. After that date, the president.
UNP—United National Party; SLFP—Sri Lankan Freedom Party; PA—People's Alliance
Source: Author's notes.

The United National Party.   The United National Party is the party of the right in Sri Lankan politics. It has generated such personalities as Don Stephen Senanayake, J. R. Jayawardene, and Ranasinghe Premadasa. Its emergence as an umbrella party from the colonial era was similar to the formation of the Indian National Congress of India (see Chapter 4) insofar as it represented a union of many different ideologies and personalities that arose from the independence movement. The domination of the party by independence movement politicians ended when President J. R. Jayawardene retired in 1988, precipitating a power struggle among party leaders.

Its first leader in the post-Jayawardene era, President Ranasinghe Premadasa, was killed in a bomb explosion in 1993. It is widely believed that the bomb was set by the guerrillas of the LTTE, but rumors persist that disgruntled members of his own party killed him.

After the UNP lost the 1994 elections, Ranil Wickremasinghe took control of the party. His rise to power was aided by the assassinations of Gamini Dissanayake and Lalith Athulathmudali, popular figures in the party who would have challenged his leadership. The party was devastated when Dissanayake was killed by a suicide bomber in October 1994 while he was campaigning for the presidency. Few leaders with clean reputations remained to challenge Ranil for party leadership. Ironically, one of the few was Anura Bandaranaike, who joined the party in 1994 after losing a power struggle with his sister for leadership of the SLFP. He returned to the SLFP after the death of his mother in 2000.

Until the 1994 elections, the UNP had been the strongest vote-getter in Sri Lankan elections. It dominated the first two elections after independence in 1947 and 1952 before losing the 1956 elections to the SLFP, and it returned to power for a brief period in 1960 after the elections in March of that year. Since those elections did not give the UNP a working parliamentary majority, it was unable to obtain a vote of confidence from parliament for its government. In the elections of July 1960 the UNP once again lost to the SLFP. It returned to power in 1965 and governed until 1970, when it lost the elections. In 1977 the UNP was returned to power with a commanding five-sixths majority in parliament. The scheduled 1983 elections were canceled after a referendum held in 1982 over the question of whether the present parliament, which had been elected in 1977, should be continued until 1989.

The 1989 parliamentary elections gave the UNP control over parliament but with a smaller majority (125 of 225 seats). In 1994 the party was in disarray under the leadership of Dingiri Banda Wijetunga, who replaced Premadasa as president in 1993. The elections resulted in a slim margin of victory for the People's Alliance, which obtained a majority by creating a wide coalition of leftist, Muslim, and Tamil parties. The UNP would gain a majority in the 2001 elections and ruled the country for two years before losing to the SLFP in the April 2004 elections.

The Other Parties

The Lanka Sama Samaja Party and Communist Party.   Sri Lanka has had a long tradition of strong leftist parties based on two traditional Marxist parties. At one time, the Lanka Sama Samaja Party (LSSP) was billed as the world's only successful Trotskyite party. (Leon Trotsky was vanquished by Joseph Stalin in the power struggle that followed Lenin's death in 1924 in the Soviet Union.) Its support came from Marxists who objected to the Communist Party's close association with the Soviet Union and thus preferred the independent Marxism of the LSSP. Moreover, it represents an independent doctrine of Marxism adapted to the culture and needs of Sri Lanka rather than the Soviet-oriented Marxism of the Sri Lanka Communist Party.[1]

After the 1947 elections the LSSP was the main opposition to the governing UNP. But the emergence of the SLFP provided many voters on the left wing of Sri Lankan politics with a moderate alternative to the Marxist LSSP and the Communist Party. The LSSP was an important element of the 1970 United Front coalition established by Sirimavo Bandaranaike. Three cabinet positions were given to LSSP MPs in the government formed after the 1970 elections, including the important ministry of finance. Since that election, the party has lost influence but remains an ally of the SLFP.

The Communist Party.   The Communist Party of Sri Lanka maintained close ideological ties with the Soviet Union. With the collapse of Soviet communism, the party has drawn closer to the LSSP. The Communist Party has received strong support in the southern regions of the country, where it has been associated with the Durawa caste. Like the LSSP, its has experienced sharply declining influence, although it still holds several seats in parliament.

The Janatha Vimukthi Peramuna.   Today, the most significant leftist party is the Janatha Vimukthi Peramuna. The JVP (known in English as the People's Liberation Front) and its founder and leader until his death in November 1989, Rohana Wijeweera, were responsible for youth-led insurrections against the government of Sirimavo Bandaranaike in 1971 and J. R. Jayawardene in 1987–1989. Formed in the late 1960s, the JVP came perilously close to overthrowing the government with a series of well-planned attacks against police stations and government positions in 1971.[2] Official estimates placed the death toll around 1,200 people, and unofficial reports placed it much higher. In addition, more than 16,000 suspected insurgents were taken into custody after the failed revolt.[3] As a result, many of the leaders and followers of the JVP were sentenced to jail. Wijeweera was sentenced to twenty years in prison; however, the UNP released him shortly after the 1977 elections.

The UNP legalized the JVP and it emerged as a leftist party dedicated to nonviolent means of changing the society. After being legalized, it contested local council elections, and Wijeweera ran for president. In the 1982 presidential elections Wijeweera polled 4.2 percent of the total vote, or about 270,000 votes. After severe anti-Tamil riots in 1983, the party was accused of fomenting the violence and was banned. After the July 1987 Indo-Lanka accords that made concessions to the Tamil insurgents in the north of the island, the JVP began a campaign of assassinating government supporters. At the height of the violence (June to August 1989), over 800 people per month were being killed. Not all of the deaths were at the hands of the JVP, however. Death squads of government supporters and security forces are believed to have been responsible for many deaths as well.

In November 1989 the government captured Wijeweera and claimed that he was shot dead by his own supporters as he led government security forces to JVP hideouts. In any case, all of the JVP politburo and most of its district leaders were captured or killed in November 1989. Since that time, the JVP has been rebuilding its organization and has disavowed violence.[4] In the 1990s, it became the third largest party in the country and elected thirty-nine members to parliament in the 2004 elections. The party has become more nationalist, adopting an anti-Tamil position and opposing efforts to resolve the civil war peacefully.

The Tamil Party System

In Sri Lanka (as in India), some regional minority groups have formed their own political parties. The Sri Lanka Tamils, for example, have consistently supported their own parties and tried to win the support of the Sri Lanka Muslims. As a result, there is a separate party system operating in areas where the Sri Lanka Tamils are in the majority. The Sri Lanka Tamil party system is in a state of transition because of its transformation by the ethnic conflict that developed into a civil war in the 1980s.

Immediately after independence, there was only one important Tamil party in Sri Lanka—the Tamil Congress (TC), led by G. G. Ponnambalam. The TC cooperated with the UNP in the first government after independence, when the Indian Tamils were denied citizenship and the right to vote. Several members of the TC deserted their party in opposition to its support of this action and formed a new party called the Federal Party. Under the leadership of S. J. V. Chelvanayagam, this party demanded a federal system in Sri Lanka, with home rule for the Tamils in the eastern and northern parts of the island.

The Federal Party soon replaced the TC as the dominant party among the Sri Lanka Tamils. Shortly after the 1970 elections, the Tamil parties, comprising both the Indian and the Sri Lanka Tamils, came together in a coalition to form the Tamil United Liberation Front (TULF). A significant element of the TC opposed the union and reappeared as the Tamil Congress after the 1977 elections.

The TULF increased its demands for regional self-rule in 1976 and began demanding an independent state (Eelam) for the Tamil people. In the 1977 general elections, and in the local council and presidential elections in the early 1980s, the TULF received the overwhelming backing of the Sri Lanka Tamils in the north and along the east coast.

The call for Eelam, accompanied by the increasing violence by Tamil youths in the north and east of the island, led the government to pass the Sixth Amendment to the constitution in 1983. This amendment specifically banned the advocacy of separatism. All of the sixteen TULF MPs were expelled from parliament for failing to recite a loyalty oath disavowing separatism as required by the amendment. The government then refused to hold by-elections in the areas represented by these opposition members because of the youth-led violence, and the Sri Lanka Tamils remained without representation in parliament until 1989. During their five-year absence from parliament, the radical LTTE replaced them as the dominant political force among the Tamils.

The TULF originally included the largest Indian Tamil political organization, the Ceylon Worker's Congress (CWC). After the 1977 elections, however, the leader of the CWC was offered a cabinet post in the UNP government. As a result, the CWC disassociated itself from the TULF. In any case, the calls for Eelam are largely ignored by the Indian Tamils, who reside outside the territory that has been claimed for the state of Eelam.

As the tension between the Sinhalese and the Sri Lankan Tamils increased, Sri Lanka Tamil youths resorted to violence and joined several political groups commonly called "tigers." These organizations challenged the leadership position of the TULF in the Sri Lanka Tamil community and became the dominant force in Sri Lankan Tamil politics in the 1980s.

Although there were a large number of tiger groups, only a few were important as political forces. The larger groups had sophisticated training camps in southern India, and most were financed by the proceeds from bank robberies in Sri Lanka and drug sales in Europe as well as by donations from wealthy Tamils living in the United States and Great Britain.

The political strength of the tigers became apparent after the July 1987 Indo-Lanka accords calling for a cease-fire between the tigers and the government, with the Indian army acting as a peacekeeping force. The accords also established a system of provincial councils. All but one of the major tiger groups went along with the treaty and turned over their arms and became legal political organizations. The one exception was the group with the most powerful military, the Liberation Tigers of Tamil Eelam (LTTE), which continued to fight against the Indian forces.

The other armed groups have formed into democratic political parties, joined by the Eelam Peoples Democratic Party and the Tamileelam Makkal Viduthalai Pulikal (TMVP), a breakaway faction of the LTTE also known as the Karuna faction. These other groups have not been able to win strong support from Tamil voters, and most elections have been dominated by the TULF.

The TULF split in 2004 when the largely ceremonial president of the party, Anandasangaree, refused to accept an electoral agreement with the LTTE. As a result, the rest of the party leadership formed the Tamil National Alliance and ran in the 2004 elections with a mix of TULF leaders and Tamil candidates selected by the LTTE. They elected twenty-two members to parliament.

Until the next election, there is no way to determine how much support the Tamil parties have. It appears that the TNA is still the strongest party, but the EPDP, led by a cabinet minister in the Rajapakse government, and the TMVP both have bases of support.

The Muslim Party System

The Muslims have shifted their support between the UNP and the SLFP, with most voting for the UNP. In 1988, the Sri Lanka Muslim Congress (SLMC) was formed and almost immediately gained majority support among Muslim voters, especially in the Eastern Province. The SLMC was formed by the charismatic M. H. M. Ashroff, who died in a suspicious helicopter crash in 2002. The party then broke up into a number of factions. These factions have shifted and their leaders have created alliances with other Muslim faction leaders. Currently, the two most powerful factions are the SLMC, led by Rauff Hakeem and Ashroff's widow, Ferial Ashroff, who leads the National Unity Alliance.

Party Systems in Change

The many changes in the party system in Sri Lanka since 1977 have created a highly volatile situation that could pose a serious threat to the political system. Among the Tamil parties, a new generation of leadership has emerged. The TULF, representing the older generation of leadership, appears to have recovered from a near fatal blow with the LTTE assassination of its leader, A. Amirthalingam, in July 1989. The younger generation of leaders, represented by the tigers, appears to have taken a leading role in Tamil politics. Many of the older generation of Tamils appear to have acknowledged that the "boys," as the guerrilla fighters have been called, have earned the right to lead the Tamils because of their sacrifices for the Tamil people. However, the "legal" tiger groups (such as the EPDP and the TMVP) have not been able to win support from the Tamil people. How much electoral support the LTTE would have is unknown. Government propaganda claiming that the LTTE has no support among the Tamil people does not appear to be true.

The Sinhalese party system has also been in a state of change, especially in regard to the apparent demise of the Sri Lankan "old left," which consists of the Communist Party and the LSSP and its allies. Since the 1977 parliamentary elections, the parties of the old left have not been able to run competitively with the UNP and the SLFP. The growth of the JVP, especially among young people, appears to reflect the inability of the LSSP and the Communist Party to win youth support as they did in the 1950s and 1960s.

Change has not been confined to the parties of the left. The SLFP and the UNP have both experienced pressure for change. The retirement of Chandrika Kumaratunga allowed a non-Bandaranaike to take over the leadership of the party. The new leader, Mahinda Rajapakse, severed ties to Kumaratunga and has placed his own loyalists in charge of the party. Although Chandrika's brother Anura Bandranaike is still a minister in the Rajapakse government, he has been marginalized.

President Rajapakse has also lured a number of prominent UNP MPs to cross over and support his government, most of whom were dissatisfied with the party leadership of Ranil Wickremasinghe. They have formed a bloc in the Rajapakse government voting with his government but maintaining their identity as a UNP faction. The departure of these MPs has weakened the UNP, and the future ability of the party to win national elections is in doubt.

The rise of the SLMC and other Muslim parties has also threatened the UNP's base of support. Traditionally Muslims living in Colombo and other urban centers of the Sinhalese areas supported the UNP. Now the Muslim parties are drawing votes away from the UNP.

The next few years will be very important to the future of democracy in Sri Lanka as the party system struggles with the forces that have been changing it. The nature of the changes is still not known, although their consequences will have a major impact on the structure that Sri Lankan politics takes in the future.

Interest Groups

National Groups

Many have argued that the emergence of broad-based national interest groups is a part of the development process that third world democracies are undergoing.[5] Interest groups provide governmental representation for the various interests in the society. In Sri Lanka interest groups are unorganized and weak and do not exert significant pressure on lawmakers and bureaucrats. Their weakness can be attributed to several factors.

First, many interest groups do not find it worthwhile to approach the elected members of parliament with their demands. Hence they try to influence the administrative rather than the policy-making process. Public policy in Sri Lanka is the result of a party's election platform and its ideology. Many groups know in advance that the government's ideology is not favorable to their demands, and so they direct their demands to the administrators, who may be more responsive and can circumvent the rules to meet their demands. But this practice is limited by a general sense of hostility among the governing Sri Lankan political parties toward what they call "sabotage by public officials" hostile to the governing party's policies.[6] Attempts are frequently made to transfer or suspend bureaucrats who may be sympathetic to the opposition party. Many politicians believe that bureaucrats work for one or the other of the major parties. As a result, elected politicians try to limit the amount of policy interpretation exercised by the bureaucrats. This limits the influence the interest groups can exert over government decisions by approaching the bureaucracy.

A second factor is that the major parties establish interest groups they can control. In fact, most interest groups are closely connected with either the government or an opposition party and thus do not need access to politicians. Interest groups in Sri Lanka are frequently extensions of political parties. This is especially the case among trade unions, in which the electoral triumph of the union's party is believed to lead to the achievement of the union's political objectives—hence the all-or-nothing view of the political process by the unions.[7] If the wrong party is in power, the unions do not expect to receive government cooperation and benefits. There is little bargaining and compromise between the government and the interest groups. The interest group either receives what it wants from its party when the party is in power or it is denied its objectives.

A third factor is that policy-making power is concentrated in a few important ministries, and therefore the number of people who may influence policy is limited.[8] The domination of Sri Lanka by a few charismatic personalities has resulted in a small inner circle consisting of people who hold significant policy-making power.

A fourth factor is the nature of power and influence in Sri Lanka. Much pressure is exerted through family networks and friends. As noted earlier, Sri Lankans tend to view power in personal terms; thus, when an individual, no matter how unimportant, goes to a person with power, he or she expects to be granted a personal meeting with that official.[9] No mere representative of that official would be acceptable. Access to power is indeed a personal affair.[10] Consequently a lobbyist in Sri Lanka is effective only if he or she establishes a set of personal contacts. At the same time, the highly partisan nature of politics in Sri Lanka makes it very difficult for an individual to maintain close personal contacts with powerful members of both parties.

A fifth factor is that interest groups tend to be ad hoc.[11] Groups may rise around an emotional issue, but once their initial objectives have been achieved or the issues lose their emotional appeal, the groups become inactive and disappear. This is especially the case with village-level interest groups. For instance, an important person in the village with a demand may gather some of his clients and go to the government official as a delegation representing the village. Many of the clients go with him because of the opportunity to present their own demands if the opportunity arises. Thus the important person's demand appears to reflect a broader segment of the village population than it actually does.

Nevertheless, the people in positions of power do not generally feel pressured by these groups since they are usually dealing with friends who are leading the groups.[12] This practice has been reinforced by the creation of ministries that cater to a specific clientele, such as the Ministry of Cultural Affairs, which was set up to deal with the demands of the All-Ceylon Buddhist Congress, or the Ministry of Regional Development, which was established to deal with the Tamil ethnic group in the eastern and northern parts of the island.

In short, the relationship between national interest groups and people in positions of power is not one of compromise and bargaining but rather one of cooperation and accommodation. These groups' ability to affect policy, although limited by poor organization, is enhanced by close ties to the political parties as well as by the personal relationships created by the leaders of the groups with people in positions of power.

These limitations, however, have not completely hindered the development of interest groups. Several Buddhist organizations have utilized their connections to powerful individuals in the government and mobilized mass support for their initiatives. In recent years they have been extremely active in trying to influence peace negotiations with the LTTE.

Local Groups

Local interest groups function in a different way and are more influential than the national organizations. South Asian life revolves around the village. More than 78 percent of the Sri Lankan population lives in rural areas. The average villager is very active in village-level organizations, and a large number of village-level organizations have developed. These include development-oriented organizations such as rural development societies, religious societies, parent-teacher associations, cooperatives, and occupational groups, which are quite active and vigorously lobby for policies and government actions that will benefit their group.

These organizations are dominated by a small elite of the village-level society and often revolve around one or two important people in the village. Villagers in Sri Lanka often look to people with high economic standing, good background, the right caste, educational attainment, and religious piety to lead them. Many of the organizations in the village often have the same people leading them, thus limiting the influence and input of the villagers themselves.[13]

In addition, these groups tend to be highly politicized, with their leadership allied to one of the major political parties. After elections, the leaders are often replaced by people acceptable to the newly elected national leaders or MPs. There have been cases in some rural development societies in which the old leaders have refused to yield power in the organization after a national election and the government has recognized a new organization led by the supporters of the government. On the whole, however, the village-level groups tend to deal with village-level concerns—new roads, village electrification, bridges, development projects, and so on. The amount of influence they exert depends, once again, on how closely they are aligned with those who wield power.

Individual Demands

Most demands on the Sri Lankan political system are made by individuals. Many Sri Lankans expect government representatives to respond to their personal needs, and the benefits they receive are called particularized benefits. Sri Lankan members of parliament set aside time to meet personally with their constituents. As a result, they are inundated by constituents with highly personalized requests for such things as jobs for their children or themselves. The average member of parliament may meet with more than 700 people a week, and the ministers, who have a large number of patronage jobs available to them, may see several thousand constituents each week.[14] The constituents begin lining up outside the meeting place before sunrise and wait for hours for their opportunity to speak to the member of parliament. The MP will usually deal with each request quickly and move on to the next petitioner. Ministers are assisted by staff people who type letters of recommendation, call government servants who have refused to act on a government form, and take down information to follow up on requests.

The most frequent request received by MPs is for help with employment.[15] The petitioner, his or her son or daughter, or another relative may request help in finding a job, obtaining an employment transfer to a better location, or getting an improved appointment. Beyond this, the member of parliament may be faced with requests to resolve family feuds or even speak to a husband who has been sleeping with other women. Rarely do the demands deal with national issues or questions of community development. Even then they often involve projects that personally benefit the petitioner, such as a paved road past his house or a new irrigation canal to his fields. Another important aspect of these demands is that both men and women come to make them, with women composing more than 40 percent of the petitioners.[16]

The members of parliament have a limited number of jobs and other benefits to provide to their constituents. They base their decisions on patronage. Almost all government jobs are given on the basis of personal connections rather than merit. The patronage system has undergone considerable expansion since the 1960s, which has resulted in increased constituent demands and expectations as well as dissatisfaction from the supporters of the opposition parties.

The net consequence of this pressure for personalized treatment is overburdened legislators who spend most of their time dealing with petitioners' requests. In fact, the legislators are often left feeling that their time should be spent on more important activities, such as development work and national issues. Efforts to reduce the constituent pressure on legislators have not been successful. During the Jayawardene years the creation of a computerized "job bank" to dispense government jobs turned into a fiasco that rewarded those with access to the computer "bank." The creation of proportional representation was intended to be a means of controlling job seekers. However, the use of the preferential ballot requires that members of parliament be popular in their electoral districts. The main effect of the change was to enlarge the size of the electoral district to include a whole administrative district.

*   *   *

In sum, interest articulation and demands, like other aspects of Sri Lankan society, is a highly personalized process. Government representatives frequently respond to people's personal needs, and most people expect this. Yet the most important part of this system of demands and government responses is its high level of institutionalization and effectiveness, especially where individual demands are concerned. Sri Lankans have access to their leaders, and they take advantage of this access.

NOTES

1. For a thorough description of the early history of the party, see George Jan Lerski, *The Origins of Trotskyism in Ceylon* (Stanford, Calif.: Hoover Institution, 1968).

2. Robert N. Kearney and Janice Jiggins, "The Ceylon Insurrection of 1971," *Journal of Commonwealth and Comparative Politics,* March 1975, pp. 40–65; A. C. Alles, *J.V.P.: 1969–1989* (Colombo: Lake House Investments, 1990).

3. Gananath Obeyesekere, "Some Comments on the Social Backgrounds of the April 1971 Insurgency in Sri Lanka (Ceylon)," *Journal of Asian Studies* 33 (1974): 367–384.

4. For an insider's description of the insurrection, see C. A. Chandraprema, *Sri Lanka, The Years of Terror: The JVP Insurrection, 1987–1989* (Colombo: Lake House Bookshop, 1991). For a journalist's view from the outside of the movement, see Rohan Gunaratna, *Sri Lanka, A Lost Revolution: The Inside Story of the JVP* (Colombo: Institute of Fundamental Studies, 1990).

5. Gabriel A. Almond and G. Bingham Powell, *Comparative Politics: System, Process, and Policy,* 2d ed. (Boston: Little, Brown, 1978), pp. 196–197.

6. Robert N. Kearney, *Trade Unions and Politics in Ceylon* (Berkeley: University of California Press), pp. 83–84.

7. Kearney, *Trade Unions,* p. 2.

8. Robert C. Oberst, "Democracy and the Persistence of Westernized Elite Dominance in Sri Lanka," *Asian Survey,* July 1985, pp. 760–772.

9. Janice Jiggins, *Caste and Family in the Politics of the Sinhalese, 1947–1976* (New York: Cambridge University Press, 1979); James Jupp, *Sri Lanka: Third World Democracy* (London: Frank Cass, 1978), p. 174.

10. Robert C. Oberst, *Legislators and Representation in Sri Lanka: The Decentralization of Development Planning* (Boulder: Westview, 1985), pp. 34–35.

11. Urmila Phadnis, *Religion and Politics in Sri Lanka* (New Delhi: Manohar, 1976), p. 273.

12. Oberst, *Legislators and Representation,* pp. 40–41.

13. Oberst, *Legislators and Representation,* pp. 41–44.

14. Oberst, *Legislators and Representation,* p. 59.

15. Oberst, *Legislators and Representation,* p. 37.

16. Oberst, *Legislators and Representation,* chap. 3.

22

Conflict Mediation:
Ethnic Conflict and War

Since the late 1970s, no issue has dominated Sri Lankan society as much as the conflict between the Liberation Tigers of Tamil Eelam (LTTE) and the government. The conflict grew out of a long-standing sense of deprivation felt by the country's Tamil population. During the British era the Tamils adapted to the English language and British cultural mores more readily than the Sinhalese. As a result, the British rewarded them with important places in the colonial bureaucracy. After independence, however, the Sinhalese attempted to assert a dominant role in the society, and conflict resulted.

At first the Tamil leadership sought more control over Tamil affairs. The emergence of the Federal Party as the dominant party in the Sri Lanka Tamil areas was the result of its strong advocacy for federalism and regional autonomy for the Tamils. Its success in replacing the Tamil Congress as the dominant Sri Lanka Tamil party can be attributed to this advocacy. Until the 1970s the Federal Party demanded a federal system of government in Sri Lanka so that the Tamils could control their own affairs. In the mid-1970s, with the creation of the Tamil United Liberation Front (TULF), the Federal Party escalated its demands to include the creation of an independent state for the Tamils.

The Federal Party's demands for greater autonomy were fueled by several concerns. The first was the language issue. As long as the British ruled Sri Lanka, an alien language—English—was imposed on the people. As soon as the British left the island, the issue emerged as an important point of contention. When the Official Language Act of 1956 specified Sinhala as the sole official language of Sri Lanka, Tamils feared being denied employment in government jobs, which would now require proficiency in Sinhala; they also feared that they would be unable to understand government legal proceedings, which would now be held in Sinhala, and that they would be left out of the commercial life of the society, also conducted in Sinhala. The government responded by passing a resolution allowing the use of Tamil in government transactions involving people who spoke Tamil. The resolution also provided government employees whose mother tongue was Tamil time to learn Sinhala. However, these requirements, which were passed in 1959, have not yet been fully implemented. Many government communications to Tamil-speaking people still appear in Sinhala. Moreover, although the constitution of 1978 gave the Tamil language special status in some government dealings, it maintained the superiority of Sinhala in the society; in addition, its designation of Tamil as a "national language" while Sinhala remained the only "official language" failed to placate the Tamil leadership, and the problem remains a point of conflict.

A second concern has been education. As noted in Chapter 19, Sri Lankans know the importance of education. Admissions to university education are limited and coveted. After independence, admissions were determined on the basis of examinations in the three languages used in the country—Sinhala, Tamil, and English. Only those receiving the highest scores were admitted. For many years the number of students admitted on the basis of the Tamil language exams exceeded the number that would have been expected from this group on the basis of their percentage of the population. Many Sinhalese felt that the Tamil examiners were inflating the scores so that more Tamil students would be admitted to the universities. In the 1970s the United Front government of Sirimavo Bandaranaike became concerned with the superior performance of the Tamil students. Quotas based on the size of each ethnic community were set, and university exams became a disputed issue. The UNP sought to defuse the issue by altering the system to one based on both quotas and merit, but this effort was slow to ease resentment.

A third concern pertains to employment. The government sector is the main source of high-status jobs. As Sinhala has become more important as the language of government, Tamil speakers have become more concerned with the access of their community to government employment. But there has been a severe shortage of jobs for educated young people from all ethnic communities since the early 1960s. The lack of jobs has been cited as a cause of the youth insurrections led by the JVP in the early 1970s and late 1980s. These uprisings involved many more Sinhalese youths than Tamil youths. The government's language and education policies helped to create a sense of deprivation among the Tamil youths, who now also had the Sinhalese and the government to blame for their plight. They also fueled the guerrilla warfare that has engulfed the northern and eastern regions of the country.

A fourth concern has been the Sinhalese colonization of traditional Tamil areas. In Trincomalee, Vavuniya, and Batticaloa districts, recently irrigated lands have been opened for settlement. In many areas, especially Trincomalee, the lands have been given to Sinhalese. This has had the effect of reducing the Tamil percentage of the population in these areas. The problem has been amplified by the Mahaweli development project, which has opened up newly irrigated lands at a rapid pace. Most of the irrigated farmland created by the Mahaweli project has been distributed to Sinhalese settlers.

A fifth concern is the central government's neglect of the north and east. Both areas have been largely ignored in the government's development plans. The highly centralized Sri Lankan government has tended to focus its attention on the southwestern areas of the country. The rural areas of the north and east are much more traditional than other parts of Sri Lanka.

The sixth concern has been regional autonomy or control over significant policy decisions directly affecting the Tamils. One of these decisions is on the number and type of development projects in Tamil areas. The Tamils feel that they have not received their fair share of the projects available. This was especially the case with the Jayawardene government's two major development initiatives—the Mahaweli project, which, for the most part, affects Sinhalese areas, and the free trade zones, which are located in the Sinhalese areas. In short, the Tamils believe that they are not benefiting from the income and jobs generated by these projects.

A second issue raised by the question of regional autonomy concerns the maintenance of law and order. The majority of police and armed forces in the Tamil areas are members of the Sinhalese ethnic group. Many of the attacks carried out by the "tiger" groups were directed against the Sinhalese police and soldiers. Since 1977, police and soldiers have sporadically rioted and attacked innocent bystanders. Several of these security force actions have resulted in over 100 civilians being killed. These attacks became common during the 1980s and early 1990s. Despite efforts by the Kumaratunga government to control these abuses, they still occur. In addition, since the UNP came to power, the country has suffered major outbursts of anti-Tamil rioting (in 1977, 1981, and 1983). Once again, large numbers of Tamils have lost their lives and personal belongings. Moreover, some Tamil leaders have claimed that the police cooperated and assisted the rioters in their attacks against the Tamils.

Probably the most important issue related to regional autonomy is the question of what area should be included in the "Tamil region." The TULF and the LTTE have supported the union of the Eastern and Northern provinces. This proposal has been criticized because of the large numbers of Sinhalese and Muslims in the Eastern Province. Most Muslims are concerned about a regional government controlled by the Tamils. They fear that their influence would be diluted in such an arrangement.

The Sinhalese population of the east poses another problem. Over the past fifty years there has been a large influx of Sinhalese settlers into the Eastern Province. This growth was accelerated after 1977 when the Mahaweli project opened up land in Ampara, Batticaloa, and Trincomalee districts to Sinhalese settlers. These settlers fear a Tamil-dominated regional government.[1]

These five concerns led Tamil leaders to intensify their demands for an independent state, and the Tamil youths to encourage further violence. Communication between the Sinhalese and the Tamils broke down, and the militant tiger leaders gained more influence in the Tamil community.

From 1984 until 1987, the two sides negotiated, with the Indian government acting as an intermediary. These negotiations met with little success. In July 1987 the Sri Lankan and Indian governments signed the Indo-Lanka accords, which brought Indian troops to Sri Lanka to enforce a cease-fire. The tigers were never involved in the negotiations, and the LTTE never agreed to the accords. Open warfare between the Indian peacekeeping forces and the LTTE erupted in October 1987 and continued until the Indian departure in March 1990.[2]

In 1989 President Premadasa began the first direct negotiations between the Sri Lankan government and the LTTE and reached an agreement with them in June 1989 to lay down their arms, renounce separatism, and negotiate further on regional autonomy. He then asked the Indian troops to leave the country by the second anniversary of their arrival. They refused and continued their war against the LTTE.

Indian troops finally left Sri Lanka in March 1990. Their departure was followed by a brief period of peace between the government and the LTTE. However, in June the LTTE began an offensive against police stations in the north and east. The civil war evolved into a bloodier conflict as the LTTE increased its attacks against Muslim and Sinhalese civilians and the government used air power to bomb targets in Tamil areas. By the end of August 1994 the government controlled the cities of the Eastern Province and some of the countryside but failed to conquer the mainland of the Jaffna peninsula in the north. The war had become a bloody stalemate.

President Kumaratunga and her government were elected on a platform of negotiating an end to the conflict in 1994. Kumaratunga took the courageous position of offering to grant regional autonomy to the Tamils. For the first time since independence, a Sri Lankan government acknowledged that the political system was not providing the Tamils with a fair role in the system.

President Kumaratunga began negotiations with the LTTE in January 1995. These talks became a comedy of errors as the LTTE was insulted by the limited power and stature of the government negotiators and the government was angered by the LTTE's demand that before negotiations on substantive issues such as the devolution of power could occur, the problems and suffering of the Tamil people must first be alleviated.

After four months the negotiations had failed to achieve any progress. The LTTE finally gave the government a series of ultimatums and threats about pulling out of the negotiations. Finally, on April 19, 1995, the civil war began again when the LTTE followed through with their threats.

The Kumaratunga government was stung with criticism of its trust of the LTTE and the concessions it had offered to them. Despite this, it promised to continue to propose and implement its devolution proposal to give the Tamils autonomy. In addition, it embarked on a massive military offensive against the LTTE.

The Sri Lankan military was expanded and the government sought to capture the LTTE capital, Jaffna. In December 1995 the Sri Lankan army raised the Sri Lankan flag over Jaffna and claimed to have reconquered the Jaffna peninsula. For the first time in nearly ten years, Jaffna was largely under Sri Lankan government rule.

The LTTE was embarrassed by its loss of the Tamil heartland, but it was not defeated militarily. Its members retreated to the dense jungles of the Vanni region to the south of Jaffna and set up a new capital in Killinochi.

In anger and frustration, the LTTE struck back at the government by blowing up the Central Bank building in Colombo on January 31, 1996. Nearly 100 people died and over 1,400 were wounded in an explosion, destroying the euphoria and celebration of the Sinhalese people over the fall of Jaffna. The bombing was a symbolic attack by the LTTE, but more significantly, it destroyed any realistic opportunity for the two sides to seek a negotiated settlement to the conflict. Sinhalese positions on the conflict hardened, and the government became resolute in its position that the LTTE must be militarily hurt before it would ever return to the negotiating table.

After this the war took new turns as the LTTE captured the Mullaitivu army base in July 1996, killing over 1,000 government troops and capturing tons of ammunition and supplies. The government responded by capturing Killinochi in September, which drove the LTTE into the jungles. The LTTE no longer controlled any major towns. In May 1997 the government began an operation to open a land route to Jaffna through the LTTE-controlled Vanni.[3] Success would have helped to normalize life in Jaffna and dealt a humiliating defeat to the LTTE. This maneuver resulted in another stalemate, however, as the government troops bogged down trying to consolidate their gains about halfway along the road to Jaffna.

In the spring of 2000, the LTTE launched a series of attacks on the Elephant Pass army camp at the entrance to the Jaffna peninsula. The camp was captured in May as LTTE troops began pushing the government troops to the outskirts of Jaffna. With the imminent collapse of the government forces, the Sri Lankan government sought outside help. In response to their pleas, Israel provided massive supplies of armaments, including air power, and, as a result, the LTTE offensive was stopped. Once again the conflict entered a period of stalemate as the Sri Lankan army gradually recaptured small amounts of the seized territory at great cost to both sides.

In the late 1990s, the Sri Lanka government asked the Norwegian government to act as an intermediary between the LTTE and the government. For the first time in over twenty years of conflict, the two sides would communicate with each other on a regular basis. The Norwegian efforts resulted in a cease-fire agreement in February 2002. The agreement followed a publicly announced willingness by the LTTE to consider a solution that did not involve independence. In the December 2001 parliamentary elections, the UNP ran on a platform to accept the LTTE's willingness to negotiate and cease hostilities. The LTTE stopped hostilities almost immediately after the election and an official ceasefire agreement was signed in February 2002.

The agreement called for the two sides to control the territory they held at the time of the agreement and normalize relations. For the first time in twenty years, the country was at peace. A massive effort was begun to rebuild the war-torn north and east.

However, the cease-fire agreement was not accepted by all within the government. The JVP opposed the agreement along with a significant segment of the SLFP. The Norwegian-brokered negotiations between the two sides showed no progress and in April 2004 the SLFP, with the support of the JVP, was able to form a minority government. Many of the government ministers appointed by the party had originally opposed negotiations with the LTTE. In November 2005, Mahinda Rajapakse, the new leader of the SLFP, was elected president and immediately began to dismantle the peace accords. The party began a policy of localized offensives against the LTTE, attacking them at the extremities of their control and gradually reducing their area of control. This policy was coupled with an alliance with a breakaway faction of the LTTE in the Eastern Province. This faction, led by Colonel Karuna, began a program of attacking unarmed LTTE political operatives working in government-held areas and kidnapping Tamils in the east and elsewhere. In addition, the Eelam People's Democratic Party (EPDP), an ally in the Rajapkse cabinet, began a campaign of attacking the LTTE and other Tamils.

The program would reap success with the LTTE effectively eliminated from the Eastern Province after a series of military victories in 2006 and 2007. In mid-2007, the government began to attack LTTE outposts in the Northern Province.

In January 2008, the government officially announced that it was pulling out of the cease-fire agreement.

Along with the military policy was a series of severe human rights abuses as journalists, aid workers, and opposition members of parliament have been targeted by the government or its allies.

The year 2008 began with government claims that the LTTE leader Prabhakaran would be killed during the year and the "terrorist" threat of the LTTE ended. Although these claims have been made many times before, the military victories of 2006 and 2007 for the first time implied that the government might finally be able to end the civil war. Beyond the LTTE losses is the reality that the conditions which led to the civil war have not been addressed. Evidence from the Eastern Province where the LTTE was eliminated indicates that the government has allowed the armed cadres of the Karuna faction to intimidate, murder, kidnap, and threaten the local population.

NOTES

1. For a somewhat dated but still relevant analysis of the homeland issue, see Chelvadura Manogaran, *Ethnic Conflict and Reconciliation in Sri Lanka* (Honolulu: University of Hawaii Press, 1987). S. L. Gunasekera, in *Tigers, "Moderates," and Pandora's Package* (Colombo: S. L. Gunasekera, 1996), presents a Sinhalese nationalist position.

2. Ketheshwaran Loganathan, in *Sri Lanka: Lost Opportunities* (Colombo: Centre for Policy Research and Analysis, 1996), presents a good description of the history of negotiations between the two sides.

3. A special issue of the *Harvard International Review* entitled "Conflict and Cohesion: Identity and Politics in South Asia," Summer 1996, carried two opinions about the conflict: Chandrika Kumaratunga, "A New Approach: The Democratic Path to Peace in Sri Lanka"; and Robert C. Oberst, "Tigers and the Lion: The Evolution of Sri Lanka's Civil War."

23

The Search for Prosperity

As serious as they are, Sri Lanka's economic problems have been overshadowed by the ethnic conflict between the Tamils and Sinhalese. In the summer of 1984 the country entered a period of open warfare between the Tamil guerrilla fighters and the government. The Jaffna, Vavuniya, Mannar, Batticaloa, Ampara, and Trincomalee districts became a battleground, with almost daily clashes between the Tamil guerrillas and the Sinhalese soldiers, and the conflict has continued since that time.

Because of the war Sri Lanka's economic needs have been neglected by recent Sri Lankan governments. Sri Lanka remains a low-income country. In 2005 its per capita income was US$1,196 per year. Although this is still low, GNP per capita grew at a rate of 3.7 percent per year between 1990 and 2005. This compares to a world rate of growth of 1.5 percent over the same period.[1] This relatively strong growth is complemented by significant gains in the quality of life. As already mentioned, life expectancy is high and infant mortality, at 15 deaths per 1,000 births, is low.[2] This standard of living is aided by high standards of education.

The search for economic development has been a difficult one for Sri Lanka. The high standard of living was produced through a series of programs begun by S.W.R.D. Bandaranaike in the 1950s that provided every Sri Lankan with a guaranteed measure of food and free health care. These programs were expensive and ultimately were discarded in favor of programs aimed at increasing the productive capacity of the population rather than improving the quality of life of the citizens.

The conflict that Sri Lanka has faced since the 1970s is closely tied to the economic problems the country is facing. The alienation and anger among Tamil youths is fostered by the economic stagnation of the Tamil areas, and the JVP insurrections of 1971 and 1987–1990 reflect the discontent of Sinhalese youths. Both insurrections relied on the large number of educated youths produced by the Sri Lankan school system over the past thirty years who failed to find jobs commensurate with their education.

The two JVP insurrections reflected these problems. The 1987 Indo-Lanka accords and the 1989 Indian refusal to leave the country stirred Sinhalese nationalist emotions. The JVP, which had been organizing for armed struggle since 1983, emerged with a campaign of assassinations against supporters of the government and the accords. The JVP found a large number of potential followers among the ranks of the unemployed. This campaign was intensified in June, July, and August 1989 after the Indian refusal to leave the country. By 1989 the JVP insurrection had become bloodier than the Tamil conflict, with an estimated 20,000 to 50,000 people dying in the two-year period. In addition, progovernment death squads emerged and by July and August 1989 were responsible for most of the deaths that year. Thousands of low-caste youths and university students were murdered during the summer and fall of 1989 by the death squads, which consisted of off-duty security personnel and UNP supporters. In November the leader of the JVP, Rohana Wijeweera, and most of the JVP leaders were captured. Most were killed shortly after their capture or during it, and the violence subsided.

Since that time, the JVP has become a legal political party and has been contesting elections and mobilizing its followers. The discontent that led to the two earlier insurrections has not disappeared. The forces that led to the creation of the JVP remain despite the demise of its leadership. There is a strong sense of alienation among members of the younger generation in Sri Lanka. The extensive death squad killings and torture of Sri Lankan young people, especially university students, angered many members of the younger generation. Even government supporters among the youths have found it difficult to support the brutality of the death squads' indiscriminate attacks. The damage done by the extralegal methods employed by the government to eradicate the JVP will take a long time to repair, but the economic conditions that fostered the uprising have proved even harder to control.

The search for a solution to the country's economic problems has focused on three major efforts: a massive irrigation scheme to increase agricultural production, a liberalization policy to increase investment in the economy, and an effort to devolve power to regional governments.

The most aggressive effort to develop the agricultural sector has been the Mahaweli development project. The plan is an example of both the potential success of major development projects and the unintended problems they generate. The project has sought to irrigate the vast dry zone of northern and eastern Sri Lanka, recreating the massive irrigation systems of the Anuradhapura and Polonnaruwa eras. The massive irrigation scheme was first envisioned in the

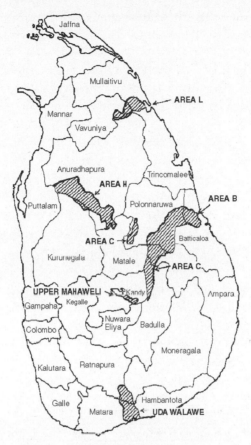

Jaffna

Mullaitivu

AREA L

Mannar

Vavuniya

Anuradhapura

AREA H

Trincomalee

Puttalam

Polonnaruwa

AREA B

AREA C

Batticaloa

Kurunegala

Matale

AREA C

UPPER MAHAWELI

Kandy

Ampara

Gampaha

Kegalle

Colombo

Nuwara
Eliya

Badulla

Moneragala

Kalutara

Ratnapura

Galle

Matara

Hambantota

UDA WALAWE

MAP 23.1   Mahaweli project areas

1950s, but little work was done on it until the United Front government of the 1970s planned a thirty-year effort to implement the plan.

The UNP government that came to power in 1977 planned an accelerated Mahaweli project, scaling it down to four major dams and several irrigation zones and calling for completion of the system in five years instead of thirty. As the reservoir projects were completed, water was diverted to the dry zone in the north and east. The government then planned the infrastructure to support the increased population drawn to these areas by the offer of free land. Unfortunately, the project has required the diversion of large amounts of resources to its construction in addition to the large national debt created as a result of the international loans used to fund it. However, the project has had a major impact on the economy of Sri Lanka. More than 146,000 families have been settled in the newly irrigated lands (see Map 23.1), including both farmers and nonfarm families providing services to the farming community.[3]

The Mahaweli lands now provide 22 percent of Sri Lanka's rice production, 13 percent of the chilies, 31 percent of the Bombay onions, and 14 percent of its electrical power.[4]

The settlers in the newly irrigated lands have been selected from the densely populated southwestern portion of Sri Lanka as well as from the Kandyan hill country. The program has provided free land to settlers who can now earn a reasonable income.

However, the project's success has been limited by the creation of social and economic problems that now require resources for resolution. In 1979, when the project was just getting under way, malaria was nearly eradicated in Sri Lanka. Today the disease is common and has been joined by hemorrhagic dengue fever and Japanese encephalitis. The massive movement of families to new homes in the dry zone has created a host of social problems as well. These problems have been exacerbated by the logistical problems of setting up schools, shops, and other support facilities for the settlers. The social problems have included familial violence and alcoholism. In addition, these areas have been a breeding ground for JVP supporters.

Another problem is related to the ethnic composition of the settlers. Over 96 percent of the families (121,268) are Sinhalese.[5] The Mahaweli areas are in the sparsely populated region that is the buffer between the Tamil areas to the east and north of the Sinhalese settlements. With the exception of Area H, which is in traditionally Sinhalese areas, the settlement of Sinhalese colonists has exacerbated the disillusionment of Tamils.

No other Mahaweli area reflects this more than Area L, which straddles Mullaitivu and Vavuniya districts. It is situated at the front lines of the ethnic war and is located in two districts that were almost exclusively populated by Tamils before the civil war. The settlements create a line of heavily fortified farming communities, some located a few miles from important LTTE bases. Much of the money spent on Area L has been used to build roads and wells that support the military more than the 3,364 families who have settled there. The conflict has led to nearly 1,400 of these families leaving the area out of fears for their safety.[6]

Despite the problems created by the Mahaweli project, agricultural production has increased and the population and job pressures of the populated southwestern sector of the country have been alleviated.

The cornerstone of the Jayawardene administration (1977–1989) was its effort to create a free market economy. In 1977 Sri Lanka embarked on an effort to reduce the government role in the economy through a number of programs, including the creation of an "investment promotion zone" or free trade zone, the sale of government-owned enterprises, the reduction of economic regulations on doing business, and easier convertibility of currency. The creation of the free trade zone reflects the view of both domestic and foreign investment. A 180-square-mile area was set up north of the capital city of Colombo adjacent to the city's international airport. In an effort to lure multinational corporations, it offered potential investors several benefits:

1. The right to import all equipment and inputs duty free.
2. No taxes on all royalty payments.
3. Exemption from taxes on the income of all foreign personnel attached to the project.
4. Exemption from taxes on all dividends paid to all foreign and Sri Lankan investors in the project.
5. A tax holiday for up to ten years, depending on the nature of the project.
6. An additional period of reduced taxes after the ten-year tax holiday.[7]

The program got off to a slow start given the limited number of foreign corporations that took advantage of the tax holidays. The original export promotion zone near the Katunayake International Airport has grown to nine zones, most of which are near Colombo. At the end of 2006, the zones employed 227,000 people and resulted in about $1.5 million a month in exports.[8] Most of the exports are garments made for markets in Western Europe and North America.

The program also sought to privatize government-run corporations. This effort has included the development of a private bus system, telephone companies, and television stations as well as the sale of many government-run corporations. The Kumaratunga government angered some of its leftist allies by adopting and continuing many of the Jayawardene free enterprise policies. It is still too early to determine if President Rajapakse will change Kumaratunga's policies.

As mentioned in Chapter 20, decentralization or devolution has been used to increase the power of local governments. It has also been used to enhance development projects. Serious attempts to decentralize development administration were begun in the 1970s, when a scheme later called the decentralized budget (DCB) was created. This was a plan to provide each of the members of parliament with block grants for development projects in their electoral districts. A council called a district ministry (known the political authority under the SLFP government from 1970 to 1977) was created in each district and headed by the district minister (or political authority). The district ministry reviewed the projects of the MPs and gave them final approval. The MPs were in charge of project selection, administering the project once it was accepted by the technical staff undertaking the work, and ensuring that the project was completed properly. In many cases, the projects involved small-scale development works that were not feasible for the centralized government departments. Many projects were turned over to villages to complete, and some were done with volunteer labor.

Since the creation of the DCB, other attempts have been made to decentralize development work, including the District Development Committees and a scheme to carry out development work at the district level by means of an integrated district-level plan. These projects offer Sri Lankan villagers hope for more realistic development projects and greater influence over the government actions that directly affect their lives.

The creation of provincial councils by the government has also helped to decentralize power. However, the future of the provincial councils and any decentralization efforts to reduce the problems of the ethnic conflict depends on new constitutional solutions adopted by the Sri Lankan government.

The Boxing Day Tsunami

The 2002 cease-fire agreement gave the economic development reforms an opportunity to foster economic growth in the economy. The GDP growth rate was negative 2.5 percent in 2001. It would increase to 3 percent in 2002 and 5.1 percent in 2003.

On December 26, 2004, an earthquake with a magnitude of 9.3 on the Richter scale off the coast of Aceh province on the Indonesian island of Sumatra sent a shockwave across the Indian Ocean. A wall of water traveled nearly 1,600 miles beneath the Indian Ocean and smashed into the eastern and southern coasts of Sri Lanka. The hardest hit areas were along the east coast, especially in Ampara district. The World Bank estimated that 35,322 died.[9] This total does not include over 19,000 deaths claimed by the LTTE in its territory and not included in Sri Lankan government totals.

The tsunami destroyed or damaged all buildings within five kilometers of the sea and left 500,000 without homes.[10] Roads and bridges were washed away. Although an outpouring of aid came from the rest of the world, the economic impact on those living near the sea or relying on the tens of thousands of boats that were washed away was massive. However, the Sri Lankan economy is largely based on garment exports and the economy of the Colombo area, which was largely untouched. The end result was that the country did not experience a major economic downturn because of the tsunami. The inflow of aid and the fact that the main engines of the economy were left untouched by the wave resulted in economic growth (5.1 percent in 2005 and 6.3 percent in 2006).

While the economic effect of the tsunami appears to have been relatively limited, the increased fighting in Sri Lanka is expected to lower economic growth rates and especially foreign investment. Through the end of 2007, the economy was growing at a robust 6–7 percent a year, although down from 7.7 percent a year at the end of 2006.[11]

Although reform and development efforts have helped create a good record of economic growth, poverty and malnutrition persist in Sri Lanka and major changes must still be implemented. With the return to war, however, the economic future of Sri Lanka remains uncertain.

NOTES

1. United Nations Development Program, *Human Development Report,* http://hdrstats .undp.org/buildtables/#.

2. Ibid.

3. Mahaweli Authority of Sri Lanka, *Statistical Bulletin 2006,* www.mahaweli.gov.lk/ Other%20pages/SB_mahaweli/2006%20SB/menue.htm.

4. Mahaweli Authority of Sri Lanka, *Statistical Bulletin 2006,* www.mahaweli.gov.lk/ Other%20pages/SB_mahaweli/2006%20SB/2005–2.htm.

5. Ibid., p. 11.

6. Mahaweli Authority of Sri Lanka, *Statistical Bulletin 2006,* www.mahaweli.gov.lk/ Other%20pages/SB_mahaweli/2006%20SB/2005–46.htm.

7. Government of Sri Lanka, *A Guide to the Foreign Investor* (Colombo: Ministry of Finance and Planning, n.d.), p. 2.

8. Sri Lanka Board of Investment, Free Trade Zones, www.boi.lk/boi2005/content.asp?content=about5&SubMenuID=36.

9. *Daily Mirror,* "World Bank Tsunami Fact Sheet on Sri Lanka," December 19, 2005.

10. Research Center for Disaster Reduction Systems (Kyoto), "The December 26, 2004 Earthquake Tsunami Disaster of the Indian Ocean," www.drs.dpri.kyoto-u.ac.jp/sumatra/index-e .html#lk.

11. Department of Census and Statistics, *Bulletin of Quarterly National Accounts, 3rd Quarter 2007,* Table 1b, www.statistics.gov.lk/national_accounts/Quarterly%20Bulletin%202007% 20Q3.pdf.

24

Modernization and Development: Prospects and Problems

This final chapter on Sri Lanka examines the effectiveness of the Sri Lankan government in resolving the problems facing it. Three serious problems stand out. The first is the search for economic development discussed in the preceding chapter. The second is the crisis of political development and the difficulty maintaining a democratic system. The third is the need to resolve the civil war that has engulfed the country since 1983. Each of these problems poses a serious threat to stable and representative government in Sri Lanka.

Maintaining Democracy

Most of the political systems of the third world are facing a political development crisis: trying to meet the needs of their societies with limited resources and government institutions which are incapable of achieving goals. The irony of Sri Lanka is that twenty years ago, the country appeared to have developed those institutions. Today, after twenty-five years of war, it is no longer certain that Sri Lanka can maintain its democratic institutions.

Chapter 22 discussed some of the human rights issues that have arisen during the Rajapakse presidency. While these issues pose a serious threat to democratic governance in the Tamil areas, the problems extend beyond the Tamil community.

The first issue has been the increasing levels of violence in Sri Lankan elections. Prior to 1988, Sri Lanka elections were remarkably peaceful with only rare instances of violence. During the 1970s, violence began to appear after elections as supporters of the winning candidates attacked their political opponents. In the 1989 parliamentary elections, the JVP threatened to kill anyone who voted. Consequently vigilante groups attacked suspected JVP supporters. Hundreds of people died during the electoral violence.

In elections that followed the 1989 elections, it has become common for the supporters of the major parties to attack their opponents during the campaign and on election day. Hundreds of civilians have been killed in elections since the 1980s. In 2004, the government banned the pasting of election posters on public property and the level of violence declined but did not go away. Party supporters who put up election posters create an ideal opportunity for their opponents to attack them. Banning the posters reduced the violence but did not end it.

Election violence is part of a broader decline of civility in Sri Lankan politics. Many politicians now have armed body guards who protect them. The seriousness of the threat has led some politicians to make deals with criminal groups to provide security for them in return for protection from the police. For example, Nalanda Ellawala, an SLFP member of parliament from Ratnapura district, died on February 11, 1997, when his vehicle was stopped by a UNP member of parliament and a gunfight ensued. The UNP MP, Susantha Punchinilame, and UNP mayor of the city of Ratnapura, Mahinda Rathnatilake, were arrested for killing Ellawala and his police bodyguard and wounding SLFP MP Dilan Perera.

Punchinilame is still awaiting trial for the Ellawala murder as well as for a murder he is accused of committing in 1989 when men in his vehicle kidnapped three men from the streets of Ratnapura. Their burned bodies were found the next day fifty miles away. Despite the charges against him, the UNP nominated him for parliament. Ironically, he changed parties from the UNP to the SLFP in 2007 and became a minister in the Rajapakse government. This led Minister of Justice and Law Reform Dilan Perera, the member of parliament injured in the Ellawala shooting, to symbolically resign from the SLFP. Many believe that the party change accompanied an agreement to drop the murder charges against him.

Electoral fraud is also growing as all major parties have resorted to using fake identification to vote. In the 2004 parliamentary election, this author was an election monitor in Ampara district in the Eastern Province. I personally observed electoral ID cards being handed out to men in front of a UNP office. In another area, a man flagged our vehicle down and asked to be given a ride to a polling station so that he could vote for a third time. The problem was so serious that even one of the drivers of the agency carrying out the election monitoring had bragged about not needing to vote because he had given his electoral card to his wife to give to the SLFP to distribute to a voter who would impersonate him.

Beyond the electoral fraud, the Ampara election also included a government minister leading members of the police commando unit who fired gunshots into the air while masked men attacked homes in one neighborhood. In another incident, I paused to let an independent candidate leave a polling station ahead of me. As he stepped out onto the street, he was attacked by a man with a brick. Almost immediately, a police van came and the assailant jumped into the van and left.

During the Rajapakse presidency there has been a growing intolerance towards media outlets that criticize the government. While there have been many attacks against Tamil-language newspapers, journalists, and media men, the attacks have also targeted Sinhalese-language news media. Media that criticize the government commonly experience police raids on their offices, arrests, or brief detentions of their employees and in some cases violent attacks.

The most serious threat to democracy has been efforts to intimidate members of parliament. Members who vote against the government have had their security removed. On January 1, 2008, UNP MP T. Maheshwaran, a Tamil, was shot in Colombo while praying in a Hindu temple. His security detail had been reduced from eighteen to two guards after he voted against the government budget in parliament on December 14. Shortly before the vote, TNA MPs were told that kidnapped relatives would be murdered if they voted on the budget. The relatives were released unharmed after the MPs failed to show up at parliament to vote.

Rising violence and intimidation in Sri Lankan politics have, for the first time in the post-independence period, threatened the future of the democratic institutions of the country. While the reasons for the violence are complex, the violence accompanying the civil war appears to be an important contributor. Twenty-five years of civil war have desensitized the population to the violence in their society.

The Search for a Political Solution

The Norwegian peace initiative began under the leadership of President Kumaratunga and resulted in a cease-fire under the leadership of UNP Prime Minister Ranil Wickremasinghe. While the negotiations between the two sides did not result in a permanent cease-fire, the country prospered during the brief period of peace (2002–2004).

As noted in Chapter 22, a significant group of Sri Lankans opposed the cease-fire. The election of an SLFP government in 2004 and SLFP President Rajapakse in 2005 led to a change in the attitude about what to do to resolve the civil war. Many in the Rajapakse government believe that the war can be ended by force. At the core of their position is the belief that the conflict is not a civil war but rather a war between the government and a group of power-hungry terrorists who seek to take over the country.

This belief has led them to think they can militarily defeat the LTTE. Many of these leaders have believed that the LTTE has been close to defeat for the past twenty-five years. Obviously they were wrong in the past. Recent events, however, lead them to believe that this time they are correct.

First, the LTTE is believed to have lost thousands of fighters to the 2004 tsunami that ravaged LTTE-controlled areas. Second, when Colonel Karuna split from the LTTE, the organization lost one its best commanders and its position in Batticaloa and Ampara districts was seriously weakened. Finally, the Sri Lankan security forces were strengthened during the cease-fire. They now have better technology, better training, and better hardware. The United States has been supplying the military and training them.

These changes led the government to adopt a coordinated strategy to defeat the LTTE. It involves several major programs:

- The enlistment of Karuna and his supporters to attack the LTTE. Initially this involved attacks against unarmed LTTE political cadres operating offices in government-controlled areas under the provisions of the cease-fire. Later it involved military attacks against the LTTE in their own territory. The security forces provided safe haven to the Karuna forces at military bases and provided logistical support.

- A strategy to attack the LTTE in limited operations at the extremities of their control. These operations focused on limited objectives, gradually capturing small areas from the LTTE while maintaining the "cease-fire."

- A program of arrest and intimidation of potential supporters of the LTTE. The Prevention of Terrorism Act, which had been suspended during the cease-fire, was reinstated, allowing troops to arrest and hold anyone for no cause. Coupled with this was a program of kidnappings and murders of Tamil civilians that usually preceded the limited military operations described above.

- An increased diplomatic effort to persuade foreign nations to restrict and prevent the LTTE from raising funds and procuring armaments. This included increased efforts by the U.S., British, and European Union governments to restrict the LTTE.

- A decentralization plan to provide more self-governance to the Tamil areas. This plan resulted in the proposal to implement the much maligned Thirteenth Amendment to the constitution. This amendment was part of the Indo-Lanka accords of 1987 and never fully implemented. It calls for the creation of provincial councils, which most observers have called inadequate to effectively devolve power to the north and east of the island.

The military elements of the strategy have been extremely successful, as the government security forces have now surrounded the LTTE in the north and limited their control of land to a small area including the Mannar, Vavuniya, Kilinochchi, and Mullaitivu districts. The government began 2008 with boasts that the LTTE and its leadership would be eradicated by the end of the year. However, the official end of the cease-fire on January 15, 2008, was marked by widespread LTTE bombings across the country.

The Rajapkse administration has chosen the same strategy to end the war that was taken by President Jayawardene in the 1980s—war. It is still uncertain if the military approach will be any more successful in 2008 than it was in the 1980s. The political elements of the strategy have been widely rejected by Tamil leaders as inadequate and may have no impact in resolving the complaints of the Tamil population.

The Future of Democracy in Sri Lanka

The future of Sri Lanka is still clouded by both LTTE violence and the increasing violence by the followers of the established Sinhalese parties. Communication has broken down between the two major ethnic groups, the Sinhalese and the Sri Lanka Tamils, and between the youth of Sri Lanka and the older generation. It is still uncertain whether the government will be able to resolve these problems and address the economic problems facing the country.

Sri Lanka's future depends on ending the violence in the country. However, after peace is established, the nation will face the prospect of building its economy. In the long run the economic issues will be the key to Sri Lanka's future. The youth-led civil wars have been fueled in part by the inability of the economy to provide jobs and a secure future to Sri Lanka's educated youths. The failure to accelerate economic development may lead to another JVP insurrection in the future and an unending ethnic crisis.

SUGGESTED READINGS

Bandarage, Asoka. *Colonialism in Sri Lanka.* New York: Mouton, 1983.

Chandraprema, C. A. *Sri Lanka, The Years of Terror: The JVP Insurrection, 1987–1989.* Colombo: Lake House Bookshop, 1991.

DeSilva, Colvin R. *Ceylon Under the British Occupation, 1795–1833: Its Political, Administrative, and Economic Development.* 2 vols. Colombo: Colombo Apothecaries, 1962.

DeSilva, C. R. *Sri Lanka: A History.* New Delhi: Vikas, 1987.

DeSilva, K. M. *A History of Sri Lanka.* Berkeley: University of California Press, 1981.

———. *Managing Ethnic Tensions in Multi-Ethnic Societies: Sri Lanka, 1880–1985.* Lanham, Md.: University Press of America, 1986.

DeSilva, K. M., ed. *Sri Lanka: A Survey.* Honolulu: University of Hawaii Press, 1977.

Dubey, Swaroop Rani. *One-Day Revolution in Sri Lanka: Anatomy of the 1971 Insurrection.* Jaipur: Aalekh, 1988.

Fernando, Tissa, and Robert N. Kearney, eds. *Modern Sri Lanka: A Society in Transition.* Syracuse, N.Y.: Maxwell School, Syracuse University, 1979.

Gunaratna, Rohan. *Sri Lanka, A Lost Revolution: The Inside Story of the JVP.* Colombo: Institute of Fundamental Studies, 1990.

Gunasekera, S. L. *Tigers, "Moderates," and Pandora's Package.* Colombo: S. L. Gunasekera, 1996.

Jiggins, Janice. *Caste and Family in the Politics of the Sinhalese, 1947–1976.* New York: Cambridge University Press, 1979.

Kearney, Robert N. *Communalism and Language in the Politics of Ceylon.* Durham, N.C.: Duke University Press, 1967.

———. *Trade Unions and Politics in Ceylon.* Berkeley: University of California Press, 1971.

———. "Territorial Elements of Tamil Separatism in Sri Lanka." *Pacific Affairs,* Winter 1987, pp. 561–577.

Kearney, Robert N., and Janice Jiggins. "The Ceylon Insurrection of 1971." *Journal of Commonwealth and Comparative Politics,* March 1975, pp. 40–65.

———. *Internal Migration in Sri Lanka and Its Social Consequences.* Boulder: Westview, 1987.

———. "Women's Suicide in Sri Lanka." In *Women and Health: Cross-Cultural Perspectives,* ed. Patricia Whelehan. Granby, Mass.: Bergin & Garvey, 1988.

Kearney, Robert N., and Barbara Diane Miller. "The Spiral of Suicide and Social Change in Sri Lanka." *Journal of Asian Studies,* November 1985, pp. 81–101.

Knox, Robert. "An Historical Relation of Ceylon." *Ceylon Historical Journal,* July 1956–April 1957.

Loganathan, Ketheshwaran. *Sri Lanka: Lost Opportunities.* Colombo: Centre for Policy Research and Analysis, 1996.

Manogaran, Chelvadurai. *Ethnic Conflict and Reconciliation in Sri Lanka.* Honolulu: University of Hawaii, 1987.

Matthews, Bruce. "District Development Councils in Sri Lanka." *Asian Survey,* November 1982, pp. 1117–1134.

Oberst, Robert C. *Legislators and Representation in Sri Lanka: The Decentralization of Development Planning.* Boulder: Westview, 1985.

———. "Democracy and the Persistence of Westernized Elite Dominance in Sri Lanka." *Asian Survey,* July 1985, pp. 760–772.

———. "Federalism and Ethnic Conflict in Sri Lanka." *Publius,* Summer 1988, pp. 175–193.

———. "Tigers and the Lion: The Evolution of Sri Lanka's Civil War." *Harvard International Review,* Summer 1996, pp. 32–35, 80.

Pfaffenberger, Bryan. *Caste in Tamil Culture: The Religious Foundations of Sudra Domination in Tamil Sri Lanka.* Syracuse, N.Y.: Maxwell School, Syracuse University, 1983.

Rogers, John. "Social Mobility, Popular Ideology, and Collective Violence in Modern Sri Lanka." *Journal of Asian Studies,* August 1987, pp. 583–602.

Ryan, Bryce. *Caste in Modern Ceylon.* New Brunswick, N.J.: Rutgers University Press, 1953.

Tambiah, S. J. *Ethnic Fratricide and the Dismantling of Democracy.* Chicago: University of Chicago Press, 1986.

Wilson, A. Jeyaratnam. *The Gaullist System in Asia: The Constitution of Sri Lanka.* 1978. London: Macmillan, 1980.

PART V

NEPAL

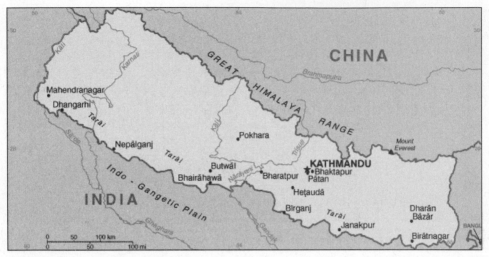

NEPAL

25

Political Heritage
and Culture

Nepal is the oldest state in South Asia and one of the few developing countries that was never colonized.[1] However, it is still struggling with building a democratic state. In fact, during the late 1990s and at the turn of the century, the spectacle of becoming a failed state was often mentioned in public and academic discourse.[2]

Nepal was territorially consolidated in the eighteenth century by Prithvi Narayan Shah (1722–1775), a dynamic king of Gorkha, a small princely state in the western hills. In the 1814–1816 war with the British rulers of India, Nepal suffered a defeat and lost considerable territory. However, it gained British recognition of its sovereignty in return. Even though Nepal was never colonized by the British, it was rarely in a position to assert its complete independence. The Nepali rulers in the nineteenth and first half of the twentieth century safeguarded their despotic rule by maintaining a good relationship with the British. After India became independent in 1947, Nepal, too, freed itself from the century-long oligarchic hereditary Rana premiers in 1951. A review of governance and politics of the country will shed light on the causes of Nepal's problems as well as other challenges it faces.

Geography

Nepal is a country the size of the state of Illinois, with an estimated population of about 27 million in 2006. It is landlocked and sandwiched between two giant neighbors, the People's Republic of China (Tibet autonomous region) in the north and India in the east, south and west. It has access to the sea only through Indian territories (see opposite map). It has open borders with India, while the massive Himalaya massif makes travel to China difficult.[3] Linked with both China and India by all-weather roads, Nepal today occupies a strategic position on the South Asian subcontinent.

Within a strip of land that ranges from 145 to 241 kilometers in width and 885 kilometers in length, Nepal contains a diverse topography. While the snow-clad Himalayas in the north contain eight of the world's ten mountains higher than 8,000 meters (including Mount Everest, the highest in the world), the southern Tarai is a tropical plain strip just a few hundred feet above sea level. In between lies the Mahabharata range, Siwalik hills, and the valleys between them. This topographical variation produces diverse weather, flora, fauna, and people. Rivers flow south from the Himalayas, irrigating the land in the hills and the Tarai. The Kosi, the Gandaki, and the Karnali are the three major river systems in Nepal, which eventually flow to the Ganges in north India. The three river basins form three distinct watershed regions from east to west.

The northern Himalaya and the plains north of it are mostly infertile, rugged, and dry. They occupy around 25 percent of the country's landmass. The altitude ranges from 3,000 to 8,848 meters. People in the Himalayas are pastoralists and traders. The valleys north of the Himalayas receive little rain. Monsoons from the Bay of Bengal generally bring more rain to southeastern Nepal. Rain clouds come from the Arabian Sea to western Nepal but bring less rain. The population density is sparse in the Himalayas. The temperate weather also does not support agriculture. The culture and lifestyle of the residents of this region are similar to that of Tibetans. Many are Buddhist and speak Tibeto-Burman languages.

The Mahabarat range south of the Himalayas and Siwalik hills south of it form the heartland of the country. The height ranges from 600 to 3,000 meters. The regions occupy around 50 percent of the landmass between the plains (Tarai) and the Himalayas. The people of this region have ruled the country for its entire modern epoch. Large areas of the land are not fertile, but valleys, terraces, and river basins irrigated by the rivers produce ample amounts of food. Kathmandu valley is very fertile and supports a rich, artistic civilization.

The fertile Tarai has become the food basket of the country. Once dense forests have been cut down to make way for agricultural land. By the beginning of the twenty-first century, around half of the population lived in the Tarai. The region also boasts more infrastructure and industries than the mountain and hill regions. The latest immigrants to the Tarai are the hill people who descended there after malaria was eliminated in the 1950s. Tharus, Dhimals, Rajbansi, and Santhal are the native people of the region. Madhesi, who have a similar culture and lifestyle to inhabitants of north India, are believed to have migrated to the region before and after the conquest of the region by the Gorkhalis.

Inner Tarai are the valleys between the Mahabaharat and Siwalik ranges. This region is fertile and subtropical. The Tarai and Inner Tarai occupy around 25 percent of the landmass. The region has been increasingly populated by migrants, mostly from the hills. Udayapur, Chitwan, and Dang are the largest and best known of the Inner Tarai valleys.

Social and Political History

Before being conquered by the Shah dynasty, Nepal was divided into small principalities and autonomous indigenous republics.[4] The Karnali basin had the Baise, or twenty-two principalities, and the Gandaki region had the Chaubise, or twenty-four principalities. The region east of Kathmandu and the Koshi region had autochthonous native communities. The Kathmandu valley had three rich Malla principalities, which were supported by the fertile land as well as the India-Tibet trade route through the valleys.

The Gopalas are believed to be the first people to found a kingdom in Kathmandu. Gopalas were cowherds; beyond that not much is known about them, including their reign period. They are believed to have established their capital in Matatirtha in the western part of the Kathmandu valley. They used primitive agricultural technology. The Kiratas ruled Kathmandu and the surrounding region after the Gopalas. The Kiratas are believed to have moved from the east, but they also ruled the western hills. They introduced dry rice cultivation and a sedentary agricultural lifestyle. Yelamber, the Kirata king, is mentioned in the Mahabharata, the Hindu epic. The Kiratas established their capital in Gokarna in the eastern part of the Kathmandu valley. Kirata rule is believed to have been established during the early first millennium B.C., lasting for a thousand years.

The Khasa established an empire in the Karnali basin around A.D. 1100. The empire controlled around 142,000 square kilometers at its zenith and ruled parts of Kumaon in India and southwestern Tibet. The Khasa, initially Buddhists, were later Hinduized. The Khasa occasionally raided the Kathmandu valley. Even though the latter Khasa adopted the title of Malla, they were not related to the Newar Malla of the Kathmandu valley. The Khasa supposedly arrived in western Nepal in the first millennium B.C. They displaced the Kiratis when they came into contact. The Khasa learned dry rice cultivation and sedentary agriculture lifestyle from the Kiratas. They were pastoralists and spoke an Indo-Aryan language.

The Licchavis ruled the Kathmandu valley after the Kiratas. The Licchavis left more documentation than other people. From the first century to the tenth century, the Lichhavis ruled alternately with the Guptas. Both were of Indo-Aryan background. A caste system was introduced to the valley during this period but was confined mostly to the rulers. The people largely remained immune from it. Amsuvarma is one of the well-known Licchavi rulers. The Licchavis promoted urban culture, craftsmanship, and trade with Tibet and India. During most of the Licchiva period they observed Shaivism, Mahayana Buddhism, and Vaisnavism with equal respect. However, during the end of the Licchavi period the Sanakaracharya convinced Shiva Deva to destroy Buddhist culture and monasteries.

The Mallas began to dominate the Kathmandu valley beginning in the fourteenth century. The Mallas promoted Hinduism and mistreated Buddhism and Buddhist monasteries. However, they were more tolerant than the Hindus of the western hills, who conquered and ruled the valleys after them. Jayasthiti Malla (1295–1382) enforced a caste order among the Newars, the Kathmandu valley inhabitants. Following that, the society became rigid. The Mallas developed literature, fine arts, architecture, wood carving, and metal casting.

The Tarai also had several kingdoms during the ancient period. Lumbini, Kapailvastu, Devdah, Janakpur, and Simaraungarh were prominent sites in the Tarai. Kapilvastu emerged as a Buddhist center after Siddhartha Gautama Buddha established the religion around 400 B.C. These kingdoms had connections with both the Gangetic plains and the hills. Most of these kingdoms were decimated by disease and plundered by invading armies, and eventually were reforested.

Modern Nepal's History

The history of present-day Nepal begins with the conquest of the Kathmandu valley in 1968–1969. The period before 1951, when democracy was first established, can be divided into two periods: the conquest period and Rana regime.

The Conquest Period, 1768–1846

After conquering the Kathmandu valley, Prithvi Narayan Shah moved his capital to Kathmandu and began his expansion to the east. He either conquered principalities and tribal chiefs or brought them under the Gorkhali realm through treaties. The treaties gave some groups (e.g., the Limbu) considerable autonomy. He was successful in extending the border of his kingdom to eastern Tarai and the Tista River, including much of modern Sikkim.[5] Prithvi Narayan Shah was successful in his campaigns because he attracted a large number of land-hungry hill residents to the army by developing a land-military complex. The soldiers were given land in the conquered areas as compensation for their services. This strategy attracted a large number of people to the army, as the expansion required.[6]

Prithvi Narayan died in 1775, but the mission of conquest continued. After Pratap Singh took the throne, Nepal witnessed increasing factionalism, conspiracies, murder of courtiers, and governmental instability. After Pratap Singh died in 1777, his wife Queen Rajya Laxmi and his brother Bahadur Shah vied for power and court politics became factionalized. Bahadur Shah was expelled, and Rajya Laxmi (1777–1785) became the regent of the infant king, Rana Bahadur, until she died in 1785. During this period, Nepal continued its westward expansion and conquered some Chaubesi principalities.

Bahadur Shah (1785–1794) became the regent after Rajya Laxmi's death. Nepal's conquest continued west to the Karnali basin and Kumaon region. King Rana Bahadur dismissed regent Bahadur Shah and assumed full power in 1794 after coming of age. Bahadur Shah was incarcerated and died in prison in 1797. Rana Bahadur abdicated in favor of Girvana Yuddha, his two-year-old son by an illicit union with a Maithali Brahmin widow, Kantivati. Palace infighting then intensified among different queen mothers, Rana Bahadur, and courtier factions who sought to control the kingdom through regency. Rana Bahdur was killed by his half brother (1806). The administration stabilized after Tripura Sundari became the regent and Bhimsen Thapa (1806–1837) became prime minister in 1806. Before that Queen Rajarajeshvari (twice), Queen Suvarnaprabha, and Rana Bahadur Shah became regent. A culture of eliminating court enemies developed during the period, which helped Janga Bahadur capture political power within his family.

This first phase was characterized by a feudalistic society in which the landed aristocracy occupied key positions in the court, the army, and the administration. The bhardars, or courtiers, were confined to families from Gorkha that helped Prithvi Narayan in the conquests. During the period, the court was further centralized. In his long rule, Bhimsen Thapa consolidated central control and strengthened caste barriers.

From the period of Rana Bahadur Shah, the British East India Company took an increasing interest in Nepal. The Kirkpatrick mission to Kathmandu came in 1793, and Captain Knox became the British resident in 1802. Nepal and the British East India Company finally clashed in the 1814–1816 war. Nepal lost the war and the resulting Sugauli treaty confined Nepal to roughly its present-day territory. Nepal's expansion was finally halted. The British returned Western Tarai to Nepal for helping repress the Indian Mutiny against the British in 1857.

The Oligarchic Rana Regime, 1846–1951

The king was reduced to titular head of the state by Janga Bahadur Kunwar, who later changed his family surname to Rana. In 1846 Janga Bahadur and his seven brothers killed thirty influential courtiers and noblemen during the Kot massacre, which was the culmination of a series of intrigues, conspiracies, and assassinations among the nobility and royal family members that began with the junior queen's desire to crown her son king in place of the wayward Crown Prince Surendra, the son of the late senior queen. Around 600 family members of the killed courtiers were expelled after the Kot massacre.

In 1856, Janga Bahadur made himself the maharaja (great king) of Lamjung and Kaski, further strengthening his position. Upgrading his caste to Thakuri with adoption of the Rana surname allowed him to marry his children into the royal family. This further consolidated his hold on power. The effective power passed into the hands of the Rana family, who provided the various hereditary prime ministers of the country. The Kunwar, an upper-caste Chhetri that participated in the conquests of the House of Gorkha, made the position of prime minister hereditary after 1856. The premiership was made to pass on by agnate succession. Janga Bahadur's brothers were to succeed him, followed by his sons and nephews. Even though the succession order set by Jang Bahadur was often manipulated by succeeding Rana premiers to bring their children higher in the succession line, the Rana family occupied the key positions in the court, the administration, and the army. Efforts by the kings to break out of this order and to establish themselves as effective rulers of the country always ended in failure prior to 1951. The Ranas exercised despotic power and left no room for democratic reforms.

The Rana period, like earlier years, did not see attempts to develop the country and society. These rulers aimed to exploit the peasantry as much as possible, since agriculture was the government's main source of income. With the borders settled after the 1816 Sugauli treaty, additional agricultural lands were no longer available. This resulted in further taxation of the peasants, not only to maintain the government structure but also to sustain the lavish lifestyle of the ruling elite.[7]

The Ranas, following the earlier established policy of discouraging interaction with foreigners, tried to keep Nepal isolated. However, a social and cultural revival in India and the rise of the nationalist movement under the Indian National Congress deeply influenced the emerging Nepali middle class. The Rana regime's suppression of the modernist aspirations of the educated classes gave birth to an anti-Rana movement. In 1936 the Praja Parishad, the first political party to be established in Nepal, began as an anti-Rana campaign. Several Praja Parishad leaders were killed and imprisoned in 1941, and the organization was brutally repressed.

Many educated young Nepalese living in India in the early 1940s were influenced by Indian socialist leaders like Jaya Prakash Narayan and Ram Manohar

Lohia. Close contact with the freedom movement in India encouraged young Nepali leaders, such as B. P. Koirala and D. R. Regmi, to organize political parties. The Nepali National Congress and the Nepali Democratic Congress were formed in 1947 and in 1948 respectively. They merged into the Nepali Congress in 1950, which spearheaded the anti-Rana movement and demanded the democratization of Nepal.

The Ranas, unaware of the extent of middle-class alienation, responded with increased suppression. The break for the Nepali nationalists came in 1950 when King Tribhuvan and his family sought asylum in India. Various anti-Rana organizations joined under the banner of the Nepali Congress and launched an armed struggle against the Rana regime. The king's flight deprived the Ranas of their legitimacy. Faced with this popular upsurge and the tough attitude of the government of newly independent India, which was sympathetic to the aspirations of both the Nepali Congress and King Tribhuvan, the Ranas yielded. The 1950–1951 resistance brought an end to the Rana regime.

Hindu Kingdom

Until 2006, Nepal was constitutionally a Hindu kingdom, with the king recognized as the protector and promoter of the Hindu religion. The provisions of the 1959, 1962, and 1990 constitutions declared Nepal a "Hindu kingdom." For instance, the 1990 constitution stipulated that "the ruler must be an adherent of Aryan culture and a follower of Hindu religion."[8] The central place of Hinduism in Nepal's political setup has been increasingly challenged by different segments of the society, especially indigenous nationalities and those who belong to extremist revolutionary groups. This challenge gained momentum after King Gyanendra dismissed the elected government in 2002 and usurped power directly in 2005.

As discussed above, Hinduism entered Nepal during the Khasa reign in the west and during the Licchavi period in the Kathmandu valley. However, it was mostly confined to the ruling families and courtiers. The names of places inscribed during the Licchavi period clearly demonstrate that non-Hindu influence was common among the people.

Jayasthiti Malla, as noted before, formalized a caste system within the Newar in the Kathmandu valley. During the period, the rulers of the western hills also followed Hinduism. King Privthvi Narayan Shah, the conqueror of Nepal, also proclaimed Nepal as "asali [real] Hindustan." Janga Bahadur Rana introduced a civil code in 1854 that formally introduced a caste system into Nepal and imposed it among non-Hindus as well.

The reinstated parliament after the successful second people's movement in 2006 declared the state as secular. However, many laws and public policies still

TABLE 25.1   Religious Diversity in Percentage, 1952/1954–2001

Religion	First Reported Census	1952/54	1961	1971	1981	1991	2001
Hindu	1952/54	88.9	87.7	89.4	89.5	86.5	80.6
Buddhist	1952/54	8.6	9.3	7.5	5.3	7.8	10.7
Muslim	1952/54	2.5	3.0	3.0	2.7	3.5	4.2
Christian	1961	-	-	-	-	0.2	0.5
Jain	1961	-	-	-	0.1	0.0	0.0
Kiranti	1991	-	-	-	-	1.7	3.6
Sikh	1991	-	-	-	-	-	0.0
Bahai	2001	-	-	-	-	-	0.0
Others or Unstated	-	-	0.1	-	2.4	0.2	0.4
All	-	100	100.0	100.0	100.0	100.0	100.0

Source: Mahendra Lawoti, *Towards a Democratic Nepal: Inclusive Political Institutions for a Multicultural Society* (New Delhi: Sage, 2005).

promote the Hindu religion and its followers. The cow, a Hindu deity, is still the national animal and killing it is punishable by twelve years of imprisonment. Many public holidays are on Hindu festivals. Likewise, the interim prime minister regularly attended Hindu religious ceremonies as head of state, in place of the king, conveying the government and ruling group's preference for the religion.

Ethnic and Religious Plurality

Nepal is a multireligious, multilingual, multiethnic, and multiracial society. The 2001 census recorded 106 languages and dialects. Most of the languages belong to Indo-Aryan and Tibeto Burman families, but a few are Mundra and Dravidian as well. Followers of Hinduism, Buddhism, Islam, Kirant, Animism, Jainism, Sikkhism, and Christianity live in the country. Hindu is the largest religious group, with 80.6 percent of the population according to the 2001 census, but its proportion has been declining since 1991 because many ethnic groups began to reassert their identity and religion after the polity opened in 1990. On the other hand, the Buddhist, Muslim, Kirati, and Christian groups have grown as a proportion of population between 1991 and 2001 compared to the 1981 census (see Table 25.1).

The ethnic composition of Nepal and its cultural heritage have been deeply influenced by India and Tibet. Its population is divided into two predominant racial groups, Caucasoid and Mongoloid. The Caucasoids possess predominantly Indo-Aryan traits because their ancestors migrated to Nepal mainly from north India. In the twelfth and thirteenth centuries, frequent Muslim invasions

TABLE 25.2   Population of Major Ethnic/Caste Groups, 2001

Group	Population	Percentage
CHHE (Bahun, Chhetri, Thakuri, and Sanyasi)	7,023,220	30.89
Indigenous Nationalities	8,271,975	36.31
Mountain	190,107	0.82
Hill*	6,038,506	26.51
Inner Tarai	251,117	1.11
Tarai	1,786,986	7.85
Unidentified Indigenous Nationalities	5,259	0.02
Dalit	3,233,488	14.99
Hill Dalit	1,611,135	7.09
Madhesi Dalit	1,622,313	6.74
Unidentified Dalit	88,338	0.76
Madhesi**	3,778,136	16.59
Caste Madhesi	2,802,187	12.30
Muslim	971,056	4.27
Churaute Muslim***	4,893	0.02
Others	265,721	1.16
Total	22,736,556	100.00

* Newar, an indigenous nationalities group from the hill, which is doing well economically, make up 5.48 percent (population: 1,245,232) of the population.
**Madhesi becomes 32.29 percent (population: 7,438,552) if Madhesi Dalit and indigenous nationalities are added to it.
***All Muslims have been added to the Madhesi category.

Source: Adapted from Krishna B. Bhattachan, *Indigenous Nationalities and Minorities in Nepal* (London: Minority Rights Group International, 2003), Appendix A-1, pp. 48–51.

of India spurred Hindus to migrate to Nepal. The Malla dynasty ruled the Kathmandu valley from the thirteenth century until 1769, and the Shah dynasty migrated from India seeking shelter in Nepal to save their religion from Muslim onslaughts. The number of Caucasoids increased when population pressure forced many north Indians to seek land and livelihood in the Terai area of Nepal. The ancestors of the people of Mongoloid origin in Nepal came mainly from the east and Tibet and the southern provinces of China before the Indo-Aryans.

The Nepali population of both racial stocks can be subdivided into four major subgroups. The sections below describe them along with women and the problems they face.

The Dominant Group: Caste Hill Hindu Elite

The Caste Hill Hindu elite (CHHE), or the "upper-caste" hill Hindus, made up of Bahun (hill Brahmin) (12 percent), Chhetri (hill Kshatriya) (17 percent), Thakuri (1 percent), and Sanyasi (1 percent), is the dominant subgroup. The CHHE captured the state and defined Nepali nationalism and state institutions with its cultural and religious elements. The group has imposed its values, lifestyles and dress, and mother tongue, the Khas-Nepali (earlier known as Khas kura, now popularly called Nepali) language, and its hill version of Hinduism on the rest of the society.

The CHHE is dominant in almost all spheres of the state, society, and market. Collectively, they constitute less than 31 percent of the population but their hold on different government branches and influential civil society sectors is overwhelming, ranging from 60 to 90 percent (Neupane 2000; Lawoti 2005). The group's dominance began with the conquest of Nepal and it consolidated further with the consolidation of Nepal.

The Indigenous Nationalities

Indigenous nationalities, or the adibasi janajati, are generally the Tibeto-Burman speaking groups.[9] In Nepal, they are popularly believed to belong to the Mongoloid stock. They are found in the mountains, hills, Inner Tarai, and Tarai. There are more than sixty such groups, varying in population from a few hundred to more than a million. Collectively they constitute around 37 percent of the population.[10] They differ in terms of sociocultural conditions. Some, like the Raute and the Chepang, still live in isolation from the larger society, while a group like the Newar are found in urban communities and doing fairly well socioeconomically. The common thread that binds the indigenous nationalities is cultural discrimination, such as the linguistic and religious discrimination they face at the hands of the state and the dominant group. Most of the groups generally face discrimination in accessing state and societal resources as well.

Nine of the indigenous groups had populations of more than 100,000 in 2001. The Magar, Gurung, Rai, and Limbu have produced Nepal's famed Gurkha soldiers. Some of these groups (Limbu, Rai, Yakha, Sunuwar) consider their religion to be Kirati and possess a distinct ethnic identity based on their language and religious affiliation. The Sherpas are Buddhists and are well-known for their mountaineering skills. They often serve as guides on expeditions into the Himalayas. The Tamangs are a tribal group of Tibetan origin and follow Buddhism. The Newar constitute another important subgroup, with both Hindus and Buddhists among their ranks. The Newar are highly literate, internally caste stratified, and urbane, and they dominate Nepal's trade and commerce.

Over the years many of the indigenous nationalities were Hinduized by assimilation policies of the state. Some of the groups gave up their customs and gradually embraced the dominant Nepali culture based on Hinduism. However, especially after 1990, these groups have begun to reassert their non-Hindu identities. The Federation of Indigenous Nationalities (NEFIN), an umbrella organization of indigenous nationalities, defines the groups as Non-Hindus.

The Madhesi

The Madhesi, many of whom are the Indo-Aryan people living in the Tarai, the fertile southern plains, is a regional community group. The Tarai is home to indigenous groups like the Tharu and Dhimals, lower-caste Hindu groups like Dalit, upper-caste Brahmin and Kshyatriya, middle-caste Yadav, and Muslims. Collectively, their population is slightly more than 32 percent. They speak various languages and dialects, including Maithali, Abadhi, and Bhojpuri. Some of them, especially the caste groups and Muslims, bear close resemblance and share culture and traditions with people of northern India. The identity and problems faced by indigenous nationalities and the Dalit of the Tarai overlap with hill Dalit and indigenous nationalities. Thus some prefer to identify as Madhesi while others as indigenous nationalities or Dalit; still others identify both as Madhesi as well as indigenous nationalities or Dalit, depending on context and issues. One must bear in mind this complex overlap of identity while counting the population of different marginalized groups as well as analyzing the problems faced by different groups. The Madhesi Dalit and indigenous nationalities face double discrimination: first, as a Madhesi, and second, as a Dalit or indigenous nationalities.

The state of Nepal and the dominant hill society did not fully recognize the rights of Madhesi citizens. For instance, millions of Madhesi were deprived of citizenship certificates until 2007, effectively hindering the Madhesi from enjoying the rights of citizens. The hill community perceives them as immigrants from India and questions their loyalty toward the Nepali state. This perception is fueled by the acquisition of Nepali citizenship by many Indians over the years.[11] In reality, however, many Madhesi used to live in the Tarai before the Gorkha conquest. The racist attitude toward the entire Madhesi community, whether upper-caste Brahmin, Dalit, indigenous nationalities, or Muslims, has united the Madhesi community despite considerable intragroup differences. The Madhesi face linguistic, religious, and cultural domination, marginalization, and exclusion from the state. For instance, the Madhesi presence in the security forces is negligible.

The Dalit

The Dalit comprise the groups made up of the traditional untouchable castes, following orthodox Hindu tradition: Madhesi, hill, Himalayan, and Newar Dalit. They made up 14.99 percent of the population, according to the 2001 census; 7.09 percent and 6.74 percent of Dalit live in the hill and Tarai respectively.[12] Newar Dalit associations recently renounced their Dalit identity, and in 2003 the National Dalit Commission dropped them from the list of Dalit.

However, some Newar Dalit organizations are demanding inclusion in the Dalit list, especially after the government announced a reservation for the Dalit in civil administration and admission to educational institutions.

The Dalit face severe social discrimination. They undergo the inhumane treatment of untouchability, such as denial to enter houses of upper-caste groups and some temples. All groups are considered to be above the Dalit in caste hierarchy and discriminate against them. The group has a low literacy rate and very limited access to economic resources. They are the most excluded group in accessing political, economic, and social resources. Social exclusion is more severe for the Madhesi Dalit because Tarai society is very conservative. Even though the hill Dalit do not face linguistic and religious discrimination, they do face severe discrimination based on religious traditions.

Women

Women, across almost all groups, face domination, exclusion, and discrimination. Patriarchal discrimination is stronger among the high-caste Tarai Hindus and Muslims. Gender relation is more egalitarian among the indigenous nationalities. Dalit women face less gender discrimination compared to "high caste" women because there is less significance attached to the concept of purity among Dalit and there is an absence of significant land holdings, which sustains patriarchy.[13] The indigenous nationalities, Madhesi, and women from religious minority groups face religious, linguistic, and cultural discrimination. The dominant ethnic/caste women do not face linguistic and religious discrimination; rather, the discrimination they face is based on the cultural practices that emanate from the religion they follow.

As Table 25.3 shows, women's socioeconomic status compared to men's is quite low. Their literacy and purchasing power are about half that of men. Women's participation in the parliament and administration never exceeded 10 percent. Women's presence in the cabinet even after 1990 has been at a token level (one or two or even none). Thirty-five percent of members elected to the Constituent Assembly in 2008 were women.

The demands of the women's movement include an end to gender discrimination in the constitution, laws, public policies, and everyday life. They have also demanded reservation in education, administrative services, and public offices, and an end to patriarchy, chauvinism, sexist stereotyping, women's trafficking, violence against women, implementation of the Convention on the Elimination of All Forms of Discrimination Against Women (CEDAW), equal property rights, and control over resources. Indigenous women within the movement have demanded an end to cultural discrimination based on language, religion, and culture, while women of both Dalit and indigenous nationalities have demanded that positions reserved for women be reserved within the group for them.

TABLE 25.3 Select Indicators of Women's Status

Year	1981 Male	Female	1991 Male	Female	2001 Male	Female
Literacy (percent)	34	12	54.1	24.7	65.1	42.5
Human Development Index (percent)	0.328		0.416		0.49	
Gender Development Index (percent)			0.312			0.47
Per capita purchasing power parity (US$)					1,752	880

Year	1986/87	1991/92	2000
Parliament (percent)	5.7	3.8	6.4
Number of women in cabinet	1	2	2
Government administration (percent)	2.87	N. A.	7.8
Professional and technological human power (all sectors, census 2001, percent)	16.6	15.1	19

Source: Meena Acharya, *Efforts at Promotion of Women in Nepal* (Kathmandu, Tanka Prasad/Acharya Memorial Foundation/Friedrich-Ebert-Stiftung, 2003).

The women's movement has been generously supported by INGOs (international nongovernmental organizations). As a result, among the different social justice movements, women have produced the most impressive conference papers, reports, and documents in support of their demands. However, they have not been very effective politically. Their campaigns mostly consist of petitioning political leaders, government agencies, INGOs, and international agencies and forums. Because they have not threatened the electoral prospects of politicians by mobilizing grassroots women, the male-dominated political leadership has been able to ignore them. The mainstream women's movement has also not been able to incorporate the issues of Dalit, Madhesi, and indigenous nationalities women.

Caste System and Fatalistic Political Culture

Despite its legal abolition, the caste system is widely practiced in Nepal, even though it is slowly losing its grip, especially in the urban areas. Its prevalence can be ascertained from the fact that Dalit are denied access to public places like temples. Preference for endogamous marriages even among modern "high-caste" groups and the practice of ritual purity in private and public functions and ceremonies is helping to perpetuate the practice.

As Hinduism spread in Nepal, the caste system became more prevalent. It is generally accepted that the caste system entered the region through Rajputs and Brahmins who were running away from the Muslim onslaught in northern India. The caste system practiced in Nepal varies slightly from India and there are differences within Nepal as well. First, the caste system was imposed by the state in

Nepal, whereas it was only practiced socially in India. Caste-based discrimination was practiced in Nepal with the backing of law until 1963. Lower-caste groups received more punishment for the same crimes compared to high-caste groups.[14] Second, the artisan castes such as Vishwakorma (blacksmiths) and Pariyar (tailors) were considered Dalit and a part of the fourfold Varnashram (Brahmin, Thakurs, Vaisya, and Sudhra) in Nepal. In India and Nepali Tarai, the Dalit are outside the Varnashram. Third, Thakuri, the warrior caste, were put above non-Upadhya Bramin in the Nepali caste system backed by the civil code. Madhesi Brahmin were put below hill Brahmin groups and Chhetris.[15] This clearly signified the political manipulation of the caste system by the ruling families.

The caste system affected Nepal's political culture tremendously. By definition a caste system privileges some groups while discriminating against others, socially as well as economically. The caste system socializes people into respecting and obeying older people, upper-caste men, and authorities. It is not an egalitarian value system. Hence it has contributed to undermining democracy by fostering a nonegalitarian political culture.

The prominent anthropologist Dor Bahadur Bista has argued that the caste system and the rigid and fatalistic attitudes it introduced undermined development in Nepal. He labels the phenomenon as Bahunism, indicating the religious ideology of the hill variant caste system propounded by the Bahun religious advisers of its rulers. The phenomenon undermined values of physical work ethics and explained away achievements based on a fatalistic norm determined by one's prior life activities. The system of *afno manche* (one's circle) that was often determined by family, caste, and loyal friendship group favored ascription based mobility rather than an achievement-oriented system. It contributed to undermining competence, hard work, and independence. The caste-based fatalistic culture has hence impeded attempts to democratize and develop the country.

NOTES

1. Some sections of Chapters 25–29 draw liberally from Mahendra Lawoti, ed., *Contentious Politics and Democratization in Nepal* (Los Angeles: Sage, 2007); Lawoti, *Looking Back, Looking Forward: Centralization, Multiple Conflicts, and Democratic State Building in Nepal* (Washington, D.C.: East-West Center, 2007).

2. Ali Riaz and Subho Basu, *Paradise Lost? State Failure in Nepal* (Lanham, Md.: Lexington, 2007).

3. Nepalis and Indians do not need a passport to travel to the two countries.

4. This section draws on Dor Bahadur Bista, *Fatalism and Development: Nepal's Struggle for Modernization* (Hyderabad: Orient Longman, 1991); John Whelpton, *A History of Nepal* (Cambridge: Cambridge University Press, 2005).

5. Kumar Pradhan, *The Gorkha Conquests: The Process and Consequences of the Unification of Nepal, with Particular Reference to Eastern Nepal* (Calcutta: Oxford, 1991).

6. L. F. Stiller, *The Rise of the House of Gorkha* (Ranchi: Patna Jesuit Society, 1973).

7. Mahesh C. Regmi, *Thatched Huts and Stucco Palaces: Peasants and Landlords in 19th-Century Nepal* (New Delhi: Vikash, 1978).

8. HMG Nepal, *Constitution of the Kingdom of Nepal* (Kathmandu: Ministry of Law and Justice, Law Books Management Board, 1990).

9. "Indigenous nationalities" is a term coined to create solidarity among various ethnic groups, generally speaking Tibeto-Burman languages. Many of them are indigenous peoples as well, whereas a few groups are nationalities but not indigenous.

10. See Dor Bahadur Bista, *Peoples of Nepal*, 7th ed. (Kathmandu: Ratna Pustak Bhandar, 1996), for coverage of major ethnic groups in Nepal.

11. Harka Gurung, "Nepali Nationalism," in *Nepal Tomorrow: Voices and Visions*, ed. D. B. Gurung (Kathmandu: Kosele Prakashan, 2003).

12. Krishna B. Bhattachan, *Indigenous Nationalities and Minorities of Nepal: A Final Report Submitted to the Minority Rights Group International* (London: Minority Rights Group International, 2003).

13. Mary M. Cameron, *On the Edge of the Auspicious: Gender and Caste in Nepal* (Urbana-Champaign: University of Illinois Press, 1998).

14. Nancy E. Levine, "Caste, State, and Ethnic Boundaries in Nepal," *Journal of Asian Studies* 46, no. 1 (1987).

15. A. Hofer, *The Caste Hierarchy and the State in Nepal: A Study of the Muluki Ain of 1854* (Innsbruck: University Press, 1979).

Suggested Readings

Bista, Dor Bahadur. *Fatalism and Development: Nepal's Struggle for Modernization*. Hyderabad: Orient Longman, 1991.

_____. *Peoples of Nepal*. 7th ed. Kathmandu: Ratna Pustak Bhandar, 1996.

Cameron, Mary M. *On the Edge of the Auspicious: Gender and Caste in Nepal*. Champaign-Urbana: University of Illinois Press, 1998.

Gurung, Harka. "Nepali Nationalism." *Nepal Tomorrow: Voices and Visions*, 1–31. Ed. D. B. Gurung. Kathmandu: Kosele Prakashan, 2003.

Hofer, A. *The Caste Hierarchy and the State in Nepal: A Study of the Muluki Ain of 1854*. Innsbruck: University Press, Wagner, 1979.

Lawoti, Mahendra, ed. *Contentious Politics and Democratization in Nepal*. Los Angeles: Sage, 2007.

_____. *Towards a Democratic Nepal: Inclusive Political Institutions for a Multicultural Society*. New Delhi: Sage, 2005.

Levine, Nancy E. "Caste, State, and Ethnic Boundaries in Nepal." *Journal of Asian Studies* 46, no. 1 (1987): 71–88.

Pradhan, Kumar. *The Gorkha Conquests: The Process and Consequences of the Unification of Nepal, with Particular Reference to Eastern Nepal*. Calcutta: Oxford, 1991.

Regmi, Mahesh C. *Thatched Huts and Stucco Palaces: Peasants and Landlords in 19th-Century Nepal*. New Delhi: Vikash, 1978.

Stiller, L. F. *The Rise of the House of Gorkha*. Ranchi: Patna Jesuit Society, 1973.

Whelpton, John. *A History of Nepal*. Cambridge: Cambridge University Press, 2005.

26

Political Institutions and Governmental Processes

The history of political transformation and institutional development in Nepal can be divided into five phases after Nepal obtained freedom from the Ranas: the first democratic period (1951–1960), the panchayat period (1969–1990), the second democratic period (1990–2002), the royal interregnum (2002–2006), and the post-2006 transitional phase.

The First Experimentation with Democracy, 1951–1960

The end of despotic Rana rule in 1951 and the return of King Tribhuvan as effective ruler of the country raised hopes for democratic reforms. The second phase in the institutional development of Nepal started with the interim constitution of 1951 that was promulgated after the successful 1950–1951 resistance against the Ranas.[1] The interim constitution promised free elections and set up a coalition government consisting of the representatives of the Nepali Congress and members of the Rana family. The king was to serve as the head of state. King Tribhuvan was not an activist monarch; indeed, he aroused hope that power would soon be transferred to the people's representatives. The hope evaporated, however, with the disintegration of the coalition between the Nepali Congress and the Ranas, and the ongoing bickering among political leaders and political parties.

The Nepali Congress, the main reformist and modernist party in the country, became divided into various factions and could not provide united leadership. Amid the quarreling political parties, politicians, and factional squabbles, political stability became elusive. The period witnessed several governments headed by Mohan Shamshere Rana, Matrika Prasad Koirala (twice), Tanka Prasad Acharaya, Dr. K. I. Sing, and Suvarna Sumshere, in addition to direct rule by the king with a council of advisers. Due to continuous squabbling among the political leaders, the people viewed the monarch not only as the symbol of national unity but also as the savior of the country.[2]

King Mahendra, who succeeded his father in March 1955, promulgated a modified form of parliamentary government through the 1959 constitution. This new constitution provided for a bicameral legislative body consisting of the Pritinidhi Sabha (representative assembly) with 109 members to be elected directly on the basis of universal suffrage and the Maha Sabha (great assembly), the upper house, consisting of thirty-six members. The Maha Sabha was to be a permanent body with partly elected and partly appointed members serving terms of six years, one-third of whom would retire every two years. The new constitution also provided for a cabinet responsible to both the parliament and the king.

In the first free elections to parliament, held in February 1959, the Nepali Congress won an absolute majority with 74 of 109 seats. Gorkha Dal became the opposition party with nineteen seats. The Communist Party of Nepal (CPN) won four seats. Nepali Congress leader B. P. Koirala became the prime minister and formed a cabinet consisting of other Congress members. Nepal's experiment with parliamentary government did not last long, however. On December 15, 1960, King Mahendra dismissed the Koirala government on charges of failing to maintain law and order, being corrupt, and encouraging antinational elements; he then arrested the prime minister as well as his cabinet colleagues.

Nepal remained basically a feudal society. Traditional ruling elites still occupied powerful positions in the army and the administration. The Nepali Congress leaders lacked not only solidarity but also an extensive organizational network to mobilize the masses against members of the landed aristocracy when they sporadically resisted national authority. The king was concerned about stability in the country and could not afford to alienate the landowning segment of the society, which had held power for such a long time. King Mahendra and his prime minister also had serious personal and political differences. The king feared that a popular prime minister backed by a popularly elected parliament might impose severe restraints on his personal power and reduce him to a figurehead. The idea of a constitutional monarchy did not appeal to the king.

The Partyless Panchayat System, 1960–1990

Like many rulers in third world countries, King Mahendra believed that a democratic system and parliamentary government were products of the Western cultural milieu and thus not suitable for societies such as Nepal. At the same time, he found it hard to rule without some sort of popular association. The panchayat (council) system, which was argued to exist in Nepali society in the past, was considered more suited for its people than the representative institutions of Western societies. In 1962, therefore, the king introduced a new constitution with new popular institutions based on an indirect system of election. The panchayats were to be elected at the village, town, district, and national levels; but only the lowest level, the village and municipal panchayats, were to be directly elected by the people. At the national level stood the Rashtriya Panchayat (national council or parliament), which was to be elected indirectly by the members of the lower panchayats as well as by the members of professional and class organizations. A council of ministers, to be selected from the members of the national parliament, was to serve as an advisory body to the king. The panchayat system was an attempt at a guided democracy and the real power remained with the king, who had the authority not only to amend the constitution but also to suspend it by royal proclamation during emergencies. Another important feature of the constitution was the abolition of all political parties.

King Mahendra introduced several socioeconomic reforms. The caste system and untouchability were formally ended by the new civil code in 1963. The Land Reform Act, passed in 1964, provided some rights to tenant farmers and landless peasants but actually took away some rights from some groups. It took communal ownership of land (kipat) from Limbus and Rais, kiranti communities that had enjoyed these rights from the time of Prithvi Narayan Shah, and facilitated alienation of land from indigenous groups like the Tharus in the Tarai. King Mahendra also attempted to modernize the country and foster development. Education was expanded throughout the country, a bureaucracy was created to steer development, and the communication system was strengthened.

The period was also significant for promoting Khas hill nationalism. One language, one religion, and one dress code and lifestyle were promoted over diverse languages, religions, and lifestyles. This policy was promoted in earlier years as well but became more effective during the panchayat period with expansion of education and instruction in Khas-Nepali, as well as expansion of communication and the bureaucracy.

King Mahendra's efforts, however, failed to satisfy the politicians, the intellectuals, or the students—the most articulate segments of Nepali society. The demonstrations that ensued, often leading to considerable unrest, finally forced King Birendra, the successor to King Mahendra, to call for a nationwide referendum to determine the future form of Nepal's polity in May 1979. The referendum gave two choices to the people: a partyless panchayat system with the prospect of future reform, or a multiparty system. Although multiparty system was not clearly defined, it was implied to stand for a parliamentary system of government run on a party basis.

The supporters of the panchayat system and of the multiparty system were provided ample opportunity to campaign for their preferred form of government. The referendum was held on May 2, 1980, with 67 percent of eligible voters participating. The reformed panchayat system won by a narrow majority with 54.7 percent of the vote, showing that there was still considerable support for the free operation of political parties and a parliamentary system of government.

Even though the new institutional system created after the 1980 referendum failed to lift the ban on political parties, it nevertheless represented a significant departure from the constitutional arrangements existing since 1962. Under the new system, the 112 members of the Rastriya Panchayat were elected directly by the people on the basis of universal adult suffrage. Furthermore, the prime minister was elected by the Rastriya Panchayat, from which he selected the council of ministers. Both held office as long as they enjoyed the parliament's confidence. The constitutional reforms, however, did not alter the status of the king, who still held sovereign power in the kingdom of Nepal. At the societal level, more pluralism came into existence. More freedom of the press was tolerated than before 1980 and various social and cultural organizations, such as ethnic associations and fronts, began to emerge. Following the referendum of 1980, the people's participation in the political process increased.

Elections to the Rastriya Panchayat were held in 1981 and 1986. In the absence of officially sanctioned parties, groups and factions organizing around powerful members of the national parliament became common. Even though the political parties could not contest the elections, their leaders were not restricted to seeking seats in the national legislature. Some former party leaders were elected to the Rastriya Panchayat and some of them began to demand more political rights.

Second Democratic Experience, 1990–2002

In February 1990 the Nepali Congress, joined by the Leftist United Front and human rights activists, launched a movement to legalize political parties and restore a parliamentary system of government. Public pressure from the popular movement finally forced the king to replace the thirty-year-old panchayat system with a new constitution. Promulgated in November 1990, it provided for a parliamentary system of government, gave fundamental rights to the citizens, and introduced a system of multiparty democracy based on universal suffrage. The constitution created a bicameral parliament consisting of a lower and an upper house, with 205 and 60 members respectively. The lower house was directly elected by the people, and it held real power. The upper house was partly nominated and partly elected indirectly by the lower house and representatives of lower governments from the different development regions in the country. Ten members were nominated by the king. Executive power was vested in the prime minister and the cabinet, and the king served as the constitutional head of state.

Despite the political transformation, the polity remained highly centralized. It continued with a unitary structure despite a demand for federalism among different ethnic and regional groups. The first-past-the-post electoral method also helped centralize political power by creating artificial majorities. For instance, the Nepali Congress received less than 40 percent of votes in 1991 and 1999 but received a majority of seats in the lower house.

The Central Government

The political system between 1990 and 2002 was parliamentary, but most of the central power remained with the cabinet. Cabinets generally are more powerful in the parliamentary system because the most powerful leaders of the ruling party join the government and the parliament passes what the government pushes. This made the Nepali cabinet extremely powerful and the parliament very weak. Most of the legislation was introduced by the government, as only the government could introduce legislation with budgetary provisions. The parliamentary committees were not powerful and except for the Public Accounts Committee other committees rarely held the executive accountable. Further, the parliament did not enjoy the right to screen nominees to executive agencies and constitutional commissions.[3]

The executive was supported by the bureaucracy, which was recruited through merit-based examination. However, the bureaucracy was not autonomous. It was politicized by the ruling political parties, eroding its competency and independence. The whole administration, consisting of bureaucrats and the police force, was directly controlled by the central government. As a result, the bureaucrats were more loyal to central authorities than responsive and accountable to local needs and aspirations.

People elected 205 parliamentarians, and the parliamentarians elected the prime minister. The head of state was the king. Even though the king was designated a constitutional monarch, he remained commander in chief of the army. The king's power lay in the army's loyalty to him.

The judiciary was powerful to some extent. A Supreme Court at the center was followed by appellate courts and district courts. The cabinet authorized the budget and personnel for it. A cabinet minister also remained in the judicial council that recommended promotion of justices. Hence, despite the judiciary's exemplary role in protecting individual rights and press freedom, it was sometimes accused of being influenced by the executive.

The Local Governments

Decentralization in Nepal began in the 1960s, but minimal power was delegated, since effective decentralization was not compatible with the centralized panchayat system. Local governments were provided with some power and resources after 1990. However, the fact that the local governments do not control civil and police administration, which is still directly under the center, demonstrates that they do not enjoy much power. The village development committees (VDC) and municipalities are the lowest tiers of local governments. At present there are 3,913 VDCs and 58 municipalities. These bodies are directly elected. The district development committees (DDC) form the middle tier, and they are elected by members of the VDCs and municipalities. They are responsible for the development of the seventy-five districts.

The Local Self-Governance Act of 1999, even though weak in political and fiscal decentralization, provided a legal framework for administrative decentralization (providing services). Over the years different governments transferred resources to the local governments. The minority CPN-UML government in 1994 provided block grants to the village development committees. The funds increased the local governments' capacities as they conducted surveys of development activities, made plans, implemented projects, kept accounts, and mobilized communities to generate additional resources. The local governments have built schools, roads, and bridges, constructed drinking water projects, managed trails, and initiated many other development work. During the second local election in 1997, the CPN(UML) dominated coalition government ensured 20 percent reservation for women in local bodies. It enabled thousands of women to be elected to the local bodies.[4]

Governance Crises, 1990–2002

Nepal witnessed major governance crises during the period. Power abuse, corruption, and governmental instability occurred. The Maoist insurgency began during this period and expanded rapidly. This will be discussed in detail in Chapter 28.

Pervasive Corruption and Culture of Impunity

Power abuse, corruption, and politicization of the bureaucracy and the police, popularly described as Congressikaran (when NC was involved) or Amalekaran (when CPN[UML] followed), became widespread after 1990. The ruling

parties often appointed, transferred, and promoted bureaucrats and police officers based on partisan and personal interests. They also often appointed political cadres to public corporations and other influential public offices. These
activities undermined the autonomy of the bureaucracy and the police, lowered
the morale of the administration, increased nepotism, eroded meritocracy, and
effectively undermined the rule of law.

Corruption occurred both at the highest political level, involving millions of
rupees, and the everyday arenas that directly affected the common people.
Bribes became common for normal transactions in many public offices, including obtaining driving licenses and passports. Corruption occurred in many sectors with the complicity of government officials: goods were smuggled into
Nepal without paying taxes after bribing customs officers, fraudulent medicines
were openly sold in markets and distributed through public health agencies, vehicles stolen in India were sold in Nepal under the nose of the administration,
mineral water companies sold regular bottled water, and so on. Media reports
allege that street bureaucrats like the police abused their position to collect regular and irregular funds from businesses as well as small entrepreneurs.[5]

Corruption became institutionalized as the ruling political parties began to
collect huge sums for party organization and elections by awarding lucrative
government contracts and taking commissions from infrastructure and service sector projects. Newspapers and opposition political leaders alleged that
some cabinet ministers even permitted gold smuggling through the airport
and took a cut from it. Corruption occurred at the policy level as well. Cabinet decisions were beyond the purview of agencies due to the protection of
the confidentiality law. A law to declassify cabinet decisions was not legis-
lated, resulting in all cabinet decisions remaining beyond public scrutiny.
Some powerful ministers preferred to have the cabinet decide to avoid being
questioned and investigated.[6]

Not only did the political parties not take action against their corrupt colleagues but sometimes they defended leaders who were implicated in corruption. The China Southwest Airlines scandal investigated by the Public Accounts
Committee of the parliament is a good example. The CPN(UML) censured
members of the Public Accounts Committee, which had taken action against
the party's cabinet member.

As corrupt politicians went scot-free, others followed suit and corruption
became pervasive. The inaction against corruption and protection of colleagues by political parties fostered a culture of impunity and fueled further
corruption.[7] People saw many ruling political leaders change their lifestyles
overnight from paupers to millionaires. The perception of increased corruption became widespread, perhaps more than in practice. Many Nepalis

thought that most politicians were corrupt, and this perception eroded the legitimacy of the democratic polity.

After getting power to the people or their representatives, the challenge for democratization is to ensure that power does not get abused. No one, even the most powerful person of the land, should be above the law. "In framing a government . . . the great difficulty lies in this: you must first enable the government to control the governed; and in the next place oblige it to control itself."[8] This is a challenge in all societies because power can be abused by anyone who has it, including leaders elected by the people. Once power is given to elected public officials in new democracies, it is necessary to develop mechanisms to hold them accountable in case they abuse it. This was a serious shortcoming in Nepal.

An important accountability mechanism is periodic free and fair elections. However, power is abused between elections, and unless those abuses are addressed, the problems could grow. Hence power holders have to be held accountable between elections as well. Different government branches and agencies must be powerful in their area of jurisdiction and independent from the institutions they are supposed to supervise. Autonomy is ensured only if an agency that is supposed to hold another agency accountable is free from the latter's influence. For instance, the executive should not have power to influence other "independent" central agencies like the Election Commission and anticorruption agency through appointment, budget allocation, and personnel assignment.

The constitutional commissions, such as the Commission for Investigation of Abuse of Authority (CIAA) and the Election Commission, were not empowered to question or restrain the abuses of the executive, nor were they independent of it. The imbalance of power between the powerful executive and the weak constitutional commissions became a problem because the executive is usually the one that abuses power and the commissions were unable to hold the executive branch accountable. Further, the executive directly and indirectly influenced the constitutional commissions. First, the ruling party had disproportionate influence in the constitutional council that recommended names of the constitutional commissioners. The five-member constitutional council consisted of the prime minister, the chief justice, the speaker of the lower house, the chairperson of the upper house, and the opposition leader in the lower house. The ruling party with a majority could command the majority in the council because the speaker of the lower house and chairperson of the upper house along with the prime minister could belong to the same party. Except during the hung parliament when the upper house elected a chair from a minority party and the prime minister kept changing, the ruling party held the majority in the constitutional council and nominated commissioners loyal to it. Second, the executive allocated the budget for the commissions, and it could reduce (or increase) or delay the budget allocation. It was in the interest of the commissions to not irritate the cabinet. Third, the cabinet also assigned personnel to the commissions.

Absence of autonomy and executive influence meant that the commissions often did not hold members of the executive accountable. For instance, the executive-dependent CIAA in the 1990s did not act against powerful ruling political leaders whose party may have been instrumental in the appointment of the commissioners and who could become handy in extending tenure or providing other benefits.

Only with empowerment in 2002 did the CIAA begin to investigate powerful political leaders of the dominant parties. The CIAA is still not independent, however, as nomination of its commissioners, its budget, and personnel deputation are still decided or influenced by the cabinet. It has been charged with being politically motivated. Its actions do not help to demonstrate its independence either. The CIAA dropped corruption charges against G. P. Koirala after he became the prime minister following the success of the people's movement. The question is whether charges were labeled against him through political motivation or dropped because he had become the prime minister.

Other branches of government were also unable to check the power abuses of the executive because they were powerless or dependent on the executive. The parliament and its committees were weak and were not in a position to hold the executive accountable, except perhaps through changing the government or the threat of doing so. Similarly, even the powerful judiciary, which was less dependent, was constrained in holding the executive accountable. The court protected the people from unlawful imprisonment and ruled in the mid-1990s that the CIAA could investigate and prosecute cabinet members but the court could not intervene in day-to-day administration, the avenue of frequent power abuse and corruption. Thus the role of the judiciary is limited in controlling power abuse and corruption in the administration except through the empowerment of nonexecutive agencies when interpreting the constitutional articles. The power through interpretation also became limited because the constitution clearly made the executive powerful and other agencies weak and dependent on it.

Governmental Instability

Nepal witnessed twelve governments between 1990 and 2002, on average one government per year. The frequent government changes occurred not only during the hung parliament of 1994–1999 but also during the other two parliaments with a majority party. Rapid government changes interrupted policy formulation, implementation, and the overall administration. The political elite devoted less time and energy on formulating new policies for development and betterment of the people and the country. They were busy breaking and forming governments most of the time. The frequent government changes also promoted an unethical political culture and practices. Legislators were bought and sold for parliamentary votes, to support existing governments as well as to vote against them.

One positive aspect of the frequent governmental changes could have been the induction of new faces in government and changes in policies. However, this did not occur. For instance, the position of prime minister has been a game of musical chairs among half a dozen individuals. The alternation often occurred so rapidly that the incumbent governments had no time to formulate and implement new policies.

The incongruence between the multiparty reality of the country and the design of a majoritarian parliamentary system suitable for a two-party system and alternation of government contributed to the instability. The majoritarian parliamentary system works better in countries without diverse ideological and cultural cleavages that produce multiple political parties. If the state structure had been designed to share power among various political parties in Nepal, the incompatibility between the empirical political reality of multiple political parties and structure would have been less. For instance, in many established consensus democracies, major political parties participate in coalition governments. The question of frequent government changes does not arise when all the major parties join the cabinet. Power sharing is enabled to some degree by the expectation of multiple political parties due to the proportional representative electoral method. A power-sharing structure would probably have meant less instability because not only the formal structures would have promoted stability but even the political leadership could have been socialized with a power-sharing culture.

Nepal also witnessed frequent strikes, bandhs (shutdowns), dharnas (sit-ins), and chhaka jams (traffic blockade). The strikes became so frequent that they were nearly in regular political repertoires. Nepal witnessed thirty-nine bandhs in 2002 alone.[9] The Maoists alone called fifty-three Nepal and Kathmandu valley bandhs between 1996 and 2002.[10]

Protests are an inherent part of democratic practice, but in Nepal many of the protestors, especially the activists of political parties and their sister organizations like the student associations, employed coercion and threats to implement the calls. The protesters vandalized and destroyed public and private properties like shops and government offices, vehicles, and roadside fences while implementing their calls. Occasionally people were murdered. These activities, in the name of expressing dissent, often undermined the individual right of common people to go about their daily life unobstructed.[11] They crippled normal life and the economy incurred a huge loss. Dhruba Kumar estimated the economic costs of Maoist bandhs, strikes, and so on to be 100 billion rupees.[12] Schools and colleges have been shut down for long periods, including during centralized exams, wasting valuable time and resources and eroding the educational system.

One major reason for bandhs is the unresponsiveness of governments. The governments understood that the opposition could not formally obstruct their policies or hold them accountable. Thus they did not respond to the demands of the opposition and social justice movements. The opposition and movements had to rely on coercive public protests to force the government to respond and change policies. The opposition perceived that it had no other options.

The bandhs were to some extent the legacy of the opposition's obstructionist politics during the panchayat period. However, the higher frequency of bandhs after 1990 suggests that opposition powerlessness and government unresponsiveness contributed significantly. If the opposition had a role in governance, their priorities and energies would probably have been spent on affecting policy changes through formal channels.

Successful Sectors During 1990–2002

The post-1990 democratic years were not only plagued by problems; they also witnessed successes in many arenas. A boom in print, radio, and electronic media occurred after the 1990 democratic change. The government removed restrictions the previous regime had imposed on the media and awarded licenses to FM radio and TV stations. Before 1990, Nepal only had government-owned English and Nepali broadsheet dailies. By the end of the 1990s, there were several Nepali and English broadsheet dailies. The Press Council reported that 217 dailies, 1,132 weeklies, and 186 fortnightlies were registered between 2002 and 2003 (all of them do not publish regularly, however). The readership and circulation also rose sharply. Sagarmatha Radio became the first private radio to operate in South Asia in 1997. By July 2003, twenty-six private radio stations were broadcasting from different towns and rural areas. Several private TV channels began operation after the turn of the century.[13]

Community forestry efforts are reforesting Nepal's hills. The process began when the government started to return forest management to the communities in 1978, but the trend gained momentum after 1990 with new legislation (the Forest Act 1993; Forest Regulations 1995) that gave community groups more rights. By 1999, community user groups in Nepal were managing more than 6,200 square kilometers of forests; 8,500 community forest groups comprising nearly a million households existed. New user groups were formed at the rate of nearly 2,000 a year in the 1990s. The gradual reversal of earlier deforestation sharply contrasts with the trend of large-scale deforestation after 1957, when the government of Nepal nationalized the forests.[14] The government was unable to protect and manage the nationalized forests, whereas local communities no longer had the authority to do so. The Nepali experience shows that when governments transfer rights to communities, user groups can craft appropriate institutional arrangements to manage common pool resources that reduce the threat of environmental degradation due to population boom.[15]

Another sector that witnessed remarkable growth after 1990 is the civil society. Over 11,000 NGOs were registered by the year 2000 compared to only a few hundred in 1990.[16] Some NGOs focus on delivering services whereas others target protecting the rights of citizens and advocating social justice. Social justice movements of the Dalit, indigenous nationalities, Madhesi, and women also exploded during the 1990s. Even though they have not been able to uproot discrimination and inequality, they have increased awareness, mobilized marginal groups, and sensitized the society and the government to the injustice and inequality.

A common factor in all the successful sectors is the withdrawal of the central state. For instance, the media grew because the government permitted the sector to operate more or less without restrictions. Forestry efforts grew when nationalized forests were returned to the communities. The government gave back considerable power to the communities, including the power to access, manage, and exclude nonuser groups from common resources. With some power and resources in the 1990s, local governments performed better. The financial sectors expanded and became more efficient after the state further liberalized. Likewise, the government encouraged NGOs and tolerated social justice movements, leading to their explosive growth. When the state gave space to operate, different actors used those opportunities to perform and deliver. This suggests that if given space, people work to deliver in arenas of their interest and expertise.

This comparison between problematic and successful sectors makes it clear that the central state's excessive intervention created problems whereas different sectors successfully functioned when the central state gave up restrictive power. This does not mean that the state should completely withdraw, though. It can play a positive role as facilitator, regulator, arbitrator, and so on.

The Royal Interventions, 2002–2006

On the night of June 1, 2001, King Birendra's entire family was massacred, presumably by Crown Prince Dipendra. King Gyanendra, Birendra's surviving brother, became the king. King Gyanendra was more assertive and ambitious than the late king. On October 4, 2002, after the government failed to hold scheduled parliamentary elections, the king dismissed the elected government of Sher Bahadur Deuba.

King Gyanendra formed a government headed by Lokendra Bahadur Chand consisting of different ethnic groups and civil society. Within a year he formed another government headed by Surya Bahadur Thapa. As a movement against the king began to gain support among the people, he again reinstated Sher Bahadur Dueba. This strategic move seemed to take the wind out of the opposition movement as two large parties, the Nepali Congress (Democratic) and the Communist Party of Nepal (United Marxist Leninist), participated in the government. The king however, dismissed the Deuba government on February 1, 2005, and formed a cabinet under his own chairpersonship. The royal interregnum saw an increase in the militarization of politics, both in its attempt to repress the Maoists and the parliamentary political parties. This pushed the Maoist rebels and the parliamentary political parties together. The seven political parties that had launched a movement against the king and the Maoists agreed to launch a joint movement. The civil society movement also mobilized broader support. The king was finally forced to give up power after nineteen days of huge mass demonstration in the Kathmandu valley in April 2006.

The Second People's Movement (2006) and Beyond

Girija Prasad Koirala, as the leader of the movement against royal rule, became the prime minister, leading a coalition government of the seven political parties in April 2006. The Maoists and the interim government signed a comprehensive peace treaty in November 2006. An interim constitution drafted by representatives of the seven political parties and the Maoists was promulgated in January 2007 by the parliament, paving the way for Maoists to enter the interim parliament, which they joined in April 2007. These events generated hope in the war-torn society.

Several traditionally marginalized ethnic groups protested against the interim constitution and its provisions. Many discriminatory provisions toward the marginalized groups were eliminated but others remained. The positive aspects are declaring a secular state and ending discrimination in regard to citizenship. Remaining discrimination includes the ban on ethnic parties, keeping the cow (a Hindu deity) as national animal, unequal treatment toward Nepali women's foreign spouses in acquiring Nepali citizenship, and so on. The first issue was addressed by an amendment to the interim constitution, but the issue of administrative and ethnic federalism has not been resolved. Major ethnic groups want ethnic autonomy, while the ruling elite seem reluctant to award it.[17]

The transition has not been smooth, especially when initial optimism evaporated after several months. The Madhesi movement in early 2007 led to nearly fifty deaths. The indigenous nationalities have also launched movements. Some of the Madhesi groups are engaged in violent revolt as well. They are engaged in extortions, abductions, and killings of political activists, civil servants, and common people. The Young Communist League of the Maoists is still engaged in extortions and abductions. They have occasionally killed people, including journalists. Likewise, the Maoists have not returned private property they seized despite promises to do so. In fact, they continue to take forcefully the private property of people they deem enemies.

The election for Constituent Assembly was finally held in April 10, 2008, after being postponed twice. Its mandate is to craft a new Constitution to build a "new" Nepal. As no party secured a majority, the process will probably be based on consensus. As a result, the document would probably be acceptable to more people.

NOTES

1. It is the second constitution. The first was promulgated by Padma Sumshere Rana in 1948 to appease the rising movement for democracy.

2. Bhuwan Lal Joshi and Leo E Rose, *Democratic Innovations in Nepal: A Case Study of Political Acculturation* (Berkeley: University of California Press, 1966).

3. Mahendra Lawoti, *Looking Back, Looking Forward: Centralization, Multiple Conflicts and Democratic State Building in Nepal* (Washington: East-West Center, 2007).

4. Rabindra Khanal, *Local Governance in Nepal: Democracy at Grassroots* (Kathmandu: Smriti, 2006); Damodar Adhikari, *Towards Local Democracy in Nepal: Power and Participation in District Development Planning, Spring Research Series* (Dortmund: University of Dortmund, 2006).

5. Basanta Thapa and Mohan Mainali, eds., *Dharap: Taskari, Hinsa Ra Arajakatako Katha* (Lalitpur: Khoj Patrakarita Kendra, 2001–2002; Basanta Thapa and Mohan Mainali, eds., *Abyabastha Ra Aniyamata: Bhrastachar Sambandhi Khojmulak Lekhharu* (Lalitpur: Khoj Patrakarita Kendra, 2003).

6. Binod Bhattarai, Jogendra Ghimire and Mohan Mainali, *Excesses Unlimited: A Study on Impunity in Nepal* (Lalitpur: Himal, 2005).

7. Bhattarai, Ghimire, and Mainali, *Excesses Unlimited.*

8. Andreas Schedler, "Conceptualizing Accountability," in *The Self-Restraining State: Power and Accountability in New Democracies,* ed. Andreas Schedler, Larry Diamond, and Marc F. Plattner (Boulder: Lynne Rienner, 1999).

9. Tejasuee Rajbhandari and Pooj Shrestha, "2002 AD, a Year with 39 Days of Bandhs," *Kathmandu Post,* January 1, 2003.

10. Dhruba Kumar, "Consequences of the Militarized Conflict and the Cost of Violence in Nepal," *Contributions to Nepalese Studies* 30, no. 2 (2003).

11. Genevieve Lakier, "Illiberal Democracy and the Problem of Law: Street Protest and Democratization in Multiparty Nepal," *Contentious Politics and Democratization in Nepal,* ed. Mahendra Lawoti (New Delhi: Sage, 2007).

12. One U.S. dollar was equal to 63.65 rupees in December 2007. Kumar, "Consequences of the Militarized Conflict."

13. Pratyoush Onta, "The Print Media in Nepal Since 1990: Impressive Growth and Institutional Challenges," *Studies in Nepali History and Society* 6, no. 2 (2001); Bharat Dutta Koirala, "The Role of the Media in Nepal," in *The Maoist Insurgency in Nepal: A Monograph; Causes, Impact, and Avenues of Resolution*, ed. Shambhu Ram Simkhada and Fabio Oliva (Geneva: PSIO, 2006).

14. Arun Agrawal and Elinor Ostrom, "Collective Action, Property Rights, and Decentralization in Resource Use in India and Nepal," *Politics and Society* 29, no. 4 (2001).

15. Agrawal and Ostrom, "Collective Action."

16. Saubhagya Shah, "From Evil State to Civil Society," in *State of Nepal*, ed. Kanak Mani Dixit and Shastri Ramachandaran (Lalitpur: Himal, 2002).

17. Mahendra Lawoti, ed., *Contentious Politics and Democratization in Nepal* (Los Angeles: Sage, 2007).

SUGGESTED READINGS

Adhikari, Damodar. *Towards Local Democracy in Nepal: Power and Participation in District Development Planning. Spring Research Series.* Dortmund: University of Dortmund, 2006.

Agrawal, Arun, and Elinor Ostrom. "Collective Action, Property Rights, and Decentralization in Resource Use in India and Nepal." *Politics and Society* 29, no. 4 (2001): 485–514.

Baral, Lok Raj. *Oppositional Politics in Nepal.* New Delhi: Abhinab, 1977.

Baral, Lok Raj, ed. *Election and Governance in Nepal.* New Delhi: Manohar, 2005.

Brown, T. Louise. *The Challenge to Democracy in Nepal.* London: Routledge, 1996.

Chauhan, R. S. *Society and State Building in Nepal.* New Delhi: Sterling, 1989.

Dhruba Kumar. *State, Leadership, and Politics in Nepal.* Kathmandu: CNAS, 1995.

Joshi, Bhuwan Lal, and Leo E. Rose. *Democratic Innovations in Nepal: A Case Study of Political Acculturation.* Berkeley: University of California Press, 1966.

Khanal, Rabindra. *Local Governance in Nepal: Democracy at Grassroots.* Kathmandu: Smriti, 2006.

Lawoti, Mahendra, ed. *Contentious Politics and Democratization in Nepal.* Los Angeles: Sage, 2007.

———. *Looking Back, Looking Forward: Centralization, Multiple Conflicts, and Democratic State Building in Nepal.* Washington, D.C.: East-West Center, 2007.

Malla, K. P. *Nepal: Perspectives on Continuity and Change.* Kathmandu: CNAS, 1989.

Parajulee, Ramjee P. *The Democratic Transition in Nepal.* Lanham, Md.: Rowman & Littlefield, 2000.

Shah, Rishikesh. *Politics in Nepal: 1980–1991.* New Delhi: Manohar, 1993.

27

Political Parties, Elections, and Leaders

Political Parties

With the 1990 constitution and free elections, Nepal joined the growing number of new third world democracies. However, like other third world democracies Nepal also experienced political instability. Political parties have played an important role in bringing about democracy and then restoring it after it has been taken away. However, they have faced problems in maintaining it. Partly as a result of misgovernance by political parties, democracy has been derailed several times in Nepal.

Political parties are supposed to articulate and aggregate interests, and engage in electoral mobilization, candidate nomination, issue structuring, societal representation, and forming and sustaining governments.[1] This section evaluates the Nepali political parties based on how they perform some of these functions.

History of Formation of Political Parties

The political parties were established in Nepal with the aim to abolish the Rana regime (1846–1951). The Prachanda Gorkha, a political movement, was formed in 1931. The first political party, the Praja Parishad (People's Council), was formed in June 4, 1936, in Kathmandu. Tanka Prasad Acharya was the president and Dasarath Chand was the vice president. The three other founding members were Ram Hari Sharma, Dharma Bhakta, and Jeev Raj Sharma. Ganesh Man Singh and others joined the party soon afterward (Fisher 1998, 36). Praja Parishad began engaging in activities such as distributing pamphlets and hatching conspiracies to overthrow the Ranas. It also contacted King Tribhuvan, who was kept under close surveillance, and gained his support. However, the Ranas discovered their activities and brutally repressed the party. Four members of Praja Parishad were apprehended and hanged by the Ranas in 1941. Others were sentenced to life imprisonment.[2]

Several political parties were set up in India in the late 1940s by Nepali exiles and Indian domiciled Nepalis. The All-India Nepali National Congress and the All-India Gorkha Congress, set up in Calcutta and Varanasi respectively, were merged in 1947 to form the Nepali National Congress. The Nepali National Congress (B. P. Koirala) and the Nepal Democratic Congress (M. B. Shah) merged to become the Nepali Congress in 1950.[3] The Communist Party of Nepal (CPN) was also formed in India in 1949. The Nepali Congress launched an armed movement against the Ranas in November 1950.

Ideological Orientation of Nepali Parties

Political parties in Nepal can be broadly categorized into leftist, centrist, rightist, and identity oriented. Some of the parties have engaged in violent movements as well. One of the interesting features of the Nepali party system is that despite the decline of the communist ideology after the collapse of the Soviet Union and the Warsaw Pact, the Nepali communist parties are still very strong. Table 27.1 shows that if the communist parties had a united front with common candidates they probably would have defeated the Nepali Congress in 1999, the largest noncommunist party to form a government. In the 2008 Constituent Assembly election, the communist parties collectively polled 57 percent of popular votes. For the first time in Nepali electoral history, they obtained a majority of votes and seats.

The Communist Parties

The left parties in Nepal, including the ones that have embraced parliamentary democracy, call themselves communist parties. Some are still critical of the parliamentary system and hope to launch a violent movement in the future when the time is ripe for revolution to establish communism. The Communist Party of Nepal-United Marxist Leninist (CPN-UML), a party that became more moderate in the 1990s, was the main opposition or ruling party during the 1990s. The Communist Party of Nepal (Maoist) (CPN-Maoist), a party that espoused radical communist ideology, grew rapidly after it launched an insurgency in 1996. The trend of both the moderate and extremist communist parties growth during the 1990s demonstrates the contradictory tendencies within the communist movement and their supporters in Nepal.

The communist movement in Nepal has been deeply influenced by the Communist Party of India. Many young Nepali intellectuals residing in Bengal came

TABLE 27.1   Votes and Seats Received by Communist and Noncommunist Parties in the 1990s

Political Parties	1991 Vote %	1991 Seats	1994 Vote %	1994 Seats	1999 Vote %	1999 Seats
COMMUNIST PARTIES						
Communist Party of Nepal(UML)	27.75	69	30.85	83	30.74	68
Nepal Workers Peasants Party	1.25	2	0.98	4	0.55	1
United Peoples Front Nepal	4.83	9	1.32	-	0.84	1
Communist Party of Nepal(D)	2.43	2	-	-	-	-
National Peoples Front	-	-	-	-	1.37	5
Communist Party of Nepal(ML)	-	-	-	-	6.00	-
TOTAL	36.26	82	33.15	87	39.51	75
NONCOMMUNIST PARTIES						
Nepali Congress	37.75	110	33.38	83	36.14	113
National Democratic Party(C)	6.56	3	-	-	3.33	-
National Democratic Party(T)	5.38	1	-	-	-	-
National Democratic Party	-	-	17.93	20	10.14	12
Nepal Sadhvawana Party	4.10	6	3.49	3	3.13	5
TOTAL	53.79	120	54.8	106	52.74	128

Only parties that secured seats in the parliament are listed.

Source: Mahendra Lawoti, *Towards a Democratic Nepal: Inclusive Political Institutions for a Multicultural Society* (New Delhi: Sage, 2005).

under the influence of Indian Marxists, whose guidance in 1949 helped them found the Nepali Communist Party in Calcutta. The CPN was banned in January 1952 for supporting the rebellion by Dr. K. I. Singh.[4] The ban was lifted in April 1956, when Tanka Prasad Acharya was prime minister, after the party agreed to engage in "peaceful movement and accept constitutional monarchy."[5]

Like their counterparts in India, the Nepali communists looked on the Nepali Congress leaders as willing tools of international imperialism. They called for a broad-based alliance of progressive forces to fight the Nepali Congress and an expansionist India. The establishment of people's democracies, relentless opposition to the king (some factions, however, worked indirectly with the monarchy), his feudalistic regime, and radical social and economic reforms are the hallmarks of the party's program.

Not unlike the communist movement in India, the Nepali communist movement suffers from factional conflicts and ideological schisms that have produced deep divisions within its leadership. In addition to its various minor splinter groups, the Communist Party was divided into pro-Moscow and pro-Beijing factions, the two largest ideological groups, until the end of the cold war.[6]

The Communist Party of Nepal-United Marxist Leninist

The CPN(UML) emerged out of the merger of CPN(ML) (Marxist Leninist) and CPN(M) (Marxist) in January 1991. The former brought a mass-based organization and the younger generation of communist leaders, whereas the CPN(ML) provided well-known leaders from the mainstream communist movement. The former CPN(ML) leaders controlled the united party.

The CPN(ML) was formally launched through a convention on December 28, 1976. The organization was the culmination of the Jhapa Resistance, a movement that aimed to physically eliminate class enemies launched in the Jhapa district in southeast Nepal in 1971. The movement was brutally repressed by the government but it was successful in organizing and expanding. In June 1975, it held a secret conference to establish the All-Nepal Revolutionary Coordination Committee (Marxist Leninist). It changed the name to CPN(ML) subsequently.[7]

CPN(UML) is an organization that maintains a stable base in the country. It is able to maintain its support because it has a strong hold on peasants and workers, and it recruits new cadres through its student union. It projects a progressive image by raising issues of inequality. The party briefly ruled alone for nine months in 1994 as a minority government. While in power it provided block grants to village development committees and ensured one female representative out of five members in the ward committees of the VDC.

In the 1990s, especially after 1993, the CPN(UML) moderated its ideological stance. It has accepted a market economy and parliamentary democracy despite holding on to the communist name. During the 1990s it also accepted the constitutional monarchy and even joined the government formed by King Gyanendra under Prime Minister Sher Bahadur Deuba in 2004. During the 1990s it also formed various coalition governments with centrist, rightist, and ethnic oriented political parties. It transformed itself into a democratic parliamentary party in the 1990s despite its name.

The CPN (Maoist)

The CPN (Maoist) was formed in 1995 by a faction of CPN (Unity Center) headed by Prachanda. It expanded rapidly after launching an insurgency against the parliamentary democracy in 1996. With the peace accord in November 2006, the Maoists seemed to accept some form of multiparty democracy. However, contradictory rhetoric by different Maoist leaders at different times raises the issue that their real objective is attaining a communist republic. They took part in the Constituent Assembly election and won 220 seats out of 575 contested seats (twenty-six seats would be nominated), being the largest party. We will examine the Maoists in detail in the next chapter regarding conflict in Nepal.

The Fringe Left Parties

There are several other small communist parties. The Nepal Peasant Workers Party, the CPN (Unity Center), the CPN (Mashal), and their factions are communist groups that have some representation in parliament. Several other marginal communist parties exist that did not have representation in parliament. Some leaders of these parties are partially underground (do not appear in public). Most of these fringe parties lie between the CPN (Maoist) and CPN(UML) in their ideological orientations.

The Centrist Party: The Nepali Congress

Nepali Congress is one of the oldest and best-known political parties of Nepal. As an umbrella organization founded in 1950 by the anti-Rana intellectuals residing in India, it sought to overthrow the Rana regime and democratize the society. After the 1950 revolution the Nepali Congress became the ruling party for a short period. Under the leadership of the charismatic B. P. Koirala, however, it survived as a major political force in the country even after its government was dismissed and its leaders jailed in 1960.

The party is a moderately socialist, reform-oriented organization that seeks to liberalize Nepali society along democratic lines. In the 1980 referendum it supported the multiparty option in opposition to the panchayat system. Although Koirala himself was ambivalent toward the new institutional setup of the postreferendum period, his party decided to boycott the 1981 Rastriya Panchayat elections. Thus the Nepali Congress adopted a rejectionist posture toward the new regime.

On July 22, 1982, B. P. Koirala died. His death created a void in the Nepali Congress and in politics generally, because he had played a central role in national politics since 1950. He was also a moderating force within his party during his later years and consistently advocated for a policy of national reconciliation in Nepal. Although his death left the Nepali Congress without a widely accepted leader, the party maintained its support among the different sections of the population in the country. Ganesh Man Singh, Krishna Prasad Bhattarai, and Girija Prasad (G. P.) Koirala, the youngest brother of B. P., collectively led the Nepali Congress after B. P.'s death.

The Nepali Congress formed majority governments in 1991 and 1999 but could not maintain a stable government due to internal fighting. It frequently participated in the ever-changing coalition governments between 1994 and 1999. The Nepali Congress in the 1990s did not introduce major reforms during its rule, except for market-oriented reforms that the World Bank and IMF forced on Nepal. Thus it has increasingly projected an image of a status quo party.

After 1990 the Koirala clan led by G. P. Koirala began to dominate the party. Ganesh Man Singh and K. P. Bhattarai were eased out of the party over the years. In 2002 the Nepali Congress split into the Nepali Congress led by G. P. Koirala and Nepali Congress(Democratic) led by Sher Bahadur Dueba. The split resulted from a power struggle between Koirala and the opposition faction led by Sher Bahadur Deuba. The two Congresses merged in 2007 as a run-up to the Constituent Assembly. Today the Nepali Congress is led by G. P. Koirala and Sher Bahadur Deuba, among others.

The Rightist Parties

The Gorkha Dal emerged as the conservative party in the 1950s, representing the interests of the Ranas and their supporters. However, after King Mahendra dismissed the Nepali Congress government in 1960 and ended the multiparty system, it merged with the Nepali Congress. Thereafter, the ruling panchayat system carried the torch of conservatives in Nepal.

Two conservative parties with the same name, the National Democratic Party, were formed by the former panchas (politicians active during the panchayat period) in 1990 after the restoration of democracy. The parties have merged and split several times since then. As a combined outfit it received 17 percent of the votes in 1994 and elected twenty members to parliament. It captured fewer seats and votes when it contested elections as separate parties.

The NDP is close to the royal palace. A major splinter group supported King Gyanendra when he directly ruled the country after 2005. Two factions opposed the king's direct rule but supported constitutional monarchy. The central committees of the NDPs are better balanced ethnically than those of the Nepali Congress and CPN(UML), and they receive considerable support from ethnic/caste groups. Despite this, the parties are conservative in raising the issues of the marginalized groups compared to the communist parties.

The Ethnically Named Parties

Explicitly ethnic oriented political parties emerged between 1951 and 1960.[8] The Nepal Tarai Congress, whose major demand was autonomy for the Tarai, received 2.1 percent of the popular votes but did not win any seats in 1959. More ethnic parties emerged after the restoration of democracy in 1990. Most of the ethnic parties have not performed well during the elections. Except for the Nepal Goodwill Party (NGP) of the Madhesi, no ethnically oriented party elected representatives to parliament in the 1990s. NGP was transformed into a political party from the Goodwill Forum by Gajendra Narayan Singh, the champion of the Madhesi cause. It has been raising the problems the Madhesi are facing such as the lack of citizenship certificates, domination of hill people in the governance of country, and discrimination against Madhesi languages, dress codes, and values. Among its major demands are making Hindi a lingua franca in the Tarai, federalism, and inclusion of the Madhesi in governance. NGP received the highest percentage of votes and seats in the 1991 election: 4 percent of votes and six seats respectively. Since then, its vote share has declined. Major reasons for this decline could be its inability to mobilize resources during elections compared to the larger parties, its inability to represent all subgroups of the Tarai, especially the larger groups like Muslims and Tharus, and its inability to deliver even after it joined the government during the coalition years. The Madhesi Peoples Right Forum (MPRF), which transformed into a political party after successfully leading a movement in 2007, emerged as the largest Madhesi party in the Constituent Assembly by winning fifty-two seats. The Tarai Madhesh Democratic Party (TMDP), a party formed by Madhesi leaders who quit mainstream political parties to raise the Madhesi cause, emerged as the second largest party with twenty seats.

Among the indigenous nationalities parties, the National People's Liberation Party (NPLP) has received around 1 percent of votes. It steadily increased its vote share since 1991 but was not able to elect a member to parliament under the first-past-the-post electoral system. Some specifically ethnic-named parties like the Mongol National Organization and National Nationalities Party were denied registration by the Election Commission in 1990 following the constitutional provision that bans ethnic parties.[9] The indigenous nationalities parties have demanded federalism, declaration of a secular state, equality among native languages, and inclusion in governance, among other things. Even though the indigenous nationalities parties did not win any seat in the FPTP election, they won five seats through the proportional representative method in the Constituent Assembly.

Problems in the Party System

Political Exclusion of Women and Marginalized Ethnic/Caste Groups

One major failure of the major political parties has been their inability to include various ethnic and caste groups and women. All major political parties are dominated by the CHHEM. For instance in 1999, CPN(UML), despite its progressive rhetoric, was dominated by the CHHE by 87 percent in its central committee. The same group dominated the Nepali Congress by 71 percent and the NDPs by around 45 percent.[10] The presence of women in the central committees of the political parties, including small and ethically named ones, has also been negligible, with a few women at most. The expansion of the Maoist insurgency, on the other hand, indicates that substantial numbers of people, especially the poor and the downtrodden, do not feel represented by the major parties. The Maoist party has emerged as the most inclusive party even though its top leaders also hail from the dominant group.

Party Factionalism and Splits

Almost all political parties in Nepal have witnessed fragmentation. This problem has plagued parties of all ideological persuasion and sizes. However, the frequency of split is much higher among the communist parties. During the cold war, the communist parties fragmented along Russian and Chinese lines. When King Mahendra took power in 1960, they also split between those who sympathized with the king and those who opposed him. They have also differed with regard to adopting violent or peaceful strategies for revolution. At other times, the communists tend to split over differences involving interpretation of terms, concepts, and ideology. At any given time since the 1970s, there have been around a dozen communist parties in Nepal.[11]

However, the communist voters tend not to be as divided. Especially after 1990, a large number of communist factions have tended to vote for the CPN(UML). It always polled more than 30 percent of votes during the elections in the 1990s. However, the rapid expansion of the Maoists after 1996 have come at the cost of CPN(UML). The election to the Constituent Assembly has proved that.

The Nepali Congress did not experience such frequent splits, but it was plagued by intense intraparty factionalism. Sometimes opposition factions worked to undermine official candidates in the elections. At other times, members of parliament opposed their own government proposals. As noted above, the Nepali Congress went through a major split in 2002, but the two factions merged again in 2007.

The conservative National Democratic Party and ethnic parties like the NGP and the NPLP have also frequently split. The NDP has generally merged after being routed in subsequent elections, but that does not seem likely to prevent splits in the party again. The splits in these parties have often been due to personality clashes of the leaders as well as the fight for spoils when party leaders joined government.

Lack of Intraparty Democracy

Almost all the political parties lack internal democracy. Most parties have been dominated by one leader for long periods, whether rightist, centrist, parliamentary, revolutionary communist, or fringe parties that have not been able to elect members to parliament. The Nepali Congress, CPN(UML), and CPN (Maoist) or smaller ones like the Nepal Workers and Peasant Party (NWPP) or Nepal Goodwill Party (NGP) have been governed by a dominant leader with unprecedented power for long periods. The top leaders frequently ignore party rules and procedures and often govern based on personal whims. They undermine intraparty democracy by not holding regular meetings and conventions, even when legitimately called by dissenting factions. In parties like the Nepali Congress and the NDP factions, major party decisions often have been made by the top leaders outside formal party forums. In the case of communist parties, the dissenting factions, on the other hand, have often been hounded out or forced to split for challenging the establishment.

The political parties and leaders have been able to monopolize political power because most agencies and institutions, which are supposed to wield countervailing power or hold the political forces accountable in democracies, like the media, trade unions, professional associations, human rights groups, and civic organizations, either are under the influence of the political parties or are weak. For instance, many civil society organizations and nongovernmental organizations (NGOs), including human rights groups with independent facades, have a close affiliation with specific political parties beyond ideological affinities. The few civil society organizations that are independent, on the other hand, find it challenging to be effective because political parties, through their cadres and supporters working in government agencies, NGOs, and donor organizations, influence distribution of resources and rewards.[12] As political loyalty and affiliation seem to pay off more than being independent, many in the media, professions, and academia nurture their relationships with political parties. This becomes a problem where the civil society is small and a large proportion of it has partisan affiliations. The civil society was often uncivil and failed to hold political parties accountable.[13]

The sociopolitical structure in Nepal has not been conducive to the development of a sound party system. With political and administrative life dominated by a few high-caste families, the caste system, nonegalitarian culture, power-aggrandizing attitudes among top leaders, and the monarchy's hostile attitude toward parties and political leaders, the growth of a responsible competitive party system in the country has been slow. The public behavior of the party leaders and continual interparty conflicts have led to a poor image of party leaders in Nepali society.

Elections: Local and Central

Electoral History

Elections to a few village councils and municipalities were held during the later part of the Rana regime, but the first democratic election in Nepal was held to

TABLE 27.2   Seats and Votes Obtained by Political Parties in the 1959 Election

Party	Seats won	% of Total Seats	% of Total Votes
Nepali Congress	74	67.9	37.4
Gorkha Parishad	19	17.4	17.3
United Democratic Party	5	4.6	9.9
Nepal Communist Party	4	3.7	7.2
Praja Parishad (Acharya)	2	1.8	2.9
Praja Parishad (Mishra)	1	0.9	3.3
Nepal Tarai Congress	0	0	2.1
Nepali National Congress	0	0	0.7
Prajatantrik Mahasabha	0	0	3.3
Independents	0	0	16.7

Source: John Whelpton, A History of Nepal (Cambridge: Cambridge University Press, 2005), p. 96.

elect the Kathmandu municipality in 1953. The CPN won the most seats (6), followed by Nepali Congress (4), Praja Parishad (4), Gorkha Parishad (1), and independents (4).[14] The first general elections were held in 1959 to elect a parliament. King Tribhuvan's promise to elect a Constituent Assembly when the Rana regime fell was never realized. The Nepali Congress won an overwhelming majority in the first election, even though it received less than 40 percent of the votes. The communist party won only four seats, whereas the conservative Gorakha Parishad won nineteen.

The panchayat system (1960–1990) held partyless elections. The king ruled directly, aided by different levels of governments. The sovereignty rested with the king and he handpicked the prime minister and the cabinet. Political parties could not field candidates and the candidates competed individually against each other. Further, before the referendum in 1980 to decide the fate of panchayat, elections were direct only at the local levels. People voted for village and municipal offices and the elected officers elected district level officers who, in turn, elected the members of the Rastriya Panchayat. Village, district, and zonal panchayats were organized below the Rastriya Panchayat. An important contribution of the panchayat period was the extension of village panchayats or village units across the country and conduction of elections to elect the office bearers. Less than 800 village units were established in 1956, whereas the panchayat period established 3,999 units.[15]

The referendum held in 1980 to choose between panchayat with reform and multiparty democracy mobilized people extensively. The referendum itself was the work of the student movement against the panchayat regime. The panchayat with reform side won the referendum narrowly. The elections held during the 1980s were based on universal adult franchise. However, political parties were still banned and candidates to the Rastriya Panchayat had to fight

TABLE 27.3   Local Election Results (Percentage of Seats)

Parties	1992			1997		
	VDC	Municipalities	DDC	VDC	Municipalities	DDC
Nepali Congress	50.24	50.84	64.80	29.47	28.92	14.32
CPN(UML)	26.05	22.33	17.94	50.10	55.98	68.05
NDP	9.73	10.32	7.63	12.22	8.15	9.94
NGP	2.94	3.38	1.96	1.21	1.59	1.42
NPF	5.09	1.50	3.54	-	-	-
Independents and other parties	5.93	11.63	4.10	4.93	5.36	6.27

VDC = Village Development Committee, DDC = District Development Committee

Source: Adapted from Krishna Hacchethu, "Political Parties and Elections," in *Elections and Governance in Nepal*, ed. Lok Raj Baral (New Delhi: Manohar, 2005), p. 165.

the elections independently. The Nepali Congress boycotted both the 1981 and 1986 parliamentary elections but participated in the local election. Some communist parties participated in the local and parliamentary elections. CPN(ML) fielded candidates in thirty-two districts and elected six members to the parliament. CPN(Manadhar) and NWPP also elected one candidate each in 1986.[16]

Elections During the 1990s

The 1990s witnessed three general elections and two local elections. The results of the general elections are given in Table 27.1. The centrist Nepali Congress and the leftist CPN(UML) emerged as the two major political parties. The Nepali Congress won a majority of seats in 1991 and 1999 but could not maintain stable governments. The CPN(UML) won the largest number of seats in the hung parliament of 1994. Table 27.3 shows the results of the local elections in 1992 and 1997. The Nepali Congress won a majority of seats in 1992 while the CPN(UML) won a majority in 1997. Both the local elections saw massive mobilization of state resources by the parties that controlled the home ministry, the Nepali Congress in 1992 and CPN(UML) in 1997.

The electoral trend shows that the communists grew significantly in the 1990s compared to the 1959 election, when they won only four seats and 7 percent of votes. This was because their organization building during the panchayat period remained underground while the Nepali Congress leaders were mostly in exile. The electoral results also show that the rightist parties have not done well, never receiving 20 percent of votes during the entire electoral history of Nepal. This is partly because they were associated with the previous autocratic regimes. The ethnically named parties have also appeared in the electoral fray but have not fared well. However, their performance was better in the

1990s than in the 1950s. The explosive growth of identity politics since 1990 also suggests that parties with ethnic names may fare better in the future.

Erosion of Electoral Institutions

Nepal witnessed the erosion of the electoral process between 1990 and 2002. Most of the major parties attempted to influence the elections in whatever ways they could. The ruling party usually had more leverage because it enjoyed the coercive power of the state as well as its vast resources. The degree of government influence on elections can be assessed by the election results. The two political parties that controlled the government won the two local elections. The party that controlled the government also won two of the three parliamentary elections. The 1994 election was an exception due to the high level of factional infighting in the ruling party, the Nepali Congress. That the major parties desired to conduct elections when they were in power implicitly acknowledges the advantages of leading the government during elections. This tendency became especially clear during the five-year hung parliament (1994–1999), when governments faced with the threats of no-confidence votes dissolved parliament in order to conduct fresh elections. The ability of the ruling party to influence elections is also a reason for the parties to go to extreme lengths, including unethical means, to retain power or topple the government.

The tendency to vote for the ruling party in exchange for patronage is also a factor that increases the incentive to be in power to conduct elections. It also underlines the importance of capturing the center to distribute goods and benefits before and during elections, and being in government when fulfilling promises appears more plausible. Governments distributed resources, whereas the opposition could not because the parliament did not control budget.

The ruling party could influence elections partly because the horizontal accountability mechanisms were not strong. The Election Commission, even though termed "independent," was not in fact independent, nor powerful enough to restrain the government from abusing power to influence elections. Like other central constitutional commissions, the cabinet influenced the appointment of commissioners to the Election Commission. The candidates were never publicly screened. This meant that the cabinet could often appoint party minions. The appointees also understood the dynamics of their appointments.

As a result of the weak Election Commission, vertical accountability was undermined as the unpredictability of the elections diminished. The ruling parties abused the administration, police, state media, and other resources to influence elections. State-owned Radio Nepal effectively spread the ruling party's views, news, and propaganda because it reached every nook and cranny of the country, unlike other media. The ruling parties also collected a disproportionate

TABLE 27.4   Seats Won in the Constituent Assembly, 2008

Name	FPTP	PR	Total	Name	FPTP	PR	Total
CPN(Maoist)	120	100	220	NPPP	0	3	3
Nepali Congress	37	73	110	NPLP	0	2	2
CPN(UML)	33	70	103	CPN-United	0	2	2
MPRF	30	22	52	NGP-A	0	2	2
TMDP	9	11	20	Nepali Peoples Party	0	2	2
NGP	4	5	9	FDNF	0	2	2
NDP	0	8	8	SDPPN	0	1	1
CPN(ML)	0	8	8	Dalit Nationalist Party	0	1	1
PFN	2	5	7	Nepal Family Party	0	1	1
CPN(Joint)	0	5	5	Nepa: National Party	0	1	1
NDP(N)	0	4	4	NDSP	0	1	1
NPF	1	3	4	CBNUPN	0	1	1
NWPP	2	2	4	Independents	2	0	2

Source: Election Commission, Nepal homepage, www.election.gov.np/reports/CAResults/reportBody.php.

CPN(ML)—Communist Party of Nepal(Marxist Leninist); PFN—People's Front Nepal; CPN(Joint)—Communist Party of Nepal (Joint); NDP(N)—National Democratic Party (Nepal); NPF—National People's Front; NWPP—Nepal Workers Peasant Party; NPPP—Nepal Peoples Power Party; CPN(United)—Communist Party of Nepal(United); NGP(A)—Nepal Goodwill Party(Anandidevi); FDNF—Federal Democratic National Forum; SDPPN—Socialist Democratic Peoples Party Nepal; NDSP—Nepal Democratic Socialist Party; CBNUPN—Chure Bhawar National Unity Party Nepal

amount of funds through government contracts and licenses. They transferred and deployed civil servants and police officials and distributed development projects and funds to improve electoral prospects. The Election Commission, weak and lacking independence, was often not in a position to intervene and stop the abuses.

The Election to the Constituent Assembly

Despite some misgivings the election to the Constituent Assembly was held reasonably successfully on April 10, 2008. Even though it was the most violent election in Nepal's history, compared to other post-civil war societies, it can be deemed to be reasonably well executed under the circumstances. Allegations of intimidation and violence have been brought against the Maoists and MPRF by other parties as well as the election observers and human rights organizations.

The elections produced some major surprises. The Maoists emerged as the largest party at the cost of established parties. Likewise, nationalist parties, especially the Madhesi, have also won a considerable number of seats. The votes clearly show that people voted for movement parties and they were seeking change. The Constituent Assembly will become the most inclusive legislature to date partly because the large parties have to distribute seats won under the proportional electoral method proportionally along ethnic/caste and gender lines. The Maoists also fielded many candidates under the FPTP from the marginalized groups.

Political Leaders

This section will discuss political leaders who have made significant contributions to Nepali politics and changed the direction of the polity, such as leading mass movements, beginning new trends through establishing political parties during the Rana regime, establishing ethnic parties, and so on.

The Conservative Leaders

Prithvi Narayan Shah (1722–1775).　　Prithvi Narayan Shah, who succeeded his father Narbhupal Shah as king of Gorkha, a small principality in the West central hills in 1743, established the Shah dynasty by conquering Nepal. In his bid to conquer the Kathmandu valley, he first defeated small principalities surrounding the valley. He finally conquered the Kathmandu valley kingdoms (1768–1769) after a campaign of two decades. Thereafter he conquered the kingdoms and republics in the east as far as Sikkim and the Tista River.

Prithvi Narayan was an ambitious king and a shrewd tactician. He conquered valley kingdoms that had greater resources than did his small principality of Gorkha. He established a standing army, which did not exist in other Himalayan principalities during the period, and used it to facilitate his conquests. He devised a land-military complex to increase his conquering force. The land-hungry hill peasants who joined the army were given land from the conquered regions.[17] In addition, he employed tactics that went against the standard warfare of the time, such as attacking opponents during festivals.

He lived a frugal life and dictated *Dibya Upadesh,* his treatise on governance, before he died. The treatise protected local products, discouraged dependence on foreign goods, and discussed the challenge Nepal faced in trying to survive between two large countries. However, the treatise also upheld the caste system and facilitated caste-based domination. He also introduced the more intolerant version of Hinduism in the valley that went on to become the state policy in subsequent centuries.

He became known as the father of the nation after 1951, when his descendants regained power. However, that position was challenged after democracy was restored in 1990, and more so after the 2006 second people's movement.

Janga Bahadur Rana Kunwar (1817–1877).　　Janga Bahadur eclipsed the kings by capturing effective political power. He was appointed prime minister in

1846 following the Kot massacre, in which his troops killed most other contenders for power. He exploited the extreme factionalism in the court, which resulted from a weak king, a wayward crown prince, and a junior queen who wanted to install her son on the throne. Janga engineered the replacement of King Rajendra by Crown Prince Surendra but kept real control in his and his family's hands. He assumed the title of maharaj (great king) in 1856. He established a hereditary prime minister based on a transfer of power to his brothers and their children thereafter. The family ruled autocratically over Nepal for a century, tightly controlling power within the family and repressing political awareness and mobilization.

He assumed the name of Rana to upgrade his caste to the ruling family. This allowed him to marry his children into the royal family, further consolidating his power. Janga Bahadur assisted the British in suppressing the Indian Mutiny in 1857–1859. The British, as a reward, returned the western Tarai, which was ceded to the East India Company in 1816 after defeat in the Anglo-Gorkha war. He introduced the new civil code in 1854 that formally stratified the society into a caste system and imposed Hinduism on the indigenous population.

King Mahendra Bir Bikram Shah (1920–1972).   King Mahendra succeeded his father King Tribhuvan in 1955. He was ambitious and wanted a more active role for the monarchy in the governance of the country. He organized the first parliamentary election in 1959 but removed the elected Prime Minister B. P. Koirala and his Nepali Congress government in December 1960. He introduced a panchayat constitution in 1962 that provided for an active monarchy. He introduced indirect elections in the panchayat system—an experiment with guided democracy. The panchayat system was a facade of representative democracy, since the power remained within the royal palace.

He promulgated a new civil code in 1963 that dropped the caste system. He attempted to modernize the kingdom through development programs, such as industrialization, administrative reforms, and infrastructure construction like the building of the East-West Highway. The period also witnessed an active assimilation policy of the diverse ethnic and linguistic groups through the public education system instructed in the Khas-Nepali language. It also saw the promotion of hill Hindu nationalism. Both the constitutions (1959 and 1960) sponsored by King Mahendra declared the state as Hindu.

The Centrist Leaders

Tanka Prasad Acharya (1910–1992).   Tanka Prasad Acharya was the founding president of the Praja Parishad, the first political party in Nepal. Although many other parties were established in India, Praja Parishad was launched in

Nepal. As a Bahun (hill Brahmin) he escaped the death penalty in 1940 for anti-Rana resistance but was imprisoned for life. Thus he is considered a "living martyr." He was freed after the end of the Rana regime in 1951. In the early 1950s he drew close to the communists and flirted with Marxism. He was also a nationalist who criticized Indian interference in Nepali politics and supported a constitutional monarchy to bolster nationalism.[18] He served as prime minister in 1956–1957, but his party won only two seats in the 1959 general election. He formally revived the party after 1990 but did not contest the 1991 elections.

Bishweshwar Prasad (B. P.) Koirala (1915–1982).   B. P. became the first elected prime minister of Nepal in 1959. He played a leading role in setting up the Nepali Congress in India to revolt against the Rana regime in the 1940s. After the 1950–1951 armed resistance, he became the home minister in the 1951 Rana-Congress coalition that was formed after India brokered a settlement in New Delhi between the Ranas, the king, and the Nepali Congress. He frequently bickered with his elder stepbrother Matrika Prasad Koirala, who was made prime minister twice by King Tribhuvan.

B. P. was the party's chief ideologue and a charismatic leader. B. P. briefly flirted with communist ideology in his youth but later became a socialist and persuaded the Nepali Congress to adopt the socialist ideology. He participated in the Indian independence movement and was close to Indian socialist leaders. He is an established vernacular novelist as well.

B. P.'s government was dismissed and he was imprisoned by King Mahendra from 1960 until 1968. He went into exile in India thereafter and organized an armed resistance but later on returned to Nepal under the slogan of national reconciliation and opposed the Panchayat system peacefully.

Girija Prasad (G. P.) Koirala (1925–).   G. P. Koirala led the movement against King Gyanendra's takeover in 2002. A rabid communist hater initially, he went on to negotiate an understanding with the Maoists in 2005 to oust King Gyanendra. Since King Gyanendra gave up power in 2006, he has led the coalition government formed by the parties that launched the movement, including the Maoists. Younger brother of B. P. Koirala and M. P. Koirala (former prime ministers), he was the junior troika member that led the Nepali Congress after B. P.'s death. He went on to become the sole leader of the Nepali Congress, relegating Krishna Prasad Bhattarai and Ganesh Man Singh to the sideline. He led several governments of the Nepali Congress as well as coalition governments during the 1990s. His clash with Sher Bahadur Deuba led to the split of the Nepali Congress in 2002. G. P. has been a controversial leader, admired for taking a firm stand against King Gyanendra's intervention in 2002 but criticized for nepotism and condoning alleged corruption under his rule.

The Communist Leaders

Pushpa Lal Shrestha (1924–1978).   Pushpa Lal Shrestha was the founding father of the communist movement in Nepal. Brother of Ganga Lal Shrestha, one of the Praja Parishad martyrs executed in 1940 by the Ranas, he was the first general secretary of the Communist Party of Nepal (1947–1949). He remained on the radical wing of the party as it witnessed many splits. He called for restoring the parliament when King Mahendra dismissed it. In 1968 he split from the Tulsi Lal group and formed his own communist party. He advocated for a joint movement with the Nepali Congress against the monarchy, but his colleagues and the Nepali Congress did not heed his policy during his lifetime. When the Nepali Congress and a communist front finally emerged and launched a joint movement, the king was forced to bow down in 1990.

Madan Bhandari (1952–1993).   Madan Bhandari helped found the Communist Party of Nepal (Marxist-Lenninist) in 1978, which emerged as the largest communist party after 1990. He became the general secretary from 1989 until his death in 1993 in a controversial accident when the jeep he was travelling in plunged into a river. CPN(ML) and CPN(M) merged in 1991 to become CPN(United Marxist-Leninist). Bhandari led the party and transformed it into a parliamentary party by revising its ideological line into "multiparty people's democracy," formally adopted at the party convention in 1993. The new party line went on to accept multiparty parliamentary democracy, constitutional monarchy, and a market economy.

Prachanda aka Pushpa Kamal Dahal (1956–).   Prachanda was the general secretary of the CPN(Maoist) party that launched a violent insurgency in 1996. A small extremist party, it spread its influence throughout the country within a decade. Prachanda has kept the party united even in a communist culture in Nepal that tends to split over small disputes.

Prachanda became an underground communist activist in 1971. He worked with Mohan Bikram Singh, a doyen in the communist movement in the CPN(Fourth Convention) and CPN(Mashal) (different manifestation after splits). He broke away from Mohan Bikram in 1985 to set up CPN(Masal) (different from Mashal). His new party merged with the Fourth Convention in 1990 to form the Unity Center, which was part of the United People's Front, a second communist front during the 1990s people's movement. He established the CPN(Maoist) in 1995 and has been in firm control of it ever since.

He became party chairman in 2001, and the party adopted "Prachanda path" as its official ideology in the same year. The Maoists reached an understanding with the seven parliamentary parties to fight against King Gyanendra and subsequently signed a comprehensive peace agreement with the government that was formed after the success of the movement in 2006. Although the Maoists joined the interim parliament and government, Prachanda did not join the parliament and government.

Ethnic and Women Leaders

Gajendra Narayan Singh (1930–2002).   Gajendra Narayan Singh was a democrat and a champion of the Madhesi cause. He began his politics in the Nepali Congress but formed a Madhesi front and political party after the Nepali Congress failed to address the problems faced by the Madhesi, despite receiving significant votes from the Tarai.[19]

He participated in the 1950–1951 resistance against the Ranas and was imprisoned by King Mahendra in 1960–1961. He was again imprisoned in 1985 briefly for setting up the Nepal Sadhvawana Parishad (Nepal Goodwill Council) to fight against discrimination faced by Madhesi, including discrimination in citizenship. He was first elected to the parliament (Rastriya Panchayat) in 1986. He launched the Nepal Goodwill Party (NGP) in 1990 advocating regional autonomy and inclusion of Madhesi in the government. He headed the NGP until his death and served in various coalition governments from 1995 onward.

Shaileja Acharya (1944–).   Shaileja Acharya, niece of three prime ministers, rose to become the deputy prime minister, the first woman to reach that position. She was initiated into politics when very young. She was one of the few people who protested when King Mahendra dismissed B. P. Koirala's elected government in 1960. She spent many years in prison and in exile in India. She became minister after 1990 and deputy prime minister in 1998. She was considered a noncorrupt leader but close to India and Indian leaders. During her tenure as agriculture and water resource minister, she favored small-scale projects following her socialist background. Her role in the party hierarchy diminished in the later years because she did not openly come out against the royal rule after King Gyanendra took power.

Gore Bahadur Khapangi (1945–).   Gore Bahadur Khapangi is a communist turned ethnic activist. Born in Udayapur in eastern Nepal, he set up an indigenous nationalities party after being disenchanted with the CPN(Marxist Leninist) politics that was dominated by Bahuns who ignored the aspirations of indigenous nationalities despite the party's progressive rhetoric. He is a good orator who toured many regions of the country to spread ethnic awareness. In 1990 he launched the Rastriya Janamukti Party (National People's Liberation Front) to champion the cause of the indigenous nationalities. He was unsuccessful in electoral politics, but in 2002 he joined the royal government under Lokendra Bahadur Chand. He currently heads the Democratic People's Liberation Party, after a split from NPLP.

NOTES

1. Richard Gunther and Larry Diamond, "Types and Functions of Parties," *Political Parties and Democracy*, ed. Larry Diamond and Richard Gunther (Baltimore: John Hopkins University Press, 2001).

2. James F. Fisher, *Living Martyrs: Individuals and Revolutions in Nepal* (Delhi: Oxford University Press, 1998); Krishna Hachhethu, *Party Building in Nepal: Organization, Leadership, and People* (Kathmandu: Mandala Book Point, 2002).

3. Rishikesh Shah, *Modern Nepal: A Political History, 1769–1995* (Delhi: Manohar, 1996).

4. Dr. K. I. Singh had been imprisoned for opposing the 1951 settlement between the king, Nepali Congress, and the Ranas brokered by India. He rebelled in January 21, 1952, from prison with the assistance of his supporters in the Rakshya Dal, the paramilitary police force formed from the military wing of the Nepali Congress during the rebellion against the Ranas. Bhuwan Lal Joshi and Leo E. Rose, *Democratic Innovations in Nepal: A Case Study of Political Acculturation* (Berkeley: University of California Press, 1966), 100–101.

5. Bhim Rawal, *Nepalma Samyabadi Andolanko: Adbhav Ra Bikash* [Communist Movement in Nepal: Rise and Development] (Kathmandu: Pairavi Prakashan, 1991), p. 36.

6. Narayan Khadka, "Factionalism in the Communist Movement in Nepal," *Pacific Affairs* 68, no. 1 (1995); Rawal, *Nepalma Samyabadi Andolanko*.

7. Rawal, *Nepalma Samyabadi Andolanko*.

8. The mainstream political parties are dominated by CHHE and primarily promote the interests of that group; hence they can also be termed ethnic parties on that basis (Lawoti 2005).

9. Susan Hangen, "Between Political Party and Social Movement: The Mongol National Organization and Democratization in Rural Nepal," *Contentious Politics and Democratization in Nepal*, ed. Mahendra Lawoti (New Delhi: Sage, 2007).

10. Govinda Neupane, *Nepalko Jatiya Prashna: Samajik Banot Ra Sajhedariko Sambhawana* [Nepal's National Question: Social Composition and Possibilities of Accommodation] (Kathmandu: Center for Development Studies, 2000), 71.

11. Rawal, *Nepalma Samyabadi Andolanko*; Khadka, "Factionalism in the Communist Movement in Nepal"; K. C. Surendra, *Nepalma Communist Andolanko Itihas* [The History of Communist Movement in Nepal] (Kathmandu: Vidhyarthi Pustak Bhandar, 1999).

12. Krishna B. Bhattachan, "Manab Adhikar Ra Nepalko Pratibadhatta," Seminar organized by Nepal Foundation for Advanced Studies (NEFAS) and Friedrich-Ebert Stiftung, Nepal (Kathmandu: 1999).

13. Saubhagya Shah, "From Evil State to Civil Society," *State of Nepal*, ed. Kanak Mani Dixit and Shastri Ramachandaran (Lalitpur: Himal, 2002).

14. Rawal, *Nepalma Samyabadi Andolanko*, 37.

15. Rabindra Khanal, *Local Governance in Nepal: Democracy at Grassroots* (Kathmandu: Smriti, 2006).

16. Rawal, *Nepalma Samyabadi Andolanko*, 131.

17. L. F. Stiller, *The Rise of the House of Gorkha* (Ranchi: Patna Jesuit Society, 1973).

18. Fisher, *Living Martyrs*.

19. Vedananda Jha established the Nepal Tarai Party to raise the issues of the Madhesi in the early 1950s, but later he joined the panchayat system and the party was not revived.

SUGGESTED READINGS

Fisher, James F. *Living Martyrs: Individuals and Revolutions in Nepal.* Delhi: Oxford University Press, 1998.

Hachhethu, Krishna. *Party Building in Nepal: Organization, Leadership, and People.* Kathmandu: Mandala Book Point, 2002.

Hangen, Susan. "Between Political Party and Social Movement: The Mongol National Organization and Democratization in Rural Nepal." In *Contentious Politics and Democratization in Nepal,* ed. Mahendra Lawoti. New Delhi: Sage, 2007.

Joshi, Bhuwan Lal, and Leo E. Rose. *Democratic Innovations in Nepal: A Case Study of Political Acculturation.* Berkeley: University of California Press, 1966.

Khanal, Rabindra. *Local Governance in Nepal: Democracy at Grassroots.* Kathmandu: Smriti, 2006.

Neupane, Govinda. *Nepalko Jatiya Prashna: Samajik Banot Ra Sajhedariko Sambhawana* [Nepal's National Question: Social Composition and Possibilities of Accommodation]. Kathmandu: Center for Development Studies, 2000.

Rawal, Bhim. *Nepalma Samyabadi Andolanko: Adbhav Ra Bikash* [Communist Movement in Nepal: Rise and Development]. Kathmandu: Pairavi Prakashan, 1991.

Shah, Rishikesh. *Modern Nepal: A Political History, 1769–1995.* Delhi: Manohar, 1996.

Stiller, L. F. *The Rise of the House of Gorkha.* Ranchi: Patna Jesuit Society, 1973.

Surendra, K. C. *Nepalma Communist Andolanko Itihas* [The History of Communist Movement in Nepal]. Kathmandu: Vidhyarthi Pustak Bhandar, 1999.

Whelpton, John. *A History of Nepal.* Cambridge: Cambridge University Press, 2005.

28

Class and Identity Conflicts

Nepal seems to be on the way to settling the Maoist insurgency that has raged for a decade, even as ethnic conflicts are turning more violent. The Maoist insurgency began in 1996 and the settlement process, though not always smooth, began after November 2006 with the signing of the comprehensive peace agreement between the government and the Maoist rebels.[1] Ethnic conflicts existed prior to the Maoist insurgency but were largely nonviolent. Violent ethnic conflicts have become more frequent since the Maoists joined mainstream politics. This chapter will discuss the nature and dynamics of the two conflicts.

The Maoist Insurgency

The Maoist insurgency, launched by a small extreme communist party, expanded rapidly. During the insurgency, more than 13,000 people were killed, thousands were injured and displaced, and millions were affected psychologically, economically, and politically. The death toll increased dramatically after the second round of talks failed in November 2001, as Figure 28.1 shows. The Maoists attacked an army barracks after the talks ended and the army was finally mobilized against the insurgency. Human rights groups accused both the Maoists and the security forces of gross human rights violations.

The insurgency grew to such an extent that almost all of the seventy-five districts of the country were affected within a decade.[2] The Maoists initially attracted popular support by initiating popular activities like punishing moneylenders and local well-off people they labeled as exploiters. Many social activists and political opponents also fell victim to their wrath. They increased their domination in many parts of the country by terrorizing people who opposed

421

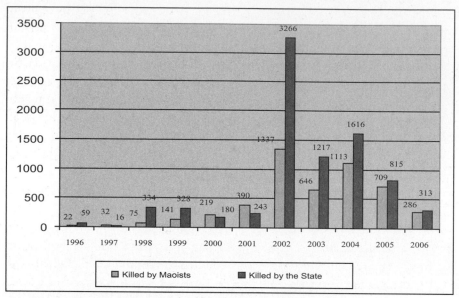

FIGURE 28.1   People Killed During the Maoist Insurgency

Source: "No. of Victims Killed by State and Maoist in Connection with the 'Peoples War.'" Kathmandu: INSEC, November 25, 2007.

them into submission with threats of dire consequences. The strategy worked because of the state's failure to provide security to the people.

The Maoists demanded a republic, an all-party government, and an election to the Constituent Assembly to design a new constitution. Other prominent issues addressed class inequality, marginalized ethnic/caste groups, women's rights, and concerns about Nepal's sovereignty. The Maoists, however, have strategically highlighted different demands at different times depending on context. Since the Maoists launched the insurgency when the parliamentary democracy was running, the overall objective of the Maoists was to form a Maoist communist state—a people's democracy. With the signing of a comprehensive peace accord, they have at least formally given up on that objective.

Economic Inequality and the Maoist Insurgency

The literature on insurgency and civil strife has identified income inequality as a major cause of violent conflict.[3] Relative deprivation or the gap between expected and achieved well-being can increase alienation and push groups toward violent conflict. The inequality thesis has been discussed widely with regard to the Nepali Maoist insurgency. Bray, Lunde, and Murshed point out the relatively low level in human development indicators (HDI) in the Maoist strongholds.[4] They also found that inequality was significant across districts in Nepal.

Nepal is not only poor but has become a more unequal society in terms of material well-being.[5] In the 1990s, Nepal was the most unequal country in South Asia. It had the highest Gini Index of 0.426. Inequality, as measured by the Gini Index, was lower in the 1980s in Nepal (0.300) than India (0.312), Sri Lanka (0.341), and Pakistan (0.326).[6] Inequality is rising despite the improvement in overall human development indicators (HDI) in the 1990s. Growth in a few select areas and stagnation in others led to this ironic situation of rise in inequality despite a moderate rise in HDI. Inequality in Nepal exists among different sectors: ethnic and caste groups, geographic regions (mountain and hills and Tarai and East to West), gender, and rural and urban areas.

The stagnation of the rural regions during the 1970s was portrayed vividly in the book *Nepal in Crisis,* which shows the neglect of the rural regions, the increasing pressure on limited land in the hills, and the erosion of traditional jobs and sources of income.[7] Different economic and demographic indicators demonstrate the continuous neglect of the rural regions. This neglect contributed to the rise of inequality in the 1990s in various spheres. Poverty levels were 33 percent in 1976–1977 but rose to 42 percent by 1995–1996. The "income share of the top 10 percent of the people increased from 21 percent in the mid-1980s to 35 percent by the mid-1990s, while the share of the bottom 40 percent shrank from 24 percent to 15 percent by the mid-1990s."[8]

Some regions in Nepal face greater inequality. Poverty levels are significantly higher in rural areas (44 percent) than in urban areas (20 percent). Poverty is also more widespread in the mountains, where the incidence of poverty is 56 percent, compared with around 40 percent in the hills and plains. The incidence of poverty in the rural central (67 percent) and mid and far western (72 percent) hills and mountains far outweighs that in eastern (28 percent) and western (40 percent) regions.[9]

Poverty and economic stagnation had a more detrimental impact on rural residents (87 percent in 2001) because they depend on agriculture, which has stagnated. Annual growth rates of agricultural output (major crops) declined from 1961–1962 to 1991–1993. The growth rate was negative 0.07 percent for all crops in Nepal during the period while other South Asian countries witnessed an increase. The stagnation in agriculture was due to the government policy of import substitution industrialization, following which it attempted to industrialize urban areas at the cost of peasants and rural areas. This neglect occurred despite the importance of agriculture as a major source of employment and national income. Sharma (2006) writes that agriculture, in which more than 80 percent of the people are engaged, "has not received more than 26 percent of development expenditure in any development plan since the mid-1950s . . . Nepal, which had the highest agriculture yield (per

hectare) in South Asia in the early 1960s fell significantly behind other countries by early 1990s."[10]

Landownership patterns also contribute to inequality. Despite the relatively
low levels of landownership, the inequality reflects the persistence of the feudal
system: "44 percent of households in the country are marginal landowners
[0–0.5 hectare], but this group only accounts for 14 percent of total privately
owned agricultural land. In contrast, the 5 percent of agricultural households
who own plots greater than 3 h[ectares] account for around 27 percent of total
agricultural land."[11] MacFarlane's ethnographic study also supports the pictures
painted by the broad aggregate data. In a hill village in central Nepal, where he
has frequently returned, a wage earner could buy a chicken with a day's wages
in the late 1960s, whereas in the mid-1990s it took eight days' wages.[12]

The deregulation of the market since the mid-1980s led to an improvement
in some economic indicators such as GDP, growth in output, and exports and
international reserve. These were mainly brought about by an expansion of the
urban-based modern sector and did not close the inequality gap. For instance,
the nominal income of the people living in urban areas increased by 16 percent
per annum (from US$126 to US$285) between 1988 and 1996, compared to
only 4 percent for the rural population (from US$95 to US$125). Sharma argues that "when the average annual rate of inflation is taken into consideration,
the growth in rural income is in fact negative. This not only increased poverty
in the rural areas but also increased rural-urban inequality."[13] Large parts of the
rural areas stagnated while the urban centers, especially the Kathmandu valley,
developed into centers of wealth. The growth in urban areas and stagnation in
the rural areas may have further increased the perception of inequality among
rural residents.[14]

The neglect of the rural regions and the poor by a centralized state is nothing
new for a student of Nepali history. The Nepali state-building process involves
extracting great amounts from the peasantry by the state and ruling groups.[15]
The state gave land as jagir (compensation) and birta (tax-free land grants) to
various central government and military functionaries as rewards and compensation for their services. The peasantry had to turn in a large proportion of their
products to these often distant landholders. The elite extracted as much as they
could from the peasantry, often to build stucco palaces. During wars the peasantry had to cough up extra taxes and provide free labor services for carrying
weapons and war supplies.

State neglect of the peasants continued after 1990. The 1990 changes, despite
formally ushering in the fundamental rights of expression and organization, primarily ended up expanding the ruling group.[16] The state is still controlled by an
elite caste that has largely failed to represent the peasantry, the poor, and mar-

ginalized ethnic and caste groups. The needs and aspirations of the rural poor have rarely been represented in the corridors of power and decision-making processes. Consequently deep economic inequality continues, as the elite monopolize economic resources through political domination.

The continued marginalization of the peasantry in the 1990s is ironic because one of the major political parties was a communist party (the Communist Party of Nepal-United Marxist Leninist: CPN-UML) that claims to speak for the poor. However, which segments of the poor the CPN(UML) and other parliamentary communist parties represent is another question. In terms of other large mainstream parties, they represent the less well-off, but their core constituency is not the poorest of the poor. The trade unions, college students, and primary and high school teachers who form their core constituency are relatively well-off in an impoverished country like Nepal. Only the village elite can send their children to college. The claim to represent the downtrodden is not sufficient; they have failed to take action. The attraction rural people feel to the Maoist insurgency, which promised radical transformation, shows that the parliamentary communist parties failed to win the hearts of the poor. The inequalities in different sectors and regions and neglect of the periphery contributed to the dissatisfaction among the rural people, especially the youth, and created a fertile ground for the rise of the Maoist insurgency.

The Democratic Political Process and the Rise of the Maoist Insurgency

The predecessor of the Maoists participated in the first general elections in 1991 and won nine seats. However, they boycotted the second parliamentary election in 1994 and eventually launched the insurgency.[17] Events and activities between 1991 and 1996 helped push the Maoists to violent insurgency.

The Maoists began putting demands on different governments beginning in the early 1990s. The forty-point demands they submitted to the Sher Bahadur Deuba government before they launched the insurgency was their final list; they had expanded the list each time they submitted to a new government. The different governments from 1991 to 1996 were not responsive to the demands. Further, the persecution of the Maoist cadres in their western hill strongholds forced their cadres to go underground. Subsequently the Maoists launched the insurgency.[18]

Majoritarian democratic processes contributed to the alienation of the Maoists. In Nepal, democracy was defined in narrowly majoritarian terms during the 1990s. The notion that the majority has the right to rule in whatever way it pleases, often abusing the state machinery and resources for partisan purposes, was prevalent. Such a conceptualization encouraged the executive to undermine other branches of state agencies and other political actors. O'Donnell terms the problem as "delegative democracy." One of the consequences was that politicians in the nonruling political party and citizens felt impotent because they were unable to affect policies. Perpetual street demonstrations by the opposition intended to force the government to respond showed that the formal political process was not working effectively.

Significant numbers of people participated in the insurgency, showing their perception that the political process would not meet their aspirations. This perception could have been fueled by the abuse of power by the ruling political leaders and cadres. The growth of corruption at local and central levels and the negative attitudes of the government and the constitution toward minorities also may have alienated people. The absence of public policies to address the problems of the poor, weak, and disadvantaged also may have contributed to the alienation.

State Incapability

The coercive capability of the state can make a difference in repressing civil strife, even though it may just postpone the conflict if the underlying causes are not addressed.[19] In Nepal, one could argue that the Maoists grew rapidly due to the incapability of the state. When Maoists began attacking rural police posts and government offices, the state agencies were withdrawn to district centers and other safer areas. These withdrawals allowed the Maoists to consolidate their hold in the rural regions with less effort. Likewise, local governments collapsed when the Maoists threatened them. They had little power, despite the rhetoric of decentralization. Even the people who opposed their ideology did not resist the Maoists because the state could not guarantee their security. Further, as the state had not done much for the people, a large segment of the population did not care, at least initially, if the state or the Maoists dominated the rural areas.

The incapability of the state can be demonstrated by analyzing the Maoist forces and their weaponry. According to security expert Ashok Mehta, the Maoists had few weapons, most of them looted from the police and the army.[20] Including homemade guns, shotguns, and .22-caliber rifles, the Maoists had fewer than 3,000 weapons at the turn of the century. Photos of Maoist army training show that not all combatants held arms. The arms submitted by the Maoists in the cantonment approximate this number. Not every Maoist guerrilla (estimated by Mehta at 4,000 as of 2004) had a weapon.[21] This raises the question of why the army of 90,000, along with additional police and armed forces, was not able to undermine the Maoist insurgency—the state was internally weak and could not effectively mobilize its resources. Mehta argues that the ceremonial nature of the Royal Nepal Army (RNA), its lack of preparation for internal insurgencies, absence of war experience, and absence of motivation were some of the reasons for the failure of the RNA to contain the Maoist insurgency.[22]

The state was incapacitated for other reasons as well. The centralization of power in Kathmandu and within the executive at the center rendered different sectors of the state ineffective because they had no power to formulate and execute public policies. The centralized state did not penetrate the countryside partly because it did not care much about the periphery except to extract resources from it. On the other hand, concentration of power in the executive meant that its scope was wide, making it impossible to focus on any priority issue. As a result the state was not effective in many realms.[23]

Violent Ideology, Agency, and Strategies of the Maoists

The Maoist call to arms attracted a large number of people into their fold. Why was the violent ideology so attractive to a large number of Nepali people? The Communist Party of Nepal(United Marxist Leninist) (CPN-UML), the main opposition party in 1991 and 1999 and the largest party in 1994, also grew significantly after it launched a violent uprising in the 1970s, eclipsing the mainstream factions. Likewise, the Nepali Congress, which led the violent anti-Rana movement in 1950–1951, also emerged as the largest party. The attraction to violent parties is probably due to the promise of total transformation in an extremely poor and unequal society.

Maoist leaders played a significant role in the growth of the insurgency as well. Not only did they risk their lives but also they avoided party breakup for more than a decade, unlike most communist parties in Nepal and the Maoists in India. Some commentators reason that Prachanda, the top leader, is skilled in balancing different leaders and incorporating issues raised by others into the official party line.

The Nepali Maoists have formulated policies that brilliantly exploit the societal conditions and divisions among other political actors. At the societal level, in addition to class issues they have raised identity and cultural issues to attract the indigenous nationalities, Dalit, and women. At the political level, the Maoist strategies have effectively played on the fault lines and divisions among their enemies. Initially, the Maoists selectively attacked the cadres of the ruling Nepali Congress. The moderate communist factions and rightist groups did not care much about attacks on political opponents who were abusing political power. When the moderate left formed the government, the Maoists began attacking their cadres. This turn of events pleased the Nepali Congress and the royalists. When the Maoists targeted the rightist cadres, the NC and CPN(UML) seemed to be least bothered.

The competition and conflict of interests within mainstream political forces kept the army from being mobilized until November 2001, after the Maoists looted substantial arms and ammunition in an attack on army barracks. Mehta argues that the Maoists have been successful at psychological war because they did not have competitive military strength.[24] In the initial years of the insurgency, when the Maoists were much weaker, they avoided direct confrontation with the army.

The Maoists began to highlight their republican demands after King Gyanendra began intervening in politics. The mainstream political parties were allowed to operate more freely in rural areas by the Maoists after that. The political parties then moved closer to the Maoists. The Maoists have to be applauded for their well thought out plans and effective strategies. Their policies, however, have been successful because other actors have played to their tunes. The lust for power among the political forces (the king and different political parties) produced divisions among the political forces, including attempts to use the Maoist card to capture and retain power.

The Ethnic and Gender Dimensions of the Insurgency

The Maoist insurgency has seen considerable participation by indigenous nationalities, the Dalit, and women (as well as the Madhesi in later years). Their participation was much wider than in the mainstream political parties and the state.[25] In fact, the Maoist insurgency was launched from the land of Kham Magars, an indigenous group. The region was a Maoist stronghold, where leaders and the retreating people's army took shelter after attacks. The significant participation of the indigenous and other ethnic/caste groups in a class-based insurgency was ironic. The participation of women, including in violent activities, is also interesting because women had not received such widespread public exposure and political role in Nepal prior to the insurgency.

The Maoists incorporated the demands of marginalized groups, for example, for a secular state, self-determination rights, and an end to the imposition of Sanskrit in schools, which attracted those groups to the Maoists. The Maoists also formed ethnic/national fronts to mobilize the marginalized groups.

The mainstream political parties, ethnic political parties, and mainstream identity movements failed to stop the flow of marginalized groups to the Maoists. The mainstream political parties did little to raise, address, and accommodate the marginalized groups' demands. The ethnic parties, on the other hand, despite raising the issues vociferously, were ineffective due to the inexperience of their organizations. The failure of ethnic parties and identity movements to get concessions from the state and dominant society alienated many marginalized groups from the political process.

The National/Ethnic and Caste Conflict

Nepal was portrayed as a peaceful country prior to the Maoist insurgency. However, major violent ethnic resistance occurred in the last quarter of the eighteenth century, when the House of Gorkha was consolidating its domain. The Limbu, Khambu, and Tamang also engaged in resistance. Violent ethnic resistance occurred sporadically. Historical accounts record more than two dozen ethnic rebellions and violent conflicts before 1990.[26] Many more non-violent conflicts and mobilization occurred during the period. Some of these occurred as resistance to appropriation of the land and resources of the indigenous people.

Violent ethnic and religious conflicts increased after democracy was restored in 1990, but they were eclipsed by the Maoist insurgency, partly because they did not directly threaten the state and society (see Table 28.1). The identity movements gained momentum and became more visible after 1990. National/ethnic and caste and regional groups are fighting for equal recognition of their language, religion, and culture, as well as for equal opportunities in the polity, economy, and society. The movements in the early 1990s were mostly peaceful in nature, but violent discourse and practice has been increasing, partly due to the frustration that has resulted from the nonresponsive state and partly after the violent strategies of the Maoists succeeded. Activists began to discuss taking up arms against the state if their demands went unmet. The beginning of change in discourse is significant because Apter and colleagues argue that the discourse of violence legitimizes violence when it occurs.[27]

Table 28.1 lists violent conflicts in Nepal after 1990. There have been several Hindu-Muslim conflicts, riots targeted against the Muslim community, and riots against and involving the Madhesi. Nepalgunj witnessed five violent conflicts between Hindus and Muslims from 1992 to 1997, but it seems to have petered out since 1997. The KNF, which subsequently joined the Maoists, launched an ethnic insurgency demanding autonomy for the group in 1999. The Mongol National Organization (MNO) has threatened violent rebellion and has announced the formation of an army.[28] The Dalit, on the other hand, have faced numerous violent backlashes in their struggle toward equality.

As noted above, the table shows that more groups have been involved in violent ethnic protests and conflicts after 2006. This is partly due to the transition period when different discontented groups may mobilize to have their grievances fulfilled.[29] Among the mobilized groups, except for some Madhesi groups, the identity movements have not demanded secession, interpreting self-determination rights as a demand for autonomy. If the movements are not addressed well, they could turn more violent and become protracted conflicts.

TABLE 28.1   Non-Maoist Violent Conflict (Riots and Insurgencies) in Nepal Since 1990

Year	Events/Actors	Location
October 1992	Hindu-Muslim riots during Deepawali	Nepalganj
November 3–4, 1994	Hindu-Muslim riots during parliamentary election	Nepalganj
December 3–9, 1994	Hindu-Muslim riots during well renovation at a temple	Nepalganj
October 25–28, 1995	Hindu-Muslim riots during Deepawali	Nepalganj
May 1997	Hindu-Muslim riots during local elections	Nepalganj
December 26–27, 2000	Hritik Roshan riots: Hill people versus Madhesi	Kathmandu and Tarai
Since 1999, increased in 2001–02	Khambuwan insurgency	Khotang, Bhojpur, Solukhumbu, Okhaldhunga
September 1, 2004	Riots against Muslims (reaction against killings of Nepali workers in Iraq)	Kathmandu
Ongoing since January 2005	Madhesi insurgency	Mid and East Tarai
December 2006	Hill people versus Madhesi riots	Nepalganj
2007	Madhesi People's Rights Forum–led movement	Middle and East Tarai
2007	Autonomy movements of Limbu, Khambu, Tamang, and Tharu	East and Middle Nepal and Southwestern Tarai
2007	Chure-Bhawar movement	Middle and East Tarai, around and north of the East-West Highway

Source: Mahendra Lawoti, Looking Back, Looking Forward: Centralization, Multiple Conflicts, and Democratic State Building in Nepal (Washington, D.C.: East-West Center, 2007).

Ethnic Domination

Ethnic conflicts have resulted due to the hegemonic CHHE domination.[30] Political, economic, social, and cultural power is monopolized by the CHHEM (caste hill Hindu elite males) in Nepal. Neupane found that the CHHEM overwhelmingly dominated twelve influential sectors he investigated in 1999: the executive, judiciary, constitutional councils, civil administration, parliament, political party leadership, local government heads, and leadership of industrial and commercial, academic, professional, cultural, science and technology, and civil society associations (see Table 28.2 for details).[31]

Except for a Newar, only Bahun and Chhetri have become prime ministers in the history of Nepal. The dominance is so great that even ideological opponents

Table 28.2. Ethnic/Caste Representation in Governance, 1999

Institutions	CHHE		Dalit		Madhesi		Newar		Indigenous Nationalities		Other		Total
	No.	%	No.	%	No.	%	No.	%	No.	%	No.	%	
Judiciary: Supreme, appellate, district	181	77	0	0	18	7.7	32	13.6	4	1.7			235
Constitutional bodies and commissions	14	56	0	0	3	12	6	24	2	8			25
Cabinet	20	62.5	0	0	5	15.6	3	9.4	4	12.5			32
Parliament: Lower and upper houses	159	60	4	1.5	46	17.4	20	7.6	36	13.6			265
Public administration, police, army elite	190	77.6	0	0	9	3.7	43	17.6	3	1.2			245
Central members of national political parties	97	58.8	0	0	26	17.8	18	10.9	25	15.2			166
District Development Committee chair/vice, mayor/deputy mayors	106	55.5	0	0	31	16.2	30	15.7	23	12			190
Industry/commerce association leadership	7	16.7	0	0	15	35.7	20	47.6	0	0			42
Education: Administrative and academic elite, and teachers association leadership	75	77.3	1	1	7	7.2	11	11.3	2	2.1	1	1	97
Culture: Institutions and associations leadership	85	69.1	0	0	0	0	22	17.9	6	4.9			113
Science/tech: Institution and association leadership	36	58.0	0	0	6	9.7	18	29	2	3.2			62
Civil society association leadership	41	75.9	0	0	4	7.4	8	14.8	1	1.9			54
Total	1011		5		170		231	15.1	108	7.1	1	0	1526
Percentage (a)	66.25		0.3		11.1		15.1		7.1		0		100
Population %, 1991 (b)	31.6		8.7		30.9		5.6		22.2		1.0		100
Difference % (a,b)	+34.65		-8.4		-19.8		+9.5		-15.1		-1.0		
Domination ratio (a/b)	2.1		0.03		0.36		2.69		0.32		0		

Source: Govinda Neupane, *Nepalko Jatiya Prashma: Samajik Banot Ra Sajhedariko Sambhawara* [Nepal's National Question: Social Composition and Possibilities of Accommodation] (Kathmandu: Center for Development Studies, 2000), 82.

hail from the same group. The presence of groups like the indigenous nationalities in some of the institutions even decreased during the 1990-2002 democratic era compared to the panchayat and the first parliamentary democratic
(1959–1960) periods.[32] The gap between the dominant and other groups has
further widened in the bureaucracy. In 2001–2002, the dominant group, which
consists of around 30 percent of the population, made up nearly 90 percent of
the civil service exam graduates. Not a single Dalit was inducted into the cabinet between 1990 and 2002.

CHHE has dominated mainstream civil society as well. The CHHE and
Newar dominated around 90 percent of the top positions in prominent Nepali
NGOs and human rights groups in 1999.[33] Onta and Parajuli found that
CHHE made up 80 percent of media elite (editors, publishers, and colum-
nists). It shows that most power, both at the state and civil society, is effectively
enjoyed by CHHE.[34]

Some of the larger ethnic groups are less marginalized or even dominant in
areas of their origin, but once they come into contact with the center or its representatives at district levels they face domination. Studies have shown that
local CHHE use their caste networks with CHHE at district and national levels to enhance their economic, political, and social positions and defend their
interests.[35] Cultural imperialism, or imposition of the dominant group's language, religion, and values on the rest of the society, is a consequence as well as
cause of ethnic domination. The CHHE perform better in schools taught in
their native language and their social standing is enhanced because their culture
and values have been projected as superior by the state.[36] Likewise, the poor
CHHE get opportunities for social mobility from central policies. For instance,
a poor, hard-working Bahun boy can get free residential education in Sanskrit
up to the Ph.D. level fully supported by the state, while similar opportunities
are not provided to women or members of other ethnic groups.

In addition to political, social, and economic domination, marginalized
groups also face discrimination in the cultural sphere, formally as well as infor-
mally. Even well-off groups like Newar and Thakalis face cultural discrimination. The Hindu state discriminates against other indigenous and
nonindigenous religions. Khas-Nepali has been given special privileges, whereas
other native languages have not been. Citizenship discrimination occurred
based on racial markers. More than 3 million adult Nepalis, mostly Madhesi
but also Dalit and indigenous nationalities, were denied citizenship prior to
2007, according to the government Citizenship Commission.[37] Obtaining citizenship also is based on language. Only foreigners who learn Khas-Nepali are
permitted to acquire Nepali citizenship; similar privileges are not awarded to
those who learn other native languages.

Discrimination against the various groups is capped by the constitutional ban on forming ethnically named political parties. The disadvantaged marginalized groups form political parties based on their identity because they have been discriminated based on it. If Nepal's 1990 democratic constitution were followed, the Christian Democratic Union and Christian Social Union in Germany and various political parties in India (Telegu Desam, Muslim League, etc.), for example, would be banned.

Group-Related Conflicts

The cleavages in Nepal are based on religion, language, ethnicity/caste, race/physical differences, negative historical memories, norms against inter-group marriages, region, class, and gender. The many cleavages and conflicts in the country add complexity to identifying domination and exclusion. However, a deeper analysis of the conflicts show the CHHE or the Bahun-Chhetri as the dominant group in almost all the influential spheres, making ethnicity/caste the most salient and widespread basis for exclusion and conflict. Exclusion along ethnicity/caste occurs within religious, linguistic, community, and gender groups.[38] The conflict exists because the prevalent caste system based on Hindu traditions considers CHHE a high-caste group and others as low-caste and less pure. The conflict is further aggravated by the capture of the state by the CHHE, resulting in effective exclusion of all other groups from the state. The caste system has been used as a political tool to impose the ruling group's domination. For instance, the CHHE, as rulers, put the Tarai Brahman and Kshetriya below the hill Bahun and Chhetri in the 1854 civil code, even though Hindu tradition generally considers Brahman above Chhetri/Kshetriya. Likewise, the caste system in Nepal also attempted to incorporate the indigenous nationalities as low-caste, even though the indigenous nationalities were originally not part of it. The caste system also defines non-Hindu groups like Muslims and Christians as impure.

Indigenous Nationalities Movement and Conflicts

Ethnic conflicts in Nepal are as old as the Nepali state. The conflicts occurred as the House of Gorkha and its Chhetri rulers conquered other peoples and territories. Violent resistance occurred more frequently during the last quarter of the eighteenth century, as demonstrated by several Limbu, Khambu, and Tamang rebellions. Ethnic rebellions and protests lessened during the nineteenth century as the autocratic regime of the period became more successful in repressing the movements. However, attempts at reviving language and religion and other forms of resistance continued.

Ethnic movements arose more frequently during open periods, including during the 1950s, when several ethnic organizations were formed such as Tamang Bhasa Samskriti Bikas Samiti, Tamu Dhi Pariwar, Langhali Pariwar Sangh, Tharu Kalyan Samaj, Rai Limbu Sudhar Samaj, Thakali Sudhar Samaj, and Gurung Kalyan Sangh. Some of the groups formed an umbrella organization called the Pichhadieko Bargiya Samgh (Backward Class Organization). Eventually it included twelve ethnic groups.[39] The groups became less active during the panchyat years but resumed activities in 1979 after the polity became more open in preparation for the referendum in 1980. The Kirat Dharma Tatha Sahitaya Sangh (Society for Promotion of Kirat Religion and Literature) and the Nepal Bhasa Manka Khala, an organization to promote the Newar language, were established in 1979. Various groups like the Tharus organized mass meetings during the period.[40] In 1986 an umbrella organization of the indigenous nationalities, the Nepal Sarvajatiya Adhikar Manch (Forum for the Rights of All Ethnic Peoples in Nepal), was formed to work for the rights of indigenous nationalities.

The indigenous movement saw a huge spurt after democracy was restored in 1990. Since 1990 the indigenous nationalities have organized and mobilized considerably by establishing ethnic associations (such as Kirat Yakthung Chumlung, Nepal Tamang Ghedung, Nepal Sherpa Association, Nepal Magar Association) where activists from different political parties and nonparty activists work together.

Major indigenous nationalities groups came together to form the Nepal Federation of Nationalities (NEFEN) in 1990 to fight for group rights.[41] As of 2007, fifty-four ethnic groups and several allied organizations are associated with NEFIN (the name was changed to Nepal Federation of Indigenous Nationalities). One major success of this movement has been the development of a common identity of indigenous nationalities among the diverse linguistic and ethnic groups. However, the indigenous nationalities have failed to form an effective ethnic political party, failed to create an effective political mobilization within mainstream political parties, and failed to persuade the state to fulfill their major demands. The indigenous nationalities established political parties but have not elected members to the parliament.

The indigenous nationalities have demanded the declaration of the state as secular, sociocultural equality among different ethnic/caste groups, equality among native languages (protection and promotion of native languages, schooling in native languages, and a three-language policy), and proportional distribution of resources (proportional electoral method, reservation in education, administration, and political offices). Their demands also include cultural and political autonomy (federalism, House of Nationalities), right to self-determination, an end to the assimilation policy of the state and society, the right to traditional land and natural resources, and recognition as an indigenous people.

The indigenous nationalities began to engage in violent conflict from the end of 1990s. The Khambuwan National Front (KNF) launched an insurgency demanding autonomy. Its activities resulted in the deaths and destruction of public property. Eventually it merged with the CPN(Maoist).[42] The Mongol National Organization has also threatened to launch a violent insurgency. Since late 2006 the federal Limbuwan State Council has become active in organizing many protests and bandhs. Political organizations of Khambu, Tamang, and Tharu have also joined the group to fight for their autonomy.

Madhesi Movement and Violent Conflicts

The Madhesis have also organized themselves since the early 1950s. The Nepal Tarai Congress (NTC), a regional party demanding autonomy for the Tarai and recognition of Hindi as a second language, received 2.1 percent of popular votes in the 1959 general election. However, it did not win any seats to the parliament. The Madhesi also opposed the imposition of Khas-Nepali as a medium of instruction in public schools in the late 1950s.[43] During the panchayat period, Gajendra Narayan Singh established the Nepal Goodwill Council (NGC) (1985) to raise the issues of the Madhesi. The NGC was transformed into a political party in 1990 and it has won several seats in the parliament in all the elections since 1990.

The Madhesi movement has a regional characteristic because most constituent groups hail from the Tarai.[44] However, all residents of the Tarai, like the hill migrants, are not included in the movement. The Madhesi movement was, to a considerable degree, against the "internal colonization" of the Tarai by the hill people.

Among the different social justice movements, the Madhesi movement is the most mobilized but the least recognized by the state. The government did not form Madhesi commissions, unlike for women or the Dalit or an academy for the indigenous nationalities. The government also did not provide reservations for the Madhesi when it announced reservation policies for the Dalit, women, and indigenous nationalities in 2003.

The Madhesi organized around the Nepal Goodwill Party (NGP) and various linguistic associations in the 1990s. The NGP-led movement has focused on the political inclusion of the Madhesi. The NGP has elected representatives to the House of Representatives (HOR) regularly, though never getting more than 5 percent of the seats. Madhesi demands include rightful citizenship, reservation (especially in security forces), cultural autonomy, regional federalism, linguistic rights, socioeconomic equality, and an end to the neglect of the Tarai, mandatory daura suruwal ("Nepali" dress), and racist stereotyping.[45]

Some Madhesi organizations began a violent movement in 2005 after the CPN(Maoist) Madhesi front split from its mother party. The factions continued violent activities even after the Maoist-government settlement. Since then other violent organizations (e.g., Tarai Cobra, Madhesi Tigers) have sprouted in the Tarai. Some of the groups have demanded separation as well. In the meantime, the MPRF launched a movement against the interim constitution in 2007 that generated widespread participation among the Madhesi people. Around fifty people died during the course of the protest and the movement was successful in forcing the government to amend the constitution to accommodate the demand for federalism. In early 2008, MPRF, NGP, and TMDP jointly launched another successful movement that forced the government to concede to some more Madhesi demands.

Dalit Movement

The Dalit have been fighting to end untouchability and establish social justice. Three Dalit organizations came up in Kathmandu, Baglung, and Sunsari in 1947–1948.[46] Pragati Nari Sangh, an organization of Dalit women, was established in 1955–1956. The Dalit continued to organize during the panchayat period even though the closed environment was unfavorable. The Nepal Rastriya Dalit Jan Vikash Parishad was formed with the involvement of prominent Dalit activists in 1967–1968. It opened branches in many districts. With the polity gearing up for a referendum, a Dalit organization named Samaj Sudhar Sangh was formed in 1979–1980. Jati Bibhed Unmalan Manch was formed in 1987–1988 in the relatively open period after the 1980 referendum.[47]

The Dalit have organized around numerous political parties and nongovernmental organizations (NGO) in the post-1990 multiparty Nepal. No effective Dalit political party, whose aim is primarily to represent the Dalit, exists. Most of the mainstream political parties did not have a Dalit in their central committees during the 1990s.

The Dalit movement is riddled by chronic infighting among its leaders. Some commentators opine that one reason for the infighting is their division along major political parties. International NGOs have been providing support to the Dalit movement since the 1990s, but some commentators say that this has contributed to the infighting as Dalit groups and leaders compete for funds.

The Dalit oppose Brahmanism, untouchability, stereotyping of their group, and restriction from public places such as temples. Their demands include reservation in education, administration, and political offices; an end to untouchability; social, economic, and political empowerment of Dalit community; and secularism. Since the 1990s the Dalit have engaged in many public protests and movements to allow them to enter Hindu temples, sell milk to dairies, use water from public taps and wells, and refuse to engage in traditional work such as carcass disposal. Many of these activities led to conflict with members of local dominant groups.[48]

NOTES

1. The government and the Maoists sat down twice in 2001 and 2003 for negotiations to settle the conflict through dialogue, but the talks failed.

2. By 2004, only Mustang and Manang, two mountainous districts inhabited by indigenous nationalities, had no insurgency-related deaths.

3. Edward N. Muller and Mitchell A. Seligson, "Inequality and Insurgency," *American Political Science Review* 81, no. 2 (1987); Ted Robert Gurr, "A Causal Model of Civil Strife: A Comparative Analysis Using New Indices," *American Political Science Review* 62, no. 4 (1968).

4. John Bray, Leiv Lunde, and S. Mansoob Murshed, "Economic Drivers in Nepal's Maoist Insurgency," in *Political Economy of Armed Conflict Beyond Greed and Grievance*, ed. Karen Ballentine and Kake Sherman (Boulder: Lynne Rienner, 2003).

5. This section draws liberally from Lawoti Mahendra Lawoti, "Contentious Politics in Demcratizing Nepal," *Contentious Politics and Democratization in Nepal*, ed. Mahendra Lawoti (Los Angeles: Sage, 2007).

6. Udaya R. Wagle, *Inclusive Democracy and Economic Inequality in South Asia: Any Discernible Link?* (School of Public Affairs and Administration, Western Michigan University, 2006).

7. Piers Blaikie, John Cameron, and David Seddon, *Nepal in Crisis: Growth and Stagnation at the Periphery* (Delhi: Oxford, 1980).

8. Kishor Sharma, "The Political Economy of Civil War in Nepal," *World Development* 34, no. 7 (2006): 1245.

9. Sonali Deraniyagala, "The Political Economy of Civil Conflict in Nepal," *Oxford Development Studies* 33, no. 1 (2005): 52.

10. Kishore Sharma, "The Political Economy of Civil War in Nepal," *World Development* 34, no. 7 (2006): 1241–1242.

11. Land ownership, on the other hand, may hide poverty in the hills and mountains: "over 40 percent of medium and large landowners in the hills were classified as 'poor' in 1996." Deraniyagala, "Political Economy," 54–55.

12. Alan Macfarlane, "Sliding Down Hill: Some Reflections on Thirty Years of Change in a Himalayan Village," *European Bulletin of Himalayan Research* 20, no. 1 (2001).

13. Sharma, "Political Economy of Civil War," pp. 242–1243.

14. Deraniyagala, "Political Economy."

15. Mahesh C. Regmi, *The Land Tenure and Taxation in Nepal*, Vol. 3: *The Jagir, Rakam, and Kipat Tenure Systems* (Berkeley: Institute of International Studies, 1965); Mahesh C. Regmi, *Thatched Huts and Stucco Palaces: Peasants and Landlords in 19th-Century Nepal* (New Delhi: Vikash, 1978).

16. T. Louise Brown, *The Challenge to Democracy in Nepal* (London: Routledge, 1996).

17. In contrast, another extremist communist group boycotted the 1991 elections but participated in the subsequent elections.

18. Deepak Thapa and Bandita Sijapati, *A Kingdom Under Siege: Nepal's Maoist Insurgency, 1996 to 2003* (Kathmandu: Printhouse, 2003); Mahendra Lawoti, *Towards a Democratic Nepal: Inclusive Political Institutions for a Multicultural Society* (New Delhi: Sage, 2005).

19. Ted Robert Gurr, *Minorities at Risk? A Global View of Ethnopolitical Conflicts* (Washington, D.C.: United States Institute of Peace Press, 1993).

20. Ashok K. Mehta, *The Royal Nepal Army: Meeting the Maoist Challenge* (New Delhi: Rupa, 2005).

21. The approximate strength of the Maoists according to Mehta (p. 94) was as follows: armed guerrillas 4,000; militias trained as guerrillas 5,000; unarmed militias 20,000; political activists 14,000; supporters 24,000 and sympathizers 200,000. The total was 267,000.

22. Mehta, *Royal Nepal Army*.

23. Mahendra Lawoti, *Looking Back, Looking Forward: Centralization, Multiple Conflicts, and Democratic State Building in Nepal* (Washington: East-West Center, 2007).

24. Mehta, *Royal Nepal Army*.

25. Mahendra Lawoti, "Maoists and Minorities: Overlap of Interests or the Case of Exploitation?" *Studies in Nepali History and Society* 8, no. 1 (2003).

26. Kumar Pradhan, *The Gorkha Conquests: The Process and Consequences of the Unification of Nepal, with Particular Reference to Eastern Nepal* (Calcutta: Oxford, 1991); Mahesh C. Regmi, *Kings and Political Leaders of the Gorkhali Empire, 1768–1814* (Hyderabad: Orient Longman, 1995); Lawoti, "Contentious Politics in Democratizing Nepal"; Neupane Govinda Neupane, *Nepali Samajko Rupantaran* [Transformation in Nepali Society] (Kathmandu: Center for Development Studies, 2001) lists over a dozen peasant resistances and half a dozen student mobilizations between 1950 and 1990 that were often brutally repressed.

27. David Apter, ed., *The Legitimization of Violence* (New York: New York University Press, 1997).

28. Susan Hangen, "Between Political Party and Social Movement: The Mongol National Organization and Democratization in Rural Nepal," *Contentious Politics and Democratization in Nepal*, ed. Mahendra Lawoti (New Delhi: Sage, 2007).

29. Ted Robert Gurr, *Peoples Versus States: Minorities at Risk in the New Century* (Washington, D.C.: United Institute of Peace Press, 2000).

30. This section draws from Lawoti, *Looking Back, Looking Forward*.

31. Govinda Neupane, *Nepalko Jatiya Prashna: Samajik Banot Ra Sajhedariko Sambhawana* [Nepal's National Question: Social Composition and Possibilities of Accommodation] (Kathmandu: Center for Development Studies, 2000).

32. NESAC, *Nepal Human Development Report 1998* (Kathmandu: NESAC, 1998). Neupane, *Nepalko Jatiya Prashna*; Mahendra Lawoti, *Towards a Democratic Nepal: Inclusive Political Institutions for a Multicultural Society* (New Delhi: Sage, 1998).

33. Neupane, *Nepalko Jatiya Prashna*.

34. Praytoush Onta and Shekhar Parajuli, eds., *Nepali Mediama Dalit Ra Janajati* (Kathmandu: Ekta, 2001–2002).

35. Lionel Caplan, *Land and Social Change in East Nepal*, rev. ed. (Kathmandu: Himal, 2000); David Holmberg, "Violence, Non-Violence, Sacrifice, Rebellion and the State," *Studies in Nepali History and Society* 11, no. 1 (2006).

36. Bryan Maddox, "Language Policy, Modernist Ambivalence, and Social Exclusion: A Case Study of Rupendehi District in Nepal's Tarai," *Studies in Nepali History and Society* 8, no. 2 (2003).

37. Dhanpati Upadhaya, *Report of the High Level Citizenship Commission-2051* (Kathmandu: HMG Nepal, 1995).

38. See Dor Bahadur Bista, *Fatalism and Development: Nepal's Struggle for Modernization* (Hyderabad: Orient Longman, 1991), for an early theorization of conflicts of interests among different groups.

39. Cited in Susan I. Hangen, "Making Mongols: Ethnic Politics and Emerging Identities in Nepal," (Ph.D. diss., University of Wisconsin, 2000).

40. Hangen, "Making Mongols."

41. It was renamed in 2003 as the Nepal Federation of Indigenous Nationalities (NEFIN). It indicates the group's increasing self-identification as indigenous peoples.

42. The KNF began violent activities in Sawan in 1997 by planting a bomb in a Sanskrit school in Dingla, Bhojpur. Since then it killed opponents, looted an agricultural bank, destroyed a power station, kidnapped opponents, and expelled Bahun-Chettris from the area of their influence. The KNF merged and split with the Maoists several times. In Asoj in 2001, the KNF and Limbuwan National Front (LNF) were merged by the Maoists to form the Kirant National Front. The violence by KNF increased during 2001 and 2002 even though it had been killing opponents since April–May 1999. Sudheer Sharma, *The Ethnic Dimension of the Maoist Insurgency* (Kathmandu, 2002); Damber Krishna, Shrestha, "Kirant Rastriya Morcha Ra Maobadi Gathbandhan," in *Bandukko Bojh*, ed. Rajendra Dahal and Mohan Mainali (Lalitpur: Himal, 2004).

43. Frederick H Gaige. *Regionalism and National Unity in Nepal* (Delhi: Vikas, 1975).

44. The Madhesi movement incorporates some of the Muslims' sociocultural and political demands. However, Muslim religious demands are not incorporated by the Madhesi movement. On the other hand, Muslims may not mobilize for the foreseeable future because they fear a Hindu backlash if they do so.

45. The NGP and other pan-Madhesi movements demand the declaration of Hindi as a medium language and an end to hegemony of Khas-Nepali language, whereas regional language activists favor the promotion of Maithili, Bhojpuri, and Abadhi.

46. Fifty-six years and eight and a half months should be deducted to get a Gregorian date from a Vikram Sambat (v.s.) date.

47. Hira Biswakorma, "Nepalko Dalit Andolanma Dalit Sangathanko Bhumika," *Nepalma Dalit Utthanka Rananiti*, ed. Haribansa Jha (Kathmandu: CETS, 2000).

48. Neupane, *Nepali Samajko Rupantaran*.

SUGGESTED READINGS

Bhattachan, Krishna B. "Ethnopolitics and Ethnodevelopment." In *State, Politics, and Leadership in Nepal*, ed. Dhruba Kumar. Kathmandu: CNAS, 1995.

Bista, Dor Bahadur. *Fatalism and Development: Nepal's Struggle for Modernization*. Hyderabad: Orient Longman, 1991.

Blaikie, Piers, John Cameron, and David Seddon. *Nepal in Crisis: Growth and Stagnation at the Periphery*. Delhi: Oxford, 1980.

Brown, T. Louise. *The Challenge to Democracy in Nepal*. London: Routledge, 1996.

Caplan, Lionel. *Land and Social Change in East Nepal*. Rev. ed. Kathmandu: Himal, 2000.

Deraniyagala, Sonali. "The Political Economy of Civil Conflict in Nepal." *Oxford Development Studies* 33, no. 1 (2005): 47–62.

Dhruba Kumar, ed. *Domestic Conflict and Crises of Governability in Nepal*. Kathmandu: CNAS, 2000.

_____. "Proximate Causes of Conflict in Nepal." *Contributions to Nepalese Studies* 32, no. 1 (2003): 51–93.

Gaige, Frederick H. *Regionalism and National Unity in Nepal*. Delhi: Vikas, 1975.

Gellner, David N. *Resistance and the State: Nepalese Experience*. New Delhi: Social Science Press. 2003.

Gellner, David N., Joanna Pfaff-Czarnecka, and John Whelpton, eds. *Nationalism and Ethnicity in a Hindu Kingdom: The Politics of Culture in Contemporary Nepal*. Amsterdam: Harwood Academic, 1997.

Holmberg, David. "Violence, Non-Violence, Sacrifice, Rebellion, and the State." *Studies in Nepali History and Society* 11, no. 1 (2006): 31–64.

Hutt, Michael, ed. *Himalayan People's War: Nepal's Maoist Rebellion*. Bloomington: Indiana University Press. 2004.

Lawoti, Mahendra, ed. *Contentious Politics and Democratization in Nepal*. Los Angeles: Sage, 2007.

———. *Towards a Democratic Nepal: Inclusive Political Institutions for a Multicultural Society*. New Delhi: Sage, 2005.

Lecomte-Tilouine, Marie, and Pascal Dolfus, eds. *Ethnic Revival and Religious Turmoil*. New Delhi: Oxford University Press, 2003.

Maddox, Bryan. "Language Policy, Modernist Ambivalence, and Social Exclusion: A Case Study of Rupendehi District in Nepal's Tarai." *Studies in Nepali History and Society* 8, no. 2 (2003): 205–224.

Mehta, Ashok K. *The Royal Nepal Army: Meeting the Maoist Challenge*. New Delhi: Rupa, 2005.

Mishra, Chaitanya. "Locating the 'Causes' of the Maoist Struggle." *Studies in Nepali History and Society* 9, no. 1 (2004): 3–56.

NESAC. *Nepal Human Development Report 1998*. Kathmandu: NESAC, 1998.

Neupane, Govinda. *Nepalko Jatiya Prashna: Samajik Banot Ra Sajhedariko Sambhawana* [Nepal's National Question: Social Composition and Possibilities of Accommodation]. Kathmandu: Center for Development Studies, 2000.

Onta, Praytoush, and Shekhar Parajuli, eds. *Nepali Mediama Dalit Ra Janajati*. Kathmandu: Ekta, 2001–2002.

Pradhan, Kumar. *The Gorkha Conquests: The Process and Consequences of the Unification of Nepal, with Particular Reference to Eastern Nepal*. Calcutta: Oxford, 1991.

Regmi, Mahesh C. *Kings and Political Leaders of the Gorkhali Empire, 1768–1814*. Hyderabad: Orient Longman, 1995.

———. *The Land Tenure and Taxation in Nepal: Vol. 3, The Jagir, Rakam, and Kipat Tenure Systems*. Berkeley: Institute of International Studies, 1965.

———. *Thatched Huts and Stucco Palaces: Peasants and Landlords in 19th-Century Nepal*. New Delhi: Vikash, 1978.

Thapa, Deepak, and Bandita Sijapati. *A Kingdom Under Siege: Nepal's Maoist Insurgency, 1996 to 2003*. Kathmandu: Printhouse, 2003.

29

Modernization and Development: Problems and Prospects

Nepal is a poor county. According to the UNDP its gross domestic product (GDP) per capita in purchasing power parity (PPP) was US$1,490.00 in 2004.[1] Its human development index (HDI) was 138 out of 177 countries in the world, life expectancy was 62.1 years, and the adult (ages fifteen and older) literacy rate was 48.6 percent. The infant mortality rate (under one year) was 56 per thousand and the under-five mortality rate was 74 per thousand in 2005.[2] Much of the Nepali population suffers from serious malnutrition. Nepal, however, has been trying to overcome the problem of poverty through economic development and modernization.

Late Start in Modernization

Nepal began its modernization attempt late in the 1950s. At the time of independence from the Ranas in 1951, Nepal did not possess any significant infrastructure for modernization. There was no drivable road linking Nepal to the outside world, only a few industries existed, literacy was at 5 percent between 1952 and 1954, and only twenty-five telephone lines existed in the country.

The dismal level of infrastructure and development at the time was due to the Rana regime's policy of not promoting economic development for fear of rebellion against its autocratic rule. They restricted establishment of schools for fear of raising awareness. The regime limited outside contact to maintain control over the population. It was a regime that did not care about the welfare of the people. It extracted resources from peasants to support its luxurious lifestyle and build palaces. It did not invest back in the people. Ironically, a country that was not colonized did not build infrastructure before 1950, while the colonial British built infrastructure such as the railway and postal system and higher educational institutions in the colonized India.

Since 1956 Nepal has launched various economic development plans. Nepal has expanded its roads, airports, and postal services, and it has enhanced power generation capacity and increased irrigation facilities. Nepal has also built several higher educational institutions to develop technically skilled manpower and has improved its health care facilities.

Nepal has received economic and development aid from its two giant neighbors, India and the People's Republic of China, which continue to competitively woo the Himalayan kingdom. In addition, Nepal has benefited from development assistance provided by the United States, Japan, and the former Soviet Union. Despite these efforts, Nepal's economic growth continues to be dismal. According to the World Bank's *World Development Report* for 1987, "Nepal's economic growth on a per capita basis was only 0.1 percent per year during 1965–85, with a per capita income of $160 in 1985, the fifth lowest in the world." The 1995 per capita income was reported to be $200, whereas in 2006 it was $290. Nepal's GDP per capita growth in 2005 was 0.7 percent. As a result of the dismal performance, Nepal's attempts have been termed "failed development."[3]

Problems in Modernization and Development

Nepal's long-term economic development prospects depend on continuous political stability, population control, and the cooperation of its neighbors. The path toward modernization and development has not been easy for Nepal. Various factors have hindered its attempts. Historical factors, mentioned above, played a role. The lack of infrastructure meant that Nepal had to begin from the very beginning. Absence of educational institutions and low literacy rates meant that Nepal lacked human resources and institutions to produce them. Hence Nepal had to overcome a vicious circle of constraints.

Geographic factors also contributed to Nepal's underdevelopment. Three-fourths of the country is mountainous, and the northern mountains are very rugged and steep. Good agricultural land is limited and irrigation is difficult. Further, due to the ruggedness of the territory, development cost per unit area is expensive. Infrastructure development costs increase because of the need for bridges, and so on. The cost of imports and exports is high due to large transportation costs. Population settlements are dispersed throughout the mountain and hills, also increasing the cost of providing services.

The landlocked condition of the country has also hampered development. Nepal is practically surrounded by India, and as the massive Himalayan range and valleys that border China (Tibet Autonomous region) make travel and trade with China difficult and limited. Access to sea via China is long and not feasible. Though the open border with India has facilitated movement, it has also promoted smuggling and so on. On the other hand, since Nepal has to conduct trade to third countries through Indian soil and ports, Nepal has to rely on the goodwill of the Indian government. Such a condition has allowed India to negotiate favorably in its dealing with Nepal, often harming Nepali interests. As a result Nepal has been a backwater market of India. Nepal is flooded with Indian goods, but India often hampers the export of Nepali goods to its territories. Thus the Nepali manufacturing sector and industrialization policy has been affected negatively. In the words of some critics, Nepal was a semi-colony of India during the British Empire and it continues to be so.[4]

Sociologists have also pointed to the fatalistic attitude of the society as a cause of underdevelopment. Bista has argued that the caste system, which provides status and privilege to high caste and socializes people to caste-based norms, has eroded the work culture.[5] People think that their current position is due to the past life. The ascriptive caste system also denies a large section of the people equal opportunities to develop. Fatalistic and caste-based attitudes mean that achievement and work-oriented values receive less importance, resulting in the socialization of clerical values among educated sections of the society.

Development Policies

Nepal adopted mixed development policies in the mid-1950s with the initiation of five-year plans. The state established large corporations to produce and distribute goods and to monitor the private sector through licensing small-scale enterprises. The government established cement factories, agricultural implement industries, a national airline, brick factories, and a national trading center. Small industries were allowed to be operated by the private sector but they had to get license, which was a cumbersome process. The industrialization policy was based on the principle of import substitution—producing goods and services in the country to become self-reliant.

The focus on industrialization led to neglect of the agricultural sector. As noted in an earlier chapter, no five-year plan spent more than 26 percent of the development budget in agriculture, which employed more than 80 percent of the people. Hence the agricultural growth rate did not meet the population growth rate. A net agricultural export country in the 1960s, Nepal had become net a importer of food products by the 1980s.[6]

The industrialization policies failed to make the country self-reliant in manufactured products. Due to the license system, free competition did not occur.

As a result, inefficiency grew and many corporations lost money. They had to be sustained by state subsidies and consequently the national debt grew. In the mid-1980s the state had to borrow funds from the IMF and the World Bank to address the deficit problem. The agencies attached a condition for structural adjustment on the loans they forwarded. As a result, a liberalization process began in the mid-1980s.[7]

Economic liberalization, initiated in 1985 and expanded in the early 1990s, increased the economy's efficiency in some sectors. Private domestic airlines, which went into operation after the promulgation of the open air policy in the early 1990s, provide reliable services to more destinations, reversing the inadequacy and unreliability of the previous system. Total passengers on domestic flights increased from 228,000 in 1989–1990 to 1,209,000 in 2002–2003.[8] The banking sector also improved dramatically. The number of commercial banks, development banks, insurance providers, finance companies, and saving and credit cooperatives increased, and the economy grew. There were 148 financial institutions in 2004, compared to seventy-three in 2000 and five in 1990. With regard to commercial banks, seventeen were operating in 2004 compared to thirteen in 2000 and five in 1990.[9] Liberalization also benefited the education sector. Educational opportunities expanded at all levels. Approximately thirty engineering colleges and a dozen medical colleges, most of them established through private initiative after 1990, provided higher technical education.[10] Liberalization also resulted in the availability of affordable consumer goods. These varieties of goods would never be available under a state-controlled or mixed economy. People's opportunities to engage in different entrepreneurial activities also expanded. The deepened economy meant more jobs.

Resources

Nepal does not have extensive mineral resources but is rich in water resources. Its hydropower potential is estimated to be the second highest in the world at 83,290 megawatts, after Brazil.[11] The rivers that flow from the steep mountains have very high potential for the generation of electricity. Nepal has been trying to develop hydro power to export but the only viable external market is India. Nepal has not been able to reach an electricity selling agreement with India to build large hydro power projects that would benefit Nepal. Thus the potential has not been exploited. In such a context, the best chance for Nepal may be to develop smaller hydroelectric projects to meet its needs and sell remaining amounts for profit.

Tourism is another sector with potential due to Nepal's diverse flora and fauna. The country is extremely beautiful and the people are very hospitable. Tourism was developing steadily, but instability and law-and-order problems that emerged with the advent of the Maoist insurgency hindered its growth. As tourism declined, many hotels and tourism-related businesses went bankrupt. After the settlement of the Maoist insurgency, tourists have begun to arrive.

Since the 1980s, Nepal developed a carpet industry and since the 1990s has expanded its garment industry. However, due to the lack of quality control and fickle international trends, both these sectors began to decline in the late 1990s.

A remittance economy has supported Nepal for a long time. Earlier, the Nepalis working in the British and Indian armies and the Singapore police sent in remittances. People working in India also contributed. During the late 1990s, people increasingly began to go to East Asian countries like Malaysia and Korea and the Gulf countries for work. The trend increased as young people fled the villages to escape being forcefully recruited by the Maoists or being perceived as Maoist sympathizers by the security forces.

Challenges

Nepal has witnessed success in various sectors. Literacy has risen. Infant mortality has decreased. Life expectancy has risen. More roads have been built, more telephone lines distributed, more people have access to drinking water, and so on. However, many challenges remain. As noted above, one-third of the people still live under the poverty line. Rural people, members of marginalized groups, and women face higher poverty and inequality. Many people do not have access to the benefits of development. Some regions still occasionally witness famine and starvation.

When the Maoists and the government settled their disagreements in 2006, a lot of hope was raised. A new constitution is to be drafted by representatives elected by the people. Major parties do not seem to be sensitive to the demands made by traditionally marginalized groups like the Dalit, indigenous nationalities, Madhesi, and women. Some of these groups have launched movements to make the government accept their demands. Some factions have even initiated violent insurgencies. If the state continues to disregard major demands of the marginalized communities, more groups may begin violent movements. Hence the challenge during the transitional phase is to include all groups in the process of charting out consensual guidelines for a "new Nepal." If that is not done, then Nepali democracy may again witness conflicts that will eventually undermine it.

NOTES

1. UNDP, *Nepal: The Human Development Index: Going Beyond Income*, 2007, http://hdrstats.undp.org/countries/country_fact_sheets/cty_fs_NPL.html.

2. UNICEF, Nepal Statistics 2007, www.unicef.org/infobycountry/nepal_nepal_statistics.html#23.

3. Devendra Raj Panday, *Nepal's Failed Development: Reflections on the Mission and the Maladies* (Kathmandu: Nepal South Asia Center, 1999).

4. Piers Blaikie, John Cameron, and David Seddon, *Nepal in Crisis: Growth and Stagnation at the Periphery* (Delhi: Oxford, 1980).

5. Dor Bahadur Bista, *Fatalism and Development: Nepal's Struggle for Modernization* (Hyderabad: Orient Longman, 1991).

6. Kishor Sharma, "The Political Economy of Civil War in Nepal," *World Development* 34, no. 7 (2006); Sonali Deraniyagala, "The Political Economy of Civil Conflict in Nepal," *Oxford Development Studies* 33, no. 1 (2005).

7. Meena Acharya, Yubaraj Khatiwada, and Shankar Aryal, *Structural Adjustment Policies and Poverty Eradication* (Kathmandu: IIDS, 2003).

8. Ram Sharan Mahat, *In Defense of Democracy: Dynamics and Fault Lines of Nepal's Political Economy* (New Delhi: Adroit, 2005).

9. Mahat, *In Defense of Democracy*; Acharya, Khatiwada, and Aryal, Structural Adjustment Policies.

10. Mahat, In Defense of Democracy.

11. Vinod Prasad Shrestha, *A Concise Geography of Nepal* (Kathmandu: Mandala Book Point, 2007).

Suggested Readings

Acharya, Meena, Yubaraj Khatiwada, and Shankar Aryal. *Structural Adjustment Policies and Poverty Eradication.* Kathmandu: IIDS, 2003.

Bista, Dor Bahadur. *Fatalism and Development: Nepal's Struggle for Modernization.* Hyderabad: Orient Longman, 1991.

Blaikie, Piers, John Cameron, and David Seddon. *Nepal in Crisis: Growth and Stagnation at the Periphery.* Delhi: Oxford, 1980.

Deraniyagala, Sonali. "The Political Economy of Civil Conflict in Nepal." *Oxford Development Studies* 33, no. 1 (2005): 47–62.

Mahat, Ram Sharan. *In Defense of Democracy: Dynamics and Fault Lines of Nepal's Political Economy.* New Delhi: Adroit, 2005.

Panday, Devendra Raj. *Nepal's Failed Development: Reflections on the Mission and the Maladies.* Kathmandu: Nepal South Asia Center, 1999.

Seddon, David. *Nepal: A State of Poverty.* New Delhi: Vikash, 1987.

PART VI

SOUTH ASIA

30

The Future: South Asia as a Region and a Player in the World System

Over the past twenty-nine chapters, we have examined each of the major nation-states of South Asia. In this final chapter we will look at the region as a whole and discuss the major issues facing it. As South Asia emerges as an important actor in world affairs, the region must address the most serious issues that can harm its development and growth. The first and foremost of these is its relationship with the rest of the world. This will be followed by a discussion of two major conflicts between the countries of the region. The final sections will examine the continuing efforts to create a national identity in the region and the rise of militant Islam.

Foreign Affairs

The strategic location of South Asia makes it an area of importance in the world system. Pakistan is almost as much a part of Southwest Asia as it is of South Asia, given its proximity to the Persian Gulf and its border with Iran. It is also a neighbor of Afghanistan and looks beyond that country toward a major role in Central Asia and that region's newly independent states. India, as the second most populous nation in the world, is important not only in terms of its geographic location but also as a huge market, as a destination for foreign direct investment, as a rapidly growing technological power, as a longtime leader among third world nations, and as an active and effective participant in Asian economic, strategic, and cultural activities. Both India and Pakistan, as nuclear powers, are important players in the diplomacy of nuclear and missile proliferation and nonproliferation. Sri Lanka, which extends south into the Indian

Ocean, sits across some of the world's important shipping lanes and is the center of an intractable and destructive civil war that has defied efforts toward a peaceful resolution. Bangladesh lies adjacent to the volatile eastern regions of India. Despite efforts to entangle Bangladesh in the rise of global Islamic militancy, barring sporadic incidents inside the country, it has been able to avoid becoming embroiled in it. At the same time it has actively pursued an international peacekeeping role for itself.

The region sits astride the sea lanes of the Indian Ocean that are critical for oil trade between Asia and the Middle East and for peaceful commerce in the Indian Ocean area that involves Africa and Australia as well as interests of key U.S. allies in the vast area. The Indian Ocean is a pathway for the military, air and naval movement of the major global and regional powers during wars and crises (e.g., in Afghanistan and Iraq), and humanitarian disasters (e.g., tsunami in 2004). Two major U.S. military commands—the Pacific and Central commands—maintain access to the Indian Ocean, since the area is a part of their operational jurisdiction.

Growing interregional interactions between South Asia and its neighborhood suggest that political, economic, military, and cultural boundaries of the cold war era no longer make sense. Then it made sense to place Central Asia as a part of the Soviet Union, Iran as a part of the Middle East, Afghanistan, and Burma (now Myanmar) as parts of the Middle East and Southeast Asia respectively on the basis of the pattern and intensity of interactions among members of each region. In the twenty-first century this pattern no longer prevails. Terrorism, illicit drug trade, and weapons proliferation as well as changing patterns of intensity of interactions between South Asian states and those in Central Asia, Southeast Asia, China, and the Indian Ocean area indicate that territorial borders are no longer working as boundaries or limits of state and nonstate actions. For example, Chinese rail and road links in the Tibetan region are planned for extension into Nepal and Pakistan, while China and India plan to revive the World War II Stillwell Road through Myanmar that ferried Western supplies to fight Japan's military expansionism. NATO's expansion into Afghanistan and the U.S. military expansion into Central Asia indicate that contemporary wars and crises make interregionalism the basis of academic and policy analysis in the twenty-first century. We also see the growth of the presence of nontraditional players in the South Asian, Middle Eastern, and Indian Ocean scene, for example, the buildup of Israeli-Indian diplomatic and defense ties; Saudi Arabia's growing interest in checking extremist influence within the kingdom and its neighborhood in South Asia and the Gulf; and Japan's buildup of its economic and strategic ties with India and its naval presence in the Indian Ocean. These changes appear irreversible and indicate a sea change in the politics and policies in the region, and are indicative of a rapidly changing international environment.

India's Relations Outside the Region

It is interesting to note that India rejected dominion status within the British Commonwealth of Nations in its Lahore resolution of 1930 but accepted a similar offer at independence in 1947. When India became a republic under the constitution of 1950, the pattern of the Commonwealth was altered. Previously, all members of the Commonwealth had accepted the British monarch as monarch of the respective newly independent states as well (as in the case of Canada or Australia). But in India's case it was agreed that India would remain a member of the Commonwealth as a republic but accept the British monarch as occupying a symbolic position as head of the Commonwealth. The pattern applied to India has been followed by a large number of the members of the Commonwealth that have become independent since World War II, including Pakistan, Bangladesh, and Sri Lanka.

India had already set another precedent for the colonies of Great Britain by organizing a political party that looked beyond the achievement of freedom to the creation of a polity, economy, and society to follow the initial step of independence. Many of the parties in other colonies used the word "Congress" to denote a party seeking freedom. Relations between the Indian National Congress and other freedom movements were often close—a situation India could build on after independence to assert its leadership in what was called the third world. Nehru, who participated in the Bandung (Indonesia) Conference in 1955, is credited with being one of the three principal leaders involved in forming the Nonaligned Movement (the other two being Gamal Abdel Nasser of Egypt and Marshal Josef Broz Tito of Yugoslavia).

Nonalignment was a part of Nehru's creed. To him it meant avoiding alignment with either of the two blocs led by the superpowers, the United States and the Soviet Union. What it did not mean was neutrality. Nehru maintained that India reserved the right to take whatever position on an issue that best served India's interests. However, such interests often seemed to U.S. governments as favoring the Soviet view over the American. During the cold war India tilted toward Moscow on a number of important diplomatic issues such as the Korean War and the China question, and appeared to blame the United States for the cold war and saw the Soviet Union as inclined toward peace. Nehru was ambivalent about Soviet interventions in Eastern Europe (e.g., Hungary, 1956) and lost the moral high ground in Western eyes as a result. That India benefited by Soviet diplomatic and military support on Kashmir, Pakistan, China,

Nehru's economic socialism, and the military buildup after 1962 showed that despite Nehru's declarations about nonalignment, he tilted toward Moscow.

The stance on nonalignment that Nehru had advocated for India was further eroded after his death when his daughter, Indira Gandhi, signed a treaty of friendship with the Soviet Union in 1971. The agreement stated that the two countries would consult with each other when either was threatened by a third party. This treaty formalized the India-Soviet Union alignment and it was an alliance in all but name. India under Nehru had protested strongly when Pakistan joined the Central Treaty Organization (CENTO) and Southeast Asia Treaty Organization (SEATO) alliances with the West in the 1950s on the grounds that the alliance arrangements would bring one of the superpowers into the subcontinent. This argument apparently did not concern Indira Gandhi in 1971. The treaty was renewed in 1991, and the Soviet Union collapsed shortly thereafter.

The Soviet Union was by far the largest supplier of military equipment to the Indian military as well as an important trading partner. It also provided both diplomatic and military support during India's conflict with China in 1962. India, however, maintained a somewhat more neutral stance during its leadership of the Nonaligned Movement beginning in 1983. For instance, India favored the Soviet withdrawal from Afghanistan but continued to support the Soviet puppet regime that was left behind in that country. After the Soviet Union collapsed, India found itself looking to the industrialized countries (especially the United States) for much-needed technology and investment in contrast to earlier reliance on the Soviet Union for military and technical assistance. Indian relations with the United States improved during the Clinton presidency. When India conducted its nuclear tests in 1998, the Clinton approach was to engage in a nuclear dialogue, separating the nuclear issue from other issues, while building areas of convergence. President George W. Bush went even further. His agreements with India announced in 2005 and 2006 recognized the need to bring India into the global economic and strategic mainstream by recognizing its nuclear energy needs and the value of international nuclear cooperation with India.

India's relations with China appeared to be close after communist forces gained power in 1949. The slogan *Hindi-Chini bhai bhai* ("Indians and Chinese are brothers") was frequently heard. However, relations cooled when India discovered that China had built a road between Sinkiang and Tibet across the Aksai Chin in Ladakh, which India believed to be its territory. China also disputed the legitimacy of the border in the northeast, demarcated by the 1914 McMahon Line. Accordingly, China claimed much of northeast India, all of Bhutan, and parts of Nepal, Kashmir, and Uttar Pradesh. In October 1962 war broke out between China and India, and Indian forces suffered a humiliating defeat—especially in the Northeast Frontier Agency (now Arunachal Pradesh). China withdrew unilaterally but made it clear to all that India had been given a "black eye." Diplomatic and trade relations between the two states have since improved (e.g., ambassadors have once again been exchanged and visits at high levels have taken place). But until recently China treated India as a subregional power. Now, following India's economic growth, its nuclear weapons status, and its strategic partnership with the United States, China has started to negotiate seriously with India on many important issues such as the border and China's nuclear and missile aid to Pakistan. China no longer wholly champions Pakistan's position on Kashmir, and urges a bilateral and peaceful settlement. However, mistrust remains. China opposes the U.S.-Indian nuclear energy supply deal and insists on India's denuclearization. India remains adamant in its demand that the territory occupied by China in the Aksai Chin be returned to India. China has proposed the application of the "watershed principle" in both the northeast (i.e., essentially the McMahon Line) and in the Aksai Chin.

India and the United States have had a love-hate relationship. Historically, U.S. investment in India has been modest. The opening up of the Indian economy in the 1990s, however, has greatly increased investment in India from the United States as well as from other developed countries. India, as mentioned earlier, strongly opposed the U.S. relationship with Pakistan, especially its provision of sophisticated military equipment to Pakistan. The United States still supplies arms to Pakistan but now the context is different. Washington is sensitive about Indian fears of Pakistani military adventurism and its "misuse" of U.S. arms, and the United States has developed robust defense ties with India in the context of the view that India should be built up as a major global power. Moreover, with growing military capacity, India can absorb changes in Pakistan's conventional military arsenals since it is not seen as changing the balance of power. With growing self-confidence and political maturity India no longer brackets itself with Pakistan and sees itself as an emerging power in a changing global context.

Indeed U.S.-Indian relations have improved markedly in recent years. President Clinton visited India for several days in March 2000 and Vajpayee visited the United States in September of that year. Besides formal talks with Vajpayee in New Delhi, Clinton also visited an important technological center in Hyderabad and the financial center in Bombay, signifying the growing importance of economic relations between the two countries. President G. W. Bush stunned the world in 2005 by waiving economic sanctions that the United States had imposed on India following its testing of nuclear weapons in 1998. This exemption required major changes in U.S. nonproliferation laws and international nuclear trading regulations.

Pakistan's Foreign Relations

Faced with the disadvantage of being the new country following the partition of India and of being in conflict with its larger coinheritor of the British Raj, Pakistan believed that it had to look outside the subcontinent for possible allies in defending itself against what it thought would eventually be an Indian bid to reunify South Asia.

Pakistan lobbied for and accepted Western offers to join the ring of security pacts built in the 1950s to close the gap between U.S. commitments in Europe (through the North Atlantic Treaty Organization, NATO) and those in East Asia (following the Korean War). Pakistan in 1955 joined SEATO along with Thailand and the Philippines, and CENTO along with Iraq (briefly, until 1958), Iran, and Turkey. Its negotiations with the United States also brought U.S. military assistance through agreements initiated in 1954. This assistance met with strong objections from India, which perceived that the purposes of the United States and Pakistan were very different—Pakistan accepted the weapons as protection against India, whereas the United States provided them in an effort to build strength against possible Soviet or Chinese action. (For details of Pakistani-U.S. relations, see Chapter 13).

Pakistan's relations with the Soviet Union, never very close to begin with, were severely damaged by the Soviet invasion of Afghanistan in 1979. With the breakup of the Soviet Union, however, Pakistan looks toward the Central Asian republics as an area for economic expansion, though for the time being this possibility is stymied by the continuing war in Afghanistan. By contrast, Pakistan has had close and valuable relations with China, owing in part to the chronic rift between India and China. The Chinese supported Pakistan diplomatically in 1965 and 1971, and China has provided important military aid. Moreover, Pakistan played a key role in facilitating the visit of Henry Kissinger to China in 1971 that led to the opening of Sino-American relations. China has been a staunch supporter of Pakistan, given their common enmity with India and given Pakistan's utility as a pathway for China's influence in the Gulf and Middle Eastern Muslim world. But the convergence of interests between the two countries is not total. And as China has sought to rebuild its commercial, political, and strategic links with India, the triangularity of the China-Pakistan-India linkage has weakened. Since the 1960s Beijing saw South Asia through Islamabad's eyes. Now its perspective has become more balanced and is fluid.

Since 1971, Pakistan has expanded its ties with the Islamic countries of the Middle East. The religious ties are close, but the economic ties have been of even greater importance. Trade has expanded greatly, and Pakistani migrant workers have found employment in the Gulf States. Remittances from workers abroad account for the largest single item in Pakistan's foreign exchange earnings. Pakistan also has had military relationships with several countries, including Saudi Arabia, Jordan, Oman, and the United Arab Emirates.

Bangladesh Emerges

At independence Bangladesh found itself in close association with India and the Soviet Union and was subject to delayed recognition by the United States and China. Relations with India are defined by the party in power in Bangladesh, with relationships becoming more friendly during Awami League governance and distant when the Bangladesh Nationalist Party is in power. Since January 2007 Bangladesh has pursued a steadier and more balanced relationship with India. Relations with Russia have generally remained correct if not particularly cordial throughout.

The United States recognized Bangladesh in early 1972, and the anger that resulted from the U.S. tilt toward Pakistan in the liberation war has largely dissipated. U.S.-Bangladeshi relations are now built on bilateral assistance and the U.S. need to prevent China from becoming the dominant power in Bangladesh as well as commercial preferential treatment sought by Bangladesh for its textile products.

China's recognition of Bangladesh followed that of Pakistan. The Chinese have provided some economic assistance as well as a small amount of military aid, primarily for the air force. In 2000, Bangladesh agreed to purchase MiG-29s from the Soviet Union. China has developed its defense ties because of its strategic location and as a line of pressure against India's northeastern areas, just as Pakistan has served as a line of pressure on India's western and Kashmir fronts.

Bangladesh's location has prompted it to reach out to Southeast Asia while its majority religion has drawn it close to the countries of the Middle East. Southeast Asia provides a limited market and is a source of open market purchases of rice, whereas the Middle East has been a source of economic assistance and is an outlet for migrant workers from Bangladesh. Bangladesh receives economic assistance from many other sources as well, Japan being the largest donor. The discovery of natural gas is a positive development for its economy and its eastward economic orientation involving Myanmar and other Southeast Asian states is a promising channel for its development pending settlement of controversies with

India, and in its internal political arrangements. With India and Pakistan embroiled in regional and strategic positioning, Bangladesh carved out its own sphere of influence in two areas. It gained regional influence in the mid-1980s by pushing for regional cooperation and is currently seeking a global strategic role by becoming the critical country involved in international peacekeeping operations. The award of the Nobel Prize to a Bangladeshi citizen, Muhammad Yunus, for his innovative work with nongovernmental microlending points to the importance of civil society work in Bangladesh and further lends credence to its international role in this arena.

Nepal: From Isolated Kingdom to Major Player in the Region

Nepal's international affairs have largely focused on India and China. Many of its concerns have dealt with questions of trade and transit and defense. Regarding the latter issue, India has had troops stationed in Nepal to monitor Chinese movements across the Himalayas in the Tibet region of China. This arrangement has ended, however, as Nepal (which tries to maintain equal relations with its two neighbors) objected. As well, there is a psychological dimension in the relationship. Nepal is a predominantly Hindu kingdom, but nationalism among the Nepalese centers on the fear of Indian domination and a resentment about India's attitude. India, however, gives Nepal a special status by its policy of an open border with Nepal, recruitment of Nepalese Gorkhas into the Indian army, and a commitment to Nepal's development. India's difficulties with China and the buildup of Chinese road and rail links in Tibet ensure that Nepal is of long-term geopolitical value in Indian security planning and diplomacy.

The trade and transit issues have created strains in Indo-Nepalese relations, particularly in the 1980s. India and Nepal assumed treaty obligations concerning trade and security which in part are meant to ensure Nepal's buffer status vis-à-vis China. A key provision was that Nepalese defense requirements would be met by arms imports from India. In 1987 Nepal toyed with the idea of Chinese arms importation. India questioned the need, asked Nepal to either abandon its special links with India or maintain India's special position regarding its defense ties with Nepal. India imposed a trade embargo on Nepal. A nasty spat followed, the Nepalese king and his advisers realized that China could not replace India in meeting Nepal's needs, and the treaty relationship was confirmed.

Nepal has emerged as a major player in the region and a center of action and change that involves the attention of Pakistan, China, India, and the West. Pakistan, China, and Bangladesh played on the anti-Indian sentiments among Nepalese public opinion. India alleges that Pakistan's ISI has used Nepal as a base of insurgency against Indian targets. As well, a powerful Maoist uprising emerged in the last decade with a program to establish a Maoist republic and undermine the monarchy. Along with the West, India played a role in building the political process so as to diminish the power of the palace, bring Maoist guerrillas into the democratic political process, and strengthen the position of Nepal's weak party system. Despite the difficulties in Indo-Nepali relations, the open border remains a sign of a unique relationship and the recognition of the importance of assured mutual dependency. It should also be noted that the border between China and Nepal is such that commerce is severely restricted by topographical factors.

Nepal does have leverage in one respect that is of importance to India and potentially to Bangladesh: the rising of many key tributaries of the Ganges in Nepal. Storage and hydroelectric dam sites in Nepal can regulate the flow of the Ganges and can provide power for export from Nepal to India. They could also be part of a long-term solution to the Farakka barrage problem between Bangladesh and India.

Sri Lanka: From Model Colony to Civil War

After independence, Sri Lanka, under the leadership of the United National Party of D. S. Senanayake and Sir John Kotelawala, generally maintained close ties with the West, especially with Great Britain, which provided the largest market for Sri Lankan goods and also maintained a naval base at Trincomalee. The somewhat leftist regimes of the two Bandaranaikes ended the naval arrangement, and Sri Lanka began to associate more closely with the East, including close trade ties with China. This was the view of many in the West, although Sri Lankans would aver that Sri Lanka was actually moving toward a stance of more balanced nonalignment. Sri Lanka annoyed India in 1962 by joining in a third world proposal to end the Sino-Indian War—calling for mediation rather than an acceptance of the Indian view. Sri Lanka also became the leader of the Nonaligned Movement in 1976 and gained greater recognition of its position in the world. Sri Lanka has greatly opened its economy and is using its highly educated labor force to serve as an offshore manufacturing base.

The civil war in Sri Lanka has dominated its relations with the rest of the world. The Liberation Tigers of Tamil Eelam (LTTE) have established an international network of fund-raising activities. These have included extensive activities in Great Britain, France, Canada, and the United States where they raise money from the well educated Tamil expatriate community. In addition, the LTTE has operated a merchant fleet that usually transports legal products but also transports any product for any group that pays the money. They have also sold their expertise and have been involved in training groups in Nepal, India, and Bangladesh. In response to the international reach of the LTTE, the Sri Lankan government has established close military relations with potential military suppliers. In recent years, the United States has provided both armaments and training to the Sri Lankan military. The government has tried to obtain international support against the LTTE and for them by stressing the fact that the LTTE is on many of the world's terrorism lists, including the U.S. State Department's list of terrorist organizations.

The Sri Lankan case illustrates the importance of subnational grievances leading to the growth of militancy and transnationalism from an island that has the character of paradise on earth in terms of its geography and was expected to be a point of westernized civilization after it gained independence in 1948.

Interests of the Major Powers

U.S. interests in South Asia fall into five categories. First, the United States would like to see the nations of South Asia settle disputes through negotiation rather than open conflict. Second, the United States supports democratic regimes responsive to the wishes of the people in each nation. Third, the United States supports economic development of each nation with the goal of reasonable standards of living for all. Fourth, the United States neither seeks a position of primacy in the area nor wishes to see any other outside power gain such a position. Finally, since 2001 the United States has added the importance of pursuing the "global war on terror" in the region.

China's interests have been seen as generally compatible with those of the United States. China feared an expanded Soviet presence in South Asia and accused both the Soviet Union and India of seeking "hegemony" in the region. China therefore worked closely with Pakistan and Bangladesh on many issues, such as Afghanistan. China maintained that it was prepared to negotiate its outstanding border problems with India, but negotiations produced only ritualistic declarations until recently. Indian-Chinese relations have improved significantly in recent years.

The Soviet Union anchored its policy toward South Asia on its close relationship with India. In return, it received diplomatic support from India on a wide variety of issues ranging from Afghanistan to Kampuchea. India found the alliance useful, as not only did the Soviets constitute a good market for its exports but also, and more importantly, they supplied military equipment. At the same time, many Indians believed that the former Soviet Union was far behind the West in industrial and military technology. Following the collapse of the Soviet Union, the South Asian states—especially India—are in the process of sorting out relationships with Russia and the other countries of the former Soviet Union. Russia is reemerging as a major power in European, Middle Eastern, and Far Eastern affairs, and Indian strategists are aware of its growing importance and of the value of maintaining substantial military and economic links with Russia even as the world is eyeing the rapid rise of China.

Regional Affairs: South Asian Association for Regional Cooperation

In August 1983 the seven South Asian nations signed an agreement in New Delhi formally establishing the South Asian Regional Cooperation (SARC). The group was renamed when the 1983 agreement was ratified at a summit meeting in Dhaka in December 1985. It is now known as the South Asian Association for Regional Cooperation (SAARC).

SAARC was founded through the efforts of Bangladesh president Ziaur Rahman, who was the first head of government to visit each of the other four major states of South Asia (India, Pakistan, Sri Lanka, and Nepal). Ziaur Rahman preached the importance, as he saw it, of the states coming together to work on economic, social, and technological matters as a prelude to political cooperation. India resisted at first, as it saw SAARC as a limitation on its strength; Pakistan also had misgivings as it feared that India would dominate the group. However, both were eventually persuaded that the formation of a regional group would be advantageous to all.

SAARC generally avoids political matters and shuns strictly bilateral issues, but it has agreed to explore a wide range of social, economic, environmental, and technological matters. Though it is a far cry from a common market, it has established a South Asian Preferential Trade Area (SAPTA) under which each country at its discretion can lower tariffs on specific goods. This is thought by some to be a prelude to a South Asian Free Trade Agreement (SAFTA), but such an agreement appears to be at best a distant hope. Trade among the countries of South Asia (with the exception of trade between Nepal and India) is quite limited; each nation trades more with developed countries than with its neighbors. If trade within South Asia were to expand, however, India would surely benefit the most. Further, the annual summit meetings provide a means for private discussions between heads of government.

The formal establishment of SAARC raised the hope that disputes within the region would be moderated and solutions found—in short, that there would be no repetition of the three wars fought between India and Pakistan in 1948, 1965, and 1971. Arguably this goal has been achieved. However, the economic links between the member countries have remained minimal inasmuch as intraregional trade is infrequent (Indo-Nepali and Indo-Bhutanese trade being exceptions). Cultural links are also minimal, as the three largest states have been separated from each other for more than sixty years. Kolkatra, for instance, is no longer the prime magnet for Bangladeshi Bengalis, nor is Lahore for Indian Punjabis; and although there are many Islamic pilgrimage sites in India and some Sikh shrines in Pakistan, they are important to only a small number of people. Still, SAARC plays a great potential role in such areas as technology, tourism, meteorology, and trade.

The twenty-first century is likely to see the growth of regionalism on a pan-Asian basis. Many Asian countries—from Japan to India, including China and the Southeast Asian nations—are involved in an interstate dialogue to develop economic and cultural links on a pan-Asian basis. Such a movement is likely to place subregional rivalries into a narrow box of manageable controversies. The challenge before South Asian leaders is to think outside the box and create new situations that produce paradigmatic changes.

Regional Conflicts

As South Asia emerges as an important actor in world affairs, it must resolve the major issues that prevent regional unity. While there are many issues, there are several that are serious and have defied resolution. Most important are the conflicts between Pakistan and India and the chronic dispute between Bangladesh and India concerning water resources. While there are other important regional conflicts, space considerations limit us to a brief discussion of these two.

Conflict Between India and Pakistan

The issue of contention between India and Pakistan that has caused the greatest difficulty and drawn the most international attention is that involving Kashmir. In brief, at the time of independence in 1947, the ruling princes of the Indian states (see Chapter 1) were given the choice as to which of the two successors, India or Pakistan, they wished their states to join. Joining at this early stage meant the cession of powers over defense, foreign affairs, and communications to one or the other state; as it turned out, it would eventually mean full integration into the new state chosen. All but three of the more than 500 princes decided quickly to accede to one state or the other, taking into consideration primarily the geographic location of the state and the religious majority of the people of the state. The two states that delayed—Hyderabad (the most populous of the princely states, whose Muslim ruler desired independence even though Hyderabad was surrounded by Indian territory) and Junagadh (a small state with a Muslim prince who acceded to Pakistan despite its majority Hindu population)—were eventually merged with India by means of force.

The third Kashmir remains a problem that has not been formally and finally settled. Had the princely states been subject to partition as the provinces were, Kashmir might have been divided inasmuch as its minority Hindu population lived in a clearly defined area bordering India. Moreover, the majority Muslim community and its also fairly well defined area could have joined Pakistan, although that would have left a sparsely populated Buddhist area, Ladakh, on the Chinese border to be argued about. The maharaja, however, wished to retain control of the state and desired independence; the British were not willing to consider this an option. The maharaja then concluded "standstill" agreements with both India and Pakistan. These agreements stipulated that official services, such as posts and transport, would continue unhindered. The maharaja also faced internal demands for constitutional rule from the multicommunal party known as the National Conference, led by Sheikh Muhammad Abdullah, a close friend of Nehru.

In October 1947 Muslim tribesmen from Pakistan began a series of raids into Kashmir and detached some of the northern and western areas of the state as "governments" independent of the ruler in the capital of Srinagar. The northern areas have since been in a de facto sense incorporated into Pakistan; and the western areas, including Muzaffarabad, have been designated as the "independent state" Azad Kashmir (free Kashmir), an entity not recognized by any country except Pakistan. The threat to Srinagar caused the maharaja to appeal to India for assistance, which was given only after the maharaja acceded to India on October 26, 1947. The accession was accepted by the government of India the following day with the proviso that the will of the people would be ascertained after conditions in the state had returned to normal.[1] The maharaja subsequently installed a new government under Sheikh Abdullah. Because Indian troops were involved, Pakistani troops also entered the war.

India brought the matter of what it called "Pakistani aggression" to the United Nations in January 1948. Resolutions of the Security Council in August 1948 and January 1949 made provisions for a Pakistani withdrawal and the withdrawal of the bulk of the Indian troops preparatory to the holding of a plebiscite under United Nations auspices. A cease-fire became effective on January 1, 1949. A United Nations peacekeeping force was set up in the area (and, though small, remains to this day). Several attempts were made by Security Council representatives to implement the plebiscite agreement, but all failed. In 1954 Prime Ministers Jawaharlal Nehru of India and Muhammad Ali Bogra of Pakistan met in an attempt to resolve the difficulties, but they too were unsuccessful. Earlier, in 1953, Abdullah had been removed as prime minister of

Jammu and Kashmir and arrested on the charge that he was in opposition to the integration of the state into the Indian Union. Abdullah was released in 1964 and returned to the state as chief minister in 1975—a post he held until his death in 1982. In 1958 another meeting was held between Nehru and Pakistani Prime Minister Firoz Khan Noon, but this also failed to produce a mutually satisfactory settlement of the issue.

The question of Kashmir continues to plague Indo-Pakistani relations. Pakistan still demands that the plebiscite be held, as required by the Security Council resolutions. India in turn maintains that the regular elections in the state have returned parties favoring integration with India and that these elections have served as a surrogate for the plebiscite; in the view of many observers, however, the elections were far from "free and fair." India has thus responded that the only issue still to be resolved is the "vacation" of the Pakistani "aggression" in the northern area and in Azad Kashmir. Neither country has yet publicly recognized that these nonnegotiable demands are unrealistic and that only a compromise agreement can ultimately resolve the issue.

In the summer of 1965, disturbances in Kashmir signified (falsely, as it turned out) to the Pakistanis that Muslim Kashmiris in the Srinagar area were prepared to rebel against Indian rule and that, with some help from Pakistan, they would be successful. Apparently at the urging of the foreign minister, Zulfiqar Ali Bhutto, President Ayub Khan authorized Pakistani troops to cross the 1949 cease-fire line and to invade Indian-held Kashmir. The result was a disaster for Pakistan. The Pakistanis had initially caused the Indian military situation in the Vale of Kashmir to become difficult by threatening the key land communications line, but India responded by attacking Pakistani Punjab at Lahore and Sialkot in early September. Within two and a half weeks, a cease-fire was arranged. Ayub and Indian Prime Minister Lal Bahadur Shastri met under the auspices of Soviet Prime Minister Aleksey Kosygin at Tashkent in January 1966 and arranged for a mutual withdrawal both in Kashmir and along the international boundary.

Kashmir also played a limited role in late 1971 when India entered the Bangladesh liberation war. The cease-fire in December covered both the eastern (Bangladesh) and western (Kashmir and the Punjab) fronts. The 1949 cease-fire line was modified to a limited extent by the 1972 line of control (LOC) that separates the territories administered by India and Pakistan (or Azad Kashmir). The issue continued to fester. No Pakistani politician can publicly accept the status quo in Kashmir and expect to survive politically, whereas India could perhaps accept the present line of control as an international boundary. In 1989 and 1990 dissident Muslims in the Indian part of Kashmir raised demands, often violently, that the government of Farooq Abdullah, the sheikh's son, be dismissed. The then Indian prime minister, V. P. Singh, dismissed Farooq, but this did not quiet the situation. Civil order unraveled rapidly and the ensuing violence between the Indian military and Muslim Kashmiri militants (many of whom advocated secession from India and Kashmiri independence) claimed thousands of lives. There was clear "moral" and material support for the militants from Pakistan, with Pakistan officially claiming that such support was unofficial and in any case justified by the draconian repression by the "Indian occupation forces" of the "freedom-loving peoples" of Kashmir. India held a different view—that Pakistan was the main cause of the conflict and was sponsoring "cross-border terrorism" against the legitimate government of Jammu and Kashmir (see Chapter 11). Numerous attempts have been made by both Pakistan and India to quiet the Kashmir dispute subsequently. The most promising initiative to date was the unprecedented visit of Prime Minister Vajpayee to Lahore in February 1999 that resulted in the Lahore Declaration, which among other things called for a just settlement of the Kashmir conflict. But such hopes were dashed when Pakistan decided to occupy parts of "Indian-occupied Kashmir" in the spring of 1999—the so-called Kargil Operation. India strenuously contested the occupation and a bloody if limited war erupted between India and Pakistan. India, with the diplomatic support of the United States, eventually prevailed and the Pakistani forces were obliged to leave their positions, suffering many casualties as a result. The debacle of Kargil weakened the civilian government of Nawaz Sharif and was a contributing factor to Musharraf's military coup in October (see Chapter 12). It also effectively ended for the time being diplomatic efforts to solve the Kashmir dispute.

The Kargil Operation furthered the decline of relations between India and Pakistan, which reached their nadir in December 2001, following the attack on the Lok Sabha in Delhi by Islamic militants, whom India claimed were officially sponsored by the Pakistan government. Pakistan denied such involvement, but in subsequent months both India and Pakistan conducted threatening military exercises on their common border. Many worried about the prospect of a fourth war between India and Pakistan—and the first war between two states possessing nuclear weapons. Cooler heads and skillful international diplomatic intervention prevailed, but the optimistic days of the Vajpayee-Nawaz Sharif accord on Kashmir have so far not returned. Kashmir remains unsettled, episodic violence still is chronic in the state, and the unresolved dispute continues to poison Pakistan-India relations.[2]

Other unresolved issues also continue to plague Pakistani-Indian relations, including Hindu-Muslim relations (each state claims that the other mistreats its respective minorities), and perhaps the world's longest lasting pointless international conflict—the Siachin glacier dispute.

One major dispute was resolved successfully, however, through international intervention—the division of the waters of the Indus River system. Immediately after partition the rivers from which irrigation canals branched were those running through India (i.e., the Ravi, the Sutlej, and the Beas rivers), but the areas using the water were principally in Pakistan. India naturally wished to use these waters to develop and expand its irrigation systems, but in doing so (beginning in the late 1940s) it would leave the Pakistan areas without water. In response, Pakistan threatened to go to war. The flow was restored, but the Indian desire to use the waters was clearly communicated. During the 1950s the World Bank became involved and offered the two countries several plans for solving the problem. A treaty was signed by Nehru and Ayub Khan in 1960 under which the waters would be divided and international donors, including the World Bank, India, and most Western nations, would finance the building of replacement works in Pakistan. These works included two large storage dams at Mangla on the Jhelum and Tarbela on the Indus, several barrages designed to divert the waters of those two rivers and the Chenab, and a series of link canals to carry the water from the western rivers into the irrigation system formerly supplied by the eastern Ravi, Beas, and Sutlej. In turn, India was permitted to use the waters of the three eastern rivers. The plan, which was completed by the end of the 1960s (except for the dam at Tarbela), has worked exceptionally well. It has also demonstrated that the application of engineering solutions to a problem not charged with communal issues (as is Kashmir) could lead to a settlement that would meet most of the interests of each party.[3]

India and Bangladesh: Water Problems and Other Issues

In its initial period of independence, Bangladesh expressed strong gratitude for India's aid in the civil war. But this feeling dissipated quickly, despite the twenty-five-year treaty signed in March 1972.[4] Bangladeshis felt that the Indians were staying on too long after the war, especially in the Chittagong Hill Tracts, to the extent that they had almost become an occupying army. India, the Bangladeshis claimed, had taken charge of the prisoners and had removed almost all of the captured Pakistani military equipment. And the Indian building of the Farakka barrage on the Ganges River, which was completed in 1975, aroused strong anger toward India as well as toward Mujibur Rahman, who seemed to some to be unable to do anything to protect Bangladeshi interests.

During most of any given year the flow in the Ganges is sufficient that India's withdrawal of 90,000 cubic feet per second (cusecs) makes no significant impact on the flow received downstream in Bangladesh. But during the low-flow period in April and May, such a withdrawal would all but dry up the Ganges below Farakka in Bangladesh. Clearly the needs of both India and Bangladesh could not be met during this low-flow period.

It might be thought that the upper riparian/lower riparian conflict could be settled along the lines of the Indus Settlement. The political differences involved made that unlikely, however. According to the terms of the Indus Settlement, India and Pakistan have almost total control over the rivers that are assigned to them. But this solution could not be applied to the Ganges waters, even if the Brahmaputra waters were taken into account, because both rivers then would be subject to Indian control. The Indians have proposed building a link canal that would run from the Brahmaputra at a point just inside India, then across about 150 miles of Bangladeshi territory, and then empty into the Ganges just above Farakka in India. Bangladesh objected on the grounds that this plan would give India control of the intake on the Brahmaputra as well as the outflow on the Ganges and would also displace a large number of Bangladeshis.

In turn, Bangladesh has proposed that the flow of the Ganges be controlled by means of storage dams in Nepal on tributaries of the river. But India has objected on the grounds that, as the matter is bilateral, a third party should not be introduced into the discussions. The issue was the subject of regular meetings of a joint rivers commission, but it was not until 1997 that a long-term agreement was signed that provides for division of the waters during the dry season, a division that each side has termed as "equitable," despite opposition by the Bangladesh Nationalist Party, which sees the agreement as an Awami League sellout to India. The polarized party politics of Bangladesh and its external policies reveal a rising trend toward Islamic militancy within Bangladesh, and its effect in Islamizing India's northwest. As well, Bangladeshi poverty and a porous border with India have stimulated mass illegal migration into India's northeast and the demographic changes have increased prospects of political, economic, and social instability in the region.

The Growth of Terror and Extremism

While South Asia has struggled to democratize, the rise of Islamic extremism has posed the newest threat to the growth of democracy in Pakistan, Bangladesh, and Nepal and threatened to destabilize the Muslim communities in India and Sri Lanka. This has been added to the problem of developing national identities in each of the states.

South Asia is home to a number of organizations that appear on the U.S. terrorist list. These include al-Qaeda, the Liberation Tigers of Tamil Eelam, and the Communist Party of Nepal (Maoist). Both the LTTE and CPN(Maoist) have focused their activities within their own countries, while al-Qaeda has sought to create an international network of Muslims.

The Soviet invasion of Afghanistan in 1979 led President Carter's national security adviser, Zbigniew Brzezinski, to try to make Afghanistan into Moscow's Vietnam. The Mujahideen, or freedom fighters, opposed to the Soviet Union were trained in military tactics and were well funded by the United States, China, and others. The Carter administration identified Pakistan as a frontline state and provided economic and military assistance to Pakistan and military supplies to the Afghan Mujahideen. During the war more than 3 million Afghans fled to Pakistan and perhaps another million to Iran. Pakistan, despite international assistance, found the cost of supporting these refugees to be a great burden on its economy and on its political and social systems. It worked through the United Nations in an effort to find a means by which Soviet troops could be removed from Afghanistan and a nonaligned government free of outside interference established in Kabul. The first of these goals has been met, as the Soviets completed their withdrawal in 1989. But the fall of the Muhammad Najibullah government in 1992 led to another civil war in Afghanistan, in which the Taliban movement (literally, students movement) gained ascendancy and sought to recreate Afghan society along lines they imagined were countenanced by the Quran.

Following September 11, 2001, the United States launched a massive military campaign against the Taliban after they refused to expel al-Qaeda (blamed for the 9/11 attacks) from the country. The U.S. military action drove the Taliban from power, but both al-Qaeda and the Taliban regrouped in southern Afghanistan and along the tribal frontier of Pakistan. Also, since 2001 Pakistan has been obliged to join the United States in its "global war against terror." Consequently Pakistani authorities have killed or captured thousands of "Muslim insurgents" (mostly Afghans, Arabs, Uzbeks, or Tajiks) and turned many of them over to U.S. and coalition authorities. Also, since 2005 Pakistan has engaged in increasingly large-scale military operations which have targeted the Federally Administered Tribal Agencies (FATA), especially North and South Waziristan. The blowback from such military operations has been associated with the alarming rise of civil disorder within the settled areas of state. In 2007, Pakistan suffered the effects of over fifty suicide bombings and the deaths of over 3,500 associated with acts of terrorism.

NOTES

1. The text of the maharaja's letter of accession and Lord Mountbatten's reply on behalf of the government of India are contained in Josef Korbel, *Danger in Kashmir*, rev. ed. (Princeton: Princeton University Press, 1966), pp. 80–83.

2. Robert Wirsing, *Kashmir in the Shadow of War: Regional Rivalries in a Nuclear Age* (New York: Sharpe, 2003). For a useful discussion of attitudes of Indians and Pakistanis toward the Kashmir dispute, see Kashmir Study Group, *The Kashmir Dispute at Fifty: Charting Paths to Peace* (Livingston, N.Y.: Kashmir Study Group, 1997).

3. Aloys A. Michel, *The Indus Rivers: A Study of the Effects of Partition* (New Haven: Yale University Press, 1967).

4. The treaty was not renewed when it expired in 1997.

SUGGESTED READINGS

Baxter, Craig. *Bangladesh: From a Nation to a State.* Boulder: Westview, 1997.

Bhutto, Zulfikar Ali. *The Myth of Independence.* Lahore: Oxford University Press, 1969.

Carnegie Endowment for International Peace. *Nuclear Weapons and South Asian Security.* Washington, D.C.: Carnegie Endowment for International Peace, 1988.

Choudhury, Dilara, *Bangladesh and the South Asian International System.* Buckhurst, U.K.: Scorpion, 1992.

DeSilva, K. M. *Regional Powers and Small State Security: India and Sri Lanka, 1977–90.* Washington, D.C.: Woodrow Wilson Center Press, 1995.

Dutt, V. P. *India's Foreign Policy.* New Delhi: Vikas, 1985.

Ganguly, Sumit. *The Origins of War in South Asia.* Boulder: Westview, 1986.

Hagerty, Devin T. *The Consequences of Nuclear Proliferation: Lessons from South Asia.* Cambridge: MIT Press, 1998.

Hardgrave, Robert L., Jr. *India Under Pressure: Prospects for Political Stability.* Boulder: Westview, 1984.

Jalal, Ayesha. *Democracy and Authoritarianism in South Asia: A Comparative and Historical Perspective.* New York: Cambridge University Press, 1995.

_____. *The State of Martial Rule: The Origins of Pakistan's Political Economy of Defense.* Cambridge: Cambridge University Press, 1991.

Kohli, Atul. *Democracy and Discontent: India's Growing Crisis of Governability.* Cambridge: Cambridge University Press, 1990.

Kux, Dennis, *Estranged Democracies: India and the United States.* Thousand Oaks, Calif.: Sage, 1993.

Lamb, Alastair. *Crisis in Kashmir, 1947–1966.* London: Routledge & Kegan Paul, 1966.

_____. *Kashmir: A Disputed Legacy, 1846–1990.* New York: Oxford University Press, 1991.

Lu, Chih H. *The Sino-Indian Border Dispute.* Westport, Conn.: Greenwood, 1986.

Mansingh, Surjit. *India's Search for Power: Indira Gandhi's Foreign Policy, 1966–1982.* Beverly Hills, Calif.: Sage, 1984.

Maxwell, Neville. *India's China War.* London: Jonathan Cape, 1970.

Michel, Aloys A. *The Indus Rivers: A Study of the Effects of Partition.* New Haven: Yale University Press, 1967.

Palmer, Norman D. *The United States and India: The Dimensions of Influence.* New York: Praeger, 1984.

Rizvi, Hasan Askari. *Internal Strife and External Intervention: India's Role in Civil War in East Pakistan Bangladesh.* Lahore: Progressive, 1981.

_____. *The Military and Politics in Pakistan.* 3d ed. Lahore: Progressive, 1986.

Rose, Leo E., and John T. Scholz. *Nepal: Profile of a Himalayan Kingdom.* Boulder: Westview, 1980.

Talbot, Ian. *Pakistan: A Modern History.* London: Hurst, 1998.

Thomas, Raju G. C. *Indian Security Policy.* Princeton: Princeton University Press, 1986.

Vertzberger, Yaacov Y. I. *The Enduring Entente: Sino-Pakistan Relations, 1960–1980*. New York: Praeger, 1983.

————. *Misconceptions in Foreign Policy Making: The Sino-Indian Conflict, 1959–1962*. Boulder: Westview, 1984.

Wirsing, Robert. *Kashmir in the Shadow of War: Regional Rivalries in a Nuclear Age*. New York: Sharpe, 2003.

————. *Pakistan's Security Under Zia*. New York: St. Martin's, 1991.

Ziring, Lawrence, ed. *The Sub-continent in World Affairs: India, Its Neighbors, and the Great Powers*. New York: Praeger, 1982.

STATISTICAL APPENDIX

(Data 2005 unless otherwise noted)

	India	Pakistan	Bangladesh	Sri Lanka	Nepal
Population (in millions)	1,134.40	158.1	153.3	19.1	27.1
Area (in 1,000s of square miles)	1269.3	310.4	55.6	25.3	56.8
GDP per capita (2006)	784	913	437	1,425	290
GDP per capita (PPP US$)	3,452	2,370	2,053	4,595	1,550
Average annual GDP per capita growth (1990–2005)	4.2	1.3	2.9	3.7	2
Average annual growth rate in GDP (2006):					
Agriculture	17.6	9.8	9.8	12.0	1.7
Manufacturing	8.1	3.8	3.1	8.7	2.2
Retail Trade	6.5	3.4	5.6	12.4	3.9
Total GDP (2006) (in millions of US$)	90,3226	146,888	68,220	27,373	8,012
Distribution of GDP (2006):					
Agriculture	20	22	20	15	38
Industry	28	26	27	31	20
Services	53	52	53	54	41
Percent of population without electricity	42.9	45.0	62.8	35.1	66.8
Merchandise Trade (percent of GDP) 2006:					
Exports	22	16	18	33	19
Imports	26	25	26	44	38
Balance (in millions of US$)	-36,143	-13,132	-5,152	-3,247	-1,537
Official development assistance per capita (in US$)	1.60	10.70	9.30	23.50	7.40
External debt (in millions of US$)	123,123.0	33,675.1	18,934.5	11,443.9	3,284.7
Debt service ratio as percent of GDP	3	2.2	1.3	1.9	1.6
Foreign direct investment as percent of GDP	0.8	2	1.3	1.2	(.0)
Human Development Index	0.619	0.551	0.547	0.743	0.534
Gender Related Development Index	0.6	0.525	0.539	0.735	0.52
Population Growth, average percent:					
1975–2005	2	2.8	2.2	1.1	2.3
2005–2015 estimated	1.4	1.9	1.6	0.4	1.9

(continues)

	India	Pakistan	Bangladesh	Sri Lanka	Nepal
Urbanization (2005)	28.7	34.9	25.1	15.1	15.8
estimated 2015	32	39.6	29.9	15.7	20.9
Infant mortality (per 1000 births)	56	79	54	12	56
Percent of population with access:					
Births attended by skilled health					
professional	43	31	13	96	11
Improved water source	86	91	74	79	90
Improved sanitation	33	59	39	91	35
Life Expectancy:	63.7	64.6	63.1	71.6	62.6
Male	62.3	64.3	62.3	67.9	62.1
Female	65.3	64.8	64	75.6	62.9
Adult Literacy (1995–2005 average):	61.0	49.9	47.5	90.7	48.6
Male	73.4	64.1	53.9	92.3	62.7
Female	47.8	35.4	40.8	89.1	34.9
CO_2 Emissions per capita (tons)	1.2	0.8	0.3	0.6	0.1
Inequality measures, ratio of richest 10					
percent to poorest 10 percent	8.6	6.5	7.5	11.1	15.8
Central government expenditures as percent					
of GDP:					
Defense	2.3	4.1	1.2	2.5	1.5
Education (2002–2005)	3.8	2.3	2.5	---	3.4
Health (2004)	0.9	0.4	0.9	2	1.5

Sources: UNDP, *Human Development Report*, http://hdrstats.undp.org/indicators/indicators_table.cfm, United Nations Statistics Division, http://unstats.un.org/unsd/default.htm, and CIA, The *CIA World Fact Book* https://www.cia.gov/library/publications/the-world-factbook/.

INDEX